THE OXFORD HAN

FILM MUSIC
STUDIES

THE OXFORD HANDBOOK OF

FILM MUSIC

STUDIES

Edited by

DAVID NEUMEYER

OXFORD

UNIVERSITY PRESS

OXFORD
UNIVERSITY PRESS

Oxford University Press is a department of the University of Oxford.
It furthers the University's objective of excellence in research, scholarship,
and education by publishing worldwide.

Oxford   New York
Auckland   Cape Town   Dar es Salaam   Hong Kong   Karachi
Kuala Lumpur   Madrid   Melbourne   Mexico City   Nairobi
New Delhi   Shanghai   Taipei   Toronto

With offices in
Argentina   Austria   Brazil   Chile   Czech Republic   France   Greece
Guatemala   Hungary   Italy   Japan   Poland   Portugal   Singapore
South Korea   Switzerland   Thailand   Turkey   Ukraine   Vietnam

Oxford is a registered trade mark of Oxford University Press
in the UK and certain other countries.

Published in the United States of America by
Oxford University Press
198 Madison Avenue, New York, NY 10016

Library of Congress Cataloging-in-Publication Data
The Oxford handbook of film music studies / edited by David Neumeyer.
pages cm
Includes bibliographical references and index.
ISBN 978-0-19-532849-3 (hardcover : alk. paper); 978-0-19-025059-1 (paperback : alk. paper)
1. Motion picture music—History and criticism. I. Neumeyer, David, editor of compilation.
ML2075.O93 2014
781.5'42—dc23
2013010582

Contents

PART III INTERPRETATIVE THEORY AND PRACTICE

PART IV CONTEMPORARY APPROACHES TO ANALYSIS

PART V HISTORICAL ISSUES

Contributors

Rick Altman, Professor of Cinema and Comparative Literature in the College of Liberal Arts and Sciences, The University of Iowa

Julie Brown, Reader in Music, Department of Music, Royal Holloway, University of London

James Buhler, Associate Professor of Music Theory, Sarah and Ernest Butler School of Music, The University of Texas at Austin

Marcia J. Citron, Martha and Henry Malcolm Lovett Distinguished Service Professor of Musicology, Shepherd School of Music, Rice University

Annabel Cohen, Professor of Psychology, University of Prince Edward Island

Johannes C. Gall, Free University, Berlin, member of the editorial staff of the Hanns Eisler *Complete Edition* (*HEGA*), published by Breitkopf & Härtel; board member of the International Hanns Eisler Society

Daniel Goldmark, Associate Professor of Musicology, Case Western Reserve University

Julie Hubbert, Associate Professor of Music History in the School of Music, University of South Carolina

Kathryn Kalinak, Margaret Tucker Thorp Professor of English and Film Studies in Rhode Island College

Lawrence Kramer, Distinguished Professor of English and Music, Fordham University

Marianne Kielian-Gilbert, Professor of Music Theory, Jacobs School of Music, Indiana University, Bloomington

Neil Lerner, Professor of Music, Davidson College

Cari McDonnell, PhD candidate in music theory in the Sarah and Ernest Butler School of Music, The University of Texas at Austin

Julie McQuinn, Associate Professor of Music, Conservatory of Music, Lawrence University

Mitchell Morris, Associate Professor of Music, Department of Musicology, The UCLA Herb Alpert School of Music

Scott Murphy, Associate Professor of Music Theory, School of Music, University of Kansas

David Neumeyer, Marlene and Morton Meyerson Professor of Music and Professor of Music Theory, Sarah and Ernest Butler School of Music, University of Texas at Austin

Michael Pisani, Professor of Music, Vassar College

Nathan Platte, Assistant Professor of Musicology, School of Music, The University of Iowa

Ronald Rodman, Dye Family Professor of Music, Carleton College

Peter Schweinhardt, Instructor of music, politics, history, and ethics in the Babelsberger-Filmgymnasium, Potsdam, Germany; board member of the International Hanns Eisler Society

Jeff Smith, Professor of Film in the Department of Communication Arts, University of Wisconsin, Madison

Robynn Stilwell, Associate Professor of Music, Georgetown University

THE OXFORD HANDBOOK OF

FILM MUSIC
STUDIES

CHAPTER 1

....

OVERVIEW

....

DAVID NEUMEYER

THE *Oxford Handbook of Film Music Studies* charts the current state of, and prospects for, scholarly work focusing on one element of audiovisual aesthetic experience. Music's role over time has by no means been simple or obvious—either to producers or consumers of audiovisual art—and it is both the contested territory and the range of creative, industrial, and critical responses that are the objects of our inquiry here.

FILM STUDIES AND FILM MUSIC STUDIES

....

From its beginnings more than a century ago, film as a commercial and artistic medium has provoked not only practice-oriented writing but also aesthetic-critical manifestos and technical or technological studies (the last significantly concerned with issues relating to sound recording and reproduction). As a cultural phenomenon, film has long been supported by extensive review and fan literatures, as well, the best of which offered—and still does offer—a great deal of insight and specific scholarship. It was, however, the combination of the influence of the circle of French filmologues surrounding André Bazin (and linked to the journal *Cahiers du Cinema*) and the rapid expansion of colleges and universities in the 1950s and 1960s, especially in the United States, that brought film into literature departments, where feature films as adaptations of stories and novels (and to a lesser extent films on historical topics) lent themselves naturally to pedagogical use. Films also, of course, assisted with language training and gave insight into national cultures. At the same time, American studies programs, established both outside the United States (mainly in Europe) and within the country, contributed to an increasing focus on film, whether directly or indirectly through the critical study of contemporary American culture. From a practice standpoint, the simplification and reduced cost of production materials and processes— first and foremost among them magnetic tape, which became commercially available in the late 1940s, and the portable cameras that magnetic tape made practical—quickly led to widespread experimental use of film, independent shorts and even features, and before long the establishment of specific radio, television, and film departments in many tertiary educational institutions, a development that dovetailed nicely with then current ideas of technological progress and educational outreach.

On a broader platform still, film—specifically the full-length feature—has been the predominant art form in most of the world's cultures for nearly a century now. Its historical ties to existing arts practices and repertoires vary from country to country but in general are complex and, to a surprising extent, still obscure (see, in this volume, Pisani, Chapter 22, on links to nineteenth-century theater, and Kalinak, Chapter 24, on some international practices). The entire range of film genres, but particularly avant-garde (or experimental) film, filmed performances, and the familiar narrative feature film, have been implicated at one time or another in two central debates of arts cultures in the twentieth century: the high/low (or serious/popular) binary and the status of recorded sound. Thus, in addition to the familiar and deeply entrenched position of film in everyday cultural commerce, there are not only historical but also strong theoretical and ideological dimensions to the study of film.

Music has wound its way in and out of these debates and their literatures almost from the beginning. Periodicals and practical manuals served the professional and semiprofessional musicians who performed for early film exhibition. Serious theoretical issues were pushed to the fore with the coming of sound, in part because of rapid technological changes, in part because an established tradition of film production and exhibition already existed by that time, against which the emerging practices of the sound film could be judged (for more on this, see Buhler and Neumeyer, Chapter 2). Already by the mid-1930s, attention was turning to composer-auteurs (by analogy with the director-auteur), that is, the creative musicians who worked in studio music departments and who fashioned original symphonic underscore to classic-era films in the United States and elsewhere. The status of this underscore came into question only in the early 1960s, as a broader range of musics came to occupy, and often to dominate, both performances and underscore in feature films—sometimes also in the typically hour-long filmed television dramas that derived directly from the feature-film tradition. The introduction of the Dolby noise-reduction system in the early 1970s changed the nature of the soundtrack—and music's position in it—nearly as radically as had the coming of sound more than forty years earlier. The composer-auteur was partially displaced by the sound designer, a soundtrack-auteur who created the subtle and detailed mix of soundtrack elements with which we are all familiar in the present day. When directors acted as their own sound designers, composers might be shut out altogether.

Along with these changes in practice, the gradual incorporation of film studies into the academy after the Second World War led to a new type of discussion of film and the soundtrack. Before that, studies of music and the soundtrack tended to be oriented toward industry professionals in the form of manuals and technical articles and toward general audiences in the form of books and newspaper and magazine articles on general film aesthetics, histories, and stars. Rarely were studies of film music oriented toward methodological or critical concerns that would in turn promote scholarly production.

This situation began to change as film criticism became more sophisticated (as noted earlier), film studies emerged as an academic discipline, and methodological options and priorities became overt (on film theory and criticism in this period, see Buhler, Chapter 7).

In 1977, the year that the premiere of *Star Wars* solidified the Dolby system's position in film exhibition (as theaters realized that screenings with Dolby sound were attracting far larger audiences than those without), Roy Prendergast's textbook/tradebook *Film Music: A Neglected Art* was published, offering a nostalgic but also affronted view of an art done wrong. Although the book's accounts are even-handed in many respects, Prendergast clearly spoke for composers of the traditional symphonic underscore, who felt they deserved respect (that is, their craft was mostly ignored, neglected) but who also feared that the tradition they represented was in danger of disappearing under the combined onslaught of popular music, sound design that took away much of music's traditional role in guiding and supporting narrative, and directors who "composed" underscore by dropping in preexisting recordings (on this last, see Hubbert, Chapter 11). A decade later, Claudia Gorbman's *Unheard Melodies: Narrative Film Music* (1987) might have appeared to play into this narrative with its initial adjective, but in fact the book is a historical, theoretical, and methodological survey of symphonic underscore in the classical Hollywood system, where "unheard" refers to the conceptual and functional subordination of music to the imagetrack and its primary sound element, speech (or dialogue). Among its distinctive contributions, the book brings together French and American scholarly programs in film and applies them to music (Gorbman began her career as a professor of French literature).

The very titles of Prendergast's tradebook and Gorbman's academic monograph, then, crystalized two long-standing issues of aesthetics and practice. Two words— "neglected" and "unheard"—encapsulate, respectively, the question of film music's status in the world and the question of music's status in the soundtrack; they are now the longest-running tropes in the scholarly literature. The first word has cultural-ideological implications (Neglected by whom? To whose advantage?). The second has philosophical (aesthetic) and practical, creative implications (Unheard in relation to what?), but, equally, implications that are historical, critical, and methodological in a field where the classical model of the narrative feature film is understood by most to hold sway into the present, despite the many changes over the years in production structures, directorial priorities, exhibition venues, and textual (commodity) form.

FILM MUSIC STUDIES AS A DISCIPLINE

The rise of film music studies closely parallels the recent commodity history of feature films. The widespread availability of VHS tapes in the 1980s encouraged some initial steps, as it suddenly became possible to acquire films and play them repeatedly, thereby setting up the most basic necessary conditions for close study of an individual film and its soundtrack. The ability to record from television with a VCR, along with a gradual ramping-up of commercial releases of both historical and contemporary films, greatly facilitated style studies as well. Gorbman's book appeared at a very opportune moment in this process and is generally understood as the first—and now classic—text of film music studies as an academic area of study. It is, indeed, a treatise so sturdy in its historical and aesthetic arguments that, even in the present, the only real blemishes one might point to are a reliance on a dated psychoanalytic suture theory and the relative obscurity of the films in the chapters devoted to case studies.

Almost immediately thereafter the pace of publication began to pick up, starting with a cluster of monographs published between 1992 and 1994 that moved the field forward quickly: Caryl Flinn, *Strains of Utopia* (1992); Kathryn Kalinak, *Settling the Score* (1992); Royal S. Brown, *Overtones and Undertones* (1994); and George Burt, *The Art of Film Music* (1994). Journal articles and books continued to appear sporadically throughout the decade, with the latter especially widening the field of serious inquiry beyond the general questions of description and interpretation that were the focus of the earlier literature. Nicholas Cook's *Analysing Musical Multimedia* (1998) offered a framework for analysis of all manner of music's combinations with other media, including not only the familiar audiovisual media but also song, opera, and dance. Martin Marks, in *Music and the Silent Film* (1997), applied the tools of musicological research to case studies of music in early film. Jeff Smith's *The Sounds of Commerce* (1998) emphasized the interpenetration of industrial, commercial, and aesthetic practices. Anahid Kassabian's *Hearing Film* (2001), concerned with an updated interpretative model for music in relation to questions of gender, identity, and agency, also advanced repertorial breadth by reading music in films of the 1980s and 1990s, where most earlier studies had focused on the classical sound film. By the end of the decade, the literature had advanced to the point where a thorough critical review could be entertained: Robynn Stilwell's "Music in Films" (2002) covers the period 1980–1996. Since the year 2000, as Pool and Wright correctly observe, "writing on film music has exploded" (2011, xv). Kate Daubney initiated a series of single-volume case studies with her study of Max Steiner's music for *Now, Voyager* (2000). Journal articles and anthologies of case studies quickly proliferated. Isolated articles on film music topics appeared in a variety of journals, but since 2000 three academic journals have been established with a focus on film music and closely related subjects (*Music and the Moving Image* [University of Illinois Press, for the Film Music Society]; *Music, Sound, and the Moving Image* [University of Liverpool]; and the *Journal of Film Music* [Los Angeles]). Representative essay anthologies include *Music and Cinema* (2000), ed. James Buhler, Caryl Flinn, and David Neumeyer; *Film Music: Critical Approaches* (2001), ed. K. J. Donnelly; *Between Opera and Cinema* (2002), ed. Jeongwon Joe and Rose Theresa; *Changing Tunes: The Use of Pre-existing Music in Film* (2006), ed. Phil Powrie and Robynn Stilwell; and, among the more recent entries, *Wagner and Cinema* (2010), ed. Jeongwon Joe and Sander L. Gilman. Textbooks followed in short order, including histories by Mervyn Cooke (2008), Laurence MacDonald (1998), Roger Hickman (2006), and James Wierzbicki (2009); three anthologies of source readings edited by Julie Hubbert (2011), Mervyn Cooke (2010), and

James Wierzbicki, Nathan Platte, and Ian Cross (2011); and an introduction to analysis of music in the soundtrack, in the context of a technological history of film sound, by James Buhler, David Neumeyer, and Rob Deemer (2010). Julie Brown (2009) has written a thoughtful chapter-length students' introduction to research questions in music for film and television, and very recently, Warren Sherk (2011) and Jeannie Pool and Stephen H. Wright (2011) have published book-length guides to research.

As this brief and selective historical account of the literature suggests, film music studies are now firmly established in the humanities, and I note with satisfaction that the number of scholars, particularly younger scholars, who are devoting time and effort to the field continues to increase. Nevertheless, film music studies do not constitute a distinct and separate discipline. They are, instead, a node between disciplines, principally film studies, language and literature studies, media (communication) studies, and musicology (or music studies). Others include especially philosophy (aesthetics) and psychology (cognitive studies; on this, see Cohen, Chapter 5). The material of that node, of course, is the huge repertoire of the cinema—more than a century's worth now—and its catalogue of musical practices, as augmented after 1950 by television, documentary videotape and films of performances, and, more recently, by computer-enabled formats, notably video games and internet-based digital video, both professional and amateur (on music in television, see Rodman, Chapter 21; on music and digital platforms, see Smith, Chapter 10, and Hubbert, Chapter 11; on music in the early history of video games, see Lerner, Chapter 12).

Of these bodies of audiovisual art, scholars have given by far the greatest attention to feature films, with a disproportionate concentration on commercial American films, to a smaller extent European, Russian, and Japanese films, and only in the past decade or so films from other nations and cultural groups, including the so-called "transnational cinemas," which consciously adopt the format and methods of American and European film production but with themes and cultural priorities that may well differ. Television has been represented mainly by long-running series, particularly those from the 1980s and later. Internet studies, not surprisingly, have steadily gravitated toward social media and YouTube and its competitors.

Even if they are not—and they are not likely to become—a separate discipline, film music studies do require their experts. For the individual interested in criticism and interpretation, the scholarly literature of film music is, even now, by no means too large to survey in a reasonable amount of time. Pool and Wright do note that the Library of Congress catalog now lists 150 books on the topic of film music history ("85 of them published since 1980") (2011, xv), but that number is still minuscule compared with the volume of published work in most established disciplines. On the other hand, if one adds, as one should, the scholarly literatures of sound and film studies, extended by the trade-book literature on studios, genres, national cinemas, directors, and stars, then the literature with which the scholar needs to be familiar, even if much of it may often be used opportunistically, is indeed substantial.

Even more demanding than the literature for the historian and for the analyst of style is the size and variety of the repertoire, which does demand a large commitment of time in itself. Accordingly, a small body of scholars has arisen whose main focus of research is music for film. For those in academic positions, institutional homes are mostly in music studies, with a very few in film studies departments. In music, the positions tend to be slots for American music or twentieth-century music, with a few outliers in other areas, especially in music theory (in part because of that discipline's traditional association with music composition and thus its long-standing interest in recent and contemporary musics, in part because music theorists often carry out style studies based on detailed textual analysis).

For film studies or communication departments, film history has been the typical placement for scholars, but that is changing as a rapidly advancing trajectory toward greater attention to sound studies continues. The great majority of those who have presented and published film music analyses and interpretations to date have had backgrounds and specific expertise in music studies. Film studies scholars have begun to bypass the modes requiring highly specialized musical knowledge and jargon by moving toward sound studies, which take the formal unit of the soundtrack as their object and admit of a wider range of methods for audiovisual analysis. Since music is one element of the film soundtrack, along with human speech (dialogue) and special effects (all sounds other than music and speech), a highly focused study of music in a film can be faulted for skewing attention in ways that do not always or automatically yield the most productive or richest results for interpretation. Furthermore, the focus on music tends to encourage historical narratives that isolate music as a special case, a long-standing problem for music in relation to other arts. In the future, one might well expect that areas, divisions, or even departments will coalesce around groups of practitioners, sound/music theorists, and historians, with an emphasis on cultures of reproduced sound, in particular sound film and contemporary musical and social practices that depend on reproduced sound.

The rapid rise of sound studies and music media studies promises to reconfigure historical narratives of twentieth-century arts and music in ways that were hard to imagine as little as ten years ago. If so, the future trajectory of film music studies may very well be toward a position as a subfield of a broadly construed discipline of sound studies. How such a discipline will fit into—or, better, transform—traditional institutional structures remains to be seen. In the meantime, film music studies are in a charmed moment. For film studies scholars, a substantial and focused literature on music in film is finally available. For music studies scholars, generational change is breaking down barriers to serious study of music outside the traditional classical canon and is rapidly naturalizing pluralism within the music studies community. In this environment, we have a better chance than ever of writing adequate historical narratives of music in the past century, narratives that do not cling to a nostalgic musical textuality based on the written score but acknowledge that recorded sound is the elephant in the room for a proper history, as it has generated the first truly musical texts, which fundamentally changed both music making and concepts about music, and did so from early on in the twentieth century. Sound film is deeply embedded in that change.

THIS *HANDBOOK*

It is through television, video games, and internet-based audiovisual media that film music studies engage with—and by and large pass over to—cultural studies and sociology or anthropology-based media studies. This *Handbook* is not directly concerned with those areas of inquiry; the focus here is on the priorities and interests of history, literature, and performance arts—that is to say, on historical research, analysis and criticism, and the construction of historical narratives. Understood this way, film music studies begin from and always revolve about their repertoire base, whether that foundation is taken narrowly as the dominant form of the feature film or in more inclusive terms as an audiovisual repertoire.

Determining the boundaries of the repertoire is one issue, whether in the context of an ontology (for example, if film is an art, what is required to distinguish this art from ephemera such as home movies?) or of exhibition history. In the sound film, music's questions are subsumed by those relating to the entire text, since the sound strip is a physical part of the film (or, more recently, an integral but still distinct part of the digital file). In the pre-sound-film era, however, the situation was completely different. Not only were films typically shown in programs that included live or recorded musical and stage performances, but the sound that accompanied a film varied widely, according to the status of the program in a theater's weekly schedule, to the status of the theater itself (as a neighborhood theater, a small-town opera house or vaudeville theater, or a big-city picture palace), or to the performance forces at hand (from none at all to an amplified gramophone record, lone pianist, organist, or percussionist, to a vaudeville orchestra of eight to ten players or a symphonic orchestra of anywhere from fifteen to sixty musicians). In other words, the history of production and exhibition, fundamental to the study of film, is no less important for its music.

Given the rapidly changing and globally expanding situation of audiovisual media now, any volume like the present one must appear either conservative—in the sense of describing an established set of interests and practices—or else highly speculative, extrapolating to a variety of possible futures. The former was obviously the better choice for this *Handbook*, not only because it offers greater depth and clarity in treatment but also because scholars' interests and the literature they have generated from their research have now advanced to the place where, for the first time, summaries, surveys, and historical essays on topics broader than case studies are not only desirable, as they have long been, but are also more firmly grounded. From that newly possible moment of grounding, a plausible future for ideas and interpretation can also be more easily and more productively read, and we can leave technology to make its own impact through the whirlwind development it has undergone since the early 1920s, from the moment of the rapid rise of electricity, commercial radio, and shortly thereafter the sound cinema.

PART 1: FILM MUSIC: CENTRAL QUESTIONS

In the introductory Chapter 2, James Buhler and I focus on a crucial moment in the history of cinema—the transition decade (roughly 1925–1935)—and specifically on the move from sound in silent film performance practices to music in the soundtrack of the sound film. We do not reject the traditional narrative emphasizing the break between silent and sound film (the ontology of the sound film is indeed fundamentally different), but we argue that there are continuities in the treatment of music that have important consequences for the integrated soundtrack of the classical Hollywood sound film, which is the benchmark for sound feature films generally.

Marcia Citron's chapter on opera and film, Chapter 3, brings together these two venerable audiovisual forms and shows, first, what happens in the most direct hybrid, the filmed opera or opera-film, and, second, how opera is integrated into and how it can signify in wide-circulation dramatic feature films. Her chapter "Opera and Visual Media" in a companion volume, *The Oxford Handbook of Opera*, surveys and describes the issues. "Opera and Film," in the present *Handbook*, focuses on opera's embedding in film narratives.

Rick Altman explores graphical representations of film sequences in Chapter 4. He argues that such visual aids are essential to detailed and accurate analysis; that, in the form of frame enlargements, which became common in the 1980s, they "set a new standard for intellectual discussion and argumentation on cinema issues"; but that they also exacerbated a prior tendency to favor the visual over the aural. Altman discusses several historical examples that combine drawings or screen grabs with musical notation, beginning with a well-known diagram by Sergei Eisenstein (for *Alexander Nevsky*), and somewhat similar examples from Manvell and Huntley 1957 and Gorbman 1987, and moving on to forms that he and his students have developed over the past decade with an aim of expressing a broader range of features of the soundtrack.

Annabel Cohen, like Marcia Citron, has provided a discussion, Chapter 5, that is complementary to others she written for recent volumes in the series: *The Oxford Handbook of Music Psychology* (2009) and *The Oxford Handbook of Music and Emotion* (2010). Where these reviewed, respectively, psychological studies relevant to the role of music in electronic and live artistic multimedia contexts and music as one of the primary sources of emotion in a film, the current chapter takes a broader view of the psychology of film music. Cohen describes the relevant literature in cognitive science, both theoretical and experimental, that forwards an initiative to explain why music is important to film and also how music functions in film, providing empirical grounding for practices of description and interpretation.

In a wide-ranging essay, Chapter 6, Peter Schweinhardt and Johannes C. Gall examine the life and work of Hanns Eisler, a powerful film, film music, cultural, and political node in himself, and one uniquely important in the history of film music and film music studies. Excepting perhaps the Russians Shostakovich and Prokofiev, Eisler covered more cultural and political ground than any prominent composer in the twentieth century—from the end of the Austrian Empire to Weimar-era Germany, then to an itinerant life ranging across Europe in support of Communist causes, abruptly to the United States and, through deportation, back to Europe following hearings of the House Un-American Activities Committee.

Eisler wrote concert and stage music throughout his career, but the authors emphasize that he also wrote music for films in virtually every year of his adult life (from 1927 on). Still, he is best known among film scholars for the book *Composing for the Films* (1947, coauthored with Theodor Adorno), the "foundational work of critical theory on film music [that] in a very real way prepared the ground for much recent scholarship on film music" (Buhler, Chapter 7 *infra*). The authors contextualize the book through a survey of Eisler's experience as an early practitioner in sound film, including an experimental Film Music Project that laid much of the ground-work for the book, whose famously convoluted writing and publication history is then unravelled. The final section of the chapter summarizes the motivations and methods associated withwhat the authors call Eisler's "lifelong film music project."

Chapter 7 is the first of three (the others being Chapter 14 and Chapter 15) in which James Buhler surveys the development of film theory and criticism after the Second World War. Here he offers an account of the development of film studies in the period roughly 1950–1990, relying for its frame on Francesco Casetti's three-stage model (ontological, extra-disciplinary, and disciplinary [or field]). Buhler positions music and sound within each of these paradigms, for the last of them devoting particular attention to the opposed views of formalism and critical theory (including ideology critique).

PART 2: GENRE AND PLATFORM

The first two chapters of Part 2 offer historical-critical accounts of one genre where music has been central to production from nearly the beginning—animated films—as well as another where music must necessarily play a significant role—the musical. After that, we look to establishing contexts for analysis of the feature film by venturing outside, as it were, to questions of the interaction of the film and music industries, the history of the compilation score, and music in the early history of video games.

Daniel Goldmark provides a succinct historical account of animated films and their musics in Chapter 8. Working with shorts and animated features as well as television shows, Goldmark traces a path running from Disney's *Steamboat Willie* (1928) to *The Fairly Odd Parents* (2001–) and emphasizes the variety of early studio practices, the centrality of production for music, and the effects of technological changes after 1950.

Cari McDonnell discusses the film musical in Chapter 9, centering her discussion on the problem of a long-standing critical bias toward the integrated musical (in which narrative considerations, rather than performance opportunities, are primary). Summaries and critiques of genre theory and conceptions of the integrated musical are followed by a reversal: a consideration of film genres or subgenres that are not normally considered part of the repertoire of the film musical but which arguably belong there. As a case study, McDonnell looks at singing cowboy films of the 1930s, in particular those starring Gene Autry.

Jeff Smith turns attention to music in film commerce in Chapter 10 by surveying the history of interactions between the film and music industries. He argues that this history shows a pattern of several long-term business cycles, each of which he associates with a specific point in time: 1927, 1958, 1975, and 1999. In each of these years the cycle was prompted to turn by an important change, either in film technology, music technology, industry structures, or in some combination of these.

Julie Hubbert also brings the work into the present in Chapter 11, exploring the phenomenon of the compilation score, a device not unknown in earlier decades (indeed, it closely resembles some characteristic silent-film-era methods) but which emerged as an important practice in the 1960s and has remained so since. Where earlier uses of recorded music were primarily stock library cues, in the 1960s directors drew on commercially available recordings of all types. There were economic reasons (cost, effects of studio reorganization, popular-music tie-ins), production reasons (director control of the soundtrack), and cultural reasons (in the era of the stereo LP, listeners' relationships to music had changed). Hubbert argues that compilation practices were not static; she charts three stages in a process of change, roughly according to decade and—as with the business cycles discussed by Jeff Smith—closely aligned with significant technological changes.

Neil Lerner looks at the early history of video games in Chapter 12, primarily arcade games in the period 1977–1983. The topic may seem far removed from the feature film, but Lerner demonstrates that it is not the tangent it might at first appear to be. He uses familiar methods of description and comparison to get at what he calls "the stylistic distinctiveness that occurs in the history of video game music," and in so doing he locates a thread that ties early video games to early film music practices, a parallel history that finds video games "adopting many of the same strategies for fitting music to screen action."

PART 3: INTERPRETATIVE THEORY AND PRACTICE

Part 3, then, turns to issues of interpretation. In Chapter 13, Lawrence Kramer draws connections between music (particularly classical music) and the representation of the human body onscreen. He begins from and explores both implications and limitations of four theses: cinema is about moving images of bodies, those cinematic bodies are "primarily or originarily erotic," classical music is particularly adept in enabling the cinematic embodiment that screen images alone cannot, and, finally, music so enables through a contradiction that it "cultivates without having either the capacity or, for the most part, the intent to resolve…between the body as sensorial and the body as form or figure."

James Buhler continues his examination of critical theory and interpretation (which began in Chapter 7) with a survey of the literature and arguments around film, sound, and music with respect to gender and sexuality (Chapter 14) and psychoanalysis and subjectivity (Chapter 15).

In Chapter 16, Robynn Stilwell introduces two case studies—characteristically for the field, each focuses on a single film—by arguing for the foundational importance of the practice, its role as a thorough-going way to "recapitulate the experience of encountering a film." In the first of these studies, Chapter 17, Mitchell Morris traces the connections between a prevailing mode of "authenticity"—a familiarizing naturalism—in Cecil B. DeMille's *The Ten Commandments* and the music Elmer Bernstein wrote for the film. In Chapter 18, Julie McQuinn explores ways in which the compilation score for Terry Gilliam's *12 Monkeys* supports the film's thorough intermingling of present and past, natural and artificial, sane and insane. As Stilwell puts it in summing up, "[m]usic, one of the most potent cues for memory, [becomes] a pivot point for recollection, nostalgia, and delusion."

PART 4: CONTEMPORARY APPROACHES TO ANALYSIS

In Part 4, the focus is on descriptive analysis, but the view offered is deliberately prismatic, three quite different approaches to understanding music in audiovisual media.

Scott Murphy shows, in Chapter 19, how the tools of contemporary music theory can provide a context for sound qualities particularly common in film music since the early 1980s. These harmonic progressions are pairs of chords (in this case, triads) related in ways that are considered "distant" in traditional tonal theory (the model that is intended to cover eighteenth- and most nineteenth-century styles in European concert music). There are forty-eight possible such pairs, which Murphy names "tonal-triadic progression classes" or TTPCs. He demonstrates that the TTPCs can be readily explained and grouped using neo-Riemannian theory, and that these groupings can not only furnish a tool for stylistic analysis (to connect and tally like progressions in different films) but also offer a key to interpreting the narrative and expressive roles of these progressions in specific film sequences.

Marianne Kielian-Gilbert, in Chapter 20, explores some particular and very concrete phenomenal issues with respect to the potential of "vivid listening" for music's temporal figurations in and of material contexts (music/film, audiovisual). She focuses on "how listening in film becomes a problem for analysis, and how recontextualizing music in cinematic settings (moving images) interacts with experiences of their (music/filmic) temporal unfolding."

Ronald Rodman offers a survey of literature and analytical approaches in the study of television music (not only series shows but also commercials) in Chapter 21. He distinguishes between a composer-based "auteurist" model and "agency"-oriented models that focus on communication and audience response, then discusses television as commodity (especially music in television commercials) and the distinctive character of music video, and he assesses the current state and prospects for television music research.

PART 5: HISTORICAL ISSUES

Part 5, even more than many earlier chapters in the *Handbook*, emphasizes the fundamental importance of basic historical research to film music studies. The chapters in this section demonstrate how the work can be done and the kinds of results that can be obtained, but in so doing they also highlight how much work remains to be done in cinematic precedents, production and performance practices, and the history of film and film music criticism—not only for the United States but also for other national cinemas. The essays are arranged roughly chronologically by topic.

Michael Pisani discusses precedents for film music practices in the nineteenth-century theater in Chapter 22. Making liberal use of archival documents, Pisani demonstrates that the soundscape of the theater was considerably richer and more varied than might be suggested by a retrospective history (that is, a narrative that reads backward from silent film to earlier theatrical practices, assuming film's continuity with the theater). Although there was undeniably a strong strain of continuity, Pisani shows that techniques of the nineteenth-century melodrama also leapt beyond the silent film to influence underscoring practices in the sound film of the 1930s and 1940s.

Julie Brown explores the surprisingly complex set of questions surrounding silent films and their musics in Chapter 23. She emphasizes the empherality (that is, performative rather than textual character) of exhibition practices for the silent film. To do this, she focuses on the reconstruction and exhibition of "special scores," the small minority of musical accompaniments that were composed for individual films.

In Chapter 24, Kathryn Kalinak offers the reader a glimpse of the diversity in international practices during the same period, before the "enforced" standardization that arose with the commodity-text of the sound feature film. Ranging around the globe, from South America to India, Kalinak provides a new sense of what the sound of a cinema was like, offers a broader context in which to consider American practices at the time, and also makes suggestions about how research in these areas can be forwarded.

Nathan Platte (Chapter 25) follows the history of orchestral performance from early silent film (where reactions to orchestral playing could be surprisingly negative) through the picture-palace era and early Vitaphone shorts and features well into the sound film era. A case study of short films of symphonic performances from the 1950s allows Platte to make observations about the role of the orchestra not only in the cinema but also more broadly in American culture.

ACKNOWLEDGMENTS

I am grateful, first and foremost, to the authors for their contributions to this volume—and also for their patience and cooperation throughout the several stages of the writing and editing process. Norm Hirschy initiated the idea for this *Handbook* and overcame my reservations about whether a large essay anthology on this topic was even possible (the present volume, I am pleased to report, has obviously proved me wrong). He has been steadfast in support and prompt with advice and counsel from the first day till now. I am also grateful to others at Oxford University Press, especially Lisbeth Redfield, assistant editor, and Michael Durnin, copyeditor. The production managers at Newgen, Balamurugan and Saranya Rajkumar, worked with us with both courtesy and efficiency. Thanks to my frequent coauthor James Buhler for many conversations about design and priorities; to Margaret Fons for her work regularizing formatting and checking film titles and release years; to Christopher Husted for engraving music examples in two of the chapters; and to several rights holders for permission to reuse material from published work.

BIBLIOGRAPHY

Brown, Julie. 2009. "Music in Film and Television." In *An Introduction to Music Studies*, edited by J. P. E. Harper-Scott and Jim Samson, 201–218. Cambridge: Cambridge University Press.

Brown, Royal S. 1994. *Overtones and Undertones: Reading Film Music*. Berkeley: University of California Press.

Buhler, James, Caryl Flinn, and David Neumeyer, eds. 2000. *Music and Cinema*. Hanover, NH: University Press of New England.

Buhler, James, David Neumeyer, and Rob Deemer. 2010. *Hearing the Movies: Music and Sound in Film History*. New York: Oxford University Press.

Burt, George. 1994. *The Art of Film Music: Special Emphasis on Hugo Friedhofer, Alex North, David Raksin, Leonard Rosenman*. Boston: Northeastern University Press.

Cook, Nicholas. 1998. *Analysing Musical Multimedia*. New York and Oxford: Oxford University Press.

Cooke, Mervyn. 2008. *A History of Film Music*. Cambridge: Cambridge University Press.

——. 2010. *The Hollywood Film Music Reader*. New York: Oxford University Press.

Daubney, Kate. 2000. *Max Steiner's Now, Voyager*. Westport, CT: Greenwood.

Donnelly, K. J., ed. 2001. *Film Music: Critical Approaches*. Edinburgh: Edinburgh University Press.

Eisler, Hanns, and Theodor Adorno. 1947. *Composing for the Films*. New York: Oxford University Press. [On later editions and authorship, see this volume, chapter 6.]

Flinn, Caryl. 1992. *Strains of Utopia: Gender, Nostalgia, and Hollywood Film Music.* Princeton: Princeton University Press.

Gorbman, Claudia. 1987. *Unheard Melodies: Narrative Film Music.* Bloomington: Indiana University Press.

Hickman, Roger. 2006. *Reel Music: Exploring 100 Years of Film Music.* New York: W. W. Norton.

Hubbert, Julie. 2011. *Celluloid Symphonies: Texts and Contexts in Film Music History.* Berkeley: University of California Press.

Joe, Jeongwon, and Sander L. Gilman, eds. 2010. *Wagner and Cinema.* Bloomington: Indiana University Press.

Joe, Jeongwon, and Rose Theresa, eds. 2002. *Between Opera and Cinema.* New York: Routledge.

Kalinak, Kathryn. 1992. *Settling the Score: Music and the Classical Hollywood Film.* Madison: University of Wisconsin Press.

Kassabian, Anahid. 2001. *Hearing Film: Tracking Identifications in Contemporary Hollywood Film Music.* New York and London: Routledge.

MacDonald, Laurence E. 1998. *The Invisible Art of Film Music: A Comprehensive History.* New York: Ardsley House.

Manvell, Roger, and John Huntley. 1957. *The Technique of Film Music.* New York: Hastings House.

Marks, Martin Miller. 1997. *Music and the Silent Film: Contexts and Case Studies, 1895–1924.* New York: Oxford University Press.

Pool, Jeannie, and Stephen H. Wright. 2011. *A Research Guide to Film and Television Music.* Lanham, MD: Scarecrow.

Powrie, Phil, and Robynn Stilwell, eds. 2006. *Changing Tunes: The Use of Pre-existing Music in Film.* Aldershot, UK, and Burlington, VT: Ashgate.

Prendergast, Roy. 1977. *Film Music: A Neglected Art: A Critical Study of Music in Films.* New York: W. W. Norton. 2nd ed., 1992.

Sherk, Warren. 2011. *Film and Television Music: A Guide to Books, Articles, and Composer Interviews.* Lanham, MD: Scarecrow.

Smith, Jeff. 1998. *The Sounds of Commerce: Marketing Popular Film Music.* New York: Columbia University Press.

Stilwell, Robynn. 2002. "Music in Films: A Critical Review of Literature, 1980–1996." *Journal of Film Music* 1 no. 1: 19–61.

Wierzbicki, James. 2009. *Film Music: A History.* New York: Routledge.

Wierzbicki, James, Nathan Platte, and Colin Roust. 2011. *The Routledge Film Music Sourcebook.* New York: Routledge.

PART 1

....

FILM MUSIC: CENTRAL

QUESTIONS

....

....

CHAPTER 2

MUSIC AND THE ONTOLOGY OF THE SOUND FILM: THE CLASSICAL HOLLYWOOD SYSTEM

....

JAMES BUHLER AND DAVID NEUMEYER

THE invention of the phonograph in 1877 and its cultural dissemination in the 1880s and 1890s changed the nature of sound; recording transformed it into a text, a "tangible object," as Mark Katz puts it (2004, 9). Before that, sound had been conceptually "silent," a chaos of unique, unrepeatable events. Music in the cinema repeats this history: up to the sound era, music was likewise "silent," a heterogeneous set of performance practices; in sound film, by contrast, music became tangible, part of a physical object, a "text." Music began to "sound" as part of the projected film strip.

The historical bifurcation of film music with the introduction of sound film, although broadly true, is nevertheless misleading insofar as it covers over several distinct stages on the historical path. These include music's essential role *outside* the film in nickelodeon programs (before 1910); the emergence of narrative music (and the concept of "harmony" with the picture) alongside continuity editing around 1910; the attempts at solutions to the problem of "synchronizing" sound and music in the early to mid-1920s and during the transition years (roughly 1927–1933); and the emergence of a sound design anchored in what Michel Chion calls "sync points" (1994, 58–60), which not only enabled dialogue underscoring but also allowed the development of new narrative functions for nondiegetic music and clarified other musical narrative functions inherited from theatrical traditions, including the silent cinema itself.

In what follows, we will trace these stages through the broader history of silent and early sound film, with particular emphasis on music's passage into—and its role within—the soundtrack. By rethinking music this way, we do not reject the historical narrative of film music that is structured around the dramatic changes inspired by the sound film, the projected film with recorded sound. Not only is the significance of synchronized sound one area of agreement between film- and music-oriented scholars of film music, but it is also undeniable that sound film markedly transformed nearly every facet of filmmaking. Yet the emphasis on a break between silent and sound practice has incurred some costs, the most obvious being a tendency to downplay real continuities between silent and sound musical styles and scoring practices, a tendency promulgated especially by the first generation of Hollywood composers who needed to establish the importance of their work to increase their leverage in the studio system. The scholarly literature has often simply appropriated this account as the basis of the historiography of this period (Neumeyer 1995, 64), even as it has ignored the many other challenges—economic, technological, cultural, and aesthetic—of negotiating a place for music on the recorded soundtrack.

Music and Silent Film Sound

Already in the early days of the sound era, Irving Thalberg was telling anyone who would listen that the silent film consisted of more than just images: "There never was a silent film. We'd finish a picture, show it in one of our projection rooms and come out shattered. It would be awful. Then we'd show it in a theatre with a girl pounding away at a piano and there would be all the difference in the world" (quoted in Boller 1985, 99). Music, Thalberg's story suggests, was a crucial component not just of silent film exhibition but of the industry as a whole. Rick Altman reminds us, however, that this story enchants precisely because it is nostalgic, that Thalberg's memory was selective (Altman 2004, 193). In fact, the practice of accompanying film was never monolithic in the silent era. Even in the 1920s, when performance practices had become relatively codified, acceptable accompaniment was still extremely varied, ranging from the full orchestra and mighty Wurlitzer organ for the evening show in a deluxe house to a lone pianist, a phonograph, or even silence during an early or dinner show at a small rural theater.

Before 1905, film exhibition was dominated by vaudeville and itinerant showmen.[1] Thus we can say, at least, that musicians were present in most venues where films were screened in those early days, but as Altman points out, we can conclude little about the early practice of accompanying film from the mere presence of musicians (Altman 2004, 195–96). There was nothing particularly remarkable about that presence, since even public lecturers typically hired a pianist to provide music. What musicians played—how they interacted with the film—would have been mediated largely by the institution of the venue in which the screening took place. As part of a vaudeville show, for instance, film would be handled like an act on the bill, at first as a technological marvel, later as a purveyor of news and other important or interesting views, but music would relate to the film as music did for any act: primarily incidental, providing flourishes, representational sounds, march tunes, and dances.

The shift to the storefront theater, or nickelodeon, around 1905 allowed a new mode of accompaniment to appear.[2] The shows themselves typically oscillated between screening of films and performances of illustrated songs—popular songs of the day accompanied by lantern slides concluding with an audience sing-along (Altman 2004, 182–94; Abel 2001, 143–55). Besides accompanying the illustrated songs, music served primarily as an adjunct to the film: entrance and exit music for the show and ballyhoo to attract passers-by to the theater. To what extent music was played with the film remains uncertain, but it seems clear that musicians primarily served the theater. The trade papers at the time discuss music as "an added attraction," noting that music could improve atmosphere, lending the theater an ambience of refinement. Music might add "pep," as in vaudeville,[3] or enhance presentation values for the film, but it remained mostly indifferent to the images. The player played to and for the audience, not to and for the film.

As measured by number of feet of film sold, narrative film took the lead by 1904,[4] and by 1910, continuity editing had established itself as a specifically cinematic mode of narration, a mode that shifted filmmaking from what James Lastra calls an "ontology of recording" to a "pragmatics of representation" (2000, 65, 82–91). The ontology of recording conceived narrative film as a species of recorded drama. It reduced the filmic (what is depicted on film) to the profilmic (what lies before the camera): the film is conceived simply as a recording of what passed before the camera lens. This conception was useful in stabilizing the ontological status of film, for it construes the camera as a recording device that objectively captures the action that lies before it. That action may represent something fictional, but that fictive status is a property of the action rather than the camera. These films, in other words, were merely recorded theater. Continuity editing challenged this conception by constructing a diegetic world reducible neither to the filmic nor the profilmic. Instead, the action was staged for how it would represent an imaginary diegetic world. The essential tools of continuity editing, framing and edited shots, were turned more and more to the task of constructing this diegetic space, based on the principle of an intelligible displacement of one shot by another in order to structure a series of shots into a narrative sequence.

The sound of the cinema quickly changed in response. Earlier, sound and music had been oriented around decoding the images "topologically," that is, reading the images for sonic possibilities (Burch 1990, 154). A bird would appear onscreen and the musicians or drummer (that is, the sound effects person) would imitate a birdcall, whether or not the presence of the bird was integral to the film (Bottomore 2001, 133). With the emergence of the diegetic world, however, the accompanying sound evolved by about 1912 to one based primarily on music, because it provided a layer of continuity, a ground against which a series of discrete shots could be constituted as larger units of structure. By contrast, sound effects, although common, remained merely supplementary to the mature silent film: nothing fundamental depended on their presence, even if the spectacle of sound could become a draw in its own right, such as for the famous production of *Wings* (1927), which included recorded effects of airplanes crashing, propellers whirling, and engines roaring midflight (Crafton 1997, 134–35). The oscillation of synchronous and nonsynchronous sound so common in structuring sound film, although it was obviously useful for enhancing dramatic effect in silent film, could not be structural, a determinative element in the film, for the simple reason that the exhibitor rather than the studio controlled the sound: sound belonged to performance rather than the film per se.

Sound in the silent era, in other words, did not articulate the image so much through points of synchronization as through musical continuity. The fundamental function of music in the later silent era was to underscore the underlying narrative structure of the film by establishing a musical unit of structure, the musical cue, that extended across individual shots, binding them together into a larger unit of narration, the sequence. Music then was certainly not indifferent to the images—in the language of the time, music was "fit" to the image—but the prevailing metaphor for guiding the interaction of music and image was harmony rather than redundant identity. Even at this early stage, a familiar priority of music's functions in narrative film was quickly being established: it was less an issue of mimicking the image than of complementing it, of drawing out narratively pertinent aspects of a sequence of images. George Beynon, writing in 1921 after the system had been fully codified, puts it this way: "The secret of synchrony lies not so much in careful timing of the selections as in the accurate judgment of the musical director." That judgment consists, not in merely cutting music "to fit the situation," but instead in a particular mode of musical continuity: "If care be taken in the finishing of phrases, the musical setting becomes cohesive—one complete whole that conveys to the audience that sense of unity so essential to plot portrayal" (Beynon 1921, 102).

Music's role was to convince the audience that a continuity of thought, a narrative line, existed in the film, and that the audience could also discern this line (Buhler 2010, 34–37). The relation between sound and image might be symbolic in a simple sense of mood and atmosphere. Music might signify a battle, a storm, love—all the standard topics and moods represented in published collections of music for film performance—but the use of such musical symbols was guided instead by the taste and judgment of the musical director with respect to a perceived harmony with the sequence. Music, Beynon said, was most effective when it respected its own integrity, completed its phrases, followed its own logic, without becoming merely indifferent to the images. In other words, this symbolism was not structured primarily by a synchronization conceived as sound film later would, in terms of sync points.

If music substituted for the missing voice of the silent cinema, it did so as allegory rather than symbol: it stood precisely for a failure of the voice to pass the membrane of the screen (Buhler 2010, 38). The shadows that flitted across the screen remained deaf to the sound of the theater and the patrons in the theater likewise remained deaf to the sounds of the screen, and this negative reciprocity established an absolute, unbridgeable distance between the two worlds. Music of the silent film belonged to the world of the audience, the world of live performance, rather than the world of the film. Sound effects, though often "synchronized," were also performed in the theater; they were understood as representations of screen sound rather than mimetically related to it. Diegetic music, too, although sometimes synchronized, was understood fundamentally as cue music, not as source music in the manner of sound film. In this sense it was not yet "diegetic": it was a sound effect, and like other sound effects it was not mistaken for part of the apparatus. Its sound belonged to the theater rather than the image. This is one reason why it was never overly important that sound effects or music closely match the sounds they represent; the most important criterion was harmony with the image—a harmony evaluated externally from the theater—rather than synchronization, a filmic figure that would allow the screened world to appear to sound in itself.

THE CONCEPT OF SYNCHRONIZATION IN SOUND CINEMA

Although it is sometimes represented in these terms, the transition from silent film to sound film did not occur over night. Indeed, the idea of mechanically synchronized sound goes back to the very origins of cinema. As nearly every textbook on the cinema reminds us, Edison's guiding idea in developing the motion picture camera was to do for the eye what the phonograph did for the ear. Edison's main assistant in developing the moving picture camera, W. K. L. Dickson, managed to make a number of synchronized films prior even to the commercial release of the Kinetoscope, which inaugurated the medium of the motion picture.[5] There were numerous attempts at synchronizing film and phonograph over the years—most successful were Gaumont's Chronophone and Edison's Kinetophone—but none gained more than novelty status, due to difficulties maintaining synchronization and a lack of adequate amplification. It was only with widespread commercial availability of radio tubes after the First World War that an effective means of amplification was developed.[6] Even when commercially viable sound film did emerge in the late 1920s, silent film did not immediately disappear. *The Jazz Singer* (1927) did not constitute a radical break in the terms of filmmaking.[7] The production of pure silent film basically stopped in Hollywood by the second half of 1929, but studios continued releasing silent versions of most films through at least 1931 in order to service those theaters, both international and domestic, not yet wired for sound. These silent versions included intertitles and often contained separate footage, different direction, and occasionally even different stars.

During the transitional period, roughly 1926–1932, feature films were made using basically three different approaches to sound, plus one prominent hybrid type (Buhler, Neumeyer, and Deemer 2010, 295):

1. the "pure" silent film—silent film with live accompaniment;
2. the "talking" or "100% talking" film—sound film with synchronized dialogue and effects;
3. the "synchronized" film—sound film with recorded music and sound effects (but little or no dialogue);
4. the "part-talkie"—hybrids that were essentially synchronized films containing interpolated talking sequences as novelties.

Under this typology, *The Jazz Singer*, though often called the first talking feature film, would have been considered a part-talkie, but *Wild Orchids* (1929) was considered "synchronized," despite the interpolation of several closely synchronized dance sequences, because none of these involved dialogue.

Sound film, the mechanical linking of recorded images and sound, inevitably won out because it offered huge economic advantages and gave studios better control over the distribution of their products. These changes benefited both producers (in giving them more control over the product) and exhibitors (who could reduce the expense of live performers and musicians). Still, there was nothing on the surface that made it inevitable the *talking* film would become the dominant form. Initially, executives and creative personnel at most studios, including Warner Bros. (which released *The Jazz Singer*), thought that dialogue and synchronized onscreen musical performances would, like color, remain a special effect and that synchronized rather than talking film would become the dominant form of sound film. Hindsight allows us to see that this assessment was radically mistaken because it ignored the structural shift in the relations between image and sound that occurred with the introduction of mechanically synchronized sound, most obviously with dialogue but even more profoundly with music. As Paolo Cherchi Usai reminds us, the aesthetic of silent cinema was based on maintaining "a clear distinction between an apparatus producing images and a sound source in front of or behind the screen" (Usai 1994, 52). Most characteristically, of course, this sound source was an orchestra or an organ. Kurt London noted similarly how absolutely crucial the pit is to the presentation of opera. "The operatic stage keeps its spell only when it is symbolically removed from the audience by the orchestra pit: thus it retains the air of 'once upon a time', the element of the extraordinary" (London 1936, 140). This sort of fantasy space was also open to the silent film with its live music in a way that would be denied the sound film. Indeed, the synchronized film eroded this distinction—music, dialogue, and effects were all emitted from the loudspeaker—making the placement of music and sound uncertain.

This ambiguity of position explains the uncanny effect of synchronized sound and music in a late silent film such as *Wild Orchids* (Figure 2.1), where the realistic sound of the crowd in the opening sequence seems to hover oddly above the film, as though it does not quite belong to the image.[8] The loose synchronization and the lack of change in the sound with respect to the images—the sound level for the shots on the pier is the same as that for the shots on the ship, for instance, and crowd sounds continue across the intertitles—give the sense that this is a background that is oddly indifferent to the images, despite the presence of several overt sync points. The term "generic sound" is sometimes used to describe this effect (Altman 1992, 250), but such generic sound is not yet an ambience in the sense of a sound that emanates from the diegetic space. This sound is part of the apparatus but has not been fully assimilated into the film. No doubt the sound of this opening was modeled on the deluxe performance tradition; yet the production of the sound effects live within the theater constructs a different relation to the image than does recorded sound. If sound effects in a theater do not seem to emanate from the diegetic space of the film, it is easy to attribute them to the space of the

FIGURE 2.1 a–c: *Wild Orchids* (MGM, 1929) uses generic sound of a crowd greeting disembarking ship passengers to set the scene, but the sound seems to float unanchored above the image.

theater—the sound is produced for us, however effective the illusion. When recorded, however, these sounds occupy an uncertain space: they belong neither fully to the diegetic screen world nor to the theater. The "synchronized" film is thus acutely disembodied: it has extracted the performing body from the theater but not yet placed it into the film.

Music that has been "synchronized" to a silent film—recorded and then used as a soundtrack—occupies a position similar to that of generic sound. Displaced to the soundtrack, the music no longer stands on our side of the screen; nor—even more than sound effects—is it part of the diegetic world. Its displacement to the soundtrack has in many respects attenuated its prime function in the silent theater: it no longer registers a visible presence as mediator. Music has become a sign, perhaps, but it stands above all, as with the earlier use of the phonograph in the theater, as a sign of the absent labor of performance.[9] In this sense, the synchronized musical soundtrack is ideologically problematic, and surely more so for audiences of the time than for audiences today, who have become largely inured to the displacement of living labor by machines. In a context dominated by the practice of silent cinema, the audience would have registered this displacement acutely through the empty orchestra pit yawning between seats and the screen. Only the most callous viewer would not have been sensitive to the plight of performers being pushed out of the theater by the machine, and synchronization in itself could do little to compensate for the loss of live performance in the deluxe houses, which is why it demanded some sort of supplementation to persuade the audience that synchronization could mean something more than a loss of presence. Given the social situation, the mechanical reproduction of sound inevitably required a transformation in the ontological commitments of the cinema.

The lure turned out to be famous performers and news events. In these cases, sound film was not immediately threatening to the practice of the silent feature because it was understood as a replacement for some aspects of the show, in particular the expensive prologues and vaudeville, and as an attractive enhancement to others, such as newsreels. Movietone, for instance, was developed not for feature films but for newsreels, for bringing the sight and sound of important public events to the theater. Political speech was a particular favorite, and what was important here was the spectacle of synchronization: seeing the figure of political speech, hearing the speech of the political figure.

Vitaphone, the other principal method for sound synchronization, was used from the moment of its commercial introduction for synchronizing music and sound effects to the feature, but it was initially developed as a means of recording famous acts to be used as shorts in place of live prologues. The Vitaphone shorts therefore did not in themselves challenge the priorities of the silent feature: they "belong[ed] to a mode of representation significantly different from the norms of classical cinema—one dedicated to the absolutely faithful duplication of real acoustic perceptions" (Lastra 2000, 195). Conceived as recorded vaudeville—itself a throwback to the days when the nickelodeon was sold as "electric vaudeville"—these sound shorts were understood as transcriptions of performances, as "phonograph records with visual accompaniment" (Wolfe 1990, 62). The editing of the images followed the soundtrack, which was inviolate, in order to display the spectacle of synchronization: "What tends to be emphasized through cutting and camera work in all cases is the *source* of the sound within a broader spatial field. The films presume—and structure—an interest in closely viewing the human figure as agent of sound, positioned frontally before a camera and centered within the frame" (62–63). In fact, Michael Slowik argues that concern for the sound source was not always the overriding factor in these films, especially in slapstick comedy shorts; instead, he says that a more generalized spectacle of synchronization that emphasized the continuity of action and required the ability to perform an elaborate routine in one take was at least as important. Issues of synchronization, he says, "encouraged the selection of material in which the actors could reliably perform everything in one try" (Slowik 2010, 69). For acts focused on dialogue or singing, however, where the spectacle of synchronization consisted in the synchronized talking or singing body—and these constituted a large number of the shorts in the early sound period—editing was secondary to the integrity of the soundtrack; it served to display the source of the sound, to give the illusion that the sound recording was embodied in the image. Consequently it is arguable whether the relatively distant shot scale—early Vitaphone performances rarely used anything closer than a medium shot—was primarily a function of multiple camera shooting (Bordwell 1985, 305) or rather, whether a relatively consistent distance was also required to give the illusion that the sound was embodied in the image. When shot scale shifted markedly, from, say, a long shot to a close-up, sound could either follow the scale of the image or not. If sound followed the image scale, however, it would necessarily draw attention to the cut; but if sound did not follow image scale, the illusion of embodiment would be imperiled. In this sense, the restriction of shots to various positions in the orchestra seats served as a compromise that allowed some degree of editing with a single take audio recording while also preserving the illusion of embodiment, the sense that the sound resided in the image.

As the Vitaphone process was applied to the feature film, little seemed to change on the surface. *Don Juan* (1926), the first feature film Warner Bros. made using Vitaphone, is a silent film with a musical score that simply reproduces mechanically what an audience might have heard from a live orchestra in a big-city deluxe theater. Even *The Jazz Singer* a year later offered less a direct challenge to the aesthetic of silent film than a means of supplementing it. Indeed, many critics at the time wrote of the film as "vitaphonized," meaning that it merely had Vitaphone sequences dropped into what was otherwise seen as a relatively mundane family melodrama exploring themes of entertainment and assimilation. The fact that *The Jazz Singer* was also released relatively successfully as a silent film testifies to the supplemental status of its Vitaphone sequences, famous though they may be.

SYNCHRONIZATION AND AN ONTOLOGY OF SOUND FILM

Although many of the early difficulties of sound film were technical, the problems of cutting and constructing scenes through editing could not be solved by increasing the fidelity of the recording. Ironically, solving such problems entailed breaking the spell of authenticity, the regression to an ontology of recording wherein sound film was a faithful recording of the world, to win back its ability to construct its own representation of reality—and, in this, music turned out to be both a sign of the basic problem and an important aspect of the solution. Films that immediately followed *The Jazz Singer* used music, of course. Countless pictures were advertised as "all talking, all dancing, all music," but these films were, as the slogan implies, musicals. One important conceptual advantage of the musical at the time was that it permitted music to be plausibly motivated consistent with the premise that sound film entailed recording a performance rather than constructing a representation. Music could appear as part of a show, as the films tended to be about actors putting on a show. The films were therefore often bifurcated into stage show and backstage life. The stage was in a sense about the presentation of a fantasy space, a state emphasized by the use of music and (sometimes) color in the "production numbers," as in the famous "Wedding of the Painted Doll" sequence from *Broadway Melody* (Barrios, 1995, 73, 122–25).[10] Backstage sequences remained in black and white and generally the music that occurred here was confined to rehearsals or gatherings of the actors for some "real world" diversion. Operettas, such as Rudolf Friml's *The Lottery Bride* (1930), were an exception: taken more or less straight from the stage tradition, they retained dialogue underscoring for lead-ins to the numbers and more general underscoring for melodramatic sequences, the difference being that actors fit their lines and actions around the music, as they would do onstage, rather than the other way around, as mature sound film would do.

By 1931, however, musicals had fallen out of favor, and the weight of studio production shifted to dramatic films, which were, like the musicals and Vitaphone shorts, also at first modeled after theatrical performance, whether as rather literal adaptations of stage plays or as original productions. Essentially film once again was conceived as recorded theater—as early film prior to the codification of continuity editing had been. These constraints were partly due to recording processes that restricted both camera work and editing because of unpredictable sound dropouts on rerecording, but much of it was simply due to the difficulty of conceiving what sound film should be other than a recording of the world (Jacobs 2012).

Writing in 1928, Rudolf Arnheim argued that the talking film was irreducibly mimetic—"The impression that this is not a copy but a living being is completely compelling" (Arnheim 1997, 30)—not the least because of the way synchronization foregrounded whatever was synchronized, vectorized time, and so unbalanced all attempts at nonsynchronous sound. "The unity of sound demands I also keep the picture unchanged" (31). Although Arnheim would later come to recognize the viability of nonsynchronous sound, he thought the mimetic quality of sound film, its literal realism, placed a severe limit on its potential due to the inherent ambiguity of any sounds not firmly anchored in the image. The attraction of the image was sufficiently strong, Arnheim thought, that any nonsynchronous sound was liable to be assumed to be off-screen and in close proximity. Mixing sound and image that represented distinct places (whether physical or conceptual) threatened confusion. In 1934, he could still believe the following caution was warranted: "The danger always exists that the viewer will misunderstand such a montage of image and sound and expect the sound to come from the scene." Thus, for example, "when the drunkard at the bar hears the warning voice of his far-off wife, the viewer will quite likely look around for the woman in the picture, assuming that since he can hear her, she must be nearby" (51).

If Arnheim here no longer insisted that sound film was inherently committed to strict synchronization, he nevertheless still presumed the image served as its ultimate anchor, that nonsynchronous sound would be understood in the first place as offscreen sound, and that such offscreen sound set up a strong expectation for synchronization. The problem extended to music as well: "In many cases this danger also exists with musical accompaniment that suddenly sets in; the viewer connects it to the scene of action, and, should he even hear the voice of a young girl sitting alone in the forest accompanied by a large orchestra, he quite rightly wonders how such luxury comes to exist in the wilderness" (Arnheim 1997, 51). If synchronized sound appeared redundant to the image in the sound film—all sounds had visual correlates, even dialogue had its moving lips—music without a clear source in the image appeared extraneous, superfluous, and even potentially confusing to the regime of sound film. Since recorded music not synchronized to the image was neither of the theater nor of the world screened, the question arose: where precisely was its place in the film? That is, it was difficult to conceive a place for music not motivated by the diegetic world, a nondiegetic register of sound that belonged neither to the theater nor the world of the image.

In 1931, even Max Steiner, who would soon do much to establish the place of nondiegetic music, expressed deep skepticism over music that came from "some mysterious source." In his role as music director at RKO, Steiner committed the studio to music with "logical" motivation from the image.

> When music is found in Radio films, it will be secondary to the plot action and the movement of the story itself. Music will be largely incidental, and often atmospheric. It will not come into a picture from some mysterious source (the orchestra pit?) but by some logical, and, if possible, visual means—such as the turning-on of a radio or a phonograph in a scene, or a glimpse of an orchestra or chorus. (quoted in Wierzbicki 2009, 124)

In a retrospective account of the transition to sound film written in 1937, Steiner told a somewhat different tale, a story recalling Arnheim's situation of the girl in the forest that also pointed to the difficulty music had in earning a place on the soundtrack. "A constant fear prevailed among producers, directors and musicians, that they would be asked: Where does the music come from? Therefore they never used music unless it could be explained by the presence of a source like an orchestra, piano player, phonograph or radio, which was specified in the script" (Steiner 1937, 218).

In fact, some early sound films did feature a large amount of music that could not be easily situated in the image, including *The Lights of New York* (1928), the first feature-length talking film, where the music not only does not have a source in the image but also, judging from the mutual indifference of music and dialogue during many of the scenes, even seems to have been synchronized during postproduction—as the Vitaphone silent films were at the time—using some rudimentary process of rerecording. Indeed, throughout the transitional era, Warner Bros. deployed music more extensively than did other studios, perhaps because the disc-based Vitaphone system in use there required developing rerecording skills and technology in order to do any sound editing at all (Jacobs 2012, 11). But Steiner no doubt told the story because it captured real anxieties about the early sound period while also setting in relief the artistic superiority of the recently stabilized system that accommodated a substantial place for musical scoring. Yet understood this way, it is clear that the "fear" Steiner spoke about referred less to producers and directors committed to an ideal of fidelity than to musicians who had no way of justifying the presence of music in the face of recorded drama. Steiner deflects these anxieties onto the amusingly absurd figure of the "wandering violinist," according to his tale a ubiquitous character in early sound film, though in actuality not that common. "They began to add a little music here and there to support love scenes or silent sequences. But they felt it necessary to explain the music pictorially.... For instance, a love scene might take place in the woods, and...a wandering violinist would be brought in for no reason at all." Regardless of such precautions, ambiguity of diegetic and nondiegetic arose quickly: "Or, again, a shepherd would be seen herding his sheep and playing his flute, to the accompaniment of a fifty-piece symphony orchestra" (Steiner 1937, 219).

As suggested above, the anxieties here belong not so much to the filmmakers as to the musicians, and Steiner pulls something of a rhetorical sleight of hand, since removing the wandering musician from the scene eliminates the narrative absurdity but also the justification for the music. That Steiner felt it necessary to make this sleight of hand suggests that the newly won consensus still remained somewhat precarious in 1937 and that the conceptualization that made it possible had a less than rigorous intellectual defense. In this respect it is entirely characteristic that, later in the same article, Steiner defended his score for *King Kong* (1933) on the basis of its effect of verisimilitude, that it "made the artificially animated animals more life-like, the battle and pursuit scenes more vivid" (Steiner 1937, 220).

This problem of conceptualizing a place for music basically rested on the underlying ambiguity of offscreen sound: since on an abstract formal level relations between film and soundtrack are essentially oppositional—they may be synchronized or not—nonsynchronous sound tells us only that the source of the sound is not in the image; but a lack of synchronization tells us nothing of a sound's relation to the narrative world. How was sound to negotiate this inherent ambiguity?

At its most basic level, nonsynchronous sound simply extends the screened world: we hear what we do not see and assume that the world continues beyond the edge of the frame. Sound in this sense operates much as does a cut: it reveals a world beyond any particular image of it. Both offscreen sound and the cut commit film to a version of philosophical realism: the world does not require my viewing for its existence; no representation of the world can be complete; there is more to the world than can be seen. The image can motivate a cut through a match on a look (eyeline match), on action, and so forth, but in such matches our attention is guided outside the image by a subject that in some way transcends the frame. But this transcendence is only ever partial, successive, with one view displacing another. The frame edge thus remains always as a defined limit of our view, however close or distant that view might be, or indeed however many views we may be given.

Nonsynchronous sound, unlike the cut, is "transparent": it reveals the world beyond the image to be coterminous with the image. When image and sound are not synchronized, we quickly note the disparity and seek to explain it. This does not mean that sound film was always synchronized—obviously it was not—nor that silent film used only nonsynchronous sound—it did not—but rather that the structure of sound film is governed fundamentally by a relation of image to sound based on the expectation of sync points.[11] A sound is emphasized in the absence of the image precisely to create an enigma that the image before us cannot solve. Nonsynchronous sound thus becomes symbolic rather than allegorical: it marks a determinate lack in the image. Under the ontology of sound film, the presence of a sound without a corresponding image is precisely that: it stands for something or someone not present. In the silent film, by contrast, a similar sequence would typically be rendered with a brief close-up shot of the knocking itself, as happens in *Don Juan*, for example. Defining offscreen space through the representation of hearing is not by any means unknown in the silent era (Raynauld 2001), but the sound film gives this space audible definition and thus effects the representation of a diegetic world that exceeds the image.

In sound film, sync points establish pertinence and so also help delineate the soundtrack into hierarchical layers of foreground and background. A good example of this occurs in the opening scene to *Romance* (1930), which features a symphony of street noise. A comparison with the scene from *Wild Orchids* discussed above, where the sound seems to float above the scene, is instructive. In *Romance*, the sync points and use of sound perspective serve to anchor the whole soundscape to the image (Figure 2.2). Although this handling of the soundtrack provides for a neat transition from background to foreground that seems to ground all the sound in the image, it remains consistent with a conception of nonsynchronous sound that presumes an identity between nonsynchronous sound and offscreen diegetic space. To secure music's place on the soundtrack meant breaking down this identity and dividing nonsynchronous sound into diegetic and nondiegetic registers (Buhler, Neumeyer, and Deemer 2010, 302).

There was nothing inherent in the nature of sound film that required that filmmakers develop the conceptual distinction between diegetic and nondiegetic sound in the way they did. As pit music, the presence of music might even have been reconciled with the conception of recorded theater. What seems to have forced the issue, as Steiner astutely noted, was the need to reconcile the love scene with dramatic sound film. Absolutely crucial to Hollywood production since it typically forms either the primary or secondary line of action, romance was not an element that filmmakers could easily dispense with. Yet, according to various publications at the time, love scenes proved exceedingly awkward to depict in early sound films. "Having so much smouldering sexiness," *Variety* wrote of *The River* (1929), "it is occasionally liable to laughter. . . . Coming from the women mostly there may have been a factor of overflowing tension expressing itself as tittering" (quoted in Crafton 1997, 504). Here is exposed the difference between the

FIGURE 2.2 *Romance* (MGM, 1930) opens with a striking symphony of street sounds that uses coinciding aural and visual close-ups to anchor the sound to the image.

physical distance of the theatrical stage and the intimacy of film: the close-up in particular seemed to force viewers to intrude on the film's diegetic world. They had the uncomfortable sense that they were overhearing intimate conversation. In 1929, *Motion Picture Classic* published a set of readers' responses to the talkies. One writer complained: "Some of the love scenes [in the talkies] aren't so effective when the actors are putting their emotions in words. This is especially true when the hero pleads with the heroine for her love. While she is deciding what the answer will be, we hear nothing but the whispering, coughing audience and the suspense is terrible" (quoted in Crafton 1997, 504).

Besides the issue of intimacy, audience discomfort may also have been the product of the scenes becoming difficult to read without music, which could not, as in the silent era, guide an audience interpretation. In *Behind Office Doors* (1931), for instance, Mary (Mary Astor) and her boss, Jim (James Duneen), return to her apartment after a giddy night of dancing. He makes sexual advances (Figure 2.3), which she declines, apparently reluctantly. Without music underscoring the scene, however, Mary's actions in this sequence are difficult to decipher with confidence, and the result is an intense unease over her response that would likely produce precisely the audience whispering and coughing mentioned above. We might claim that a lack of music allows the audience a richer experience of the scene because, without music suggesting to the audience how Mary feels over the course of the scene, viewers are allowed to decide for themselves

FIGURE 2.3 In *Behind Office Doors* (RKO, 1931), the lack of underscore makes it difficult to determine how Mary feels about Jim's advances.

how to interpret her actions. Without discounting this objection, we should also recognize that, because the audience was open to form its own interpretation, viewers were more likely to have a dawning awareness of their own voyeurism. Though not couched in exactly these terms, the contemporary press indeed found the public display of such private intimacy embarrassing. Writing for *Motion Picture Classics* in 1930, George Kent Shuler noted: "An old observation has it that nothing seems so silly to a man as another man's love-letters. But there is something sillier, it would seem; not only public, but audible, love-making. It appears to be the consensus of opinion that all love scenes should be silent—unless comedy is intended" (quoted in Crafton 1997, 504). The call to return to the silent film for love making is instructive, for in the silent film such scenes were accompanied with a music that seemed to authorize the presence of the audience. In the sound picture, too, the presence of music proved orphic, controlling this laughter, guiding the audience into a "proper" interpretation of the scene, allowing it to indulge once more its fantasy of romance. Thus, it was the love scene in particular that seemed to demand a return to music.

Nondiegetic music was not, of course, the only way to manage audience reaction to love scenes—Greta Garbo was particularly adept at playing emotional scenes without music—and such scenes did not single-handedly win a place for it in the sound film, but nondiegetic music was generally more effective than poorly located diegetic music (such as offscreen radios or phonographs), attempted revivals of stylized silent-film practices, or continuous, undifferentiated background music (as was tried in *Lights of New York* in 1928 and a few Paramount films in 1931). Love scenes, along with other dialogue scenes that had strong emotional components, thus fostered underscoring, first as an expedient for controlling audience reception, then more broadly, once filmmakers became used to its presence and began to conceptualize it apart from the recording of reality into the representation of a diegetic world.

The invention of nondiegetic music went hand in hand with the separation of the soundtrack into foreground (usually dialogue) and background, where music and effects were both added during postproduction and both served to set off the dialogue as foreground. If music was generally associated with nondiegetic space and effects with diegetic background, music could also cross the boundary depending on whether its function was to represent the appropriate sound of the location (dance music) or underscore the mood or emotion of scene, in a sense registering the *feeling* of the action rather than its *sound*. And the determination as to whether music or sound would serve as background became a function of whether the scene's action was primarily concerned with representing the interior or the exterior. Underscoring is in effect the place where the concept of nondiegetic music was forged, an invention of sound film with certain affinities to such theatrical forms as melodrama, operetta, and silent film, but whose narrative function is not reducible to any of them (Neumeyer 1995). This place for music was really possible only once sound had been fixed on sync points (rather than general synchronization), on markers of a diegetic rather than prophonographic concept of sound use. Only when representation of the diegetic had clearly formed could one distinguish between symbolic modes of offscreen sound: diegetic (foreground/background) and nondiegetic (background only). As a result, dialogue underscoring could appear in a way that would not be confused with offscreen sound, and it could divide the character planes into inner and outer—diegetic the outer, nondiegetic the inner—thus achieving a new kind of musical "synchronization" that registered the flickering interior of the character around the dialogue. Credit for realizing an effective dialogue underscoring technique goes to Max Steiner, in a series of films for RKO during 1932 and 1933.

MAX STEINER AND NONDIEGETIC MUSIC

At the beginning of 1932, Steiner was perfectly positioned to develop quickly a distinctive technique for underscoring dialogue. Although technological improvements in rerecording had made it possible for scenes dominated by speech to be supplemented effectively with music (Jacobs 2012), filmmakers seemed reluctant to take full advantage of it, and soundtrack practices throughout that year remained almost as heterogeneous as in the two previous years. Financial matters were an element—prestige productions tended to have more music (and more complex uses of music) than did B-productions—and policy on music varied extensively by studio, but in principle all films by now could be heavily scored, even if that meant nothing more than inexpensive

stock music. At Paramount, for example, studio policy continued to encourage extensive use of music; one of the most striking results in this year was *Blonde Venus*, a
Marlene Dietrich vehicle for which Franke Harling (and three colleagues) produced
a complex score that runs the gamut from the main-title overture to quickly shifting
thematic music in the silent-film manner (even quoting Mendelssohn) to mood-setting
underscoring to Dietrich's extended diegetic song performances. Music covers just over
fifty of the film's ninety-three-minute runtime. Harling and his collaborators were by no
means afraid to make extensive use of nondiegetic music, including music behind dialogue, but they were unable to resolve the tension between that music and the diegetic
world: the music still seems related to but detached from that world, in the manner of
the "musical synchronizations" of later silent-film practice. At Warner Bros., which had
always used music more extensively than other studios, policy had also changed to substantially increase underscoring. MGM, however, remained committed to restricting
music to situations with a strong onscreen motivation, as did RKO (Wierzbicki 2009,
123–24). *Red Dust* (1932), which stars Clark Gable, Jean Harlow, and Mary Astor, is typical of MGM's practice at the time. After the logo, music starts during six seconds of black
screen before the main title; at that point, the dramatic allegro turns strongly thematic;
it exits very abruptly on a negative stinger thirty-five seconds later. Fully eleven minutes
later, Vantine (Harlow) briefly hums a folk melody. After this, the only music appears
a few seconds before the end title. Thus music is restricted to the typical formal functions of beginning and ending plus a very brief motivated diegetic performance. Even
at MGM, however, actual practice varied by film, and *Grand Hotel* from the same year
uses music under dialogue extensively (roughly forty-seven of its 112- minutes runtime
have music). Sometimes this music is clearly diegetic (as in the bar where the Baron
[John Barrymore], Flaemmchen [Joan Crawford], and Kringelein [Lionel Barrymore]
meet as a dance band plays), sometimes it is vaguely motivated by location (as in the
hotel lobby), but often it lacks a plausible diegetic anchor (as in the soulful music that
accompanies Grusinskaya [Greta Garbo] or the comic music that mimics Kringelein's
drunkenness in his room).

  Thus, although by 1932 the technology was in place to accommodate music and dialogue together on the soundtrack and although a number of Hollywood productions
used music more extensively that year, composers and music directors still had difficulty
in moving beyond earlier practices. Steiner is the composer who made the decisive contribution. To grasp his accomplishment, it will help to identify a hierarchy of musical
synchronization, as follows:

  1. very tight synchronization ("mickey-mousing," stingers, naming);
  2. close synchronization (Steiner);
  3. general "overall" synchronization (mood; "harmony");
  4. "unsynchronized" musical number behind dialogue.

In early sound-film practice, individual musical cues tend to serve just one of these
functions. The score of *Lights of New York*, for instance, uses three of these types, but

segregates them fairly strictly according to function. Type 1, in fact, appears only as music for dancing in the speakeasy and it never occurs under dialogue. In this film, tight synchronization signifies foregrounded sound linked to onscreen action. When dialogue appears in these scenes, the music either continues into type 4 on the cutaway from the dance floor or the scene shifts to an inner office, which features a sonically impenetrable door (Figure 2.4). Most of the musical cues of the film fall under types 3 and 4. Type 3 is used for emotional or dramatically intense scenes: Eddie asking his mother for money to go to New York; the establishing scene in New York and the murder of the police officer; the love scene between Eddie and Kitty; the murder of Hawk; and the climax. Type 4 is also used for a number of scenes, sometimes, as in the hotel, where it might plausibly be interpreted as lobby music, but other times seeming to provide nothing but a neutral musical backdrop. Generally, the music seems to follow the conventions of silent film, with music chosen on the basis of the overall mood of the scene and little thought given to local sync points: the music does not even take account of the two killing gunshots, although both of those scenes feature heavy music in anticipation of the deaths. The only exception to musical sync points occurs in the office, where opening and closing the door has the inadvertently comic effect of turning on and off the music of the club (Altman, Jones, and Tatroe 2000, 351).

The musical practice that Steiner developed after 1933, on the other hand, tends to move fluidly between these functions at different moments *within* cues, and he was

FIGURE 2.4 A sonically impervious door in *Lights of New York* (Warner Bros., 1928) creates inadvertent musical sync points whenever it opens and closes.

careful to scatter dramatically pertinent sync points throughout to stick his music to the action, whether physical, emotional or dramatic. In essence, this meant that Steiner forged dramatic dialogue underscoring (type 2, close synchronization) by combining two staples of silent film practice: mickey-mousing, that is, stinger chords and comedic gags, and tightly focused naming (type 1, tight synchronization) on the one hand, an empathetic point of view determined by the narrative situation (type 3, general overall synchronization) on the other. In addition, he drew on the theatrical models of melo-drama and Wagnerian parlando (Neumeyer 1995, 65)[12] to organize the play between these types of synchronization, and all of it had to be worked out in the split timings required for recorded sound. He also incorporated into the system even the "unsyn-chronized" musical number (type 4) by treating its entry, exit, and temporal duration in terms of high-level sync points through a process of what we have elsewhere termed "structural spotting" (Buhler, Neumeyer, and Deemer 2010, 328–31). The key to his sys-tem of dialogue underscoring, in other words, was recognizing each of the four items in the list above as a layer in a hierarchical system of sync points. (That he understood the distinctiveness of his contribution—and enjoyed the work—is clear from *Gone with the Wind* [1939], whose massive music requirements prompted Steiner to enlist the help of no fewer than five composer colleagues, to whom he gave such plums as the main-title and prologue cues while reserving for himself great patches of dialogue underscoring.)

Steiner might well have developed his methods in any case, but he found positive encour-agement in David O. Selznick, who was RKO chief executive from October 1931 until he returned to MGM in early 1933 and who, according to David Thomson, "encouraged Steiner toward large-scale scores.... Steiner worked on most of David's RKO pictures, and with *Symphony of Six Million* [1932], *Bird of Paradise* [1932] and *King Kong* [1933], especially, he established a role for movie scores that has scarcely altered in sixty years" (Thomson 1992, 131). The overstatement in this last claim misleads: what Steiner did was to establish and confirm a central role for music in Selznick's notion of the "art film" or prestige produc-tion. Primary to accomplishing this task was to cover a large part of the film with music, in a manner that evoked the deluxe theater orchestral performances of the 1920s but that also took account of the peculiar requirements of recorded sound. *Symphony of Six Million* is not unique for 1932 in that about half of its ninety-three minutes have music, but it is strik-ing in that almost all of that music is nondiegetic and most of it underscores dialogue. *Bird of Paradise* is an extreme case: virtually the entire film has music. Although these films cer-tainly look ahead to the later 1930s, in films such as *The Garden of Allah* (1936), *The Charge of the Light Brigade* (1936), and—most notably—*Gone with the Wind*, for their own time they are exceptions: most of Steiner's films in 1932 have scores ranging from twenty to thirty minutes, at most (such as *The Conquerors*) and a few have very little music at all, including (inexplicably) *Bill of Divorcement*, in whose production Selznick was personally involved and whose marquee actor (John Barrymore) plays a composer. But the music-laden pres-tige films were laboratories for underscoring, as the impulse to cover the film with music necessarily involves writing much accompaniment for dialogue. We should point out, how-ever, that the most famous of those early films, *King Kong*, is another exception: although it has a great deal of music, most of that accompanies action rather than dialogue.

Given all this, it is ironic that Steiner's first fully effective examples of dialogue underscoring occur not in music-laden films like *Symphony of Six Million* or *Bird of Paradise*, but in other more modest productions of 1932 and early 1933. A comparison of Steiner's technique in scoring two dialogue scenes, one drawn from *Symphony of Six Million*, the other from *The Conquerors*, is instructive. In a scene about a third of the way into *Symphony of Six Million*, Felix (Ricardo Cortez), who has trained as a doctor but is working in a ghetto clinic, is confronted by his mother (played by Anna Appel); she has been pressured by her other children into telling Felix to move uptown and establish a money-making private clinic. An appropriately sad solo cello melody starts up as she sits alone contemplating her unwelcome task, and the music continues in a slow dance as she and Felix talk (Figure 2.5). A sudden, unmotivated flourish appears about a minute in, followed by an equally unmotivated return to the slow dance. When she becomes visibly upset, a solo violin enters briefly as though in response, but this is undercut immediately. At the end the music rises as she finishes and he responds. Our last view of her alone brings a nice parallel moment in the music, but an abrupt cut to Felix in his room brings an equally abrupt appearance of the main theme (which names him)—this builds appropriately to a climax as he struggles over the decision. When he reaches the window and looks out, the music switches to ethnic ghetto music (from early in the film).

The technique in *The Conquerors* is, by contrast, much more assured. Early in the film, Roger Standish (Richard Dix) and his wife Caroline (Ann Harding) are settlers heading

FIGURE 2.5 Felix and his mother talk in *Symphony of Six Million* (RKO, 1932).

west on the Missouri River. As the scene changes, a fanfare fragment accompanies an insert map of the Great Plains. This cues a shift to a pastoral music for their river journey; as the couple, in good spirits, flirt with each other, a romantic version of the film's main theme plays and comes to a clean cadence, which, along with a shift in camera position, suggests the scene is coming to an end (Figures 2.6, a–c). Instead, bandits fall out of an overhanging tree—a sudden misterioso/agitato cue sounds, and music synchronizes

(a)

(b)

(c)

FIGURE 2.6 a–c: Roger and Caroline flirt, then bandits appear in the Missouri River scene from *The Conquerors* (RKO, 1932).

with one of the bandits touching Mrs. Standish, her husband's resistance, a shot, and his fall. Music goes out with the fall.

If the music for the conversation between Felix and his mother still seems uncertain in its methods, the river scene from *The Conquerors* has all the assurance of much later, famous underscoring cues from *Gone with the Wind*, *Casablanca* (1943), and Bette Davis films such as *Dark Victory* (1939) and *Now, Voyager* (1942). Although the scene from *The Conquerors* has the advantage of being partially a montage and partially an action scene, the types of synchronization fluctuate fluidly between type 3 general establishment of mood (as in the pastoral music) and type 1 tight synchronization (in two modalities: the device of naming for the statement of the main theme and mickey-moused sync points with physical action for the robbery and shooting), with quick but fluent musical transitions—not merely cuts—between segments. This skill in transition between types and points of synchronization—which is not a part of silent-film practice and had little value in the early sound musicals—is essential to scoring both dramatic scenes and montages. Montages were very common in early sound film, in both comedy and drama—*The Conquerors* is an extreme case, as it uses seven montage scenes to depict financial boom and bust cycles and passage of time in the family's history. Music for a slow-moving montage (that is, with brief scenes as well as individual shots of action or graphics) can be almost indistinguishable from closely synchronized dialogue underscoring.

That his dialogue underscoring methods have more affinity with type 1 (tight synchronization) than with type 3 (general synchronization) is plain from Steiner's own comment in 1940 that he wrote music intended to "fit the film like a glove" (quoted in Neumeyer 2000, 15). It would be a mistake, however, to claim that any of the four synchronization classes disappeared, even in Steiner's practice. Although composers were rarely responsible for writing music of pure type 4, songs that unfolded indifferently behind the dialogue—a preexisting song from the studio's back catalog or a song writer would be called in—music of a neutral, undistinguished, and uncommitted nature was frequently required, and Aaron Copland at one point even claimed that Steiner was particularly proficient at writing this kind of music. "For certain types of neutral music, a kind of melody-less music is needed. Steiner does not supply mere chords, but superimposes a certain amount of melodic motion, just enough to make the music sound normal, and yet not enough to compel attention" (Copland 1940, 147). There is no question about the influence of Steiner's practices arising from the works discussed above and a string of film scores after 1932, including several Katharine Hepburn vehicles (*Morning Glory*, *Christopher Strong*, and *Little Women* [all 1933]; *The Little Minister* [1934], and others) and culminating in *The Informer* (1935), which won the first Academy Award for a dramatic film score. By that time, all composers in the major studios had assimilated the core of Steiner's methods into the basic technique of film scoring. We should also make note of Steiner's assistant/associate Roy Webb, who was already at RKO when Steiner arrived in 1929. Webb, who continued to write film scores into the late 1950s, quickly adopted Steiner's methods and proved equally adept at dialogue underscoring, as his music for *Topaze* (1933) already shows clearly.

CONCLUSION

David Bordwell argues that film style clearly changed in response to the coming of sound but that the formal system of narrative filmmaking was itself never seriously challenged, that Hollywood's adoption of sound in fact required only adjustments to, not a fundamental shift in, the prevailing paradigm of film production. "Sound cinema," he writes, "was not a radical alternative to silent filmmaking" (Bordwell 1985, 301). The economic foundations of the industry depended on the ability to make films that preserved through editing the underlying systems of narrative coherence (causality, space, and time). "Given the centrality of editing within the classical paradigm, the coming of sound [did] represent ... a threat. For both economic and stylistic reasons, the option of editing had to be preserved. The task became that of inserting sound into the already existing model of filmmaking" (301). Thus, sound film, even in Hollywood, remained at base a *cinéma du découpage*, and possibilities opened up by mechanical synchronization of sound were immediately circumscribed by this need to preserve the possibility of editing. For example, although "the shot lengthened to accommodate the speaking of lines" (304), its duration remained relatively short, rarely averaging more than eleven seconds for a film. In other words, according to Bordwell, "what is remarkable about the transitional films is not how long the takes are but how relatively short they are; although the technology permitted a shot to be drastically prolonged, Hollywood remained a cinema of cutting" (304). The end result was that, "by 1933, shooting a sound film came to mean shooting a silent film with sound" (306).

For Bordwell, the basic functions of music in sound film remain what they had been in the silent era: underscoring mood and character; providing suitable diegetic sound when required (fanfares, songs, dances, and so forth); and (especially) ensuring continuity. Thus, music, like sound itself, is essentially "pleonastic"—supplemental, merely added, sounding what is already apparent in the image. Bordwell's historiographic emphasis on aesthetic continuity during the transition of sound is an important corrective to self-serving histories that composers constructed at the time and that have been uncritically accepted in the secondary literature. As one of us once cautioned in this spirit, we should take care not to claim "that Steiner 'invented' sound-film underscoring, as if a wholly separate silent-cinema practice died with *The Jazz Singer*, then came a hiatus (roughly 1927–1931), then came Steiner" (Neumeyer 1995, 64). The composer himself may have had reason to promote such a history, but "in fact a very strong continuity obtained between the musical practices of the silent and sound cinemas." An historiography of the cinema can recognize basic continuities, whether in cutting or musical style, at the same time that it emphasizes significant shifts both within and among practices. Bordwell is correct, for instance, that recorded speech did in many respects replace the function of the silent film's dialogue intertitle. But it is less clear what to make of the presence of music in sound film, where its location is no longer secure once it has been assimilated to the apparatus. The mechanizing of music's functions brings them under the control of production, but more importantly it also changes the place from where music does its work—and so also the work it can do. On the soundtrack, the relation of music to effects and dialogue is always already constituted through mixing: *this* dialogue and *these* sounds and *this* music have been brought together to produce the sound of *this* film. But just as the formal relationship among the elements of the soundtrack is triangulated by the world we see screened, the soundtrack is also more than a recording of that world. Synchronized sounds are of the image, the sounds of the screen; nonsynchronous sounds, by contrast, have no place in the image: their place is offscreen, imaginary; and that imaginary need not be of the world screened. Paradoxically, it is only when sound is conceived not as a recording but as a representation of diegetic space that it becomes possible to think of music as belonging to another register entirely.

We have argued for an important break in the scoring practice of sound film—the invention of nondiegetic space as conceptually distinct from offscreen space and its practical construction through Steiner's development of close dramatic underscoring based on musical sync points and structural spotting—but one with deep roots, especially stylistic, in previous practice. Given that music became a tangible object when it entered the recorded soundtrack and that it lost its ubiquity once dialogue established itself as the dominant element of the soundtrack, music could not simply exist as it did in the silent era. The crisis in the musical practice arose most profoundly, however, not with the coming of synchronized sound but with the commitment that sound film would be understood as fundamentally continuous with silent film, once it became clear, in other words, that sound film would be construed as representation rather than reproduction.

But what kind of representation? Here, Steiner in fact made a decisive intervention. Steiner's technique of close dialogue underscoring tapped into the very structuring principle of sync points that was coming to define the construction of the soundtrack. From the presumption of such sync points were ultimately derived the three basic oppositions of image and sound that would characterize the practice of classic Hollywood sound film: onscreen/offscreen, diegetic/nondiegetic, and foreground/background. Just as sync points guide the layering of foreground and background sound so that the background sounds seem to belong to the image rather than float above it, so too music finds correspondences in voice and bodily movement that allow it to find an analogue in the image without having an image source for the sound. Music in this way becomes symbolic; it "grants insight into what must otherwise remain unseen and unsaid: psychology, mood, motivation" (Buhler 2001, 47). Ironically perhaps, the control permitted by the mechanical soundtrack gave to music a power it had never held before.

NOTES

1. See Musser 1994, 273–76, 303, 444–47; Musser and Nelson 1991; Altman 2004, 95–115.
2. On the nickelodeon, see Bowers 1986; Musser 1994, 449–89; Bowser 1994, 1–20: Altman 2004, 181–226.
3. On the role of the musician in vaudeville, see Christensen 1912, 38–39.
4. See Musser 1984, 24–44, esp. 39; Musser 1994, 338, 375.
5. See Loughney 2001; Musser 1997, 178; Musser 1994, 88.
6. See Altman 2004, 157–78.
7. Indeed, *The Jazz Singer* was not even the most popular film over the course of its New York run. That honor went to *Wings*. See Crafton 1996, 468–72; Crafton 1997, 516–31, esp. 522–23; and Koszarski 1994, 33.
8. Similar generic sound of a crowd can be heard in the Paris café performance in *The Jazz Singer* and in the extended restaurant scene in the second reel of Hitchcock's *Blackmail* (1929).
9. On the displacement of labor, see Geduld 1975, 252–60; Kraft 1996, passim; Crafton 1997, 218–21; Hubbert 2011, 115–16.
10. On the structure of backstage musicals in general, see Altman 1987.
11. These sorts of gestures, basic to the syntax of classic sound film, also serve as the basis for analyzing the soundtrack in terms of suture theory. See Buhler, Chapter 15, below.
12. See also Neumeyer 2010 for further discussion.

BIBLIOGRAPHY

Abel, Richard. 2001. "The Most American of Attractions, the Illustrated Song." In *The Sounds of Early Cinema*, edited by Richard Abel and Rick Altman, 143–155. Bloomington: Indiana University Press.

Abel, Richard, and Rick Altman, eds. 2001. *The Sounds of Early Cinema*. Bloomington: Indiana University Press.

Altman, Rick. 1987. *The American Film Musical*. Bloomington: Indiana University Press.

——, ed. 1992. *Sound Theory/Sound Practice*. New York: Routledge.

——. 2004. *Silent Film Sound*. New York: Columbia University Press.

Altman, Rick, with McGraw Jones and Sonia Tatroe. 2000. "Inventing the Cinema Soundtrack: Hollywood's Multiplane Sound System." In *Music and Cinema*, edited by James Buhler, Caryl Flinn, and David Neumeyer, 339–359. Hanover, NH: University Press of New England.

Arnheim, Rudolf. 1997. *Film Essays and Criticism*. Translated by Brenda Benthien. Madison: University of Wisconsin Press.

Barrios, Richard. 1995. *A Song in the Dark: The Birth of the Musical Film*. New York: Oxford University Press.

Beynon, George W. 1921. *Musical Presentation of Motion Pictures*. New York. G. Schirmer.

Boller, Paul F. 1985. "The Sounds of the Silents." *American Heritage* 36, no. 5. http://www.americanheritage.com/content/sound-silents (accessed May 23, 2012).

Bordwell, David. 1985. "The Introduction of Sound." In *The Classical Hollywood Cinema: Film Style and Mode of Production to 1960*, edited by David Bordwell, Janet Staiger, and Kristin Thompson, 298–308. New York: Columbia University Press.

Bottomore, Stephen. 2001. "The Story of Percy Peashaker: Debates about Sound Effects in the Early Cinema." In *The Sounds of Early Cinema*, edited by Richard Abel and Rick Altman, 129–142. Bloomington: Indiana University Press.

Bowers, Q. David. 1986. *Nickelodeon Theatres and their Music*. Vestal, NY: Vestal Press.

Bowser, Eileen. 1994. *The Transformation of Cinema, 1907–1915*. Berkeley: University of California Press.

Buhler, James. 2001. "Analytical and Interpretive Approaches to Film Music (II): Interpreting Interactions of Music and Film." In *Film Music: Critical Approaches*, edited by K. J. Donnelly, 39–61. Edinburgh: Edinburgh University Press.

——. 2010. "Wagnerian Motives: Narrative Integration and the Development of Silent Film Accompaniment, 1908–1913." In *Wagner and Cinema*, edited by Jeongwon Joe and Sander L. Gilman, 27–45. Bloomington: Indiana University Press.

——, Caryl Flinn, and David Neumeyer, eds. 2000. *Music and Cinema*. Hanover, NH: University Press of New England.

——, David Neumeyer, and Rob Deemer. 2010. *Hearing the Movies: Music and Sound in Film History*. New York: Oxford University Press.

Burch, Noël. 1990. *Life to Those Shadows*. Berkeley: University of California Press.

Cherchi Usai, Paolo. 1994. *Burning Passions: An Introduction to the Study of Silent Cinema*. Translated by Emma Sansone Rittle. London: BFI Publishing.

Chion, Michel. 1994. *Audio-Vision: Sound on Screen*. Translated by Claudia Gorbman. New York: Columbia University Press.

Christensen, Axel W. 1912. *Vaudeville Piano Playing*. Chicago: [n.p.].

Copland, Aaron. 1940. "Second Thoughts on Hollywood." *Modern Music* 17, no. 3: 141–147.

Crafton, Donald. 1996. "*The Jazz Singer*'s Reception in the Media and at the Box Office." In *Post-Theory: Reconstructing Film Studies*, edited by David Bordwell and Noël Carroll, 460–480. Madison: University of Wisconsin Press.

——. 1997. *The Talkies: American Cinema's Transition to Sound, 1926–1931*. New York: Scribner.

Geduld, Harry. 1975. *The Birth of the Talkies: From Edison to Jolson*. Bloomington: Indiana University Press.

Hubbert, Julie, ed. 2011. *Celluloid Symphonies: Texts and Contexts in Film Music History*. Berkeley: University of California Press.

Jacobs, Lea. 2012. "The Innovation of Re-Recording in the Hollywood Studios." *Film History* 24, no. 1: 5–34.

Katz, Mark. 2004. *Capturing Sound: How Technology has Changed Music*. Berkeley: University of California Press.

Kraft, James P. 1996. *Stage to Studio: Musicians and the Sound Revolution, 1890–1950*. Baltimore: Johns Hopkins University Press.

Koszarski, Richard. 1994. *An Evening's Entertainment: The Age of the Silent Feature Picture, 1915–1928*. Berkeley: University of California Press.

Lastra, James. 2000. *Sound Technology and the American Cinema: Perception, Representation, Modernity*. New York: Columbia University Press.

London, Kurt. 1936. *Film Music*. Translated by Eric S. Bensinger. London: Faber and Faber.

Loughney, Patrick. 2001. "Domitor Witnesses the First Complete Public Presentation of the [Dickson Experimental Sound Film] in the Twentieth Century." In *The Sounds of Early Cinema*, edited by Richard Abel and Rick Altman, 215–219. Bloomington: Indiana University Press.

Musser, Charles. 1984. "Another Look at the 'Chaser Theory.'" *Studies in Visual Communication* 10, no. 4: 24–44.

——. 1994. *The Emergence of Cinema: The American Screen to 1907*. Berkeley: University of California Press.

——. 1997. *Edison Motion Pictures, 1890–1900*. Washington, DC: Smithsonian Institution Press.

——, with Carol Nelson. 1991. *High Class Moving Pictures: Lyman H. Howe and the Forgotten Era of Traveling Exhibition, 1880–1920*. Princeton: Princeton University Press.

Neumeyer, David. 1995. "Melodrama as a Compositional Resource in Early Hollywood Sound Cinema." *Current Musicology* 57: 61–94.

——. 2000. "Introduction." In *Music and Cinema*, edited by James Buhler, Caryl Flinn, and David Neumeyer, 1–29. Hanover, NH: University Press of New England.

——. 2010. "The Resonances of Wagnerian Opera and Nineteenth-Century Melodrama in the Film Scores of Max Steiner." In *Wagner and Cinema*, edited by Jeongwon Joe and Sander L. Gilman, 152–174. Bloomington: Indiana University Press.

Raynauld, Isabelle. 2001. "Silent Sound Screenplays: What Actors Really Said." In *The Sounds of Early Cinema*, edited by Richard Abel and Rick Altman, 69–78. Bloomington: Indiana University Press.

Slowik, Michael. 2010. "'The Plasterers' and Early Sound Cinema Aesthetics." *Music, Sound, and the Moving Image* 4, no. 1: 55–75.

Steiner, Max. 1937. "Scoring the Film." In *We Make the Movies*, edited by Nancy Naumberg, 216–238. New York: W. W. Norton.

Thomson, David. 1992. *Showman: The Life of David O. Selznick*. New York: Alfred A. Knopf.

Wierzbicki, James. 2009. *Film Music: A History*. New York: Routledge.

Wolfe, Charles. 1990. "Vitaphone Shorts and *The Jazz Singer*." *Wide Angle* 12, no. 3: 58–78.

CHAPTER 3

....

OPERA AND FILM

....

MARCIA J. CITRON

OPERA and film have enjoyed a fruitful and fascinating relationship since the beginning of cinema. In the early years opera helped legitimize film by injecting cultural cachet into the mass medium. A legendary *Carmen* of 1915 epitomizes what opera was doing for film at the time. Directed by Cecil B. DeMille, the film stars Geraldine Farrar, a leading light of the Metropolitan Opera. Like most early filmic versions, this is not Bizet's opera but a story based on the opera's source, the novella by Mérimée. The music consists of a loose arrangement of the score, keeps very little singing, and has only cursory connections with the action. It was wildly successful and ensured that other filmic *Carmen*s would soon follow. As of this writing, there are more cinematic versions of *Carmen* than of any other opera.

Another landmark of silent film is Robert Wiene's 1926 version of Richard Strauss's *Der Rosenkavalier*, arranged for the screen by the composer himself working along with the opera's librettist Hugo von Hoffmansthal. Following a growing trend over the past decade, orchestras have offered the restored print of this movie in concert halls with the synchronized live performance that Wiene and Strauss assumed. At one such presentation, by the Houston Symphony in 2009, I was struck by the idea that the opera's creators could tailor their work so imaginatively for another medium.

Both *Carmen* and *Der Rosenkavalier* demonstrate the potential richness of the opera/film interaction. The subject is vast, and scholars have approached it in diverse ways. A general discussion of the field appears in my essay "Opera and Visual Media," written for *The Oxford Handbook of Opera* (Citron forthcoming). The present chapter serves as a companion piece to its Handbook cousin and is more targeted in scope, centered on opera's musical functioning in film (since the present volume stresses music). The treatment here will be selective and depend on which elements and films have received attention in the literature. Although the focus is mainly on the contributions of musicologists, many disciplines have produced exciting work on the opera/film encounter. This eclecticism is an important context for understanding the interdisciplinary texture of the research and musicologists' debt to scholars in other fields.

Exploration of opera and film began outside musicology. Jeremy Tambling, a scholar of comparative literature, authored the first serious monograph in 1987. Entitled *Opera, Ideology and Film*, the study is a thinly veiled Marxist critique of opera and its reactionary values (Tambling 1987). Although it skirts engagement with music, *Opera, Ideology and Film* became the seminal study of opera and film and, perhaps unintentionally, established a modest canon of full-length films of opera. Musicology picked up the thread in the 1990s, a move that coincided with disciplinary expansion into film music and popular music. My article on Zeffirelli's *Otello* (1986) is an early musicological study devoted to an opera-film (Citron 1994). A few years later, *Opera on Screen* explored additional opera-films and grapples with the aesthetic challenges of the hybrid encounter (Citron 2000). *Between Opera and Cinema*, a collection edited by Jeongwon Joe and Rose Theresa, launched a new stage of research (Joe and Theresa 2002). Here the scope expands to opera in film, that is, opera's appearance in ordinary films (mainstream films), not just opera filling an entire film (opera-films). Although organized by musicologists, the volume embraces perspectives from many fields. In the past decade, then, scholars have explored both types of repertoire (opera in film and opera-film), and matters of genre, definition, and ontology have taken a backseat to aesthetics and interpretation. In recent years, however, opera in film has attracted much more attention than opera-film. There is considerably more repertoire to explore, most of the major opera-films having been studied. Beyond practical factors, however, the preference for mainstream film aligns with musicology's intense interest in film music generally. In this way, the study of opera and film does more than tie in with opera research: it figures in the field's attraction to film music in all its forms.

Other important studies include Tambling's edited volume *A Night in at the Opera*, which covers television formats as well as film but unfortunately had limited distribution (Tambling 1994). More recently, Michal Grover-Friedlander homes in on the voice's affinity for absence and death; she shows its centrality to the mutual attraction of opera and film (Grover-Friedlander 2005). My study *When Opera Meets Film* argues that opera can reveal something fundamental about a film, and vice-versa, and applies the concept of intermediality (Werner Wolf's version) to promote an understanding of the relative roles of the media when they combine (Citron 2010). Also published very recently, the one other major publication on opera and film is *Wagner and Cinema*, edited by Jeongwon Joe and Sander Gilman (Joe and Gilman 2010). This essay collection evinces an interesting shift towards media studies clustered around a figure. Wagner is not just any figure, of course, but a composer whose *Gesamtkunstwerk* lays the groundwork for film and for its interaction with opera. Moreover, Wagner is arguably the most influential classical composer on Hollywood film-scoring practices.

This chapter consists of two main sections. The first discusses important opera-films that have attracted scholarly attention. I will treat them individually and explore salient musical issues that help us understand the hybrid encounter. In the second part, opera in mainstream film takes center stage. Here the organization proceeds thematically as individual films illustrate key concepts involved in opera's musical disposition in cinema.

OPERA-FILMS

Scholars have approached the music in opera-films in myriad ways. No one model has emerged, largely because of the variety of the filmic styles and the operas chosen for cinematic treatment. Directors have come to opera-films from different backgrounds. Some, like Franco Zeffirelli and Jean-Pierre Ponnelle, are renowned directors of staged opera; others, including Francesco Rosi, Ingmar Bergman, and Michael Powell, are noted film directors. These differences suggest that a variety of preferences will be brought to the medial combination and when you consider the range of geographical and chronological provenance, it becomes clear that many variables enter into the picture (literally). Nonetheless, a helpful, if obvious, theme emerges across the studied repertoire: the style of the operatic music influences the way it is used in the film, and also the very nature of the film. As we will see, scholars have had an eye fixed on the premise that certain musical styles fit certain filmic treatments. In most cases the filmmakers also seem aware of this issue, and it appears to be a key reason why a given opera was chosen. In a few cases, however, a mismatch has led to unusual results. Although such films have generated controversy, the contested issues have led to productive insights into the glories and pitfalls of opera on film and have advanced the conceptual framework of the field.

Zeffirelli's *Otello*

Zeffirelli's 1986 *Otello* film provides a look at the challenges of adaptation from opera to film. The movie scored a hit with art-house audiences, especially in France, but fared less well with musicians and opera fans. Sensing criticism from professional quarters, the director barred music critics from the film's premiere. He had reason to do this, for the movie does some unconventional things with Verdi's music. In what follows I will present my published views on the musical problems (Citron 1994; 2000, 69–111). Then we will see a very different interpretation, by Grover-Friedlander (2005, 53–80), who proposes a positive rationale for their use.

Zeffirelli makes numerous cuts to Verdi's score. Not only do they involve entire numbers, such as the "Fuoco di gioia" chorus (Act I) and Desdemona's Willow Song (Act IV), but a substantial amount of connective material. Unlike earlier Verdi operas such as *La Traviata*, *Otello* (1887) is linear in its musical construction. The flow is basically continuous, each musical moment leads into the next, and the semideclamatory syntax binds the whole together. Otello's growing jealousy is carefully paced out in the timing and placement of musical events. In the film, Zeffirelli's cuts cause the jealousy to erupt earlier, and this exacerbates the problem of motivation that already inheres in the opera (and Shakespeare's play). These cuts also affect characterization, and the figure of Iago seems more casual than in many productions. Besides the many bits of critical musical dialogue between Otello and Iago that are omitted, the start of Act IV undergoes extensive revision that amounts to recomposition. First is a passage from several pages in, then a jump back to the opening, then a leap forward to something else, and so on. The whimsical cut-and-paste method verges on the cynical—not because of cuts per se, but because they subvert the musico-dramatic spirit of this particular opera.

Zeffirelli had reasons for the cutting and rearranging of the music. One involves the length of the film. He claims that he wanted a commercially viable movie and that meant trimming the opera so that the film came in at two hours. Although this sounds reasonable, it loses some credibility when one considers that Zeffirelli added music to the film, notably the ethnic dances that Verdi provided for the Paris production of 1893 (in the film they are in Act I). The more important reason entails Zeffirelli's aesthetic sensibilities. A designer as well as director, Zeffirelli is known for an emphasis on visuality that approaches excess, not only in filmic ventures such as *Romeo and Juliet* (1968) but in his staged operas. In his *Otello* film, the disposition of the operatic music conforms to the visual needs of his treatment, but at the same time one can argue that the visual excess reduces the success of the filmic opera. The relationship can also be expressed in theoretical terms that apply to cinema. The issue revolves around the compensatory function of one filmic element for another. The underlying premise is that cinema as a medium constitutes a lack—reality does not appear on the screen but a manufactured world that attempts to pass for it. Scored music becomes a way to compensate for that fundamental lack. Yet when the music itself has holes, as in Zeffirelli's film, music arguably is unable to do what it is supposed to do in film. As a result, viewers may be left with an uneasy feeling with respect to the visual component as they watch the movie.

To a great extent the key issue is what sort of opera is suitable for what sort of filmic treatment—or in this particular case, the cinematic implications of continuous opera *versus* number opera. A sense of verticality replaces the linearity of Verdi's continuous score and produces "a luxuriating in the moment: an aesthetic that ties in well with the filmmaker's propensity for the visual" (Citron 2000, 82). Zeffirelli appears to convert Verdi's opera to number opera, and in the process the aesthetic rhythm approaches that of the film musical. Ultimately, as I suggested above, one has to ask if the result is successful. Although I am seduced by the visual beauty, I believe that the director could have expended his luxurious urges more productively on another opera. Actually, he had already done that in his extremely successful film of *La Traviata* (1982), whose score of individual numbers lends itself to Zeffirelli's visual opulence (see Tambling 1987, 176–93).

In contrast, Grover-Friedlander (2005, 53–80) views the *Otello* film in a positive light. In her monograph on voice, loss, and death, a chapter is devoted to Zeffirelli's movie. She characterizes Verdi's opera as "the quest for perfect song" and contends that the film achieves this in some respects and not in others. Addressing the director's cut and paste methods, Grover-Friedlander refutes my objections. In her opinion, the cuts and rearranging pose little problem because they are not the essence of "song" that she considers special to the opera. These transitional passages, or "little songs," do not convey essential information, and thus the new connections that result from the changes do not harm the more fully formed sections of song. What is kept in the "little songs" is sufficient to impart what needs to be conveyed. I am not sure whether this refers to music, plot, or the larger point about the stylistic goal of song. But even if inferred generally, the interpretation glosses over the awkward seams at the junctures and implies that the larger musical moments are what we should focus on. Perhaps Grover-Friedlander is right. In the event, however, the seams loom larger because of the clumsy reconnections, much like a badly compiled film score. Of course, this raises the question of what is attended to in a film of an opera with a continuous score. Much of this may depend on musical knowledge and the extent to which the visual occupies one's attention over the aural.

When Grover-Friedlander turns to the eliminated Willow Song, a defining number in Verdi's work, one that epitomizes "perfect song," and thus a stumbling block to her theory, she reads its omission in technical terms. She argues that although it is cut, some of the aria is present in the snippets inserted elsewhere in the rearranged score at the start of Act IV. This presence acts to confirm the opera's emphasis on interruptions. It also means that "the vocal narrative is sustained by not sounding the singing voice" (Grover-Friedlander 2005, 79). Not coincidentally, the stress on absence is thematic across the volume.

Beyond our divergent views, it is fair to say that the beauty of Zeffirelli's *Otello* renders it an appealing visual experience. But its success as an opera-film is less certain because of the unconventional, and arguably cavalier, treatment of the music.

Syberberg's *Parsifal*

Syberberg's *Parsifal* (1982) is a very different opera-film from *Otello*. Taking aim at Wagner and Wagnerism, it trades in ideology and deploys postmodernist methods to convey its message. In the process, operatic performance and its conventions are subverted in basic ways. It could be argued that the challenge to opera is Syberberg's main goal, but I see it as one of several strategies to deconstruct and critique Wagner. Tambling had it right when he wrote that "the composer is on trial" in the film (Tambling 1987, 196). And since Wagner represents an iconic operatic figure, it makes sense to challenge operatic conventions as part of the critique. I stress music here, but the larger ideological apparatus probably represents the most striking aspect of the film and the one that has attracted the most attention (Tambling 1987, 194–212; Nattiez 1993, 290–91; Joe 1998, 136–87; Citron 2000, 112–19, 141–60). As we will see, however, the musical issues are inseparable from ideology.

Actors fill most of the main roles and lip-sync to the recorded voices of singers. The character Parsifal is depicted by two actors in succession. In the most sensational feature of the film, the second Parsifal is played by a woman, who takes over from the first Parsifal after he spurns Kundry's sexual advances in Act II. Interestingly, the gender of the two Parsifals moves towards an androgynous position in the middle because of the ambiguous definition of the actors: Michael Kutter looks feminine, and Karin Krick masculine—see Figure 3.1. Another intriguing element characterizes these figures. They are not actors, but people Syberberg met at a dinner party. This avoidance

FIGURE 3.1 Syberberg's *Parsifal* (1982), androgyny of the two Parsifals.

of professionals demonstrates the director's remarkably casual attitude towards performance and opera. Amateurs suffice, and the polish of professionals is irrelevant or even dishonest. Syberberg cast amateurs in other films, which are similarly long disquisitions on Germanic guilt. In *Parsifal*, the bodies of the dualistic title role serve as receptacles for the voice. This arrangement illustrates Carolyn Abbate's notion of ventriloquism, a useful concept introduced into musicology to characterize performative relationships that entail a voice whose source is housed in another body or is ambiguous (Abbate 1991). Furthermore, the two Parsifal bodies are tethered to one voice. In contrast to typical Wagnerian practices, a light tenor voice (Reiner Goldberg) sings the role instead of a massive *Heldentenor*, and its androgyny blends with the visual emitters onscreen. Still, viewers are jolted when they hear the male voice "sung" by the female body. Vocal performance is further subverted by horrible lip-syncing—opinions run the gamut on whether it was intentional. As all these features suggest, the film thematizes separation and the fragmentation of performance elements typically found in opera and filmic opera.

In contrast to the amateurs, professional actress Edith Clever portrays Kundry. She gives a sophisticated gestural performance and is very aware of the "listening body" as a separate entity from the emitting voice. Thomas Elsaesser has noted how the slight hesitations between the vocal sound and Clever's lip-syncing make the sometimes animal-like character more believable (cited in Citron 2000, 152–53). Amfortas is depicted onscreen by the conductor, Armin Jordan, who exhibits the same inexperience with the lip-syncing. In Act III the actor and the conductor combine in the filmic space. During the Good Friday music, Jordan's image appears on the screen as he conducts the moving instrumental passage. This intrusion into the fiction implies that the music requires work for its realization and allows Syberberg to interrupt the hypnotic power of Wagner's art. In this way it contributes to the film's deconstruction of the Wagnerian myth.

Finally, I would like to comment on the astonishing opening sequence on the soundtrack. Consisting entirely of instrumental music, it forms a three-part layering process that moves from chaos to coherence. First come disjunct primal sounds that arise out of nothingness and prefigure Kundry's moans later in the work. Then there are fragments of the orchestra rehearsal, which sound over images of historical destruction as real and imagined ruin appears in photos strewn behind the title credits. In the third stage we get fully formed music. As the glorious Prelude intones, Syberberg enacts a minidrama that shows the prehistory and foretells what is to come. A flashback to Parsifal as a boy has him watching a puppet show of Kundry's seduction of Amfortas and Klingsor's wounding him. Then time flashes forward as a puppet of the grown Parsifal wounds a swan. Besides contributing to visual time, the theatrical events keep Wagner's music grounded and assist in Syberberg's demythification of the composer. Musically, the director's tripartite structure resonates with the Prelude in an important way. Just as the three sections progress from chaos to coherence, so Wagner's Prelude moves from formative musical material to its realization. Syberberg's preview of the process through compiled musical material becomes a creative way to launch his critique of Wagner.

Rosi's *Bizet's Carmen*

Francesco Rosi's movie from 1983, during a decade when many *Carmen* films appeared, is one of the most satisfying opera-films ever made. One reason involves the film's musical treatment, which accords extremely well with the needs of cinema and the style of the film. I discuss this in *Opera on Screen* (Citron 2000, 161–204), but there are other important studies that explore the film (Tambling 1987, 13–40; McClary 1992, 141–46; Leicester 1994). Although ideology draws some attention in my inquiry, the other studies place it at the center and use it as an organizing theme. Like many opera-films by movie directors, such as Syberberg's *Parsifal*, Rosi's movie presents a point of view and uses the opera to express it. Here it is class and society, not the composer or the opera, that is under interrogation. In the process the director celebrates Bizet's music while simultaneously diminishing its status as opera. This may seem contradictory, but no such conflict emerges in the film. *Bizet's Carmen* works magnificently as opera, as cinema, and as opera-film.

The music comes across as film music more than as opera music; *Carmen's* score is conducive to that sort of treatment. As *opéra comique* it consists of individual numbers that are separated by dialogue. The close connection with spoken drama, especially popular theater, nudges the work toward the dramaturgy of mainstream film. In addition to musical pieces and spoken text, *Carmen* includes idioms that blend the two discourses, especially melodrama, where dialogue appears over instrumental music. Of course, this refers to Bizet's first version rather than the all-music version made for Vienna in late 1875, although some differences between them are not so clear-cut. The music features a wonderful discursive mobility as it transitions from one idiom to another, and the flexibility suits the cinematic needs very well. Meanwhile, with an abundance of tuneful melodies, regular phrase structure, homophonic accompaniments, and strophic form, the score displays a delightful popular style. In many places it borrows from cabaret and pointedly departs from high-opera style. We need only think of the iconic "Habanera" or "Gypsy Song" to appreciate *Carmen*'s roots in rhythm and dance, topoi that have figured in cinema since the start of sound.

These features enable Rosi's film to feel like a film musical much of the time, no doubt a key reason for the movie's success at the box office. Rick Altman's concept of the "audio dissolve," which he sees as a central aspect of film musicals (Altman 1987, 62–73), figures in several places in *Bizet's Carmen*. The audio dissolve describes a situation in which full-blown music is approached or left by a more remote or skeletal musical element, such as a tune on a radio or the rhythm of clapping. This device allows musical numbers to blend into the prevailing discourse of the film, namely speech, and this promotes a sense of realism. In the Rosi, several numbers are approached or left with an audio dissolve. Although many devolve to the discursive mobility of Bizet's score, some numbers feature an added transitional element, for example the clapping of the dancers after the conclusion of the Habanera and the Gypsy Song.

Another way in which the film works well cinematically involves its approach to opera. Basically, *Bizet's Carmen* downplays opera. Important moments in opera-film are typically rendered by camerawork that expresses their operatic significance. Rosi's film, however, disrupts such support in order to blunt the operaticness of opera. For example, in the Love Duet of Act I between Don José and Micaela, at the culminating final cadence the camera remains at an objectified remove and we see a donkey pass in front of the figures. Not only is this an affront to the supposed love between the two, but it implicitly mocks opera's high-minded ideals. Elsewhere, many numbers feature a heavy dose of noise that competes with the music—an effect that H. Marshall Leicester terms "the musicalization of the noise track" (Leicester 1994, 269). In a sense, Altman's audio dissolve is being applied simultaneously to discursive elements, not successively. This arrangement might seem to be a slap to opera, but in fact the opposite is true: opera's "suppression" leads to a brilliantly successful opera-film. One of the reasons is that Rosi recognizes the musico-dramatic implications of Bizet's populist score and fashions an utterly appropriate cinematic treatment around it.

Powell and Pressburger's *The Tales of Hoffmann*

From several decades earlier comes another populist opera-film: Michael Powell's *The Tales of Hoffmann* (1951), made in collaboration with screenwriter Emeric Pressburger (the team was called the "Archers") (see Babbington and Evans 1994, Citron 2000,

112–41, 158–60, and Stern 2002). *Hoffmann* represents a sequel to the Archers' hit movie *The Red Shoes* (1948), a dance film that influenced blockbuster musicals such as *An American in Paris* (1951) and *The Band Wagon* (1953). *Hoffmann* also foregrounds dance, to the point where opera-film becomes ballet-film. It reprises the leading dancers of *Shoes*, including Moira Shearer, Léonide Massine, and Robert Helpmann, who fill most key roles of the opera, with the exception of Hoffmann and Antonia, portrayed by singers. As in Rosi's movie, *Hoffmann* takes on qualities of mainstream film, but here opera yields to dance and fantasy. Its whimsical visual look shows the influence of the animated classic *Fantasia* (1940) and the surrealist style of 1920s German expressionism. The presentation of *Tales* in English translation also serves to dilute operaticness and heighten the appeal to Anglo-American audiences.

Like *Carmen*, Offenbach's opera is perfectly suited to this type of treatment. *Les Contes de Hoffmann* belongs to a popular genre (here *opéra fantastique*) and represents a blend of dialogue and interspersed numbers that betrays its roots in theater. Although not as light as his operettas that captured the spirit of the *belle époque*, *Contes* sports a musical style that is tuneful and pleasing. The Archers' film conveys this by avoiding heavy voices on the soundtrack. Even Robert Rounseville (Hoffmann), who appeared in musicals onstage and onscreen, produces a sound that is closer to Mario Lanza or Nelson Eddy than to a big-name opera singer—another way that *Tales* situates itself within popular cinema.

As a ballet-film that uses opera, *Tales* places a spotlight on performance. Lesley Stern coins the term "operality" to describe the "histrionic" quality of the film's emphasis on performance (Stern 2002). Stern, a scholar of visual arts, applies operality to many opera-films—she seems to view the genre collectively against the backdrop of cinema—but the Archers' film is decidedly over the top in the way it presents performance. Whereas Syberberg's *Parsifal* gives us actors as receptacles for the detached voice, the dancing bodies of *Tales* take ventriloquism to another level. Not only does the physical movement "compete" with the heard music, but the voice often occupies an ambiguous location in the filmic space because it frequently is not mouthed by the dancing characters. This sort of separation typifies the centrifugal tendencies of *Tales* that made it a postmodernist work *avant la lettre*. The so-called Doll Number, Olympia's aria "Les oiseaux dans la charmille" ("Birds in woodland ways are winging" in this rendition), illustrates the fascinating dynamic between voice and dance (Citron 2000, 131–33). The coloratura piece displays its virtuosity in the choreography as much as in the music, and when Shearer's steps get difficult she stops mouthing the words. At that point a free-floating vocal signifier seems to comment on what she is doing. We could call the effect voiceover, but that term does not account for the proliferation of personas as the voice assumes a distinct narrative position and interacts with dance, dancer, and the character Olympia. The separation also implies that Olympia may hear the voice when she does not mime the words. In fact, at one point Olympia cranes her neck as if she is listening to something. Of course, another element behind the separation is that much of the melismatic music lacks words, and the absence of substantive meaning allows the music to float and hook up with other narrative functions.

Throughout *Tales* the emphasis on movement is akin to mime. In some places, especially Helpmann's depiction of the four villains, movement turns highly stylized and takes on the melodramatic gestures of silent film. Powell had worked in silent movies when he was young, and he likened the soundless environment of shooting an opera-film to the earlier era. Without the need to synchronize sound and image on the set, both idioms afford an expanded range of visual possibilities. In *Tales*, for example, a few places show the sort of accelerated movements seen in silent films. The director summed up his appreciation for the increased freedoms by dubbing *Tales* "the fully composed film" (Citron 2000, 116). The term also acknowledges the convenience of a preexistent sound stream that allows for the visual experimentation. Playback becomes an advantage, not a drawback.

Most of Offenbach's score does appear in *Tales*, but the film omits several numbers and rearranges others to fit the scenario. Many changes appear in the Prologue and Epilogue, which were modified for the new emphasis on dance. Unlike Rosi's film, Powell and Pressburger's movie does not deploy the version of the opera with spoken dialogue. As we have seen, *Tales* depends on other devices to tamp operaticness and create a populist film.

A dazzling explosion of color and effect, the Archers' *Tales of Hoffmann* is arguably one of the most original films of the 1950s in any genre. Martin Scorsese, a big fan of Powell, is effusive in his praise of *Tales* and notes that it made a huge impact on him as an aspiring director (Scorsese 1992). This is a fitting tribute to the exhilarating opera-film, which is now part of the Criterion Collection of classic films.

Ponnelle's Opera-Films

We close this portion of the chapter with a look at the opera-films of Jean-Pierre Ponnelle. Made for European television in the 1970s and 1980s, Ponnelle's films rely heavily on music to structure image (Citron 2010, 97–135). Ponnelle was a famous opera director, and as a trained musician he regularly consulted the orchestral score during rehearsal. His most cinematic opera-films—*Madama Butterfly* (1973), *Le nozze di Figaro* (1976), and *Rigoletto* (1983)—show music as a major impetus for visual decisions. For example, cuts between shots often occur at key musical divisions. Sometimes a musical procedure that marks growth, such as a crescendo or an approach to a cadence, is rendered by a zoom or tracking shot; or an important arrival point in the music is articulated by a major change in the visual language. Such effects occur in every opera-film, but what is striking about Ponnelle's practices is how often they appear. The director acknowledged that visual elements of camerawork correspond to specific musical effects and that this sort of thinking guides his visual decisions. Another aspect of his musically centered films involves a multiplication of narrative strands. Much of that entails the use of "interior singing"—heard music on the soundtrack that lacks moving lips of the character associated with it. For example, in the Countess's aria "Dove sono" in *Figaro* or the start of the Love Duet in *Butterfly*, interior singing expands the subjective realm of the character by showing thinking or some other layer of interiority. Ponnelle makes judicious use of the device and lets musical affect, text, drama, and interpretation guide the decision of when to use it.

On the whole, Ponnelle's emphasis on music takes precedence over other sorts of aims, especially the sort of social criticism and filmic experimentation seen in other opera-films. As a result he has been passed over as an auteur, for the term typically designates an avant-garde figure. Ponnelle's opera-films are revelatory from a musical standpoint and deserve more attention than they have received (Citron 2010, 134–35). That having been said, they are cinematically conservative in comparison with many opera-films and have had little impact on other filmmakers of opera.

OPERA IN FILM

Because opera has been used in so many ways in mainstream film, it is difficult to articulate a theme with broad application to the repertoire. One possible way to theorize opera in film is the extent to which opera reveals something fundamental about the movie. In some films, opera is so integral that it provides access to the very nature and meaning of the film—what Marc A. Weiner perceptively dubs the "interpretive key" (Weiner 2002, 75). In others, opera is more incidental and serves a decorative role. In the following discussions I will organize the material thematically and elaborate with specific films. As we will see, in most of these movies opera plays an integral role and contributes something essential to the tone or identity of the film. Perhaps it is a matter of self-selection that scholars have been drawn to movies in which opera is a critical element. Or perhaps it suggests quality, that better movies use opera with care and purpose, and scholars instinctively recognize this and want to work on thoughtful encounters of the media. Indeed, this became the impetus for the choice of repertoire in *When Opera Meets Film* (Citron 2010), which thematizes the idea that opera can offer access to the core of some films. A few of these movies will be treated here.

The Opera Visit

The opera visit has been a staple of cinema and has provided attractive opportunities for the development of narrative and expression of meaning. It has helped to define character, signify high culture, culminate an operatic element that pervades the film, present a parallel to the movie's plot, furnish a platform for cultural criticism, and supply an emotional climax for the film.

A famous early example is the Marx Brothers' hilarious send-up in *A Night at the Opera* (1935) (Kramer 1994; Grover-Friedlander 2005, 33–51). Verdi's *Il trovatore* undergoes comedic deconstruction in a climactic sequence that creates a happy ending for the Brothers and the romantic couple they help, who are aspiring opera singers. The opera house becomes a "site of anarchy" (Koch 1986, 25–26) as class and ritual are undermined by the scrappy outsiders. The performance receives a lot of attention. First there are the antics in the pit before the performance. As the orchestra plays the overture, Harpo smacks a line-drive with a violin to "Take Me Out to the Ballgame," whose score was inserted into the parts at the end of the slow introduction. At that point Groucho dons a vendor's uniform in the aisle and hawks peanuts to the crowd (a.k.a. audience)—see Figure 3.2. Once the action starts, several numbers are presented, with malice afoot to dent the self-importance of the work and the ritual. Chico and Harpo frolic onstage in gypsy costumes; who can forget Chico's lusty clank-clank in the Anvil Chorus or Harpo's stripping the skirt off a female dancer. Whereas these acts comment on the kitsch quality of the number, others subvert performance and operatic seriousness. For example, Harpo's manipulations of the backdrop confuse performer and audience when a battleship descends during "Di quella pira," the tenor's big aria (Figure 3.3), and Harpo literally climbs the scenery and steals the show. In this subversive display music is not criticized, only the elitist artifice behind it. Yet even as opera is mocked in this visit, the film displays a big dash of affection for the art form (Kramer 1994, 257).

Opera serves important dramatic ends in the visit in *The Godfather: Part III* (1990), the final installment of Coppola's epic of the Corleone family (Citron 2010, 19–57; also Franke 2006, Greene 2000). The scene is perhaps *the* iconic opera visit in film. Parts I and II of Coppola's trilogy are suffused with an operatic sensibility in tone, pacing, and ritual; Part III actualizes it through performed opera in the climax at the end. Not coincidentally, the work is Mascagni's *Cavalleria rusticana*, an opera about Sicilian

FIGURE 3.2 *A Night at the Opera* (1935), Groucho "at the ballpark."

FIGURE 3.3 *A Night at the Opera* (1935), *Il Trovatore* with battleship scrim.

codes of justice. These codes echo themes in the saga and affirm the Sicilian roots of the Corleones, whose ethnic identity assumes form in the nostalgic tone of the films. The performance venue, the opera house in Palermo, further affirms the significance of Sicily. Opera is intimately linked to the family through son Anthony, who sings the lead role (Turiddu) and is the reason they are there. Opera's exaggerated musical style, especially in the *verismo* aesthetic of Mascagni, captures the grand emotions associated with the fortunes of the family. More specifically, opera affords the needed majesty for the over-the-top sequence in which scores are settled at the highest level. Parts I and II end with blowout scenes of violent carnage intercut with cold normality that seemingly could not topped. But opera accomplishes just that in the finale and demonstrates its ability to resolve cinematic drama on the largest scale.

Several numbers of the opera appear, although not always in sequential order. That is of little consequence, for what matters is the dramatic power of the editing between the stage and other events. These include actual and threatened violence in the hall, public spaces, and locations in Rome, including the Vatican. We do hear Mascagni's music when the stage is shown, but it also often sounds when other places are shown. Meanwhile, events onstage and in the filmic story are connected. For example, after the Pope is found dead we see the parade of penitents onstage; and after the Archbishop is murdered we hear operatic cries that Turiddu has been killed. The most sensational musical effect comes when Nino Rota's scored music is layered atop the opera music. Just as the opera visit actualizes the saga's operatic tone, so this extraordinary combination affirms the operatic quality of Rota's evocative score, a key factor in the success of Parts I and II.

The real climax of the opera scene and the trilogy occurs on the steps of the theater after the performance. Here, instrumental music and the absence of voice supply the ultimate meaning. The Intermezzo from Mascagni's opera accompanies Michael's devastation (and ours) after daughter Mary is murdered before his eyes. Utterly moving, it reinforces the Romantic idealization of instrumental music as the best vehicle for emotional transcendence. In this way it hearkens back to the "voiceless" operatic style of much of the saga as feeling trumps substantive meaning through words. As the lush music continues, the past also appears in flashbacks to happy times in his life. It is interesting that the instrumental impulse serves to bookend the opera visit, which began with the mystical Prelude that opens Mascagni's work. This suppression of the vocal is expressed in another striking element of the scene: Michael's emitting a forceful silent scream before he can vocalize it. The glorious mix of presence and absence, sound and silence, that shapes the scene testifies to the power of opera to register what is special about a special movie.

Something entirely different happens in the opera visit in *Quantum of Solace* (2008) (Citron 2011). The film presents a performance of Puccini's *Tosca* at a real location, the Bregenz Opera Festival situated at the edge of the Bodensee (Lake Constance) in Austria. It is the scene in which Bond and his foes come together in a public space. This is no ordinary space, but an open-air arena whose stage literally floats on the water. It comes to symbolize the trope of detachment that characterizes the scene. Although most opera visits idealize the genre and convey its idealizing powers, *Quantum*'s visit promotes separation and blunts what can be termed operatic subjectivity—the narrative, performative, and communicative elements that characterize the genre. Bond and the other main characters are present in the hall, but no one is watching the performance. Instead, they are engaged in private conversations via earpieces. In the second part of the scene they are in adjacent spaces, and the super-fast montage during a restaurant chase precludes subjective connection with the flashes of performed opera. The production also contributes to the detachment. The backdrop set, which is always enormous at Bregenz given its super-size stage, features a huge eye that signifies Big Brother in a postmodern age (Figure 3.4). It suggests that the usual specular dynamic of opera is reversed, as now the stage watches the audience instead of the other way around. Bond's position atop the set as he scans the audience for the villains and snaps their photo affirms the arrangement; meanwhile, Bond himself is being watched by a monitor at MI6's headquarters in London. Opera almost becomes superfluous.

The disposition of the music adds to the detachment. An introductory section, with repetitive music by the film's composer, David Arnold, gives us a dry sound environment that separates Bond from the reality around him and sets up his subjective isolation during the opera proper (Figure 3.5). Part 1 of the performance, inside the hall, presents the massive concerted Te Deum that ends Act I. At some places the operatic voice disappears to allow the conspirators' conversation to be heard (by us). This rebalancing among sound elements has been a standard feature of film since the start of the sound

FIGURE 3.4 *Quantum of Solace* (2008), the floating stage.

FIGURE 3.5 *Quantum of Solace* (2008), Bond alone in a crowd.

era (Altman, Jones, and Tatroe 2000). Here it interrupts operatic communication and nudges the musical functioning towards underscoring, as all we hear is accompanimental instrumental music. In part 2 the separation from opera becomes more apparent. Against fractured image and breakneck visual speed, the section uses extremely slow music. It is the melodramatic instrumental passage that occurs in the opera after Tosca has killed Scarpia (a similar passage also accompanies earlier action). Not only is there a disconnect between the slow music and the fast image, but the music promotes detachment in other ways. For one thing, it takes on a hyperreal feel because of the extremely dry sound environment around it, which is more pronounced than in the introductory part of the scene. Yet the music itself is highly resonant and seems more melodramatic and lurid than usual. This relates to the second aspect of the music's detachment: it functions as filmic underscoring. With hardly any of the performed opera shown, and that only in microsecond flashes, Puccini's music is effectively detached from the opera. These cinematic uses of the opera confirm Puccini's reputation as a composer of strong cinematic bent. Peter Franklin, for one, characterizes the score of *Tosca* as movie music in everything but name (Franklin 1994, 84).

Quantum of Solace is certainly an action-thriller, and it is striking to find an opera visit in this genre. In light of this, it would be a mistake to conclude that *Quantum's* reconception of the event represents a new way that all will follow. Its disposition of the opera visit resonates powerfully in an age of medial experimentation, and it brilliantly uses opera to capture the sense of alienation in modern culture. But *Quantum* probably represents only one among many future paths. Filmic genre and interpretive goals will continue to determine how the opera visit is rendered in film.

OPERA ON THE SOUNDTRACK

Opera has appeared on the soundtrack in numerous forms and films, and I can only scratch the surface here. An interesting arrangement of opera on the soundtrack involves the diegetic use of an operatic number. Two films that have received critical attention organize a pivotal scene around an operatic piece: *The Shawshank Redemption* (1994) and *Philadelphia* (1993). In both cases the scene stands apart from the prevailing narrative and has been identified as a high point of the film.

The Shawkshank Redemption, directed by Frank Darabont, is about an innocent man, Andy (Tim Robbins), who is sent to prison for the murder of his wife. Supportive of his fellow inmates, he forms a close relationship with Red (Morgan Freeman), and the two slowly dig an escape tunnel. In the midst of the numbing prison routine, Andy finds an LP of Mozart's *Le nozze di Figaro* in the warden's office—see Figure 3.6. He places the Letter Duet on the phonograph and moments later broadcasts it over the prison's PA system. This becomes a transfixing experience for the inmates, who stop what they are doing as they succumb to the magic of Mozart's music. Red narrates the effect of the music in voiceover: although folks didn't know what it was and couldn't make out the words, they felt the specialness of the moment as music transported them to another place: "And for the briefest of moments every last man at Shawshank felt free" (quoted in Hunter 2002a, 94). In Mary Hunter's characterization, the piece creates a "culture of feeling" that is central to the film, which trades in sentiment much more than the novella that inspired it.

The duet forges other connections with the film, although none is particularly obvi-ous (Hunter 2002a, 97–106, the basis of this paragraph). In Mozart's opera, the Letter Duet marks an important moment in the relationship between Susanna, the lady's maid, and the Countess, her mistress. It is here we see musical expression of their rather equal relationship and close friendship. The Countess is dictating a letter that Susanna writes down, and the musical line the Countess proffers is repeated by Susanna. The musical equivalence expresses their dramatic equality, which represents a radical concept for the late eighteenth century (see Allanbrook 1983). In the Duet's recapitulation, where the musical similarities are more exact, a striking role reversal occurs as Susanna takes

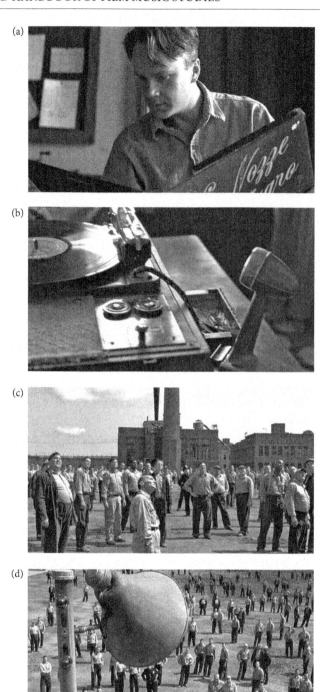

FIGURE 3.6 a–d: *The Shawshank Redemption* (1994), Mozart over the PA system.

the lead and the Countess follows. Hunter contends that this unlikely friendship resonates with the interclass and interracial relationship in *Shawshank*: Andy is white, professional, and highly educated, while Red is black, poor, and barely educated. The duet
symbolizes their special bond. Another parallel, though more remote, entails the pastoral feel of the piece. Building on the work of Wye Allanbrook, who considers the opera
a pastoral, Hunter sees a connection between the pastoral quality of the Duet and the
movie's ending on a remote beach with Red and Andy reunited. Of course, on a basic
level the very idea of doubleness is expressed by the Duet, and that plays out in Andy and
Red's reactions to the music.

Hunter goes further in her interpretation of what the piece accomplishes in the film.
She argues that the prisoners' communal wonderment as they listen means that the
piece taps into ideals of "universality and fraternity" (Hunter 2002a, 103). Although an
appeal to the universal may be too broad—the label runs the risk of effacing nuances
of class, race, and narrative—Hunter is on the mark when she points out how the piece
stops time in the film. The leisurely quality of the pastoral mode and the beauty of the
blended voices, which often sing in thirds, combine to put listeners both inside and outside the film into another zone. Mozart's glorious music will do that, as we will see later
in the discussion of *Sunday, Bloody Sunday* (1971).

A similar suspension of time occurs in *Philadelphia* when opera is invoked (Weiner
2002). Jonathan Demme's film of 1993 tells the story of Andrew Beckett (Tom Hanks),
a gay lawyer at a high-end firm who conceals his sexuality but discovers he has AIDS.
When the law firm finds out it fires him, Andy mounts a lawsuit charging discrimination.
Andy hires Joe Miller (Denzel Washington), an ambulance-chasing attorney, to make
the case. Andy eventually loses and dies, but his battle is inflected with an extraordinary
scene that involves opera. In the middle of the film Joe visits Andrew's house to review
strategy. Distracted and somewhat uncooperative, Andrew wants to show him what's
important in life. He puts on an LP of Maria Callas singing the aria "La mamma morta"
from Giordano's *Andrea Chénier*. In what Mitchell Morris describes as a cross between
"a music appreciation lecture, a translation (from the music and from the Italian), and a
lip-synch" (Morris 1994, as quoted in Weiner 2002, 76), Andrew conveys aloud what is
happening in the music. The scene is completely different from the rest of the film: the
camera shoots from on high, the visual look is heightened through strong colored filters,
Andrew's face is bathed in sweat as he gesticulates, and his movements are captured in
a swirling pattern as if he is a performer. Synaesthesia overtakes reality in the surfeit
of sensation. Callas's voice engulfs everything, especially with the increased volume as
the scene progresses. Andrew seems to merge bodily with the mystical attraction of her
voice, enacting the metaphorical sexual process described by Wayne Koestenbaum in
The Queen's Throat: Opera, Homosexuality, and the Mystery of Desire (1993).

Marc Weiner, a scholar of Germanic Studies, explores the cultural and aesthetic
meanings of this scene. His main point is that the sequence embodies phantasmagoria: Adorno's term for a hypnotic aesthetic experience that effaces reality and takes one
to a fantastic and dangerous realm. This charge was leveled not only by Adorno, but also

by Nietzsche and others against Wagner, but Weiner in no way condemns the film for the effect. In fact, in explaining how phantasmagoria works in the scene, Weiner implicitly praises its impact. Meanwhile, he notes how phantasmagoria acts to suspend time, creating an atemporality that is so strong that the aria appears to extend well past its literal length. Further ambiguity resides in the scene's ideology. Weiner is persuasive when he contends that opera seems to undergo contradictory impulses in the film. On the one hand, its ephemeral nature and its ability to efface reality appear to be criticized. On the other hand, the very fact of a striking presentation of opera serves to buttress the genre. I would add that another potential problem is that Giordano's *verismo* aesthetic is quite different from Wagner's operatic disposition. Nonetheless, Weiner is right when he argues that the filmic disposition of the operatic music is Wagnerian, or rather, Wagnerian in terms of how Adorno and others have interpreted his aesthetic. Thus, although Weiner's critique omits musical style, it captures what is significant about this extraordinary scene.

The film *Sunday, Bloody Sunday*, directed by John Schlesinger, offers another fascinating example of opera on the soundtrack (Citron 2010, 212–45). Here one operatic number occurs several times and becomes a signature leitmotif for the movie. It is the stunning trio "Soave sia il vento" from *Così fan tutte*, a number that has probably elicited more commentary than any other in that opera. Described as the embodiment of the trope of beauty (Hunter 1999, 286–87, 296–98) and a piece that suspends time (Goehring 2004, 186–87), "Soave" symbolizes the elusiveness of desire in Mozart's enigmatic work. It is but a short step to Schlesinger's film about the vagaries of desire in a romantic triangle that has a young man in simultaneous relationships with a middle-aged man and woman. Before we discuss it further, it is worth noting that other films also use the Trio, including Mike Nichols's *Closer* (2004) (Citron 2010, 212–45) and the French movie *Comme une image* (2003), directed by and starring Agnès Jaoui. In my view this is not coincidental, for the Trio's sensual quality enables it to serve the needs of other artistic media, especially cinema.

The first of the six cues in *Sunday* is diegetic. Daniel, a fifty-ish physician, gently drops an LP on the turntable and "Soave" begins. The piece establishes Daniel as an orderly person with refined tastes and at the same time places quotation marks around the piece. The event is ritualized by a close-up of the disc dropping and the needle being engaged, all this before a note is heard. We see Daniel listening to the music, and as he does so his artistic senses are heightened by gazing at his lover Bob's installation of water-filled tubes in the backyard. The image is a pun on the music: "Soave's" text eulogizes wafting winds and gentle waves, and the main musical gesture consists of undulating figures in the strings. Daniel's sensory world is expressed in the piece.

In most of the other cues, "Soave" accompanies a gaze of sexual desire. Sometimes it is Alex, the female lover, who looks with longing at the elusive love object who is Bob; and sometimes it is Daniel who focuses on Bob. Rarely does it emanate from Bob himself, who is immature, irresponsible, and incapable of forming a deep relationship. At the same time that "Soave" charts the ironies of unfulfilled desire, it resonates with the practicality of the older characters. Daniel in particular is guided by reason in his highly ordered world. This parallels another major feature of the Trio: its roots in Baroque rationality in features such as the cut-time pulse, the basso-continuo-like bass, and the imitative and essentially a cappella section that provides the main tension of the piece (Citron 2010, 216–24). In other words, the character of Daniel—and to some extent Alex—is reflected in the musical makeup of "Soave," and its subtle mix of desire and reason beautifully expresses the emotional agonies experienced by the older figures.

Except for various diegetic entertainment pieces and a hearing of a Schubert Impromptu on an LP, "Soave" is the only music on the soundtrack. This presents an interesting situation, for Mozart's music runs the risk of being desensitized through the repetition. It might come to seem less operatic, less intense, less fraught with emotion, after multiple hearings. It is true that each time the piece is played it begins and ends at a slightly different place in the music, and only over the final credits is the number complete. But I do not believe the average viewer would notice the starting and ending points, nor would this affect their sense that the same music is used repeatedly. The music functions like a leitmotif, and each appearance registers the psychological state of desire at that moment. This acts to preclude a dilution of the music's powerful affect. In fact, the viewer's growing familiarity with the music probably adds to its effectiveness. For in this film with little in the way of plot, feeling matters most. The self-destructive impulses of Alex and Daniel are close to the surface throughout the film, and each time "Soave" sounds that emotional state is crystallized for us. That in itself is operatic, and the Trio does not lose its powerful affect. The diegetic status of the first iteration defines the number as opera, and the impression stays with us through the film.

THE OPERA-IMITATION SCORE

In some movies, the underscore riffs on real opera pieces to produce "faux" opera. Usually this happens in a film where opera also makes an appearance. A marvelous example is *Prizzi's Honor* (1985), directed by John Huston (Hunter 2002a). A wacky film that Pauline Kael likens to "*The Godfather* [1972] acted out by the Munsters" (Kael 1994, 1065), *Prizzi* uses "a daring comic tone" to tell the story of a Brooklyn mob family and the charged yet goofy relationship between Charley Partanna (Jack Nicholson), the Prizzis's main hit man, and Irene Walker (Kathleen Turner), his new WASP wife who turns out to be a freelance assassin. Hovering ghoulishy is Maerose Prizzi (Angelica Huston), a gaudily stylish figure who was dishonored by Charley but still has feelings for him. Opera appears in literal form a few times. Puccini's "O mio babbino caro" (from *Gianni Schicchi*) is heard in the background from a radio, as Maerose lies to her prim father in his dining room about what Charley "did to her" sexually—see Figures 3.7a–b. The choice of aria is telling. *Schicchi* parallels the film's plot of shady dealings involving money, honor, and family, and has a similar air of far-flung parody. Parody also inheres in the irony of the opera's aria of filial persuasion in the name of ideal love appearing in a place of such deceit in the film. Later, Don Corrado (William Hickey), the shriveled head of the clan, listens to another operatic work, "Questo o quella" from *Rigoletto*.

(a)

(b)

FIGURE 3.7 a, b: *Prizzi's Honor* (1985), Maerose and her father. "O mio babbino caro" sounds in the background.

Prizzi's blurring of real and fake resonates in the film score. The overtures to Rossini's *La gazza ladra* and *The Barber of Seville* make literal appearances, but they are riffed many other times to the point where they are as much North's music as they are Rossini's. As if to confuse things further, a saccharine motif with lamenting stepwise appoggiaturas features prominently on the soundtrack. In its exaggerated sentiment it seems operatic, but it functions as scored music because of its brevity, rhythmic character, and incessant repetition in many places. Yet this is the main instrumental motif of Puccini's *Gianni Schicchi*. North performs a witty musical trick: he makes literal opera music sound like scored music that sounds operatic. This sleight of hand is possible because *Gianni Schicchi* is a relatively unfamiliar work, and the borrowed ostinato idea is mainly accompanimental in the opera. Another Puccini work confuses what is borrowed and what is new: the little-known *Crisantemi* (1890), written for string quartet. It appears frequently on the soundtrack. I have not come across any identification of it in the literature on the film, and the credits do not list the borrowed pieces. My sense is that people have assumed it is new music by North—an understandable inference given its excessively affective style.

Whereas *Crisantemi* appears in literal form or close to it, North succumbs to composerly virtuosity when he combines two operatic numbers with each other: the rhythmic tag of the overture to *Barber of Seville* is layered over the habanera rhythm from Bizet's *Carmen*. This effect marks a moment of absurdity when Irene approaches a meeting with Maerose's father, who will hire her to kill Charley. The same music appears at length over the final credits. Not only does it sum up the film's operatic impulses, but artfully encapsulates the lopsided parody and dark humor that define *Prizzi's Honor*.

Another film that riffs off (rips off?) its operatic content is Mark Joffe's comedy *Cosi* (1996) (Hunter 2002b). As the title suggests, the movie has something to do with Mozart's opera. The plot concerns a young man, Lewis (Ben Mendelsohn), who finds work as a recreation director at a lovable institution for mentally ill people in Australia. He discovers he is in over his head, for the residents insist on mounting a production of *Così fan tutte*. Lots of pratfalls happen along the way, but in the end the performance, such as it is, marks a triumph for the patients and for Lewis. Meanwhile, the challenges on the job parallel those in his relationship with live-in girlfriend Lucy (Rachel Griffiths). The vagaries of love enfolded in Mozart's opera are played out by the "sane" pair and by the patients in their ties with outside loved ones.

Besides the performance proper, where a few numbers are played on an LP and the patients deliver some convoluted storyline, the soundtrack frequently presents scored music that is closely related to the opera. The most obvious is the one we hear the most: a theme with the same rhythm and ascending arpeggio that opens the Overture at the start of the slow introduction—that is, a C major arpeggio starting on the fifth (G), consisting of half-note, two quarter-notes, then a held note on the top. In addition, at a few places the soundtrack offers brief glimpses of a vocal number from the opera. The effect of this musical blending throughout the film is to erase the boundary between diegetic and nondiegetic functions. Whether it is literal or varied, the *Così* "sound" is with us as content or commentary, a persistent presence that contributes to our acceptance of the fantastic feat that is pulled off in the plot.

Sometimes an underscore variant of opera appears in a film without opera, for example, in *Trading Places* (1983, directed by John Landis), a comedy in which a black ghetto hustler (Eddie Murphy) and a rich white commodities trader (Dan Aykroyd) are switched as pawns in a bet to see how breeding holds up when social roles are reversed. Composer Elmer Bernstein supplies instrumental riffs on a few numbers from *Le nozze di Figaro*—the opera's overture and Figaro's arias "Se vuol ballare" and "Non più andrai." In fact, the opening credits roll over Mozart's overture in its original form. The literal version establishes a tone of formality that will continue in Bernstein's riffs and serve to satirize the pompous world of privilege that Aykroyd inhabits at the start. Musically the overture forms the linchpin of several classical-music knockoffs devised by Bernstein. These include, among others, a riff on the chorale passage from the last movement of Brahms's Symphony No. 1, and a variation on the start of Mendelssohn's Italian Symphony. It is as if Bernstein plays a private joke on the film, and possibly on classical music, by including so many parodies of real pieces. Of course, this treatment fits nicely with the parodic spirit behind the film and the inside bet that sets the story in motion. The prominence of *Saturday Night Live* (1975–) legends such as Aykroyd and Murphy, as well as Al Franken and James Belushi in minor roles, tells you a lot about the film. Unlike *Cosi* and *Prizzi's Honor*, the operatic riffs in *Trading Places* could easily be replaced by other classical-era pieces and not change anything fundamental about the film.

VOICE, MUTENESS, AND AURAL REMAINS

As mentioned earlier, Grover-Friedlander's study *Vocal Apparitions: The Attraction of Cinema to Opera* represents a new way of approaching the opera/film encounter (Grover-Friedlander 2005). Always subtle and often metaphorical, the book views the voice, especially the operatic voice, as a critical link between the two media. She argues that the voice need not be present to connect the two, and in fact does some of its most important work when it is absent. Even when the singing voice is present, its ephemeral nature means that its absence, in other words its death, is ontologically part of its existence. Although in some ways a pessimistic theoretical framework, it has great potential to elucidate the behavior of many films that engage opera. One attractive element involves the notion of aural remains: the idea of some vocal element that outlasts other phenomena, be they material, visual, or narrative. To elucidate how aural remains can be applied, I will discuss Grover-Friedlander's interpretation of a Fellini movie and then my take on a movie by Chabrol.

Grover-Friedlander's chapter "Fellini's Ashes" explores Fellini's film *E la nave va* (*And the Ship Sails On*, 1983) (Grover-Friedlander 2005, 131–52). The story takes place in 1914 and concerns a dead opera singer, a diva named Edmea Tutua, whose ashes are taken by ship to be scattered at sea. The ceremony will be a grand ritual, and the ship features an exotic mix of artists and fans who will share in the event. Tutua's voice lives on through her gramophone recordings, which are played aboard ship. Grover-Friedlander calls these vocal remains the singer's afterlife, a theme she pursues in other work (Grover-Friedlander 2011). But as the chapter's title suggests, the main focus is on the ashes—the meaning of the remains of the singer's body. This is broadened out to the real-life case of Maria Callas. Fellini strongly implies the link through the filmic diva's first name, Edmea, which is an anagram of "Medea," a role Callas played on screen after she had lost her voice and turned to roles in cinema. Metaphorically, the diva's ashes in the film relate to the ashes of Callas's body after she was cremated, an event that caused considerable controversy and a huge media circus. Through several rhetorical moves, Grover-Friedlander contends that the fictional and real ashes stage a phoenix-like rebirth of cinema. And why would cinema need a rebirth? The answer comes from the start of the chapter: Fellini was worried that cinema was dead, that the anemic attendance at movie houses spelled the "end of cinema" (Grover-Friedlander 2005, 131). The essay plays out the idea that the film's staging of the death of the prima donna's operatic voice also stages the threat of the demise of cinema. But at the end, which is also the end of the book, an optimistic note is sounded: "As a phoenix, a bird miraculously reborn from its own ashes, film, without allowing opera to die in its place, rises from the ashes of opera" (152).

Claude Chabrol's *La Cérémonie* (1995), considered by many his best film, is mainly a work of social criticism (Citron 2010, 136–70). Unfolding on the coast of Brittany, the story concerns the well-heeled Lelièvre family, who love art and classical music, and the building resentment of their maid, Sophie (Sandrine Bonnaire), and her explosive friend, the *postière* Jeanne (Isabelle Huppert). When Sophie's shameful secret that she cannot read is discovered, her quiet reserve is turned into deadly violence by her friend. One evening, the family are brutally murdered by the women as they watch a televised broadcast of *Don Giovanni*. After the carnage the women quietly exult in their work: Jeanne leaves with the family's portable tape recorder and Sophie cleans up. But Jeanne is killed when a car plows into her vehicle. As the police sift through the wreckage, operatic music wafts through the air from the tape recorder, which daughter Melinda (Virginie Ledoyen) set up to record the broadcast. Over a long camera shot the gunshots are heard with the family's cries, followed by the murderers' calm "Ça y est; on a bien fait" ("It's done; we did well"). These aural remains serve to represent the event, having replaced the visual as the means to truth. The implication is that this aural version of the crime will lead the police to arrest Sophie, although at film's end she walks off and we don't know what will happen. The valorizing of hearing aligns with a major aim of Chabrol in *La Cérémonie*: the critique of television, a visual medium, for its mindless entertainment and its encouragement of passive acceptance of bourgeois values. Yet lest we infer that Chabrol completely rejects the visual in favor of the aural, it is important to note that Chabrol's visual mastery behind the camera served him well in crafting subjective relationships that express his critical view of class. The triumph of the aural over the visual in *La Cérémonie* demonstrates how Chabrol trades in irony in his films, and how this elusive filmmaker is not easy to pin down.

MORE COMPLEX SITUATIONS

The movie *Moonstruck* (1987) brings a smile to the face of many filmgoers. Part of its success comes from the incorporation of opera on multiple levels, to the point where opera pervades the very fabric and essentially defines the film (Citron 2010, 173–211). Pauline Kael rightly calls *Moonstruck* "an honest contrivance" (Kael 1994, 1164), and opera's mix of feeling and artifice is key to its special tone. The plot turns on Italian-American culture in Brooklyn, where Loretta, a no-nonsense bookkeeper, becomes engaged to Johnny Camareri, a mama's boy. When he goes on a trip she meets his younger brother Ronny, a poetic baker who is both brutish and a big opera fan. They instantly fall in love, and Loretta's resistance eventually crumbles when they go to the Met to see *La Bohème*. The rest of the story plays out like an *opera buffa*, where feuds, identities, and far-flung strands are resolved. Although the *buffa* tone permeates John Patrick Shanley's off-kilter dialogue throughout, it isn't allowed to stand alone. It mixes with Puccinian *verismo* as many cues come directly from *Bohème*, some as literal quotes, others as arrangements. All are brought to a head in the film's major diegetic engagements with Puccini's music. At the opera visit, a small portion of Act III is presented onstage—the reunion of Mimì and Rodolfo when they officially part. This echoes the filmic plot, for this is supposed to be the last time that Loretta and Ronny see each other. The performed music also picks up on an important diegetic moment seen earlier. When Loretta and Ronny first meet (the day before!) and she goes to his apartment to talk, the very same music inaugurates the scene as it plays on Ronny's turntable. We see him at the phonograph, and his connection with opera is sealed (the camera had just panned down a poster of *Bohème* before it trained on the apparatus). The phonographic disposition of opera—opera on the phonograph—is something we have seen in other films (*Shawshank Redemption*; *Philadelphia*; *Sunday, Bloody Sunday*). Phonograph culture has important meaning for the way opera has been presented in film, and this is something that could be explored further. As a hint of its riches, Robynn Stilwell's essay on gender and phonograph culture in popular music (Stilwell 2006) helped me to situate Ronny's relationship to the apparatus and how that helps to explain his obsessive attraction to opera. Of course, when one thinks of operatic obsession one is reminded of the "opera queen" and its ties to homosexuality and desire (see Koestenbaum 1993). Yet just as Ronny's heterosexuality undermines this stereotype, so his refined tastes counter the image of the Italian-American working-class male. This unusual opera fan is key to the film's tone of honest contrivance.

Although the opera visit acts as the turning point, the film's real climax comes at the second encounter with opera on the phonograph. After a night together following the Met visit, Ronny is splayed out in his apartment, alone, listening to *Bohème*. As a big climax approaches—where Mimì and Rodolfo come together in ardent octaves in the Act I Love Duet—Ronny cranks up the volume and the scene shifts sharply to Loretta at the musical resolution. This is the famous image where she kicks a can down a street with her red pumps. Not only does this reprise the music from the first phonograph encounter, when Ronny carried her to his bed, but it marks the first time that opera music is tied solely to Loretta. She is opera-struck: the old Loretta is gone. It is especially extraordinary because she appears to be hearing the music, to be reacting to its magic. The effect resembles what Michel Chion dubs the *acousmêtre*, the situation in which a filmic sound has no visible source (Chion 1994, 127–31). But we know the source—it is Ronny's phonograph. Ronny's manipulation of the volume seems to be for the purpose of allowing Loretta to hear the music from afar. When that happens Ronny and Loretta are fused, and she enters the affective realm where operatic emotion resides.

A different kind of complexity attends *Aria* (1987). Conceived and produced by Don Boyd, *Aria* is a self-conscious operatic project intended to infuse opera with popular culture and to make it accessible. MTV was on the rise at the time, and the film borrows several of its features. The most obvious entails the basic construction. A collection rather than a narrative, the movie consists of ten short segments based on the music from different operas, each rendered by a different director. Boyd told the directors to use their imagination, and most of the stories have little to do with opera. Many foreground fantasy. Most of all, actors figure in the scenarios and, except for two segments where they mouth others' singing, the heard vocal music is not performed by the figures we see. The visuals seem to accompany the music, as in MTV, although they lack the genre's emphasis on star power and the promotion of the number. As Jeongwon Joe explains, a variety of narrative strategies appears among the ten (Joe 1999). The diversity led Boyd to insert a narrative thread to provide unity. Interestingly, it emphasizes operatic performance by showing a man enter an opera house, don clown make-up, and lip-sync onstage to *Pagliacci* to end the film. Throughout *Aria*, all the heard music comes from the backlist of RCA, which was a major sponsor. Although the film does include some formidable stars, such as Jussi Bjoerling, the limitations on repertoire also mean that some numbers have unusual casting. For example, the great Leontyne Price, whose voice soars majestically in a Verdi segment, unfortunately does not do herself justice in Wagner's *Liebestod*, a style foreign to her talents.

Nonetheless, Franc Roddam's segment on the *Liebestod* is arguably the most success-ful part of *Aria* (Citron 2010, 58–76). A director with little knowledge of opera but exten-sive experience with youth culture, Roddam renders Wagner's mystical Love-Death in an unforgettable way. His segment acts out the concept simply and directly. Two teen-agers, played by Bridget Fonda and James Mathers, drive through glitzy Las Vegas and become disillusioned by what they see. They have sex in a cheap hotel, then slit their wrists in the bathtub. The events are coordinated closely with the key musical events, and so the scenario seems to visualize the charged course of the music. Fred Elmes's cin-ematography creates a strong synaesthetic effect by using filters and soft focus at impor-tant moments. The sensual interplay of music and image becomes so heady that we feel as if the characters are hearing the music, just as Isolde's text focuses on hearing and the senses. As things build musically the camera zooms in to the bathtub, and at the climac-tic musical resolution the razor pierces the skin and their dying begins. The ethereal musical coda is visualized by way of fantasy as the two seem to drive off into the desert, which is where we saw them at the start. In typical MTV style we are meant to wonder if they are transfigured in some afterlife, if the whole thing was a dream, or if they consid-ered suicide but did not carry it out.

Roddam's segment forms the high point in the arc of the film. It will be followed by a death-and-resurrection narrative in Ken Russell's segment on Puccini's "Nessun dorma" (from *Turandot*), in which a car-crash victim is restored to life (Citron 2010, 76–93). Afterward *Aria*'s narrative focuses on memory and decline, including the idea of opera as an outdated medium. This is interesting in light of the fact that *Aria* was intended to help revivify opera—a hope on which the film did not have much effect one way or the other. Nevertheless, *Aria* represents an important experiment and reflects contempo-rary anxiety over the future of opera. Ironically, this was the same time that opera-film was flourishing, and perhaps Boyd conceived *Aria* as a corrective. Beyond historical coincidence, both types of film constitute landmarks of opera on film.

CONCLUDING COMMENT

The study of opera and film promises to expand as technology offers new ways for opera to be reproduced on screen. Of course, television, the Internet, and portable devices are already engaged with opera, a nexus that lies beyond the scope of this chapter. Future movies will continue to find imaginative ways to involve opera, as suggested by the postmodern opera visit in *Quantum of Solace*. We can only look forward to such encounters and to their investigation by scholars.

BIBLIOGRAPHY

Abbate, Carolyn. 1991. *Unsung Voices: Opera and Musical Narrative in the Nineteenth Century*. Princeton: Princeton University Press.

Allanbrook, Wye Jamison. 1983. *Rhythmic Gesture in Mozart: "Le nozze di Figaro" and "Don Giovanni"*. Chicago: University of Chicago Press.

Altman, Rick. 1987. *The American Film Musical*. Bloomington: Indiana University Press.

Altman, Rick, with McGraw Jones and Sonia Tatroe. 2000. "Inventing the Cinema Soundtrack: Hollywood's Multiplane Sound System." In *Music and Cinema*, edited by James Buhler, Caryl Flinn, and David Neumeyer, 339–359. Hanover, NH: University Press of New England.

Babbington, Bruce, and Peter Evans. 1994. "Matters of Life and Death in Powell and Pressburger's *The Tales of Hoffmann*." In *A Night in at the Opera: Media Representations of Opera*, edited by Jeremy Tambling, 145–168. London: John Libbey.

Chion, Michel. 1994. *Audio-Vision: Sound on Screen*. Edited and translated by Claudia Gorbman. New York: Columbia University Press.

Citron, Marcia J. 1994. "A Night at the Cinema: Zeffirelli's *Otello* and the Genre of Film-Opera." *Musical Quarterly* 78, no. 4: 700–741.

——. 2000. *Opera on Screen*. New Haven: Yale University Press.

——. 2010. *When Opera Meets Film*. Cambridge: Cambridge University Press.

——. 2011. "The Operatics of Detachment: Tosca in the James Bond Film Quantum of Solace." *19th-Century Music* 34, no. 3: 316–340.

——. forthcoming. "Opera and Visual Media." In *The Oxford Handbook of Opera*, edited by Helen M. Greenwald. New York: Oxford University Press.

Franke, Lars. 2006. "*The Godfather Part III*: Film, Opera, and the Generation of Meaning." In *Changing Tunes: The Use of Pre-existing Music in Film*, edited by Phil Powrie and Robynn Stilwell, 31–45. Aldershot, UK, and Burlington, VT: Ashgate.

Franklin, Peter. 1994. "Movies as Opera (Behind the Great Divide)." In *A Night in at the Opera: Media Representations of Opera*, edited by Jeremy Tambling, 77–112. London: John Libbey.

Goehring, Edmund J. 2004. *Three Modes of Perception in Mozart: The Philosophical, Pastoral, and Comic in "Così fan tutte"*. Cambridge: Cambridge University Press.

Greene, Naomi. 2000. "Family Ceremonies; or, Opera in *The Godfather* Trilogy." In *Francis Ford Coppola's "The Godfather" Trilogy*, edited by Nick Browne, 133–156. Cambridge: Cambridge University Press.

Grover-Friedlander, Michal. 2005. *Vocal Apparitions: The Attraction of Cinema to Opera*. Princeton: Princeton University Press.

——. 2011. *Operatic Afterlives*. New York: Zone Books.

Hunter, Mary. 1999. *The Culture of Opera Buffa in Mozart's Vienna: A Poetics of Entertainment*. Princeton: Princeton University Press.

——. 2002a. "Opera *in* Film—Sentiment and Wit, Feeling and Knowing: *The Shawshank Redemption* and *Prizzi's Honor*." In *Between Opera and Cinema*, edited by Jeongwon Joe and Rose Theresa, 93–120. New York: Routledge.

———. 2002b. "*Così fan tutte* and Knowledge." Paper presented at Rice University.

Joe, Jeongwon. 1998. "Opera on Film, Film in Opera: Postmodern Implications of the Cinematic Influence on Opera." PhD diss., Northwestern University.

———. 1999. "Don Boyd's Aria: A Narrative Polyphony between Music and Image." *Journal of Musicological Research* 18, no. 4: 347–369.

———, and Sander L. Gilman, eds. 2010. *Wagner and Cinema*. Bloomington: Indiana University Press.

———, and Rose Theresa, eds. 2002. *Between Opera and Cinema*. New York: Routledge.

Kael, Pauline. 1994. *For Keeps: 30 Years at the Movies*. New York: Dutton.

Koch, Gerhard R. 1986. "Vom Nutzen des Grenzgängerischen: Wie sich Oper und Film befruchten." In *Oper, Film, Rockmusik: Veränderungen in der Alltagskultur*, edited by Hans-Klaus Jungenheinrich, 15–38. Kassel: Bärenreiter.

Koestenbaum, Wayne. 1993. *The Queen's Throat: Opera, Homosexuality, and the Mystery of Desire*. New York: Poseidon.

Kramer, Lawrence. 1994. "The Singing Salami: Unsystematic Reflections on the Marx Brothers' *A Night at the Opera*." In *A Night in at the Opera: Media Representations of Opera*, edited by Jeremy Tambling, 253–266. London: John Libbey.

Leicester, H. Marshall. 1994. "Discourse and the Film Text: Four Readings of *Carmen*." *Cambridge Opera Journal* 6, no. 3: 245–282.

McClary, Susan. 1992. *Georges Bizet, Carmen*. Cambridge: Cambridge University Press.

Morris, Mitchell. 1994. "Aspects of the Coming-Out Aria." Paper presented at the Annual Meeting of the Modern Language Association, San Diego, California.

Nattiez, Jean-Jacques. 1993. *Wagner Androgyne: A Study in Interpretation*. Translated by Stewart Spencer. Princeton: Princeton University Press.

Scorsese, Martin. 1992. Introduction to *Million Dollar Movie: The Second Volume of His Life in Movies*, by Michael Powell, ix–xiii. New York: Random House.

Stern, Lesley. 2002. "*The Tales of Hoffmann*: An Instance of Operality." In *Between Opera and Cinema*, edited by Jeongwon Joe and Rose Theresa, 39–58. New York: Routledge.

Stilwell, Robynn. 2006. "Vinyl Communion: The Record as Ritual Object in Girls' Rites-of-Passage Films." In *Changing Tunes: The Use of Pre-existing Music in Film*, edited by Phil Powrie and Robynn Stilwell, 152–166. Aldershot, UK, and Burlington, VT: Ashgate.

Tambling, Jeremy. 1987. *Opera, Ideology and Film*. New York: St. Martin's.

———, ed. 1994. *A Night in at the Opera: Media Representations of Opera*. London: John Libbey.

Weiner, Marc A. 2002. "Why Does Hollywood Like Opera?" In *Between Opera and Cinema*, edited by Jeongwon Joe and Rose Theresa, 75–92. New York: Routledge.

CHAPTER 4

···

VISUAL REPRESENTATION OF FILM SOUND AS AN ANALYTICAL TOOL

···

RICK ALTMAN

CAREFUL consideration of the history of the discipline of film studies reveals an interesting pattern. Far from developing in a continuous manner, film studies have alternated between periods of intensive growth and relatively fallow moments. Growth spurts may be attributed to three separate categories of event, two of which are well known, the other rarely mentioned. One important condition has been a periodic substantial increase in access to films. In one sense, expanded film distribution has been a constant concern of all those associated with the cinema, from filmmakers to exhibitors. But the development of film studies as a discipline has been spurred not only by broad public distribution of films, but also by an increase in film availability to fans and scholars. Before and after the Second World War, the film-club movement depended heavily on the availability of so-called substandard film technology. Access to 16mm copies of commercial and independent films regularly nourished the thinking and writing of those responsible for creating the discipline of film studies. Several decades later, film studies bounded forward with the application of video technology to filmic materials. Videotape, starting in the late 1970s, followed by videodiscs and DVDs in the 1990s, gave fans and scholars access to a much broader selection of films (often in better condition) than had previously been available.

A second important contributing factor in the development of film studies lies in the rapid expansion of film-related publication. Beginning in the 1970s, with the inauguration of many new journals and book series, academic and commercial publishers alike created important new avenues for the dissemination of general information and specialized scholarship on film topics. Not only did expanded publication possibilities increase communication among film scholars, but the prestige of the presses engaged in publishing film-oriented books, along with the aura associated with peer-reviewed journal publication, also lent the discipline the seriousness necessary to secure a permanent home in the academic world.

A third factor in the rapid expansion of film studies deserves a level of attention that it has not yet received. One of the most important catalysts for intensified development of the field of film studies has come from the creation of devices fostering extended and accurate discussion of films. Until the late 1970s, publications on cinema were rarely illustrated with carefully chosen frame enlargements designed to illustrate or support an analysis or argument. Typically, the only visual material included in a film article or book—if any—would be still photographs selected from an archival collection (often from the Museum of Modern Art collection in New York). At the time, publishers were still unsure about the copyright status of film frame enlargements, but they remained convinced that reproducing production stills was allowable. Since these photographs were taken on the set during production (rather than being actual frames from the film), they were of limited usefulness for encouraging extended discussion or careful analysis. During the 1980s, the exponential expansion of publishing on film topics, along with progressive clarification of the copyright issue, opened the way for scholars to illustrate their film publications with frame enlargements, at first painstakingly made from 16mm or 35mm film originals, and eventually (with the development of videodiscs and DVDs) more easily produced from video copies. In a sense, these scholars were simply reiterating the work of Eadweard Muybridge, who a century earlier had already understood the analytical potential of breaking continuous movement into a series of stopped images.

It would be hard to overestimate the impact of carefully chosen frame enlargements on the growth of film studies as a discipline. Though publishers probably saw these illustrations primarily as salable attractions, academics quickly found that the frequent use of frame enlargements set a new standard for intellectual discussion and argumentation on cinema issues. In conjunction with the freeze-frame capacity that videotape introduced during the 1980s (as well as the analyzer projectors acquired by many film studies programs during this period), published frame enlargements made it easy to discuss the basics of film analysis in great detail. From shot scale to mise-en-scène and from lighting to depth of focus, every aspect of the film image was suddenly available for detailed consideration. The ability to conduct microanalyses of film frames had an enormous impact on the teaching of cinema. Using illustrated articles by French scholars (Raymond Bellour, Thierry Kuntzel, Marie-Claire Ropars-Wuilleumier) and their American followers, we began to practice—and to require of our students—a level and type of film analysis not previously witnessed (but quite obviously influenced by the recent New Criticism vogue of literary close analysis). The effect on published film analyses was massive and virtually immediate. Accompanied by the newly available range of films on videotape, the frame-enlargement revolution set entirely new standards for detail and accuracy.

This newly acquired ability (and responsibility) to subject films to extremely close analysis came at a price. Providing the materials and technology required for careful examination of film images, published illustrations and video freeze-frames simultaneously reinforced a long-existing tendency to define and analyze cinema through its images, with little or no attention to the soundtrack. This tendency to nudge film studies toward image analysis is especially regrettable given sound's inherent inability to follow the image into the realm of still photographs and freeze-frames. Given the impossibility of slowing or stopping sound to make it easier to understand and analyze, sound-sensitive film fans and scholars sought alternative ways of emulating the period's vogue of frame enlargements and freeze-frames, eventually giving rise to a long series of attempts to represent sound visually. Designed to make up for sound's fundamentally time-based nature, these visual representations of film sound are the heirs of a long tradition. Indeed, it can reasonably be claimed that attempts to counter and arrest sound's fleeting nature lie at the very heart of civilization itself. What is written language, if not an overt attempt to transcribe and store oral language, frustratingly elusive and thus in need of a less fleeting record? Similarly, while also serving as a recipe for the production of music, the conventions of musical transcription also facilitate the creation of a permanent record of performances that otherwise would exist only in the all too volatile domain of human memory. Modern technology offers multiple methods of achieving similar results. From basic oscilloscopes to the most sophisticated digital systems, every method of representing sounds offers increased opportunities for extending and refining our analysis of those sounds.

If film studies received a substantial impetus from the representation of moving images as still frames, then what benefits might we expect from a similar approach to sound? Indeed, just what would constitute a "similar approach to sound?" Two radically disparate answers might reasonably be proposed. On the one hand, the reproduction of frame enlargements involves quoting a portion of the film itself: the film is made up of discrete visual frames, so—like latter-day disciples of Muybridge—we reproduce those frames separately in order to facilitate image analysis. As is readily apparent, this approach involves using one form of visual information (the frame enlargement) to provide privileged access to another form of visual information (the film's entire imagetrack). The parallel strategy in the domain of film sound would involve quoting a small snippet of film sound as a point of entry to the soundtrack as a whole. In a sense, this is what we do when (using relatively recent technology) we play the same passage over and over, to make sure that students are hearing (for example) the reduced volume and increased reverb that identify a particular passage as offscreen sound. As pedagogically necessary as this approach may be, it fails to capture one essential aspect of the frame-enlargement strategy. While the frame-enlargement model depends on representation of one aspect of the film by another version of that same aspect (the film's imagetrack being represented by a subset of that imagetrack), and as such might suggest representing a film's soundtrack by a (recorded) subset of that soundtrack, this approach loses sight of the frame enlargement model's ability to represent a moving, time-bound, aspect of the film through a stable, two-dimensional visual device. The benefits of representing sound through sound are obvious and not to be ignored, but they must not keep us from recognizing the equally important advantage of a model whose visual nature and two-dimensionality would make it easily consultable and eminently discussable. Just as written language and the conventions of musical transcription spatialize and visualize phenomena that are time-bound and aural in nature, thereby facilitating the analysis of speech and music, so visual representations of film sound might reasonably be expected to permit a new level of detail and accuracy in the analysis of film sound.

A THUMBNAIL HISTORY OF FILM SOUND DIAGRAMS

Virtually every filmmaker or scholar who has written extensively about sound has at one point or another offered a visual representation of the scene and/or aural phenomena under analysis. Having built an entire film theory on the relationship between succeeding shots, Sergei Eisenstein found himself seriously challenged by the entirely different structures characteristic of synchronized sound film. In the context of his lengthy consideration of his 1938 film *Alexander Nevsky*, Eisenstein handled this challenge by coining the expression "vertical montage." Taking the orchestral score as his model, with its obvious connections between instrumental parts that are both separate and simultaneous, Eisenstein imagined a graphing technique that would operate as a simple extension of the multipart musical score:

> When we turn from this image of the orchestral score to that of the audio-visual score, we find it necessary to add a new part to the instrumental parts: this new part is a "staff" of visuals, succeeding each other and corresponding, according to their own laws, with the movement of the music—and *vice versa*. (Eisenstein 1942, 74)

In previous articles, in order to explain various aspects of his montage-based film theory, Eisenstein had repeatedly resorted to diagrams ranging from simple contrasts to the complexity of Chinese pictograms. Now, in order to represent the "polyphonic structure" of sound films, which "achieves its total effect through the *composite sensation of all the pieces as a whole*" (Eisenstein 1942, 77; emphasis in original), Eisenstein sensed the need to offer a new kind of diagrammatic representation.

> In order to diagram what takes place in *vertical montage,* we may visualize it as *two* lines, keeping in mind that each of these lines represents *a whole complex of a many-voiced scoring.* The search for correspondence must proceed from the intention of matching both picture and music to the general, complex "imagery" produced by the whole. (Eisenstein 1942, 78; emphasis in original)

The results of Eisenstein's reflections on his graphic representation needs are evident in Figure 4.1, Eisenstein's celebrated visual rendition of the "audiovisual correspondences" in the Battle on the Ice sequence from *Alexander Nevsky*.

This fascinating and complex visual representation—combining thumbnail frame enlargements, two musical staffs, and storyboard-like pictorial diagrams, along with a

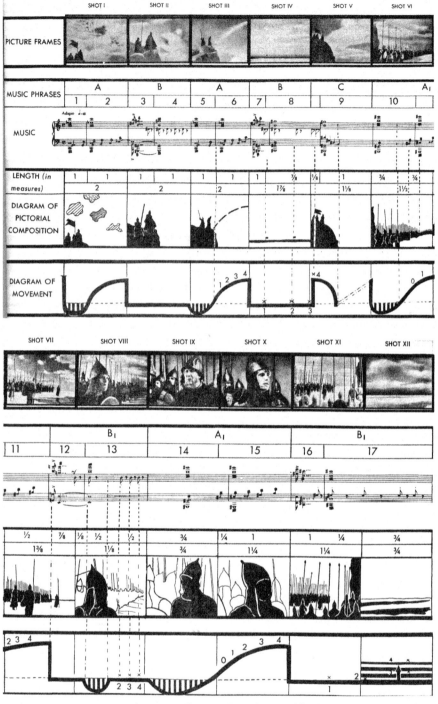

FIGURE 4.1 Sergei Eisenstein (1942, 175ff.): Visual rendition of "audiovisual correspondences" in the Battle on the Ice sequence from *Alexander Nevsky* (1938). From *The Film Sense* by Sergei Eisenstein, translated by Jay Leyda. Copyright 1942 by Houghton Mifflin Harcourt Publishing Company. Copyright (c) Renewed 1969 by Jay Leyda. Reprinted by permission of Houghton Mifflin Harcourt Publishing Company. All rights reserved.

somewhat cryptic line labeled "diagram of movement"—raises several important questions. In order to stress the montage nature of the film's structure, Eisenstein makes a point of presenting music and image separately before graphing them in a single series of vertical correspondences, so as to hammer home the importance of analyzing each line separately, according to its individual inner structures, before jumping to analysis of the vertical correspondences between different lines. When presented separately, Prokofiev's film score precedes representation of Eisenstein's images, but when vertical correspondences are configured in the composite diagram occupying the lower half of the double-page figure, it is the images that receive priority. The terminology used and the divisions created within Eisenstein's graph are thus systematically image-based.

It is worth noting that Eisenstein's graph is not generated by a desire to produce an accurate picture of a random scene. On the contrary—as one would expect from Eisenstein—the graph is produced as a key portion of an *argument* regarding audiovisual correspondences and their essential role in the creation of a vertical-montage-based polyphonic structure. As usual, Eisenstein is less interested in film analysis than he is in film theory. If he bothers to create a new form of graphic representation, it is primarily to exemplify his theoretical claims, and only secondarily as an aid to analyzing *Alexander Nevsky*. In the pages to come, we will repeatedly have occasion to recognize how important the author's theoretical program is to the constitution of each film sound graph.

Only a few years after Eisenstein, Pierre Schaeffer offered a less grandiose, but highly instructive, graph of a sequence from Jean Grémillon's 1944 film, *Le ciel est à vous* (Schaeffer 1946, 46). More than Eisenstein's idiosyncratic and somewhat ostentatious diagram, Schaeffer's graph (Figure 4.2) prefigures the approach reflected in sound-sensitive charts in the years to come. Working within the limits of the technology available to him in the immediate postwar era, Schaeffer must forgo the privilege of reproducing frame enlargements or musical transcriptions. In compensation, Schaeffer's graph goes beyond the two lines (image and music) that provide the framework for Eisensteins's diagram. By decomposing the soundtrack into three lines, Schaeffer offers a four-part harmony (image, dialogue, sound effects, music) that we will have occasion to observe more than once in later years. As with Eisenstein's approach, Schaeffer carefully lines up all analyzed aspects along the same time line, thereby facilitating "vertical" analysis. Whereas Eisenstein subordinates his numbering system to the visual sequence of separate shots, however, Schaeffer sticks instead to the more neutral yardstick of elapsed time.

In spite of obvious differences between Eisenstein's and Schaeffer's diagrams, several important resemblances deserve attention. First, both authors base at least a portion of their analysis on privileged access to preproduction materials that don't necessarily match the finished film. Eisenstein's diagram is based not on careful listening, but on Prokofiev's score. Similarly, Schaeffer's graph is not a record of careful viewing and listening, but a reproduction of Grémillon's own outline, produced "simultaneously with the scenario and before the actual sound mix" (Schaeffer 1946, 46). However obvious the dangers of depending on privileged access to preproduction materials provided by one of the film's collaborators, the analysis of film sound (and especially music) has often

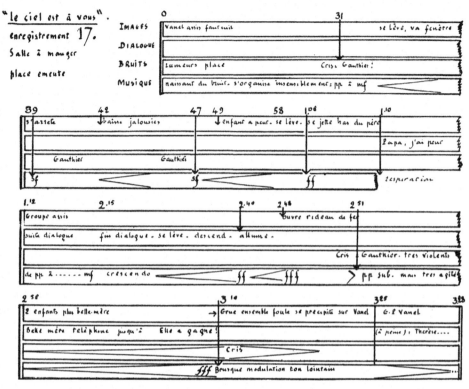

FIGURE 4.2 Pierre Schaeffer (1946, 46): Graph of a sequence from *Le ciel est à vous* (1944). From "L'élément non visuel au cinéma: (I) Analyse de la bande son." *Revue du cinéma* 1, no. 1: 45–48. Reprinted by permission of Éditions Gallimard. © Éditions Gallimard.

given in to the apparent benefits of this approach. Until recently, books on film music were based primarily on printed or manuscript copies of the original score—whether or not that score was actually performed as written and preserved intact in the film's final mix. It seems so obvious that there is something to be gained from access to the composer's own version of the score that generations of film music critics have regularly turned a deaf ear to the equally evident dangers of such an approach.

It is perhaps worth noting that Schaeffer, like Eisenstein, opts to produce this particular diagram not because it is complete or all-encompassing, but because it permits him to make an analytical point. The imagetrack is represented by only minimal description (whereas, even if frame enlargements were technically impractical, more complete description and information about shot scale and camera movement could have easily been included), only the opening words of each dialogue passage are provided (yet the entire dialogue could readily have been transcribed and included), sound effects are treated schematically (omitting, for example, information about whether the apparent sound effect sources are onscreen or offscreen), and only dynamics are mentioned in the description of the music (but even a musically untrained listener could provide additional information about such details as instrumentation and frequency range). As useful as all this supplementary information might appear to viewers interested in the structure of Grémillon's film, it would not have added to Schaeffer's basic point—that a modulation in the score and the scene's loudest music occur simultaneously with the scene's most important narrative action.

The broadest spectrum of visual representations of film sound may be found in an important manual by Roger Manvell and John Huntley: *The Technique of Film Music* (1957). Several scores for silent films are presented not just for their musical value, but also to demonstrate the many ways in which silent film sound was engineered to guarantee specific sound–image correspondences. A page from the *The Birth of a Nation* (1915) score by Joseph Carl Breil (systematically misspelled "Briel" throughout the book) reveals handwritten cues for careful placement of musical passages with respect to narrative action (Manvell and Huntley 1957, 57). Exemplary of the many cue sheets distributed with (or for) films in the latter half of the 1910s and throughout the 1920s, a page of Arthur Dulay's musical suggestions for George Melford's 1929 film *Sea Fury* identifies the exact screen action and/or intertitle text that serve as musical cues, along with a brief indication of the style of music called for (58). A page from Wolfgang Zeller's score for Lotte Reiniger's 1926 silhouette animation film *The Adventures of Prince Achmed* goes one better than these examples, providing an actual silhouette frame at the appropriate cue point on the musical score (60). Whereas these examples feature no more than a few cues (that is, clear indications of music/image correspondence), Edmund Meisel's score for Walter Ruttmann's 1927 *Berlin: Symphony of a Great City* offers much tighter cueing, with image information written over nearly every measure of the music (62).

Later in their book, Manvell and Huntley offer a new approach to image–sound graphing that has served as the model for many more recent diagrams. Devoting several pages to each film analyzed, Manvell and Huntley sandwich written descriptions of the action, dialogue, and sound effects between frame enlargements of the image and a three-staff representation of the music. A page from their treatment of Carol Reed's 1947 film *Odd Man Out* provides a good example of their approach (Figure 4.3; Manvell and Huntley 1957, 140–41). As with Eisenstein and Schaeffer, Manvell and Huntley are careful to line up all corresponding aspects vertically: action, dialogue, sound effects, and music. Frame enlargements are provided, but not lined up with the other elements. Where substantial camera movement occurs within a shot, multiple frame enlargements are reproduced. Further facilitating imagetrack analysis, shot scale is indicated, along with a shot description that includes information about the film's ample camera movement. In addition to the notes themselves, the musical transcription includes information about instrumentation and exact placement of sound effects. In comparison to all previous image/sound diagrams, Manvell and Huntley's *Odd Man Out* treatment is less selective in its choice of materials to present. While Manvell and Huntley clearly have a point to make, regarding the importance of sound–image correlations, they do not limit the information they provide to the minimum needed to make that point. Consequently, readers find themselves empowered by the variety of information provided. With access to a full roster of images, camera movements, dialogue, sound effects, and music, readers can easily follow the film—not just as a narrative, but as a

I

ACTION   L.S. Approach to Dock Square through a covered way. Father Tom catches up with Shell, who is wrestling with a shoe that has come off in the snow.

DIALOGUE   *Shell:* "Father Tom, me shoe came off
Father Tom: "Where is she?"
Shell : "The lace busted; she went on."
Father Tom: "Which way?"
Shell: "I couldn't keep up with her, but we'll get her now."

EFFECTS

FIGURE 4.3 Manvell and Huntley (1957, 140–41): Analysis of a sequence from *Odd Man Out* (1947), first two pages (of ten).

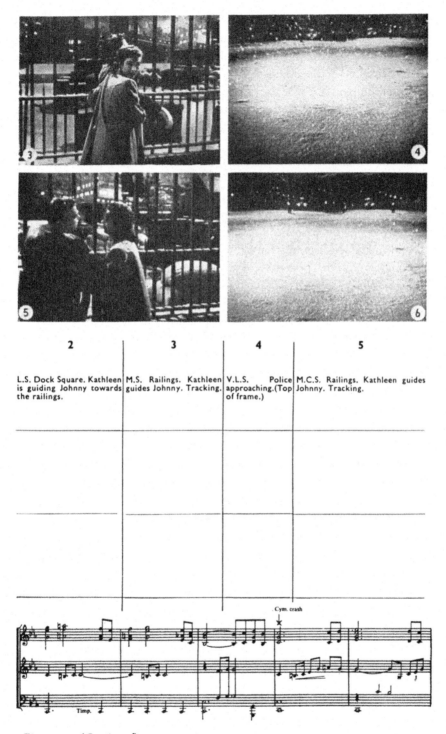

Figure 4.3 (*Continued*)

multifarious text featuring complex sound-to-sound and sound-to-image correspondences. Instead of sticking solely to the relationship between image and sound, Manvell and Huntley's approach makes it possible also to note connections between and among the different portions of the soundtrack.

Claudia Gorbman's (1977) representation of the images and music used in Jean Vigo's 1933 film *Zéro de conduite* deserves mention here if only because the music that she provides comes not—as it does in so many other film music analyses—from the author's privileged access to the score written for the film but from her careful listening to the music that actually occurs in the film's final mix. As Figure 4.4 reveals, the music Gorbman presents is spare as compared with the scores offered by other film music analysts. But it has the important quality of being the sound actually heard in the film. It is equally worth noting that the continuity in Gorbman's presentation, the through-line, is maintained not by the sequence of frame enlargements that parade across the top of most sound and image diagrams, but by the music itself. Instead of squeezing the music to fit the images, Gorbman follows normal musical practice of making each system the same size (four bars per line), with the frame enlargements inserted at the point where they occur in the music, rather than vice versa. For scholars interested in foregrounding sound rather than image, this arrangement offers clear benefits.

Recent Experiments in Sound Graphing

For some years now, I have been experimenting (and encouraging my students to experiment) with varying methods of representing film sound graphically. Like my predecessors, I have found myself regularly divided between two equally important goals. The first of these is to use a sound diagram as appropriate evidence in support of a theoretical or analytical argument. Purely verbal descriptions of film sound systematically fail to capture—and to communicate—the specificity of the sound under consideration. I have found that my audiences, whether students or colleagues, understand my claims much better when they are able both to experience the film passage in question and to study the schematic diagram I present as supporting material. But often I am not in a position to play a film clip for my audience. Perhaps in the not too distant future it will be commonplace for books and articles to include multimedia examples, but over the course of my career it has simply not been possible to provide exemplary film clips for my readers. By using a series of film sound diagrams, I make it possible for readers to imagine (or remember) more easily the scenes that I am analyzing.

Note that any diagram that is used to support an argument will almost certainly be skewed by the limits of that argument. Eisenstein's purpose was to analyze music–image relationships, so he not only selected a scene where music dominates the soundtrack, but he produced graphs that ignore all sounds other than music. This must not be understood as a failing on Eisenstein's part, but as part and parcel of all discourse. In order to make a point we regularly stress one film over another, one scene over another, one part

FIGURE 4.4 Gorbman (1987, 118–19): Images and music used in a sequence from *Zéro de conduite* (1933). Reproduced by permission of the author. © 1987 Claudia Gorbman. All rights reserved.

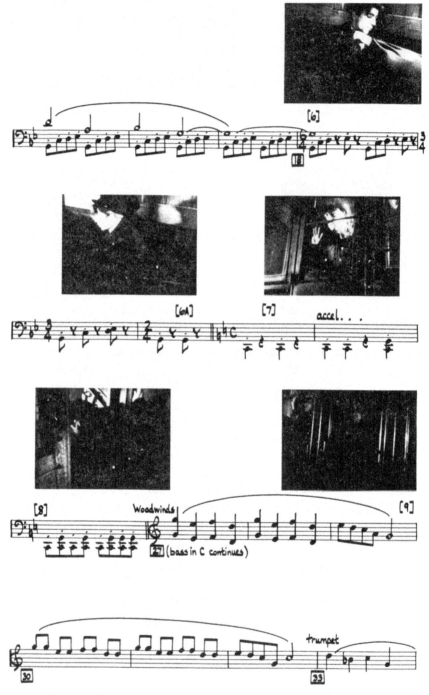

FIGURE 4.4 (*Continued*)

of a scene over another. This is not only normal, it is a virtually necessary part of our process of making sense of cinema (or anything else, for that matter). In any given film or scene there is simply too much material to represent, either verbally or graphically. We must make decisions about what is worth representing, or find ourselves condemned to producing diagrams that are so crowded and busy that we have trouble understanding them ourselves, let alone using them to communicate clearly with others.

My second goal in producing film diagrams is to slow down the process of consuming film sound, thereby making it easier to discuss that sound. Whereas diagrams that satisfy the first goal are often spare and single-minded, this second goal requires broad enough information for viewers/listeners to reach their own conclusions about the passage in question. It is worth pointing out that visual representations of film sound offer double benefits. The process of preparing a film sound diagram requires close, continued contact with the scene's soundtrack, thus forcing the preparer to listen both repeatedly and extremely carefully. There is no better teacher of sound characteristics than the need to track changes in the volume and reverberation of dialogue, sound effects, and music, as well as correspondences with the image. But the benefits of representing film sound visually are by no means limited to those who do the graphing. In my classes, I have found that students who have little to say in response to repeated film-clip viewings and listenings suddenly find their voices when offered a chance to discuss a visual representation of that same clip. For decades now, sound-oriented film scholars have been lamenting the fact that the world we live in and the languages we speak depend so heavily on sight. Instead of cursing the wind, it is time we built windmills. Knowing that our audiences are prejudiced in favor of sight, we need to take advantage of every possible visual device to lure those audiences into more active interaction with film sound. Visual representations of film sound constitute one of the most successful methods of extending the amount of time that audiences are willing to devote to the analysis of film sound.

When I began to listen carefully to the sound of *Citizen Kane* (1941) I found that it often operates more like Welles's rather idiosyncratic radio programs than according to the realist descriptions which at the time were taken as gospel. On the one hand, I found Welles's (and his chief soundman James Stewart's) ability to manipulate volume and reverb nothing short of astounding, but, at the same time, I noted that *Citizen Kane*'s approach to sound served realist purposes only intermittently, leaving ample room for passages where rhetoric outpaced realism. Yet, in spite of a well-established cottage industry devoted to publications about *Citizen Kane*, no published materials offered an appropriate basis for close analysis of *Kane*'s sound. In response, I appended to my article on "Deep Focus Sound: *Citizen Kane* and the Radio Aesthetic" what I called a "sound-sensitive description" of the film's Colorado sequence (Altman 1996, 116–21). Unlike other versions of the film's script, dialogue, or action, this short addendum concentrates on one aspect of the image (shot scale) and two related aspects of the sound (volume and reverb), thus allowing clear recognition of the soundtrack's careful (and rhetorically satisfying) manipulation of apparent distance. Figure 4.5 reproduces one page from this "sound-sensitive" description, specifying approximate

Shot #	Camera/ Speaker	Volume (1–10)	Description/dialogue
172			(8 feet 6 frames/ Voyager videodisc frame 27783) Charles on sled (begins as dissolve)
	--	7–8	Volume of music increases as Charles rides sled and throws snowball.
173			(3′ 13f/ Voyager videodisc frame 27949) Snowball hits sign above porch: MRS. KANE'S BOARDINGHOUSE
	8	10	Music spike synced to snowball's impact.
174			(I58′ 10f/ Voyager videodisc frame 28004) Charles throws snowball whose impact makes no sound
	4	3r	Charles: Come on boys. The Union forever…
			Camera tracks back, revealing Mother in left foreground
	2	6	Mother: Be careful, Charles.
	2	5	Thatcher (off): Mrs. Kane…
	4	6	Mother: Pull your muffler around your neck, Charles.
			Camera tracks back, revealing Thatcher in right foreground
	4	5	Thatcher: Mrs. Kane, I think we shall have to tell him now.
	4–6	5	Mother: Yes. I'll sign those papers now, Mr. Thatcher
			Camera continues to track back; Charles is intermittently visible through window
	4–8	5	Father: You people seem to forget that I'm the boy's father.
	4	5	Mother: It's going to be done exactly the way I've told Mr. Thatcher.
			She sits at foreground table; Thatcher sits next to her; Father approaches

FIGURE 4.5 Altman (1996, 116–17): First page of appendix, "'sound-sensitive description' of *Citizen Kane*, Colorado sequence."

Does not include all effects or music. The first figure in each line provides the approximate camera-to-speaker distance in feet. The second figure provides the approximate volume, on a scale of 1–10; noticeable reverb is indicated by an "r." Shot numbers and lengths are taken from *The Citizen Kane Book* (1971).

camera-to-speaker distance, volume on a scale of one to ten, the presence of reverberation (r), camera movement, action, and dialogue. While detailed charting of volume and reverb levels effectively supports the points made in the body of the article, this form of presentation is hardly user-friendly. Published at a time when illustration was still at a premium, this article cries out both for graphic presentation of volume and reverberation variations and for the corresponding frame enlargements. Together, these additions would have substantially increased the usefulness of this "sound-sensitive description."

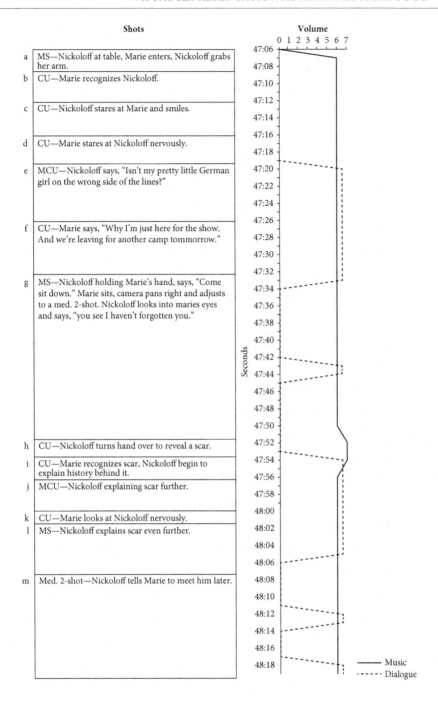

	Shots
a	MS—Nickoloff at table, Marie enters, Nickoloff grabs her arm.
b	CU—Marie recognizes Nickoloff.
c	CU—Nickoloff stares at Marie and smiles.
d	CU—Marie stares at Nickoloff nervously.
e	MCU—Nickoloff says, "Isn't my pretty little German girl on the wrong side of the lines?"
f	CU—Marie says, "Why I'm just here for the show. And we're leaving for another camp tommorrow."
g	MS—Nickoloff holding Marie's hand, says, "Come sit down." Marie sits, camera pans right and adjusts to a med. 2-shot. Nickoloff looks into maries eyes and says, "you see I haven't forgotten you."
h	CU—Nickoloff turns hand over to reveal a scar.
i	CU—Marie recognizes scar, Nickoloff begin to explain history behind it.
j	MCU—Nickoloff explaining scar further.
k	CU—Marie looks at Nickoloff nervously.
l	MS—Nickoloff explains scar even further.
m	Med. 2-shot—Nickoloff tells Marie to meet him later.

FIGURE 4.6 Altman (2000, 344–45): Analysis of a scene from *Noah's Ark* (1928).

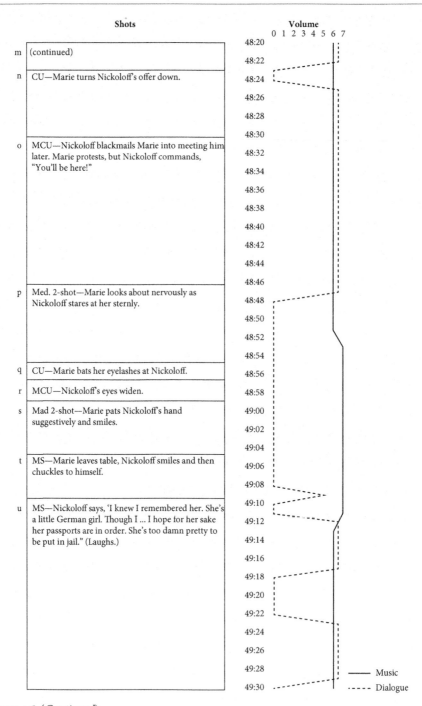

FIGURE 4.6 (Continued)

A later article took up the challenge of providing a more satisfactory graphic representation of film sound (Altman, Jones, and Tatroe 2000, 339–59). Arguing that early Hollywood sound films were still in the process of creating the notion of a "soundtrack"—this transitional stage being easily recognizable by the clash of differing types of sound simultaneously striving to dominate the soundtrack—I offered a scene from Michael Curtiz's 1928 extravaganza *Noah's Ark* as evidence (Figure 4.6). As this diagram readily reveals, the intermittent dialogue remains at a theatrically high level throughout, while the music continues to obey the rules of silent film accompaniment: when an exciting event takes place (Marie's recognition of Nickoloff's scar) the music crescendoes, in this case covering and thus obscuring the concurrent dialogue. In the years to come, Hollywood would find several solutions to this competitive approach to sound, but while the industry was still experimenting with approaches borrowed from existing models cohabitation remained difficult. A simple diagram makes this point easy to communicate or to understand, even without the frame enlargements that would have substantially improved the process. Several other diagrams in the same article offer similar benefits.

Several dedicated students have contributed to the development of more satisfying diagrams. Jay Beck was among the first to combine sound graphing techniques with thumbnail frame enlargements. His article on Jonathan Demme's 1991 *Silence of the Lambs* (Beck 2000) includes a seven-page treatment of the film's penultimate sequence, Clarice's discovery of Buffalo Bill (Figure 4.7 reproduces the last page of the diagram). Covering no fewer than nine separate domains (frame enlargements, elapsed time, amplitude graph, shot description, dialogue transcription, nondiegetic music, diegetic music, sound effects, ambient sound), Beck's verbal and visual presentation challenges readers to relive the sequence in all its audiovisual complexity. Because Beck provides so much information, users of his diagrams have the opportunity to analyze the sequence with greater attention to the details of film sound than if they were limited either to Beck's prose text or to Demme's film.

Over the past few years, working with graduate research assistant Andrew Ritchey and undergraduate research assistant Caitlin Bryant, I have developed what has now become a fairly standard method of representing the sound of a film sequence. Whereas I initially sought to present every possible aspect of every scene I graphed, I have learned that for communication purposes legibility is often more important than completeness. The chart of a portion of a scene from Lewis Milestone's 1930 classic *All Quiet on the Western Front* offers a particularly spare, and thus especially clear, example (Figure 4.8). In the midst of battle, German soldier Lew Ayres finds himself sharing a bomb crater with the dead Frenchman he has just killed. Taking place in the midst of a noisy battlefield, but dependent on dialogue details, this scene perfectly exemplifies the problems faced by early soundmen: how to make space for two different types of sound while simultaneously respecting both current standards of realism and period expectations regarding volume, reverberation, and frequency range. In one sense, this scene offers a microcosmic representation of the basic problem that Hollywood grappled with throughout its first decade of synchronized sound: which should be privileged,

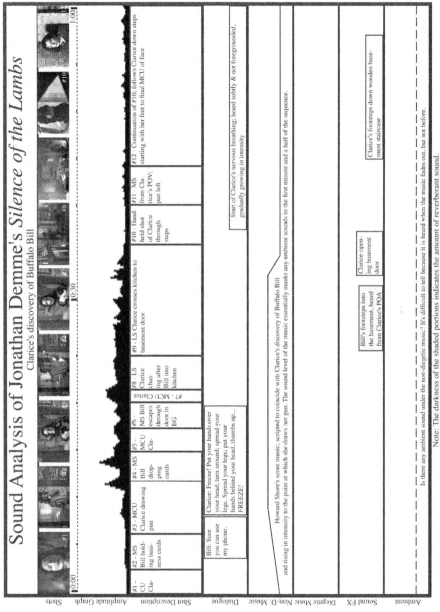

FIGURE 4.7 Beck (2000, 291): *Silence of the Lambs* (1991), penultimate sequence, Clarice's discovery of Buffalo Bill (last page only). Reproduced by permission of the author.

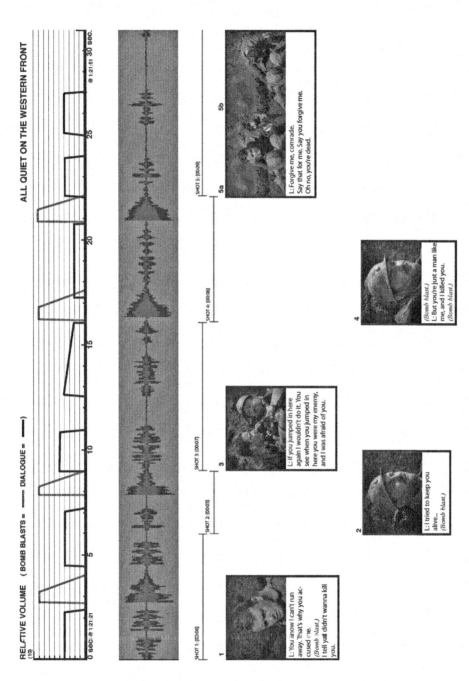

FIGURE 4.8 Altman, with Ritchey and Bryant, sequence from *All Quiet on the Western Front* (1930).

intelligibility or realism? As noted previously, early Hollywood sound films like *Noah's Ark* were not always successful in solving this problem. In *All Quiet on the Western Front*'s bomb crater scene, however, an effective solution is applied. Instead of privileging either intelligibility or realism, the scene is built around carefully engineered and precisely timed alternation. As the graph makes abundantly clear, the scene's repeated bomb blasts are all precisely placed between dialogue passages. Though the diagram covers only thirty seconds of a longer scene, it amply demonstrates not only the film's general strategy of alternation, but also the fraction-of-a-second accuracy of the sound mix. What would have been impossible with the sound systems available in 1927–1928 (including the Vitaphone sound-on-disc direct recording used for Warner's *Noah's Ark*) now became entirely feasible thanks to technical advances in both recording and rerecording.

It is perhaps worth pointing out a few practical details exemplified by Figure 4.8. Relative volume is determined by careful listening, on a scale of 0 (silence) to 10 (the film's loudest sound). Far from scientifically accurate, this measurement is necessarily subjective and imprecise. In particular, a quick look at the wave form shows that the dialogue passages do not in fact retain continuous volume throughout, but regularly include short periods of silence. Were the purpose of this graph to exemplify variations in dialogue volume, far greater accuracy in plotting dialogue volume would be required. For practical purposes of reference, discussion, and location within the film as a whole, the chart offers two time references, location within the entire film (the sequence starts at 1:21:21 and runs to 1:21:51) and location within the represented sequence (0 to 30 seconds). The wave form (now easy to produce on a home computer using easily accessible software) offers an extremely useful independent measure of volume. Here, for example, we note the realistic presentation of the sound envelope characteristic of bomb blasts—a sharp attack followed by a slow but nearly straight-line decay. Though the diagram as a whole privileges sound, the image information provided offers ample opportunities to analyze sound–image relationships. For example, we discover that dialogue is sometimes presented with an onscreen source, but at times also allowed to emanate from an offscreen space. In order to facilitate analysis of onscreen *versus* offscreen sound sources, offscreen dialogue is presented in italics. We also note that the scene combines a sound–image correspondence system that by 1930 was becoming outdated (each change of sound corresponding to a change of shot, as we observe at the beginning of shots 3, 4, and 5) with a new mixing standard (using continuous sound to cover cuts in the image, as with shots 1 and 2, to which we cut in the middle of Ayres's dialogue).

If I have dwelt on this diagram somewhat at length, it is in order to demonstrate to readers just how useful a representation of this type can be for communicating not only with those who have recently seen and heard the sequence diagrammed, but even with those who have never (or not recently) seen the film. I dare suspect that hardly any readers of this chapter have taken the time to locate and play the thirty-second sequence charted here. Yet for the last several minutes you have been engaged in careful and detailed analysis of a sequence that is only thirty seconds long. This extension of time spent with the soundtrack is in fact the very goal that I (and all the others who have

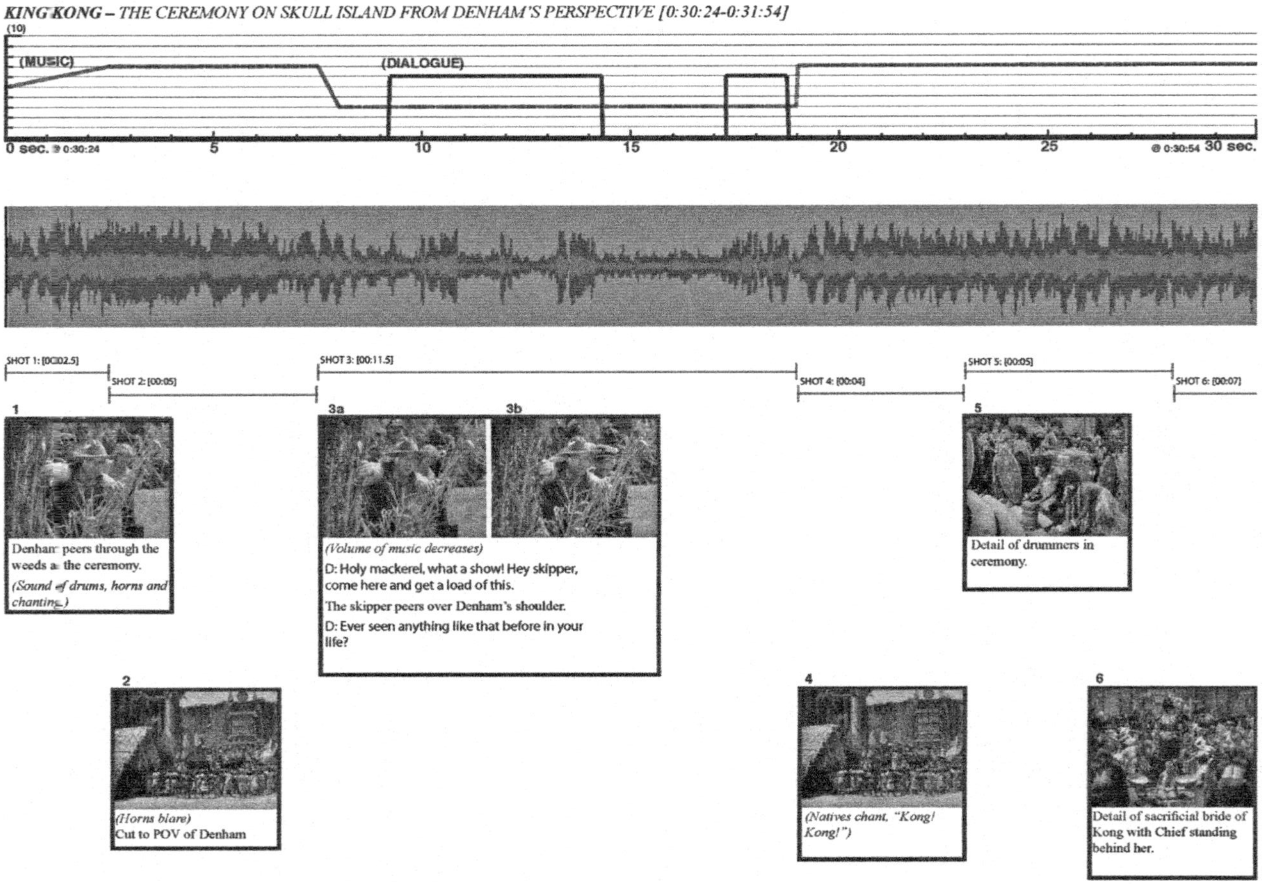

KING KONG – THE CEREMONY ON SKULL ISLAND FROM DENHAM'S PERSPECTIVE [0:30:24-0:31:54]
(10)

[MUSIC]
(DIALOGUE)

0 sec. @ 0:30:24   5   10   15   20   25   @ 0:30:54   30 sec.

SHOT 1: [00:02.5]   SHOT 2: [00:05]   SHOT 3: [00:11.5]   SHOT 4: [00:04]   SHOT 5: [00:05]   SHOT 6: [00:07]

1
Denham peers through the weeds at the ceremony.
(Sound of drums, horns and chanting.)

2
(Horns blare)
Cut to POV of Denham

3a   3b
(Volume of music decreases)
D: Holy mackerel, what a show! Hey skipper, come here and get a load of this.
The skipper peers over Denham's shoulder.
D: Ever seen anything like that before in your life?

4
(Natives chant, "Kong/ Kong!")

5
Detail of drummers in ceremony.

6
Detail of sacrificial bride of Kong with Chief standing behind her.

FIGURE 4.9 Altman, with Ritchey and Bryant: *King Kong* (1933), sequence on Skull Island.

produced similar soundtrack diagrams) seek to accomplish with charts that are by their very nature imprecise.

When watching a film sequence with complex sound, we are most often hard pressed to attend to more than a single aspect of the soundtrack. Repeated hearings certainly offer the possibility of discovering additional details and new correspondences, but the process is at best slow and often impeded by the overwhelming influence of an initial hearing. Because they offer a wide spectrum of information in an easily consultable format, visual renditions of a soundtrack segment invite the critic to analyze not only in greater depth but also with attention to a greater variety of concerns. Figure 4.9 represents the memorable scene in Merian C. Cooper and Ernest B. Schoedsack's *King Kong* (1933) where the ship's crew members happen upon the Skull Island natives' preparation for a sacrifice. The overall shape of the sound graph reveals what has now become a soundtrack standard: the volume of the music is dipped so that the dialogue may be heard. Unlike the *All Quiet on the Western Front* bomb crater example, which depended on alternation of sounds in order to secure dialogue intelligibility, the *King Kong* sequence uses a layering strategy that will become more and more common throughout the 1930s. Yet, fascinatingly, we note that the dipped music is diegetic music, played by the natives and heard by the crew members. Shouldn't diegetic music follow the standards of realism normally applied to other diegetic sounds? Why is the music louder when it accompanies a distant point-of-view shot of the natives (shots 2 and 4) than when we see the crew members in medium shot (shots 1 and 3)? Is the dip in musical volume attributable to an increase in distance from the sound source, a change in camera orientation, or some form of psychoacoustic motivation? And how does it happen that the cut-in from the extremely distant point of view in shot 4 to a medium shot of the drummers in shot 5 produces no change in the music volume? In fact, this anomaly is immediately repeated in the cut from shot 5 to shot 6, where we move from a medium shot of the drummers to a long shot of the sacrificial bride and her court without a change in volume. The diagram of course provides no answers to these questions. But it does make it more likely that these important questions will be asked.

However useful these black-and-white diagrams may be, they pale in comparison to the multicolor graphs easily produced on a computer screen or printed by even the most inexpensive of today's printers. The use of black-and-white technology—which is what we are currently limited to in virtually all printed articles and books—sets unavoidable limits on the range of available graphing strategies. In particular, black-and-white technology severely limits our ability to produce—and reproduce—legible graphs with more than two lines, whereas the multiple colors available on computer screens provide an easily accessible method of separating competing lines. As long as our articles and books cannot be accompanied by multicolor graphs, however, we are doomed—at least for publication purposes—to a black-and-white world.

In a classroom situation, however, many things are possible that simply cannot be printed in an article or book. Recently, I challenged students in an undergraduate seminar to come up with novel ways of graphing film sound. Imagine my delight when two groups, independently, devised methods of animating their sound graphs, so that the graph advanced on the screen at the same speed as the accompanying sound and the moving image above. Though this approach sacrifices the important benefits of having a stable diagram to work with, it produces an effect that is nothing less than exhilarating.

Bottom line: we need to recognize openly that film sound is not easy to work with, and to devise as many ways as possible to overcome the difficulties of working with sound. Visual representations of film sound can play an important role in this process, because they are capable of providing an important tool for film analysis.

Bibliography

Altman, Rick. 1996. "Deep-Focus Sound: *Citizen Kane* and the Radio Aesthetic." In *Perspectives on Citizen Kane*, edited by Ronald Gottesman, 94–121. New York: G. K. Hall. A longer version of this essay was published earlier under the same title: *Quarterly Review of Film and Video* 15, no. 3 (1994): 1–33.

———, with McGraw Jones and Sonia Tatroe. 2000. "Inventing the Cinema Soundtrack: Hollywood's Multiplane Sound System." In *Music and Cinema*, edited by James Buhler, Caryl Flinn, and David Neumeyer, 339–359. Hanover, NH: University Press of New England.

Beck, Jay. 2000. " 'Rewriting the Audio-Visual Contract': *Silence of the Lambs* and Dolby Stereo." *Southern Review* (Australia) 33, no. 3: 273–291.

The Citizen Kane Book. 1971. Boston: Little, Brown.

Eisenstein, Sergei. 1942. *The Film Sense*. Translated by Jay Leyda. New York: Harcourt, Brace.

Gorbman, Claudia. 1977. "Vigo/Jaubert." *Ciné-Tracts* 2: 65–80.

Manvell, Roger and John Huntley. 1957. *The Technique of Film Music*. New York: Hastings House.

Schaeffer, Pierre. 1946. "L'élément non visuel au cinéma: (I) Analyse de la bande son." *Revue du cinéma* 1, no. 1: 45–48.

CHAPTER 5

....

FILM MUSIC FROM THE PERSPECTIVE OF COGNITIVE SCIENCE

....

ANNABEL J. COHEN

THIS chapter is complementary to two others that I have written on film music for the Oxford Handbook series, the first for *The Oxford Handbook of Music Psychology* (Hallam, Cross, & Thaut 2009) and the second for *The Oxford Handbook of Music and Emotion* (Juslin & Sloboda 2010). The former chapter is entitled "Music in Performance Arts: Film, Theatre and Dance." It reviews psychological studies relevant to the role of music in electronic and live artistic multimedia contexts and considers a developmental psychological perspective in which minds develop throughout the lifespan. The latter chapter considers music as one of the primary sources of emotion in a film. It argues that the emotion produced by film music is real emotion, as defined by the psychologist Frijda's (1986) laws of emotion. Both chapters presented my Congruence-Associationist Model, and this provides common ground with the present chapter, though in all chapters, the model is treated in slightly different ways. In contrast to the former chapters, the present chapter is more extensive and takes a foundational and focused approach to the psychology of film music in general. Though they were written earlier, the previous two chapters might be considered as specialized branches that stem from the present chapter.

The human mind makes film and film music possible, but by the same token the mind constrains those possibilities. Understanding these mental proclivities and limitations would seem crucial to scholarship in film and film music. Obtaining such understanding entails turning to a body of knowledge known as *cognitive science,* the scientific study of the mind (Bermúdez 2010). This field addresses many issues associated with mental processes, including the treatment of audio and visual information and the representation of music and emotion. The knowledge generated often arises from controlled experiments with human participants. A few of these experiments have been conducted specifically on the role of music in the context of film. It must be said at the outset, however, firstly, that understanding the mind is one of the most complex problems facing science, and, secondly, that although recent progress is illuminating, much remains unknown. Placing the role of film music in the context of current cognitive science can certainly help to explain not only why music is so important to film but also how music functions in film. At the same time, discourse on film music in the context of cognitive science can both reveal unexplored features of mental function and point to specific questions that future research in cognitive science ought soon to address.

1. COGNITIVE SCIENCE AND THE COGNITIVE PERSPECTIVE

The field of cognitive science originated in the 1950s (cf. Boden 2006, for review). It has flourished, however, only since the 1980s. Its focus on mental activity, such as thinking, memory, and imagery, marked a change from prior decades (beginning around the 1920s) that were dominated by behaviorist psychology. Behaviorism focused on observable behavior (such as a rat's learning to press a bar for a food pellet on hearing a tone), taking inspiration initially from the success of Pavlovian conditioning which appeared to reveal basic laws of learning. The movement was further bolstered by operant conditioning, made famous by B. F. Skinner. Laws of learning derived from studies of rats and pigeons, however, proved to be less generalizable to human complex behavior than was originally envisioned: behavioral research ultimately failed to account for such abilities as language and reading acquisition, handwriting and speech recognition, and other higher thought processes.

Cognitive science is an endeavor that involves all disciplines that focus on mind or human behavior, including psychology, philosophy, computer science, neuroscience, linguistics, and anthropology (Thagard 2005; Von Eckardt 1995). Since its inception, activity in cognitive science has coincided with developments in computer science. There are two primary reasons for this. First, the ability of computers to process, store, and access enormous amounts of data provided a model of human information processing and thus inspired theories of human information processing and the creation of computer programs to simulate how the brain might carry out certain mental tasks. The second reason is that computers have been essential to running complex controlled experiments and analyzing the resulting data. Linguists contribute to neuroscience through their understanding of language, the most complex of all human mental abilities. Anthropology provides a universal and cultural perspective. Philosophy addresses issues of consciousness, mental representation, and meaning. Cognitive psychology focuses on explaining and describing the general principles underlying the mental activity of individuals. It stands out in its applicability to understanding film music due to its theories of mental processing that can be tested in experiments (Cohen 2000). Closely related to cognitive psychology, the field of cognitive neuroscience more directly studies brain function. Scholarship in music cognition and music cognitive neuroscience is reflected in specialized journals such as *Music Perception, Musicae Scientiae, Psychology of Music*, and *Psychomusicology:Music, Mind & Brain*, in the activities of dedicated societies and professional meetings, and also in a recently established Masters of Science program in Music and Neuroscience offered at Goldsmiths, University of London (Cohen & Graziano 2009).

From the cognitive scientific perspective, scholarly and lay assumptions and proposals about perception and reception of music and film can be treated as hypotheses testable through experiments. In humanities disciplines, including film theory and musicology, logical argument and compelling narrative advance understanding, but the sciences ask for objective evidence that is replicable. Cognitive psychology takes this latter approach to hypotheses or assumptions about mental activity.

Here are three examples of common assumptions about film music held by film directors, composers, and audiences: (1) music adds meaning to film; (2) music accompanying visual images in a film forms a bond in memory; and (3) music engages an audience in a film. Few would argue with any of these assumptions, but when we probe further, particular questions arise whose answers are not straightforward. Take item (1) above: music adds meaning to film. If music adds meaning to a film, then is the meaning of the music by itself reflected directly in the meaning of the film when the film and music are combined? Does the music simply add meaning to the film as opposed to creating a new emergent whole? Or take item (2): If a mental connection or association between music and film is formed in one presentation, then, afterward, the music, when presented by itself, should prime the memory of the associated film excerpt that occurred originally with the music. This is the basic notion of leitmotif, originating from opera, but what is the time course of such leitmotifs? Does the connection form in just one presentation? And, finally, item (3): if an *appropriate* music soundtrack engages the interest of an audience in a film, then this soundtrack should reduce detection of events extraneous to the film more than would an *inappropriate* music soundtrack because the latter would make the film less engaging and leave more attention to spare for extraneous material. This latter hypothesis assumes that the amount of attention of an audience member is finite and that attentive engagement to a film takes mental capacity. If so, does music processing take processing resources away from visual information and speech and sound effects? Or, is it possible that music might even enhance processing in other modalities, like visual scenes and speech, and if so under what conditions?

Scholarship and discourse on film music often entail assumptions and hypotheses like these. Cognitive psychology can turn them into experiments from which objective answers can arise. Cognitive science—here I am speaking about cognitive psychology and cognitive neuroscience in particular—thereby allows scholarship to go a step further than verbal or symbolic argument by testing whether in fact the hypotheses can be supported when examined in controlled conditions.

It is often challenging to design studies to test assumptions that would first seem to be easily addressed—for example, the assumption that music adds meaning to film. Any single study can focus on only a small set of circumstances or conditions, and, in spite of all the care that is taken, for example, in finding optimal examples and testing large numbers of participants who will be asked to give a response on a large number of trials, the results may not turn out as expected. Regardless of whether the study supports or fails to support an hypothesis, much can be learned. Support for the tested hypothesis gives strength to the original explanation of the film music phenomena in question. Lack of support leads to examination of the experiment—which may have been either ill conceived or poorly executed—and perhaps to reexamination of the underlying theory, which might need revision or extension.

As a simple practical example of the use of —and need for—a cognitive scientific approach to film music, consider a brief sequence from *Avatar* (Cameron 2009), the science fiction film that relied on computer graphics as never before to create the experience of being in the extraterrestrial realm of Pandora, which is populated by the Na'vi, who live in harmony with spectacular flora and fauna. Jake Sully, a former US marine, has been recruited to take part in the Avatar program, through which, by lending his consciousness to a Na'vi Avatar replica, he is poised to obtain scientific information needed by his human support team and ultimately his country back on Earth.

On his first mission to Pandora, Jake becomes separated from his team while escaping the pursuit of a six-legged giant sturmbeast, all to the accompaniment of a dramatic full orchestral cue composed by James Horner. The music ends on a loud sustained chord as Jake throws himself over a cliff and survives a descent through a gushing waterfall. Now in apparent safety off the bank of the water, Jake makes a spear from a branch. Bass notes reminiscent of an ultra-slow heartbeat suggest that safety will in fact be short lived. Overhead, a Na'vi princess, Neytiri, has spied the interloper. She is about to release a lethal arrow from her bow (see Figure 5.1a) when suddenly a delicate high-pitched descending sequence of notes introduces a wood sprite, an equally delicate floating floral creature descending over the arrow. Neytiri's gaze follows the wood sprite (see Figure 5.1b, c). Interpreting the wood sprite as a positive sign that Jake is good, Neytiri lowers the bow and arrow. The audience also senses this goodness from the simple melody in the high range. With the end of the melody and the disappearance of the wood sprite, the music changes to a more ponderous diminished triad arpeggio theme as the next shot depicts the departure from Pandora of the helicopter that would have taken Jake back to safety.

In this short sequence of barely a minute, four contrasting music cues parallel distinct activities in the film—the orchestral music associated with the chase, the heart-beat music foretelling danger, the delicate music associated with the wood sprite and Jake's goodness, and the ponderous diminished triad music associated with the departure of the helicopter. Can there be disagreement that these contrasting music selections elicit mental associations that add meaning to the film? Surely not. In this example, film music clearly helps the audience interpret the rapidly changing actions.

Suppose we now play back only the music track from the excerpt. The music might conjure up images (past visual associations) of the chase with the sturmbeast. The sustained chord might bring to mind the descent down the waterfall. The high-pitched

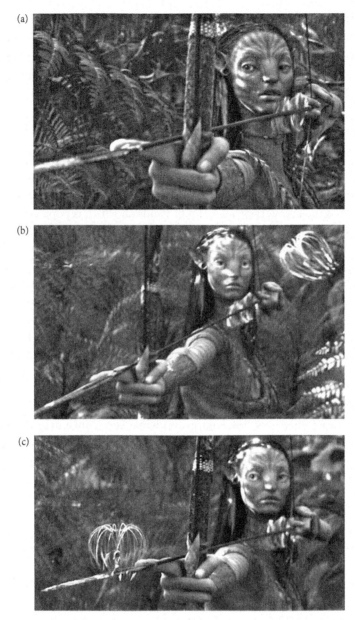

FIGURE 5.1 a–c. *Avatar* (2009), images from the segment referred to as "The Sign," at approximately 0:25:00. A high-pitched musical cue accompanies the movement of the wood sprite, the eye movement of Neytiri, and the change in the bow-and-arrow and arm movement.

descending melody would remind us of the intervention by the delicate wood sprite, and the broken diminished chord would remind us of the departing helicopter. Thus a second role of music is to aid the audience in remembering parts of the film, reinforcing the connection among film events and eliciting associations.

This examination of a brief, representative excerpt from a modern Hollywood film points to three major functions of film-music: (1) music interprets and adds meaning; (2) it aids memory; (3) it engages the audience. What I wrote a decade ago in a summary of the cognitive perspective on film music at that time still applies:

> it is one thing to postulate these functions of film music speculatively and another to subject the postulates to convincing empirical tests. Here is where the methods of cognitive psychology prove useful. With its reliance on controlled experiments, cognitive psychology can place a provocative but speculative theory on solid psychological foundation. Empirical evidence from psychology experiments helps complete our understanding of how music aids the audience's comprehension of a film. (Cohen 2000, 361–362).

Just over a decade later, cognitive research on film music continues to help us understand how music aids the audience's comprehension of a film, but now cognitive psychology is complemented by developments in cognitive neuroscience.

The remainder of this chapter is divided into four sections. Section 2 reviews experiments that examine the influence of music on the three major functions: meaning, memory, and engagement in film. For each function, research prior to 2000 will be briefly reviewed and developments in the last decade will be highlighted. Section 3 focuses on neuroscience, explaining a little about brain structure and function, ways of imaging the active brain, and findings relevant to understanding film music. We will discuss whether brain activity takes place in separate modules or whether holistic activity across the entire brain contributes to the role of music in film. The applicability of the *mirror neuron system,* a concept that has attracted much attention in the last decade, will be discussed with respect to film and film music. Section 4 presents a descriptive model that emphasizes structural and associationist mental coding principles in its account of the effects of film music. This Congruence-Associationist Model (C-A M), which I have been developing and refining for over two decades, conceptualizes a process of optimal synthesis whereby the physical elements of sound and light presented by the film, along with the mental memories and story grammars that the audience brings to the film situation, culminate in a "working narrative," or one's conscious experience of the film. The model helps to address such issues as whether music simply adds information to the film experience or whether it leads to new emergent properties of the film experience by virtue of the audiovisual combinations. The model also sheds light on the issue of the level of consciousness at which music operates in the film, in particular, accounting for the fact that the emotional component of music seems to be extracted from the music acoustic signal for the story (diegesis) while the acoustical aspect of the signal is often left behind. The concluding Section 5 reviews the value of the cognitive approach to the understanding of film music and encourages future collaborations among musicologists and film theorists and others involved in the many disciplines of cognitive science.

2. INFLUENCES OF MUSIC ON MEANING, MEMORY, AND ENGAGEMENT: EXPERIMENTAL EVIDENCE

2.1 Meaning

Meaning can be a very difficult concept, but here we will consider meaning of an event in terms of all the thought processes, associations, and emotions that the event brings to mind. In discussing the meaning of events, be they visual or auditory, two types of meaning can be contrasted—that which relates to the external world (external meaning and associations) and that which relates to the structural relations of sound and visual patterns (internal meaning). Each of these will be discussed in turn.

2.1.1 *External Meaning: Associations*

Film theorists generally assume that musical soundtracks influence the interpretation of images on the screen (for example, Brown 1994, 54; Burt 1994, 4; Winter 2008, 3), and they offer compelling examples and subjective statements as evidence. Another source of evidence for meaning created by musical soundtracks is provided by experiments that systematically collect judgments from many persons about the music and visual components alone as well as from the music and visual information when combined. A comparison of these measures of individual musical and visual meanings with the measure of the combined audiovisual condition can reveal whether the addition of the music to the visual information produces a very straightforward result. Indeed, a number of studies show a rather simple, additive relation between the meaning of the music and the meaning of the film. Simply stated: Sad music plus a neutral scene produces a sad scene, whereas the opposite happens if the music is happy.

In a clear example reported in my 2000 paper, one of my experiments investigated one dimension of emotional meaning (happy–sad) as a product of the interaction between a monophonic melody and one moving object presented on a screen. The musical examples were repeating broken triads (*do mi sol mi do*) that differed in two respects: tempo and pitch (an additional variable—major/minor quality—is not relevant to the present discussion). These musical examples were presented at a slow, moderate, or fast tempo and were low, medium, or high in pitch. Previous work had revealed that these two physical dimensions controlled listeners' judgments on a five-point happiness–sadness rating scale (Trehub, Cohen, & Guerriero 1986). In other words, low pitch on average led to a rating below 3 and high pitch led to a rating above 3. Slow and fast tempo led to low and high numerical judgments respectively. The visual stimulus in the audiovisual experiment was a computer-generated ball that bounced at one of three heights and at one of three speeds. Again, perhaps surprisingly, these dimensions also led to systematic judgments on the happy–sad dimension. Low, slow bounces were judged as sad, and high, fast bounces were judged as happy. It may well seem odd that people reliably judge whether a bouncing ball is happy or sad or something in between, but the experiment shows that indeed they do.

As might be expected, the experiments show that when the auditory and visual dimensions are the same (that is, low, slow bounce paired with low, slow pitch; high, fast bounce paired with high, fast pitch), the judgment is consistent with the presentations of either audio or visual modality alone. When the levels on the audio and visual dimensions differ (low, slow, melody paired with high, fast bounce), however, the judgment represents neither the audio or visual dimension alone but rather a combination derived from both dimensions. A low and slow melody, for instance, produced judgments of the high-fast ball that were lower (less happy) than they were in the absence of the music. Even though the participants were asked to focus on the meaning of the ball, they seemed unable to resist the systematic influence of music on their interpretation of the image. This suggests that, in the simplest case, film music communicates by adding together the associations or meanings mentally generated by the different film and music components. Similar effects were observed in a study of the role of music on the judged degree of friendliness or aggressiveness of social interactions of wolves (Bolivar, Cohen, & Fentress 1994).

A recent study by Van den Stock, Peretz, Grèzes, and de Gelder (2009) also produced a straightforward pattern of results for judgments of human happy and sad actions when accompanied by happy or sad classical music excerpts. In this study, ten visual examples of actors who were depicted drinking a favorite drink that makes one happy and ten examples of drinking from a glass that makes one sad were paired once with an example of happy classical music and once with sad classical music, with each excerpt lasting three seconds. All emotional meanings of the music and visual stimuli were validated prior to the main study. The excerpts were presented in blocks of music only, motion picture only, and music and motion picture together.

The task was simply to categorize the stimuli as happy or sad. The percentage of correct identification of the actor's intended emotion for each condition was tabulated. It was found that when the meaning of the music matched that of the visually depicted intension, there were more correct responses than when the music and visually depicted intension differed in meaning. The authors provided several neurocognitive accounts, to be reviewed later, and the data contribute to the findings of direct additivity of music and visual meanings, but it should be noted that this clear-cut pattern of results is not always found.

Using a short video animation involving three geometric objects, a small circle, and a small and a large triangle, Marshall and Cohen (1988) measured multiple scales of affective meaning (rather than one scale as in the previous studies). Specifically they employed the classic semantic differential technique of Osgood, Suci, and Tannenbaum (1957) which results in ratings on three dimensions of affective meaning: evaluative (for example, good–bad), potency (for example, strong–weak), and activity (for example, fast–slow). The motion picture had been developed originally by Heider and Simmel (1944) to study stereotypical attitude formation. Typically viewers interpreted the action of the inanimate objects in a stereotypic and anthropomorphic way; for example, reporting a large bully (the large triangle) persecuting a loving, innocent couple (the small triangle and circle). In the experiment by Marshall and Cohen (1988), two contrasting musical scores, A and B, were judged by different groups of listeners respectively on multiple rating scales. Another group judged the film only. Then, with either music A or music B playing, two other groups judged the film overall and each of the three geometric characters in the film. The ratings of the film overall differed for the two music soundtracks, as might be expected, but of special interest was that the effect of music extended to judgments of the geometric objects, but in different ways. The small triangle, but not the other two characters, was judged as more active with one of the musical scores. It was proposed that structural *congruence* between the temporal patterns of the music and the motion of the geometric figures drew attention to the small triangle, which permitted musical meanings to become linked with the small triangle. The idea led to postulation of the "Congruence-Associationist framework," which is discussed in its current form as the C-A M in Section 4 below.

The point introduced by this study, which measures the meaning of several visual objects at once, is that a simple additive model is not sufficient to account for how film music alters meaning. The music did not affect the three film "characters" in the same way. At least two processes must be considered—the associations that the music brings to mind and the structuring in time (tempo, rhythm, and how various attributes such as intensity in both auditory and visual domains change in time). A third aspect became apparent in another study that used live action films (Cohen 1993). Here, two video excerpts—in one, a woman runs from a man, in the other, two men fight—were selected from a film made by an amateur director. Two contrasting music selections were used in the study. Once again the film and two music selections were evaluated by independent groups of viewers. The results were mixed: although music had a strong straightforward effect on the excerpt that depicted the male–female chase, the music for the fight scene did not strongly affect viewer interpretation. In retrospect, it was clear that the influence of music depends to a large extent on the degree of visual ambiguity. The fight scene was much more highly determined than the male–female interaction, which could be interpreted as representing either an aggressive interaction or amorous play. In this case, music resolved some of the ambiguity of the latter situation but had relatively little impact on the unambiguous fight scene.

Shevy (2007) presented a short realistic video with two kinds of rock music. One music excerpt was cheerful, and the other was described as neutral. Participants heard one of these excerpts or no music while watching the film and subsequently provided ratings of the film overall, the main character, and the mood of the film. The results indicated significant influences of the music on all three items rated, but the direction of change did not reflect straightforward addition of the meaning of the music to the meaning of the visual elements, similar to the results of Marshall and Cohen (1988).

Whereas in all examples described so far, the music accompanied the film portion of interest, Boltz, Schulkind, and Kantra (1991) presented music either before or during a target scene. The similarity in the meanings of the music and the target scene was manipulated such that the music either matched the mood or contrasted with it. This manipulation of meaning affected memory for the target scene. Tan, Spackman, and Bezdek (2007) focused not on memory but on the time course of the influence of music on interpretation of the visual event. Excerpts of 15 seconds of music chosen to represent four emotions (happiness, sadness, fear, and anger) were paired with four film clips of a film character, with a neutral expression, carrying out an activity. Music was presented either before or after the character appeared and overlapped for only a few seconds. Music in both pre- and post-film positions systematically altered the interpretation of the film characters' emotions, as indicated by an analysis of the one-word emotion labels and rating scales of eight emotions. Following the judgments of emotion, the participants rated the extent to which each of nine film factors (including presence of music) contributed to the depiction of the emotion of the film character. Participants ascribed their own judgments to two factors primarily: to the music and to the facial expression of the film character, even though the facial expressions were neutral and had been presented with all four music emotions. (Incidentally, this points to the potential fallibility of introspection.) Participants also rated aspects of the character's apparent physiological responses that were felt to portray emotion. These results clustered along two dimensions termed by the authors *action readiness* (reflecting the participant's remembered impression of the character's alertness and having a racing heart) and what the authors term *valence* (capturing the remembered impression of the character being *energized* and *trembling-shaking*). Although there may be some tolerance of asynchrony between the onsets of a visual and musical event, the results of Tan et al. (2007) add to the evidence of Boltz et al. (1991) that the same piece of music presented at different times during an action can lead to different interpretations. In addition, they showed that, music had more interpretive impact when presented prior to as opposed to after an ambiguous scene.

Taking another twist on meaning in the context of music and film, Boltz, Ebendorf, and Field (2009) turned the tables and presented music with neutral affect in the context of visual information that had clear meaning. They showed that the music took on the meaning of the visual information, such that the same music was recalled as having characteristics associated with the visual meaning to which the viewer-listeners had been exposed. This result reveals that the associations of a visual stimulus can be extended to a musical stimulus that has neutral meaning. Generally, in media contexts, the audio source modifies the visual information, but Boltz et al., (2009) showed that the reverse occurs in the case of material such as music videos in which the music dominates.

2.1.2 Internal Meaning: Congruent Structure

Associations with real-world events and emotions brought to mind by music or film were referred to above as "external meaning." Another aspect of meaning arises simply from patterning or structure, quite independent of connections to the world, and is thus referred to as "internal meaning." Internal meaning derived from pattern and relations alone can apply to any stimulus, and visual patterning in the film is no exception. A redundant visual pattern—for example, an undulating line created by an actor running across the film screen—would have more internal meaning than a line with random changes in direction. The relation between the internal meaning of the music and the internal meaning of the film may or may not be congruent. For example, congruence would arise when the melodic contour matches that of the visual pattern on the screen, or when the tempo of the music mirrors the tempo visually depicted of the pace of a person walking, an army marching, a leaf blowing, or—as in *Avatar*—a wood sprite landing on an arrow. The extent to which the audience is sensitive to such temporal congruence has received attention in a few experiments.

Bolivar et al. (1994) showed that participants could reliably distinguish between synchronous and asynchronous audiovisual combinations of wolf interactions and music excerpts. Lipscomb (2005) more precisely contrasted judgments of audiovisual sequences in which phase and tempo of the audio and visual sequences were controlled. The judged effectiveness of the audiovisual pairs was highest for the condition of the synchronized accents (same tempo and phase). Iwamiya (1994) showed that desynchronizing the music of short clips of a music video by 500 milliseconds altered several rating scales of the audio and visual information. Pursuing this line of research farther, Kim and Iwamiya (2008) studied the motion patterns of animated text (as might appear in television advertising) and accompanying music. Sets of these moving letter patterns—known as Telops in Japan—and sound patterns were combined arbitrarily. Telops and sound combinations that were temporally congruent (referred to as formal congruence) were judged as congruent. Two aspects of formal congruency were distinguished. The first, synchronization of temporal structures, depended on the synchronized onsets of similarly changing audio and visual patterns. The second depended on the type of change, for example, gradually rising loudness or pitch of sounds and the pictorial expansion of a Telop pattern.

In a similar vein, Kendall (2005a, 2005b, 2010) has explored the fit between music and visual structures. In one study, animations in two-dimensional space were created consisting of a circle that moves in x-y space. Patterns of ascending and descending ramps, arches, and undulations were superimposed. These were accompanied by two-part pitch patterns consisting of ascending and descending chromatic scales and diatonic scales ascending and descending from a C5 tonic. The stimuli were 2.5 seconds in duration (as an example, see Figure 5.2). Results demonstrate participant matches based on direction and contour of pitch for monophonic patterns; complications appear in polyphonic pitch patterns with visual stratification. Rather than view association and congruence as two different categories of meaning, he suggests a continuum bounded by these two concepts and mediated by the concepts of iconicity and stratification. In addition to his studies with abstract, formal materials, as above, he has demonstrated that musicians have been able to use this continuum (abstract to iconic to association) systematically in judging the relation between music and video clips from films.

Both film and music are organized in hierarchical units. For music we may consider motive, phrase, period, section, movement, and for film, there is shot, scene, sequence, act (Buhler, Neumeyer, & Deemer 2010). The units of music typically do not parallel the units of film. What is parallel is the notion of segment in both domains. Both listeners

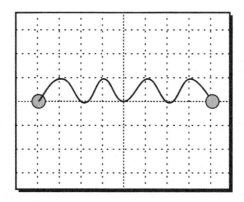

FIGURE 5.2 The visual arch starting at the center and extending only above the center line is hypothesized to match pitch pattern contours that move away from and back to the tonic (but not below it). From Kendall (2005a, 146).

and viewers are able to report when a meaningful unit has occurred (for example, for music, Frankland & Cohen 2004; for music and filmed ballet, Krumhansl & Schenk 1997). A question currently is whether the unit structure of music influences the segmentation of a film.

Krumhansl and Schenk (1997) explored whether structure and expression could be similarly represented in visual and music aspects of classical dance. The material was a film of George Balanchine's choreography of a movement of Mozart's Divertimento no. 15. Balanchine choreographed the dance with the aim of representing the musical structure; hence, it might not be surprising that breakpoints (judged phrase endings) for the two modalities corresponded. In the experiment, participants rated the music, the visual ballet, or the music plus ballet in terms of phrase endings, new ideas, levels of tension, and emotion. The results for the music–dance condition could be predicted from the ratings for the music and dance independently obtained, with greater weight contributed by the music. In the context of understanding the role of music on film meaning, this study shows an effect of music on film interpretation on several dimensions including segmentation into phrases and expressiveness. An additive (that is, statistically noninteractive) relation was found. What this means is that music has a direct effect on film in a straightforward way, but there may be more complex situations in which the additive relation is not obtained. The authors, however, note that a similar finding of additivity had been obtained for the contribution of pitch and rhythm to judgments of music alone (Krumhansl & Schenk 1997, 78).

Yet, in studies of the role of visual information in a performance of solo clarinet repertoire by Stravinsky, the role of music and visual information in conveying performers' intentions were dependent on the presence of the visual information along with the music (Vines, Krumhansl, Wanderley, Dalca, & Levitin 2011). Enjoyment levels reached highest levels only with both music and visual sources. Emotional judgment was found to be based on an interaction between the music and visual information. Earlier work by Vines had examined judgments of phrasing of this same musical material, and here the contribution of visual information exceeded that of the music information. Examples such as that from *Avatar* described earlier, of coinciding onsets of new film and music themes and styles, suggest that music may play a role in establishing discontinuities. Thompson, Russo, and Sinclair (1994) showed that music influences judgments about perceived closure in a film narrative. Related research is underway in which participants are asked to segment a film with or without music. Segmentation of the music is also obtained. The research aims to determine the extent to which the segmentation of the music influences the segmentation of the film (Hamon-Hill, Cohen, & Klein 2010).

2.2 Memory

David Fincher, director of the acclaimed film *The Social Network* (2010), speaks on a DVD supplement about his decisions regarding the score (which, incidentally, received both the prestigious Golden Globe Award and the Academy Award for best original score in 2011). Fincher speaks about the decision to replay the main theme at two critical points later in the film. The decision was based on the assumption that the audience will recall the theme presented some time earlier and will pick up on the slight changes in the repeated theme that illustrate character development. The director clearly is counting on the audience's memory for the opening theme, such that it can be recognized on subsequent presentations. Similarly, film-music theorist Claudia Gorbman (1987, 93) states that one comes gradually to associate a particular highly repeated music theme with the protagonist Mildred Pierce, in the 1945 film by the same name. Here, Gorbman also makes an assumption about how musical memory works. The approach from cognitive science would aim to determine how reliable audience memory actually is.

The most extensive work on the role of film music on memory has been conducted by Marilyn Boltz. Boltz et al. (1991) found that music marks images for conscious attention, but the extent to which it does so depends on timing and congruence in meaning. In this study, the music either accompanied a scene's outcome and thereby accentuated its affective meaning, or foreshadowed the same scene and thereby created expectations about the future course of events. The background music was either congruent or incongruent with the episode's outcome. In a subsequent recall task, when the film violated expectations foreshadowed by the music, memory was facilitated more than it was in the foreshadowing condition in which expectations were met, whereas conditions in which the film ending was correctly foreshadowed by the music accompaniment led to better memory than the incorrect foreshadowing by the music accompaniment. Results from a recognition task further revealed that music helped participants in the study recall scenes they did not otherwise remember. The background music thus manipulated visual attention depending on whether the music either preceded or accompanied the visual image, and whether its meaning was consistent or inconsistent with that of the image.

Boltz (2001) presented three ambiguous film clips with happy, sad, or no music background. In a surprise recognition task a week later, the items remembered from the films differed as a function of the music background. For example, those who heard happy music accompanying a particular film tended to remember flowers as opposed to a black car, whereas the opposite was true for those who heard the sad music. The results supported Boltz's view that associations from the music help to provide an explanatory schema to make sense of the information presented in the film. In her use of *schema*, Boltz borrows a concept fundamental to much research literature in cognitive science that focuses on memory and comprehension.

In a further set of experiments (Boltz 2004), participants viewed a set of music/film clips that were either consistent or inconsistent in their emotional meaning (mood). Selective attending was also systematically manipulated by instructing viewers to attend to and remember the music or the film, or both in tandem. The results from tune recognition, film recall, and paired discrimination tasks revealed that mood-congruent pairs led to a joint encoding of music/film information as well as an integrated memory code. Incongruent pairs, on the other hand, resulted in an independent encoding in which a given dimension, music or film, was remembered well only if it was selectively attended to at the time of encoding. A second experiment extended these findings by showing that tunes from mood-congruent pairs were better recognized when cued by their original scenes. Music from incongruent pairs was better remembered in the absence of scene information. Such evidence validates the assumption that music and the visual scene it accompanies may be linked in memory after little exposure but primarily when the emotional meanings of the music match that of the visual information. The assumption underlying leitmotif is thus supported by Boltz's (2004) findings, if the leitmotif and the visual scene make a reasonable match. The results lend support to the assumptions of theorist Gorbman and director Fincher. Indeed there is evidence that an audience member will remember a music/visual pairing presented once (actually in Boltz's studies, presentations are made twice); however, Boltz's studies imply that such memory breaks down with the incoherence or inconsistency of the meanings of the music and film pair.

2.3 Engagement

My review of film music research (Cohen 2000) discussed the assumed contribution of music to the sense of engagement in a film. The discussion was speculative. In spite of the enormous contribution of music to this aspect of film experience, there was no research on this topic. I proposed a specific hypothesis, in part attributable to the insight of James Buhler, that the less realistic the images in a film the more must music contribute so as to retain audience engagement; for example, music is more likely needed in a cartoon than in a documentary. I noted in 2000 that the idea admitted to testing, and I later executed a small program of research to explore this idea (cf., Cohen 2009). We began with short excerpts from five types of film ranging from cartoon animation to news broadcast. We presented these with appropriate music background and without any music at all. Participant's own ratings of their sense of absorption in the film were higher under the music condition for all but the news broadcast condition. We extended the study to include 11 examples representing degrees of film realism ranging from animation to TV broadcast. The results were similar.

To determine whether the effect was attributable to sound in general or to the music track specifically, in another study we created three different kinds of soundtracks for a single short movie clip. Two film clips were used: one from the film *Witness* (1985) and the other from the film *The Day of the Jackal* (1973). Three soundtracks were created for each: one solely music, one solely sound effects, and one solely speech. For *Witness*, the music track was the original score at that point in the film (the soundtrack otherwise lacked sound effects and speech). For *Jackal*, the music comprised other music for the film. Participants saw the film with only one combination of material and they were asked to rate their degree of absorption, the sense of realism of the film, and the level of professional quality of the material presented. The music led to the highest rating of absorption in the *Witness* film, as compared to either the speech or sound-effects tracks, supporting the view that music can influence absorption in a film. One problem with this study is that measures count on participants being able to assess their own level of absorption. As mentioned earlier with reference to the study by Tan et al. (2007), although people sometimes provide useful information through introspection, it is always well to obtain complementary objective measures.

To get a more objective measure of the extent to which music engages absorption in a film, a methodology was developed in which the participant's behavior would *indirectly* reflect the level of absorption in the film. The visual material was the silent film *The Railrodder* (1965), a film produced the by National Film Board of Canada and starring Buster Keaton, whose character rides the rail lines from coast to coast in Canada in a small motorized vehicle and carries out all kinds of curious activities along the way. The film was accompanied either by its original music, composed by Eldon Rathburn, or by a contrasting instrumental piece. Over the course of the 20-minute film presentation, at approximately one-minute intervals, an extraneous "X" appeared in one corner of the screen, and the participant was required to detect this and press a key on a computer keyboard as quickly as possible. The participant received the condition twice, with the first considered as a "warm-up." For the data from the second presentation, detectability of the Xs was on average slower for the appropriate music than the no-music condition, and this supported the notion that appropriate music increases engagement in a film. This was the evidence we were seeking, of course. The effect was complicated because it did not appear equally for each of the items (i.e., film excerpts) probed. The methodology, however, lends itself to many variations for future studies, which may well be aided by new brain imaging techniques as well as by the revival of an older technique, electro-encephalography (EEG), to be described in the next section.

3. FILM MUSIC AND NEUROSCIENCE

Cognitive neuroscience aims to elucidate how the brain supports mental activity. Its progress in the last decade is due in large part to recent developments in brain imaging technology. Such functional tools as electroencephalography (EEG) and positron emission tomography (PET) scans provide information about the temporal dynamics of certain regions of the brain active during ongoing cognition. Information about the location and timing of brain activity that takes place while experiencing a film could greatly help reveal how film music influences film perception. It could distinguish between the following possibilities: music and video activate independent brain sites, overlapping brain sites, or different brain sites when presented simultaneously as compared to nonsimultaneous presentation. Brain imaging tools could also indicate whether the time of brain activity during music and video is simply a linear addition of the activity from either stimulus alone, or whether together the signal is sooner or later, or larger or smaller, than would arise from simple addition. To date, however, only one study of brain imaging has combined the presentation of film and music. Happily, much important groundwork has been laid in the last decade by brain imaging studies of music alone, visual presentation alone, music and static images together, and speech and film together. Before these are reviewed, it will be useful to describe some aspects of the brain itself.

3.1 Background

The basic unit of the brain is the neuron. The human brain contains about 100 billion of them (Edelman & Tononi 2000). A neuron can be regarded as a tiny conductor of an electrical signal, but also a site in which a chemical reaction can take place. Neurons are massively interconnected through dendrites which bring information to the neuron and through axons which direct activity away from the neuron. Drawing energy and oxygen from the blood supply and influenced by the surrounding bath of electrochemical forces, electrochemical impulses within the neuron (referred to collectively as an *action potential*) are generated and travel down the axon. These action potentials or, in other words, impulses, constitute the neural code that is at the base of all mental function. Bundles of axons comprise nerves. The number of neurons in the brain is very large, but there are only 30,000 axons in the auditory nerve, which runs from the inner ear to the first way-stations along the path to the higher centers of the brain. One of the main higher centers is the auditory area of the cortex located in the temporal lobe, just above the ear.

There are four lobes of the cortex, on the surface of the brain (revealed when the skull is removed). Greatly oversimplifying, the occipital lobe, at the back of the brain, is activated by vision. The temporal lobe (or temporal cortex) is activated by speech and language and some music functions. The frontal cortex represents meanings, associations, and is the source of decision making and thinking. The parietal cortex, a band at the top of the brain, controls body movement and represents sensation. These four lobes find representation on both sides of the brain because the brain consists of two almost symmetrical halves. The functions of the left brain are generally but not completely paralleled by the right. The departure from symmetrical function is seen particularly for linguistic and music functions, with linguistic functions located primarily in the left hemisphere. Some locations specialized for music reside in the right hemisphere. Stewart (2011) provides some evidence in persons who have music deficiencies. Earlier studies showing right hemisphere localized music functions include those by Kester et al. (1991), Kimura (1964, 1967), Milner (1962), Samson and Zatorre (1991), Zatorre and Halpern (1993). It needs to be emphasized that both hemispheres are involved in representing music and speech, and that only some functions are localized in a particular hemisphere. Some aspects of artistic and creative behavior have been reported as a right-hemisphere function, and focused and fine motor tasks may in part be carried out by the left hemisphere, but again, these characterizations are overly simplistic given the hundreds of anatomical sites in the brain.

The interactivity of neurons referred to above as *massive* is captured by the concept of neural network. Neurons influence and are influenced by adjacent neurons but also by those that are quite remote. The response of individual neurons has been measured directly in animals but in humans this is seldom possible for ethical reasons. Verbal response to direct electrical stimulation of the brain has taken place on rare occasions for medical reasons (Penfield 1950), revealing, for example, localization of very vivid memories in the frontal lobe, and representation of body areas in the parietal lobe. In this case though, groups of neurons were probed, not an individual neuron. Today, again always in rare medical situations, single-cell recording in awake humans is possible (Mukamel & Fried, 2012).

Electrical activity of millions of neurons combine to establish a signal that is measurable outside the skull through electrodes using a technique such as electroencephalography (EEG), first demonstrated for humans in the 1930s. The activity pattern can be analyzed in terms of electrical wave oscillations ranging from 1 Hz (cycle per sec) to over 100 Hz. Different bands of frequencies represent different brain states or activities. The slowest frequencies, 3 Hz and below, are called delta waves. Theta waves lie between 3 and 8 Hz. Alpha waves are between 8 and 12 Hz, and above these are beta waves. Waves higher than 30 Hz are referred to as the gamma band. As an example, alpha waves are associated with a wakened state with the eyes closed. Gamma has in recent years been implicated in memory and consciousness. Through computer analysis, the source inside the brain of this EEG brain activity can be roughly localized.

Another informative aspect of the EEG wave is that portion evoked in the first second (that is, 1000 milliseconds) after the presentation of a physical stimulus such as a sound or light pattern. It is known as the *evoked potential*, or when many such epochs are averaged, the *evoked response potential* (ERP). It is described at the millisecond level and reflects unique cognitive activities at particular time periods within this range. For example, an increase in amplitude at about 300 ms into the wave reflects detection of an unexpected event, as shown by the *oddball* technique. In such a procedure, one event, such as a low tone, is repeated frequently and another, such as a high tone, infrequently. While the participant in the study pays attention to another task, a *P300* component in the ERP typically arises, indicating that the brain registered an unexpected event around 300 milliseconds after the onset of the unexpected tone. Other tasks involving knowledge of meaning will show a different kind of wave earlier than the P300. This wave is called *mismatched negativity* (MMN), because it results in a lower amplitude in the electrical activity than would otherwise be produced at that point (cf., Trainor & Zatorre 2009). Detection of a grammatical violation additionally may appear at around 600 milliseconds. The ERP provides precise information about the timing of different kinds of brain activity and how these change across the lifespan.

Newer brain imaging techniques provide more precise spatial information about the location in the brain that is active during the particular mental activity of interest. Magnetoencephalography (MEG), like EEG, picks up surface electrical activity, although it is limited to activity of neurons oriented in a particular direction, due to the magnetic current that is actually measured. MEG has the advantage of being able to measure signals from many sites without applying contact electrodes to the scalp. Positron emission tomography (PET) scans entail tracking brain activity upon injection of a radioactive dye. Functional magnetic resonance imaging (fMRI), on the other hand, measures the time course of the blood oxygenation level (BOLD) during various mental activities. An fMRI does not require injection, but it entails the presence of an extremely loud noise of the magnet. This noise requires wearing hearing protection and makes a study of film music rather unnatural. Nevertheless, studies with music alone and with music and images have been conducted by presenting the stimuli during short silent periods and measuring the activity that has resulted in the subsequent noisy period when the magnet is activated. None of these imaging techniques offers a complete picture, but employing more than one technique to the study of one phenomenon has recently been found to be very informative. For example, EEG provides high temporal resolution that can complement information from fMRI, which provides a high resolution spatial image of brain activity (Koelsch 2012, 43 & 79–83). Each technique, however, requires expensive equipment as well as operating costs, and using two techniques in the same study augments the cost even further. The equipment often primarily serves life-saving clinical functions, and is in high demand for that reason, which accounts for why the number of brain imaging studies involving music or film have been more limited than we might have hoped.

In spite of the evidence for localized function for some aspects of speech, music, and vision, the last decade of brain imaging has shown that music, perhaps even more than any other stimulus, engages a great proportion of the brain (Overy & Molnar-Szakacs 2009). Massive brain activity is, however, associated with any cognitive activity

(Edelman & Tononi 2000). Overlapping brain activity has been shown in tasks sensitive to music and linguistic syntax, that is, tasks requiring sensitivity to harmonic progression and language grammar (Maess, Koelsch, Gunter, & Friederici 2001). Consistent with the evidence for this overlap and with similar hierarchical structuring required for generation of rule-governed sequences in music and speech, Patel (2008) put forward the *shared syntactic integration resource hypothesis* (SSIRH).

SSIRH proposes that limited processing resources are shared by both music and language for the purpose of integrating distinct elements into hierarchically organized sequences. Thus, music and language elements to be integrated may be represented in unique respective locations in the brain, but the syntactic process that generates the sequences for both music and language is found in the same brain space. In support of this hypothesis, Slevc, Rosenberg, and Patel (2009) presented sentences word by word or in short phrases one by one on a computer screen and asked participants to press a computer key after reading the word or phrase. Some target words or phrases created syntactic challenges, others contained semantic ambiguities. Simultaneously with each word, a musical chord was presented. The chords generally followed normal rules of musical syntax, but in some cases a chord that violated the key (Experiment 1) or a chord with an altered timbre (Experiment 2) accompanied the linguistic violation (Experiment 1). The chord violation was regarded as a violation of music syntax in contrast to the timbre violation which was considered like a semantic violation. The combined effect of the music and linguistic syntactic violations was greater than the effect of either alone. This nonlinearity did not appear for the combined semantic violations. The significant interaction between music and linguistic syntactic processes supported SSIRH. The proposed syntactic activity may take place in Broca's area, which lies in the inferior (lower) frontal lobe near the temporal (auditory) lobe of the brain, and in its homologue on the right side of the brain (Maess et al. 2001).

3.2 Studies relevant to film music

One recent MEG study presented seven participants with short clips of matched or mismatched film and speech segments from the film *Dumb and Dumber* (1994) (Luo, Liu, & Poeppel 2010). The general purpose of the study was to understand how the brain integrates information from audio and visual modalities, in this case speech and scenes from the film. The more specific purpose of the study was much more complex and focused on a very exciting proposal of how information from audio and visual sources can be combined into a smooth unitary percept.

Earlier I mentioned that the brain generates electrical waves ranging from 1 to over 100 Hz. It has been proposed that the temporal synchrony arising from audio and visual information having the same physical source (for example, someone speaking) would produce synchronous waves, and that the wave produced by the auditory cortex would be influenced by the temporal parameters of simultaneously presented visual information and vice versa. If the audio and visual information were synchronized, the resultant electrical wave would be more clearly defined than if the two modes were asynchronous. Luo et al. (2010, 8) argue that "multisensory integration may use cross-modal phase modulation as a basic mechanism to construct temporally aligned representations that facilitate perceptual decoding of audiovisual speech."

While in an MEG scanner that extracted brain wave activity from 157 channels, each participant was presented with 15 repetitions of three 30-second clips of the film, as well as 15 repetitions of three combinations of mismatched film and speech tracks. The particular focus was the slow EEG wave band from 2 to 7 Hz, the delta and theta bands. The potentially groundbreaking findings revealed a mechanism in the early cortical path for audition and vision "continuously tracking natural audio-visual systems, carrying dynamic multi-sensory information, and reflecting cross-sensory interaction in real-time" (Luo et al. 2010, l). Further "auditory and visual modalities can mutually and actively modulate the phase of the internal low-frequency rhythms in early sensory cortical regions and that such cross-sensory driving efficiency depends on the relative audiovisual timing" (9). The authors direct attention to the fact that the typical timing (frequency) of syllables, is about 4 per sec (4 Hz) and falls within the delta-theta band. In the context of film music, however, it can also be pointed out that the majority of music tempos fall within the delta-theta range (for example, andante exceeds 1 beat per sec (> 1 Hz); allegro typically exceeds 2 Hz; the fastest of music tempos, prestissimo, is in the range of 3.5 Hz). Clearly the beat of film music could serve (possibly even better) the same function as syllable timing. However, this is all highly speculative given that the results of Luo et al. (2010) would need to be repeated and then extended to a study which included film music, and film music tempo, as a variable for examination.

Another study using MEG also explored audiovisual signals, though much more abstractly than in the study by Luo et al. (2010). Besle et al. (2007) presented an "odd-ball" task to ten participants in which two audiovisual pairs (A1V1 and A2V2) were each presented approximately 44% of the time and two other pairs A1V2 and A2V1 were each presented approximately 6% of the time (for a total of 100%). As typical of this procedure, the task of the participant was to ignore the AV stimuli and to indicate the disappearance of a visual fixation cross. The audio stimuli consisted of a tone having two overtones and a fundamental (low frequency) of 500 Hz that ascended to either 540 Hz (for stimulus A1) or 600 Hz (for stimulus A2). The visual dimension was a circle that changed to either a horizontal (V1) or vertical (V2) ellipse. A follow-up study revealed that the discrimination of the stimuli was difficult; hence, it was not surprising that not all participants in the main study showed any significant effect of the *oddball* infrequent stimuli. The group data, however, revealed an oddball response that appeared as both a change in the temporal (auditory) lobe and occipital (visual) lobe sites. This study has many problems due to the difficulty of the task for many of the participants, but the methodology, nevertheless, is clearly amenable to further studies of brain function with this sophisticated brain imaging technology that can measure over 300 brain sites with high temporal accuracy (to 1 millisecond). The authors concluded that the results of the study suggested that bimodal events are represented in modality specific cortices (temporal lobe for auditory and occipital lobe for visual, as would be expected) and that their conjunction may also be represented, in that, for example, the audio response followed rather than preceded the occipital response, which is to some extent counterintuitive in that auditory processing is the faster sense generally, as compared to vision. Film music provides a future opportunity for this MEG application.

A recent study of film perception alone by Whittingstall, Bartels, Singh, Kwon, and Logothetis (2010) reports methodology for collecting EEG and fMRI simultaneously. In this study, participants, in an fMRI machine, wore a cap fitted with 64 electrodes. They were presented with 25 repetitions of one two-minute excerpt of a James Bond film. Seven participants saw one of two excerpts. The results revealed that the combination of the EEG and fMRI measure enables very precise localization of brain activity that occurred over the two minutes while watching the excerpt. The paper is entitled "Integration of EEG source imaging and fMRI during continuous viewing of natural movies"; however, what the researchers refer to as "natural movies" would differ from what the average person would view as watching a film in a natural context. They measured particularly the response to changing light patterns during the two-minute film clip and localized the response to an early cortical area called V6.

Before leaving the discussion of the EEG signals, it is well to mention interest in the gamma band, signals of 30 Hz or more. Gamma-band activity is understood to reflect the process of binding the representations of object features together (as described by Herrmann, Munk, & Engel 2004). Coherent activity in the gamma-band is enhanced during attentional selection of sensory information (Herrmann et al. 2004, 349). Gamma-band activity is also implicated in matching of attended objects with working memory (Herrmann et al. 2004, 350). The authors' *match-and-utilization model* imputes gamma-band activity with the ability to establish consciousness of some of the material in working memory. There has been in general increasing evidence that conscious brain activity is supported by synchronized firing across many brain structures (Crick & Koch 1990; Edelman & Tononi 2000; Revonsuo & Newman 1999).

Turning to another important theoretical shift in the last decade, Rizzolatti and his colleagues in Italy discovered and reported that neurons in an area of the macaque monkey brain responded both when the macaque enacted or watched an action such as grasping an object (as reviewed by Rizzolatti & Fabbri-Destro 2010). These neurons which responded to either executing or observing the same action were termed *mirror neurons*. The same neural activity was found in homologous structures of the human brain—the premotor and inferior parietal regions—in response to action of the self or observing such action carried out by another individual. The basic concept has been extended to the much more general notion that the brain is sensitive to intentional messaging of self and other. This also forms a basis for empathetic behaviors. A *mirror system hypothesis* has also been proposed for the acquisition of language (Arbib 2005, 2006).

Extending the mirror neuron system theory to music, Overy and Molnar-Szakacs (2009, 492) propose that the human mirror neuron system may provide "a domain-general neural mechanism for processing combinatorial rules common to language, action and music, which in turn can communicate meaning and human affect." They further propose the *shared affective motion experience* (SAME) model that assumes that music is perceived not only in terms of its auditory signal but also "in terms of the intentional, hierarchically organized sequences of expressive motor acts behind the signal" (492). They pinpoint the brain structure known as the anterior insula as the "neural conduit" between the mirror neuron system and the limbic (emotional brain) system that ultimately accounts for the emotional response to music. It is noted that the insula lies close to the auditory cortex (in the temporal lobe) and is also near the amygdala, a site known to support emotion. They emphasize that at its core, music is a stimulus associated with production—for the untrained musician production through vocal or percussive (for example, clapping) activity, and for the trained musician production through training on any of a variety of instruments. It is only in the very recent era of electronic music that the link between action and music has been to some extent broken.

The theory of the mirror neuron system encourages consideration of music in terms of a reflection of motion, and in particular bodily motion. This is relevant to the role of music in film, in that film can visually present information about body motion (see also Rosar 1994 for parallels with earlier notions of physiognomic perception). A link between music and emotional body language was shown in the study by Van den Stock et al. (2009) already described in Section 2.1.1 on meaning. It will be recalled that in that study, classical music that was compatible with the actors' intentions (drinking associated with happiness or sadness) led to increased correct judgments of the actors' intentions. The authors suggest several accounts for their data, one of which draws a parallel between the mirror neuron system in the monkey premotor and motor structures and the proposed human mirror neuron system in the premotor cortex in humans (Van den Stock et al. 2009, 219). Based on research of Lahav, Saltzman, and Schlaug (2007) and that of Grèzes, Pichon, and de Gelder (2007), which respectively have revealed activation of the right premotor structures for music in nonmusicians and emotional body language, Van den Stock et al. highlight the possibility that this neural structure may account for the influence of music that had clear meaning on the interpretation of the visually depicted intentions of the actors. They also note the importance of the amygdala in the processing of emotional information, particularly in the left hemisphere. They refer to their accounts to explain the significant impact of the music from Richard Strauss's *Also Sprach Zarathustra* at the beginning of Stanley Kubrick's film *2001: A Space Odyssey* (1968), which shows an ape-man discovering that a bone can be used as a tool or weapon. The emphasis on bodily motion as the basis of the impact of film music has been promoted by Danish communication theorist Iben Have (2008) in her discussion of the role of music in a documentary about Pia Kjaersgaard, a Danish politician.

In its response to situations of empathy and more broadly social behavior, the mirror neuron system seems tailor-made for the movie theater which one attends for the prime purpose of watching action, and, according to some film and literary theorists, for the purpose also of identifying and empathizing with the characters and engaging in the story. Overy and Molnar-Szakacs (2009) talk about the mirror neuron system supporting the music listening experience as the result of being communicated to, sung to, or performed for. They also relate the decoding of music to the level of performance that one is capable of (for the nonmusician, the ability to sing or clap in time). It would follow that film music potentially would be interpreted as either the narrator communicating the emotional meaning of a scene, or as direct information about the protagonists emotional state with which the audience empathizes, by means of the mirror-neuron system.

Other research has focused on the basis of pleasure and has shown that music engages the same neural reward system that supports other pleasurable activities such as eating and the more extreme cases of addictions (Salimpoor, Benovoy, Larcher, Dagher, & Zatorre 2011). Participants in the study were asked to provide music that gave them chills, because such a response produces physiological changes that can be objectively measured. Positron emission tomography (PET scan), which typically measures cerebral blood flow elicited by brain activity, was used in this case to measure the level of dopamine produced during the presentation of the music. Radioactive dye was injected before the experimental trials so that dopamine production (dopaminergic activity) could be measured. Dopamine is associated with the seeking and finding of pleasure and had been implicated previously as a source of the pleasure that music produces (for example, Menon & Levitin 2005), though the idea had not been directly tested. In addition, the participants were also submitted to functional magnetic resonance imaging (fMRI) for the purpose of measuring the time course of the blood oxygenation level (BOLD) response in relation to the dopamine activity. The participants also indicated when their peak experience of chills occurred so that this could be correlated with both the dopamine and the BOLD response.

A question of interest to the researchers was whether dopamine was released in anticipation of pleasure or at the time peak pleasure occurred. Results for both pleasurable and neutral music were contrasted for each participant. Anticipation epochs were defined as 15 seconds before the peak experience was reported. Note that this is the same duration that Tan et al. (2008) had employed in their study of the time of influence of film music prior to and after the presentation of a visual event. A clear outcome was obtained. Anticipation was associated with greater dopamine release in the *caudate*, and peak experience was associated with greater dopamine in the nearby *nucleus accumbens*. Both of these structures are close to the primary auditory cortex in the temporal lobe. The activity took place primarily in the right hemisphere, and the dorsal and ventral subdivisions of the striatum were most involved in anticipation and peak emotional responses during music listening respectively (Salimpoor et al., 2011, 260). This evidence for the endogenous (self-produced) generation of dopamine via music, though preliminary and in need of replication, is groundbreaking; as the authors themselves say, "The results further speak to why music can be effectively used in rituals, marketing or film to manipulate hedonic states" (262).

Using fMRI, Eldar, Ganor, Admon, Bleich, and Hendler (2007) showed that emotional music, combined with neutral film images (12 sec duration) that were rich in real-world detail, increased activity in several brain areas (amygdala, hippocampus, and lateral prefrontal areas) as compared to the activity elicited by the unimodal stimuli. At the time of writing, this is the only brain imaging study that has controlled both music and film in the same experiment, and it shows how the two types of information are complimentary in engaging the brain's emotional structures. The findings are consistent with those of Baumgartner, Lutz, Schmidt, and Jäncke (2006) who used fMRI to study the response to emotional pictures and music. Their study showed that combination led to greater activation of the same emotional centers identified by Eldar et al. (2007), and that the pictures alone elicited activity associated with a more "cognitive mode of emotion perception" (Baumgartner et al., 151). The work of Spreckelmeyer, Kutas, Urbach, Altenmüller, and Münte (2006), which investigated ERP recordings during simultaneous presentation of emotional pictures and affectively sung notes, also merits consideration in this context, although the results are less clear and tend to focus on additivity of meaning as well as "emotional coherence as a binding factor" (Spreckelmeyer et al. 2006, 166).

The studies described above focus on sites that are activated through integration, but film music also encourages us to consider the extent to which domains of experience are represented in unique locations by the brain. Fodor (1983) proposed a celebrated theory of modularity of the mind. It starts with fairly obvious facts of physiology: for example, the peripheral visual system encodes activities that take place at the retina, not at the cochlea, and so on. Our perception of reality is a construct to the extent that it appears integrated. In the 25 years since, neurophysiological and psychological studies have provided evidence on the extent of separable mental processes, some of which has been reviewed above. Separate, independent systems for verbal and musical information have been implied by early psychological studies of short-term memory showing that tones were processed independently of verbal information, spoken numbers in the case of Deutsch (1970). On a larger scale are the longstanding and influential views of Howard Gardner (1983, 1993), who has argued for eight types of intelligence, music being one. Other intelligences relevant to the present discussion are linguistic, spatial, and—in light of the mirror neuron theory—kinesthetic, interpersonal, and intrapersonal.

4. CONGRUENCE-ASSOCIATIONIST MODEL (C-A M) FOR UNDERSTANDING FILM MUSIC

The Congruence-Associationist Model was first introduced in the study reported by Marshall and Cohen (1988) to account for the fact that the attitudes toward three geometric film characters were affected differently by background music. The model is presented in the following as a means of integrating some of the preceding material and to help in the design of future studies in cognitive science of film music. The framework is essentially a flow diagram that highlights certain aspects of the independent and interactive processing of five primary media in cinema, as identified by film theorist Christian Metz (1974)—two visual channels (visual scenes and text) and three audio channels (music, speech, and noise or environmental sounds). In consideration of recent studies on the mirror neuron system, a sixth sensory channel, representing bodily motion or kinesthetic information is added to this model (see Figure 5.3, Level A, where the 6

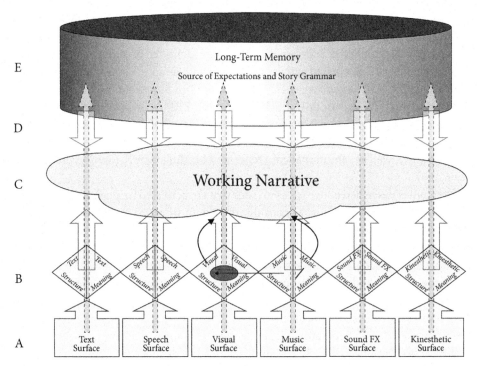

FIGURE 5.3 Congruence-Associationist Model (C-A M) for understanding film-music communication. Information flow diagram of mental activity underlying the joint processing of continuous media. Level A represents the physical surface features of each of the six physical/sensory domains. Information quickly processed after A is sent along the pathway indicated by dotted lines that travel to level E. This fast (rough) processed information provides cues to initiate activity at E. At B, the surfaces are similarly analyzed into structural and meaning (associationist) components. Music structural information combines with similar structural information from other domains (here visual scene domain similarity depicted by the lower horizontal arrow), such that corresponding information patterns (here visual information in the dark oval) receive priority for inclusion in the working narrative at C. Note that information from music meaning (at B) also travels to the working narrative at C (depicted by the ascending arrow from music meaning moving up to C). Information from B selected for the Working Narrative at C is matched with information originating from long-term memory (LTM) at E through channels at D. Hypotheses based on experience and story grammar at level E are generated at D to make sense of the 6 channels of information received at C. Some of this information admitted to the working narrative at C may travel back to LTM (level E) to form new long-term memories. See text for further explanation.

physical/sensory surfaces begin). The addition of the sixth kinesthetic channel was first proposed by Cohen (2009, 449) in a developmental context in speculation which is now better supported by more recent evidence, as has been mentioned (for example, Overy & Molnar-Szakacs 2009).

Figure 5.3, Level B, also illustrates that through structural congruence, depicted by the arrow directed from music structure to the dark grey oval within the visual structure/

meaning diamond, music directs specific attention to particular aspects of the visual scene depicted. The structural aspect of music, however, could be congruent with any of the other channels at Level B, for example, speech has rhythm (Luo et al. 2010), and text may be presented as an animation with temporal properties parallel to those of the music (Kim & Iwamiya 2008). In other words, arrows from music structure could be directed to any of these other domains. Structural congruencies might be activated for other surfaces, as well, such as speech and visual (Luo et al. 2010).

Regarding music meaning, the arrow moving from music meaning Level B to Level C reflects that music conveys meaning or associations as described in Section 2.1 above (Boltz 2004; Cohen 1990, 1993; Shevy 2007; Tan et al. 2007) that may get represented in the conscious experience of the film, called here the Working Narrative (Level C). Because of the pervasive use of the concepts of congruence (internal structure) and association (external structure) by which all of the six physical/sensory information channels are or can be analyzed, the framework is referred to as the Congruence-Associationist Model or C-A M.

Within the film or media context, C-A M portrays that music is a vehicle transporting a variety of information, only some of which is relevant to a particular cinematic goal. The brain selects what is useful for the goal at hand with the help of all the information stored in long-term memory at Level E, including story grammar. The origin of knowledge of story grammar is an interesting theoretical question, but is outside the bounds of the present discussion.

The story at Level D arises from ideas generated by Level E's long-term memory and story grammar, primed by information that has leaked to Level E through fast preprocessing of the sensory surfaces at Level A. The dashed lines and arrow ascending into Level E represent the leaked cues that start at Level A. These ideas descending from E through D to C potentially comprising the story of which the audience is aware are matched against information moving more slowly from Level B analyses. The sensory information from Level B is to be matched through re-entrant involvement of Level D. This information at Level B can attain consciousness only if a decision is made at C that this information makes the best match with the story or hypotheses descending at D. This matching processes is consistent with other models of attention and consciousness (for example, Grossberg's (1995, 2007) Adaptive Resonance Theory (ART); Kintsch's (1998) Model of Comprehension; Herrmann et al.'s (2004) match-and-utilization model).

C-A M explains that affective meanings or associations from music contribute to the narrative. In serving the nondiegetic role (role outside the story), the sounds themselves are often of little concern whereas the affective meaning conveyed by the sounds is often of critical importance. The C-A M Model explains that music does not have to be either diegetic or nondiegetic but rather some information arising from one aspect can take part in the diegesis while other information of the music can be ignored, though it may be useful for some other purpose (such as selling a soundtrack album).

The diagram represents five levels of information flow, from A to E. Level A represents the surface structure—of speech, music, sound effects, text, visual scenes, and

kinesthetic information. At level B, each of these is analyzed into structural and associationist (structure and meaning) components by domain-specific systems. For the
domain of music, this means decomposition into temporal structures and emotional
meaning (affect). (There are, of course, other kinds of feature analysis that could take
place, but the diagram emphasizes these.) Level B affords the possibility for cross-modal
congruencies to take control and automatically lead preliminary attention only to a portion of the visual information (or text information, or kinesthetic information, should
there be some source of that information provided), shown here as the material within
the oval. The kinesthetic system plays no role at this point in the normal film viewing
situation. In the case of a video game, where kinesthetic information may play a role
through a motor interface, kinesthetic information would in fact be processed in accordance with the associations it may bring to mind as well as the structural patterns of the
kinesthetic information.

Cognitive psychologists have applied Gestalt principles to visual pattern—and more
recently to auditory information (for example, Bregman 1990, 1993), including music
(Lerdahl & Jackendoff 1983; Narmour 1991)—but rarely have the principles been applied
to the two domains at once (Luo et al. 2010 make the same point). When the auditory
information and visual information are structurally congruent, the visually congruent
information becomes the figure, the focus of attention. Gestalt theoretic ideas (I have
avoided the term principles, because this implies they are more precise than they actually are)are typically applied to visual or auditory domains independently, but they can
be applied productively to conjoint visual and auditory dynamic information (Saygin,
Driver, & de Sa 2008). It follows that through innate Gestalt grouping processes, music
can in theory define the visual (or speech, or text, or sound effects or kinesthetic) figure
against the audio and other sensory background; that is, music can sometimes determine what is the visual (or other sensory) focus of attention.

These ideas relate to those in the film-music literature on sensitivity to and effectiveness of structurally congruent musical and film structures. An old example is Prokofiev's
score for the "Battle on the Ice" sequence in *Alexander Nevsky* (1938), where the temporal contour of the melody mimics the static visual contour of the scene. A modern
example is that provided earlier in this chapter of the descending scalar line that is congruent with the descent of the wood sprite in *Avatar*. Notably, this scale descent is also
congruent with the eye movement and the hand movement of Neytiri. The film-music
technique of mickey-mousing could supply many other examples. In these instances,
the composer or director has intuitions that similar formal or structural congruence
between music and video patterns promote the appreciation of or the story of the film.
The C-A M framework enables research on the following questions: To what extent is
the cross-dimensional structural congruence encoded? How accurate must the structural congruence be for it to be effective? What dimensions in the auditory and visual
domains can be manipulated to establish structural congruence? To what extent does
audiovisual structural congruence focus visual attention?

Returning to the remainder of the framework of Figure 5.3, note that certain visual
information has priority of transfer; see again the gray oval at level B. Not all of the visual

information that is potentially available can be represented in the Working Narrative at level C. The affective quality of music is directed here (note again the black arrow ascending to C from the meaning section of the music diamond at B) because it is useful in determining the meaning of the scene. In order to understand how the material from B can come into conscious attention, it will be helpful to appeal to Grossberg's (1995) ART model of conscious attention, which claims that material such as that leaving level B must be matched by material in long-term memory (LTM) for survival in short-term memory. Note Baddeley's (2012) alignment of the term *working memory* with the dynamic process of short-term memory. Assuming that experiences represented in LTM include affective tone, conceivably a match at level C would take place for visual and affective information from a film, but there would be no match for the acoustical properties of the musical accompaniment that gave rise to the musical affect. In other words, material leaving B must be matched by material generated by hypotheses D from LTM at E in order for representation to occur at level C, the Working Narrative. This explains why acoustical aspects of the music would not generally be attended: the acoustical aspects of the music do not make sense to LTM (where is that background music coming from?) and no hypotheses would be generated easily to include it (unless, of course, music were part of the diegesis, for example, the protagonist attends a concert). Thus, the main phenomenal experience C is one of a narrative. Running in parallel, all aspects of the music can be processed at a conscious level (levels D and E in the music column), as simultaneous tasks can co-occur (Neisser & Becklen 1975), and background music is remembered (Boltz 2004; Boltz and others 1991). A similar process is envisioned for speech, sound effects, and text as well, but these are not the focus of the present chapter.

The C-A M framework explains a puzzling, paradoxical role of background music in film. Music adds information that is both consistent and inconsistent with the narrative. The affective quality is usually consistent; the acoustical aspect of the music is often not. Although the affective associations produced by the music seem like they belong to images, the sounds that produced those associations do not. Somehow, the brain attends to the meaning and ignores or attenuates its acoustical source. Some individuals may in fact be particularly sensitive to film music and actually attend films because of it, just as a minority of individuals have absolute pitch and are aware of note names of musical tones they hear.

5. CONCLUSION

This chapter has attempted to show how the effects of film music on meaning, memory, and the construction of a reality within a film can be addressed from a cognitive scientific perspective. With an emphasis on the fields of cognitive psychology and cognitive neuroscience, a variety of research on the role of music on the meaning, memory and engagement of film was reviewed. A specific discussion followed on recent developments in cognitive neuroscience, describing several techniques, mentioning potential EEG measures for elucidation of consciousness, evoked response potentials representing the first second of stimulation, and the pairing of techniques that offer high temporal resolution (EEG and ERP) and high spatial resolution (fMRI), and finally, a joint use of PET scan and fMRI that successfully revealed the ability of pleasurable music to produce dopamine was described (Salimpoor et al., 2011). Only one of these brain imaging studies actually explored music in the film context (Eldar et al. 2007), but more imaging studies of film music cognition are undoubtedly just around the corner.

It is premature to speculate how all of the brain circuitry fits together to account for the effects of music in film. Yet, it is helpful to have an overview of a system that includes the various physical energies that the brain represents in specific sensory channels and that takes into account that all that the audience member has going for him or her in the film theater is this information and long-term memory and story grammar. With these materials the show must go on, and the "brain is the screen," to quote the philosopher of cinema Gilles Deleuze (interview in Flaxman 2000). The Congruence-Associationist Model (C-A M) was therefore described as a basis for understanding how these bottom-up and top-down processes co-operate to create the experience of the film, the working narrative. The C-A M helps to address the puzzle of the role of film music that straddles the diegetic and the nondiegetic worlds. The C-A M provides a solution by showing that film music is not one thing, but many. It is a vehicle transporting various kinds of information. Some of that information can be packaged to assist the narrative, while another combination can be packaged to create a music hit or a bestselling soundtrack album. The proposed system is parsimonious as the same kind of decoding takes place for all sensory channels—decoding into external and internal structure, into associations and structural congruencies. There is of course more to it, but this search for regularities and parsimony is a first step. The C-A M may also serve a role in the design of experiments that will make the most effective use of the new brain imaging tools that are becoming available stimulating new research.

A notion of considering a soundtrack as one integrated acoustic signal arising from the integration of sound effects, speech, and music has been proposed by Lipscomb and Tolchinsky (2005). They suggest that "as the field continues to mature, the constituent elements that comprise the soundtrack should be studied as a whole" (401–2). Music, speech, and sound effects must be considered as one unit. At times this approach is valid, at other times it is helpful to keep the distinction between the three acoustic domains.

Conducting experiments in film music in cognitive psychology and cognitive neuroscience requires specialized knowledge in these particular fields as well as in music, statistics, research design, experimental instrumentation, and ethical procedures in behavior research. Much knowledge about conducting experiments is gained from hands-on involvement in research: formulation of the hypothesis, development of the research design (including decisions regarding the particular audiovisual materials to be used, the setting, and the characteristics of the participants to be tested), data collection from participants in the study, analysis of the data, and finally, reporting the findings. It is a daunting task for a film theorist or film-music scholar to gain the expertise described above, and conversely, for the cognitive scientist to develop the knowledge of film or film-music production and film theory that enables asking the right questions and providing appropriate interpretations of the data. The exponential growth of discipline-specific knowledge in the 21st century encourages collaborations between film-music theorists and cognitive scientists, whether they be in academic departments of music, film, psychology, computer science, linguistics, anthropology, or a film co-op, film production company, music recording studio, or a medical research center. It is hoped that this chapter might inspire specialists in one area or another to initiate and follow through on discussions with colleagues in other disciplines so as to contribute to the future understanding of the role of music in film from the perspective of cognitive science.

BIBLIOGRAPHY

Arbib, M. A. (2005). From monkey-like action recognition to human language: An evolutionary framework for neurolinguistics. *Behavior & Brain Sciences, 28*, 105–124.

Arbib, M. A. (Ed.). (2006). *Action to language via the mirror neuron system.* Cambridge: Cambridge University Press.

Baddeley, A. (2012). Working memory: Theories, models, and controversies. *Annual Review of Psychology, 63*, 1–29.

Baumgartner, T., Lutz, K., Schmidt, C. F., &Jäncke, L. (2006). The emotional power of music: How music enhances the feeling of affective pictures. *Brain Research, 1075*, 151–164.

Bermúdez, J. L. (2010). *Cognitive science: An introduction to the science of the mind.* Cambridge: Cambridge University Press.

Besle, J., Caclin, A., Mayet, R., Delpuech, C., Lecaignard, F., Giard, M.-H., & Morlet, D. (2007). Audiovisual events in sensory memory. *Journal of Psychophysiology, 21*, 231–238.

Boden, M. A. (2006). *Mind as Machine: A History of Cognitive Science.* Oxford: Oxford University Press.

Bolivar, V. J., Cohen, A. J., & Fentress, J. C. (1994). Semantic and formal congruency in music and motion pictures: Effects on the interpretation of visual action. *Psychomusicology, 13*, 28–59.

Boltz, M. G. (2001). Musical soundtracks as a schematic influence on the cognitive processing of filmed events. *Music Perception, 18*, 427–454.

Boltz, M. G. (2004). The cognitive processing of film and musical soundtracks. *Memory & Cognition, 32*, 1194–1205.

Boltz, M. G., Ebendorf, B., & Field, B. (2009). Audiovisual interactions: The impact of visual information on music perception and memory. *Music Perception, 27*, 43–59.

Boltz, M., Schulkind, M., & Kantra, S. (1991). Effects of background music on the remembering of filmed events. *Memory & Cognition, 19*, 593–606.

Bregman, A. S. (1990). *Auditory scene analysis: The perceptual organization of sound.* Cambridge, MA: MIT Press.

Bregman, A. S. (1993). Auditory scene analysis: Hearing in complex environments. In S. McAdams, & E. Bigand (Eds.), *Thinking in sound: The cognitive psychology of human audition* (pp. 10–36). New York: Oxford University Press.

Brown, R. S. (1994). *Overtones and undertones: Reading film music.* Berkeley: University of California Press.

Buhler, J., Neumeyer, D., & Deemer, R. (2010). *Hearing the movies: Music and sound in film history*. New York: Oxford University Press.

Bullerjahn, C., & Güldenring, M. (1994). An empirical investigation of effects of film music using qualitative content analysis. *Psychomusicology, 13,* 99–118.

Burt, G. (1994). *The art of film music*. Boston: Northeastern University Press.

Cameron, J., & Landau, J. (Producers), & Cameron, J. (Director).(2009). *Avatar*. [Motion Picture]. USA, Twentieth Century Fox.

Cohen, A. J. (1990). Understanding musical soundtracks. *Empirical Studies of the Arts, 8,* 111–124.

Cohen, A. J. (1993). Associationism and musical soundtrack phenomena. *Contemporary Music Review, 9,* 163–178.

Cohen, A. J. (1994). Introduction to the special volume on the psychology of film music. *Psychomusicology, 13,* 2–8.

Cohen, A. J. (1995). One-trial memory integration of music and film: A direct test. Paper presented at the Annual Meeting of the Canadian Acoustical Association, Quebec.

Cohen, A. J. (2000). Film music: Perspectives from cognitive psychology. In D. Neumeyer, C. Flinn, & J. Buhler (Eds.), *Music and cinema* (pp. 360–377). Hanover, NH: University Press of New England.

Cohen, A. J. (2009). Music in performance arts: Film, theatre and dance. In S. Hallam, I. Cross, & M. Thaut (Eds.), *The Oxford handbook of music psychology* (pp. 441–451). New York: Oxford University Press.

Cohen, A. J. (2010). Music as a source of emotion in film. In P. Juslin & J. Sloboda (Eds.). *The Oxford handbook of music and emotion.* (pp. 879–908). Oxford: Oxford University Press.

Cohen, A. J. & Graziano, A. (Eds.). (2009). Special volume "A history of music psychology in autobiography." *Psychomusicology: Music, Mind & Brain, 20.*

Cook, N. (1998). *Analysing musical multimedia*. New York: Oxford University Press.

Crick, F., & Koch, C. (1990). Towards a neurobiological theory of consciousness. *Seminars in the neurosciences, 2,* 263–275.

Deutsch, D. (1970). Tones and numbers: Specificity of interference in immediate memory. *Science, 168,* 1604–1605.

Edelman, G., M. & Tononi, G. (2000). *Consciousness: How matter becomes imagination*. London: Penguin.

Eldar, E., Ganor, O., Admon, R., Bleich, A., & Hendler, T. (2007). Feeling the real world: Limbic response to music depends on related content. *Cerebral Cortex, 17,* 2828–2840.

Engel, A. K., & Singer, W. (2001). Temporal binding and the neural correlates of sensory awareness. *Trends in Cognitive Sciences, 5,* 16–25.

Flaxman, G. (Ed.). (2000). *The brain is the screen: Deleuze and the philosophy of cinema*. Minneapolis: University of Minnesota Press.

Flores-Gutiérrez, E. O., Díaz, J.-L., Barrios, F. A., Favila-Humara, R., Guevara, M. Á., del Rio-Portilla, Y., & Corsi-Cabrera, M. (2007). Metabolic and electric brain patterns during pleasant and unpleasant emotions induced by music masterpieces. *International Journal of Psychophysiology, 65,* 69–84.

Fodor, J. A. (1983). *Modularity of mind: An essay on faculty psychology*. Cambridge, MA: MIT Press.

Frankland, B. & Cohen, A. J. (2004). Parsing of Melody: Quantification and testing of the local grouping rules of Lerdahl and Jackendoff's (1983) *A Generative Theory of Tonal Music*. *Music Perception, 14,* 55–81.

Frijda, N. H. (1986). *The emotions*. Cambridge: Cambridge University Press.

Gardner, H. (1983/1993). *Frames of mind: The theory of multiple intelligences.* New York: Basic Books.

Hallam, S., Cross, I., & Thaut, M. (Eds.) (2009). *The Oxford handbook of Music Psychology.* New York: Oxford University Press.

Gosselin, N., Peretz, I., Noulhiane, M., Hasboun, D., Beckett, C., Baulac, M., & Samson, S. (2005). Impaired recognition of scary music following unilateral temporal lobe excision. *Brain, 128,* 628–640.

Gorbman, C. (1987). *Unheard melodies: Narrative film music.* Bloomington: Indiana University Press.

Grèzes, J., Pichon, S., de Gelder, B. (2007). Perceiving fear in dynamic body expressions. *NeuroImage, 35,* 959–967.

Grossberg, S. (1995). The attentive brain. *American Scientist, 83,* 438–449.

Grossberg, S. (2007). Consciousness CLEARS the mind. *Neural Networks, 20,* 1040–1053.

Hamon-Hill, C., Cohen, A. J., & Klein, R. M. (2010). Both music and video contribute to the parsing of a short motion picture animation. Paper presented at the Twenty-Fifth Annual Meeting of the Canadian Society for Brain Behaviour and Cognitive Science, Halifax, Nova Scotia.

Have, I. (2008). Background music and background feelings: Background music in audio-visual media. *Journal of Music and Meaning, 6.* Retrieved May 22, 2011, from http://www.musicandmeaning.net/issues/showArticle.php?artID=6.5

Heider, F., & Simmel, M. (1944). An experimental study of apparent behavior. *American Journal of Psychology, 57,* 243–259.

Herrmann, C. S., Munk, M. H. J., & Engel, K. (2004). Cognitive functions of gamma-ban activity: Memory match and utilization. *Trends in Cognitive Science, 8,* 347–355.

Iwamiya, S.-I. (1994). Interaction between auditory and visual processing when listening to music in an audio visual context: 1. Matching 2: Audio quality. *Psychomusicology, 13,* 133–153.

Juslin, P. & Sloboda, J. (Eds.) (2010). *Handbook of music and emotion.* Oxford, UK: Oxford University Press.

Kendall, R. A. (2005a). Music and video iconicity: Theory and experimental design. *Journal of Physiological Anthropology and Applied Human Science, 24,* 143–149.

Kendall, R. A. (2005b). Empirical approaches to musical meaning. In R. A. Kendall & R. W. H. Savage (Eds.). Perspectives in systematic musicology. *Selected Reports in Ethnomusicology, 12,* 69–102.

Kendall, R. A. (2010). Music in film and animation: Experimental semiotics applied to visual, sound and musical structures. In B. E. Rogowitz, & T. N. Pappas (Eds), *Proceedings of SPIE, 7525, sponsored by IS & T Electronic Imaging and SPIE: Human Vision and Electronic Imaging XV.* San Jose, CA: 1–13.

Kester, D. B., Saykin, A. J., Sperling, M. R., O'Connor, M. J., Robinson, L. J., & Gur, R. C. (1991). Acute effect of anterior temporal lobectomy on musical processing. *Neuropsychologia, 29,* 703–708.

Kim, K.-H., & Iwamiya, S.-I. (2008). Formal congruency between Telop patterns and sounds effects. *Music Perception, 25,* 429–448.

Kimura, D. (1964). Left-right differences in the perception of melodies. *Quarterly Journal of Experimental Psychology, 16,* 355–358.

Kimura, D. (1967). Functional asymmetry of the brain in dichotic listening. *Cortex, 3,* 163–178.

Kintsch, W. (1998). *Comprehension: A paradigm for cognition.* Cambridge: Cambridge University Press.

Koelsch, S. (2012). *Brain & music*. Oxford: Wiley-Blackwell.

Krumhansl, C. L. (1997). An exploratory study of musical emotions and psychophysiology. *Canadian Journal of Experimental Psychology, 51*, 336–353.

Krumhansl, C. L., & Schenck, D. L. (1997). Can dance reflect the structural and expressive qualities of music? A perceptual experiment on Balanchine's choreography of Mozart's *Divertimento* n° 15. *Musicae Scientiae, 1*, 63–84.

Kveraga, K., Ghuman, A. S., & Bar, M. (2007). Top-down predictions in the cognitive brain. *Brain and Cognition, 65*, 145–168.

Lahav, A., Saltzman, E., Schlaug, G. (2007). Action representation of sound: audiomotor recognition network while listening to newly acquired actions. *Journal of Neuroscience, 27*, 308–314.

Lerdahl, F., & Jackendoff, R. (1983). *A generative theory of tonal music*. Cambridge, MA: MIT Press.

Lipscomb, S. D. (2005). The perception of audio-visual composites: Accent structure alignment of simple stimuli. *Selected Reports in Ethnomusicology, 12*, 37–67.

Lipscomb, S. D., & Kendall, R. A. (1994). Perceptual judgment of the relationship between musical and visual components in film. *Psychomusicology, 13*, 60–98.

Lipscomb, S. D., & Tolchinsky, D. E. (2005). The Role of Music Communication in Cinema. In D. Miehl, R. MacDonald, & D. J. Hargreaves (Eds.), *Musical Communication*. New York: Oxford University Press.

Luo, H., Liu, Z., & Poeppel, D. (2010). Auditory cortex tracks both auditory and visual stimulus dynamics using low-frequency neuronal phase modulation. *PLoS Biology, 8*, e1000445, 1–13.

Maess, B., Koelsch, S., Gunter, T. C., & Friederici, A. D. (2001). Musical syntax is processed in the area of Broca: an MEG-study. *Nature Neuroscience, 4*, 540–545.

Marshall, S. K., & Cohen, A. J. (1988). Effects of musical soundtracks on attitudes to geometric figures. *Music Perception, 6*, 95–112.

Menon, V., & Levitin, D. J. (2005). The rewards of music listening: Response and physiological connectivity of the mesolimbic system. *NeuroImage, 28*, 175–184.

Metz, C. (1974). *Film language: A semiotics of the cinema* (M. Taylor, Trans.). New York: Oxford University Press.

Milner, B. (1962). Laterality effects in audition. In V. B. Mountcastle (Ed.), *Interhemispheric Relations and Cerebral Dominance*. (pp. 177–195). Baltimore: Johns Hopkins Press.

Mitry, J. (1997). *The aesthetics and psychology of the cinema* (C. King, Trans). Bloomington: Indiana University Press. (Original works published 1963).

Mukamel, R., & Fried, I. (2012). Human intracranial recordings and cognitive neuroscience. Annual Review of Psychology, 63, 511–537.

Narmour, E. (1991). The top-down and bottom-up systems of musical implication: building on Meyer's theory of emotional syntax. *Music Perception, 9*, 1–26.

Neisser, U., & Becklen, R. (1975). Selective looking: Attending to visually significant events. *Cognitive Psychology, 7*, 480–494.

Osgood, C. E., Suci, G. J., & Tannenbaum, P. H. (1957). *The measurement of meaning*. Urbana: University of Illinois Press.

Overy, K., & Molnar-Szakacs, I. (2009). Being together in time: Musical experience and the mirror neuron system. *Music Perception, 26*, 489–504.

Patel, A. D. (2008). *Music, language, and the brain*. New York: Oxford University Press.

Patel, A. D., & Peretz, I. (1997). Is music autonomous from language? A neuropsychological appraisal. In I. Deliège & J. Sloboda (Eds.), *Perception and cognition of music* (pp. 191–215). Hove, UK: Psychology Press.

Penfield, W. (1950). *The cerebral cortex of man: A clinical study of localization of function.* New York: Macmillan.

Peretz, I. (1993). Auditory agnosia: A functional analysis. In S. McAdams, & E. Bigand (Eds.), *Thinking in sound: The cognitive psychology of human audition* (pp. 199–230). New York: Oxford University Press.

Phillips-Silver, J., & Trainor, L. J. (2007). Hearing what the body feels: auditory encoding of rhythmic movement. *Cognition, 105,* 533–546.

Revonsuo, A., & Newman, J. (1999). Binding and consciousness. *Consciousness and cognition, 8,* 123–127.

Rizzolatti, G., & Craighero, L. (2004). The mirror-neuron system. *Annual Review of Neuroscience, 27,* 169–192.

Rizzolatti, G., & Fabbri-Destro, M. (2010). Mirror neurons: from discovery to autism. *Experimental Brain Research, 210,* 223–237.

Rosar, W. (1994). Film music and Heinz Werner's theory of physiognomic perception. *Psychomusicology, 13,* 154–165.

Salimpoor, V. N., Benovoy, M., Larcher, K., Dagher, A., & Zatorre, R. J. (2011). Anatomically distinct dopamine release during anticipation and experience of peak emotion to music. *Nature Neuroscience, 14,* 257–262. Sammler, D., Grigutsch, M., Fritz, T., & Koelsch, S. (2007). Music and emotion: Electrophysiological correlates of the processing of pleasant and unpleasant music. *Psychophysiology, 44,* 293–304.

Samson, S. & Zatorre, R. J. (1991). Recognition memory for text and melody of songs after unilateral temporal lobe lesion: Evidence for dual encoding. *Journal of Experimental Psychology: Learning, Memory and Cognition, 17,* 793–804.

Samson, S. & Zatorre, R. J. (1994). Contribution of the right temporal lobe to musical timbre discrimination. *Neuropsychologia, 32,* 231–240.

Saygin, A. P., Driver, J., & de Sa, V. R. (2008). In the footsteps of biological motion and multisensory perception. *Psychological Science, 19,* 469–475.

Shevy, M. (2007). The mood of rock music affects evaluation of video elements differing in valence and dominance. *Psychomusicology, 19,* 57–78.

Slevc, L. R., Rosenberg, J. C., & Patel, A. D. (2009). Making psycholinguistics musical: Self-paced reading time evidence for shared processing of linguistic and musical syntax. *Psychonomic Bulletin and Review, 16,* 374–381.

Spreckelmeyer, K. N., Kutas, M., Urbach, T. P., Altenmüller, E., & Münte, T. F. (2006). Combined perception of emotion in pictures and musical sounds. *Brain Research, 1070,* 160–170.

Stewart, L. (2011). Characterizing congenital amusia. *The Quarterly Journal of Experimental Psychology, 64,* 625–638.

Tan, S.-L., Spackman, M. P., & Bezdek, M. A. (2007). Viewers' interpretation of film characters' emotions: Effects of presenting film music before or after a character is shown. *Music Perception, 25,* 135–152.

Tan, S.-L., Spackman, M. P., & Wakefield, E. M. (2008). Source of film music (diegetic or nondiegetic) affects viewers' interpretation of film. Paper presented at the Tenth International Conference on Music Perception and Cognition, Hokkaido, Japan. August 2008.

Thagard, P. (2005). *Mind: Introduction to cognitive science* (2nd ed). Cambridge, MA: MIT Press.

Thayer, J. F., & Levenson, R. W. (1983). Effects of music on psychophysiological responses to a stressful film. *Psychomusicology, 3,* 44–52.

Thompson, W. F., Russo, F. A., & Sinclair, D. (1994). Effects of underscoring on the perception of closure in filmed events. *Psychomusicology, 13,* 9–27.

Trainor, L. J., & Zatorre, R. J. (2009). The neurobiological basis of musical expectations. In S. Hallam, I. Cross, & M. Thaut (Eds.), *The Oxford handbook of Music Psychology* (pp. 171–183). New York: Oxford University Press.

Trehub, S. E., Cohen, A. J., & Guerriero, L. (1986). Development of emotional sensitivity to music. In *Proceedings of the 12th International Congress on Acoustics*. Toronto, Canada, 3, K5-4.

Van den Stock, J., Peretz, I., Grèzes, J., & de Gelder, B. (2009). Instrumental music influences recognition of emotional body language. *Brain Topography, 21*, 216–220.

Vines, B. W., Krumhansl, C. L., Wanderley, M. M., Dalca, I. M., & Levitin, D. J. (2011). Music to my eyes: Cross-modal interactions in the perception of emotions in musical performance. *Cognition, 118*, 157–170.

Von Eckardt, B. (1995). *What is cognitive science?* Cambridge, MA: MIT Press.

Whittingstall, K., Bartels, A., Singh, V., Kwon, S., & Logothetis, N. K. (2010). Integration of EEG source imaging and fMRI during continuous viewing of natural movies. *Magnetic Resonance Imaging, 28*, 1135–1142.

Winters, B. (2008). Corporeality, musical heartbeats, and cinematic emotion. *Music, Sound and the Moving Image, 2*, 3–25.

Zatorre, R. J. & Halpern, A. R. (1993). Effect of unilateral temporal-lobe excision on perception and imagery of songs. *Neuropsychologia, 31*, 221–232.

CHAPTER 6

COMPOSING FOR FILM: HANNS EISLER'S LIFELONG FILM MUSIC PROJECT

PETER SCHWEINHARDT AND JOHANNES C. GALL,
TRANSLATED BY OLIVER DAHIN

INTRODUCTION: HANNS EISLER IN MUSIC HISTORY AND FILM MUSIC HISTORY

JOHN Williams and Hans Zimmer—to name just two of Hanns Eisler's namesakes—
can no doubt be described as *film composers* without doing them or musical history
a disservice. By contrast, a label of this kind for Hanns Eisler initially seems strange,
and this despite the fact that he composed a film score nearly every year—and in some
years several—from 1927 until his death in 1962. To venture a crude comparison (and
then promptly banish it), saying "film composer Eisler" is like saying "opera composer
Mozart"—both correct and incorrect, but in any case misleading: on account of his
remarkable role as a *composer*, understanding Eisler as a *film composer* requires understanding his persona and position in the history of twentieth-century music. That history is certainly rich with complex and varied personalities, but Eisler's own colorful
artistic and political development—which he succinctly explained with the *aperçu* that
he was the son of a Viennese philosophy professor and a Leipzig butcher's daughter—
can be seen to trace a bright line through the century's upheavals, contradictions, and
conflicts. In the fields of vocal and instrumental music, as well as music for the theater and film, Eisler contributed works of a substance and originality that accord him
a prominent position in the history of each of these genres. At the same time, one has to
acknowledge what Georg Knepler describes as the "difficulties in fully grasping Eisler's

life's work," that is, the "wealth and diversity of works, . . . the variety of styles," and Eisler's particular biographical and ideological positioning (Knepler 1998, 27 and passim).

* * *

Although born in Leipzig, then the center of the German Empire, Eisler experienced the defining moments of his early life elsewhere: in the ideological-cultural primeval soup of Vienna, the Habsburg metropolis. He already stood out as "politically suspect" while at school, due to his interest in Marxist writings in the context of the Vienna youth culture movement (an interest shared by his older siblings Elfriede and Gerhart). At seventeen, this vehement opponent of war was drafted into the Imperial and Royal Army—to a Hungarian unit in order to prevent him, by dint of the language barrier, from disseminating his political views among his fellow soldiers. Instead, he wrote down the folksongs Hungarian peasants sang to him and continued his autodidactic composition. His first surviving work, a song titled "The Tired Soldier" (*Der müde Soldat*), bears the inscription "on the field August 1917," and is a fitting harbinger of what followed, as it was doubtless in solo vocal composition that Eisler ultimately left his greatest mark—his extraordinary standing as a composer for the theater is also largely due to the art of his vocal compositions.

Eisler's artistic development took a decisive turn in 1919: from then till 1923, he was a student in the exclusive circle around Arnold Schoenberg, who was convinced of the young man's talents and took him on free of charge. The compositional skills and artistic standards Eisler learned during this period remained of crucial importance for his work and aesthetic judgment. Alongside Alban Berg and Anton Webern, Schoenberg rightly regarded Eisler as his most independent and talented student, a conviction not swayed even by Eisler's abandonment, about 1925, of both the aesthetic priorities of his master and a potential career in the concert hall. Instead, Eisler took up residence in Berlin, the European metropolis of the 1920s, and reinvented himself as a political musician. Within just a few years, he had become *the* composer of the working class and placed his artistic abilities in the service of the struggle against capitalism and fascism.

Until the National Socialists assumed power, Eisler participated in the working-class music movement as a composer, choirmaster, and pianist; he was active as a journalist, especially for the communist *Rote Fahne* ("Red Flag"); and he completed an application to join the KPD, the communist party, in which both his older siblings were active. He created *Kampfmusik*, above all *Kampflieder* ("songs of struggle"; literally, "battle songs") that became icons of the genre, artistically sound and musically at least as revolutionary as the texts they set. At the same time, he explored a range of multimedial ways of using music: he worked on at least one opera (left just as incomplete as all later attempts), devised a "ballet pantomime" (which was also not completed), composed a "radio cantata," and not least wrote his first music for a film. This period of creative exploration in the late 1920s also saw Eisler's earliest artistic collaborations with Bertolt Brecht. Before long, their work together produced classics of political art in song (for example, the "Solidaritätslied" [Solidarity Song]), for the theater (*Die Maßnahme* [The Measures Taken], *Die Mutter* [The Mother]), and for film (*Kuhle Wampe oder Wem Gehört die Welt?* [Kuhle Wampe or Who Owns the World?; 1932]).

The first years of exile that followed his leaving Germany in 1933 were characterized by tireless work in the antifascist resistance: "orbiting" Germany, where he was in danger of persecution as a Jew, communist, and musical avant-gardist, Eisler took his musical and political involvement in the fight against the Nazis to the neighboring countries, as well as to the United States, the Soviet Union, the United Kingdom, and Civil War–era Spain. In the midst of all this activity, he developed a specific mode of composition marked by a return to dodecaphony, now based on the principle of the greatest possible "accessibility" and "simplicity"—achieved largely by dispensing with row transpositions and employing tonal echoes. A significant portion of Eisler's work from 1935 to 1938 pursues this idea of "simple dodecaphony": examples include the *Lenin-Requiem*, chamber cantatas, instrumental movements from the *Deutsche Symphonie*, and his score for the film *The 400 Million* (released 1939). With considerable plausibility, this synthesis of advanced compositional technique and general accessibility can be associated with the people's front politics of the Comintern, which aimed at an alliance of the working class and the bourgeoisie in the fight against Hitler.

The idea of the people's front, however, remained largely that—it could hardly prevent the political victories of the Nazis—and Eisler finally emigrated to the United States in 1938. Once again he redirected his talents: to Broadway productions and work on the Film Music Project while in New York, then, after moving to California, to film scores and one of the key works of exile music, the collection entitled the "Hollywood Songbook." In 1948 he was deported as the "Karl Marx of communism in the musical field"—these being the crude words of chief investigator Robert E. Stripling, speaking before the House Committee on Un-American Activities in September 1947. Eisler countered this distorted comparison with an ironic "I would be flattered" (*Hearings*, 25).

Eisler's return to Europe coincided with intensification of the Cold War, and the political polarizations ultimately drove him to East Berlin, where, in addition to the symbolically influential trifle of the national anthem of the DDR [East Germany], until his death in 1962 he composed works that, then as now, were considered controversial. In part, these were marked by his attempt to create an artful new simplicity, free of ideological burden, primarily associated with the premise of artistic "usefulness" promoting the development of a socialist society, but it culminated shortly before his death in a vehement call to rescue the idea of *l'art pour l'art* and an attempt to "liquidate" his previous artistic positions. His last completed composition was the *Ernste Gesänge* for baritone and string orchestra, which can be heard as a reflection on the political developments of his time and a sign of hope for a fruitful social order in which oppression and exploitation have been ended.

A Survey of Eisler's Work for Film, Part I: 1927–1944

Eisler's Film Music Project (1940–1942) and the book derived from it and written in cooperation with Theodor W. Adorno, *Composing for the Films* (1947; abbreviated hereafter as *CftF*), have contributed to the widespread perception of a dichotomy "Eisler/film music." [1] Easily readable, intellectually and stylistically appealing, the book is still a fruitful source of discussion of film music far beyond the boundaries of Eisler's own work, but ironically it has long constricted reception of Eisler himself as a film composer by encouraging reflection on his scores only in terms of their concordance with the ideas presented there. Recent research has worked to overcome this bias, to the extent that the first coauthor has asserted, "that Adorno and Eisler's theories and Eisler's screen practice are in no way always in accord is increasingly earning the well-earned character of a commonplace" (Schweinhardt 2008b, 10).

The key role nevertheless due to *Composing for the Films* is naturally also reflected in the current chapter, but we argue that Eisler's compositional and theoretical work for the Rockefeller Foundation must be understood as part of a *lifelong* film music project. Eisler was, after all, one of the pioneers of the sound film. Like many European composers of his generation, he wrote his first scores at a time when the silent film and its musical accompaniments were just becoming outdated and original compositions for the new medium were a concern of the musical avant-garde. The artistic issues involved are reflected in a publication that appeared at this moment of change but that is known mainly for presenting an extensive collection of illustrative clichés for silent film accompaniment: the two-volume *Allgemeines Handbuch der Filmmusik*, by Hans Erdmann and Giuseppe Becce, published in 1927. Its logical contradictions are apparent even in the format: the extensive library of musical snippets in the second volume is radically out of sync with the theoretical and aesthetic ideas in the first, which read like an anticipation of Eisenstein or Eisler in their demand for a planned score developed jointly by director and composer, not subsequently and randomly added. Already in his introduction, Erdmann expresses the hope that the handbook would succeed in "releasing music in film from the bounds of its arbitrariness" and "result in a stricter artistic relationship with the film scene" (Erdmann 1927, 1:iv).

It was natural that the energy with which the avant-garde engaged image and sound in the late 1920s and early 1930s would throw up new challenges. Eisler, for example, criticized the technical limitations and aesthetic stipulations that hampered his very first project, music for Walter Ruttmann's abstract film *Opus III* (1924), which had been commissioned for the Baden-Baden festival in 1927: "I was given the following job to do: with the aid of a rather inferior new invention, Blum's synchronizing apparatus [a music chronometer invented by Carl Robert Blum], I was to 'underline' all the [film's] 'rhythms'. . . . I must confess it seems idiotic to me today" (Eisler 1936a, 121). Such reservations regarding mere musical "copying" of the visual flow, however, did not diminish his interest in the artistic possibilities and the social relevance of the new medium.

Unlike many of his prominent colleagues who contributed to the early sound film—among them Dessau, Hindemith, Honegger, and Weill—Eisler remained true to the art for his entire life (Glanz 2008, 93–99). He established himself as a key exponent of progressive film music in Europe during the 1930s, a fact often overlooked in favor of his American film work but clearly reflected in a film-music monograph by Kurt London, who particularly praises the score for *Niemandsland* (No Man's Land; 1931) and places Eisler in the "foremost rank of modern creative film composers"

(London 1936, 229). In the area of rhythm, form, and above all instrumentation—this being an aspect to which London frequently returns—Eisler is praised for his innovation and for "develop[ing] a highly individualistic style for the sake of the film's reality, without any consequential sacrifice of the originality of the writing" (230). The composer expressed these views himself in an article published the same year: he criticizes the prevailing tendency of the young sound film to accept unquestioningly the "principle of illustrating...supplemented by 'sentimental' and 'picturesque' music" (Eisler 1936b, 23), then asserts that:

> A new way of using vocal and instrumental music is above all to set the music against the action in the film. That means that the music is not employed to "illustrate" the film, but to explain it and comment on it....The material prerequisites for a good film are that in preparing the scenario, the composer should be drawn in as music consultant from the beginning so that the music has the right function in the construction of the plot and the working out of the scenes....It is high time that directors consider the quality of film music with the same seriousness they give to the [other] problems of the sound film. (Eisler 1936a, 124)

Eisler himself had already benefited from the aesthetic inclination and professional openness of the directors he worked with: Victor Trivas (*Niemandsland, Dans les rues* [Song of the Streets; 1935]), Slatan Dudow (*Kuhle Wampe*), and Joris Ivens (*Pesn' o geroyakh* [Song of Heroes; 1932], *Nieuwe Gronden* [New Earth; 1934], *The 400 Million*). For example, *Niemandsland*—a film set prior to and during the First World War and with a pacifist outlook against a militant anticapitalist background—was described by Eisler as a model for his film music "principle of self-contained, structured pieces of music" (*HEGA* IX/1.1, 152) that are not related to the imagetrack in a superficially analogous, illustrative manner but are closely allied to the structure of the montage. From the very beginning, Eisler's compositions for film took their theoretical and practical justification not only from the contemporary Russian circle surrounding Eisenstein but also from contemporary ideas of epic theater on the opera and theater stage (see Dümling 2010). By the late 1920s, Eisler was increasingly occupied with various musical theater forms and on the cusp of beginning his lifelong work with Bertolt Brecht, marked by artistically and politically revolutionary works such as *Die Maßnahme*. As Tobias Faßhauer rightly says, "the structure of the first part of *Niemandsland*, essentially founded on out-and-out 'image-music numbers' (that is, sections defined both by scene content and the musical backing) with an extreme reduction in dialogue, already approaches the elevated number opera principle in epic theater: the structure of the plot itself as a graduated succession of self-contained musical states, as Weill employed for the *Mahagonny* opera" (Faßhauer 2008, 64).

Although Eisler's approach to film music absorbed the ideas of Brecht and Eisenstein, he developed them a step further on the basis of his own compositional objectives: the conscious premise that film music can and must contribute to defining the filmic content. In *Composing for the Films*, a scene from *Niemandsland* serves as an example of this basic thesis:

> A German carpenter receives the mobilization order of 1914. He locks his tool cupboard, takes down his knapsack, and, accompanied by his wife and children, crosses the street on the way to his barracks. A number of similar groups are shown. The atmosphere is melancholy, the pace is limp, unrhythmic. Music suggesting a military march is introduced quite softly. As it grows louder, the pace of the men becomes quicker, more rhythmic, more collectively unified. The women and children, too, assume a military bearing, and even the soldiers' moustaches begin to bristle. There follows a triumphant crescendo. Intoxicated by the music, the mobilized men, ready to kill and be killed, march into the barracks. Then, fade-out. The dramaturgic clarification of this scene, the transformation of seemingly harmless individuals into a horde of barbarians, can be achieved only by resorting to music. Here music is not ornamental, but is essential to the meaning of the scene—and this is its dramaturgic justification. (*CftF*, 23f.)[2]

Another key concept in Eisler's film compositions is that of dramaturgical counterpoint: "music, instead of limiting itself to conventional reinforcement of the action or mood, can throw its meaning into relief by setting itself in opposition to what is being shown on the screen" (*CftF* 26). This principle too, is illustrated in *Composing for the Films* by scenes from the films of the early 1930s: the "Prelude" from *Kuhle Wampe* (tranquil, depressing images of a Berlin "slum" *versus* rapid, piercing, formally strict polyphonic music "deliberately aimed at arousing resistance rather than sentimental sympathy" [*CftF*, 27]) and the first fight scene from *Dans les rues* (the rough brawl is complemented by calm, cool music, which "expresses the contrast between the incident and the scene, without touching upon the action. Its lyrical character creates a distance from the savagery of the event: those who commit the brutalities are themselves victims" [*CftF*, 27]). In addition to these straightforward examples, two characteristic types of dramaturgical counterpoint stand out in Eisler's early film work: (1) rousing political songs that sharpen or carry the message of a scene, groups of scenes, or even the entire film (for example, in *Kuhle Wampe, Abdul the Damned* [1935], or *Hangmen Also Die!* [1943]; in later films, the importance of this approach recedes); and (2) the abovementioned self-contained cues (found in the majority of scores from *Niemandsland* and continuing throughout his career, up to and including his final film, *Esther* [1962]).

Beyond the development of aesthetic and compositional ideas, Eisler's work for film also clearly reflects the various biographical stages of his life. His projects from *Kuhle Wampe* up until the beginning of his American exile in 1938 were international: the documentary film *Pesn' o geroyakh* (Soviet Union) and *Nieuwe Gronden* (Holland), the features *Dans les rues* (France), *Le grand jeu* (The Great Game; France, 1934), and *Abdul the Damned* (United Kingdom), and the opera adaptation *Pagliacci* (United Kingdom, 1936). At the beginning of his American exile, while in New York, Eisler succeeded in advancing his innovative film composition ideas: in rapid succession, he wrote his first entirely dodecaphonic score for *The 400 Million*, the soundtrack to a stop-motion documentary short *Pete Roleum and his Cousins* (1939), and another twelve-tone score for the short New Deal educational film *The Living Land* (1939).

And in February 1940, he commenced work on the Film Music Project,[3] which, as mentioned above, decisively set in motion the process that until today affords the composer a unique position in the artistic and scholarly examination of film music. The Rockefeller Foundation funded the project for a maximum of two years, but in January 1942 approved an application to extend support for an additional nine months. It was, however, the publication of the book *Composing for the Films* in 1947 that represented the real culmination of the work. If the Film Music Project thus proved to have a far-reaching effect—and it certainly represented a logical continuation of Eisler's previous cinematic work and intentions—its existence was largely due to the constraints and existential difficulties of exile. Eisler took on a visiting lecturership at the New School for Social Research beginning in the spring of 1938, but instead of a standard salary he drew "compensation for his teaching in the form of one-half of the tuition fees of his students" (*Hearings*, 153) because he held a visitor's visa: his attempts to obtain an immigration visa under the quota system were doomed to failure, given his communist views and affiliations. Only in the summer of 1940, when he could prove that he had worked without interruption as a professor for the previous two years (including five months at the Conservatorio Nacional de Música in Mexico City), was he granted a non-quota immigration visa for the purpose of continuing his work at the New School. The grant from the Rockefeller Foundation thus enabled Eisler to receive a salary equivalent to that of a New School professor in the time prior to receiving his immigration visa.

The Film Music Project's point of departure was the observation that film music had developed with a certain arbitrariness, had not been accorded the serious interest it warranted, and as a consequence generally lagged behind the "highly evolved technique of the motion picture" (*CftF*, 138). Even though a certain standard had in fact developed, Eisler questioned its authenticity: it appeared to be founded on limiting prejudices, and some of its elements were attributable more to bad habits than skilled craftsmanship. Hollywood practice of the time practically ordained late Romantic symphonic music as the unavoidable model, but Eisler wanted to use his project to examine the filmic potential of new music. According to his proposal for the Project (EGW III/3, 142–45), the other main issues to be explored were alternatives to the full symphony orchestra, possible forms and structures for film music, their principal functions, and their relationship to the other auditory elements of film.

The composition of innovative film scores lay at the heart of the Project. Their recording in synchrony with the film, however, was of crucial importance and had to be accurate, nuanced, and pointed. Eisler thus exclusively engaged outstanding musicians, often old friends and acquaintances who, like him, lived in American exile. Work got underway with the film *White Flood*, a documentary short for which Eisler composed original music. Footage filmed in Alaska by William Osgood Field, a geologist and member of Frontier Films, as supplemented by alpine and stock footage, was the basis of a (largely) apolitical film about the glacier ice that, as a kind of fifth element, played a key role in shaping the earth. The film was put in distribution and earned a certain amount of profit for the production company, Frontier Films, an alliance of left-wing filmmakers.[4] This was not least among the film's goals, as the company was behind schedule on its major project *Native Lands* and was in financial difficulty.[5]

Eisler's contribution to the production of *White Flood* was beneficial to all involved. He received valuable film material for the purposes of his experiments, and in turn he delivered equally valuable, stylistically advanced music for free, including the recordings that were financed using money from the Project budget. In Eisler's score, the place of the typical Hollywood symphony orchestra is taken by a soloistic chamber orchestra with fifteen players, which in addition to woodwinds, brass, percussion, and strings also includes an electric piano and a Novachord—according to Eisler the counterpart to the "'coldness' of the nature scenes" (*CftF*, 145). Although it was widely used in Hollywood during the 1940s, the Novachord must be seen as an exotic choice this early on. The first synthesizer to be offered for sale, the Novachord was an electric keyboard instrument made by Hammond; a total of just 1069 units were produced in the years 1939 to 1942. Eisler probably became aware of the instrument during the New York World's Fair, and as a member of a chamber ensemble, he had already tested its use in music for the plays *Night Music* by Clifford Odets and *Medicine Show* by Hoffmann Hays.

In addition to the pared-down ensemble and unusual timbres, advanced features of Eisler's music for *White Flood* include the consistent use of twelve-tone technique and the work's articulation into five larger, self-contained forms, a design that made it possible for him to adapt the score for the concert hall as the *Chamber Symphony*, op. 69, the form in which the music is known today.

The Project's next film experiment was *A Child Went Forth* (1941), on the issue of child-care during the war. This, again, involved a symbiotic working relationship in which the composer contributed to production. Its director, Joseph Losey, had previously commissioned Eisler to write the music for his first film, *Pete Roleum and his Cousins*, shown during the 1939 World's Fair, and he had made the initial contacts on Eisler's behalf when the latter applied for funding from the Rockefeller Foundation. *Composing for the Films* has the following to say on the form and material of the score for *A Child Went Forth*:

> The form of suite seemed most natural—in other words, not an elaborate form with transitions and maybe leitmotifs, but a sequence of small, distinct, clearly differentiated pieces, each complete in itself with an unmistakable beginning and ending.
>
> American nursery rhymes...supplied a musical raw material that was suitable because of its simplicity and associations. Eisler also wished to show that it is possible to write unconventional music even with the simplest material constructively differentiated, without the need of pretentious disguise. (*CftF*, 141f.)

The book follows this with a scene-by-scene discussion, but the cues "ball games," "mouse feeding," and "washing the dog" are described in reverse order, and the penultimate scene is termed the "finale." From this it is evident that Eisler conceived his score for a provisional cut: in addition to the reordering, the final version[6] has a new conclusion made using surplus footage, with the narrator's commentary picking up lines from

Walt Whitman's poem *There Was a Child Went Forth* and thereby forging a retrospective link to the film's opening. Although the film deals with how childcare might be managed during wartime, the filmmakers evidently did not feel they could burden the audience with too dark a summation. The revised ending demanded more music, and Eisler made do by pulling out of the drawer his String Quartet—composed in 1938 but as of then still unperformed—and underlaying the scene of the childlike "lollipop time" with the first 54 measures of its second finale, strictly twelve-tone music that contrasts with the rest of the score. For the concluding reprise of the poem's recitation, on the other hand, Eisler used the number already heard at the film's opening and later developed into the "lullaby," extending it by a few measures. He considered the result such a success that he later used that version as the final movement of the *Suite for Septet No. 1*, all of which was assembled from the music for *A Child Went Forth*.

The next film was *Fourteen Ways to Describe Rain*, undoubtedly the best-known work to come out of the Film Music Project: the twelve-tone score is described in *Composing for the Films* as the "richest and most complete... written under the auspices of the project," and its subject, Joris Ivens's 1929 cinematic poem, is a widely admired milestone in film history. Eisler dedicated the score to his revered teacher Arnold Schoenberg on the latter's seventieth birthday, and it is in fact as chamber music that the piece is most often heard. As *music in film*, however, the composition was for many years an object of speculation. Eisler apparently presented his version to the public only twice, once during his farewell concert in Los Angeles in 1947, and again in New York in 1948. Later performances, however, were problematic because the correct version of the film—which, as it turned out, was *not* the 1929 original—could no longer be located. This became clear when the synchronous original recording of 1941 was recently rediscovered:[7] it had survived as a pair of shellac records in the estates of Louise Eisler-Fischer and Arnold Schoenberg, and also as an optical sound positive in the archive of the Amsterdam Film Museum. These confirm that Eisler used an edited version of the film from 1932, created by the Dutch composer Lou Lichtveld for his own—and therefore the first—musical setting of the film. *Fourteen Ways to Describe Rain* thus represents an alternative to Lichtveld's impressionistic score for flute, string trio, and harp.[8]

Following his move to Los Angeles, Eisler recorded his newly composed cues to a scene from *The Grapes of Wrath* as the final exercise of the Film Music Project. By early 1941, he had obtained film material with separate dialogue and soundtrack from 20th Century Fox through the Motion Picture Producers and Distributors Association, the so-called Hays Office (letter from Arthur DeBra to Eisler, December 30, 1940 [HEA 4309]). He quickly composed a section of his new score (Eisler 1941, 254), the cues later titled *Sequence No. 4* and *Sequence No. 2*. Two others, *Exodus No. 1* and *Sequence No. 5*, were written in the fall of 1942. The score of *Sequence No. 3*, for which Eisler drew on his music to *Pete Roleum and his Cousins*, was also likely first worked out sometime in 1942.

The major project that followed directly out of the Film Music Project eventually became *Composing for the Films*. Given the book's fundamental character as a critical manifesto, its general thrust unambiguously directed toward the Hollywood film industry,[9] it should not be surprising if the view that Eisler's "experience in the Hollywood studio assembly line was not a happy one" (Leppert in Adorno 2002, 366) is even now still widespread. The truth of the matter, however, is more complex. To start with, it must be recalled that *Composing for the Films* was largely written between 1943 and early 1944. At this point the composer had not forgotten how he moved from New York to Los Angeles in 1942 and chased every opportunity for eight months before finally receiving a contract in December for *Hangmen Also Die!*—an anti-Nazi film revolving around the assassination of the "Deputy Reich-Protector of Bohemia and Moravia" Reinhard Heydrich. Eisler's feelings about his own situation are well reflected in a poem by Bertolt Brecht that Eisler had set to music around this time as the third "Hollywood Elegy" in his longstanding project of a *Hollywood Songbook*: "Jeden Morgen, mein Brot zu verdienen | Geh ich zum Markt, wo Lügen verkauft werden. | Hoffnungsvoll| reihe ich mich ein unter die Verkäufer" ["Every morning, to earn my bread | I go to the market where lies are sold. | Full of hope | I take my place among the sellers"]. After the release of *Hangmen Also Die!*, Eisler found himself in a similar situation in 1943, although he does not appear to have undertaken his search for work with the same energy as in the previous year. It was yet another year before he was commissioned to score the RKO film *None but the Lonely Heart* (on the recommendation of his friend Clifford Odets) and thus obtained his first credit on a production by one of the "Big Five" studios. This film also gave Eisler his breakthrough: from 1944 until his return to Europe two feature films per year were released with his music, including four further productions by RKO, which not without pride Eisler described as his "team" in a letter to Peter Lorre. The composer thus earned a total of eight feature film credits in five years— an impressive number, especially when compared to his emigrant colleagues, whose own work was frequently both supplementary and uncredited.

Eisler's success as a Hollywood film composer was quickly confirmed by the fact that his first two scores were both nominated for Oscars. In the case of *Hangmen Also Die!*, the only one of Brecht's numerous literary attempts in the world of Hollywood that made it onto the screen, this nomination is all the more remarkable in that the music's total length is just thirteen minutes. These few cues, however, are very striking:[10] generally highly chromatic, the harmony is driven to the edge of atonality, ensuring the unconventional nature and heightened efficacy of the musical expression. Overall, the score maintains a balance between its reforming or advanced elements and its appropriation of film music clichés (which, however, become fractured in Eisler's treatments).[11] There is thus, as expected, a fanfare-like trumpet call at the start of the "Main Title" cue; a "Tension Music"; diegetic restaurant music that evokes "authentic" local color as a paraphrase of a Czech folk song; and a "Finale," which is indeed unveiled in expected splendor and closes with typically epic Hollywood proportions in which the "blaring" trumpets are in full attendance. But there is also a brief dodecaphonic passage—a first in a Hollywood film—and a *Kampflied* that captures and promotes a collective political attitude.

Composing for the Films refers to the music for *Hangmen Also Die!* no fewer than six times (*CftF* 11, 25, 27f., 37, 102, 102f.), and thus the work that was Eisler's debut in

Hollywood conveniently also served to clarify a number of key theses in the book: as the counterexample to the "unobtrusiveness" to which film music is commonly submitted, as the model for an innovative relationship between film and music in general and dramaturgical counterpoint in particular, as evidence of the far-reaching expressive power of the new musical material, and as an example of the possibilities of mixing music and sounds.

A balance between innovation and appropriation also characterizes his subsequent Hollywood scores, in line with a guiding principle stated in *Composing for the Films* that the attempt should be made "to carry out as many innovations as possible within the existing framework, to serve as an eventual starting point for a fundamentally changed motion picture" (*CftF*, 125). The "unofficial tradition of genuine art [thus] formed" was the necessary first step in the struggle: "For the new motion picture cannot fall from heaven; its history, which has not yet really begun, will be largely determined by its prehistory" (*CftF*, 116).

The Intricate History of *Composing for the Films*

In his final report to the Rockefeller Foundation (antedated October 31, 1942; sent November 21, 1942), Eisler states the following: "Since all our proceedings have been carefully analyzed we have ample material at our disposal which will be evaluated in a book which is going to be published by the Oxford University Press" (Eisler 1942, EGW III/3, 154).[12] Just under five years would pass before this monograph actually appeared, but then and for a long time afterward only a small circle of insiders were aware of the full extent to which Theodor W. Adorno contributed to its drafting, editing, and translating. Indeed, the notion that Adorno and Eisler genuinely coauthored a book is widely considered suspect in some circles even today, given that the essential differences in their views can by no means be glossed over and that the polarization of views about them in postwar Germany was real and irreversible. This situation, however, obscures the fact that, despite occasional controversy, their acquaintance and friendship was of long standing, and they repeatedly reached accord on artistic and intellectual issues, stimulated and influenced one another, with just as much good reason as they applied to their disagreements.

The future coauthors first met in Vienna in 1925. Adorno, aged twenty-one, had moved there after obtaining his doctor of philosophy degree in order to perfect his musical skills among the Schoenberg circle. He studied composition with Alban Berg and piano with Eduard Steuermann, and made the acquaintance of Eisler, five years his elder, who had already completed his studies with Schoenberg and was about to leave Vienna for Berlin. Eisler had been awarded Vienna's *Künstlerpreis* for his first major work, the Sonata for Piano, op. 1, composed in March 1923 and published by Universal

Edition in 1924, but he saw few prospects for a continuing career—and was ultimately similar in this respect to Adorno, who broke off his studies after barely six months and returned to Frankfurt. During the short time that the two lived in Vienna they were able to share their compositional efforts with one another. In a letter to his mentor Siegfried Kracauer, Adorno reports a particularly favorable response from Eisler (May 19, 1925; Adorno and Kracauer 2008, 59). For his part, Eisler gave Adorno a copy of the sonata, in which he wrote: "Dedicated to Dr. Wiesengrund with the hope of closer acquaintance | Warmly | Hanns Eisler." Much later, on February 22, 1940, Adorno selected this piece to present Eisler's music on the New York radio station WNYC.

By 1940, both Eisler and Adorno were living in exile in New York. Eisler had just received the Rockefeller Foundation grant, while Adorno had been working for just under two years on sociologist Paul Lazarsfeld's Radio Research Project, another undertaking for the Foundation arising from its new field of media research. This work was now coming to an end, as further funding for the music department had been rejected. Although Adorno's critical analyses eloquently and mercilessly highlighted the ills of music on the radio, they postponed any possibility of correction to an unforeseeable future on account of their dependence on changes in society as a whole. Adorno also had no success with plans to publish his ideas in an English-language book to be titled *Current of Music*. Eisler tried to put in a good word at Oxford University Press, but Adorno reported that the trade editor, Philip Vaudrin, had rejected the project, reasoning that "the book is too 'elevated' " (July 4, 1940; Ewenz and others 2003, 171). At the end of the letter, Adorno again expresses thanks for Eisler's support: "What this means on a human level is fortunately not dependent on success or failure in the best of all worlds."

Eisler harbored hopes that his support could achieve something, as he himself had received a contract in early 1939 for a monograph on contemporary music. He had delivered only a promising outline, however, with the title *Why is Modern Music so Difficult to Understand?* (see EGW III/I, 469f.). When the Rockefeller Foundation approved the application for the Film Music Project, and it was clear that Eisler, as its director, would not have time to devote to the book, he persuaded Vaudrin to make the subject the relationship between film and music. Vaudrin agreed, setting September 1, 1941 as the deadline for submission, with the book to appear in October or November (letter to Eisler on March 5, 1940; OUP file, fol. 4–5).[13] Eisler and Vaudrin both deluded themselves with respect to the effort required in writing and translating such a manuscript: the deadline passed without the project having even been started. Throughout much of 1942, Eisler wrote "notes of excuse and delay," as he self-critically admitted to Vaudrin (letter of September 30, 1942 [*HEGA* IX/4.1, 234]), and a statement of "good news" came only at the end of November: following completion of the Film Music Project, Eisler could now dedicate the majority of his time to the book. Additionally, he could report that:

> [For] many weeks I have been collaborating with Mr. [sic] Adorno. I feel that this collaboration goes so far that it is imperative that Dr. Adorno should be mentioned as full-fledged co-author on the title page (by Hanns Eisler and T.W. Adorno). Also the royalties will be shared. The status of Dr. Adorno's co-authorship is not only

a matter of honesty but also of expediency, because I feel that without his intense collaboration the completion of the book may be considerably delayed or even endangered. (letter of November 27, 1942; *HEGA* IX/4.1, 234f.; orthography and punctuation have been standardized).

Vaudrin might very well have expressed misgivings, since he had already rejected one of Adorno's projects, but as it happened his editorial colleague Harry Hatcher sent news that he would be standing in for Vaudrin, who had been drafted for war service. Hatcher approved every aspect of Eisler's proposal, adding: "I am glad to know that the manuscript is proceeding and that you will have it finished before too long a time" (letter of December 14, 1942; OUP file, fol. 15). In contrast to his predecessor, Hatcher refrained from exhorting Eisler and Adorno with demands and deadlines, possibly because he was just a few years away from retirement.

By contrast, Adorno, who had reunited with Max Horkheimer in Los Angeles the previous year for collaborative work on what became the *Dialectic of Enlightenment*, was very pleased to be given an opportunity to contribute his ideas on mass-media music in an English-language book after all. "We have something pleasing to report," he wrote in the postscript of a letter to his parents: "Hanns Eisler, with whom I am on very good terms, . . . and who, as you probably know, [was] director of the Rockefeller Film Music Project, and now has to write a book about it, has asked me to write it together with him. . . . As I [have] made preparations long in advance, I will be able to manage it comfortably in my spare time. I think it will be a very substantial external success. Eisler is being *extremely* loyal" (December 1, 1942; Adorno 2006, 119; emphasis in original; words in brackets corrected according to the German original).

Work on the book appears to have been both harmonious and productive. In a conversation with Jürgen Schebera, Louise Eisler-Fischer, Eisler's wife at the time, recalled that in part "Eisler and Adorno dictated orally and Gretel Adorno took down the manuscript in shorthand" (Schebera 1978, 115). Eisler-Fischer also noted that, in their meetings, the two authors discussed previously prepared working papers (*c.*1977; HEA 3382). At least one of these working papers survives (FML)[14] —the *Entwurf zum Filmmusikbuch*, first published in the addendum to Adorno and Eisler (2006, 147–54). Apart from other factors, expressions such as "my childhood in Frankfurt" and "a deleted section from the original text in Popular Music" make it clear that the document can be attributed to Adorno, and, as the majority of its thoughts are elaborated in the published book, it provides unique insight—as a kind of Rosetta Stone—into the text genesis and division of work.[15] In comment for Suhrkamp Verlag in 1969, Adorno reported that the "vast majority" of the chapter "Sociology and Aesthetics of Film Music" (*CftF*, 45–88), in particular, but also the main part of the dramaturgical chapter (*CftF*, 20–23) and the introduction (*CftF*, li–liii) were his work, while Eisler was primarily responsible for the content of the first chapter, "Prejudices and Bad Habits" (*CftF*, 3–19), and the "Report on the Film Music Project" (*CftF*, 135–57).[16] As for the remainder of the book, the section of the dramaturgical chapter (*CftF*, 23–31), headed "Models" in the German edition and containing discussion of examples from Eisler's film scores, was without doubt essentially contributed by Eisler, whereas the chapters "The New Musical Resources" (*CftF*, 32–44), "The Composer and the Movie-Making Process" (*CftF*, 89–113), and "Suggestions and Conclusions" (*CftF*, 114–33) were evidently written jointly and in approximately equal share. Nevertheless, the fact that "Adorno comprehensively edited the book"—as Albrecht Betz states with primary reference to the German-language original—"can easily be seen from its style" (1982 159). Louise Eisler-Fischer also confirmed that "Adorno was happy to take responsibility for the final wordings" (c.1977).

After a full year and a half of work, the two authors had completed the provisional manuscript. Its preface, which they signed on September 1, 1944, is of particular interest because of a reference to the *Philosophische Fragmente* (as Adorno and Horkheimer initially titled their *Dialectic of Enlightenment*), which had been published shortly before in a mimeographed edition and with a print run of just 500. In the two years prior, it had been this key work of Critical Theory that had occupied Adorno's time above all else; he undertook the "study on composing for the film" against its "theoretical background" and in particular the "critique of the 'culture industry'" (Adorno and Eisler 2006, 8). Later, Adorno even claimed to have seen the film music book as "a kind of excursus on the chapter about the culture industry" in the *Dialectic of Enlightenment* (Adorno, Suhrkamp, and Unseld 2003, 670). It may indicate Eisler's influence as coauthor that the potential of *Composing for the Films* could by no means be exhausted in an excursus of this type. When Adorno stated in 1963 that the "word 'culture industry'...was first used in the book 'Dialectic of Enlightenment'" (AGS 12: 337), it must be noted that it was in fact introduced to English-language scholarly discourse by the publication of *Composing for the Films* in 1947, and this in the very first sentence of the introduction—as "cultural industry" (see *CftF*, li). Furthermore, the concept of the culture industry is immediately and effectively described in the Introduction's remaining paragraphs. The theoretical implications of the new term may, however, have initially passed virtually unnoticed because Adorno's and Eisler's preface, with its reference to the *Dialectic of Enlightenment* and its chapter on the culture industry, was not included in the English-language edition but first printed, in its original German wording, in 1969.

Three years—a surprisingly long time—passed between completion of the German manuscript and the appearance of the English edition. Adorno would later assert "that the language of this loosely formulated book is intended to facilitate an American translation and is therefore not a strictly binding German text" (Adorno 1971, 167), but the translation work in fact turned out to be unexpectedly difficult. In summer 1946, the authors wrote to John Marshall of the Rockefeller Foundation, who had enquired about the book's progress: "Publication was held up by difficulties of translation. Now, however, the English manuscript is ready to go into print as soon as a few minor changes have been agreed upon."[17]

The surviving correspondence with Oxford University Press provides a rich picture of the difficulties involved in the translation. Adorno dealt with the editorial correspondence up until printing and initially suggested that he produce a trial translation of the introduction and first chapter with the help of a secretary paid by OUP, and the Press could then decide whether the philosopher was in a position to translate the entire book (letter to Harry Hatcher, June 8, 1944; OUP file, fol. 31). Hatcher left the request unanswered, instead turning—albeit evidently at Adorno's suggestion—to George McManus, a musicologist at UCLA who had previously translated Emil Ludwig's biography of Beethoven (letter of March 5, 1945; OUP file, fol. 20). McManus agreed in a letter a month later (OUP file, fol. 23) but proved to be an unfortunate choice: when Adorno and Eisler sent his work to the publisher on August 21 (preface, introduction, and chapters 1–4) and October 2, 1945 (chapters 5–8), they stressed that the translation could in no way be seen as final. They therefore suggested the appointment of "a very competent and reliable editor" to finalize the text (letter of August 21, 1945; OUP file, fol. 35). Hatcher retired without following through on this request, but his successor, Margaret Nicholson, also acting on Adorno's recommendation, commissioned Norbert Guterman, "a free-lance associate of the Institute [for Social Research]" (Wiggershaus 1995, 386), to edit and improve on McManus' efforts (Nicholson to Adorno, November 5, 1945; OUP file, fol. 41). Born in Warsaw in 1900, Guterman was not a native speaker of English but had distinguished himself with translations of German, French, Polish, and Russian scholarly literature.

At this point the manuscript was a heterogeneous patchwork: McManus's translations of the preface, introduction, and chapters 1–3 and 6–7; the fourth and fifth chapters on the sociology and aesthetics of film music, drafted by Adorno and corrected by McManus; and the latter's draft translation of the final chapter, which had been completely reworked by Adorno.[18] An additional difficulty for Guterman was the fact that he lived in New York, not in Los Angeles. Nevertheless, work progressed relatively smoothly at first. Section by section, Nicholson sent the revised English text (chapters 1, 2–3, and then the rest) to California, with Adorno returning his and Eisler's corrections and suggested improvements. The two authors also took the opportunity to add further comments and observations (as they had also done previously with McManus), occasionally modifying their initial formulations but also drawing on Eisler's newly won experience in composing for Hollywood films. The authors wrote their additions predominantly in German on the back of the manuscripts or, where necessary, on extra pages. The 1947 edition includes not only the English equivalents of these added texts but also further passages and footnotes for which there appear to be no German originals.[19]

One further change came at the instigation of Philip Vaudrin, who had survived the war and resumed his position as trade editor in early 1946. The "Report on the Film Music Project" (the penultimate chapter in the manuscript and German editions) was moved to an appendix and provided with a longer introduction, "pointing out concretely the bearing of the project upon the main topics of the book" (Adorno to Vaudrin, June 13, 1946; FML).[20]

In addition to the complexities of work on the text and the translation, there was a further obstacle to be overcome before *Composing for the Films* could be published in August 1947: as a consequence of serious accusations leveled against his brother Gerhart, who had emigrated to the United States in 1941, Eisler found himself on the anticommunist firing line and was branded the "top red composer working in Hollywood" (title of an article in the New York *World Telegram*, October 21, 1946). To make things worse, his sister Ruth Fischer, who had also been living in the United States since 1941, brought forward further accusations. Adorno, Eisler, and OUP therefore decided to wait and see how the situation would develop. As the House Committee on Un-American Activities (HUAC) began investigations, Gerhart was prevented from leaving the country, placed under detention, and given a custodial sentence. When Hanns was subpoenaed for questioning in Los Angeles, followed by three days of hearings in Washington, Adorno acted. There was a very real danger that he and the Institute for Social Research, like other friends, supporters, and colleagues of Eisler, would be dragged into the affair. Adorno thus withdrew his coauthorship. He later offered this explanation: "I did not seek to become a martyr in an affair that still has nothing to do with me.... At that time, I was determined to return to Europe, but feared I might have difficulties in doing so. Hanns Eisler fully understood" (Adorno 1971, 167). Thus, the jointly signed preface of 1944 was extensively rewritten; Adorno's role is credited in a formulation that neither conceals the actual nature of the collaboration nor explicitly identifies it: "The theories and formulations presented here evolved from co-operation with him [that is, Adorno] on general aesthetic and sociological matters as well as purely musical issues" (*CftF*, xlix–l).

At the end of his inglorious HUAC affair, Eisler was deported and returned to his hometown, Vienna. Not least in order to reestablish himself in postwar Europe, he now felt that publication of the book in its original language would be a fruitful undertaking. Thus, on April 22, 1948, barely three weeks after arriving in Vienna, he asked his coauthor to send him the manuscript by air mail, adding: "You must only decide whether you would like your name on the title page" (Theodor W. Adorno Archive, Br. 348/1). Adorno complied with Eisler's request but in view of the escalating Cold War and the anticommunist witch-hunt in the United States, where he had become a citizen in late 1943, he still considered revealing his coauthorship as too much of a risk. The manuscript he sent to Vienna, long considered lost, was found in 2003; it had survived as part of a large private collection of Eisler materials held by the film director Wolfgang Glück. As an addition to the two copies extant in Adorno's estate, the manuscript is of particular interest in several respects. It contains previously unpublished text sections, such as the German version of the revised 1947 preface, signed by Eisler, and the German wording of the addition on the practice of arranging in the sixth chapter.[21] It also has a series of handwritten corrections by Adorno that were not included in the earlier German editions: these range from direct corrections to stylistic improvements, clarifications of meaning, and textual modifications.

The first German edition, *Komposition für den Film*, published in East Berlin in 1949, was subjected to a variety of cuts and revisions. Eisler did not himself make most of these, most likely did not review them, and seems to have tolerated them for the sake of obtaining permission for publication.[22] Anglicisms, antiquated expressions, and linguistic mannerisms were expunged, a number of words were harmonized with official Marxist jargon, and numerous changes were made in line with the aesthetic doctrine of socialist realism. These include—"following the ideologically motivated animosity toward so-called decadence" (Klemm 1977, 13)—the elimination of references to such exponents of musical modernism as Stravinsky, Schoenberg, Berg, Webern, and even Hindemith. The footnotes, which include ideas and discussions from Adorno's writings, some in longer quotation, did not fare any better: they were also cut. Thus, the German first edition no longer included any literal reference to the book's coauthor, and traces of Critical Theory as a theoretical underpinning were largely obscured. In addition, a new preface introduces "vehement anti-American invective" (Adorno, Suhrkamp, and Unseld 2003, 671) to which Adorno took particular offence. Nevertheless, he defended Eisler in his postscript ("Zum Erstdruck der Originalfassung") for the 1969 edition; the relevant paragraph was, however, withheld at the request of Eisler's widow, Stephanie Eisler, and first published in volume 15 of the *Gesammelte Schriften* (1976). "It should be remembered," argued Adorno, that Eisler, "after making his way to the GDR from America, found himself subject to severe pressure." Thus the changes were to be seen not least as a device to grant the book "whatever limited impact it may have" in the face of the "insatiable control of socialist realism" (Adorno and Eisler 2006, 136f).

Two decades later, and several years after Eisler's death, Adorno ventured to counteract the unpopular Henschel edition with a first edition of the original German manuscript bearing the names of both authors: toward the end of 1968, he learned of the intentions of the Munich publishers Rogner & Bernhard to bring out a new version of the 1949 edition as part of the series *Passagen*, and, in a letter on September 27, 1968, he suggested to Suhrkamp that it preempt this with publication of the original manuscript (Adorno, Suhrkamp, and Unseld 2003, 652). Evidently as a result of efforts by musicologist Eberhardt Klemm, however, the volume was actually released by Rogner & Bernhard, and Adorno provided an explanatory postscript. This edition, the first with the names of both authors, caused quite a sensation, especially as it occurred almost simultaneously with Adorno's sudden death—but, as he had hoped, the "apocryphal existence" (Adorno 1971, 168) of the film music book had now come to an end.

An unfortunate consequence of this renewed attention was that the followers of Eisler and Adorno immediately began efforts to deny the writers their respective share of authorship. The Babylonian confusion that prevailed in this dispute can be traced in large part to the circumstances of divided postwar Germany, where difficulties of understanding had strong ideological and political roots. A specific locus of the dispute, however, was Adorno's comment to the effect that he had written ninety or even as much as ninety-five percent of the book alone. These oft-cited percentages clearly reflect Adorno's self-perception regarding his own relevance to and even dominance of *Komposition für den Film* and enable an understanding of how painful the withdrawal from the coauthorship must have been for him (significantly, in a letter to his mother, June 13, 1947, Adorno claimed a share of ninety percent at the time [Adorno 2006, 287]). Nevertheless, the numbers are demonstrably imprecise. Even if—in line with the least favorable reading of Adorno's statement for Suhrkamp—Eisler were accorded only the first chapter, "Prejudices and Bad Habits," and the "Report on the Film Music Project," this contribution would already add up to more than a quarter of the text of *Composing for the Films*. If, on the other hand, the text sections and chapters disregarded by Adorno in his statement are included and allocated to both authors in equal measure—with the exception of the specific part of the dramaturgy chapter written by Eisler alone—the composer's share of the book comes to just under half (or forty-nine percent).

Apart from claims about authorship, a more literal form of Babylonian confusion subsists in the fact that, as we have seen, the book was published in more than one language and in versions that diverged with respect to both structure and content. Table 6.1 provides a summarizing overview of the six versions confronting English- and German-speaking readers.

Table 6.1 Versions of *Composing for the Films* / *Komposition für den Film*

1: English-language version with revised structure ("Report on the Film Music Project," as an appendix)	a. Hanns Eisler, *Composing for the Films*, New York: Oxford University Press, 1947; b. Eisler's name only: London: Dennis Dobson, 1951; c. Eisler's name only, with an English translation of Adorno's 1969 postscript: Freeport, NY: Books for Libraries Press, 1971; d. Theodor Adorno and Hanns Eisler, with a new introduction by Graham McCann (pp. vii–xlvii) and an index: London and Atlantic Highlands: Athlone, 1994; e. Adorno and Eisler: London and New York: Continuum, 2007.
2: Version of the German first edition, contains numerous abridgements and modifications.	Hanns Eisler, *Komposition für den Film*, Berlin: Verlag Bruno Henschel und Sohn, 1949.
3: Edition of the original German manuscript of 1944 with postscript, "Zum Erstdruck der Originalfassung," by Adorno	a. Theodor W. Adorno and Hanns Eisler, *Komposition für den Film*, Munich: Rogner & Bernhard, 1969; b. Adorno and Eisler: Hamburg: Europäische Verlagsanstalt, 1996.
4: As 3, with additions from Adorno's personal copy and a paragraph of his postscript withheld from 3.	Theodor W. Adorno and Hanns Eisler, *Komposition für den Film*: Theodor W. Adorno, *Gesammelte Schriften*, ed. Rolf Tiedemann, vol. 15. Frankfurt: Suhrkamp, 1976.
5: Annotated edition of 3, with the structure of 1, and with a synoptic comparison of the divergences of 1 and 2 from 3; original wording of the additions from 4 in the addendum to the editorial introduction.	Theodor W. Adorno and Hanns Eisler, *Komposition für den Film*; Hanns Eisler, *Gesammelte Werke*, series III, vol. 4, ed. Eberhardt Klemm. Leipzig: VEB Deutscher Verlag für Musik, 1977.
6: Reviewed and corrected edition of 4, extended by two further additions from Adorno's personal copy and by a "Draft for the Film Music Book" by Adorno.	Theodor W. Adorno and Hanns Eisler, *Komposition für den Film*, with an epilogue by Johannes C. Gall and a DVD, "Hanns Eislers Rockefeller-Filmmusik-Projekt," edited on behalf of the International Hanns Eisler Society by Johannes C. Gall, Frankfurt: Suhrkamp, 2006.

At first glance these versions differ primarily with regard to length and structure, but more or less serious shifts in meaning between the German original and the English translation can be observed at a number of points and should not be underestimated. If, on the one hand, David Culbert is certainly correct in warning that in view of "[t]he extraordinary amount of time Adorno and Eisler and the translators put into the American translation," it would be "a mistake to dismiss the translation as but a pale imitation of the German original" (Culbert 2008, 28), still, on the other hand, the unusually long period of time required for the translation, which particularly indicates the problems surrounding it, cannot be ignored, especially as Adorno wrote to his mother following publication of *Composing for the Films* to say that "[u]nfortunately, the translation of the book is very [mediocre]" (after November 30, 1947; Adorno 2006, 306; word in brackets corrected in line with German original). So if the English-language first edition has the undisputed advantage of including passages that do not exist in the German versions, or only in back-translation in Eberhardt Klemm's text-critical edition, the reader is nevertheless recommended a certain skepticism and a look at the German original, which may reveal a number of ideas and formulations not carried over into the translation.

A Survey of Eisler's Work for Film, Part II: 1945–1962

One Hollywood film in which Eisler's music without doubt errs on the side of stylistic convention is the Technicolor epic *The Spanish Main*—the composer's second commission for RKO. Years later, he would recall with horror the "wretched freedom film" in which "some bold seafarers [. ..] had risen up against Spanish domination" and for which he had to "compose eighty minutes of music in a shockingly short time" (EGW III/7, 84). He managed by recycling a few numbers from his film music for *Pete Roleum and his Cousins* as well as employing the services of one of the studio's arrangers, Cil Grau, for the orchestration. This latter fact is remarkable, as Eisler was convinced that splitting up the composition and instrumentation "cannot be justified either objectively or economically. [. ..] [A]ny qualified composer should be able to invent his instrumentation together with his music" (*CftF*, 105). The following passage from *Composing for the Films*, added in the course of the English translation, may refer directly to Eisler's experience in composing the music for *The Spanish Main*:

> However, this absurd procedure is almost inevitable under the present conditions in the industry. The composers often work under great pressure and have to produce enormous quantities of music—eighty minutes of accompaniment to a motion picture—so that they themselves are unable to do the considerable writing work required for a score, even if they imagine the instruments as vividly as possible in the

course of composing. It is hardly no accident that even among the highly qualified composers in Hollywood hardly anyone orchestrates his own works. (*CftF*, 105f.)

Shortly after completing his music for *The Spanish Main*, Eisler vented his annoyance in a letter to his son Georg: "It's pure nonsense, rubbish etc. I had to do it for the money. My music, however, is pretty good. But it is wasted on this nonsense" (Eisler to Georg Eisler, FML). Indeed, Frank Borzage's buccaneer film reveals itself as an example of what *Composing for the Films* has to say about such evaluations: "Fundamentally, no motion-picture music can be better than what it accompanies. Music for a trashy picture is to some extent trashy, no matter how elegantly or skilfully it has solved its problems" (*CftF*, 116f.). In this context, Claudia Gorbman considers some parts of the score for *The Spanish Main* as a case of "artistic sabotage" evidenced in "revealing exaggeration"—a possible way of approaching the "trashy" film through music that Adorno and Eisler present in their book, before immediately adding that its efficacy should in no way be overestimated (*CftF*, 117). At any rate, this would explain "why the Mickey-Mousing in parts of the *Spanish Main* becomes so overblown" (Gorbman 1991, 283).

Gorbman rightly stresses that, notwithstanding such compromises, it would be wrong "to read Eisler's Hollywood scores as failures in the light of his theoretical principles [...], for they contain some of the most intelligent, passionate and compelling original passages in American film music" (Gorbman 1991, 284). These passages may therefore be understood as a contribution to that which is demanded in the conclusions of *Composing for the Films*:

> Even at the price of daily quarrels with wretched opponents, it is of great importance that an unofficial tradition of genuine art be formed, which may one day make itself felt. For the new motion picture cannot fall from heaven; its history, which has not yet really begun, will be largely determined by its prehistory. (*CftF*, 116)

Eisler held an internationalist view of the world but in his cultural outlook was markedly occidental and humanist, and not least Marxist. Despite all the resulting ambivalence he felt towards his exile home, his life in Hollywood in the mid-1940s was not at all bad: he was doing well financially and professionally, he was well known, and he and his wife were making efforts to obtain American citizenship. As late as February 1947, when the anticommunist campaign was already in full swing, he wrote in the *Hollywood Citizens News* (very likely with honesty): "I love this country.... America has been good to me and my wife. We both hope to become citizens" (*Hollywood Citizens News*, February 19, 1947; copy HEA 2843). His efforts to establish and consolidate his livelihood by no means contradict contacts with his homeland shortly after the end of the war, but domestic political events in the United States, the anticommunist hysteria in the nascent Cold War, put an end to any remaining indecision. In September 1947, he was summoned to testify before the House Committee on Un-American Activities and left the United States a few months later—with no certainty of his future in Europe.[23]

When Eisler boarded the aircraft in New York, he left the country as a "Hollywood composer" (*Washington Evening Star*, March 27, 1943); but this view was barely in line with that of the European public when the composer disembarked in London, and even less so at his subsequent stops in Prague, Vienna, and Berlin. For some, it was the inventive Schoenberg student who had returned, for others the "composer of the working class," while those in the concert musical field saw the Eisler of the 1920s and early 1930s. Eisler himself saw things differently: his artistic balancing act following the exile years consisted of working to reconcile his seemingly disparate development over the preceding three decades while at the same time reinventing himself. In what became his most controversial creative period—from 1948 until his death in 1962—film music played a key role as a constant in his artistic work.

Indeed, his first major project was the score to *Křižova trojka* [The Mystery of the Black Rider], the debut film of twenty-five-year-old Czech director Vaclav Gajer. This entertaining but somewhat strange combination of horror film and schoolboy comedy, predominantly set in a Czech castle, could be invoked to substantiate the popular notion that mediocre films do not necessarily provoke brilliant film music; a comparison of the soundtrack with Eisler's European films prior to his emigration, however, above all reveals how keenly Eisler's film music had developed in the United States—and this not in a way that his former friends (or even many Eisler enthusiasts today) particularly appreciate. The trend in earlier research on Eisler to "excuse" those film music scores more closely married to convention, or further removed from narrative principles in the spirit of Brechtian aesthetics, as necessitated by the need to "earn a crust" must be countered for three reasons in view of efforts such as *Křižova trojka*. First, for the composer who reimmersed himself in work straight away following his return, the score was a great deal of work and not just a casual job. Of its eighty minutes' duration, almost sixty minutes of *Křižova trojka* are filled with music; the longest music-free passage lasts a little over three minutes, while the longest unbroken stretch of music—not at the beginning or end, but in the middle of the film—plays for a full thirteen minutes. Second, it is unlikely that Eisler would have worked more sloppily or with cynical distance on films that were possibly less to his taste artistically or in terms of content; this would have been neither professionally nor economically and strategically smart. In *Křižova trojka*, the fact that Eisler both reuses sections of an existing score (*Jealousy*, 1945) and would also later employ the film music as a source for future compositions (for his vocal-symphonic *Goethe Rhapsody* and the *Lied über die Gerechtigkeit* of 1949, the score for *Wilhelm Pieck—Das Leben unseres Präsidenten* [Wilhelm Pieck: The Life of Our President], 1951, and *Frauenschicksale* [Destinies of Women], 1952; see Deeg 2009, 14), accords with his common practice, usually motivated by economic efficiency, and although it can be problematized, in terms of the aesthetic of the work it appears significant as an interpretative factor in only a small number of cases. And third, Eisler also structured scores such as that for *Křižova trojka* with careful planning and a skilled sense of dramaturgy: the music for many passages is composed very precisely to fit the onscreen elements and camera work and—although Eisler could not speak Czech— reflects the mood, dynamics, and meaning of the speech and even the intonation of the actors. Harmonizing with the plot's character, which oscillates between earnestness and slapstick, the musical narration also frequently appears to be exaggeratedly parodistical, ironically highlighting standard effects (for example with a "shock chord" when the door of the mysterious attic slams shut), while then again displaying a lyrical sincerity, almost in the manner of the Czech opera tradition.

In Eisler's film music as a whole, two compositional principles clearly emerge in which film music could serve as an exemplary testing ground, especially as realized in a number of productions in the postwar period. On the one hand, Eisler sought to reconcile the poles of modernity and popularity, of artistic ambition and "intelligibility." On the other hand, he grounded his work in the premise, as formulated in the exile publication *Composing for the Films*, that a modern method of composition is possible virtually regardless of the style employed or stylistic elements introduced, in other words, that stylistic homogeneity or consistency is not a condition of the logical development of musical material. Today, several insightful readings of the film music composed at the time are available to shore up this notion.

At the beginning of his overview of Eisler's feature film music after 1948, Wolfgang Thiel cites Herbert Jhering, a renowned critic from the time of the Weimar Republic: "[The music] was the event and recalled the golden age of Russian and German film before 1933. It assailed, seized, focused the action. The usual illustrative film music we have in our ears from hundreds of films was swept away. The composer Eisler can revolutionize film music" (Thiel 1998, 85). Jhering made this assessment in November 1949, following the premiere of the first film for which the fifty-one-year-old Eisler had composed music in the just-founded DDR, the socially critical postwar drama *Unser täglich Brot* (Our Daily Bread). Jhering's enthusiasm originates in the energy and optimism, widespread at the time (though soon to be frustrated) in cultural circles of the young East German state, in building a new Germany to continue the flourishing German culture of the 1920s, effectively skipping over the twelve years of National Socialism. High hopes were associated with Eisler in particular, the protagonist of communist *Kampfmusik* in the late Weimar Republic, which he met "in a convincing and, judged by the film symphonic standards of these years, by all means 'revolutionary', albeit inconsequential way" in his first film for Deutsche Film-Aktiengesellschaft (DEFA):

> Stylistically, Eisler on the one hand returned in this film to the intonation of his *Kampfmusik* of the 1920s.... There, dotted clarinet melodies, flutter-tongue motifs in the trumpets and trombones, and the relentless beating of the side drum alla marcia ("not too fast, but always somewhat insistent") accompany the masses on their way to work. On the other hand, the titles music and the third of eight brief self-contained orchestral numbers reflect his compositional efforts to create a "new," classically-oriented style of retraction and simplicity....
>
> In contrast to his early German and French film scores, in which Eisler avoided the high strings in analogy with the neoclassical sound concept and used the instruments of the jazz band in a stylized way, for the film *Our Daily Bread* he composed a score for large symphony orchestra [...]. (Thiel 1998, 85, 86)

Indeed, it was Eisler's instrumentation practice on his return from exile that took a number of his former artistic companions by surprise. Bertolt Brecht, for example, reacted to Eisler's 1948 symphonic arrangement of their joint *Kampflied* classic the *Einheitsfrontlied* with polite astonishment. The fact that Eisler's technique of orchestration had developed and the manner in which it had done so during his time in American exile, especially in the field of film music, was not known to his European peer group. Nevertheless, despite an increased willingness to employ symphonic tuttis from the Hollywood period, Eisler's practice remained characterized by smaller, chamber-music movements, by short forms in which a few instruments create carefully composed tonal landscapes.

The musical sections in Eisler's second DEFA film, *Der Rat der Götter* (Council of the Gods, 1950), employ tonal effects highly unusual for the time. Twelve years before its use in Alfred Hitchcock's *The Birds* (1963), Eisler deploys the characteristic sound of the trautonium consistently in seven of the eight musical numbers of the film. In contrast to Oskar Sala (the inventor of the instrument) and Remi Gassmann in *The Birds*, Eisler does not primarily use the trautonium to generate ethereal sounds but, for example, writes a brief toccata—broken up by tutti orchestral sections—for the instrument in the introduction of music for the opening credits. More recent discussions of narrative but also "purely musical" aspects of this film music (Dahin 2008; Heldt 2008, 51–55) highlight the dramatic force that Eisler unleashes in this score, despite accounting for only a tenth of the film's length (and this predominantly in its first half) as well as the charm in design that analysis of the brief numbers reveals. It is not surprising that the other two films from Eisler's first DEFA contracts have attracted less attention to date. In contrast to *Our Daily Bread* and *Council of the Gods*, which despite containing elements of the reigning ideology in the DDR primarily address general issues of the time (economic difficulties in the nascent state, guilt, and denazification), *Wilhelm Pieck—Das Leben unseres Präsidenten* and *Frauenschicksale* are problematic without a certain historic tolerance for the propagandistic entrenchments of the Cold War. That discoveries can be made in both films is not in doubt, neither is their historical significance. The latter is particularly true of Andrew Thorndike's filmic biography of Wilhelm Pieck, in which the official view of history in the early DDR finds its artistically skilled expression; and the way Eisler contributes musically to the Pieck film can in turn—partially and with caution—be analyzed as a personal political compass point. (Whereas Eisler himself compiled the score for *Wilhelm Pieck* from newly composed music and preexisting works, the situation is different in the equally historically interesting documentaries *Aktion J* [Campaign J; 1961] and *Unbändiges Spanien* (Irrepressible Spain; 1962) produced in the last two years of his life, where he most likely merely sanctioned the selections used from his works. In this sense, these two films in turn represent illuminating contributions to the reception of Eisler's film music.)

Following the series of four DEFA films from 1949 to 1952, the locus of Eisler's work shifted to Vienna for a while. The background to this was conflicts with the cultural policy ideologues in the DDR, and commissions for new works provided a welcome motive. Eisler was Austrian, and the fact that he ultimately settled in East Berlin—crucially with an Austrian passport—was the consequence of political and personal circumstances as well as simple coincidence. Until the mid-1950s, however, Vienna was Eisler's primary workplace alongside Berlin—and the fact that this changed was also due to political circumstances: the withdrawal from Austria of the occupying Soviet forces in 1955 and the deepening ideological entrenchments of the Cold War.

The five Austrian film productions he worked on between 1953 and his (artistic) retreat from Vienna in 1955 can be classified in three generic categories: filmed musical theater (*Gasparone* and *Fidelio*), filmed theater (*Herr Puntila und sein Knecht Matti* [Mr. Puntilla and his Man Matti]), and dramatic feature film (*Schicksal am Lenkrad* [Fate at the Wheel] and *Bel Ami*).

Eisler himself occasionally played down or even disparaged his not always obvious involvement as musical consultant, arranger, or coauthor of the screenplays to musical theater adaptations, and this both quantitatively and qualitatively. It can be inferred from this that these productions did not quite or at all meet his aesthetic conceptions. A glance at the musical and textual sources only partly supports this impression, as it can be seen that Eisler played a significant role in these productions. For example, only about half the music for the London *Pagliacci* film—an opera that in style and content seems worlds apart from Eisler, especially in the curious adaptation by Karl Grune—was original Leoncavallo (above all the "Prologue" and "Commedia"), while the rest was edited by Eisler (typically abridged and melodramatically underlaid) or even freshly composed (see Schweinhardt, forthcoming). For *Gasparone*, too, Eisler worked as a musical arranger and also, according to the plausible but as yet not philologically verified statements by the coauthor and director Karl Paryla, wrote more than half of the screenplay. Here, he added a private joke to the script of the Millöcker operetta by inventing a "friend" for the landlord Bonozzo named, of all things, "Adorno" (see Schweinhardt 2006, 141–42). To interpret this detail with an eye to the somewhat stony relationship between Eisler and Adorno during the Cold War as anything more than a whim would, however, be to overstate the truth.

For the Beethoven adaptation, *Fidelio*, Eisler again primarily worked as a screenwriter and only then as musical arranger (the scope of his compositional work, at the time a legally controversial issue, has to date not been settled but was probably of a minor order). Although his influence on *Gasparone*, in view of the final product, was probably more extensive, he cherished greater ambitions and interest in the content and aesthetics of the *Fidelio* project. One aspect of this interest was certainly directed at the almighty Beethoven, the opera *Fidelio* itself—one of the few examples of the genre that Eisler genuinely valued—and the chance to work with director Walter Felsenstein. An additional aspect of these and the other filmic treatments of opera is Eisler's lifelong approach to the opera as a variant of the multimedial artwork. And in this light, the work on the screenplay for *Fidelio* was not just a filmic but also a film-musical test bed of a remarkable type: film, screenplay, and the numerous sketches and drafts corroborate the thesis that Eisler in a sense tested and developed his ideas on film music aesthetics—on the relationship between the acoustical and optical layers of film in reverse—by not creating music to images but rather images to the authority of Beethoven's music (for more detail, see Schweinhardt 2006). For Eisler and Felsenstein, work on *Fidelio* also involved the attempt at further aesthetic development of the "opera film" genre: the composer saw it aesthetically as a "huge project," while the director averred in the film program that *Fidelio* "cannot be realized for the opera stage" but ultimately only on celluloid.

In addition to the composition itself, Eisler's contribution to screenwriting was also an element of his most original film-musical work in Vienna, Alberto Cavalcanti's screen adaptation of Brecht's play *Herr Puntila und sein Knecht Matti* (1955). Just under half of the film's ninety-minute length is underlaid with music of highly diverse function and character: songs and incidental music, melodramas and full compositions that interpretively consolidate the expressive content of wordless scenes, musical entries of between five seconds' and five minutes' duration. The *Puntila* film presents fruitful jumping-off points for Brecht and Eisler research and film and film music analysis in equal measure (see Schweinhardt 2006, 182–268). The latter is particularly evident from the fact that musical planning was incorporated into work on the screenplay to an unusual extent for a commercial film and that the music—as with the onstage songs—even had an influence on the structure of the film; that different musical material subsets are used in the heterogeneous music levels of the films, from the folksong style to atonal soundscapes. And in view of the fact that Eisler worked on the documentary film *Nuit et Brouillard* (Night and Fog, 1956), filmed in Auschwitz, in the same year, the authority (and speed of production) with which he could master the widest range of film-musical styles and dramaturgical requirements also becomes clear. Nevertheless, Eisler's two Vienna feature film efforts may be more instructive for a detailed cross-sectional view of Eisler than the special cases of the musical theater and theater adaptations. Despite containing socially critical undercurrents, both *Schicksal am Lenkrad* (1954) and *Bel Ami* (1955) address a broad public as entertainment films, thus according with the policy guidelines of the Rosenhügel Studio in Vienna, under Soviet administration. The latter, fanned by a Cold War that also pervaded the film industry, tried to counter the economical and artistic pressure of the Hollywood productions dominating the European markets with their own entertainment products.

Schicksal am Lenkrad—the story of the upbringing of the farmer's son Franzl Pointner and his emancipation from his rural background in the face of complicating social factors—can be read as a fascinating, and in its occasional oddity easily underestimated, gloss on or rather balancing act between two genres popular at the time (in Europe): the *Heimatfilm* and the neorealistic milieu study; and the friction between the various motives, typified characters and aesthetic references reflected in the story and image level is also supported by Eisler's music (see Schweinhardt 2012). When Eisler notes in a letter that his music for *Schicksal am Lenkrad* was received positively but as rather "unusual," this may be the consequence of precisely this friction, of the not always original but ever richer film-musical palette that followed his return from the United States. In a certain sense, the score for *Schicksal am Lenkrad*, while not particularly prominent in the composer's oeuvre, can be viewed as a survey and summing up of his development up to this point in time: in terms of sound, he draws on the one hand from the experience gained in the United States (on the Rockefeller project *and* in Hollywood), but on the other explores new sonic avenues. For example, at the film's opening, the car fanatic Franzl is attracted as if by magic to the parking luxury limousine of the farmer Gruber: the affectionate softness as he moves to the car and the exaggerated acoustic commotion when the engine starts can be analyzed as practical demonstrations of the critique and definition of the notion of film music illustration in *Composing for the Films*. In those scenes that function on the socially critical level in the film, Eisler again primarily operates with in part sober, chamber-textured, in part melodramatic and elegiacally conceived strings whose diversity and use are also indebted to his work in America. And, beyond the musical dramaturgy, some passages in the film can be described in terms of "purely musical" structuring in the context of overall formal proportions—this admittedly being the most difficult area to manifest as compositional intention.

Eisler's last feature film work in Vienna, the socially critical Maupassant adaptation *Bel Ami*, was the first of four collaborations with French directors. For the director of *Bel Ami*, Louis Daquin, he would also write the music for another film based on a nineteenth-century French novel, Balzac's *La rabouilleuse*, in 1960, and he worked with Raymond Rouleau on *Les Sorcières de Salem* (The Witches of Salem; 1957), the first filmic adaptation of Arthur Miller's recently published play *The Crucible*. Other than in a few cursory remarks on *Bel Ami*, these films have to date not been accorded much film-musical interest, which is particularly regrettable in the case of *Les Sorcières de Salem*, in which the music is composed with great intensity and focus and is methodically deployed.

The fourth of Eisler's "French" films is his best-known postwar film work, the music for Alain Resnais's *Nuit et brouillard*, produced on the commission of the French Comité d'histoire de la Seconde Guerre mondiale in 1955, first shown in 1956 and awarded the Jean Vigo Prize for direction and music. Although the work may be considered an Auschwitz documentary, in its historical context and effect maybe even *the* Auschwitz documentary (even if the film does not feature images and texts just relating to Auschwitz), this does not adequately define its *raison d'être: Nuit et brouillard* wants to bear witness, lead the prosecution, call for justice and humanity; it is unsystematic but passionately "educational." The objectivity and frequent impassiveness in the images and music, evoking both admiration and confusion, is ultimately an illusion; the film—most clearly with the French narration by Jean Cayrol or the German version by Paul Celan, in combination with Eisler's music—is essentially a plea for humanity, ultimately leading to an exhortation to remember and continue caution, to images of the deserted ruins of Auschwitz:

> War has dozed off, one eye still open. Grass grows again around the blocks, an abandoned village, still full of menace.... [Who] watches to warn of new executioners? Do they really look so different from us? Somewhere among us remain undetected kapos, officers, informers. There are all those who didn't believe, or only sometimes. And those of us who see the monster as being buried under these ruins, finding hope in being finally rid of this totalitarian disease, pretending to believe it happened but once, in one country, not seeing what goes on around us, not heeding the unending cry.

Despite the scandal that erupted in 1956 when the West German government inter-
vened to prevent the screening of *Nuit et brouillard* at the Cannes Film Festival, the film
was shown a short time later in German cinemas, one year later also on television, and
soon became an integral part of film-based education. (Interestingly, inhibitions of a
cultural-political and ideological nature resulted in a delayed and far more restrained
reception in, of all places, the DDR, where the antifascist tradition was ostensibly a
key part of its founding myth; see Schebera 2005.) Since 2003, *Nuit et brouillard* has
been one of two documentary films (the other being Claude Lanzmann's *Shoah*) on a
list of films recommended for school students in Germany published by the Federal
Center for Political Education (the so-called, naturally controversial "film canon").
Nevertheless, students are often confused by a structural peculiarity in the film that
must act as the starting point for an extensive analysis: the practically uninterrupted
narrator's text and the striking music, played continuously for the entire duration of
the film. Indeed, nonstop music can otherwise be found in Eisler in only a few experimental works (*Opus III*, the Film Music Project): "This 'through-composed' film score
calls for a different kind of approach: whereas music is called upon in 'traditional'
films only at certain times, adding its voice when a second voice is needed, this kind
of composition [as in *Nuit et brouillard*]—where characters, moods, and situations
are often assigned quasi-Leitmotivs—was largely anathema to Eisler" (Dahin 2005,
17–18). To a great extent—greater than in almost any other sound film—the music in
Nuit et brouillard helps to define the message of the multimedial whole.

The elegiac string orchestra number that plays during the opening credits and, in lengthened form, the final pan across the ruins of Auschwitz (see text excerpt above) provides a
convincing example of this: Eisler's music, unusually emotional and somewhat dramatic,
appears to "speak" directly, thereby conveying a conciliatory and simultaneously heroic
tone. Connoisseurs of Eisler's other works of the time will also notice revealing semantic
links. The string number was first employed a short time earlier in the incidental music
for Johannes R. Becher's play *Winterschlacht* (premiere 1955 in Berlin). The title of the play
refers to the German defeat in the Soviet Union as one of the turning points in the Second
World War. As in Resnais's film, the number was performed in the play both as a prelude
and at the end, melodramatically to underscore the closing monologue of a Red Army
commander that can be interpreted dialectically and in the spirit of antifascist patriotism
by German communists as the "victory for German freedom." A semantic parallel with the
closing sequence of *Nuit et brouillard* is obvious—the ruins of the concentration camp as a
symbol of the defeat of National Socialist ideology and simultaneously as the condition for
a Germany freed from Nazi tyranny. Shortly afterwards, Eisler produced a kind of piano
reduction of the *Winterschlacht* prelude in which the violin melody has mutated into a
voice, the song *Horatios Monolog*. And indeed, the well-known monolog from the end
of the fifth act of Shakespeare's *Hamlet* can astonishingly be read as a possible voice-over
commentary for the end of *Nuit et brouillard*:

> And let me speak to the yet unknowing world
> How these things came about: so shall you hear
> Of carnal, bloody and unnatural acts;

> Of accidental judgments, casual slaughters;
> Of deaths put on by cunning and forc'd cause;
> And, in this upshot, purposes mistook
> Fall'n on the inventors' heads: all this can I
> Truly deliver. (*Hamlet*, 5.2.363–70)

(In his song, Eisler used a slightly adapted German translation of this passage.)

Not just in view of the temporal proximity of these three similar uses of one and the same work of music, it appears highly likely, over and above the respective "fits" of the music's expressive force, that Eisler was aiming for an intertextual semantic relationship between the three works, with the message of the two theater monologs both flanking Cayrol's text and entering into the instrumental "closing thesis" of the score to *Nuit et brouillard* (see also Dümling 1998a).

Just as much in 1955 as now, the extremely unusual musical counterpoint with the image level may indeed give rise to confusion and agreement in equal measure (or in succession). Alain Resnais reports the general "surprise" and "unease" while recording the music, because Eisler did not underlay the horrific documentary images with commercially typical effects (as for example the stock categories of *shock* and *horror* or *despair*) but used sounds that could be effectively described as *tender, loving, sensitive,* even *confident*: "The more horrible the scenes, the more friendly the music," recalled Resnais. "Eisler wanted to show that human optimism and hope could even exist in a concentration camp" (quoted in Dümling 1998a, 581). The fact that Eisler's score does not just represent a weighty statement on key issues of film aesthetics but beyond this also invites wildly diverse analytical approaches (see Dahin 2005; Wlodarski 2008) casts a revealing light on the working methods and aims of the film composer Eisler.

In this sense, Eisler's last film score (and composition of any kind) is perhaps the most notable, the music for the DEFA television film *Esther* (1962) based on the eponymous novel by Bruno Apitz: it is remarkable (without wishing to overstate this as a general trend) that three of the last four films for which Eisler composed the music were produced for the new cultural medium of television, these being *Das verlorene Gesicht* (Lost Vision, 1958), *Aktion J* (1961), and finally *Esther*; also remarkable is the fact (again without claiming to propose a creative pattern for Eisler's late work) that in addition to the work begun in exile and completed in the late 1950s, the *Deutsche Symphonie* (premiere 1959), two key works for film in his late years, *Nuit et brouillard* and *Esther*, also deal with the theme of National Socialism and especially the concentration camps (although the Nazi murder of Jews is foregrounded only in *Esther*); a final remarkable point (this being an aspect that is strongly characteristic of Eisler's film music) is the striving for simultaneous musical-dramaturgical and compositional concision and focus, pointedly presented in *Esther*. Over a film runtime of just under an hour, music is heard for a total of less than five minutes. Thomas Ahrend summarizes the structure of Eisler's music and one aspect of its linkage with the musical diegesis:

> The seven numbers of the music to *Esther* are interlinked by diverse references to the material clusters set out in No. 1. As a whole, they pursue a strategy—also

partly traced out in No. 1—from whole-tone to diatonic structures, from melodic figurations marked by intervallic jumps, systematically composed to specific patterns of direction of movement, to scale runs and thereby from tonally uncertain to contextually (undecided) tonality. The film, or rather the dramaturgical function of the music as underlining the unspoken and invisible elements in the film, provides these contrasting groupings of material with a context which identifies the material as the basis of an illustrative technique between the two antagonistic and yet related poles of the film as a whole: whole-tone structures as illustrative of mechanized horror and death, diatonic tonality as illustrating human freedom and love. (Ahrend 2008, 208–9)

IDEAS, MOTIVATIONS, AND METHODS

When looking at Eisler's overall career as a composer for films, one readily observes that, despite the marked heterogeneity of his work, there are clear and consistent ideas and interests that he applies to the art of the cinema. In the following sections, we will discuss each of these in turn.

The Political Soundtrack

A key aspect of Eisler's identity, albeit one subject to fluctuations over the decades, was the desire to be "understood" with his music and to speak to "the masses." This wish, together with occasionally fierce criticism of the bourgeois avant-garde, resulted in the symbolic controversy and partial estrangement of Eisler from his greatly admired teacher Schoenberg—but not from the latter's compositional standards or the tradition they represented—and to a reinforcement of Eisler's further artistic development through his Marxist convictions: from the mid-1920s on, the circumstances, content, and reception of his works—and consequently also their compositional make-up—are largely interwoven with the political history of the twentieth century.

Eisler's early interest in the mass medium of film, which he considered suitable for "reach[ing] the largest audience that has ever existed in the history of music" (Eisler 1939a; EGW III/1, 440), is thus hardly surprising and should be understood not as artistic vanity but in line with Marxist and communist sociomedial ideas partly modeled on contemporary Soviet practice (see also Glanz 2008, 92ff.). Also of interest in this context is the fact that his first film scores after the experimental *Opus III* were written in collaboration with Russian directors: Alexis Granovsky and Victor Trivas emigrated from the Soviet Union to Berlin in the second half of the 1920s. In the highly politicized—in all ideological directions—but extremely liberal and multicultural atmosphere of this metropolis, the composer found the ideal opportunity to commence his artistic search and reinforce his aesthetic ideas.

For Eisler, the heavily politicized debates on art and aesthetics of the time resulted in a concept of music that takes as its starting point the relationship with other media, in other words, that which Eisler, two decades later and after returning from exile, formulated as "applied music." In 1949, he wrote that "in terms of quantity, concert listening no longer has the edge. By 'applied music,' I now want to understand vocal music, i.e., opera, oratorio, cantata, songs, choruses and their hybrid forms, also theater, film, radio plays, and the possibilities of the gramophone record" (EGW III/2, 67). And, similarly, two years later, he asserted that "when music mixes with other arts... it becomes applied music, then even what is worn out is given a new meaning and thus a new usefulness" (EGW III/2, 184).

The specific genres for which he prophesies "hegemony over purely concert [music] [...], at least in a transition period" (EGW III/2, 67f.) in 1949 would ensure the primacy of comprehensibility and social effectiveness in the spirit of Eisler's social and didactic concerns. The dialectical turn, however, to which Eisler's statements on applied forms and a critique of the *l'art pour l'art* principle in his later years is testament, can already be found in *Composing for the Films*. In the German version of the text, film is indeed described—and this, tellingly, in the first sentence of the introduction—as "the most characteristic medium of contemporary mass culture," and this thought is immediately extended in a critical, dialectical manner: "The popular messages conveyed by this industry must not be conceived as an art originally created by the masses" (*CftF*, li). The translation in the English edition does not explicitly reflect this turn, as where the German has "mass culture," the English settles for "cultural industry"—which, admittedly, does already contain within itself the limitation of not having been "originally created by the masses."

Milieu, Biography, Censorship

Eisler's political outlook determined his artistic domains, his artistic milieu, and the type, objective, design, and reception of his films. When looking at Eisler's directors, collaboration with other artistic migrants is striking: following work with the Russians Granovsky and Trivas, the Bulgarian Dudow, and the Dutch Ivens, he first worked for another Austrian, Karl Grune, on *Abdul the Damned*, an entirely Austrian-dominated British production; two of his Hollywood films were also directed by exiles, the Austrian Fritz Lang and the Czech Gustav Machatý. His first production with a German (leaving aside the atypical case of *Opus III*) was *A Scandal in Paris* (1946), directed by Douglas Sirk, who was a native of Hamburg. In addition, related and substantially relevant in terms of content, the left-wing orientation of many of the directors is significant: Eisler's films with Trivas, Dudow, and Ivens, in the United States with Herbert Kline, Clifford Odets, and Edward Dmytryk all have to some degree a socially critical character. His film partnership with the equally left-leaning Joseph Losey did not operate on a political plane as openly as in their joint work for the theater, but *A Child Went Forth* does at least have a political background.

Overall, some two-thirds of the films for which Eisler composed the music have a political or socially critical undercurrent, ranging from a decidedly communist slant (as in *Kuhle Wampe* or *Pesn' o geroyakh*) through more or less unideological criticism of social circumstances (as in *Das Lied vom Leben* [Song of Life, 1931], *Dans les rues*, *None but the Lonely Heart*, or *So Well Remembered* [1947]) to clear positions taken against war and National Socialism (*Niemandsland*, *The 400 Million*, *Hangmen Also Die!*, *Rat der Götter*, *Nuit et brouillard*, and *Esther*). This rough pattern does not acknowledge that hybrid forms are more the rule, both within and beyond the films listed above, and of course it says nothing about the quality of the music or the film itself. In any case, censorship was not surprisingly a frequent problem for Eisler's film work: while he was still in Germany, for example, the first three films he worked on following the experimental *Opus III* came into conflict with the censors of the late Weimar Republic—and all three were banned a short time later on the assumption of power by the National Socialists in 1933. These were the socially critical film *Das Lied von Leben*, banned for its "sexual slant," *Niemandsland* for pacifism, and *Kuhle Wampe* for its communist perspective. Eisler's later work for film also suffered from censorship issues motivated by global politics: *The 400 Million* (censored in England and France), which addresses Japanese warfare in China; and during the Cold War the Beethoven opera film *Fidelio* (1955; banned from the Berlinale film festival in West Berlin) and *Nuit et brouillard* (screening ban at the Cannes Film Festival on the intervention of the West German government).

Kampflieder

A key question in Eisler's musical semantics is how and to what extent his music itself contributes to the politicization of the films. The most obvious and easily perceptible strategy lies in the incorporation of vocal music. In 1931, for example, Eisler contributed to Granowsky's *Das Lied vom Leben* two songs in the characteristic style of *Kampfmusik*, a genre on which he was already acknowledged as having had a formative influence (the remainder of the score was composed by Franz Waxman and Friedrich Hollander). A grotesque and superficial opening sequence has the heroine Erika Walter, in her financial plight, on the brink of getting engaged to a repulsive baron, but she flees the engagement party in disgust and is saved from suicide by a worker named Aribert Mog. This sequence flows into Eisler's "Kessellied," and thus images of a decadent upper class are set against those of machines and workers, the dizzying light music against a typical Eislerian *Kampflied* melody and rhythm (although the effect is not helped by Walter Mehring's politically ambiguous lyrics).

In *Kuhle Wampe*, the "Solidarity Song," already a communist *Kampflied* classic, not only defines the entire final part of the film musically and dramaturgically but also in essence its overall message. In the closing scene, the question in the second half of the film's title—*Wem gehört die Welt?* (To whom does the world belong?)—is modified to form the question of who might ultimately change the world. Answer: "Die, denen sie nicht gefällt" ("Those whom it does not satisfy"). After this comes the final statement of the "Solidarity Song" with alternating solo and choral passages, its closing refrain "Wessen Straße ist die Straße | Wessen Welt ist die Welt?" ("Whose street is the street? | Whose world is the world?"). The musical and scenic performance of the militant song to images of marching masses of workers answers the question unequivocally.

The closing scene of the documentary film *Nieuwe Gronden*, on the recovery of land for cultivation in the Netherlands, reverses the message. In Eisler's words, "the picture includes a harvest scene in the fields newly conquered from the sea. But it does not end in triumph: the same people who have just harvested the grain are throwing it back into the sea. This incident took place during the economic depression of 1931, when food-stuffs were destroyed to prevent the collapse of the market. Only the end of the picture reveals the true meaning of its 'edifying' part" (*CftF*, 25f.). This final scene is further empowered and rendered politically pointed by the accompanying song (which again is the film's closing song). Eisler had composed the "Ballade von den Säckeschmeißern" (Ballad of the Sack-Throwers) three years earlier but, of course, it matches the situation perfectly.[24]

It is no surprise that a militant Eisler song occupies a meaningful position in Joris Iven's documentary transfiguration of heavy industry in the Soviet Union, *Pesn' o geroyakh*; more unusual is the fact that key parts of the British production *Abdul the Damned*, released three years later with high hopes of commercial success, also build on an Eisler song. No other politicizing film song by Eisler is as strongly present as an element of the filmic structure as this "Freedom Song," which becomes the musical insignia of democratic forces in the late Ottoman Empire, who are primarily represented in the film by a group of young men.[25] The melody of the song is first heard in instrumental form at the end of the opening credits; in the course of the film, it is heard at four further points:

1. A group of young Turkish men celebrate the signing of the new constitution by the sultan, singing the "Freedom Song." Celebration and song are interrupted by the entrance of an arrest unit, but one of the young men climbs onto the table and proclaims the song's refrain with clenched fists and in wild defiance of the sultan's henchmen. His closing call for "Freedom" is interrupted by a volley of gunfire: mortally struck, he falls from the table.

2. The imprisoned men are executed in the sultan's jail, the "Freedom Song" on their lips. This "prisoners' chorus" becomes ever smaller with each volley, until finally the last solo singer falls quiet. The song, however, is acoustically and spiritually kept alive by the film's hero, sitting alone in an adjacent cell. The events and their symbolic song have aroused bitterness, anger, and the courage to resist. It is clear, incidentally, that this scene served as the model—probably at the composer's suggestion—for the musically and dramaturgically similarly orchestrated hostage execution scene in *Hangmen Also Die!*

3. Toward the end of the film, the sultan is swept away by the fury of the people. The storming of the sultan's palace is introduced by the refrain motive of the "Freedom Song," this time conspiratorially whistled.

4. As the abdicated sultan leaves the city, his coach flanked by the people celebrating their freedom, the song is heard offscreen, for the first time in its entirety and with choir and orchestral accompaniment, as in Eisler's autograph score.

The interplay between formal-dramaturgical use of the "Freedom Song" and the plot development is clear. Sung self-assurance, a vision of a new era, and opposition to the fallen state power of the old Ottoman Empire becomes a cipher for martyr-like resistance (1 and 2), a signal of overthrow (3), and finally a hymn of victory over despotism (4). At the same time, it is transferred from the purely diegetic level, as the unaccompanied functional music of the insurgents (1 to 3), at the end of the film to the nondiegetic (or not directly diegetic) sphere of symphonic commentary. Structurally, this drama of resistance and triumph is already contained in the textual and musical design of the song. The "Freedom Song," however, does not just form a dramaturgically indispensable part of two key and forceful scene complexes in the film (the arrest scenes and the prisoner executions) but also stresses their ideological background. The content and rhetoric of the message presented in the song's refrain ("Close the ranks" and "All for one and one for all") are closely related to the efforts of the international unity front, in which Eisler was also involved at the time of composition; indeed, his far better known contribution to the topic, the "Einheitsfrontlied," was composed at almost exactly the same time as the "Freedom Song"—also in London, also in late 1934.

Other Types of Political Semantics

Alongside the clear positioning enabled by the use of songs with political texts, there are less explicit forms of musical commentary that dispense with text. These include firstly *Kampflieder* in their instrumental guise—though, of course, such wordless use of well-known song melodies is no original music-historical achievement of Eisler's. The message of the text and image level in the closing scene of *Niemandsland* is generally pacifist—as mentioned above, reason enough for the film to be banned in Nazi Germany: the five men belonging to different warring factions emerge from their common hideout and break through the barbed wire entanglement to the following voiceover narration: "What is their end? They march forward. Five men. Five men who met in No Man's Land and refused to kill each other. Marching forward. Defying their common enemy—WAR." Rousing, march-like music is heard now, clearly bolstering the men's political awakening. If, however, the listener is aware that this closing music is an instrumental version of Eisler's *Kampflied* "Der heimliche Aufmarsch," the latter's militant, much more than simply pacifist message naturally resonates in the mind: "Arbeiter, Bauern, nehmt die Gewehre, | Nehmt die Gewehre zur Hand. | … Dann steigt aus den Trümmern | Der alten Gesellschaft | Die sozialistische Weltrepublik!" ["Workers, farmers, take up your weapons | take your weapons in hand. | Then will arise, out of the ruins | of the old society, | the socialist world-republic!"].

While in American exile, Eisler was highly guarded about expressing political positions in musical form. The antifascist song of resistance in *Hangmen Also Die!* is one exception to this, as it intensifies the significance of the diverse symbols that enable the political commentary to resonate through musical means. Further, complex examples can be found in the instrumental allusions to *Kampflieder* in the Film Music Project experiments (cues for *The Grapes of Wrath*) and in the Hollywood production *None but the Lonely Heart*.

On the same semantic level as the integration of wordless *Kampfmusik* in the underscore, but under contrary political premises, Eisler frequently works with stylistic quotation of "bourgeois light music" in his scores for theater and film. A number of idioms, especially from American-style dance and pop music, serve as musical reinforcements of plot developments that require socially critical views of bourgeois or capitalist decadence, partly as a consciously exaggerative stylistic parody, partly quasi-"neutral" as seemingly direct diegetic music. Dramaturgically apt examples can be found from *Kuhle Wampe* (in which marches from the time of the Kaiser dominate during the caustic "engagement party") to *Rat der Götter* and *Frauenschicksale*. In view of such polemical reductions, it appears an easy matter to reproach Eisler's take on jazz and pop for being clichéd and insufficiently alive to the complexities of the genre. It would, however, be just as simplistic not to take into account the politically polarized circumstances of the 1920s to the 1950s and Eisler's almost lifelong confrontation with entertainment music and the culture industry.

A third level is formed by commentary on the political film action using only the means of music's immanent expressivity, without textual or stylistic references. Notwithstanding Eisler's harsh critique—born of a basic anti-Romantic attitude—of a musical aesthetics guided by the concepts of expression, illustration, and mood, his music possesses a strongly expressive, eloquent component. He attempted to describe this aspect using the Brechtian term "gestural," which aims to cover a genuinely societal dimension in addition to the linguistic and spatial element: the more strictly the idea of gestural music is transferred to composition for film, the more obviously it becomes a premise for the composer to reveal social attitudes and relations in music. This dimension, hard to capture in analysis but elementary to Eisler's self-perception, coincides with his efforts to reveal the "true perspective" of the plot through exaggeration or contradiction. Examples he offers in the second chapter of *Composing for the Films* are discussed in the section on dramaturgical counterpoint below.

The Soundtrack between Absolute Music and Multimedial Collective

In the context of the strong political entwinement in Eisler's film music works, it may seem surprising that his first film composition was for, of all things, an abstract avant-garde picture, Ruttmann's *Opus III*. But there is more to be understood here than merely the fact that Eisler, at this time, was still very close to his roots in the artistically elite circle of the Viennese School (the commission to present *Opus III* in Baden Baden was on the recommendation of Schoenberg). Running parallel to his preoccupation with the political, Eisler thought highly of the way in which many of his colleagues were employing the modern technical possibilities of film as an avant-garde aesthetic platform. Early rules of thumb of film music practice were "made obsolete by the technical development of the cinema as well as of autonomous music" (*CftF*, 3); ending this disparity was one of his declared objectives. In *Composing for the Films*, the new music in question is not restrictively defined as that which was "elaborated...in the works of Schoenberg, Bartók, and Stravinsky during the last thirty years. What is all-important in their music is not the increased number of dissonances, but the dissolution of the conventionalized musical idiom. In truly valid new music, everything is the direct result of the concrete requirement of structure, rather than of the tonal system or any ready-made pattern" (*CftF*, 32f.). The argument for jettisoning a conventional late Romantic musical language is shored up with the thesis that this language is less suitable for the flexible formal and dramaturgical requirements of the film medium than are the means of musical modernism.

The combination of the two creative impulses in Eisler's work—the politically-founded alignment with a large, non-elitist audience and simultaneously an artistically progressive outlook—gives rise to a further issue that resonates with a well-known dictum by his mentor: "If it is art, it is not for all, and if it is for all, it is not art" (Schoenberg 1984, 124). Eisler's aesthetic goal was to resolve this dilemma, and his works must stand the test themselves on the question of the extent to which this is possible and the degree to which they succeed in achieving it. For his work in the mass medium of film, however, the issue acquires concrete specificity beyond its philosophical and ideological background. The idea that took shape in connection with the work on *Composing for the Films*—that the musical material, that is, many ostensibly pure musical aspects relating to the composition and style, could recede behind the dramaturgical approach (see *CftF*, 74–75)—does not imply that Eisler broke with his central idea of the filmically coordinated but nevertheless independent composition of film music. That this is the case is demonstrated not only by the extreme cases where Eisler's film compositions live a double life as autonomous concert works but also by numerous passages in his quite "normal" film music.

If an appreciable number of Eisler's film works can thus be considered in the context of a relative musical autonomy—we avoid using the term "absolute music," of which Eisler disapproved—they are nevertheless linked with his overriding interest in an artwork that absorbs all art forms within itself. Although this project of an art form between (and beyond) Wagner's *Gesamtkunstwerk* and Brecht's "collective of independent arts" occupied the composer to a greater degree in the field of musical theater, in the more tormenting than fruitful work on the opera-idea (see Schweinhardt 2005 and 2006, 340–54), it cannot be a coincidence that the "magical" expression in concrete terms of this "new art" embracing all the other arts bears the hallmarks of a film in a key scene from the unfinished opera *Johann Faustus* (Act II, Scene 5; see also Glanz 2008, 92). "A union of all the arts—the very pinnacle!" (Eisler 1952, 45, quoted in Blake 1995, 307) is how Faust extols his "magic scenes" ("Schwarzspiele": a conscious contrast to the old German term "Lichtspiel," that is, the cinema), whose fantastic illusions he can induce only with the witty and cynical help of Mephisto's charlatanism: "By means of this metal disc known as a 'mirror', we have succeeded in trapping cosmic rays from the heavens. Within this box made of electricum metallicum they cluster together and are focused upon a kind of bell. Its ringing then triggers off phenomena that we can actually see" (Blake 1995, 309).

Eisler himself—who had to make do without a Mephisto—came closest to the ideal of total multimedial design, not surprisingly, on productions where he was involved in the screenplays; but the medial collective is nevertheless strongest and most directly reflected in films where the musical layer is designed independently and is thereby a key carrier of meaning for the filmic diegesis.

COMPOSING FOR THE FILMS: CRITIQUE AND PRESCRIPTIONS

The importance of *Composing for the Films* goes without question, as a contribution to film music theory of the twentieth century, as a contribution to exile (music) research, and as a key and introduction to exploring Eisler's work. Nevertheless, and also without wishing to detract from the significance of the lasting discourse surrounding the book's ideas on a *theoretical* basis, we introduce a summary of the premises underlying Eisler's approach to film music and his prescriptions for its practice with the admonition that the book reflects only one stage in the composer's musical development. Especially given the fact that Eisler made only sporadic theoretical comments on the subject in the fifteen years after 1947, years that were marked by continued intense productivity in the field, any broadly based stylistic and critical investigation of Eisler's film music should be based on the idea of a *lifelong* film music project. Concretely, this suggests that the specific precepts of *Composing for the Films*, important as they are to historical and critical discourse, should be examined as they apply to his music, and not the other way round.

When they set out to write *Composing for the Films*, Eisler and his coauthor Adorno wanted to produce neither a theory of film music composition nor a coherent aesthetics of film music. The aim was rather primarily to formulate a standpoint arising from the critique of contemporary practice, in part shorn up with examples of artistic alternatives, in part with implicit reasoning. The title of the first chapter loses no time in revealing this starting point—its title is "Prejudices and Bad Habits"—and in the very first sentence the artistically poor quality of film music, not just in the Hollywood of the time but in principle since the very beginnings of film, is established as its dependence on "crude everyday practice." The tone of criticism in this "delightfully grumpy first chapter" (Gorbman 1987, 86) also goes beyond the musical to take aim at contemporary film aesthetics and conditions in the film industry:

> [A] number of empirical standards—rules of thumb—were evolved that corresponded to what motion-picture people called common sense. These rules have now been made obsolete by the technical development of the cinema as well as of autonomous music, yet they have persisted as tenaciously as if they had their roots in ancient wisdom rather than in bad habits. They originated in the intellectual milieu of Tin Pan Alley; and because of practical considerations and problems of personnel, they have so entrenched themselves that they, more than anything else, have hindered the progress of motion-picture music. They only seem to make sense as a consequence of standardization within the industry itself, which calls for standard practices everywhere.
> Furthermore, these rules of thumb represent a kind of pseudo-tradition harking back to the days of spontaneity and craftsmanship, of medicine shows and covered wagons. And it is precisely this discrepancy between obsolete practices and scientific production methods that characterizes the whole system. (*CftF*, 3f.)

It is clear that a constitutive critical bias underlying the Film Music Project—and perhaps also a certain pleasure in invective—shows through in a curtain-raiser of this type; in terms of their argumentation, the two authors, trained in the German philosophy of the nineteenth century, and thus in Hegel and Marx, were quite at home when tracing the aesthetic failure of current film music to a gap between obsolete artistic practice and modern means of production. These were, of course, also ideas that Adorno and Eisler pursued well outside the confines of their joint book on film music.

"Selected at random," "typical examples of these habits" are then listed and criticized. Whether it is the verve and easy accessibility of the cutting criticism, whether it is the fact that Eisler's own works given as aesthetic counterexamples were less accessible than the book: reception of the book to date has focused on the critique or limits itself to repeating it (see, for example, Gorbman 1987, 99: "Though certainly the authors' proposals for alternatives to the classical model deserve serious critical attention, here I shall only present their critique of the classical model itself"). In the following, on the other hand, we foreground the prescriptive approaches to composition thinly veiled by the publication's "negative dialectic" undercurrent, taking the implications of that criticism as a point of departure and combining it with constructive formulations and examples from Eisler's film-music practice.

Composing for the Films begins with a critique of the leitmotif technique. In the task of "composition under pressure," this technique enables the composer to "quote where he otherwise would have to invent" (*CftF*, 4; further references to the book in this section are by page number only). Leitmotifs are said to be "the most elementary means of elucidation, the thread by which the musically inexperienced find their way about." The assumption, however, "that this device, because it is so easy to grasp, would be particularly suitable to motion pictures, which are based on the premise that they must be easily understood," is contested by Eisler and Adorno on two grounds. Firstly, because the "fundamental character" of the rudimentary leitmotif requires "a large musical canvas if it is to take on a structural meaning beyond that of a signpost," yet motion picture production, which is "completely montage technique" and itself requires "interruption of one element by another rather than continuity," cannot provide the necessary freedom for compositional development: "Cinema music is so easily understood that it has no need of leitmotifs to serve as signposts, and its limited dimension does not permit of adequate expansion of the leitmotif" (*CftF*, 5). Second, in the film that seeks to depict reality there is no place for the metaphysical and symbolic meaning for which the leitmotif was invented. In brief:

> [T]he function of the leitmotif has been reduced to the level of a musical lackey, who announces his master with an important air even though the eminent personage is clearly recognizable to everyone. The effective technique of the past thus becomes a mere duplication, ineffective and uneconomical. At the same time, since it cannot be developed to its full musical significance in the motion picture, its use leads to extreme poverty of composition. (*CftF*, 5f.)

Eisler's criticism of the leitmotif in film must also be seen in the context of his longstanding and highly ambivalent attitude to the music of Richard Wagner (even if, in the passage quoted, he does describe the original use of leitmotifs as an "effective technique"). As a whole, Eisler disliked the person and aesthetics of Wagner, and the majority of his work. Underlying this was an aversion to the Romantic as an approach and style, an attitude that Eisler shared with many of his contemporaries; and this sweeping antipathy particularly increases in its stridency and compositional relevance in the field of film music, which is hardly conceivable even into the present day without the model of musical Romanticism.

A critique of nineteenth-century music also dominates the next example of "bad habits," the premise of "melody and euphony." These are understood as "conventionalized historical categories" (*CftF*, 6) that express themselves in the "uninterrupted flow of a melody in the upper voice, in such a way that the melodic continuity seems natural, because it is almost possible to guess in advance exactly what will follow" (*CftF*, 7). The concept of melody itself is seen as constricted to a "fetishism, ... which at certain moments during the latter part of the Romantic period crowded out all the other elements of music." The stylistic ideal of musical classicism and the "theme" as the "point of departure of a composition" (*CftF*, 6) is given as a counterpole to the concept of melody as a self-contained entity. For Adorno and Eisler, the idea of "natural" melody is an illusion, an "extremely relative phenomenon illegitimately absolutized, neither an obligatory nor an *a priori* constituent of the material, but one procedure among many, singled out for exclusive use" (*CftF*, 8). This thesis becomes relevant for film music in light of the subsequent verdict that such conventional demand for melody is not compatible with the "objective requirements of the motion picture" (*CftF*, 8):

> Visual action in the motion picture has of course a prosaic irregularity and asymmetry. It claims to be photographed life; and as such every motion picture is a

documentary. As a result, there is a gap between what is happening on the screen and the symmetrically articulated conventional melody. A photographed kiss cannot actually be synchronized with an eight-bar phrase....More than anything else the demand for melody at any cost and on every occasion has throttled the development of motion-picture music. The alternative is certainly not to resort to the unmelodic, but to liberate melody from conventional fetters (*CftF*, 8, 9).

Here, for the first time, *Composing for the Films* expresses a prescriptive impulse, even if only in one sentence: for structural reasons, film music must be liberated from the "conventional fetters" of melody. In the same way, the critique of the leitmotif, turned into a demand, means an abandonment of this technique.

How then might a not "conventionally melodic" film music that foregoes leitmotifs be conceived? *Composing for the Films* provides some answers in the third chapter, "The New Musical Resources." The point of departure is the thesis that the style and approach of new music at the time fulfilled their desired film music function "more appropriate[ly] than the haphazard musical padding with which motion pictures are satisfied today"; for the authors, new music is that which was "elaborated...in the works of Schoenberg, Bartók, and Stravinsky during the last thirty years," from today's standpoint the classical modernism of the first half of the century.

> In truly valid new music, everything is the direct result of the concrete requirement of structure, rather than of the tonal system or any ready-made pattern. A piece full of dissonances can be fundamentally conventional, while one based on comparatively simpler material can be absolutely novel if these resources are used according to the constructive requirements of the pieces instead of the institutionalized flow of musical language. (*CftF*, 32f.).

This idea of the "separation of the resources and their treatment" (*CftF*, 82) is a key thesis: the observation that the contemporary development of sonic structures and effects obtained from tone groupings (for example, the "emancipation of dissonance") and a constructive approach to these new sound possibilities are two common elements of the art of composition—and that a composer does not necessarily need to employ new, "unused" resources to produce an aesthetically modern work but in principle may also achieve this with conventional material. This apparently contradictory notion, which Eisler in fact frequently expressed later on, can already be found in his "Schoenberg Anecdotes" of 1924 (on the fiftieth birthday of his teacher): "Nothing is so odious to A. S. as a composition in which the author, merely to appear 'modern,' piles up dissonances and formal mishaps without ability or inspiration. In great anger, he once exclaimed: 'Listen! I'll show this fellow something and write a piece in C major!'" (*HEGA* IX/1.1, 26). In *Composing for the Films*, the third chapter ends with a related "warning by Eisler" on the "dangers of the new style," the "irresponsible use of the new resources in a hit-or-miss style, modernism in the bad sense of the word, that is to say, the use of advanced media for their own sake, not because the subject calls for them" (*CftF*, 43).

Such theoretical issues relating to musical resources are relevant in several respects to the ideas of good film music outlined in *Composing for the Films*. On the one hand, on account of their potential for appropriate, signifying semantics, the authors consider the " musical resources" more suitable than conventional means, that is, "deliberately choos[ing] the musical elements required by the context instead of succumbing to musical clichés and prefabricated emotionalism" (*CftF*, 33). Eisler and Adorno provide a number of notorious instances of such "petrified associations" that dominated the music of the nineteenth century and thus also current film music—for example, the "accented 3/4 bar suggests the waltz and gratuitous *joie de vivre*"—before then maintaining, very much on the intellectual level and in the vocabulary of Karl Marx, Arnold Schoenberg, and Bertolt Brecht: "Such associations often place the events of the film in a false perspective. The new musical resources prevent this." This is followed by the key claims about the expressive superiority of new music: "True, the new music does not represent conceptually mediated ideas, as is the case with programmatic music, in which waterfalls rustle and sheep bleat. But it can exactly reflect the tone of a scene, the specific emotional situation, the degree of seriousness or casualness, significance or inconsequence, sincerity or falseness—differences not within the possibilities of the conventional Romantic techniques" (35). By deploying the means of new music, film music can therefore achieve effects that "do not represent a stylized picture of pain, but rather its tonal record" (*CftF*, 38), a "sharpness of expression" not granted traditional music, but also "absence of expression" (*CftF*, 40).

On the other hand, in the renunciation of tonality and the resulting formal redundancy, the new music presents the opportunity to use just those musical elements and forms that the film predominantly requires:

> In [the new music], the individual musical episodes and the patterns of the themes are conceived without regard to a pre-arranged system of reference. They are not intended to be "repeatable" and require no repetition, but stand by themselves. If they are expanded, it is not by means of symmetrical devices, such as sequences or resumptions of the first part of a song form, but rather by means of a developing variation of the given original materials, and it is not necessary that these should be easily recognizable.... It is obvious that modern music is especially qualified to construct consistent precise short forms, which contain nothing superfluous, which come to the point at once, and which need no expansion for architectonic reasons.... [This] makes it possible to formulate specific musical ideas in a far more drastic and penetrating fashion, and to free the individual musical events from all unessential gewgaws.... It is because of this capacity for unfettered characterization that the new music is in keeping with the prose character of the motion picture. (*CftF*, 39)

Over and above all unease with the idea of the Romantic, Adorno and Eisler's call for a revolution in the resources of film music—away with the ingrained conventions of over two centuries of western music and on to the new—rests on the conviction that it is only the new music, with its renunciation of the meaningless and clichéd, which both focuses on the necessary and can react to the structural and semantic requirements of film flexibly and free of musical constraints. With these characteristics, it fulfils the "principle of universal planning, so fundamental for motion-picture music" (*CftF*, 83). Using the idea of the "separation of the resources and their treatment," the demand that new music be used in film is developed further dialectically and sublimated: "Thus the negation of the traditional concept of style, which is bound up with the idea of specific materials, may lead to the formation of a new style suitable to the movies" (*CftF*, 83).

Composing for the Films: Dramaturgical Counterpoint

Additional "prejudices and bad habits" named in *Composing for the Films* relate to the level of film music dramaturgy, as do the "models" given in the following chapter of the book. The first critique focuses on the idea that film music should be "unobtrusive": "Music [should] be inconspicuous in the same sense as are selections from *La Bohème* played in a restaurant" (*CftF*, 10). For authors of Adorno or Eisler's aesthetic background and approach, this practice is out of the question, its criticism self-evident, as film music of this type would either have no effect or would work at a subconscious level, allowing neither for musical ambition nor "universal planning." This section thus also generally proclaims: "The insertion of music should be planned along with the writing of the script, and the question whether the spectator should be aware of the music is a matter to be decided in each case according to the dramatic requirements of the script" (*CftF*, 11). Essential to an appreciation of the reasoning in *Composing for the Films* and for Eisler's film music approach is not that the music is prevented from receding, that it must always act in the foreground or remain audible or consciously present, but rather that the *degree* to which it can be heard or its presence in the "field of consciousness" is to be precisely planned.

The remainder of the chapter on "prejudices and bad habits" presents a critique of standardized and thus worn-out film music effects: separate sections are devoted to the use of musical set pieces from "geography and history," the practice of using "stock music," the use of all types of musical clichés, and—on a somewhat different level—the standardization of musical interpretation. Adorno and Eisler's criticism of the primacy of poor musical "illustration," a central, ambivalent, and equivocal term, is also given a whole section.

The critique of conventional illustrative techniques leads to the heart of Eisler's approach to film music and the composer's overall understanding of music and dramaturgy. Following a spirited attack on mainstream film music based on "nature in the most superficial sense of the word," consequently "conform[ing] to...stale programmatic patterns," the section continues:

> What is in question here is not the principle of musical illustration. Certainly musical illustration is only one among many dramaturgic resources, but it is so overworked

that it deserves a rest, or at least it should be used with the greatest discrimination. This is what is generally lacking in prevailing practice....Illustrative use of music today results in unfortunate duplication. It is uneconomical, except where quite specific effects are intended, or minute interpretation of the action of the picture. The old operas left a certain amount of elbow room in their scenic arrangements for what is vague and indefinite; this could be filled out with tone painting. The music of the Wagnerian era was actually a means of elucidation. But in the cinema, both picture and dialogue are hyperexplicit. Conventional music can add nothing to the explicitness, but instead may detract from it, since even in the worst pictures standardized musical effects fail to keep up with the concrete elaboration of the screen action. But if the elucidating function is given up as superfluous, music should never attempt to accompany precise occurrences in an imprecise manner. It should stick to its task—even if it is only as questionable a one as that of creating a mood—renouncing that of repeating the obvious. Musical illustration should either be hyperexplicit itself—over-illuminating, so to speak, and thereby interpretive—or should be omitted. (*CftF*, 13–14)

In his prescriptive statements on good film music, then, Eisler does not dismiss the principle of musical imitation *per se*: instead, he defines and increases the requirements placed on it: the meaning of music in film may not be simply to provide the picture with its "double." This criticism of musical supplementation arises, first, from the notion—surprising perhaps, given Eisler's anti-Romantic image—that music is actually capable of expression in the manner of images and texts and, second, as a consequence of the semiotic assertion that music (for example) is a poor image in the same way an image would be a poor poem. Adorno and Eisler thus essentially work from the principle of a film aesthetic that demands of each of the medial levels that they fully exploit their possibilities of expression, which for music means adding something to the image that it does not or cannot express. For Eisler, consequently, film music moves toward permanent interpretation, indeed toward a permanent and sophisticated illustration of filmic action. It would therefore be a mistake to investigate Eisler's film music (or "good" film music) on the basis of the absence of illustrative elements; what are worth analyzing are precisely what and how the music illustrates at any given moment.

If, in this sense, film music should provide an independent contribution to the message of the film, there are broadly three possibilities: contradiction, exaggeration, and illustration of what cannot (in principle yet or again) be seen. In their second chapter, "Function and Dramaturgy," the authors provide examples of such approaches—consciously termed "models"—from Eisler's scores. Under the heading "Sham Collectivity," a scene from *Niemandsland* shows how the "transformation of seemingly harmless individuals into a horde of barbarians" (*CftF*, 24) is achieved only through the use of music (the paragraph from which this statement is taken is quoted at greater length in the section "Eisler's Work for Film" above). The section "Invisible Community" describes the end of *Hangmen Also Die!*, in which an off-screen *Kampflied* represents "the real hero of the picture, the Czech people," as the "sensuous suggestion of something unsensuous: illegality" (*CftF*, 25). The "Visible Solidarity" section then presents a scene from *La*

Nouvelle Terre (that is, *Nieuwe Gronden*) in which the music is not confined to reproducing the "'mood' of the scene, a mood of gloom and great effort"—the workers are
shown bearing a huge steel conduit—but instead the underlying triumph of solidarity: "Although the rhythmical beat of the music synchronized with the work rhythm of
the incident on the screen, the melody was rhythmically quite free and, strongly contrasting with the accompaniment, pointed beyond the constraint represented on the
screen" (*CftF*, 26).

Adorno and Eisler then introduce the notion of "dramaturgical counterpoint."
Considering that this is perhaps the most famous and colorful term in *Composing for
the Films* and is so fundamental for an interpretation of Eisler's film music, the brevity of
the discussion is astonishing. A single introductory sentence—"The following examples
show how music, instead of limiting itself to conventional reinforcement of the action or
mood, can throw its meaning into relief by setting itself in opposition to what is being
shown on the screen" (26)—is followed by three more examples from Eisler films: the
model "Movement as a Contrast to Rest" is demonstrated with a sequence from *Kuhle
Wampe* in which the "passive" mood of the images is contrasted with sharp, brisk, and
dynamic music. The opposite situation, "Rest as a Contrast to Movement" is illustrated
with a scene from *Dans les rues* in which a bloody fight is depicted with "tender, sad,
rather remote" music (*CftF*, 27). Finally, the authors give an outline of the musical structure of a short scene in *Hangmen Also Die!* where the dying Reinhard Heydrich lies in
his hospital bed: "The music consists of brilliant, strident, almost elegant sequences, in
a very high register, suggesting the German colloquial phrase *auf dem letzten Lock pfeif-
end* (literally, 'to blow through the last hole', which corresponds to the English: 'To be on
one's last legs'). The accompaniment figure is synchronized with the associative motive
of the scene: the dripping of the blood is marked by a pizzicato in the strings and a piano
figure in a high register" (*CftF*, 28).

Eisler's formulation of a key demand of film music also relates to this last scene: "The
composer's task was to impart the true perspective of the scene to the spectator" (*CftF*,
28). If we understand this as a further prescriptive premise together with the notion of
musical illustration of the film action discussed above (that is, the demand for illustration that does not *merely double* but *interprets*), then the "true perspective" in Adorno
and Eisler's concept of dramaturgical counterpoint becomes clear—and, following from
this, so also is revealed the sum, essence, and vision of Eisler's work for film. It is in no
way the case that music is limited to permanently contradicting the image or text levels
of a film, which would then live up to neither the specific semiotic possibilities of these
levels nor even a solid understanding of the term "counterpoint"; instead, film music
qua music should achieve its dramaturgical sovereignty in a "collective of independent
arts" (in the spirit of Brecht) and thus become an indispensable and independent element of the filmic narrative. This requires planning of the content and structure across
all levels of the film from the beginning, that is, competent musical planning as early
as the script-writing stage (preferably in cooperation with the composer). Only in this
way may film music fulfil its key task, that is, to be "essential to the meaning of [a] scene"
(*CftF*, 24).

Conclusion: Eisler in Twentieth-century Discourses

As we have seen, Eisler's artistic biography is marked by the political, ideological, and aesthetic conflicts of the twentieth century. Given this circumstance, combined with his lively literary, journalistic, and cultural-political activities outside of composition, it is not surprising that he became an object of numerous scholarly and political discourses, to which other *film composers*—to use the term after all—are typically not exposed. By way of conclusion, we enumerate and briefly describe the most important of them:

Discourses on the Second Viennese School. Despite his own differences with Schoenberg, Eisler supported his teacher in the face of great resistance in the DDR. Then as now, Eisler's originality as a member of the Viennese School, that which specifically marks out his dodecaphonic work, became a matter for debate.

Discourses on the working-class music movement. In the Weimar Republic, Eisler took a polemical stand against "petit bourgeois" forms of working-class musical culture and became an icon of a new proletarian *Kampfmusik*. After his remigration, he responded with skepticism to the desire of the communist party (and attempts by young composers) to build on his classic *Kampflieder* because the historical situation had now changed: as he put it, in an allusion to Hitler's "thousand-year *Reich*," the time of the "Solidarity Song" was "over a thousand years old" (quoted in Grabs [1984], 487), and his aim was to discover new artistic solutions for music in socialist society.

Discourses of general cultural-political significance for the left-wing intelligentsia. In the debates of the 1930s to 1950s in which Eisler was involved, political scores were settled ruthlessly. These primarily included the "expressionism debate" of 1937–38, prompted by the Moscow exiles, in which the German-speaking left-wingers, proceeding from the question of the link between expressionism and fascism, attempted to reach agreement on the "correct" concept of realism. Eisler supported Ernst Bloch in the debate, conducted in international exile journals, and argued against the position of Georg Lukács for an undogmatic and productive understanding of cultural heritage. The key issues remained of significance in the postwar period and Eisler again confronted his adversaries of the 1930s, some of them advocates of Stalinism, in the DDR debate of the early 1950s, when the cultural authorities in his chosen Germany attacked him with the damning accusation of formalism—in the process contributing to the premature end of his final major opera project, *Johann Faustus*.[26]

Discourses on persecution, exile, and remigration. The working circumstances and themes of persecution and exile color key parts of Eisler's work, from film, via chamber music, to the lied. Looking back, he described the boredom of the exile—with yearning for the foreign and sarcasm in equal measure—as the ultimate source of productivity. On returning to Central Europe, however, he found that exile was seen by many who had remained as a moral stigma—a curious reversal of guilt based on an assumption of a paradisiacal life in exile. In the initially Stalinist states of Eastern Europe and also in the DDR, where exile and resistance were basic elements of national identity, there was a deeply rooted suspicion of "West emigrants" like Eisler, who were suspected of an affinity, if not outright collaboration, with their capitalist countries of exile.

Discourses on music and politics. A key stimulus for Eisler's oeuvre was his conviction that music is political and musicians—like all people—must adopt a political position. The fact that, as a Marxist, he adopted this stance with considerable bias and sometimes polemically succeeded in provoking surprise, rejection, hate, respect, and admiration in an unbroken line from the Weimar Republic onward, even into the present. The sometimes passionate emotions in the one or other direction are no doubt amplified by the fact that, as his son Georg attested, Hanns Eisler was a master of "falling between two stools," a role he occupied throughout his life, artistically and politically, in Vienna, in Berlin, in the United States, and especially in the DDR of the 1950s, as the representative composer figure of a nation whose political leadership neither understood nor shared his aesthetics. No wonder, then, that the majority of his sympathizers were in the left-wing opposition, in the East for example among the undogmatic Marxists in the DDR, in the West in the wake of the student movement.

Discourses ultimately on multimediality. With Eisler's basic aesthetic and societal stance, the musical genres beyond "absolute music," those he termed "applied music," ranked very highly. Key areas here are his works for stage and screen. Eisler's artistic ambitions in these areas, which in some productions encompassed more than his music, and his unyielding theoretical comments provide solid starting points for embedding this part of his oeuvre in discussions of musical semantics and with them multimediality.

FILMOGRAPHY

OPUS III. Silent animated film, Germany 1925; production, direction: Walter Ruttmann. For the Baden-Baden Music Festival in 1927, Eisler wrote music for this film, which he later used as the first movement of his *Suite für Orchester Nr. 1* op. 23. Lit.: Heller 1998.

DAS LIED VOM LEBEN (Song of Life). Feature, Germany 1931; production: Film-Kunst AG, Tonbild-Syndikat AG (Tobis); direction: Alexis Granowsky; screenplay: Victor Trivas, Hans Lechner, Walter Mehring. In addition to the music by Franz Wachsmann, the film includes songs by Friedrich Hollaender and H. Adams (i.e., Hanns Eisler).

NIEMANDSLAND (No Man's Land). Feature, Germany 1931; production: Resco-Filmproduktion; direction: Victor Tri vas; screenplay: Victor Trivas, after a draft by Leonhard Frank. Eisler grouped together parts of his music for this film as the *Suite für Orchester Nr. 2* op. 24. Lit.: Faßhauer 2008, 2009.

KUHLE WAMPE ODER WEM GEHÖRT DIE WELT? (Kuhle Wampe or Who Owns the World?). Feature, Germany 1932; production: Prometheus-Film, Praesens-Film; direction: Slatan Dudow; screenplay: Bertolt Brecht, Ernst Ottwalt. Eisler grouped together parts of his music for this film as the *Suite für Orchester Nr. 3* op. 26;

the film includes *Die Spaziergänge* and the *Solidaritätslied*. Lit.: Kuntze 1981, 1982; Maas 1995; Alter 2004; Heldt 2008.

PESN' O GEROYAKH (Song of Heroes). Documentary, Soviet Union 1932; production: Meshrabpom-Film; direction: Joris Ivens; screenplay: Yosif Sklyut, with the assistance of Sergei Tretyakov. Eisler grouped together parts of his music for this film as the *Suite für Orchester Nr. 4* op. 30. Lit.: Agde 2012; Thiel 2012.

DANS LES RUES (Song of the Streets). Feature, France 1933; production: Société Internationale Cinématographique (SIC); direction: Victor Trivas; screenplay: Victor Trivas, Alexandre Arnoux. Eisler grouped together parts of his music for this film as the *Suite für Orchester Nr. 5* op. 34. Lit.: Deeg 2009.

NIEUWE GRONDEN (New Earth). Documentary, Holland 1934; production: CAPI; direction, screenplay: Joris Ivens. Eisler took some of the music for this film from his *Suiten für Orchester Nr. 3/4* opp. 26/30; the film includes "Die Ballade von den Säckeschmeißern."

LE GRAND JEU (THE GREAT GAME). Feature, France 1934; production: Les Films de France; direction: Jacques Feyder; screenplay: Charles Spaak, Jacques Feyder. Eisler grouped together parts of his music for this film as the *Suite für Orchester Nr. 6* op. 40.

ABDUL THE DAMNED. Feature, Great Britain 1935; production: British International Pictures, Capitol; direction: Karl Grune; screenplay: Ashley Dukes, Warren C. Strode, Roger Burford, after a novella by Robert Neumann. Part of the film music was published after Eisler's death as the *Invention für Orchester*. Lit.: Schweinhardt 2008b, 2010.

PAGLIACCI (USA: *A Clown Must Laugh*). Opera screen adaptation, Great Britain 1936; production: Trafalgar Films; direction: Karl Grune; screenplay: Monckton Hoffe, John Drinkwater, Roger Burford, after the opera by Ruggiero Leoncavallo. Eisler arranged the original Leoncavallo score and composed some new music for this adaptation. Lit.: Schweinhardt 2010, forthcoming.

THE 400 MILLION. Documentary, USA 1939; production: History Today, Inc.; direction, screenplay: Joris Ivens, John Ferno. Eisler adapted parts of this film music for the *Fünf Orchesterstücke*, *Thema mit Variationen* ("Der lange Marsch"), and *Scherzo mit Solovioline*. Lit.: Kuntze 1981; Heldt 2008.

PETE ROLEUM AND HIS COUSINS. Animated film, USA 1939; production: Petroleum Industries Exhibition, Inc.; direction: Joseph Losey; screenplay: Joseph Losey, Kenneth White. The film also includes a song by Oscar Levant ("I have got something for you to sing").

THE LIVING LAND. Documentary, USA 1939; production: US Soil Conservation Service; scenario: Helen Hill. Eisler published this film music as his *Nonett Nr. 1*. Lit.: Helbing 1998, 2000, 2010.

WHITE FLOOD. Documentary, USA 1940; production: Frontier Films; direction, screenplay: David Wolff, Robert Strebbins, Lionel Berman; original image material by William O. Field, jr. and Sherman Pratt. Eisler published this film music as his *Kammersymphonie*. Lit.: Faßhauer 1998, 2004.

A CHILD WENT FORTH. Documentary, USA 1941; production: National Association of Nursery Educators; direction: Joseph Losey, John Ferno; screenplay: Joseph Losey. Eisler grouped together parts of his music from this film as the *Suite für Septett Nr. 1* op. 92a.

THE FORGOTTEN VILLAGE. Semidocumentary, USA 1941; production: Pan-American Films; direction: Herbert Kline; screenplay: John Steinbeck. Eisler grouped together parts of his music from this film as the *Nonett Nr. 2*; following Eisler's death, Manfred Grabs published the further *Sätze für Nonett*, also from the music to this film. Lit.: Kolb 2008, Helbing 2010; Weber 2012.

REGEN (Rain). Silent film, Holland 1929; production: CAPI; direction: Joris Ivens; screenplay: Joris Ivens, Mannus Franken. In 1941, Eisler wrote music for a revised cut of this film from 1932, which he later published as *Vierzehn Arten den Regen zu beschreiben*. Lit.: Kuntze 1981; Heller 1998; Kuntze 2001; Gall 2008; Gall 2012.

[Scenes from] THE GRAPES OF WRATH. Feature, USA 1940 (Original film music by Alfred Newman); production: 20th Century Fox; direction: John Ford; screenplay: Nunnally Johnson after the novel by John Steinbeck. Eisler wrote alternative music for selected scenes in this film in 1941/42. Lit.: Gall 2002, 2009.

HANGMEN ALSO DIE! Feature, USA 1943; production: Arnold Productions, United Artists; direction: Fritz Lang; screenplay: John Wexley; "Original Story": Bertolt Brecht, Fritz Lang. Eisler's music was nominated for a 1944 Oscar in the category "Music Score for a Dramatic or Comedy Picture." Lit.: Gorbman 1991; Gall 1998; Schebera 1998; Bick 2001, 2003, 2010–11; Gall forthcoming; Weber 2012.

NONE BUT THE LONELY HEART. Feature, USA 1944; production: RKO; direction: Clifford Odets; screenplay: Clifford Odets, after a novella by Richard Llewellyn. Eisler's music was nominated for a 1945 Oscar in the category "Music Score for a Dramatic or Comedy Picture." Lit.: Weber 1998; Heldt 2008; Schweinhardt 2008b; Weber 2012.

JEALOUSY. Feature, USA 1945; production: Republic Pictures; direction: Gustav Machatý; screenplay: Arnold Philips, after an idea by Dalton Trumbo. Lit.: Deeg 2009.

THE SPANISH MAIN. Feature, USA 1945; production: RKO; direction: Frank Borzage; screenplay: Herman J. Mankiewicz, George W. Yates, after a story by Aeneas MacKenzie. Lit.: Gorbman 1991.

DEADLINE AT DAWN. Feature, USA 1946, production: RKO; direction: Harold Clurman; screenplay: Clifford Odets, after a novella by William Irish.

A SCANDAL IN PARIS. Feature, USA 1946; production: Arnold Productions, United Artists; direction: Douglas Sirk; screenplay: Ellis St. Joseph. Lit.: Neumeyer and Buhler 2008.

THE WOMAN ON THE BEACH. Feature, USA 1947; production: RKO; direction: Jean Renoir; screenplay: Jean Renoir, Frank Davis, Michael Hogan, after a novel by Mitchell Wilson. Lit.: Weber 2012.

SO WELL REMEMBERED. Feature, USA 1947; production: Alliance Productions London, RKO; direction: Edward Dmytryk; screenplay: John Paxton, after a novel by James Hilton.

[Scenes from] THE CIRCUS. 1947. Eisler scored a number of scenes of the planned sound version of Charlie Chaplin's silent film from 1928. Chaplin ultimately released s version with his own music. Eisler published his compositions as the *Septett Nr. 2*. Lit.: Heller 1998.

KŘÍŽOVÁ TROJKA (Austria: *Das Geheimnis des schwarzen Ritters*, GDR: *Kreuz drei* [The Mystery of the Black Rider]). Feature, Czechoslovakia 1948; production: Filmové Studio Barrandov; direction: Vaclav Gajer; screenplay: F. A. Dvorak, Vladimir Tumar. Lit: Deeg 2009.

UNSER TÄGLICH BROT (Our Daily Bread). Feature, DDR 1949; production: DEFA; direction: Slatan Dudow; screenplay: Slatan Dudow, Hans Joachim Beyer, Ludwig Turek. Lit.: Thiel 1998.

DER RAT DER GÖTTER (Council of the Gods). Feature, DDR 1950; production: DEFA; direction: Kurt Maetzig; screenplay: Friedrich Wolf, Philipp Gecht. Lit.: Grützner 1974; Thiel 1998; Dahin 2008; Heldt 2008.

WILHELM PIECK—DAS LEBEN UNSERES PRÄSIDENTEN (Wilhelm Pieck—The Life of Our President). Documentary, GDR 1951; production: DEFA; direction: Andrew Thorndike; screenplay: Andrew Thorndike, Otto Winzer.

FRAUENSCHICKSALE (Destinies of Women). Feature, GDR 1952; production: DEFA; direction: Slatan Dudow; screenplay: Gerhard Bengsch, Ursula Rumin, Slatan Dudow. The film includes the song *Das Lied vom Glück* (Text: Bertolt Brecht). Lit.: Stegmann 2005.

SCHICKSAL AM LENKRAD (FATE AT THE WHEEL). Feature, Austria 1954; production: Wien-Film, Akkord-Production; direction: Aldo Vergano; screenplay: Ruth Wieden. Lit.: Schweinhardt 2012.

BEL AMI. Feature, Austria 1954; production: Projektograph Film; direction: Louis Daquin; screenplay: Vladimir Pozner, after the novel by Guy de Maupassant. Lit.: Thiel 1998; Schweinhardt 2008b.

HERR PUNTILA UND SEIN KNECHT MATTI (Mr. Puntilla and his Man Matti). Feature, Austria 1955; production: Wien-Film; direction: Alberto Cavalcanti; screenplay: Alberto Cavalcanti, Bertolt Brecht, Vladimir Pozner, Ruth Wieden, after the play by Bertolt Brecht. Lit.: Kruppke 1985; Schweinhardt 2006.

GASPARONE. Operetta screen adaptation, Austria 1955; production: Projektograph-Film; direction: Karl Paryla; screenplay: Karl Paryla, Hanns Eisler, after the eponymous operetta by Carl Millöcker. Eisler arranged the original Millöcker score and composed some new music for this adaptation.

FIDELIO. Opera screen adaptation, Austria 1955; production: Wien-Film, Akkord-Production; direction: Walter Felsenstein; screenplay: Walter Felsenstein, Hanns Eisler, after the eponymous opera by Ludwig van Beethoven. Eisler contributed to the screenplay; his merits for the arrangement are not clear. Lit.: Ralfs 1997; Schweinhardt 2006.

NUIT ET BROUILLARD (Night and Fog). Documentary, France 1956; production: Argos Films, Como Films, Cocinor; direction: Alain Resnais; screenplay: Alain Resnais, Jean Cayrol. Lit.: Colpi 1963; Dümling 1998a; Dahin 2005; Wlodarski 2008.

LES SORCIÈRES DE SALEM (*Die Hexen von Salem* [The Witches of Salem]). Feature, France and GDR 1957; production: Films Borderie, Pathé Cinema, DEFA; direction: Raymond Rouleau; screenplay: Jean Paul Sartre, after the play *The Crucible* by Arthur Miller. Lit.: Thiel 1998.

GESCHWADER FLEDERMAUS (THE FLEDERMAUS SQUADRON). Feature, DDR 1958; production: DEFA; direction: Erich Engel; screenplay: Rolf Hunold, Hans Szekely, after the play by Rolf Hunold.

DAS VERLORENE GESICHT (LOST VISION). Feature, DDR 1958; production: Deutscher Fernsehfunk; direction: Erich-Alexander Winds; screenplay: after the play *Lofter oder Das verlorene Gesicht* by Günther Weisenborn.

LES ARRIVISTES (The Opportunists; *Trübe Wasser*). Feature, Frankreich and GDR 1960; production: Nouvelles Pathé Cinema, DEFA; direction: Louis Daquin; screenplay: Louis Daquin, Klaus Wischnewski, after the novel by Honoré de Balzac.

AKTION J (CAMPAIGN J). Documentary, GDR 1961; production: Deutscher Fernsehfunk; direction, screenplay: Walter Heynowski.

ESTHER. Feature, GDR 1962; production: Deutscher Fernsehfunk; direction: Robert Trösch; screenplay: Robert Trösch, Bruno Apitz, after the novel by Bruno Apitz. Lit.: Ahrend 2008.

NOTES

1. This section and the parallel section (Part II) are based in part on passages from Schweinhardt 2006 and 2008b.

2. Text quotes from *Composition for the Films* throughout this chapter are reprinted by permission: © Theodor Adorno and Hanns Eisler, 1947, *Composition for the Films*, Continuum, an imprint of Bloomsbury Publishing Plc.

3. For a detailed historical account of the Film Music Project, see Gall 2009a.

4. In his interim report on the Film Music Project, Eisler claimed that "three editions of *White Flood* were made, one with the usual tireless narrator, the second with very limited talk, and a third that omitted every spoken syllable and used only subtitles. This last version, in my opinion, is the most effective" (Eisler 1941, 253). There is no evidence supporting his claim, but on the basis of a new recording of the score and the production of an abridged narration, the DVD supplement to Adorno and Eisler 2006 includes possible reconstructions.

5. For detailed information, see Campbell 1982, 145–274.

6. The DVD supplement to Adorno and Eisler 2006 includes a reconstruction of this provisional cut.

7. For detailed information, see Gall 2008, 87–94.

8. On the basis of the 1941 recording of *Fourteen Ways to Describe Rain* and the 1932 film cut of *Rain*, the DVD supplement to Adorno and Eisler 2006 includes a reproduction of Eisler's experimental music version of the cinépoème.

9. In connection with this, it is of interest that on June 10, 1946, toward the end of the editing process for *Composing for the Films*, the editor at Oxford University Press, Philip Vaudrin,

wrote to Adorno, criticizing the "sometimes unfortunate tone when certain people connected with the motion picture industry are referred to" (OUP file, fol. 71). Shortly thereafter (June 13, 1946), Adorno reported that a number of passages had been replaced with "more politely worded statements" (OUP file, fol. 73).

10. For an extensive analysis of the entire film score for *Hangmen Also Die!*, see Gall forthcoming.

11. Sally Bick also describes Eisler's "ability to simultaneously resist and appropriate Hollywood film score conventions" (Bick 2010a, 92), made explicit in the film music for *Hangmen Also Die!*

12. This section is based in part on Gall 2006, 160–71, and Gall forthcoming.

13. Credit goes to David Culbert for discovering the Oxford University Press correspondence file on *Composing for the Films* (see Culbert 2008). We are very grateful to him for having granted us and other interested scholars access to the file and generously providing copies of it.

14. The Theodor W. Adorno Archive and the Hanns Eisler Archive at the Academy of Arts in Berlin hold copies of the typescript.

15. In Gall forthcoming, the draft is examined more closely with regard to the genesis and respective division of work in *Komposition für den Film*.

16. See the enclosure with Adorno's letter to Siegfried Unseld, February 6, 1969, Adorno, Suhrkamp, and Unseld 2003, 670.

17. Letter from Adorno and Eisler to Marshall, July 27, 1946, Rockefeller Archive Center, Rockefeller Foundation Archives, Record Group 1.1, Series 200R, Box 259, Folder 3096.

18. See letter from Adorno to Hatcher October 2, 1945; OUP file, fol. 37.

19. The "first edition of the German original version," published by Rogner & Bernhard under Adorno's supervision in 1969, is devoid of all these additions. They were first added to the new edition included in volume 15 of AGS by Rolf Tiedemann—but with the puzzling omission of two passages, which were first published in 2006 in the special edition edited by Johannes C. Gall.

20. The salient additions present only in the English-language first edition are as follows: the footnotes in *CftF*, 6f., 55f., and 85; *CftF*, 69, from "It might enter the process of composition..." to "...the common denominator being the sequence"; *CftF*, 105f., from "However, this absurd procedure..." to "...further factor of levelling is introduced"; and *CftF*, 135–37, from "The purpose of this appendix..." to "...tendencies of modern music."
For the following additions, the original German wording was first published in volume 15 of AGS: *CftF*, 21f., footnote 1; *CftF*, 41f., footnote 2; *CftF*, 59, from "Its social function..." to "...when there is something to be seen"; *CftF*, 111f., from "It must be granted..." to "...loss of time for real rehearsing"; *CftF*, 113, from "They vent their resentment..." to "when a brilliant E-major seems felicitous"; *CftF*, 116–18, from "As regards motion-picture music..." to "the disease of the macrocosm of which it is part."
For the following two additions, the original German wording was first published in Adorno and Eisler 2006: *CftF*, 80f., from "The tendency toward planning..." to "...jeopardizes the subject expressing himself musically"; *CftF*, 111, from "Composers of cinema music are exposed to a special danger..." to "...impedes the freedom of his imagination."

21. This is the German version of the passage from "However, this absurd procedure..." to "...further factor of leveling is introduced" in *CftF*, 105f.

22. See also Klemm 1977, 12f.

23. For a detailed discussion of Eisler's remigration, see Schweinhardt 2006.
24. The unique quality of Eisler's compositional voice is shown in this comment by Andrew Tommasini, reviewing a concert by H. K. Gruber: the "Ballade" is described as "a raucous piece of agitprop, the intricate contrapuntal lines and boldly wayward harmony made clear that Eisler had been an attentive student of Schoenberg" ("Singing of Weimar Era, Subversively," *New York Times*, November 10, 2007; online archive accessed July 6, 2012). [ed.]
25. For more detail on this song and the film, see Schweinhardt 2008b, 18–22.
26. On this, see the articles in Schweinhardt 2005.

BIBLIOGRAPHY

Abbreviations

AGS Theodor W. Adorno, *Gesammelte Schriften* [Collected writings]. Edited by Rolf Tiedemann. Frankfurt: Suhrkamp, 1970–1986.

CftF Adorno, Theodor W., and Hanns Eisler. *Composing for the Films*. With a new introduction by Graham McCann. London and Atlantic Highlands: Athlone Press, 1994. Originally published in 1947.

EGW Hanns Eisler, *Gesammelte Werke* [Collected works]. Edited by Stephanie Eisler and Manfred Grabs on behalf of the Akademie der Künste der DDR. Leipzig: Deutscher Verlag für Musik, 1968–1983.

FML Hanns Eisler Collection, Feuchtwanger Memorial Library, Specialized Libraries and Archival Collections, University of Southern California, Los Angeles.

HEA Hanns-Eisler-Archiv, Archiv Akademie der Künste [Hanns Eisler Archive, Archive of the Academy of Arts], Berlin.

Hearings *Hearings regarding Hanns Eisler: Hearings before the House Committee on Un-American Activities*, House of Representatives, Eightieth Congress, First Session, Washington: United States Government Printing Office, 1947.

HEGA *Hanns Eisler Gesamtausgabe* [Hanns Eisler complete edition]. International Hanns Eisler Society. Wiesbaden: Breitkopf & Härtel, 2002–.

OUP file File on Hanns Eisler and the book *Composing for the Films*. Archive of Oxford University Press, New York.

I.1 Editions of Film Scores by Hanns Eisler

2013a. *Alternative Film Music to an Excerpt from* The Grapes of Wrath—*Film Music to* Hangmen Also Die! Edited by Johannes C. Gall. *HEGA* VI/10.

2013b. *Film Music to* Nuit et brouillard. Edited by Oliver Dahin. *HEGA* VI/23.

I.2 Relevant or Cited Writings by Hanns Eisler

1931. "[Zum Film *Niemandsland*]." *HEGA* IX/1.1, 152.

[1932] 1978. "Blast-Furnace Music: Work on a Sound Film in the Soviet Union." In Hanns Eisler, *A Rebel in Music: Selected Writings*, edited by Manfred Grabs, translated by

Marjorie Meyer, 61–63. Berlin: Seven Seas Book. [German original published in *HEGA* IX/1.1, 164–166.]

[1935] 1978. "Hollywood Seen from the Left." *Rebel*, 101–105. [German original published in *HEGA* IX/1.1, 270–274.]

[1936a] 1978. "From My Practical Work: On the Use of Music in Sound Film." *Rebel*, 121–125. [German original published in EGW III/1, 383–388.]

1936b. "Music and Film: Illustration or Creation." *World Film News.* 1, no. 2: 23.

1939a. "Music for the Film." EGW III/1, 440–442.

1939b. "Work as Composer for the Films." EGW III/3, 134–137.

1939c. "Research Program on the Relation between Music and Films." EGW III/3, 137–142.

1939d. "Music and Films: Proposed Research Project by Hanns Eisler—Prepared for the Rockefeller Foundation." EGW III/3, 142–145.

1940. Eisler, Hanns, and others. "Music in Films: A Symposium of Composers." *Films: A Quarterly of Discussion and Analysis* 1, no. 4: 5–24.

1941. "Film Music—Work in Progress." *Modern Music* 18, no. 4: 250–254. [Also published in EGW III/3, 146–151 and *Historical Journal of Film Radio and Television* 18, no. 4: 591–594.]

1942. "Final Report on the Film Music Project on a Grant by the Rockefeller Foundation." EGW III/3, 154–158. [Also published in *Historical Journal of Film Radio and Television* 18, no. 4: 595–598.]

1944. "Prejudices and New Musical Material." *Writer's Congress: The Proceedings of the Conference Held in October 1943 under the Sponsorship of the Hollywood Writers' Mobilization and the University of California*. Berkeley: University of California Press, 260–264.

c.1944. "Contemporary Music and the Film [II]." EGW III/1, 479–487.

c.1945. "Modern Music and the Film [I–II]" EGW III/1, 459–462.

1950. "Filmkomponist bei der Arbeit: Über die Musik zum DEFA-Film 'Rat der Götter.'" EGW III/2, 82f.

1952. *Johann Faustus*. Berlin: Aufbau-Verlag.

Adorno, Theodor W., and Hanns Eisler. [1947] 2006. *Komposition für den Film*. With an epilogue by Johannes C. Gall and a DVD, "Hanns Eislers Rockefeller-Filmmusik-Projekt (1940–1942)." Edited on behalf of the International Hanns Eisler Society by Johannes C. Gall. Frankfurt: Suhrkamp, 2006.

I.3 Relevant or Cited Writings by Theodor W. Adorno

1971. "Postscript." In Theodor W. Adorno and Hanns Eisler, *Composing for the Films*, 167–169. Freeport, NY: Books for Libraries Press.

2002. *Essays on Music*. Selected, with introduction, commentary, and notes by Richard Leppert. New translations by Susan H. Gillespie. Berkeley: University of California Press.

2006. *Letters to His Parents 1939–1951*. Edited by Christoph Gödde and Henri Lonitz. Translated by Wieland Hoban. Cambridge, UK, and Malden, MA: Polity.

Adorno, Theodor W., Peter Suhrkamp, and Siegfried Unseld. 2003. "*So müßte ich ein Engel und kein Autor sein": Adorno und seine Frankfurter Verleger*. Edited by Wolfgang Schopf. Frankfurt: Suhrkamp.

Adorno, Theodor W., and Siegfried Kracauer. 2008. *Briefwechsel 1923–1966: "Der Riß der Welt geht auch durch mich."* Edited by Wolfgang Schopf. Frankfurt: Suhrkamp.

II. Selected Relevant Literature

Agde, Günther. 2012. "Ein Komponist macht Geräusche. Eine Spezialarbeit Hanns Eislers für den Dokumentarfilm *Komsomol* von Joris Ivens (1932)." In: *Hanns Eisler. Angewandte Musik (=Musik-Konzepte. Sonderband)*, edited by Ulrich Tadday, 100–113. Munich: text + kritik.

Ahrend, Thomas. 2008. " 'Wir werden ihnen unser Gesicht nicht zeigen …': Eislers Musik zum Fernsehfilm *Esther.*" In *Kompositionen für den Film*, edited by Peter Schweinhardt, 185–210. Wiesbaden: Breitkopf & Härtel.

Alter, Nora M. 2004. "The Politics and Sounds of Everyday Life in *Kuhle Wampe.*" In *Sound Matters: Essays on the Acoustics of Modern German Culture*, edited by Nora M. Alter and Lutz Koepnick, 79–90. New York: Berghahn.

Amzoll, Stefan. 1976. "Dramaturgischer Kontrapunkt in der Filmmusik: Zur Konzeption von Hanns Eisler und Theodor W. Adorno." *Musik und Gesellschaft* 26, no. 11: 659–663.

Behrens, Roger. 1998. "Vers une musique prolétarienne: Hanns Eisler zwischen Theodor W. Adorno und Ernst Bloch—ein Porträt." *Weg und Ziel: Marxistische Zeitschrift* 56, no. 1: 26–29.

Betz, Albrecht. 1982. *Hanns Eisler: Political Musician*. Translated by Bill Hopkins. Cambridge: Cambridge University Press.

——. 1999. "Eisler, Brecht, Adorno: Musik, Film, Kulturindustrie." *Brecht Yearbook* 24: 68–79.

Bick, Sally. 2001. "Composers on the Cultural Front: Aaron Copland and Hanns Eisler in Hollywood." PhD diss., Yale University, New Haven.

——. 2003. "Political Ironies: Hanns Eisler in Hollywood and Behind the Iron Curtain." *Acta Musicologica* 75, no. 1: 65–84.

——. 2008. "Eisler's Notes on Hollywood and the Film Music Project, 1935–42." *Current Musicology* 86: 7–39.

——. 2010a. "A Double Life in Hollywood: Hanns Eisler's Score for the Film *Hangmen Also Die!* and the Covert Expressions of a Marxist Composer." *Musical Quarterly* 93, no. 1: 90–143.

——. 2010b. "The Politics of Collaboration: Composing for the Films and its Publication History." *German Studies Review* 33, no. 1: 141–162.

Blake, David. 1995. Compiler and editor. *Hanns Eisler: A Miscellany*. New York: Harwood.

Campbell, Russell. 1982. *Cinema Strikes Back: Radical Filmmaking in the United States 1930–1942*. Ann Arbor: UMI Research Press.

Colpi, Henri. 1963. *Défense et illustration de la musique dans le film*. Lyon: Société d'édition de recherches et de documentation cinématographiques.

Culbert, David. 2008. "How about *Composing for the Films*? The Oxford University Press Production File for Adorno/Eisler's book." *Eisler-Mitteilungen* 45: 28–31.

Dahin, Oliver. 2005. "The Pastness of the Present: Musical Structure and 'Uncanny Returns' in Eisler's Score to *Nuit et Brouillard.*" *Eisler-Mitteilungen* 38: 17–20.

——. 2008. "An Embedded Narrative. Hanns Eisler's Score for *Council of Gods.*" In *Kompositionen für den Film*, edited by Peter Schweinhardt, 143–162. Wiesbaden: Breitkopf & Härtel.

Danuser, Hermann. 1987. " 'Mittlere Musik' als Komposition für den Film: Das Beispiel Hanns Eisler." In *film—musik—video oder die Konkurrenz von Auge und Ohr*, edited by K.-E. Behne, 13–30. Regensburg: Gustav Bossc Verlag.

Daquin, Louis. 1964. ["Für Hanns Eisler"]. In *Sinn und Form: Beiträge zur Literatur—Sonderheft Hanns Eisler*, 334–335. Deutsche Akademie der Künste. Berlin: Rütten & Loening.

Deeg, Peter. 2009. "Selten gesehene Eisler-Filme." *Eisler-Mitteilungen* 47: 14, 19, 22f.

Dümling, Albrecht. 1998a. "Eisler's Music for Resnais' *Night and Fog* (1955): A Musical Counterpoint to the Cinematic Portrayal of Terror." *Historical Journal of Film, Radio and Television* 18, no. 4: 575–584.

——, ed. 1998b. [Eisler issue] *Historical Journal of Film, Radio and Television* 18, no. 4.

——. 2010. "Illustration und Überwältigung oder dramaturgischer Kontrapunkt? Zur Filmmusik-Ästhetik bei Eisenstein, Brecht und Eisler." In *Hanns Eisler (=querstand 5/6)*, 211–226. Frankfurt: Roter Stern.

Eisler-Fischer, Louise. *c.*1977. "Zur Entstehung des Buches 'Komposition für den Film' und der Zusammenarbeit von Theodor W. Adorno und Hanns Eisler." HEA 3382.

Erdmann Hans, and Giuseppe Becce. 1927. *Allgemeines Handbuch der Film-Musik*, vol. 1. Berlin: Schlesinger.

Ewenz, Gabrielle, Christoph Gödde, Henri Lonitz, and Michael Schwarz, eds. 2003. *Adorno: Eine Bildmonographie*. Frankfurt: Suhrkamp.

Faßhauer, Tobias. 1998. "Hanns Eislers's 'Chamber Symphony op. 69' as Film Music for 'White Flood' (1940)." *Historical Journal of Film, Radio and Television* 18, no. 4: 509–521.

——. 2004. "Hanns Eislers *Kammersymphonie* als Filmmusik zu *White Flood* (1940)." *Musik & Ästhetik* 8, no. 31: 30–48.

——. 2008. "Film—Musik—Montage: Beobachtungen in *Niemandsland*." In *Kompositionen für den Film*, edited by Peter Schweinhardt, 63–85. Wiesbaden: Breitkopf & Härtel.

——. 2009. "Das falsche Kollektiv in der falschen Szene. Bemerkungen zu Eislers erster großer Spielfilmmusik." *Eisler-Mitteilungen* 47: 15–18.

Fladt, Hartmut. 2010. "*14 Arten den Regen zu beschreiben*: Zur Konstituierung musikimmanenter und musiktranszendierender Semantik bei Eisler." In *Hanns Eisler (=querstand 5/6)*, edited by Albrecht Dümling, 157–169. Frankfurt: Roter Stern.

Gall, Johannes C. 1998. "'Raise the invisible torch and pass it along'! Zur Filmmusik von *Hangmen Also Die!*" *Musik von unten* 22: 15–43.

——. 2002. "Hanns Eislers Musik zu Sequenzen aus *The Grapes of Wrath*. Eine unbeachtete Filmpartitur." *Archiv für Musikwissenschaft* 59, no. 1: 60–77; no. 2: 81–103.

——. 2006. "Modelle für den befreiten musikalischen Film." In Theodor W. Adorno and Hanns Eisler, *Komposition für den Film*, 155–182. Frankfurt: Suhrkamp.

——. 2008. "A Rediscovered Way to Describe Rain: New Paths to an Elusive Sound Version." In *Kompositionen für den Film*, edited by Peter Schweinhardt, 87–122. Wiesbaden: Breitkopf & Härtel.

——. 2009a. "Früchte des Filmmusikprojekts. Neues über Hanns Eislers Musik zu *The Grapes of Wrath*." *Eisler-Mitteilungen* 47: 10–13.

——. 2009b. "An 'Art of Fugue' of Film Scoring: Hanns Eisler's Rockefeller Foundation-Funded Film Music Project (1940–1942)." In *Patronizing the Public: American Philanthropy's Transformation of Culture, Communication, and the Humanities*, edited by William J. Buxton, 132–152. Lanham, MD: Lexington.

——. 2012. "Eine wiedergefundene Art den Regen zu beschreiben. Neue Bahnen zu einer problematischen Tonspur." In: *Hanns Eisler. Angewandte Musik (=Musik-Konzepte. Sonderband)*, edited by Ulrich Tadday, 137–167. Munich: text + kritik.

——. forthcoming. *Eisler Goes to Hollywood: Das Buch* Komposition für den Film *und die Filmmusik zu Hangmen Also Die!* [working title] (=*Eisler-Studien*, vol. 4). Wiesbaden: Breitkopf & Härtel.

Glanz, Christian. 2008. *Hanns Eisler: Werk und Leben*. Wien: Edition Steinbauer.

Gorbman, Claudia. 1987. *Unheard Melodies: Narrative Film Music*. Bloomington: Indiana University Press, London: BFI Publishing.

——. 1991. "Hanns Eisler in Hollywood." *Screen* 32, no. 3, 272–285.

Grabs, Manfred. 1969. "Film- und Bühnenmusik im sinfonischen Werk Hanns Eislers." In *Sammelbände zur Musikgeschichte der DDR*, edited by Heinz Alfred Brockhaus and Konrad Niemann, vol. 1, 20–29. Berlin: Verlag Neue Musik.

——. [1984] *Hanns Eisler: Lebensbild eines unbequemen Komponisten*, unpublished manuscript. Akademie der Künste, Berlin, Hanns Eisler Archiv, HEA 7532.

Grützner, Vera. 1974. "Das Bild-Ton-Verhältnis in Eislers Musik zu frühen DEFA-Filmen." In *Hanns Eisler heute. Berichte—Probleme—Beobachtungen*, 83–85. Berlin: Akademie der Künste der Deutschen Demokratischen Republik.

Guido, Laurent 2000: "Eine 'Neue Musik' für die Massen. Zwischen Adorno und Brecht: Hanns Eislers Überlegungen zur Filmmusik." *Dissonanz/Dissonance* 64: 20–27.

Helbing, Volker. 1998. "Hanns Eisler's Contribution to the New Deal: 'The Living Land' (1941)." *Historical Journal of Film, Radio and Television* 18, no. 4: 523–533.

——. 2000. "Pastorale, zwölftönig: Anmerkungen zu einer Filmpartitur Hanns Eislers." *Musik & Ästhetik* 4, no. 14: 25–39.

——. 2010. "Einrichtung für den Konzertgebrauch oder klassizistische Glättung? Editorische Probleme in den beiden Nonetten Eislers." In *Hanns Eisler* (=querstand 5/6), edited by Albrecht Dümling, 170–184. Frankfurt: Roter Stern.

Heldt, Guido. 2008. "Grenzgänge: Filmisches Erzählen und Hanns Eislers Musik." In *Kompositionen für den Film*, edited by Peter Schweinhardt, 43–62. Wiesbaden: Breitkopf & Härtel.

Heller, Berndt. 1998. "The Reconstruction of Eisler's Film Music: *Opus III*, *Regen* and *The Circus*." *Historical Journal of Film, Radio and Television* 18, no. 4: 541–559.

——. 2010. "Eislers filmmusikalisches Wirken im amerikanischen Exil. Bericht über Forschungsarbeiten und eine USA-Reise." In *Hanns Eisler* (=querstand 5/6), edited by Albrecht Dümling, 185–197. Frankfurt: Roter Stern.

Hufner, Martin. 1998. "'*Composing for the Films*' (1947): Adorno, Eisler and the Sociology of Music." *Historical Journal of Film, Radio and Television* 18, no. 4: 535–540.

Ivens, Joris. 1964. "Monolog auf Hanns Eisler." In *Sinn und Form: Beiträge zur Literatur—Sonderheft Hanns Eisler*, 32–44. Deutsche Akademie der Künste. Berlin: Rütten & Loening.

Klemm, Eberhardt. 1977. "Zur vorliegenden Ausgabe." In Theodor W. Adorno and Hanns Eisler, *Komposition für den Film*. EGW III/4, 1–24.

Knepler, Georg. 1998. "Schwierigkeiten mit dem Kennenlernen von Eislers Lebenswerk." In *Hanns Eisler. 's müsst dem Himmel Höllenangst werden* (=Archive zur Musik des 20. Jahrhunderts 3), edited by Maren Köster, 27–33. Hofheim: Wolke Verlag.

Kolb, Roberto. 2008. "Four Ways of Describing Death: Painting, Filming, Narrating and Scoring Mexican Funeral Scenes." In *Kompositionen für den Film*, edited by Peter Schweinhardt, 211–234. Wiesbaden: Breitkopf & Härtel.

Kruppke, Annette. 1985. "Das Volksstück 'Herr Puntila und sein Knecht Matti' von Bertolt Brecht im Vergleich mit dem gleichnamigen Film von Vladimir Pozner, Alberto Cavalcanti und Ruth Wieden." Dissertation, University of Greifswald, Germany.

Kuntze, Christian. 1981. "Filmkomposition bei Hanns Eisler." Berlin: state exam thesis.

——. 1982. "Filmmusik bei Hanns Eisler." In *Hanns Eisler—Komposition für den Film: Dokumente und Materialien zu den Filmen Hanns Eislers* (=Materialien zur Filmgeschichte 12), 1–8. Berlin: Freunde der Deutschen Kinemathek.

——. 2001. "Filmkomposition bei Hanns Eisler: Praxis und Theorie." In *Film und Musik*, edited by Regina Schlagnitweit and Gottfried Schlemmer, 104–106. Vienna: Synema.

Levin, Tom. 1984. "The Acoustic Dimension. Notes on Cinema Sound." *Screen* 25, no. 3: 55–69.

London, Kurt. 1936. *Film Music: A Summary of the Characteristic Features of its History, Aesthetics, Technique; and Possible Developments.* Translated by Eric S. Bensinger. London: Ayer.

Maas, Georg. 1995. "Hanns Eislers Musik zu dem Film *Kuhle Wampe oder: Wem gehört die Welt.*" In *"Es liegt in der Luft was Idiotisches…" (=Beiträge zur Popularmusikforschung 15/16)*, edited by Helmut Rösing, 139–156. Baden-Baden: Coda.

Mayer, Günther. 1995. "Eisler and Adorno." In *Hanns Eisler: A Miscellany*, edited by David Blake, 133–158. New York: Harwood.

McCann, Graham. 1994. " Introduction." *CftF*, vii–xlvii.

Neumeyer, David, and James Buhler. 2008. *"Composing for the Films*, Modern Soundtrack Theory, and the Difficult Case of *A Scandal in Paris.*" In *Kompositionen für den Film*, edited by Peter Schweinhardt, 123–141. Wiesbaden: Breitkopf & Härtel.

Parkes, Lisa. 2003. "Composing for the Films: Adomo and Schoenberg in Hollywood." *New German Review* 19: 90–101.

Patalas, Enno. 1960. "Herr Puntila und sein Knecht Matti." *Filmkritik* 12: 352.

Ralfs, Bettina. 1997. "Die 'Fidelio'-Verfilmung Walter Felsensteins und Hanns Eislers. Kunst und Kunstproduktion im Schatten politischer Spannungen." MA thesis, University of Erlangen.

Resnais, Alain. 1964. "[Alain Resnais in Conversation with Edouard Pfrimmer]." In *Sinn und Form: Beiträge zur Literatur—Sonderheft Hanns Eisler*, 371–375. Deutsche Akademie der Künste. Berlin: Rütten & Loening.

Rosen, Philip. 1980. "Adorno and Film Music: Theoretical Notes on *Composing for the Films.*" *Yale French Studies* 60: 157–182.

Rubsamen, Walter H. 1944. "A Modern Approach to Film Music: Hanns Eisler Rejects the Clichés." *Arts and Architecture* 61, no. 11: 25, 38.

Salmon, Barry. 2008. "*[RE]Composing for the Films*: The Problem of Praxis." In *Kompositionen für den Film*, edited by Peter Schweinhardt, 247–269. Wiesbaden: Breitkopf & Härtel.

Schebera, Jürgen. 1978. *Hanns Eisler im USA-Exil: Zu den politischen, ästhetischen und kompositorischen Positionen des Komponisten 1938 bis 1948.* Berlin: Akademie-Verlag.

——. 1982. " 'Modelle zur Befreiung des musikalischen Films…': Hanns Eislers Filmarbeit in den USA 1938-1947." In *Hanns Eisler—Komposition für den Film: Dokumente und Materialien zu den Filmkompositionen Hanns Eislers*, 16–27. Berlin: Freunde der Deutschen Kinemathek.

——. 1997. "Der Filmkomponist Hanns Eisler." In *Hanns Eisler, der Zeitgenosse. Positionen—Perspektiven: Materialien zu den Eisler-Festen 1994/1995*, edited by Günter Mayer, 41–59. Leipzig: Deutscher Verlag für Musik.

——. 1998. "*Hangmen Also Die!* (1943): Hollywood's Brecht-Eisler Collaboration." *Historical Journal of Film, Radio and Television* 18, no. 4: 567–573.

——. 2005. "Cannes ohne Nacht und Nebel: Zur zeitgenössischen Rezeption des Films *Nuit et brouillard.*" *Eisler-Mitteilungen* 38: 4–11.

Schoenberg, Arnold. 1984. *Style and Idea: Selected Writings of Arnold Schoenberg.* Edited by Leonard Stein, with translations by Leo Black. Berkeley: University of California Press.

Schweinhardt, Peter, ed. 2005. *Hanns Eislers Johann Faustus. 50 Jahre nach Erscheinen des Operntexts 1952. Symposion (=Eisler-Studien 1).* Wiesbaden: Breitkopf & Härtel.

——. 2006. *Fluchtpunkt Wien: Hanns Eislers Wiener Arbeiten nach der Rückkehr aus dem Exil (=Eisler-Studien 2).* Wiesbaden: Breitkopf & Härtel.

——, ed. 2008a. *Kompositionen für den Film: Zu Theorie und Praxis von Hanns Eislers Filmmusik* (=*Eisler-Studien* 3). Wiesbaden: Breitkopf & Härtel.

——. 2008b. "Ein guter Filmkomponist? Überlegungen zur Spielfilmmusik Hanns Eislers." In *Kompositionen für den Film*, edited by Peter Schweinhardt, 11–42. Wiesbaden: Breitkopf & Härtel.

——. 2010. "'Better don't joke!' Eislers britische Filmarbeiten." *Eisler-Mitteilungen* 49: 16–19.

——. 2011. "Pastorale, Internationale, Liebeslied: Auf der Spur der schönstmöglichen Interpretation." *Eisler-Mitteilungen* 51: 33–34.

——. 2012. "*Schicksal am Lenkrad*—Hanns Eislers Beitrag zum österreichischen Heimatfilm?" In *Hanns Eisler—Ein Komponist ohne Heimat?* (=*Schriften des Wissenschaftszentrums Arnold Schönberg* 6), edited by H. Krones, 97–108. Vienna: Böhlau.

——. Forthcoming. "'My Work Was Nil.' An Attempt to Rescue Eisler's Peculiar *Pagliacci* Production" In *Hanns Eisler in England* (=*Eisler-Studien* 5), edited by Oliver Dahin and E. Levi. Wiesbaden: Breitkopf & Härtel.

Stegmann, Vera. 2005. "*Frauenschicksale*: A DEFA Film Viewed in Light of Brecht's Critique of the Opera and Eisler/Adorno's Theory of Film Music." *German Studies Review* 28, no. 3: 481–500.

Thiel, Wolfgang. 1986. "Opernverfilmungen der DEFA." *Oper heute* 9: 276–290.

——. 1997. "Vergiss, dass du Musiker bist: Notate zum Problem einer filmspezifischen Musik." In *Jeder nach seiner Fasson: Musikalische Neuansätze heute* (=*Veröffentlichungen der Musikakademie Rheinsberg*), edited by Ulrike Liedtke, 281–293. Saarbrücken: Pfau Verlag.

——. 1998. "Modern und volkstümlich zugleich? Hanns Eislers Spielfilmmusiken nach 1948." In *Hanns Eisler. 's müsst dem Himmel Höllenangst werden* (=*Archive zur Musik des 20. Jahrhunderts* 3), edited by Maren Köster, 85–100. Hofheim: wolke verlag.

——. 2001. "Ansichten zur gesellschaftlichen Bedeutung und Wirkung der DEFA- (Spiel-Filmmusik von 1946 bis 1990." *Musikforum* 94: 18–22.

——. 2010. "Hanns Eisler als Filmkomponist nach 1948." In *Hanns Eisler* (=*querstand* 5/6), edited by Albrecht Dümling, 227–234. Frankfurt: Roter Stern.

——. 2012. "Zwischen 'Hochofen-Musik' und Orchesterklängen. Hanns Eislers Arbeit als Komponist und 'Musikreporter' für Joris Ivens' Film *Pesn o Gerojach/Heldenlied/Die Jugend hat das Wort/Komsomol* von 1932." In: *Hanns Eisler. Angewandte Musik* (= *Musik-Konzepte. Sonderband*), edited by Ulrich Tadday, 82–99. Munich: text + kritik.

Viejo, Breixo. 2008. "Neue Musik für einen befreiten Film: Giovanni Fuscos Filmmusik zu Alain Resnais' *Hiroshima mon amour*." In *Kompositionen für den Film*, edited by Peter Schweinhardt, 235–246. Wiesbaden: Breitkopf & Härtel.

Weber, Horst. 1998. "Eisler as Hollywood Film Composer, 1942–1948." *Historical Journal of Film, Radio and Television* 18, no. 4: 561–566.

——. 2012. "*I am not a hero, I am a composer*": *Hanns Eisler in Hollywood*. Hildesheim: Olms.

Wiggershaus, Rolf. 1995. *The Frankfurt School: Its History, Theories, and Political Significance*. Cambridge, MA: MIT Press.

Wlodarski, Amy Lynn. 2008. "Excavating Eisler: Relocating the Memorial Voice in *Nuit et Brouillard*." In *Kompositionen für den Film*, edited by Peter Schweinhardt, 163–181. Wiesbaden: Breitkopf & Härtel.

CHAPTER 7

....

ONTOLOGICAL, FORMAL, AND CRITICAL THEORIES OF FILM MUSIC AND SOUND

....

JAMES BUHLER

IN this chapter, I will draw on Francesco Casetti's model of the development of film theory after the Second World War, which is basically an account of film studies' institutionalization and professionalization within the academy, to chart some major trends in interpretive research on the soundtrack (Casetti 1999). According to Casetti, the development of film studies is determined by the clash and (partial) displacement of three paradigms: (1) an ontological paradigm that derived from the older, prewar theories; (2) a methodological paradigm that, in a first wave of academic appropriation, approached the cinema from distinct scholarly perspectives that did not yet constitute a discipline of film studies; and (3) a field paradigm that emphasized interpretation and exhibited a pronounced ambivalence toward methodologies that seemed to require bracketing the scholar off from the object of study. Unlike the ontological paradigm, which attempted to lodge cinematic value in the essence of the filmic, the methodological paradigm did not consist in cinema-specific methodologies but rather in methods derived from other disciplines as film became an object of research from a particular point of view: most notably, for Casetti, psychology, sociology, semiotics, and psychoanalysis.

In the case of film music, we can add musicological studies to the methodological paradigms. Such studies imported—with only marginal success—a framework that understood music history as the history of the musical material. Work based on this model focused on the increasing assimilation of modern compositional technique into film scores while explaining the lag of film music's compositional practice with respect to contemporary trends as a result of film's necessary compromise with commerce. From the standpoint of the soundtrack, the result of this shift to a methodological paradigm had the effect of marginalizing the study of the soundtrack even further than had been the case under the ontological paradigm, and, if the soundtrack (or even film music) had never been quite the "neglected art" that Prendergast (1977) claimed, the method-ological theories that dominated the formative stage of film studies showed little interest in thinking through the issues of the soundtrack with anything like the rigor and atten-tion they devoted to the construction of the image, to the analysis of image editing pat-terns, and to the explication of narrative strategies.[1]

With increasing professionalization and as film studies became defined within the academy as a coherent field, the methodological paradigm came under the internal pressure of the emerging discipline, leading to the development of Casetti's field para-digm. In essence, the methodological paradigm was a transitional phase that facilitated a fundamental shift from concerns of production possibilities for films and the nature of the object under the ontological paradigm to concerns of the production of scholarly interpretation of individual films and general industrial tendencies under the field para-digm. The ontological and methodological paradigms do not so much disappear in the process of academicization as they are displaced and become absorbed as more or less central to the general concerns of the field, which focuses more and more on the pro-duction of scholarly analysis and interpretation.

With the shift to the field paradigm, the soundtrack also begins to receive more sys-tematic attention, as the field paradigm generally favors novel interpretation over sys-tematic theory, and the soundtrack's subsidiary status under both the ontological and methodological paradigms allowed it to facilitate interpretations that subvert the the-oretical premises of the dominant trends in the field. In general, the field paradigm's attention to the soundtrack has not opened new methods of research so much as it has involved enriching and complicating the work using existing methods by allowing the soundtrack to become a topical emphasis within a particular critical field.

If the ontological theories that dominated during the transition to sound and the first two decades thereafter were very much invested in the "myth of total cinema" and the realism of film (Bazin 2005, 17–22; Kracauer 1997), the field paradigm is fairly uni-form in rejecting the notion that the automatic, mechanical basis of film reproduction ensures it any kind of innate connection to the reality that it presumes to reproduce. In other words, such realism is understood first and foremost as something constructed, managed, and selected, a representational effect produced through formal techniques. This position, in fact, binds contemporary film studies to the Russian montage theorists (Sergei Eisenstein, V. I. Pudovkin, and others) as well as such early critics of the sound film as Rudolf Arnheim, who concurred that synchronized sound increased realism but saw in it a fundamental regression of cinema from its status as representational art (Arnheim 1933, 201–80). If the editing of the soundtrack is generally controlled in such a way as to be unobtrusive and so to go unnoticed, this simply reveals that the repre-sentational effect of realism—as though reality were disclosing itself—is often a goal of filmmaking, not that it is in any respect inherent in the process. It has proven more diffi-cult to dislodge claims that sound reproduction is ontologically real in a way that image production is not (Levin 1984), probably because the editing and mixing of sound can be made more or less inaudible through careful splicing and crossfades whereas the edits of the imagetrack, however strongly motivated, are always visible. Nevertheless, most contemporary scholarship readily acknowledges that the soundtrack is a construction just as much as the imagetrack, that sounds are selected for inclusion on the soundtrack on the basis of what the recorded sound represents rather than what it reproduces.

ONTOLOGICAL THEORIES AND SCHEMATIC SYSTEMS

The earliest theories of sound film attempted to determine its nature and aesthetic possibilities by asking what was specific to it. In particular, these theories responded to the basic fact that the sound film combines two sets of distinct technologies: camera, film, projector, screen, on the one hand; microphone, record, phonograph, loudspeakers, on the other. Sound on film substitutes a sound strip for the phonograph record and a sound head for the needle, but the technologies remain quite distinct even when image and sound begin to be printed together on the medium of film. Despite the fact that sound film was supposed to restore the unity of sight and sound denied in the reproductive technologies of film, phonograph, and radio, the distinctions in technology seem to prompt a theory that emphasizes the basic hybridity and so also conceptual opposition of the two sets of technologies. Thus, in their short "Statement," first published in 1928, Eisenstein, Pudovkin, and Alexandrov propose that sound film would reach its expressive potential only if sound was not simply synchronized with the image but was rather, in montage-like fashion, placed in counterpoint to it. "Sound, treated as a new montage element (as a factor divorced from the visual image), will inevitably introduce new means of enormous power to the expression" (Eisenstein 1949, 259). Counterpoint in early sound film theory thus becomes synonymous with montage and with the asynchronous use of sound. The latter also becomes the privileged mode of sound, the sound that would not be, like synchronous sound, redundant with the image.

For Eisenstein, indeed, montage leads to "a sharp concretization of the theme being made perceptible through determining details" (1975, 44). Counterpoint applies this idea of dialectical montage to the soundtrack:

> In cinema, the selection of "correspondences" between picture and music must not be satisfied with any one of these "lines," or even with a harmony of several employed together. Aside from these general formal elements the same law has to determine the selection of the right people, the right faces, the right objects, the right actions, and the right sequences, out of all the equally possible selections within the circumstances of a given situation. (Eisenstein 1975, 172)

Sound and music should be deployed in such a way that points of contrast and coordination knit soundtrack and image together on the basis of theme.[2]

One of Eisenstein's collaborators on the "Statement," Pudovkin, places a particularly strong emphasis on the potential of asynchronous sound, which, he argues, assures counterpoint between image and sound, so that the soundtrack never becomes merely redundant. Sound should be used to "augment the potential expressiveness of the film's content" (Pudovkin 1949, 156), and this can only be accomplished, he thinks, if the director anticipates the audience's reactions and prepares their psychological place in advance (160). Of course, Pudovkin's views here are not incommensurate with mature classic Hollywood sound film, where cutting follows story pertinence far more than simply showing dialogue delivery, a tendency that René Clair (1953, 94–95) notes that Hollywood had put in practice already by 1929.

Like most writers of the time, Clair, too, was drawn to the possibilities offered up by asynchronous sound, pointing especially to a couple of poignant scenes from *The Broadway Melody* (1929). In one well-known passage, he writes: "We hear the noise of a door being slammed and a car driving off while we are shown Bessie Love's anguished face watching from a window, the departure which we do not see. . . . In another scene we see Bessie Love lying thoughtful and sad; we feel that she is on the verge of tears; but her face disappears in the shadow of a fade-out, and from the screen, now black, emerges a single sob" (Clair 1953, 94). The attraction of asynchronous sound and the contrapuntal conception in general lies in how it reveals the specificity of the medium of sound film, how it opens possibilities to the sound film not previously available to other artistic media. Synchronous sound, by contrast, seems on the surface to be both more obvious and to have less potential to the extent that it simply reproduces the neutral, objective point of audition of the recording apparatus.

Yet the apparent redundancy of synchronous sound materially transforms the image, creating a much starker divide between those elements in the image that are associated with synchronized sound (foreground) and everything else in the image (background). This shift is noted by period commentators, such as Rudolf Arnheim, who points out that synchronism in the sound film parses the image for pertinence, radically altering the quality of the image in the silent film where the human world and the world of things spoke the same mute language. In silent film, the human figure is only one figure among many: "In the universal silence of the image, the fragments of a broken vase could 'talk' exactly the way a character talked to his neighbor, and a person approaching on a road and visible on the horizon as a mere dot 'talked' as some-one acting in close-up" (Arnheim 1957, 227). In the talking film, by contrast, the focus on synchronized speech elevates the human figure to a special status. Talking film, then, is for Arnheim irreducibly anthropocentric: "It endows the actor with speech, and since only he can have it, all other things are pushed into the background" (227). The humanism of the sound film is purchased at the cost of the degradation of things, which become mere props, and the limit of things places a new limit on expression. Sound film, Arnheim says, is a completely different proposition from the silent film, and his seeming hostility toward it stems less from the thing itself, which he acknowl-edges as a return to the principles of the theater, than its eclipse of the particularity and specificity of the silent film, on the one hand, and its development of a film theory—he has especially in mind Eisenstein and Clair—that runs contrary to the nature of art and perception, on the other.

Because the concept of "counterpoint" offered a means to conceptualize nonsynchronous sound, it proved an exceedingly useful term for theorizing possibilities of sound film. The formalism of the opposition that quickly developed, however, severed asynchronous sound from its conception in dialectical montage where counterpoint was deployed not so much for its nonredundancy, but rather to "concretize" the theme of the film. Instead, counterpoint was formulated as half of one principal opposition organizing the functions of the soundtrack. For instance, Raymond Spottiswoode, who published the first edition of his influential The Grammar of Film in 1935, deploys two primary oppositions to analyze the soundtrack: realistic/nonrealistic and parallel/contrastive. Spottiswoode conceives of these oppositions as scales, that is, as realized in continuities. The first opposition can be realized in two sorts of scales. The first limit of realism is found when the all sounds heard correspond exactly to sources in the image. The unrealistic end of this scale consists either in the removal of all sounds or in their replacement with sounds that seem not to match their sources. The second limit of realism is found when the intensity of the sound precisely matches that expected from the image. This limit can be breached on either end, with sound of greater or lesser intensity than the image implied. A further distinction here is whether the source of the sound lies in the image or outside the image. Spottiswoode calls the latter situation "contrapuntal," a term explicitly borrowed from Eisenstein and Pudovkin. Thus noncontrapuntal realistic sound is sound that corresponds in a realistic way with an onscreen source; "contrapuntal realistic sound," in contrast, is sound that seems to come from the world of the image but whose source is offscreen. To classify unrealistic sound, Spottiswoode introduces another opposition, subjectivity/objectivity, which is designed as a measure of narrative focalization, that is, whether the unreality of the sound is attributed to a character (subjective) or an entity such as the director outside the world depicted (objective). Objectively unrealistic sound is often realized as a commentative function, such as voiceover. The parallel/contrastive opposition is less about the source of the sound (as counterpoint is) than in the relation of sound and image to the idea of the film. When both sound and image correspond to this idea the relationship is parallel; when sound and image "present or evoke different concepts and emotions" the relationship is contrastive (Spottiswoode 1950, 180). The poles of this particular opposition, Spottiswoode notes, are rarely encountered.

Although realism does not always line up with parallelism or unrealism with contrast, realistic contrast—lively street noise indifferent to an unfolding tragedy, for instance— is less common than unrealistic contrast, as Spottiswoode finds unrealistic music particularly suitable for conveying contrast (Spottiswoode 1950, 184). Spottiswoode also classifies music by function:

Imitative—music resembling other sounds, usually in distorted fashion.
Commentative—music reflecting on the film, usually objectively as with voiceover.
Evocative—music bringing along associations of emotion (moods) or thoughts (leitmotifs).
Dynamic—music correlating with rhythm of cutting and action.

Spottiswoode's classificatory scheme is simplified and systematized to a great extent by Siegfried Kracauer, who likewise maps the terrain with a set of two primary oppositions. For Kracauer these oppositions are synchronism/asynchronism and parallelism/counterpoint, and these divide the uses of sound into four quadrants, which he calls "types." The first opposition is purely formal: it tracks whether the sound is synchronized to the image so that the image appears to be the source of the sound. Taken literally, this opposition reduces to onscreen/offscreen, which specifies whether the source of the sound lies in the field of vision shown by the image. But asynchronism in particular has a somewhat broader application that also allows it to relate to departures from realistic sound, or what Kraucauer identifies as its commentative function. Asynchronous sound is thus sound not directly evident from the image, whether it belongs to the world of the image or not, whereas synchronous sound is simply redundant with the image. Much like Spottiswoode's parallel/contrastive opposition, parallelism/counterpoint tracks whether sound and image are consistent with respect to an idea being expressed. Parallelism then specifies a sound that runs with the narrative implications of the images, whereas counterpoint specifies a sound that runs against the grain of those implications.

This set of oppositions allows Kracauer to divide sound, as mentioned, into four basic types, with each asynchronous type being subdivided, depending on whether its sound is actual (offscreen) or commentative (belonging to a different dimension). One of the primary objectives of the typology—this is true of Spottiswoode's as well—is to break the conceptual identity that would equate asynchronous sound with the contrapuntal (or in Spottiswoode's terms, contrastive) relationship between sound and image and synchronous sound with the parallel. Although this typology maps the entire terrain of the soundtrack, Kracauer curiously restricts the use of parallelism for effects to synchronism, allowing exceptions of parallel asynchronism only for certain "symbolic" uses of sound. "Sound there substitutes for language, up to a point" (Kracauer 1995, 129). In the case of music, he concentrates on the parallelism and counterpoint of the commentative function, though he recognizes that with the addition of what he calls "actual" music, music that has its source in the world of the image, music could, like dialogue, express any of the types.

Characteristic of the ontological theorists, Kracauer is also very concerned with the specificity of sound film and so takes pains to distinguish cinematic and uncinematic usage of sound and music, the cinematic naturally being the only ones proper to film.

Nicholas Cook offers a contemporary variant of these typologies derived from ontological film theory based in opposition of the media. As with the ontological theory, which emerged from the somewhat peculiar situation of sound film with its combination of image and sound recording technologies, Cook treats the media as relatively autonomous systems. The combination of these systems in instances of what he calls "multimedia" does not produce sums of effects but rather emergent properties, which are results that cannot be predicted from each medium taken separately. Cook sees this emergent property as operating by the logic of metaphor, which is also, he thinks, the means by which musical meaning emerges in general. Cook is also very concerned with the constructive aspect of music, seeing most theories of music and cinema as restricting music to a subsidiary role of "expressing" aspects of the narrative, such as characters' feelings, already presumed to be there: "In reality, music—like any other filmic element—participates in the *construction* of cinematic characters, not their reproduction, just as it participates in the construction, not the reproduction, of all cinematic effects" (Cook 1998, 86). This insistence that music is a constructive force in film means that although he questions whether music's autonomy is ever anything more than "an aesthetician's (or music theorist's) fiction" (92), he nevertheless must uphold the notion that music is a relatively autonomous system among other filmic systems. Indeed, he mostly agrees with the strong formalist proposition that music itself is only form, not content, the difference being that he believes music rarely if ever exists in such a state (that is, as music itself). Consequently, meaning is always emerging from music's propensity to enter into a relationship with almost any other medium it encounters. To the extent that this meaning cannot be reduced to that of the other medium, it is constructed by the interaction between the media.

Cook's aim is to consider music and the other media—text, dialogue, image, and so forth—independently so as "to provide an inventory of the ways in which different media can relate to one another" (Cook 1998, 98). By applying two tests, he sorts the relationships according to three models: if a similarity test shows that the two media are consistent, the model is "conformance." If the test shows the two media are coherent rather than consistent, on the other hand, he applies a further "difference" test, which finds the two media either contrary, in which case the model is "complementation," or contradiction, in which case the model is "contest" (98–106). Conformance is further divided into three subtypes: triadic, where each medium relates to the others through a third term (for example, emotion); dyadic, where each medium relates to the others in a pairwise fashion; unitary, where one medium is dominant while the others conform to it.

In terms of film, Cook's typology allows a richer understanding of the standard opposition between parallelism and counterpoint that in some respects resembles Spottiswoode. As Cook notes, unitary conformant relationships are "vanishingly rare" (Cook 1998, 102). Consequently, musical parallelism is not generally an instance of unitary conformance, of music being subordinated to the image, although it is often presented that way. Rather, parallelism is more generally an example of triadic conformance, where both music and image conform to the needs of narrative, and the individual component media slide in and out of conformance, complementation, and contest with each other. This view in turn closely resembles the dramaturgical model of music that Kracauer attributed to Kurt London and was still considered the "standard" theory of film music in 1960 (Kracauer 1997, 142).

The Hermeneutic Turn: From Methodology to the Field of Close Reading

After the Second World War, the gradual incorporation of film studies into the academy led to a new type of discussion of film and the soundtrack. Whereas before, studies of music and the soundtrack tended to be oriented toward industry professionals in the form of manuals and technical articles and toward general audiences in the form of books and newspaper and magazine articles on general film aesthetics, histories and stars. The questions asked by both sets of writers, however, tended to be pragmatic and ontological: What is film sound? How is film sound specific to the medium of sound film? Is there such a thing as film music or sound (as distinct from other music or sound)? What are the historical antecedents for film sound (especially music)? What are the proper roles of music and sound in film? Rarely were studies of the soundtrack in general or film music in particular oriented toward either methodological or critical concerns that addressed and promoted work by scholars. In fact, even if we include texts by industrial professionals—whether aimed at other professionals or a general audience—the number of books, articles, and journals devoted to film music or sound is remarkably small until the 1980s. If anything, the shift to the methodological paradigm marginalized the soundtrack even further, as methodological study of film constructed theories of film based on the analysis of image, editing structure, and narrative. This began to change as the methodologies passed from the phase of theory construction toward means of facilitating and authorizing interpretation, that is, to the field paradigm.

The methodological paradigm entailed the application of methodologies developed in other disciplines to film, resulting in a variety of scholarly approaches with film as the object of study: psychology of film, psychoanalysis of film, sociology of film, semiotics of film, and so forth. As the discipline of film studies reached full institutionalization, these approaches served as its intellectual foundations. But the methodological paradigm represented multiple research perspectives on film, and film studies had to confront the underlying antagonisms of the various methodologies in order to stabilize itself as a discipline. It is perhaps for this reason that the film theory that emerged in the 1970s proved so attractive: the so-called apparatus theory managed to combine psychoanalysis, Marxism, and semiotics into a grand synthesis that explained everything from film's overall technological development to the significance of such ubiquitous technical devices as shot/reverse-shot editing and offscreen sound (see Chapter 15 below). Although the 1980s are best known in film studies for pitched battles over film theory, the methodological tussles actually distracted attention away from the rapid shift during the decade from the methodological paradigm to the field paradigm, as the discipline unraveled into a set of loosely affiliated strands of critical theory for guiding film analysis and interpretation and gave a new emphasis to placing film in historical context. The result was that critical interpretation and analysis quickly began to eclipse theory as the dominant form of scholarly production, a situation diagnosed by Bordwell (1989), although he perceived only the monolith of ideological interpretation, not the increasing plurality (and disparity) of the methods that underlay it (Nichols 1992, 53–54).

CINEMETRICS AND FORMAL DESCRIPTION

The scholarly activity of interpretation and close reading generally requires a base level of descriptive analysis that it can presume. One particular subfield of such descriptive analysis is known as cinemetrics, which consists in everything about cinema that is empirically measurable (quantity), although in practice it has generally been confined to material aspects of the film object, most notably tracking average shot length, the number of particular types of shots and camera movements, and so forth. Cinemetrics is associated especially with the work of Barry Salt, who has traced changing historical norms for average shot length (ASL) among other topics (Salt 2006; 2009). Others who have adopted cinemetric techniques of statistical analysis for the basis of developing stylistic norms include David Bordwell (2006), Charles O'Brien (2005), Kristin Thompson (2005), and Yuri Tsivian (n.d.), who has developed a website (www.cinemetrics.lv) and a computer program to facilitate this sort of work. One general aim of cinemetrics is to establish measurable stylistic norms against which the idiosyncrasies of particular films, filmmakers, and national trends can be quite literally measured. In that respect cinemetrics is most often deployed as a rigorously empirical form of stylistics. Although cinemetrics have not been much employed for soundtrack research, there is no reason it could not be adopted to determine empirical questions such as average cue length, identifying formal types of themes, tracking tonal motions or the balance between the components of the soundtrack, and so forth. A study by Rick Altman, McGraw Jones, and Sonia Tatroe (2000) of the "multiplane system" of early sound film is an important cinemetric contribution to the soundtrack.

Another branch of descriptive analysis involves identifying formal devices and techniques and assessing them for function with respect to a system, usually that of narration. Sometimes this requires first separating sound from any semantic function in order to focus on the purely sonic properties, such as the method of "concentrated" or "reduced" listening that Michel Chion appropriates for soundtrack analysis from Pierre Schaeffer. Reduced listening is a "listening mode that focuses on the traits of the sound itself, independent of its cause and of its meaning" (Chion 1994, 29). The technique usually involves listening repeatedly to a sound so that its fine details can be analyzed and described and its properties can be assessed "as formal raw materials in themselves" (31). Transcription of music or dialogue are two basic forms that an analytical practice grounded in concentrated listening can take, though it usually involves transcribing (or describing) the sound as literally as is feasible. Abstracting sounds from their apparent causes, sources, and meanings allows the analyst to locate aspects of formal similarity and difference among sounds and so track the play of the abstracted formal properties across a film, but it can also be usefully deployed to analyze a particular sound into constituent elements, whether to reverse engineer, as it were, how a sound was composed or to describe it vividly so as to convey something of the startling, arresting effect that many film sounds have as we hear them in the moment.

Analytical and descriptive forms of reduced listening require a set of categories, concepts, and criteria in order to fix the relevant attributes of sound. The actual set used will depend on the goals of the analysis. Insofar as the categories are well defined and their definition precedes the analysis, the analysis itself will appear methodologically "neutral," because the analysis follows the preexisting criteria of the categories (Nattiez 1990, 13). It is important to recognize, however, that the neutrality of the analysis says nothing about the neutrality of the categories or of the aim. The analysis also proceeds by abstracting the sounds from their source and meaning, so the analysis reveals the constituents of the sound but only in virtue of having neutralized the meaning through abstraction. This may seem like a quibbling point, but much of the debate over the efficacy of formalism turns on the status of the material as revealed by analysis, that is, whether and to what extent the analysis and the material are neutral or meaningful.

Many of the categories for analyzing the formal acoustic properties of the soundtrack derive from music. In their standard textbook on film analysis, for instance, Bordwell and Thompson (2010, 269–311) locate three principal properties of sound: loudness, pitch, and timbre. They add to these properties three mixing and editing operations: selection, alteration, and combination. Finally, they also point to four "dimensions of film sound": rhythm, fidelity, space, and time. All of these dimensions except certain aspects of rhythm concern interactions between sound and image; thus, the analytical reduction in these cases applies not to the sounds *per se* but to audiovisual figures. To Bordwell and Thompson's three basic acoustical properties, Robert L. Mott adds harmonics (an attribute of timbre) and the temporal aspect of rhythm, which Bordwell and Thompson classify as a dimension rather than a property. Mott also considers the sound envelope, analyzing it into three components: attack, sustain, and decay. The last of these has a non-standard definition: in the commonly-used model of the envelope known by the acronym ASDR, "decay" refers to the fall off from the peak of the attack to the sustain, while "release" is more or less equivalent to Mott's understanding of "decay." Finally, he includes the component of speed, giving him nine not entirely independent components altogether (1990, 53–70). In a text I wrote with David Neumeyer and Rob Deemer (Buhler, Neumeyer, and Deemer 2010), we develop a list of five musically inspired properties of sound: tempo, rhythm and meter, volume, timbre, and texture. We consider pitch, envelope, and alteration as aspects of timbre. Like Bordwell and Thompson, we analyze spatial and temporal relations of sound with the image as composite audiovisual figures.

Although these three sets of descriptive terms all serve to analyze sound into component properties, they do not divide up sound quite the same way, and therefore the emphases in the resulting descriptions will inevitably vary somewhat. Nevertheless, they all realize their analytical reductions by treating sound in a homogeneous manner characteristic of the formalization of musical notation. Notation, Rick Altman counters, "assumes that each sound is single, discrete, uniform, and unidimensional. Stressing the formal concerns of music's internal, self-referential aspect, musical notation diverts attention from sound's discursive dimensions, concealing the fact that sound is in reality multiple, complex, heterogeneous, and three-dimensional" (1992, 16). For Altman, the formalization of sound as musical categories is a systemic (and ideological) distortion. But this distortion follows not because the formalization has neutralized meaning in isolating the sound from its narrative context. Instead, it follows because the formalization assimilates the sound to the meaning of a general category rather than being attentive to the particular context of what he calls the "sound event." What is ideological about reduced listening in musical categories, it seems, is not just the loss of particularity in analysis, but the fact that the loss itself goes unnoticed as the category is reified into a neutral property of the sound object.

Neoformalism

Music theory is a discipline, one of whose aims involves constructing formal theories and typologies for analyzing and describing music. The tools of this discipline are often encountered in analytical descriptions of music in film (for a summary see Scott Murphy's contribution to this volume, Chapter 19). Occasionally, they have been used to classify characteristic formal attributes of film music, especially as they relate to musical topic or genre (Murphy 2006, Lehman 2013, Buhler forthcoming). Ontological theories of film, especially those developed by writers who were also filmmakers, frequently proposed formal theories and typologies for film as well. In contemporary film scholarship, work on such theories and typologies generally takes place under the rubric of cinemetrics, discussed above, or those committed to neoformalist or cognitive approaches to film. A combination of neoformalist and cognitive approaches is one of the defining aspects of the so-called Wisconsin school, which coalesced with the publication in 1985 of *The Classical Hollywood Cinema* by David Bordwell, Janet Staiger, and Kristin Thompson and has since become associated most closely with the work of Bordwell, Thompson, and Noël Carroll.

Already in "The Musical Analogy" (1980), Bordwell had proposed treating film along the lines of music scholarship. Given his formalist bent, it is easy to see why Bordwell thought music a congenial analogy for the emerging discipline of film studies: music scholarship at the time offered an alternative model to the methodological paradigms, such as psychology, sociology, Marxism, semiotics, and psychoanalysis, that were then dominating the discourse of the emerging discipline of film studies. These paradigms brought with them elaborate theoretical premises that often seemed at odds with—if they did not completely efface—the element of film as an art form. The scholarly study of music, by contrast, offered a methodology and research agenda dedicated to the explication of an art form as such rather than as an instance of the application of some methodological paradigm whose origin lay outside the art form. The primary advantage that the study of music provided as a model over the methodological paradigms is that it served only as an analogy in the sense that a precise method, which grew from the study of music, was not imported; instead, Bordwell appropriated only the relation of a method to the material under investigation. The analogy also suggested certain classes of questions that could be asked and some guidelines about how a researcher might go about answering them. The irony was that Bordwell was proposing this musical analogy just as the scholarly study of music was beginning a profound change that would take it away from the formalist and positivist moorings that Bordwell found so appealing (Buhler and Neumeyer 1994, 367).

If early ontological theorists of film had also been interested in this musical analogy, that was, Bordwell noted, at least in part because the analogy forced attention on the constructive element in film; the connection to music helped underscore that however much film seemed driven along a path of realism and Bazinian total cinema, the recording of the world (Bazin 2005), it was also irreducibly a construction, a product of human choice and intelligence. "Music has become a model of how formal unity can check, control, and override representation" (Bordwell 1980, 142). Although the term "representation" in film studies is usually opposed to recording and reproduction and so associated with those who see film as an art rather than total cinema, Bordwell seems troubled by the term because it includes the presence of a structuring narrative, something that, interestingly enough, formalist studies of music have also traditionally eschewed along with hermeneutics, another scholarly trend within film studies that Bordwell (1989) finds problematic. Bordwell therefore sets up the formal properties of film, like those of music, in opposition to both the recording of reality and to narrative.

More than simply the musical abstraction from reality and narrative recommends the musical analogy. "What has made the analogy attractive are the ways in which a musical piece can be analyzed as a *system of systems*" (Bordwell 1980, 142). Although the ostensible concern of Bordwell's article is to define and explicate the appropriation of the musical analogy by filmmakers and theorists along organic and dialectical lines, he seems equally concerned with preserving the analogy as the basis for current film scholarship. Music scholarship has a rich tradition of theorizing music's formal systems, especially with respect to pitch relationships and form, and, as noted, the discipline of music theory is devoted to developing, refining, and applying such systems to musical works. Bordwell concludes the essay with the following statement: "If we want to know how cinema may work upon the social and the suprasocial, the musical analogy must persist, for it crystallizes the drive of film form toward multiple systems. But these systems must be situated within the process of cinema's heterogeneity" (156).

Bordwell's strong invocation of the musical analogy makes it worth considering the parallels between the formal systems in music and film, both of which have strong linguistic underpinnings, especially with respect to grammar. Although music theory usually deploys its terms descriptively, almost all of them originate in theories that model (rather than simply describe) musical structure and syntax. For instance, phrase structure, which is basic to musical form theory, follows the linguistic analogy closely, in fact going so far as to borrow much of its terminology from the divisions of classical grammar. Harmonic theory is likewise clearly based on linguistic models of grammatical syntax. In this respect, harmonic theory resembles the idea of a film grammar, which serves to establish and legitimize the rules of continuity editing and which still forms the basis for elementary film analysis. The pioneering study with respect to continuity editing is Spottiswoode (1950), whose approach has been expanded in two directions in the years since its original publication in 1935—to production manuals and film appreciation textbooks. (The idea of a film grammar derived from structuralist linguistics also serves to ground Christian Metz's semiotic approach to film, in a formulation that brings it extremely close to the conception of music as a language with a syntax but without a semantics. Film, Metz asserts, "possesses a grammar, up to a point, but no vocabulary" [1982, 213; see also Metz 1991]). Continuity editing is to film theory more or less what harmony is to music theory. Bordwell's theory of intensified continuity (2006, 117–89, esp. 121–38) stands in much the same relation to classical film editing as does the theory of extended chromatic harmony to diatonic harmony. Both continuity editing and harmonic theory address issues of continuity and logic of small-unit succession, and both have left a theoretical residue of covert prescription that accrues from the analogy with grammar. For the concepts of film and musical syntax, like the linguistic one on which they are modeled, presume not just to distinguish normative and nonnormative usage but also to determine correct and proper usage.

In both film studies and music studies, formalism has strong links with ontological theories focused on defining the nature and specificity of the object of study, as in both cases pragmatic and theoretical attempts to derive film language and grammar originate in ontological theories of the art form and in wider cultural appeals that both music and film are instances of universal language. Contemporary scholars sympathetic to the aims of formalist theory and analysis, whether in music or film, typically reject the universalizing claims of grammar or even dismiss the idea that cinema is a language (Carroll 1996a, 187); and they recognize relatively stable configurations of elements as defining historical styles rather than universals (Thompson 1988, 5). According to Thompson's formulation, neoformalism shares a belief in the possibility and efficacy of aesthetic theory (3), which entails a theory that art is distinct from other cultural activity on the one hand (8) and a theory of artistic relations for each artistic medium that is immanent or specific to the medium on the other (9). Formalist theory may even reject this latter so-called specificity thesis, which is basic to the ontological theories discussed above and argues that an art form is defined by encountering, acknowledging, and revealing the peculiar limits of its medium in order to make those limits expressive (Carroll 1996a, 1–74), even though refusing the specificity thesis makes locating criteria for separating art from other cultural activity more challenging. For instance, Carroll, like most formalists, nevertheless rejects the notion that artistic forms, techniques, or devices are inherently meaningful. Forms are not representational; meaning for Carroll depends on content and is a product of art's representational rather than formal power. Though an acceptance of the form–content distinction places Carroll outside the boundaries of what is usually defined as a strict formalist conception, he is merely being consistent in a way that most formalism is not when he refuses to grant the devices and forms an expressive dimension even at their limit. Expression, too, belongs to the level of content (9). More typical of formalism, Thompson, by contrast, rejects the form–content distinction, arguing that anything that enters into the artwork is transformed into a property of form. "Meaning is not the end result of an artwork, but one of its formal components" (1988, 12).

If, as Thompson argues, "Art's main concern is to be aesthetic" (1988, 36), the refusal of the specificity thesis makes it difficult to know what is to count as aesthetic. But even scholars who avoid invoking overt prescriptive maxims will often smuggle the prescription back in on the basis of stylistics by rewriting the grammar or syntax in terms of arbitrary artistic convention or cognitive norms, which simply occupy the place vacated by grammar: exceptional procedures (within a style) become "violations" or "deformations" of the basic norms (grammar), which are valorized as "expressive deviations" or "defamiliarizations" for sympathetic critics or signs that a filmmaker or composer is mannerist or does not understand the basic conventions or cognitive constraints (language) for the unsympathetic critic.

Although contemporary formalist theory in both film and music tends toward stylistics, limiting its claims to defining relatively arbitrary stylistic norms, it retains an appeal to universality, replacing the grammar of the earlier generation with an appeal to perception and cognition (Bordwell 1985; Thompson 1988, 25–35; Carroll 1988; Carroll 1996a, 127–29, 321–35), so much so that it is tempting to relabel neoformalism as cognitive formalism, where principles of cognition displace those of language as the basis for the claim to universality. In this respect, too, music theory and formalist film theory show strong affinities. The experience of art—its distinctiveness from the practical—is also presumed to be universal, although the particulars of how that distinctiveness is realized are historically and culturally specific (Thompson 1988, 9). This specificity is style and its engine of change is defamiliarization, which draws on novelty (10–11). In this way, formal description comes to underwrite and to naturalize larger interpretive claims, even as acts of overt interpretation—what Bordwell (1989) dismissively calls "making meaning"—are devalued as idiosyncratic, homogenizing, and reductive (Thompson 1988, 3–35 passim).

With this suspicion of overt hermeneutic activity, formalist analysis tends to eschew ideological readings in favor of identifying and tracking the formal devices that make the meaning and coherence of a film possible in the first place. Although according to Thompson "neoformalist" analysis is purportedly directed toward recovering what is challenging in a film and developing and refining skills for apprehending the particularity of the film (1988, 33), the need for the analysis to have general theoretical validity— "each analysis should tell us something not only about the film in question, but about the possibilities of film as an art" (6)—means that neoformalist analysis has the tendency to "hollow out" film techniques, to generalize and abstract from them the formal properties that remain once they have been emptied of the particular content and signification that any instantiation of a device would have in a particular film. "While many works may use the same device, that device's function may be different in each work" (15). In this way, it becomes possible for the device to be redeployed with a different function and so also for it to assume a different meaning. It also becomes possible to substitute one device for another on the basis of "functional equivalency" (15). Formalism yields a neutralization of the material and figures, which become arbitrary stylistic choices evaluated in terms of artistic efficacy rather than the figures having immanent ideological content of their own. "It is vastly implausible to believe that cinematic structures, like point-of-view editing, are inherently or intrinsically ideological. The use of point-of-view editing in a particular film may serve ideological purposes. But the structure itself is ideologically neutral" (Carroll 1996a, 258). The selection of shots is simply evaluated aesthetically on the basis of how well the device serves the film's "dominant," which Thompson defines as "the main formal principle a work or group of works uses to organize devices into a whole" (Thompson 1988, 43). To some extent the neutralization can be attributed to the abstractions endemic to theorization. (These objections will be engaged in more detail in Chapter 15)

Formalism tends to follow "natural" or immanent articulations of film as a basis of segmentation. In other words, it tends to view the film with the grain, that is, the way the film asks to be viewed. Occasionally, it will adopt arbitrary articulation, but in this case it will attempt to make the articulation unbiased, as a randomly selected segment. As an aesthetic theory, formalism is not, at least not primarily, a theory of communication with a message encoded in the film to be passed along to the spectator (Thompson 1988, 7–8; Carroll, however, dissents on this point 1996a, 127); in that respect, it tends to be suspicious of or at least ambivalent about hermeneutic activity, especially any systematic interpretive method that privileges a priori certain patterns of meaning over others. In particular, formalism accepts the intentional fallacy, which presumes that intention matters only to the extent that it has been realized in the material; and if it has been realized in the material then there is no reason to appeal to the category, or indeed to history (Wimsatt and Beardsley 1954). For Bordwell, the intentional fallacy manifests itself in the peculiar figure of narration without a narrator (1985, 61–62). Formalism can also lead to art for art's sake, but modern practitioners tend to emphasize the otherness of art from ordinary experience as the basis of its exceptionalism. "Art," Thompson writes, "is set apart from the everyday world, in which we use our perception for practical ends. We perceive the world so as to filter from it those elements that are relevant to our immediate actions" (1988, 8). Art in this view offers an experience like no other, an experience obtainable and definable by contemplating aesthetic forms. Art allows us to perceive what practical perception pushes to the margins, permitting us to see in new ways. Formalism begins as an aesthetic theory, a theory of art, only pushing out to social theory from the specificity of the art. Formalism also breaks with the communication model in not taking meaning as the final term, its underlying principle. Films have meaning, but this meaning and all the particles of meaning that coalesce in it, is only a component of the film. If the film is an artistic whole, the form and meaning of the whole are only themselves moments in the total artwork. Treatment is central, more so than the theme or final meaning. Consequently, interpretation—at least overt interpretation seeking meaning—is not the central activity of the formalist approach. "Neoformalism does not do 'readings' of films," Thompson says. "The main critical activity," she adds, "is 'analysis'" (Thompson 1988, 34n25).

Suspicious that thematic and ideological criticism leads to overdetermined and reductive readings that mistake connotation for denotation and so diminish the potential open-ended play of meaning, Bordwell prefers an approach that attends to how the formal elements of film serve to shape and structure the heterogeneous material in a way that resists rather than delivers a clear denotative meaning. In *Narration in the Fiction Film*, Bordwell attempts to assimilate narrative to formalism through the intermediary of cognitive science. At a crucial point in his argument, Bordwell pivots again to the musical analogy: "The sense of order whose finest grain we can glimpse but not grasp helps produce the connotative effects of which the thematic criticism records the trace. These effects arise from a formal manipulation that is, in a strong sense, *nonsignifying*—closer to music than to the novel" (Bordwell 1985, 306). Narrative aspects of film are at this level abstract, generic, and empty, resembling musical forms and structures such as sonata form or an *Ursatz* more than the concrete specificity of novelistic form. The comparison is, however, questionable—or at least not as stark as Bordwell presumes. On the one hand, novelistic form carries similar nonsignifying manipulations (which we recognize not only in experimental forms but perhaps even more in generic conventions). On the other hand, musical content, even when not overtly representational, cannot be reduced to musical forms and their manipulation despite Hanslick's attempt to enforce an identity. Forms, functions, and manipulations can certainly be abstracted from musical pieces; content can be understood as nonrepresentational (if not exactly nonsignifying); but the forms are still forms of something, the manipulations are manipulations of something. That something is the content or material, which does not simply fall into the form any more than every idea falls neatly into the form of thought that is the sentence. These resistances of content to form are often expressive. In an ascetic interpretive ethic of the sort that Bordwell advocates, the meaning of such expression remains at the level of connotation, glimpsed rather than grasped, and a thematic reading makes the expression legible and specific in a way that it is not in itself. Thus, the refusal to risk definite meaning runs the opposite danger of underdetermination, of not recognizing a concreteness in the expression, a concreteness that remains essential to adequate understanding even if it also remains strictly speaking beyond denotation.

Ultimately, formalism tends to approach music and sound as formal elements that offer filmmakers choice in how to assemble a film. The formalist is interested in function, in what the soundtrack does, not what a particular sound is. In that respect, it runs toward abstraction and so also to a certain extent has quite different aims than reduced listening. The soundtrack may perform functions particular to it, but primarily it serves to convey information that might have been presented in other ways. Character motivation, for instance, might be shown through action, reported through dialogue, or hinted at through music, and the particular choice of the filmmakers will bear on the style and form of the film.

Consistent with this functional approach, Carroll is particularly interested in what he calls "modifying music," music that "serves to add further characterization to the scenes it embellishes" (1996a, 141). One consequence of Carroll's conception is that such music remains outside the film proper, and, as in Nicholas Cook's scheme discussed above, music and film form "two different symbol systems." These symbol systems are not determined by media—that is, image- and soundtrack—since the film system "[includes] not only visuals but recorded sound, both natural and dialogic" (141), and music is construed as the complement to the filmic system: "Such a system supplies something that the other system standardly lacks, or, at least, does not possess with the same degree of effectiveness that the other system possesses" (141). The advantages of music, Carroll says, include that it "is a highly expressive symbol system" and offers "more direct access to the emotive realm than any other symbol system" (141).

Curiously, Carroll is much more interested in identifying the lacks in music's symbol system and bolstering the strengths of the film's symbol system than in assessing any actual complementation. He is particularly quick to avoid any suggestion of the ultimate inadequacy of film's symbol system, noting that we should not oppose the two systems absolutely: "It is not the case that the movie is pure representation to be supplemented by means of musical expression" (1996a, 143). In point of fact, Carroll treats music more as supplement than complement, since music for Carroll is one means, but not the only means, that film uses to clarify "the expressive quality" and "emotional significance of the action" (144). Music, it turns out, is deployed not because the filmic system is in itself inadequate but because films "are aimed at mass audiences. They aspire for means of communication that can be grasped almost immediately by untutored audiences." The clarity that music offers—the way it makes the world screened "much more legible than life"—belongs to and is a prominent marker of the economy of mass art. By emphasizing this clarifying function and restricting it to a popular appeal, Carroll insulates the general filmic system from any particular symbolic need for music. Film "needs" music only to the extent that film "needs" emotional clarity; and even if a particular film does require such clarity, film's symbol system has other means of providing it. Strictly speaking, then, music's value to film lies primarily in the way it can increase the efficiency of existing modes of communication rather in the way it might potentially open up new modes of artistic expression. In this respect, it is significant that Carroll spends a surprising amount of space outlining the supposed lacks of music's symbol system—as though the idea of music having a coherent symbol system posed some sort of unspoken ontological challenge to that of film. In particular, he emphasizes music's deficient capacity for focusing or "particularizing the feelings it projects" (141). This deficiency derives ultimately from instrumental music's lack of a body—what Carroll also calls "the logical machinery"—on which to project the emotions and thereby individuate them (142). The film's symbol system supplies this body. "The music tells us something, of an emotive significance, about what the scene is about; the music supplies us with, so to say, a description (or presentation) of the emotive properties the film attaches to the referents of the scene" (142). Ultimately, Carroll seems to argue that if film exploits music to give its narrative the appearance of emotional depth, music benefits in turn because its symbol system gains a particularity, a relation to concrete meaning, that normally escapes its purview.

As Carroll's account of modifying music illustrates, formalist film theory can approach the soundtrack both in itself, as a relatively autonomous system with respect to the conventions of its construction and the formal relationships that obtain among its parts, and more generally as a system that articulates and is itself articulated by the similar system governing the imagetrack or narrative. If formalist theory has tended to follow the general (and questionable) bias of film studies in granting the image precedence—the actual constructive precedence of commercial filmmaking lies in the narrative system, and in devices that generally maximize narrative clarity at that—nothing in the precepts of formalism demands that this precedence be followed. Nevertheless, it cannot be denied that much of the basic descriptive language, beginning with the fundamental distinction between onscreen and offscreen sound, follows and so also reinforces this visual bias (Percheron 1980, 16), and Carroll's account of modifying music likewise renders music external to the rest of the filmic system. If the soundtrack gains much of its power from its ability to represent what the film cannot otherwise show, whether that be music that registers the emotional depth of character interior or offscreen sound that registers a world that exists beyond the edge of the frame, that power is purchased only by otherwise deferring to, or seeming to defer to, the centrality of the image. More subtle, however, is its power in conjunction with the image, where the correspondence of synchronization serves to mark objects—both in the image and in the sound—as narratively pertinent: important objects are synchronized objects, and the apparent redundancy of synchronization is simply another device for ensuring narrative clarity through the schematic hierarchy it enables.

Although formalism tends to naturalize apprehension of film, it also tends to emphasize the constructed nature of film. Thompson, for instance, notes that film is a construction, not reproduction (1988, 35–36): "Films are constructs that have no natural qualities" (35). Bordwell likewise is under no illusion that the soundtrack is anything but a fabrication in the service of the story telling, and that this service to the narrative demands a recording and mixing technique that is quite distant from any realistic recording of the scene.

CRITICAL THEORIES

Whereas formalism attempts to bracket off ideology in order to concentrate on aesthetic effects irrespective of content, most contemporary scholars writing about film question whether the aesthetic can be thus separated from ideology. Aesthetics since Kant may have sought disinterested contemplation as the ground of understanding art *qua* art, but critical theory questions the conditions of possibility that make an aesthetics and the disinterested contemplation that it authorizes conceivable in the first place. What, in short, is the "ideology of the aesthetic" (Eagleton 1990)?

Although the term "critical theory" first came to prominence in the interdisciplinary work of the Frankfurt School, especially that of Theodor W. Adorno and Max

Horkheimer, the term today, at least as applied to film and other humanities, covers a wide range of interpretive methods, including under its rubric many of the most significant trends of recent scholarship: not only the "classic" forms of Marxism and psychoanalysis, but also poststructuralism, feminism, gender and sexuality, postcolonialism, race and ethnicity, semiotics, narrative and cultural studies, among others. Along with the neoformalism just discussed, these critical theories form the methodological base of film interpretation within the field paradigm.

These otherwise rather disparate interpretive methods are linked by a commitment to locating and interpreting an ideological substrate of film. The idea is that aesthetic illusion, the surface of the art work, is not only a necessary appearance as traditional aesthetics has it, but that this illusion is bound up with ideology at a fundamental rather than contingent or superficial level; moreover, one of the effects of aesthetic illusion is that it reconfigures this ideological substrate of works into novel aesthetic forms that articulate what Fredric Jameson (1981) refers to as a "political unconscious" of society so that considerable interpretive work is required to understand the relation between aesthetic illusion and ideology. This insistence on the ideological dimension of the artwork has, however, led opponents, generally associated with neoformalism, to label its practitioners as mere "ideological critics," polemically intimating that they care more about conformity to ideology (or revealing covert ideological structures) than revealing the distinctiveness of film as an art (Carroll 1988, 1996b; Bordwell 1989, 1996). While the formalist critics thus accuse the ideological critics of bad faith and enforcing "political correctness" (Carroll 1996a, 259), these formalists also ignore the way in which such interpretive methods, however reductive, admit a dimension of social content and meaning into the interior of a film (Nichols 1992).

The foundational work of critical theory on film music is undoubtedly *Composing for the Films*, first appearing under Hanns Eisler's name alone (1947) but later revealed as a collaboration with Adorno, who would subsequently make the controversial claim that he had contributed the bulk of the text (on this and other matters relating to the book and to Eisler's career, see Schweinhardt and Gall, Chapter 6). At once a diatribe against classic film music practices and a perceptive sociological analysis of the Hollywood production system of background scoring, *Composing for the Films* remains an important contribution to the theory of film music that can still be read profitably for its keen insights into contradictions endemic to producing and consuming commercial art.

The basic thesis of the book is largely negative: that music is mostly redundant in film; that film music rarely if ever exploits even the most rudimentary critical possibilities open to it; and that its presence is largely effaced so that any critical involvement that it does obtain goes mostly unheard. If much contemporary film music scholarship accepts this critical thesis largely intact, the positive suggestions for how film music might be reformulated into a more self-reflective practice have nevertheless proved remarkably ineffectual. Gorbman (1991), for instance, shows just how closely Eisler's score for the *Spanish Main* (1945) accords with standard Hollywood practice. Similarly, Gorbman (2004) questions the effectiveness of Eisler's use of atonality in *Kuhle Wampe oder Wem gehört die Welt?* (1932), arguing that the score is most likely to result in audience puzzlement. In an article I wrote with David Neumeyer (Neumeyer and Buhler 2008), we make a similar point about Eisler's music for *A Scandal in Paris* (1945). Granted, Eisler and Adorno never clarify how ideology and art are to be weighted in evaluating film music. They conclude, for instance, that Eisler's own score for *Hangmen Also Die* (1943) is effective primarily because it assures that the audience identifies with the Czech people, "the real hero of picture" rather than Heydrich, the Nazi collaborator and villain (Eisler [and Adorno] 1947, 25). Yet such identification would hardly be novel even in a standard Hollywood film (*Casablanca*, 1943, being one prominent example). The problem with their analysis of the film in the terms set out in the book is that music winds up being evaluated more on the basis of its ideological stance, its power to encourage proper audience identification, than on its contribution to the work as art (27).

Such confusions, which tend to reinforce the caricature that ideological critics simply want to reduce art to ideology—Adorno is generally careful to avoid such confusions in his other writings on aesthetics—do not greatly diminish the importance of the book. Although a product of the time when ontological theories were dominant, *Composing for the Films* in a very real way prepared the ground for much recent scholarship on film music.

A basic premise of most critical theories is that film means more that it seems, and its excess meaning is structured as ideological figures that serve as foundational cultural myths ameliorating cultural contradictions. Critical theories therefore often engage in what has been called the "hermeneutics of suspicion" (Ricoeur 1970): they read the film not so much for what it wants to say as for what it attempts to conceal. Film offers a particularly powerful myth because its verisimilitude allows it to present its fiction as if it were something real: what is ideological or historically contingent appears in film as something natural rather than the representation that it is. It is for this reason that much critical theory work has involved battling and dismantling the myth of total cinema, where realism now becomes a figure of ideological illusion. But critical theories take issue not so much with the apparent realism of the image as with how the image of that realism is constructed from codes, stylistic norms, and conventions. It is in this respect that critical theories differ from formalism, which is likewise concerned with the codes, norms, and conventions of realism. But whereas formalism wants to take these at face value, as relatively neutral stylistic markers that serve above all to organize technique, critical theories see in such a will to style and technique the marks of deep cultural ideology.

IDEOLOGY CRITIQUE

Critical theories make a fundamental shift in the basic level of analysis from content to structure, with the end result being considerable indifference to content and a focus instead on the structuring that gives rise to articulate forms. Formalism and critical theories both make this move, but the former understands the structuring as neutral, whereas the latter understands it to be traces, reflections, sites of power.

The analysis of ideology can take place at three levels: the ideology of content, the ideology of the system, and the ideology of the apparatus. The remainder of this chapter will consider each of these three levels in turn.

Ideology of Content: 1. Musical Topics and the Analysis of Stereotype

The ideology of content has long been recognized and analyzed, and its identification continues as a practice of film analysis. It is also the least controversial level of ideological critique. Carroll (1996a, 268–72), for instance, argues that it is both the most pertinent level for understanding pernicious ideological effects and largely consistent with (or at least not antagonistic to) formalist modes of film analysis.

As early as *The Birth of a Nation* (1915), one contemporary reviewer criticized the music for reinforcing the racial characterizations of the film: "Music lends insidious aid to emphasize the teaching of the screen, for the tom-tom beats from time to time convince us that the colored man, well drest and educated though he may be, came from Africa. Why is not some Asiatic instrument used to remind us that the Aryan race came from the wrong side of the Caucasus?" (quoted in Stern 1965, 108).[3] Here, the writer points to a particularly charged musical content, namely "the tom-tom beats," musical figures of the primitive that serve not only, as in this case, to insist on an African essence to "the colored man" but also to point to a non-European essence of the Native American. Similar observations have been extended to how Hollywood scores women, homosexuals, ethnicity—basically any group or character on which a film deploys music to make into an Other. What such studies indicate is the ideological force music delivers in film at the level of content, which is, more or less, the level of its signification.

Issues of race, ethnicity, and colonialism have been approached in terms of the soundtrack from two primary directions: (1) mapping out the development and deployment of musical topics in background scoring, and (2) examining the use of recordings associated with particular ethnic and racial groups (such as hip hop). In general, this work has contributed more to interpretations of particular soundtracks than to the formulation of a general theory of the soundtrack. Nevertheless, scholars sensitive to race and the dynamics of colonialism have offered an especially cogent critical reception of the theory of musical topics. A musical topic can be defined as a conventional musical sign with an unusually clear signification. It is a term derived from the field of musical semiotics and, as such, it relates specifically to the sign-like property of music (Ratner 1980, 1–29; Agawu 1991; Hatten 2004; Monelle 2006).

As scholars of film music have long noted, scores have deployed musical topics to gain clarity in signification but at the cost of resorting to and reifying pernicious stereotypes. Gorbman, for instance, shows how the use of the Indian motif in *Stagecoach* (1939) represents them as a hostile alien force (1987, 27–28; 2000, 238–39). In the set-up to the Indian attack in Monument Valley (1:09:15), a jaunty tune associated with the stagecoach traveling across the landscape is interrupted by the brutal intrusion of fortissimo brass, which is coupled with ominous shots of Indians on a hilltop. The harsh effect is one of jarring semiotic dissonance (though the actual musical materials are less dissonant than bare and modally incompatible), of a primitive music violently cutting into the "normal," untroubled musical unfolding, itself a sign of civilization expanding its influence across the landscape. The music here, as throughout the film, demonizes: "Wordless throughout the film, and virtually invisible until the climactic chase sequence on the plain, the Indians serve as the faceless antagonist, often signaled by music alone" (Gorbman 2000, 238). As David Burnand and Benedict Sarnaker note in commenting on the same passage, such music "is designed to tell an audience next to nothing about [the Native Americans] as human beings" (1999, 7). If demonization was the most common musical representation of Native Americans during the studio era, Gorbman argues that the musical codes in the genre of the western changed markedly in the post-studio era, suggesting that the musical codes dissolved along with the genre, albeit at a somewhat slower rate (2000; 2005). Michael Pisani (2005) extends these observations, carefully tracing the development and reification of the musical topic of the American Indian in the late nineteenth and early twentieth centuries. He notes the particulars of the topic, how these conform to a certain cultural image of the Native American, and how resistant the topic has become to fundamental modification once it was codified.[4]

Common musical associations of jazz with the city, whether as a site of urbanity (musicals, romantic comedies) or of dystopic fall (film noir), continue to link race, rhythm, exoticism, and primitivism in ways that are deeply problematic and only rarely problematized (Gabbard 1996; Ford 2008). In recent years, rap music has served a similar, if more overtly racialized function in film (Doughty 2009, 327). If "black music"—whether jazz, blues, gospel, rap, and so forth—is a cultural construction with little to no basis in either biology or geography, as Philip Tagg argues (1987, 2), it is likewise the case that " 'black music' is systemically deployed by the film industry to gain swift entrance into the African American condition," as Ruth Doughty replies (2009, 325). Although Doughty proposes to accept Tagg's nonracialized musical understanding, the logic of her article is one of white appropriation (if not theft) of "black music" rather than of cultural representation and construction of race through music, as Tagg proposes. Among other things, this means that she never interrogates the definition of "whiteness" she deploys (which simply becomes the other of "blackness") and whether and to what extent "Jewish" would have been constructed as "white" (or "passing" as white) at the time about which she is writing, the jazz age of the 1920s. Doughty cites Michael Rogin (1996) on this point but collapses his narrative so that the process by which the Jew becomes culturally white through the othering effects of blackface is all but lost, as are the complex cultural negotiations required of all who stood outside the charmed circle of white American culture—marginals at the time would have included not just Jews, but most ethnic types (Irish, southern and eastern Europeans, even Germans) who have since been accepted as white.

In each of the cases cited above, the musical topic is heavily marked;[5] it seizes on something that appears to stand outside the standard musical language, and this difference serves both as the ground of its signifying element and as a way to demarcate its exteriority, its resistance to assimilation to the standard in a way that allies these topical figures with exoticism. Mark Brownrigg summarizes the principles used specifically to signify (exoticized) place:

> the use of a non-Western instrument; the use of Western instruments in imitation of non-Western ones; the use of a melody associated with a specific place; the concoction of a melody shadowing a tune with a specific geographic connotations, adopting the theoretical principles of a music culture in order to produce a simulacrum of it; harnessing rhythms evocative of a certain part of the world; using genuine music and/or musicians from the country the film is interested in evoking. (Brownrigg 2007, 312)

Brownrigg is particularly concerned with colonizing appropriations of such musical topics, where the exoticism is usually tied to representing a place as distant and governed by customs alien to the "norms" of Western, tacitly white culture.

The American context, with its complicated history of colonialism, genocide, slavery, and immigration, is especially fraught with respect to definition of its national identity and with respect to its "other." As Kathryn Kalinak explains, "in America, the other is nonwhite and constructed through racial difference from that perceived norm. Thus, Native Americans, African Americans, Latinos, and Asian Americans have functioned as points of difference against which American culture defines its essential self" (2005, 156). Interestingly, the four "others" of American identity that Kalinak identifies— Native Americans, African Americans, Latinos, and Asian Americans—all have stable and strongly defined musical topics by the time the first film music anthologies were being assembled in the early 1910s, indicating the extent to which these others had been reified into theatrical types and/or stereotypes.[6] Not all topical signification is exotic in this way[7]—for Ralph Locke, exoticism generally includes a will-to-represent something that is other, to use representation to capture and objectify the other (2009, 74)—and not all exoticism is so explicitly racialized;[8] but the exoticism of racialized topics does reveal especially clearly the cultural stakes of topical signification. And it should be noted that a clear separation between the two is not easy to maintain: Kalinak points out that many of the songs associated with cowboys and the frontier originated in overtly racialized minstrel shows and that their transformation into cowboy songs and western folk music was effected through a process of deracination (2005, 152).

Locke seeks to distinguish representations of the exotic from works written in a particular style. He recognizes that the distinction is unstable but it usefully allows him to read the exotic as a mask of power relations. Although this differentiation of modes of stylistic representation leads to sensitive and remarkably insightful analysis, less satisfying is its exemption of works borrowing other "cosmopolitan" styles (such as Meyerbeer incorporating Italianate opera structures) from such power relations on the seeming basis of the exchange of pure, neutral technique. Such commerce simply reflects these power relations at a different level: it signifies the competition and exchange of the great powers, a level at which the colonialist and imperialist exploitation and expropriation (both abroad and at home) that make these exchanges possible can seem to disappear from view because they have been sublated into the power differentials among the various nation-states. This no doubt accounts for a good deal of the instability of the original distinction. Locke's awareness that the colonialist power relations are pervasive surfaces most strikingly in his comments, following Edward Said, on the way sophisticated artistic structures "occlude...the functioning of empire" (2009, 34) and on what, borrowing terms from Richard Taruskin and James Parakilas, he calls the "double bind" of "autoexoticism," the application of the colonial will-to-represent to the self.[9]

Ideology of Content: 2. The Table of Knowledge and Communicative Efficiency

Inherited from eighteenth- and nineteenth-century theatrical traditions and codified in manuals and catalogs for cinema musicians in the silent era, topics are structured as a table of figures. From a fairly early date in cinema history, the catalogs take on a tabular form, sorted according to topic and often including fields for other attributes (key, meter, tempo, duration, etc.) as well as cross-tabs to other topics. The most elaborate of these is Erdmann and Becce (1927), a two-volume work that includes a huge fold-out table placing each of more than 3000 musical compositions (all listed, with incipits, in volume 2) in relation to broad topical categories (x-axis) and intensity of expression (y-axis). As a form of knowledge a table of topics represents an attempt to catalog the world, to stabilize knowledge by stabilizing signification. The epistemological project presumes a timeless essence that determines the topic in order that it might be efficiently exploited. The "truth" of the signifier, its conformance to the actual thing in the world that it signifies, is less important than the stability of the signification.

Writing in 1951, composer Dimitri Tiomkin freely admits that "much of the [film] music that is accepted as typical of certain races, nationalities and locales, is wholly arbitrary. Audiences have been conditioned to associate certain musical styles with certain backgrounds and peoples, regardless of whether the music is authentic" (1951, 21–22). He goes on to note that in the context of films, the use of the conventionalized topic is often "compulsory."

> I have used the "Indian music" that everyone knows not because I am not resourceful enough to originate other music, but because it is a telegraphic code that audiences recognize. If while the white settlers are resting or enjoying themselves, the background music suddenly takes on that tympani beat, the effect on the audience is electrifying. All know the Redmen are on the warpath even before the camera pans to the smoke signals on a distant hilltop. If I introduced genuine, absolutely authentic Indian tribal music, it probably wouldn't have any effect at all. (Tiomkin 1951, 22)

Tiomkin's metaphors are telling: they are signs that presume and establish the regime of modernity: the Indian topic, like the telegraphic message, is a code for efficient communication; if the effect is "electrifying," this is so not due to the authenticity of the code but rather because the audience recognizes itself as the addressee of its message (placing the audience on the side of modernity) and because this culturally and arbitrarily coded message can miraculously be transmitted and decoded faster than the image. Moreover, its telegraphic quality is opposed to the smoke signals, reflecting the disparity in power of modern "arbitrary" communication technologies compared to "primitive" ones assigned to the Indians. If the smoke signals have a seemingly mysterious power to send "the Redmen…on the warpath," the musical topic, like the historical telegraph, has the power to warn efficiently of the attack, whereas the message of the authentic tribal music would be as unintelligible to the audience as the message encoded in the smoke signals. Moreover, even if this particular attack proved successful, the music inscribes any victory as temporary that does not manage to gain control over its power of communication, its representation not so much of modernity *per se*, whose signifiers are largely "arbitrary," but of its particular regime of truth, the "arbitrary" distinctions that it requires for its particular "truth" conditions to appear.

Burnand and Sarnaker, apologists for the practice of scoring on the basis of communicative efficiency, are most forthright and follow Tiomkin's line of argument. Writing of the Indian motif in *Stagecoach*, they state: "This particular musical code stereotypes 'Red Indians' as a bellicose enemy rather than a racial or cultural group. It is dramatically essential, therefore, that they *not* be represented through their own music. Indeed the real thing…would only be distracting in the context of a narrative attempting quickly and sharply to establish location, culture or provenance" (Burnand and Sarnaker 1999, 8). The musical topic reveals the formal dramatic function of "bellicose enemy," a function that is indifferent to any particular content (racialized or otherwise), requiring only that some Other satisfy the role of bellicosity. This functional indifference to the content of the representation is the flip side of the arbitrariness of the signifier. In deracializing the content to reveal the function, however, what is lost is the purpose (if not function) of the cultural insistence of a racialized appearance of the material to fill out the requirements of the dramatic form. The excessively marked content that constitutes the stereotype generally serves to obscure the power dynamic inhering in the dramatic structure that requires the representation and its efficient communication. Also bound to this excess is the particular affective quality of the topic. In this way, although the particular topic may be accepted, condemned, or simply recognized as an arbitrary convention, the structure that reproduces the power relations passes, as in Tiomkin's account or in Burnand and Sarnaker's, without comment into a (natural) property of drama. Doughty, for example, naturalizes dramatic efficiency through the imperative of time: "Mainstream films look to inform an audience in a concise and unambiguous way. Cues are given to connote location, period, setting, and characterization. These are typically communicated through visual or aural signs. Film as a medium has to rely on such devices, as there is a prescribed period of time in which a narrative can occur" (Doughty 2009, 325–26).

Although Burnand and Sanaker themselves favor arbitrary convention, presumably because it allows the excess to stand as a mark of representational artifice that underscores the difference of the narrative from the world, it is hardly "dramatically necessary" that the topic be treated this way. Excessive representation, communicative efficiency, and audience address are the key factors, and "authentic" music can easily serve this dramatic function so long as it is readily interpretable as such. As Robert Stam and Louise Spence note, "In many classical Hollywood films, African polyrhythms became aural signifiers of encircling savagery, a kind of synecdochic acoustic shorthand for the atmosphere of menace implicit in the phrase 'the natives are restless'" (1983, 18). This remains true, whether or not the polyrhythms are genuine or fabricated. Indeed, Jean-Pierre Bartoli proposes that when it comes to exotic musical figures, evaluation of authenticity, either pro or con, bears no logical connection to evaluating the effect. If "exoticism in art arrays itself along a continuum...from the most realistic...to the totally fantastic, still,...the question of the [degree of] veracity of the borrowing has no bearing on how one gauges the effectiveness of the communication established between the creator and his public. The question...is: What is the most persuasive at a given moment" (2000, 65; quoted and translated in Locke 2009, 49).

In any event, whatever the topic used and however real or imaginary it might be, what counts is its ultimate field of signification: Is it deployed to be read—to encourage the audience to read—coarsely and simplistically? Or, does it instead deepen, problematize, crystallize a dramatic moment in a way that complicates or simplifies our understanding of the unfolding situation or of the larger world?

Ideology of Content: 3. A Postcolonial Critique of Musical Topics

Whatever the origin of the material, the topical catalog remains implicated in a colonial form of knowledge. It extends what Arjun Appadurai calls the "taxonomical control over difference" to the realm of feeling, so that musical topics can be efficiently deployed in a "spectacle to domesticate difference" (1999, 227). In this respect, the power and legitimacy of the catalog derives less from a correspondence of the table to the world than from its marshaling of affective states in the service of accommodating subjects to the social hierarchies and contradictions they encounter. Once cataloged for instrumental effect, music becomes thereby an exquisite weapon of power, at least in part because its affective quality tends to dominant any discursive referent: "Signs...acquire their full ideological value—appear to be open to articulation with wider ideological discourses and meanings—at the level of their 'associative' meanings (that is, at the connotative level)" (Hall 1999, 512). Since such associative meanings are not "fixed in natural perception (that is, they are not fully naturalized),...their fluidity of meaning and association can be more fully exploited and transformed."

Seymour Stern, whose obsession with *The Birth of a Nation* seems driven by equal parts admiration and horror at the cultural work of Griffith's film, suggests that a great deal of the ideological effect of the film resides in Breil's score, which, precisely because it effectively deploys so much music from the symphonic and operatic repertoire, transforms itself into "one of the fundamental weapons of dramatic-emotional power and political propaganda in the annals of art and politics" (Stern 1965, 120). Perhaps because of his schizophrenic ambivalence toward Griffith's film or perhaps because he focuses on the score's appropriations from the classical repertoire and other preexisting music rather than on Breil's original compositions, Stern seems less concerned with pinning down the fact of the score's stereotyping than with tracing the score's mythologizing work as ideology. In this way, he moves the point of ideological analysis away from evaluating content and toward how the score mounts its various appeals to persuade its audience of its worldview. In nascent form, Stern anticipates Homi Bhabha's suggestion that "the point of [postcolonial] intervention should shift from the *identification* of images as positive or negative, to an understanding of the *processes of subjectification* made possible (and plausible) through stereotypical discourse" (1983, 18; emphasis in original). Fixation on evaluating stereotypical figures remains caught within the closure of colonial stereotypical discourse, where the stereotype works as a fetish and the only recourse to appearance seems to be moral denunciation that reinforces colonial structures of power (26). As Anne Anlin Cheng writes: "It is clear that we do not yet have a vocabulary, beyond a moralistic one, in which to examine the space between: the ambiguous middle area in the continuum between egregious *stereotypes* on the one hand and the strategic deployment of *types* (tropes by which we recognize ourselves) on the other" (2000, 36; emphasis in original). Cheng adds that understanding the play of stereotype and type requires moving beyond an "analysis on the level of moral judgment and instead work[ing] toward an analysis of the way in which the evocations of stereotypes... provoke deeper and more vexing problems surrounding the cultural signification of the object of fetish, the racial-ethnic subjects" (39). What is required is a displacement of the colonial structure, the regime of knowledge that undergirds the stereotypical discourse and produces its social subjects.

In terms of topics, this would suggest proceeding not by identifying stereotypes and/or their dramatic function *per se*, but by analyzing their operation at the level of structure—both for how the work's structure requires and enables a particular stereotypical discourse as an ideological form but also how that ideological form serves to articulate the larger social structure in all its contradictoriness. Although much basic taxonomic work on topics still needs to be done in order to understand better their articulating and structuring work, an analysis attuned to revealing such work would resemble Eric Lott's prescriptions for analyzing blackface: "Where representation once unproblematically seemed to image forth its referent, we must now think of, say, the blackface mask as less a *repetition* of power relations than a *signifier* for them—a distorted mirror, reflecting displacements and condensations and discontinuities between which and the social field there exist lags, unevennesses, multiple determinations" (1995, 8; emphasis in original). This is not a recipe for producing hermeneutic certainty but instead a call for thoughtful intervention on both the level of practice and critique. The stereotyped musical topic reveals the hegemonic power relations crystallized in the network of musical signification and as such it offers a key not to unlocking meaning, which in the case of the stereotype is all but self-evident, but to deciphering the systemic and systematic displacements by which hegemonic power reproduces itself in representational networks such as music.

Ideology of the System

Ideology can also be found at the level of the system, in the choices filmmakers make in terms of commodifying music for cross-promotion (Smith 1998, 24–68; see also Chapter 10, below), in the systemic insistence that films operate for profit rather than for art (Eisler [and Adorno] 1947), in the mode of production, especially the characteristic division of labor, for soundtrack production (Faulkner 1971, 1983; Kraft 1996), or in the habits of production, that is, the way music and sound personnel habitually position themselves and define their professionalism in terms of being unobtrusive, not drawing attention to their labor (Doane 1980). Ideological critique at the level of the system often takes the form of sociological analysis or industry history.

James Kraft argues that a managerial fantasy of control drove the introduction of sound film technology as much as did profit motive: "Substitution of capital for labor is seldom just a matter of money. Despite occasional breakdowns and problems of synchronization, sound technology was far more reliable than actors and musicians.... [The] advantages of machinery over human labor always encourage technological innovation, especially when it increases profits as it did in this case" (1996, 49). If Kraft's account recognizes that profit does not provide a full explanation for decisions, even when considered exclusively from the perspective of management, it also conforms to the managerial fantasy of automated production, of labor without workers, and as such it naturalizes the managerial desire that underwrites technological innovation as a hedge against risk. In that respect it is complicit with the ideology of the Hollywood system even if it is sympathetic to the plight of the workers displaced by the technology that serves to anchor the fantasy.

According to Robert Faulkner, the turn to freelance employment after the dissolution of the studio system had the effect of concentrating music production. The result of the reorganization of compositional work has been greater inequality of opportunity for film composers; compared to the studio era, where scoring opportunities were relatively equally distributed for those working in the industry, the turn to freelancing in the 1960s and 1970s concentrated the scoring of a large proportion of films in the hands of only a few composers. As freelancers, however, composers are hired with more explicit expectations than was the case of studio production, and because as freelancers their employment is contingent rather than secure, they find themselves being hemmed in by these expectations and becoming typecast. Faulkner concludes, however, that the particular network structure that organizes freelance composition for Hollywood film does not provide a rational assessment but an arbitrary and capricious one: once it is assumed that almost every composer who lands a job scoring even one commercial film has adequate skills for the business, actual success in Hollywood is essentially random, a "weakness-of-everything model [that means,] in any five-, ten-, fifteen-, or twenty-year period of filmmaking and hiring, every extant composer...who scores a film has an equal, constant probability of success....In sum, nothing that the free-lancer does or undergoes really affects his chances in a population-transforming and resource-allocation process" (Faulkner 1983, 265).

This model, which Faulkner says represents the self-understanding of many work-ing in the industry, habituates composers to the gross inequalities of the system since it leaves open the hope of success even in the face of constant setbacks. If composers devote time to nurturing relationships despite all the evidence that it will not positively affect the probability of success, this is but "a symptom of the instability of the freelance system," where taking the meaningless action of hustling business serves to distract from the nervous fretting of waiting for a call (Faulkner 1983, 265). At the same time, what appears highly unstable from the perspective of the composer may be anything but from the perspective of the industry writ large: "There is overwhelming evidence that much of what goes on in Hollywood persists regardless of how professional compos-ers, film producers, directors, writers, and cinematographers define it, feel about it and about each other. It may be that the comparatively stable distribution of work preserves a social order where its participants are in flux" (266).

The turn toward electronic and digital music generation has had a similarly disruptive effect. Like the sound film, the synthesizer and virtual software instruments are ambiva-lent technological innovations because they offer both new resources and artistic possi-bilities even as they change the existing mode of musical production. In particular, such instruments both save labor costs and offer distinct timbral (and so also symbolic) pos-sibilities from acoustic instruments, even when they are used as a substitute for acoustic instruments (Buhler 2009; Niebur 2010, chaps. 4 and 5). At the level of social relations, synthesizers and virtual instruments, like most technological innovations, destroy exist-ing social networks of musicians (and the cultural knowledge these networks sustain) as orchestras are replaced by banks of equipment, computer programs, digital files, and programmers. Given the way that this equipment radically disrupts these social rela-tions, it is hardly surprising that the musicians whose livelihoods are threatened should direct hostility toward it or that, along with the usual connotations of utopian rationality that advanced products of technological innovation carry, the cultural signification of the synthesizer should absorb and transform aspects of the disenchantment and dys-phoria that displaced and alienated labor projects on it.

Still another similar instance is the use of preexisting popular songs. Such songs might indeed be criticized or valorized on a number of grounds (for example, dramatic perti-nence) not immediately connected with systemic ideology, but often their presence in film has been criticized on the basis of profit motive—that their appearance is motivated only by the wish to make money for the film where other musical choices would have been better for the dramatic structure. Irwin Bazelon, for instance, writes that "pictures like *Breakfast at Tiffany's* and *A Man and a Woman*...are seemingly better suited to a songwriter's talents than a composer's. It is a debatable point whether these films and similar types have been 'scored' in the strictest sense of the word. Any one of a thousand other songs could serve the identical purpose" (1975, 11).

Embittered film composers pushed out of the industry due to changing conditions and fashion in the 1960s and 1970s were particularly prone to make this sort of criticism. In general, such criticism reveals more about the resentment of the unemployed composer than anything significant about either the industry or the profit motive, although it does have the advantage of reminding us that the music will ultimately be evaluated by the industry in terms of the economic value it adds to the product. The relationship to economics, however, is also often not as straightforward as it might seem. Even during the heyday of the compilation soundtrack album, for instance, it often cost more to license songs than the filmmakers ever expected to recoup in ancillary income, suggesting another logic besides economics was guiding the decision making.

Ideology of the Apparatus

More challenging than the levels of ideology critique that take aim at the content of the individual films or the terms of industry production is one that homes in on the very existence of film music or sound film. This mode of analysis, which resembles the postcolonial critique sketched above and which has been heavily influenced by the theory of the apparatus considered in detail in Chapter 15, looks at the presence of music or the redundancy of synchronized sound as an ideological figure.

Thus, Rick Altman, for instance, points to the "ventriloquism" of sound film and notes how the synchronization not only disguises the heterogeneous origins of sound but also serves to single out certain aspects of the image as the soundtrack's "dummy" according to the following "rule": "An individual who speaks will in all probability become the object of the camera's, and thus of the audience's, gaze" (1980b, 68). The synchronized body is an important body, and the use of synchronization to mark narrative pertinence is absolutely fundamental to sound film practice, as it underwrites the hierarchical division between foreground and background sound. Where a formalist will recognize only structuring aspects of sound (for the good or ill of the art of film), Altman underscores how the formal system in fact is itself deeply and inherently ideological, as it encourages us to ignore the heterogeneous quality of sound and so also the constructed nature of the cinema. "To say 'pointing the camera at the speaker' is to have already been deceived by the ideology of synchronized sound. 'Pointing the camera at the (loud)speaker' is precisely what does not happen in this case. Portraying moving lips on the screen convinces us that the individual thus portrayed—and not the loudspeaker—has spoken the words we have heard" (69).

Synchronization is thus key to representing a hierarchical view of the world (recall Rudolf Arnheim's opposition to sound film discussed in chapter 2 *supra* as well as the postcolonial critique of topic theory outlined above, which likewise focused on hierarchy). Crucially, synchronization serves to naturalize this hierarchy, allowing the audience a view of an idealized world that is clearer and more readable than the real one they encounter outside the theater. The "collusion" between soundtrack and imagetrack in the figure of synchronization is taken over by members of the audience, who receive confirmation of their own unified selfhood in the cinematic spectacle of synchronization: "If the human audience accepts the cinema's unity, it is because it cannot affirm its own without admitting the cinema's" (Altman 1980b, 71). Although we might dispute the necessity of the audience finding its unity in the identification with the cinema, the point is that even a simple, apparently technical procedure such as synchronization is not ideologically neutral; it is instead a tool that has been forged to reproduce certain ideological presuppositions sometimes classed under the rubric of "bourgeois perception"—a concept that dehistoricizes actual perception into a universalized state of "natural perception" (Lowe 1982).

Stephen Neale similarly notes that " 'lip-synch' functions as the pivotal point in the relation to which systems of on-screen and off-screen, diegetic and extra- or non-diegetic sound are established, and most importantly, through which sound overall is identified with, and subordinated to, the image" (1985, 98). In early sound film, the capture of dialogue was in fact the dominant concern; camera placement, the blocking of character movement, and the mise-en-scène were often compromised for microphone placement. Indeed, in the earliest period multiple cameras would typically cover a scene in order to allow the image to be edited to the soundtrack (rather than vice versa). Theoretical hostility to the soundtrack was particularly virulent in this period, with a constant worry being expressed that an emphasis on dialogue would turn film into nothing more than a species of recorded theater (Chapter 2 *supra*). The passive nature of that theoretical formulation—sound film as mere recording—suggests the extent to which the visual element of film, especially editing, was tacitly (or not so tacitly) conceptualized as the more creative, productive, and artistic. If synchronization was the technical device by which the soundtrack was subordinated to the image by making sound appear to have its source in the image, theory also countered by valorizing asynchronous sound on the basis of its potency, its active creativity. Yet theory also required the figure of synchronization to assure the hegemony of the image: sound was something added, supplemental, even redundant. "More than half a century after the coming of sound," Altman writes, "film criticism and theory still remain resolutely image-bound" (1980a, 3).

Similar arguments have been made about film music. Synthesizing a point from Eisler and Adorno with Lacanian psychoanalysis, Claudia Gorbman suggests that, like synchronization, the very presence of music in film is ideological, whatever its content. The fact that it generally goes "unheard," by which she means it is composed to be unobtrusive and so generally to pass without conscious notice, points to its function of lulling the audience into a state of psychic regression, making spectators more susceptible to confuse the fantasy figures of the screen with reality (1987, 50–64). This tendency is furthered by music's narrating functions, which like the stereotypical topics discussed above normally serve to clarify the narrative. This last point is taken up and developed by Caryl Flinn, who argues that the clarity offered by film music is falsely utopian. Hollywood film music, she argues, with specific reference to Korngold, "assuages its listeners, offering a clarity otherwise unavailable to them through the sharply demarcated motifs for 'good guys' and 'bad guys' " (1992, 109). By contrast—to return for a moment to neoformalism—Carroll's account of "modifying music" discussed above effaces this ideological dimension of film music by treating clarity as a basic economic value of mass art.

Ideology critique at all levels presumes that ideology results in distortion, a false appearance, usually as a product of so-called "false consciousness." Film, as a representational medium, is understood by ideology critics as in the business of producing illusion rather than reproducing reality; indeed, the image of reality serves primarily to convince audiences to accept the illusion.

If film cannot reproduce the real but only offer a representation of it, if film is an ideological instrument through and through, it nevertheless does not follow that film's illusion is at one with its ideology. A pursuit for a better reproduction of reality, for instance, might lead not to a lessening of the illusory aspect of film but only to a disguising of its inherent representational quality. At the other extreme, the most illusionistic film might reveal its representational qualities and so unmask the very conditions of its own production. Ideological critics tend to valorize such moments of reflexivity, because they almost always require the revelation of the terms of ideological construction at some level of the social structure, even if that reflexivity can serve to conserve the status quo (Feuer 1993, 87–122). Musicals in particular are often vehicles of social pedagogy (Knapp 2006a, 2006b; Buhler 2008): the reflexive moments are frequently in the service of this pedagogical function of instructing subjects in the terms of the prevailing ideology rather than subverting that ideology.

CONCLUSION

Casetti's developmental model of film theory traces the progressive academic institutionalization of film studies in shifts from an ontological paradigm to a methodological paradigm to a field paradigm. Each of these stages brought a diversification and systematization of methodological options, supporting both an increase in the production of interpretation and a finer grained understanding of film history. The most recent stage, the field paradigm, has retained the earlier methodological approaches but also assimilated several new ones. The resulting loose affiliation of critical theories, which range from various modes of ideology critique to approaches focused on gender and sexuality (see Chapter 14) to general synthetic approaches centered in psychoanalysis (Chapter 15), has been oriented around three broad goals: (1) enabling interpretation of individual films, that is, providing theoretic grounds for hermeneutic practice; (2) offering an explanatory system for how cinema organizes its attractions for spectators to encourage and reward particular modes of engagement and so also to produce a certain kind of social subject; (3) understanding the cultural and economic forces at work in the development of film technology and style. All three of these goals also have antecedents in formalism: the analysis of film technique to reveal immanent structures of filmic meaning; the understanding of film as a set of historically delimited conventions, sometimes called a language, for telling stories.

Translated to a study of the soundtrack, critical theories focus on how music and sound can bear particular cultural and ideological values in a film, how music and sound can fit into or resist the general filmic system of meaning, and how the historically changing role of music and sound in film reflects larger social and ideological pressures.

NOTES

1. For an account of the musicological situation during the same time period, see Buhler and Neumeyer 1994; Neumeyer 2000.
2. Julie Hubbert's claim that music served in Eisenstein's vertical montage primarily as a large-scale structural device (2008, 140–41) would be true only to the extent that the structure dialectically served the theme.
3. Jane Gaines and Neil Lerner (2001) show how Breil's score for *The Birth of a Nation* systematically deploys topics designating primitivism to demonize each and every assertion of African American subjectivity in the film.
4. Anthony Sheppard (2001) similarly argues that Hollywood composers have tended to score Japanese characters in stereotypical ways that demeaned and demonized them while also withholding from them the full measure of humanity.
5. On "markedness," see Hatten 1994, 29–66; also the summary in Hatten 2004, 11–16.
6. On the unstable relationship between social type and stereotype, especially in works of fiction, see Dyer 1993, 11–18. For an excellent discussion centering on the film version of Rodgers and Hammerstein's *Flower Drum Song* (1961) that explores some of the ambiguities and ambivalences involved in the use of racialized types and stereotypes, see Cheng 2000, chap. 2, especially 36–45.
7. On nonexotic musical topics, see Shapiro 1984; Buhler forthcoming; Ringer 1953; and Monelle 2006.
8. For examples of exoticism that is not explicitly racialized, see Lerner 2001 on the American pastoral; Brownrigg 2007, 319–22, on the Scottish musical topic; Schubert 1998 on the *Dies Irae*; Deaville 2006 on chant; Wierzbicki 2002 on the theremin and science fiction; Schmidt 2010 on electronic and atonal music and science fiction; Murphy 2006 on space and science fiction; and Kalinak 2005 on cowboy songs and Kalinak 2007 on those songs as deployed in John Ford's films.
9. On occlusion, see Said 1993; on double bind, see Taruskin 2007; on autoexoticism, see Parakilas 1998.

BIBLIOGRAPHY

Agawu, V. Kofi. 1991. *Playing with Signs: A Semiotic Interpretation of Classic Music.* Princeton, NJ: Princeton University Press.

Altman, Rick. 1980a. "Introduction: Cinema/Sound." *Yale French Studies* 60: 3–15.

——. 1980b. "Moving Lips: Cinema as Ventriloquism," *Yale French Studies* 60: 67–79.

——. 1992. "The Material Heterogeneity of Recorded Sound." In *Sound Theory/Sound Practice*, edited by Rick Altman, 15–31. New York: Routledge.

Altman, Rick, with McGraw Jones and Sonia Tatroe. 2000. "Inventing the Cinema Soundtrack: Hollywood's Multiplane Sound System." In *Music and Cinema*, edited by James Buhler, Caryl Flinn, and David Neumeyer, 339–359. Hanover, NH: University Press of New England.

Appadurai, Arjun. 1999. "Disjuncture and Difference in the Global Cultural Economy." In *Cultural Studies Reader*, edited by Simon During, 220–230. 2nd ed. London: Routledge

Arnheim, Rudolf. 1933. *Film*. Translated by L. M. Sieveking and Ian F. D. Morrow. London: Faber and Faber. Originally published in 1932 as *Film als Kunst*. Berlin: E. Rowohlt.

——. 1957. *Film as Art*. Berkeley: University of California Press.

Bartoli, Jean-Pierre. 2000. "Propositions pour une définition de l'exotisme musical et pour une application en musique de la notion d'isotopie sémantique." *Musurgia* 7, no. 2: 61–72.

Bazelon, Irwin. 1975. *Knowing the Score: Notes on Film Music*. New York: Arco.

Bazin, André. 2005. *What is Cinema?* Translated by Hugh Grey. 2 vols. Berkeley: University of California Press. Selected from *Qu'est-ce que le cinéma?* 4 vol. Paris: Éditions du Cerf, 1958-1962.

Bhabha, Homi K. 1983. "The Other Question . . . " *Screen* 24, no. 6: 18–36.

Bordwell, David. 1980. "The Musical Analogy." *Yale French Studies* 60: 141–156.

——. 1985. *Narration in the Fiction Film*. Madison: University of Wisconsin Press.

——. 1989. *Making Meaning: Inference and Rhetoric in the Interpretation of Cinema*. Cambridge, MA: Harvard University Press.

——. 1996. "Contemporary Film Studies and the Vicissitudes of Grand Theory." In *Post-Theory: Reconstructing Film Studies*, edited by David Bordwell and Noël Carroll, 3–36 Madison: University of Wisconsin Press.

——. 2006. *The Way Hollywood Tells It*. Berkeley: The University of California Press.

Bordwell, David, Janet Staiger, and Kristin Thompson, eds. 1985. *The Classical Hollywood Cinema: Film Style and Mode of Production to 1960*. New York: Columbia University Press.

Bordwell, David, and Kristin Thompson. 2010. *Film Art: An Introduction*. New York: McGraw-Hill.

Bordwell, David, and Noël Carroll, eds. 1996. *Post-Theory: Reconstructing Film Studies*. Madison: University of Wisconsin Press.

Brownrigg, Mark. 2007. "Hearing Place: Film Music, Geography and Ethnicity." *International Journal of Media and Cultural Politics* 3, no. 3: 307–323.

Buhler, James. 2008. " 'Everybody Sing': Family and Social Harmony in the Hollywood Musical." In *A Family Affair*, edited by Murray Pomerance, 29–44. London: Wallflower.

——. 2009. "Music and the Adult Ideal in A Nightmare on Elm Street." In *Music in the Horror Film: Listening to Fear*, edited by Neil Lerner, 168–186. New York: Routledge.

——. Forthcoming. "The Agitated Allegro as Music for Silent Film: Origins, Nature, Uses and Construction." In *Studies in Honor of Eugene Narmour*, edited by Lawrence Bernstein and Lex Rozin. New York: Pendragon.

Buhler, James, Caryl Flinn, and David Neumeyer, eds. 2000. *Music and Cinema*. Hanover, NH: University Press of New England.

Buhler, James, and David Neumeyer. 1994. Review of Caryl Flinn, *Strains of Utopia* and Kathryn Kalinak, *Settling the Score*. *Journal of the American Musicological Society* 47, no. 2: 364–385.

Buhler, James, David Neumeyer, and Rob Deemer. 2010. *Hearing the Movies: Music and Sound in Film History*. New York: Oxford University Press.

Burnand, David, and Benedict Sarnaker. 1999. "The Articulation of National Identity through Film Music." *National Identities* 1, no. 1: 7–13.

Carroll, Noël. 1988. *Mystifying the Movies: Fads and Fallacies in Contemporary Film Theory.* New York: Columbia University Press.

——. 1996a. *Theorizing the Moving Image.* Cambridge: Cambridge University Press.

——. 1996b. "Prospects for Film Theory: A Personal Assessment." In *Post-Theory: Reconstructing Film Studies*, edited by David Bordwell and Noël Carroll, 37–68. Madison: University of Wisconsin Press.

Casetti, Franscesco. 1999. *Theories of Cinema, 1945–1995.* Austin: University of Texas Press.

Cheng, Anne Anlin. 2000. *The Melancholy of Race: Psychoanalysis, Assimilation, and Hidden Grief.* New York: Oxford University Press.

Chion, Michel. 1994. *Audio-Vision: Sound on Screen.* Translated by Claudia Gorbman. New York: Columbia University Press. Originally published in 1990 as *L'audio-vision.* Paris: Nathan.

Clair, René. 1953. *Reflections on the Cinema.* London: William Kimber. Originally published in 1951 as *Réflexion faite; notes pour servir à l'histoire de l'art cinématographique de 1920 à 1950.* Paris: Gallimard.

Cook, Nicholas. 1998. *Analysing Musical Multimedia.* Oxford: Oxford University Press.

Deaville, James. 2006. "The Topos of 'Evil Medieval' in American Horror Film Music." In *Music, Meaning and Media*, edited by Erkki Pekkilä, David Neumeyer, and Richard Littlefield, 26–37. Imatra, Finland: International Semiotics Institute.

Doane, Mary Ann. 1980. "The Voice in the Cinema: The Articulation of Body and Space." *Yale French Studies* 60: 33–50.

Doughty, Ruth. 2009. "African American Film Sound: Scoring Blackness." In *Sound and Music in Film and Visual Media: An Overview*, edited by Graeme Harper, Ruth Doughty, and Jochen Eisentraut, 325–339. New York: Continuum.

During, Simon ed. 1999. *Cultural Studies Reader.* 2nd ed. London: Routledge.

Dyer, Richard. 1993. *The Matter of Images: Essays on Representation.* New York: Routledge.

Eagleton, Terry. 1990. *The Ideology of the Aesthetic.* Cambridge, MA: Basil Blackwell.

Eisenstein, Sergei. 1949. *Film Form: Essays in Film Theory.* Translated by Jay Leyda. New York: Harcourt Brace.

——. 1975. *The Film Sense.* Translated by Jay Leyda. Rev. ed. New York: Harcourt Brace. The first edition was published in 1942.

Eisler, Hanns [and Theodor W. Adorno]. 1947. *Composing for the Films.* New York: Oxford University Press.

Erdmann, Hans, and Giuseppe Becce, with Ludwig Brav. 1927. *Allgemeines Handbuch der Film-Musik.* 2 vols. Berlin-Lichterfelde: Schlesinger.

Faulkner, Robert R. 1971. *Hollywood Studio Musicians: Their Work and Careers in the Recording Industry.* Chicago: Aldine-Atherton.

——. 1983. *Music on Demand: Composers and Careers in the Hollywood Film Industry.* New Brunswick, NJ: Transaction.

Flinn, Caryl. 1992. *Strains of Utopia: Gender, Nostalgia, and Hollywood Film Music.* Princeton, NJ: Princeton University Press.

Feuer, Jane. 1993. *The Hollywood Musical.* 2nd ed. Bloomington: Indiana University Press.

Ford, Phil. 2008. "Jazz Exotica and the Naked City." *Journal of Musicological Research* 27, no. 2: 113–33.

Gabbard, Krin, 1996. *Jammin' at the Margins: Jazz and the American Cinema.* Chicago: University of Chicago Press.

Gaines, Jane, and Neil Lerner. 2001. "The Orchestration of Affect: The Motif of Barbarism in Breil's *The Birth of a Nation* Score." In *The Sounds of Early Cinema*, edited by Richard Abel and Rick Altman, 252–268. Bloomington: Indiana University Press.

Gorbman, Claudia. 1987. *Unheard Melodies: Narrative Film Music*. Bloomington: Indiana University Press.

——. 1991. "Hanns Eisler in Hollywood." *Screen* 32, no. 3: 272–285.

——. 2000. "Scoring the Indian: Music in the Liberal Western." In *Western Music and Its Others: Difference, Representation, and Appropriation in Music*, edited by Georgina Born and David Hesmondhalgh, 234–253. Berkeley: University of California Press.

——. 2004. "Aesthetics and Rhetoric." *American Music* 22, no. 1: 14–26.

——. 2005. "Drums along the L. A. River: Scoring the Indian." In *Westerns: Films through History*, edited by Janet Walker, 177–195. New York: Routledge.

Hall, Stuart. 1999. "Encoding, Decoding." In *The Cultural Studies Reader*, edited by Simon During, 507–517. 2nd ed. London: Routledge. Excerpted from "Encoding and Decoding in the Television Discourse," Occasional Paper No.7, Centre for Contemporary Cultural Studies, University of Birmingham, 1973.

Hatten, Robert S. 1994. *Musical Meaning in Beethoven: Markedness, Correlation, and Interpretation*. Bloomington: Indiana University Press.

——. 2004. *Interpreting Musical Gesture, Topics and Tropes: Mozart, Beethoven, Schubert*. Bloomington: Indiana University Press.

Hubbert, Julie. 2008. "Eisenstein's Theory of Film Music Revisited: Silent and Early Sound Antecedents." In *Composing for the Screen in Germany and the USSR: Cultural Politics and Propaganda*, edited by Robynn Stilwell and Phil Powrie, 125–147. Bloomington: Indiana University Press.

Jameson, Fredric. 1981. *The Political Unconscious: Narrative as a Socially Symbolic Act*. Ithaca, NY: Cornell University Press.

Kalinak, Kathryn. 2005. "How the West Was Sung." In *Westerns: Films through History*, edited by Janet Walker, 151–176. New York: Routledge.

——. 2007. *How the West Was Sung: Music in the Westerns of John Ford*. Berkeley: University of California Press.

Knapp, Raymond. 2006a. *The American Musical and the Formation of National Identity*. Princeton: Princeton University Press.

——. 2006b. *The American Musical and the Performance of Personal Identity*. Princeton: Princeton University Press.

Kracauer, Siegfried. 1997. *Theory of Film: The Redemption of Physical Reality*. Princeton: Princeton University Press. First edition published in 1960. New York: Oxford University Press.

Kraft, James P. 1996. *Stage to Studio: Musicians and the Sound Revolution, 1890–1950*. Baltimore: Johns Hopkins University Press.

Lehman, Frank. 2013. "Transformational Analysis and the Representation of Genius in Film Music." *Music Theory Spectrum* 35, no. 1: 1–22.

Lerner, Neil. 2001. "Copland's Music of Wide Open Spaces: Surveying the Pastoral Trope in Hollywood." *Musical Quarterly* 85, no. 3: 477–515.

Levin, Tom. 1984. "The Acoustic Dimension: Notes on Cinema Sound." *Screen* 25, no. 3: 55–68.

Locke, Ralph. 2009. *Musical Exoticism: Images and Reflections*. Cambridge: Cambridge University Press.

Lott, Eric. 1995. *Love and Theft: Blackface Minstrelsy and the American Working Class*. New York: Oxford University Press.

Lowe, Donald M. 1982. *History of Bourgeois Perception*. Chicago: University of Chicago Press.

Metz, Christian. 1982. *The Imaginary Signifier: Psychoanalysis and the Cinema*. Translated by Celia Britton, Annwyl Williams, Ben Brewster and Alfred Guzzetti. Bloomington: Indiana University Press. Originally published in 1977 as *Le Signifiant imaginaire: psychanalyse et cinéma*. Paris: Union générale d'éditions.

——. 1991. *Film Language: A Semiotics of the Cinema*. Translated by Michael Taylor. Chicago: University of Chicago Press. Originally published in 1968 as *Essais sur la signification au cinéma*. Paris: Klincksieck.

Monelle. Raymond. 2006. *The Musical Topic: Hunt, Military and Pastoral*. Bloomington: Indiana University Press.

Murphy, Scott. 2006. "The Major Tritone Progression in Recent Hollywood Science Fiction Films." *Music Theory Online* 12, no. 2. http://www.mtosmt.org/issues/mto.06.12.2/mto.06.12.2.murphy.html

Mott, Robert L. 1990. *Sound Effects: Radio, TV, and Film*. Boston: Focal.

Nattiez, Jean-Jacques. 1990. *Music and Discourse: Toward a Semiology of Music*. Translated by Carolyn Abbate. Princeton: Princeton University Press.

Neale, Stephen. 1985. *Cinema and Technology: Image, Sound, Colour*. Bloomington: Indiana University Press.

Neumeyer, David. 2000. "Introduction." In *Music and Cinema*, edited by James Buhler, Caryl Flinn, and David Neumeyer, 1–29. Hanover, NH: University Press of New England.

Neumeyer, David, and James Buhler. 2008. "*Composing for the Films*, Modern Soundtrack Theory, and the Difficult Case of *A Scandal in Paris*." *Eisler-Studien* 3: 123–141.

Nichols, Bill. 1992. "Form Wars: The Political Unconscious of Formalist Theory." In *Classical Hollywood Narrative: The Paradigm Wars*, edited by Jane Gaines, 49–77. Durham: Duke University Press.

Niebur, Louis. 2010. *Special Sound: The Creation and Legacy of the BBC Radiophonic Workshop*. New York: Oxford University Press.

O'Brien, Charles. 2005. *Cinema's Conversion to Sound: Technology and Film Style in France and the U.S.* Bloomington: Indiana University Press.

Parakilas, James. 1998. "How Spain Got Its Soul." In *The Exotic in Western Music*, edited by Jonathan Bellman, 137–193. Boston: Northeastern University Press.

Percheron, Daniel. 1980. "Sound in Cinema and its Relationship to Image and Diegesis." *Yale French Studies* 60: 16–23.

Pisani, Michael. 2005. *Imagining Native America in Music*. New Haven: Yale University Press.

Prendergast, Roy M. 1977. *Film Music: A Neglected Art*. New York: Norton.

Pudovkin, V. I. 1949. *Film Technique and Film Acting: The Cinema Writings of V. I. Pudovkin*. Translated by Ivor Montagu. New York: Bonanza.

Ratner, Leonard. 1980. *Classic Music*. New York: Schirmer.

Ricoeur, Paul. 1970. *Freud and Philosophy: An Essay on Interpretation*. Translated by Denis Savage. New Haven: Yale University Press.

Ringer, Alexander L. 1953. "The 'Chasse' as a Musical Topic of the 18th Century." *Journal of the American Musicological Society* 6, no. 2: 148–159.

Rogin, Michael. 1996. *Blackface, White Noise: Jewish Immigrants in the Hollywood Melting Pot*. Berkeley: University of California Press.

Said, Edward. 1993. *Culture and Imperialism*. New York: Alfred A. Knopf.

Salt, Barry. 2006. *Moving into Pictures: More on Film History, Style, and Analysis*. London: Starwood.

——. 2009. *Film Style & Technology: History & Analysis*. 3rd. ed. London: Starwood.

Schmidt, Lisa. 2010. "A Popular Avant-Garde: The Paradoxical Tradition of Electronic and Atonal Sounds in Sci-Fi Music Scoring." In *Light Years from Home: Music in Science Fiction Film*, edited by Mathew Bartkowiak, 23–41. Jefferson, NC: McFarland.

Schubert, Linda. 1998. "Plainchant in Motion Pictures: The Dies Irae in Film Scores." *Florilegium* 15: 207–229.

Shapiro, Ann Dhu. 1984. "Action Music in American Pantomime and Melodrama, 1730–1913." *American Music* 2, no. 4: 49–72.

Sheppard, Anthony. 2001. "An Exotic Enemy: Anti-Japanese Musical Propaganda in World War II Hollywood," *Journal of the American Musicological Society* 54, no. 2: 303–357.

Smith, Jeff. 1998. *Sounds of Commerce: Marketing Popular Film Music*. New York: Columbia University Press.

Spottiswoode, Raymond. 1950. *The Grammar of Film: An Analysis of Film Technique*. Berkeley: University of California Press. First edition published in 1935. London: Faber and Faber.

Stam, Robert and Louise Spence. 1983. "Colonialism, Racism and Representation: An Introduction." *Screen* 24, no. 2: 2–20.

Stern, Seymour. 1965. "Griffith: I—*The Birth of a Nation*, Part I." *Film Culture* 36: 1–210.

Tagg, Philip. 1987 [unpublished]. "Open Letter about 'Black Music', 'Afro-American Music' and 'European Music'." http://www.tagg.org/articles/xpdfs/opeletus.pdf. A somewhat different version was published in 1989 as "Open Letter: 'Black Music', 'Afro-American Music' and 'European Music'." *Popular Music* 8, no. 3: 285–298.

Taruskin, Richard. 2007–. "Nationalism." In *Grove Music Online, Oxford Music Online* http://www.oxfordmusiconline.com. Accessed December 1, 2011.

Thompson, Kristin. 1988. *Breaking the Glass Armor: Neoformalist Film Analysis*. Princeton, NJ: Princeton University Press.

——. 2005. *Herr Lubitsch Goes to Hollywood: German and American Film after World War I*. Amsterdam: Amsterdam University Press.

Tiomkin, Dimitri. 1951. "Composing for Films." *Films in Review* 2, no. 9: 17–22.

Tsivian, Yuri. n.d. "Intolerance Study," *Cinemetrics* (website). http://www.cinemetrics.lv/tsivian.php.

Walker, Janet, ed. 2005. *Westerns: Films through History*. New York: Routledge.

Wierzbicki, James. 2002. "Weird Vibrations: How the Theremin Gave Musical Voice to Hollywood's Extraterrestrial 'Others'." *Journal of Popular Film and Television* 30, no. 3: 125–135.

Wimsatt, William K., and Monroe C. Beardsley. 1954. "The Intentional Fallacy." In *The Verbal Icon: Studies in the Meaning of Poetry*, 3–18. Lexington: University of Kentucky Press.

PART **2**

GENRE AND PLATFORM

CHAPTER 8

....

DRAWING A NEW NARRATIVE
FOR CARTOON MUSIC

....

DANIEL GOLDMARK

THE overarching narrative of Hollywood film music has been written, contested, and rewritten repeatedly, ever more so since increased interest in media studies began in the 1990s. Not surprisingly, the films that fall squarely into particular genres (such as shorts, musicals, documentaries) or that embody idiosyncratic production or exhibition practices have received more attention (in some cases, more being an improvement from nothing at all) as historians question the distinctions between the mainstream and its tributaries. Animation, the very term describing a medium and (erroneously) a genre, apparently gave writers such pause that only a brave few have ever gone beyond Disney's animated features, and then mainly by dipping a toe into the most self-proclaimedly modernist or avant-garde studio scores (MGM and UPA, both only occasionally stretching beyond Hollywood's expectations for madcap music) (see Newsom 1980, and Prendergast 1977, 180–198). The result is that (even in my own earlier work) the most basic of timelines for the development of cartoon scoring in Hollywood does not exist.

As is true of most other film forms, trying to survey the evolution and changes in scoring methods with animation is a complicated task. What follows, then, is an admittedly idiosyncratic overview of some of the trends seen in animated films (shorts and features) produced as part of the Hollywood studio system,[1] both for theatrical release and those devised for television. In spite of their position in contemporary culture as a medium targeting largely at children, the vast majority of the films considered here were created by adults for audiences of all ages.[2] What this means is that, at least until television took over in the 1950s as the primary delivery vector for animated cartoons, all components of a cartoon—plot, characters, backgrounds, voices, music, sound effects— can and must be considered to be working with an adult audience in mind.

We can discern some large-scale trends in cartoon music, but each studio's idiosyncrasies prevent too much generalizing. There were some standard production practices, yet they all but disappear when we look more closely at what differentiates the studios, especially when it comes to music. That said, music in cartoons *cannot* be separated from the writing. A long-favored point for discussion in film music studies is the fact that the music usually enters the production process at the end, after the completion of shooting. Because the animators need voice tracks to which they can animate mouth movements, dialogue—and singing—must be recorded in advance. Many of the studios also worked with their composers to time out in advance the music for scenes. Each director and studio had different viewpoints on timing, but Warner Bros., Disney, and MGM were all closely wedded to the practice of close timing. At Warner Bros., for instance, the director would work with the composer to determine the specific tempo (with a metronome) of the music for each scene—and even individual gags—in relation to the ongoing pacing (frames per beat) in the animation. Through this process, the composer could go and write the music on his own, having developed a very specific chronometric roadmap of the entire cartoon.

Besides the more traditional roles of underscoring in live-action films, music in cartoons carries an additional and crucial responsibility: not only are viewers asked to see once-still images as moving, they must also make the leap and believe that static drawings and paintings actually have an innate sense of vitality! The timing of cartoons does not just facilitate the production process, but also develops perhaps the pivotal bond between the look and sound of cartoons.

Music's presence in the cartoon diegesis typically goes unnoticed, and yet the characters move, breathe, and speak with a discernible rhythm. We might therefore think of much of the music in cartoons not simply as performance, but in terms of musicking, Christopher Small's concept of making music that is, as he defines it, "to take part, in any capacity, in a musical performance, whether by performing, by listening, by rehearsing or practicing, by providing materials for performance (what is called composing), or by dancing" (Small 1998, 9). In cartoons, we can find many explicit examples of effective synchronization between visual and aural elements that fit Small's description. The success of an especially well-known early cartoon, *Steamboat Willie* (1928), for example, can be attributed in large part to the novelty of seeing the characters comport themselves humorously onscreen while a lively and familiar sounding musical score and effects track punctuate and drive home every synchronous hit. It should be no surprise that the pejorative term "mickey-mousing" appears in the early 1930s in response to the pervasive use of exact synchronization of music and action, a process that could easily call attention to the music (something that was, and is, largely forbidden in the live-action film industry that supposedly gave birth to the term [Handzo 1985, 409–410; Cohen 2009]) and that was largely inevitable in animated shorts of the time.

THE EARLY MUSICAL CARTOON

There is also the role of music within the film to consider, both in the story and in the soundtrack (or underscore). One general perception of early sound cartoons is that "all characters did was dance and play the ukulele."[3] This impression is not entirely untrue.

The desire for performance was ubiquitous in the late 1920s and early 1930s, and manifested in a variety of ways: characters singing and playing as the story progresses, characters stopping the story to stage a performance, live-action performers showing up (as in many Fleischer cartoons), caricatures of famous performers appearing. In all these cases, the spectacle of the performance is the key, as little developed storytelling is going on (Sartin 1998, 67–85). As the years went by, songs became a less essential part of the cartoon's dramatic arc—but stories still depended greatly on music to telegraph emotions to the viewer. We can see a shift, then, in animated shorts in particular, from the focus on music as performance in the 1920s and 1930s to music as underscoring in the 1940s and 1950s. These are, once again, generalizations; some of the best animated performances come in this later period.

The first cartoon to show the world how effectively music and animation could work together was Disney's *Steamboat Willie*. A parody on the Buster Keaton Jr. film *Steamboat Bill, Jr.* (Reisner, 1928), the film overflows with synchronized movements, both obvious and subtle. The establishing scene, showing the paddle-boat floating down the river, is underscored by an instrumental statement of the chorus to "Steamboat Bill" (published by F. A. Mills in 1910). The ship's smokestacks alternate belching smoke with the beat of the music. Cut to Mickey at the steering wheel, who begins whistling the song's tune. The performative element of this scene is clear: seeing his mouth move when we hear the whistling, and seeing breaths taken between each phrase of the song. The part of the animation with which the music forges a true sense of synchronization, however, includes everything *but* the whistling:

- Mickey turns the ship's wheel with a flourish, and his eyes/face change position at the end/beginning of each new phrase of the melody;
- Mickey's foot taps subdivisions of the beat throughout his performance;
- Mickey's lower torso makes a complete sway back and forth with each phrase of the melody.

The animation is not just supported by the music, then, but is entirely interdependent with the soundtrack. The music was in fact recorded after the film's completion: the soundtrack had to be recorded twice because the first attempt did not synchronize properly, costing Disney money at a time when he had resorted to selling his car to meet production costs (Barrier 1999, 51–55). Nevertheless, the degree to which the action depends on timing (which is, ultimately, telegraphed to the viewer via the soundtrack) shows how important the music was to the way people experienced this film.

The second half of the film is no less significant, as it set a standard for onscreen performances in all the sound cartoons to follow for at least a decade. Mickey and Minnie turn a billy goat, which has eaten their sheet music for "Turkey in the Straw," into a crank organ, and, in addition to the various noise-makers (pots, pans, cans) he finds around him, Mickey proceeds to use the animals on the boat as makeshift instruments: a goose's neck slides like a trombone, a cow's teeth double for a xylophone, and a sow's teats serve as the buttons to an accordion. No explanation for the appropriation of animals into instruments occurs, and none seems necessary. Unlike the various narrative conceits made in the earliest film musicals to justify the constant singing (and, typically, dancing), animated cartoons seemed to take to music much more naturally (perhaps even innately, especially considering how important music was to the very nature of a cartoon's structure, as discussed earlier), giving over a substantial portion of the film's running time to performance (Sartin 1998, 73).[4] We might consider *Steamboat Willie* doubly important, then: it became not only the first widely seen cartoon with synchronized sound (as opposed to the other two Mickey Mouse cartoons that Walt and crew were working on at the time), but far more importantly, it established a standard for what sound cartoons might do with music. Mickey's performance with his menagerie-cum-orchestra paved the way for countless future animated musical interludes. *Steamboat Willie* splits the musical responsibilities largely down the middle between background and source, unseen underscore and visualized performance. While live-action filmmakers debated and struggled with the whys and wherefores of underscore, cartoon directors apparently had no such misgivings and applied music to animation with obviously successful results.

> After two or three of the Mickeys had been completed and were being run in theaters, Walt talked with me on getting started on the musical series that I had in mind.... When I told him I was thinking of inanimate figures, like skeletons, trees, flowers, etc., coming to life and dancing and doing other animated actions fitted to music more or less in a humorous and rhythmic mood, he became very much interested. (Barrier 2002, 41)[5]

The speaker here is Carl Stalling, a film accompanist who had known Disney in the latter's days as an animator in Kansas City, Missouri, and who was the Disney studio's first musical director (although he did not work on *Steamboat Willie*). Almost immediately after the success of recorded soundtracks at Disney's (beginning with *Willie*), Stalling proposed a series of cartoons that came to be known as the Silly Symphonies (the title was also a suggestion of Stalling's). These films reversed the scoring approach Disney had used for the Mickeys, a process in which, Stalling recalled, "Most of the time, the directors and animators were free to do what they thought best to make the action most effective" (quoted in Barrier 2002, 43–44). Stalling advocated writing a story around the music, rather than having the music be tacked on after the plot and gags had been devised. If *Willie* had music that synchronized to the action, the first Silly Symphony, *The Skeleton Dance* (Disney, 1929), was animated *to* the musical score, giving everyone (especially Walt Disney himself) a much better sense of how music could be made to work with images.

The overall effect of writing the story (or in this case, the gags, as there is no real story to speak of, just the premise of skeletons rising from their graves in a cemetery at night) to the music results in an animated ballet, where the movements of the skeletons flow so well with the music that we cannot tell which came first. This especially close relationship between sound and image effectively raises the awareness of score to the level of a performance, even though the music has no apparent source—that is, until one skeleton swipes the femur bones of another and begins playing his back like a macabre xylophone. While the Fleischers' bouncing-ball cartoons had long since incorporated preexisting songs into cartoons, this was the first time a cartoon, having been written to fit a score, revealed how strongly the link between score and story could be if the music came first, opening an entirely new avenue on how to write for cartoons.

The 1930s: Musical Cartoons and Cartoon Musicals

By the early 1930s, practically every major film studio in Hollywood was distributing cartoons as part of their film packages. Some were produced with an on-site cartoon division, and some on a contractor basis. Cartoons at this time placed a strong emphasis on performance and making music. Several studios had easy access to current popular music through their parent companies or distributors, in some cases proffering incentives (financial, typically) to feature popular songs. One of the conditions of Leon Schlesinger's agreement to produce cartoons for Warner Bros., for example, was that the cartoons feature music owned by Warner's publishing division. The Fleischers' earliest success had come from promoting popular music, the Bouncing Ball shorts having been created, in part, to spotlight hit songs. By the 1930s, they had made a deal with their distributor, Paramount, that allowed them to use live-action footage of performers starring in Paramount live-action shorts in their cartoons, the same performers who were achieving current pop hits.[6] Beginning with "Minnie's Yoo Hoo," Disney also had a string of hit pop songs inspired by or presented in their shorts. Eventually, full-length feature films gave Disney their own library of pop hits that they could draw from at any time.

Thus we can say that the presence of popular songs had a profound effect on how cartoons would be structured. Many studios modeled how they used music, in part, on the example set by their distributors or parent studios. For instance, many cartoons used songs popularized within the cartoons themselves ("Minnie's Yoo Hoo" at Disney, "Woody Woodpecker" at Lantz, for example) as recurring themes, usually as opening theme songs, and even sometimes in the cartoons themselves, a practice that in turn helped drive sheet music and record sales. For Warner Bros. in particular, songs were practically the *raison d'être* for the Merrie Melodies series, whose original purpose was to promote songs owned by the larger Warner conglomerate; most of the titles for the early Merrie Melodies simply bastardized or borrowed outright the titles of Warner controlled songs: "Lady Play Your Mandolin," "Smile, Darn Ya, Smile," "Pagan Moon," "Shuffle Off to Buffalo," to name just a few.

Only occasionally did a cartoon drives a new song's popularity rather than just promoting a hit drawn from film or records; witness *Three Little Pigs* (Gillett, 1933). The featured song, "Who's Afraid of the Big Bad Wolf?", written by Frank Churchill and with additional lyrics by Ann Ronell, became an unexpected pop hit.[7] The degree to which the song was integrated into the story and the overall feel of the cartoon (as with its Silly Symphonies predecessors) make *Three Little Pigs* a veritable turning point. Everything in the cartoon moves to an implied or audible beat. The first pig sways to the beat, and kicks his hoofs in the air to the off-beat as he plays his flute. The second pig we see working on his house of sticks; his ladder bows in and out with the beat, while all of his body movements likewise synchronize to the score. When he joins his brother they begin dancing and playing their instruments together (bringing performance into the foreground). Once again, their hoof falls (when each hoof hits the ground) emphasize the off-beat, until the song's chorus begins, at which point their hooves simultaneously hit the ground on the words "big bad wolf," providing an almost subconscious reinforcement of a key phrase of the song.

To be clear, I am not suggesting that the Disney cartoons had not been highly synchronized before his time—on the contrary, they were known for their high degree of audio-visual coordination, evidenced at the very least by the rise of the term mickey-mousing (as mentioned earlier). Rather, it is the presence of a single song as a unifying concept, heard both as performance and in the underscore, that makes this cartoon a turning point, as it gives *Three Little Pigs* an unusual musical coherence. Contrary to what we might expect, the film does not begin with the song's melody, nor with a chorus of voices singing the refrain. (Then again, why would it? No one knew how popular the song would become.) Instead, we get an overture on a fragment of the song's melody, complete with Tchaikovskian conversations between a piano and the orchestra. Also surprising is that we actually hear the song's verses—twice—before getting to the chorus, and even then, it is the two pigs taunting their other brother with "You don't take no time to play," rather than the song's actual words. The chorus proper only appears when the two pigs feel sufficiently fearless of the wolf, a perfect reminder of the danger that is just outside their door.[8]

DISNEY AND THE CARTOON MUSICAL

Sometime in 1934, Walt Disney began production work on a feature-length animated film, *Snow White and the Seven Dwarfs* (David Hand, 1938) (Barrier 1999, 125). The film is part melodrama and part musical. Unlike most musicals of the 1930s, the musical numbers in *Snow White* are not reveries, dream sequences, or performances within performances (Altman 1987, 105). On the contrary, Disney merged the narratological framework of the 1930s cartoon, in particular the constant singing and non-self-aware performing, with the narrative of the Hollywood film musical. As it turned out, the characteristics of the cartoon world combined well with those of the musical (Sartin 1998, 67).

During a discussion of the scoring for *Snow White* in 1937, composer Leigh Harline brought up the major distinction between shorts and features:

In spite of its length, however, this picture is quite a relief to us in the music department. You see, in the ordinary cartoon we have to fit the music into very close limitations, for the whole character of a cartoon is based upon the coordination of musical rhythm and photographic frequency in addition to synchronizing music with action. In the case of our feature length cartoon there are many sequences where we are allowed the same liberty of composition and scoring as is the case in any major production. While we have a great deal more music to do than is customary with any other type of picture, the fact that we can get out of the straight-jacket put around us by ordinary cartoon requirements is a decidedly agreeable occasion for us. In fact, there are many sequences where the action for the picture gets quite dramatic. For these we have prepared music that is more or less symphonic—at least in instrumentation—and of a serious form. (Steele 1937, 10)

Harline and his colleagues apparently rejoiced in *Snow White*'s lack of restrictions for composing for shorts. That is, they enjoyed the opportunity to write for a feature film over a short. Does this mean Harline and company didn't like writing for cartoons, or perhaps that what they really wanted was to compose for traditional (that is, live-action) features?[9] Whatever the answer might be, we can read in his tone some anxiety about the role played by music for animated shorts.

Disney's main competitors in popularity during the mid-1930s were the Fleischers, best known for developing cartoons around newspaper comic star Popeye, as well as their own invention, Betty Boop. Not to be outdone by Disney, the Fleischer studio developed their own musical spectacular, *Gulliver's Travels* (Dave Fleischer, 1939), with songs and score by Al Neiburg, Sammy Timberg, and Winston Sharples. Another film, *Mr. Bug Goes to Town* (Dave Fleischer, 1941), followed, but by then the Fleischers were in irreversible financial straits, and Disney's success with *Pinocchio* (Ben Sharpsteen and Hamilton Luske, 1940) and *Dumbo* (Ben Sharpsteen, 1941) ensured the latter studio's ongoing cultural identification with animated films.

One film in particular from this period that stands out featured the longest original cartoon score to that date: *Bambi* (David Hand, 1942). Unlike *Snow White*, *Pinocchio*, and *Dumbo*, the setting of Felix Salten's story of a young deer in the forest was scored in the manner of a traditional Hollywood feature, with a lush orchestral score, a choir of offscreen voices singing a few scene-setting songs, and *no* musical numbers or productions to interrupt the story's flow. *Bambi* stands out as the Disney film in which the score is the primary musical feature (Care 1985). *Fantasia* (1940) and *The Reluctant Dragon* (1941), incidentally, although they were released during this period, are not traditional narrative features; the former was a series of animated visualizations of classical music and the latter was (in part) a tour of the Disney studio.

Disney's other musical landmark during this time was the exploration of classical music and popular imagery in *Fantasia* (Ben Sharpsteen, 1940), a film that can be most easily and accurately described as an extended series of Silly Symphonies, with each segment taking on a preexisting piece of classical music and fashioning a visualization of the story within. All but one of the chosen works were already quite programmatic in nature; the exception was the Bach Toccata and Fugue in D minor, played by the

236 OXFORD HANDBOOK OF FILM MUSIC STUDIES

Philadelphia Orchestra in an arrangement by Leopold Stokowski. Rather than creating a narrative for that work out of whole cloth, the studio eventually[10] chose to use entirely abstract animation, a risky gambit for the film's opening number. Disney's hope—that the film would provoke a new appreciation of animation through the universalizing popularity of classical music—was not realized with the film's release in 1940, but rather after numerous rereleases into the 1960s, by which time the domination of classical music in American popular culture had been greatly mitigated by the growth of jazz and eventually rock and roll.

THE GOLDEN AGE OF SHORTS

Cartoons in the late 1930s—like feature films—began moving away from the "All Singing! All Dancing!" format prevalent earlier in the decade, featuring stories less dominated by performance (not that it disappeared by any means). Each studio's musical profile depended entirely on the resources they had at hand and in many cases it meant adapting to budgetary restrictions. Warner Bros. and MGM continued to have easy and inexpensive access to current popular songs, although each studio used the songs to very different ends. The Lantz studio took advantage of its proximity to the thriving jazz scene in the Los Angeles area to feature local jazz stars in the Swing Symphonies series. Lantz's musical director, Darrell Calker, knew many of these players personally. Those studios that did not have such advantages made do all the same; the Terrytoon and Columbia cartoons in particular overflow with original songs written by their composers (Philip Scheib for Terry, Joe de Nat and Eddie Kilfeather at Columbia).

The studios did not move away from performance entirely, however, showing once more just how closely tied Hollywood cartoons were to the idea of making music and putting on a show (just as feature films had, similarly, not abandoned musicals, but rather reframed the manner of their presentation). Lantz introduced two series in the 1940s predicated on specific musical genres—unsurprisingly, jazz (the aforementioned Swing Symphonies) and classical music (Musical Miniatures), the long-time cultural rivals. Terry released a series of operetta-styled shorts complete with through-composed scores, sounding something like Mighty Mouse meets Wagner. Warner Bros. and MGM also produced numerous parodies of classical music and the culture of the concert hall in the 1940s and 1950s, such as *The Cat Concerto* (1947), *Johann Mouse* (1952), *Long-Haired Hare* (1949), *Rabbit of Seville* (1950), and *What's Opera, Doc?* (1957). Despite these standouts, however, the studios and audiences both seemed less interested in highlighting performance as time went on. Ultimately, rock and roll would emerge as a highly profitable performance style in the guise of animated television series such as *Pebbles and Bamm-Bamm*, *Josie and the Pussycats*, *The Archie Show*, *Jackson 5ive*, *Fat Albert and the Cosby Kids*, and many others.

At Warner Bros., Carl Stalling continued the gag-by-gag approach to scoring cartoons that he had begun with Disney and which was itself an extension of his scoring practices as a film accompanist in the 1920s. By the 1940s the studio no longer had to spotlight a song owned by Warner Bros. in each short; regardless, Stalling's method continued to combine original descriptive music with preexisting music of every genre imaginable, all of which was carefully timed out in advance to create an underlying rhythmic affect for the entire score, whether or not anything was actually moving on screen. Stalling's access to the entire Warner Bros. publishing library, along with his encyclopedic knowledge of music that could be made to fit a scene, gave the Warner cartoon scores a remarkable feeling of breadth and originality.

Across town at MGM, Scott Bradley also had a sizable collection of popular tunes owned by the studio, but he had little interest in using them. Bradley saw the cartoon score as a vast blank canvas on which composers could develop the next great movement in modern music. To this end, Bradley availed himself of a friendly environment and conducted some musical experiments within his own scores, using techniques gleaned from Bartók, Schoenberg, and other contemporary composers. Not forsaking the expectations placed on him, Bradley surrounded his modern dabblings with more traditional-sounding fare, including rich arrangements of pop tunes and gag-specific melodies that were remarkably descriptive of the action.

The independent studio UPA (formed in the late 1940s) took a very novel viewpoint on how to make cartoons, rejecting much of the stylization tending toward naturalism that had come to be the dominant practice in Hollywood at the time. Highly saturated colors, nontraditional perspective, abstract backgrounds, and limited animation all combined to give the studio's cartoons a completely unique look and feel that was quickly adapted by other studios (including Disney).[11] If UPA had a distinguishable musical sound it was its lack of a single musical style, due in part to the variety of composers that worked there, including men with backgrounds in film (David Raksin), concert music (Gail Kubik), and radio or television (Hoyt Curtin, Bill Lava). Kubik's score for *Gerald McBoing-Boing* (1951), for instance, the story of a young boy who cannot speak words but makes the sounds of an orchestral percussion section instead, is a modernist score juxtaposed against a postclassical approach to animation. The lasting effects of UPA's cartoons can still be seen and heard, as both limited animation and scoring styles were embraced by television.

LIBRARY CUES AND THE TRANSITION
TO TELEVISION

The end of the Second World War coincided with the final moments of many production practices in Hollywood. One peripheral effect of the landmark 1948 Paramount monopoly decision was that theater-owners were no longer obligated to show the animated shorts that, in past, they had been compelled to purchase weekly along with features, whether or not they would show them (Thompson and Bordwell 1994, 374–75). The concomitant rise of television led to a new exhibition method for shorts: film studios began selling packages of their cartoons to television stations to fill empty programming slots in the morning hours as fodder for children, especially when programmers realized the degree to which children were consumers for animated cartoons, even those that were not brand new.

As cartoons produced for theatrical exhibition continued to disappear, a demand quickly arose for cartoons created expressly for television. As with the theatrical product, television cartoons made numerous demands on the composer, but now more music was needed on a shorter production schedule. With the recent shifts in scoring production practices, the film studios no longer retained large in-house orchestras for composers to use as they desired. Then again, the studios producing for TV were no longer integrated units of the major movie studios, but had once again become freelance contractors, as with the Hollywood cartoons of the 1920s and 1930s. Not surprisingly, then, we find a reversion to a small-ensemble scoring style, necessitated by the shoestring budgets the productions received. Technological advances simplified the process as well. Many major film studios had begun to use stock library cues in the 1940s, and cartoons were no exception (Mandell 2002). During a brief absence from Warner Bros. in 1951, for instance, Carl Stalling's scores were replaced with the music of Eugene Poddany on a half-dozen films. Just a decade later, following Stalling's retirement and the death not long after of Stalling's successor (Milt Franklyn, who had also been Stalling's orchestrator since the late 1930s), television and B-picture veteran Bill Lava created a series of cues for the Warner Bros. cartoons that were used for the next six years. The main downside to these cues was that, in fulfilling their primary function of being consistent in mood and engagement, the formulaic, generic melodies sounded remarkably bland and unappealing when compared to Stalling's original scores.

While stock cues made the final years for theatrical cartoons sound blah, they also helped to *define* the sound of television cartoons, particularly those by pioneer TV animation studio Hanna-Barbera. Early successes like *The Ruff and Reddy Show* (1957–1960) and particularly *The Huckleberry Hound Show* (1958–1962) used library cues licensed from Capitol Records' Hi-Q Library and written by numerous composers, including William Loose, Jack Shaindlin, John Seely, and Geordie Hormel. Once Hoyt Curtin took over as composer (he initially had been writing commercial jingles), he composed new melody sets that became the musical foundations of the many new Hanna-Barbera shows to follow.[12] This approach to scoring cartoons would dominate the industry through almost a quarter of a century, until a turn to the past would bring a return to older practices.

THE NEW TRENDS: CABLE AND NOSTALGIA

From the very first piece of Mickey Mouse merchandising, all the interested parties—film studios, toy companies, and eventually television networks—knew how well cartoons could sell products. Television shows quickly appeared that were little more than animated commercials, their entire purpose being to sell a line of toys, from *He-Man* (1983–1985) to *Rainbow Brite* (1984–1986). Music in these cartoons was, at best, barely functional.

These shows represent what can be fairly described as a nadir in cartoon production during the 1970s and 1980s. A cartoon renaissance occurred in the late 1980s with a revival of interest in Golden-Age cartoons, brought about in part by Warner Bros., which commissioned a new television series, one that featured child-sized versions of their most famous characters, in an effort to take advantage of the cultural cache of their known properties. The composers for *Tiny Toon Adventures* (1990–1992), and especially its even more popular successor *Animaniacs* (1993–1998), made a conscious effort to work within Carl Stalling's now well-known musical style for these cartoons for a new generation. This rebirth coincided with—or was possibly an extension of—an unprecedented interest in the music produced for cartoons, driven largely by *The Carl Stalling Project*, two CDs of cues and complete scores taken from the hundreds of shorts Carl Stalling scored for Warner Bros. The first disc appeared the same year (1990) as *Tiny Toon Adventures* which, driven by the runaway success of the live-action/animation hybrid *Who Framed Roger Rabbit* (Zemeckis, 1988), made several generations of Americans who had been raised on classical Hollywood animation very much aware of how much they enjoyed cartoons.

As in the classic studio era, the various production houses in the late twentieth and early twenty-first centuries take widely differing approaches to scoring cartoons. While budgetary concerns remain a key factor, certain studios have made conscious decisions about the sounds that emanate from their shows. For *The Simpsons* (1989–), like other situation comedies, much of its original music occurs between scenes. The creators of the long-running show are, however, well aware of animation's legacy with musical performance; the show has been well known for years for its musical parodies (and its parodies of musicals). The show's composer, Alf Clausen, also has the advantage of a sizable orchestra, allowing for both variance in sound/timbre and the ability to reference music of varied genres easily (films, Broadway, Nashville, etc.). As the show has progressed beyond its second decade, stories increasingly feature plots based on contemporaneous events or trends. The music once again reflects the writers' preferences; shows often feature recordings of current pop artists (REM, the White Stripes), Broadway musicals (*The Lion King, Evita*), and even entire episodes that parody film musicals (*My Fair Lady* [1964] becomes *My Fair Laddy, Mary Poppins* [1964] becomes *Simpsoncalifragilisticexpiala-D'oh-cious*, etc.).[13]

Driven by the renewed interest in animation, new networks came along—specifically, Nickelodeon (in the 1980s) and Cartoon Network (in the 1990s)—that made use of the libraries of classic Warner Bros. and MGM cartoons, helping to extend the influence of films (and their scores) then thirty to sixty years old. Both networks also eventually commissioned their own animated series, so that they could build a library of properties they would own and be able to show all the time (Simensky 2004). Two series that came about from Nickelodeon's first foray into producing new properties were

Rugrats (1991–2004) and *The Ren & Stimpy Show* (1991–1998). For the former, which showed the world from the perspective of a "bunch of babies," creators Gabor Csupo and Arlene Klasky sought out a sound that composer Mark Mothersbaugh would later recall Csupo describing as "childlike" (Goldmark 2002, 214). Using a Fairlight keyboard (the first commercial digital sampler), Mothersbaugh created the show's aural palette by sampling a toy piano. While the scores became more complex over time, the show retained its simple musical signature throughout its run. The underlying aesthetic of *Ren & Stimpy* came largely from creator John Kricfalusi's love of Hollywood animation, especially Warner Bros. cartoons, and particularly those of his mentor, Bob Clampett. Rather than opting for Carl Stalling's large orchestra approach when it came to music (which Kricfalusi could not afford), his production company Spümcø licensed inexpensive public-domain recordings of classical pieces, as well as music from Capitol Records' production library (mentioned above), the latter fitting right in to Kricfalusi's love of 1950s and 1960s pop culture and giving the cartoons a distinct feel and sound of the postwar era.

Cartoon Network's series went in diverse directions as well. Among the biggest shows the company produced during their heyday in the 1990s—*Johnny Bravo* (1997–2004), *Cow and Chicken* (1995–2004), *Courage the Cowardly Dog* (1999–2002)—probably the most enduring series came from two former students from CalArts, aka California Institute of the Arts, a well-known proving ground for future Hollywood animators. Creators and directors Genndy Tartakovsky (*Dexter's Laboratory* [1996–2003], *Samurai Jack* [2001–2004]) and Craig McCracken (*The Powerpuff Girls* [1998–2004], *Foster's Home for Imaginary Friends* [2004–2009]) both parlayed student films produced at CalArts into hugely popular series. McCracken's student film, about three sweet girls with superpowers, became the late 1990s cultural phenomenon *The Powerpuff Girls*. The combination of a standard superhero storyline with several novel twists—the heroes are a trio of young girls—as well as the strong influence of 1960s design and anime stylization makes this series particularly hybrid in nature. The music combines traditional film scoring sounds with the synthesized beats of techno dance music.

Other experiments in mainstream television cartoons, including *Family Guy* (1999–) and *The Fairly OddParents* (2001–), show how well-worn conventions of music and sound effects have been used to create their own, self-reflexive humor. These few dalliances with primatizing effects and/or music show how much Hollywood loves dialogue in its cartoons. An episode of *The Fairly OddParents*, "Pipe Down!" (2003), takes a humorous stab at notions of "typical" cartoon music. The setup is that Timmy's parents and both his fairy godparents have been yelling all day—and he's sick of it. Timmy wishes for "complete and utter silence," allowing the writers to make the lack of dialogue the entire thrust of the story. At first Timmy revels in the "mute" that has been applied worldwide, but an impending comet forces him to undo his wish by means of a hurried game of charades. What we notice when the words vanish is that the vocabulary for cartoon music and sound effects—the latter frequently executed as musical stings rather than formal sound effects—has become remarkably nuanced and value-laden; the entire story works perfectly well without dialogue.

A similar effect occurs in an episode of *Family Guy*, "Family Guy Viewer Mail #1" (2002), when Peter wishes for his own theme music. For the next few minutes, we hear a variety of perfectly executed spoofs on canned music of the 1950s, not unlike the music used in the early Hanna-Barbera cartoons. (Peter refers to the music everyone is hearing on a city bus as "classic traveling music.") Again, the humor is created in this montage of characteristic scenes (shopping, romance, depressing person on the street) through the ironic use of music that is meant to tell us subtly what is happening, yet cannot be subtle when the music is essentially a caricature of itself. The combination of visual humor and a strong soundtrack allows the director to move away from spoken language—albeit briefly (in *Fairly OddParents* the words disappear for about seven minutes; in *Family Guy* the personal soundtrack lasts for about two minutes total)—creating humor by focusing on the music and sound effects.

In the feature-film arena, Disney, having established such a successful model with their early musicals, did not change their approach to music much since the 1940s. The studio's reliance on their composers is apparent in the way the studio often groups films not in obvious historical periods, but according to the musicians—specifically, songwriters—who worked on the films. Thus, the work of the Sherman brothers in the 1960s and 1970s (*The Jungle Book* [1967], *Mary Poppins*), and that of Howard Ashman and Alan Menken (*The Little Mermaid* [1989], *Beauty and the Beast* [1991]) in the 1990s, stand out. The latter men, who had had a major success with the off-Broadway musical *The Little Shop of Horrors* in 1982, wrote the music and songs for *The Little Mermaid*, *Beauty and the Beast*, and *Aladdin* (1992). The success of these features at the box office and through video sales (an increasingly important standard by which films came to be judged) helped to repopularize the notion of the animated film musical, which had been more or less abandoned in the late 1960s, after *The Jungle Book* and, not coincidentally, after Walt Disney's death in 1966.

CONCLUSION

The story regarding music for Hollywood animation might end here if not for the galvanizing effect that Pixar has had on the entire world of cartoons. The Pixar features make use of well-known Hollywood *feature film* composers (Randy Newman, Thomas Newman, and Michael Giacchino) and have deliberately avoided making a musical in the Disney mold (all the more ironic considering Disney has owned Pixar since 2006). The scores for these films are as rich, provoking, and complex as any live-action Hollywood film and yet still (occasionally) dip into some good old-fashioned cartoonisms, with bits of mickey-mousing or none-too-subtle links between a gag and a song on the soundtrack adding a bit of semiconscious humor. The Pixar shorts are far more diversified in terms of composers, sporting everyone from jazz and pop artists (Bobby McFerrin, Gus Viseur, Riders in the Sky) to more mainstream composers (J. A. C. Redford, Michael Giacchino, Scot Stafford). The scores also run the gamut of styles, from pop songs and cool jazz to scores drawing on (or parodying) standard Hollywood fare for sci-fi, comedy, and drama. The studio presents an excellent foil to the long-engrained belief that Hollywood animation could mean only Disney by showing not only how directors have continued to find new stories to tell and new ways to tell them—as shorts or features—but also that composers continue to find unusual and innovative means to amplify the emotions and ideas in these films through choices in music and sound.

APPENDIX

ARCHIVAL MATERIALS

Archival work in cartoon music can be especially challenging. As with feature-film music of the Golden Age, most major studios have either kept their scores in studio files or disposed of or destroyed the scores long ago (particularly common with cartoons due to their perceived transitory nature, like serials or other short subjects). Several important collections do exist, however, including:

Music Special Collections, University of California, Los Angeles
Scores for Walter Lantz cartoons by Darrell Calker, Frank Churchill, Walter Greene, James Dietrich, Frank Marsales, Eugene Poddany, Clarence Wheeler

New York University
Scores for Disney by Buddy Baker

University of Cincinnati
Leigh Harline papers (*Pinocchio*)

University of Oregon, Special Collections
George Steiner: Rocky & Bullwinkle/Dudley Do-Right

University of Southern California
Scores for Warner Bros. by Carl Stalling and Milt Franklyn.
Scott Bradley papers (including scores for MGM cartoons)

University of Wyoming, American Heritage Center
Carl Stalling papers (including scores for Warner Bros., Disney, Iwerks cartoons)
Scott Bradley papers (MGM cartoons)
Michael Maltese papers (including materials related to Warner Bros., MGM cartoons)

NOTES

1. For two highly effective (and very different) takes on the "Golden Age" of Hollywood animation (roughly 1928–1958), see Maltin 1987 and Barrier 1999.
2. Kristin Thompson (1980) does an excellent job explaining some of the historical trends that led to animation as being seen as "just for kids."
3. Spoken by Chester J. Lampwick in "The Day the Violence Died," episode 3F16, *The Simpsons*, original airdate March 17, 1996.

4. Sartin 1998 discusses the influence of musical revue films on the early cartoon output from Warner Bros.

5. Wilfred Jackson, the musical director for *Steamboat Willie*, recalled that Disney and Stalling disagreed vociferously about how much a role music should have in the early Mickeys (Barrier 2007, 68).

6. The Bouncing Ball cartoons were supposedly created at the instigation of Tin Pan Alley composer Charles K. Harris, as he recalled in his autobiography, *After the Ball* (1926, 365).

7. Other studios certainly had songs published based on their characters, but none ever reached the popularity of "Who's Afraid of the Big Bad Wolf"—perhaps because none of those songs tapped so well into the nation's collective psyche at a time of crisis (one explanation of the popularity of "Big Bad Wolf"). One exception might be "Der Fuehrer's Face," recorded by Spike Jones & His City Slickers (1942). Most of these songs never shrugged off the monicker of "novelty song," although "The Woody Woodpecker Song" did receive an unlikely nomination for an Academy Award for Best Song of the Year in 1948 (Maltin 1987, 172).

8. Another musical tidbit about this short is that it was orchestrated and arranged by Carl Stalling, who had left the studio in 1930 but continued to do freelance work for several years. His piano playing can also be heard when Practical Pig sits at his piano made of bricks (what else?) to accompany (and dramatize) the wolf's attempts to gain entry (Barrier 2002, 47).

9. Harline went on to write music for dozens of live-action features. See Care 1977.

10. The animation for the sequence went through numerous conceptualizations, most famously one created by pioneering animator Oskar Fischinger (Culhane 1983, 36–43; Barrier 1999, 254).

11. See Barrier 1999, 501–532; Maltin 1987, 323–342.

12. The Capitol library cues would receive a self-reflexive nod in the early 1990s in John Kricfalusi's *The Ren & Stimpy Show*, where they would be used as nostalgic kitsch, and again (with an even more obvious reference to the past) in Kricfalusi's two takes on the hi-jinks at Jellystone Park, through the eyes of Ranger Smith (*A Day in the Life of Ranger Smith* and *Boo Boo Runs Wild*, both 1999).

13. *Family Guy*, another Fox animated sitcom (which is especially derivative of *The Simpsons*), has also parodied a variety of musicals.

Bibliography

Altman, Rick. 1987. *The American Film Musical*. Bloomington: Indiana University Press

Barrier, Michael. 1999. *Hollywood Cartoons: American Animation in Its Golden Age*. New York: Oxford University Press.

——. 2002. "An Interview With Carl Stalling." In *The Cartoon Music Book*, edited by Daniel Goldmark and Yuval Taylor, 37–60. Chicago: A Cappella.

——. 2007. *The Animated Man: A Life of Walt Disney*. Berkeley: University of California Press.

Care, Ross. 1977. "The Film Music of Leigh Harline." *Film Music Notebook* 3, no. 2: 32–48.

——. 1985. "Threads of Melody: The Evolution of a Major Film Score—Walt Disney's *Bambi*." In *Wonderful Inventions: Motion Pictures, Broadcasting, and Recorded Sound at the Library of Congress*, edited by Iris Newsom, 81–115. Washington, DC: Library of Congress.

Cohen, Thomas F. 2009. "The Click Track: The Business of Time: Metronomes, Movie Scores and Mickey Mousing." In *Sound and Music in Film and Visual Media: An Overview*, edited by Graeme Harper, Ruth Doughty, and Jochen Eisentraut, 100–113. New York: Continuum.

Culhane, John. 1983. *Walt Disney's Fantasia*. New York: Abradale.

Goldmark, Daniel. 2002. "An Interview with Mark Mothersbaugh." In *The Cartoon Music Book*, edited by Daniel Goldmark and Yuval Taylor, 207–217. Chicago: A Cappella.

——. 2005. *Tunes for 'Toons: Music and the Hollywood Cartoon*. Berkeley: University of California Press.

Handzo, Stephan. 1985. "Appendix: A Narrative Glossary of Film Sound Technology." In *Film Sound: Theory and Practice*, edited by Elisabeth Weis and John Belton, 383–426. New York: Columbia University Press.

Harris, Charles K. 1926. *After the Ball, Forty Years of Melody: An Autobiography*. New York: Frank-Maurice.

Heylbut, Rose. 1940. "The Music of the Walt Disney Cartoons: A Conference with Paul J. Smith." *Etude* 58 (July): 494.

Maltin, Leonard. 1987. *Of Mice and Magic*. Revised edition. New York: Plume.

Mandell, Paul. 2002. "Production Music in Television's Golden Age: An Overview." In *Performing Arts: Broadcasting*, edited by Iris Newsom, 148–169. Washington, DC: Library of Congress.

Newsom, Jon. 1980. "'A Sound Idea': Music for Animated Films." *Quarterly Journal of the Library of Congress* 37, nos. 3–4: 279–309.

Prendergast, Roy M. 1977. *Film Music: A Neglected Art*. New York: Norton.

Sartin, Hank. 1998. "From Vaudeville to Hollywood, from Silence to Sound: Warner Bros. Cartoons of the Early Sound Era." In *Reading the Rabbit: Explorations in Warner Bros. Animation*, edited by Kevin S. Sandler, 67–85. New Brunswick, NJ: Rutgers University Press.

Simensky, Linda. 2004. "The Early Days of Nicktoons." In *Nickelodeon Nation: The History, Politics, and Economics of America's Only TV Channel for Kids*, edited by Heather Hendershot, 87–107. New York: New York University Press.

Small, Christopher. 1998. *Musicking: The Meanings of Performing and Listening*. Hanover, NH: Wesleyan University Press.

Steele, R. Vernon. 1937. "'Fairyland Goes Hollywood': An Interview with Leigh Harline." *Pacific Coast Musician* 26 (November 20): 10.

Thompson, Kristin. 1980. "Implications of the Cel Animation Technique." In *The Cinematic Apparatus*, edited by Teresa de Laurentis and Stephen Heath, 106–120. New York: St. Martin's.

Thompson, Kristin, and David Bordwell. 1994. *Film History: An Introduction*. New York: McGraw-Hill.

CHAPTER 9

GENRE THEORY AND THE FILM MUSICAL

CARI MCDONNELL

THE Hollywood musical is now among a handful of the most frequently discussed classical genres in the film studies literature, but that level of attention is a relatively recent phenomenon. As late as 1981, Rick Altman published an edited anthology of essays in order to make up for what he saw as a long-standing lack of critical scrutiny. The approaches used by contributors to that volume represented, in Altman's words, "most of the important currents of film criticism" at the time: "the auteur 'theory', ideological concerns, structuralist analysis, the ritual function of entertainment, [and] the contribution of technology" (Altman 1981, 4). Several of the book's essays have since become the cornerstones upon which an academic body of work on the film musical has been built: gender politics in the films of Busby Berkeley (Lucy Fischer), utopianism of the musical in its cultural context (Richard Dyer), narrative structure (Altman), and entertainment myths fostered by the musical (Jane Feuer).

This chapter will survey the principal topic areas in the study of the film musical, but it is also intended to set out the consequences of a historically lopsided critical attention and thereby to encourage work that would delve into some underrepresented areas, which include: (1) the style, structure, and specific musical makeup of performance numbers; (2) the relationship between character and star persona in the musical; and (3) the genre's relationship with the popular music industry and the star system.

To prepare the ground for discussion of the central issue in the critical literature—integration, or a bias toward musicals that approach the characteristics of a typical dramatic feature film—we must first address the broader question of film genre, because studies of the musical are mostly grounded in studies of genre. This chapter is therefore divided into six sections, the first of which summarizes relevant issues in genre theory within the film studies discipline. Four subsequent sections focus on how the classical Hollywood musical has been depicted in the scholarly literature and offer a critique of the historical narrative of the integrated musical, the repertoire with which almost all published work concerns itself.[1] The final section of the chapter suggests ways to achieve a more comprehensive view of the genre, especially through work in the underrepresented areas listed above.

DEFINING GENRE: THEORY AND HISTORY

As Frans de Bruyn puts it, genre is "one of the most ancient theoretical concepts in the history of criticism," but because it "raises fundamental questions about the nature and status of literary texts, there are perhaps as many definitions of 'genre' as there are theories of literature" (1993, 79). Starting with Aristotle's *Poetics*, the idea of organizing literature around stable categories according to shared characteristics of performance, textual properties, or use was a given for historians and critics:[2] it met serious opposition only in the early nineteenth century from the individualist-minded Romantics, whose dialectical relationship with existing genres quickly became intertwined with a distinction between high and low art. After the mid-twentieth century, this model became closely linked to ideological critique, to the point that genre was considered out of date or irrelevant compared to questions of identity and representation. By this time, however, semiotics and discourse studies had undermined the Romantic critique of genre by showing that individuals use generic categories as devices fundamental to communication, far beyond their status as tools for high-art or political criticism. As Fabbri and Shepherd put it, speaking specifically with reference to music, "categorizing and naming 'kinds', referring to established genres or inventing new ones" are processes that "form the basis for all human knowledge" (Fabbri and Shepherd 2003, 402).

In terms of their treatment in the scholarly literature, film texts and the repertoire of the cinema, especially feature films, are understood to be closely analogous to novels and similar literary products, and thus questions of genre inevitably arise. In addition to his well-known work on the musical, Altman is also one of the most prolific writers on film genre theory. In order to discuss the various aspects and issues involved, he has often used colorful examples, ranging from animal taxonomy (Altman 1987, 8–12; 1998, 16–17) to sports (1987, 349–50; 1999, 192–93), trips to Walt Disney World (1999, 101–2) and to the supermarket (1999, 113–15), and memorably, a stop by the nut aisle (1999, 96–99). Some of the classifications that result have clear criteria, as for example in animal taxonomy (1998, 16). Mammals and fish are clearly distinguished from each other based on specific characteristics; some may share living space, such as whales and sharks, but their generic classifications are mutually exclusive. It is possible for the boundary between two species to be unclear, but no organism can be both mammal and fish. Not all classifications—and by extension not all genres—are so clearly defined, however. Altman uses sports to discuss genre film spectatorship (he says both are based on "constellated communities, existing without physical interaction among fans" [Altman 1999, 192]). Unlike large animals, sports can be classified according to a variety of criteria. Games can be divided into winter and summer sports, for example, as in the Olympics. Basketball will be found in categories such as sports that use a ball, team sports, sports that involve scoring, sports played on a court, and both amateur and professional sports. Institutions use sports genres differently based on their institutional goals. The NCAA, a governing institution, looks at a university's sports programs in terms of men's and women's sports and individual and team sports, whereas a sporting goods retail store defines sports genres according to the merchandise and equipment needed. Unlike the NCAA, retail stores use categories based on gender only when the equipment necessarily differs, as in apparel, footwear, or golf clubs. The differentiation between team and individual sports is rarely relevant in such a store.

If animal taxonomy and sports are taken as the two options, it is clear that film genres are much more like the latter than the former—that is to say, films should not be regarded as having a proper generic identity that needs only to be discovered (an essentialist view), but as capable of being classified in many different ways (a functionalist view). From the screenwriter to the advertising copy writer to the media store manager, everyone connected in some way to the film industry uses genre categories, but because the needs of these users vary, there can be no consensus as to what determines a film genre: as in sports, genres in film can feasibly have any number of things as their defining characteristics. The Academy of Motion Picture Arts and Sciences, to cite the example of one prominent institution, uses categories for their annual awards based on length (feature length versus short subject), medium (animated versus live-action), language, and even literary class (fiction versus nonfiction). The definitions are functional and utilitarian.

Scholars have shown that such multiplicity is of long standing in the history of the film industry. Both Tino Balio (1993) and Thomas Schatz (1988, 1997) explain that, for studio executives in the 1930s and 1940s, films were grouped according to their budgetary needs, markers that in turn dictated a particular set of filmmaking personnel and also determined the marketing strategy. Schatz demonstrates that at MGM, the most consistently successful company during the studio era, executives usually categorized films according to "star units," or star vehicles that required budgets of a particular size. Advertising personnel in the studio era also made extensive use of genre, as Steve Neale (2003) and Rick Altman (1998) have shown. Neale points to generic iconography present in studio-era movie advertisements, and Altman uses both the language and iconography in these ads to call attention to the range of genres often present there.

Janet Staiger (2003) finds this kind of multiplicity in film reviews as well. For the advertisers, at least one goal of the generic discourse was to draw attention to the many relationships a particular film might have with other financially successful films and filmmaking patterns. In a straightforward example, the poster advertisement for the 1937 MGM picture *Captains Courageous* uses imagery appropriate for a child-focused nautical adventure story, while the text links the film to MGM's 1935 Oscar-winning drama *Mutiny on the Bounty*. The generic identification is not enough to ensure audience interest; the advertisement must also link the film with another similar successful film.

Finally, Lincoln Geraghty and Mark Jancovich have demonstrated that filmmakers even exploited generic language in order to please censors while still appealing to exhibitors. They offer as an example MGM's 1941 release *Dr. Jekyll and Mr. Hyde*, which was presented to the Production Code Administration as a literary adaptation while being pitched to exhibitors as "horror, melodrama or romance"—whichever "draws best at your box office" (Geraghty and Jancovich 2008, 4–5).

Altman (1999) and Andrew Tudor (1973) both assert that scholars often have in mind a "predefined genre and corpus [of films]" (Altman 1999, 24) when they begin doing genre analysis. Geraghty and Jancovich characterize this predetermined group of films as "key works that are either claimed to be the artistic high points, the markers of key shifts within historical development, or are taken to represent key features, periods or tendencies within the genre" (Geraghty and Jancovich 2008, 1)—or virtually the definition of "canon," which can thus be understood as a slice through the possible generic categories that includes only the best in each. The vast majority of these "key works" discussed by scholars are what industry executives would have classified as prestige pictures or A-class pictures, the films with the largest budgets and most extensive advertising campaigns. Low-budget and B-class films have tended to garner attention mainly from amateur scholars and tradebook writers, rather than from academics—a curious thing, perhaps, considering these films were so numerous and were often extremely formulaic, a trait that should make generic definition easy. It may, of course, be exactly that ease of definition that limits interest for the academic scholar, yet the potential rewards can be substantial, as Peter Stanfield has demonstrated with his thorough study of 1930s Hollywood Westerns (Stanfield 2001) and John Mundy with his look at the dance-craze films of the early 1960s (Mundy 2006). Defining a genre in terms of a predefined group of films, however, clearly suffers from circularity: a set of films believed to be Westerns or musicals or gangster films becomes the basis for defining an entire genre that may consist of hundreds of films (Tudor 1973, 135). A tendency to define genres according to aesthetic criteria—that is, aspects of representation, both visual and aural, as well as those of characterization, narrative logic, and plot structure—compounds the problem: conclusions drawn from analysis of a small group of A-class films are at best too narrow to be applied to other films that could be considered part of the genre and at worst a misrepresentation of the genre (Neale 2000, 207–30).

Staiger (2003), Neale (2000), and Altman (1998, 1999) all point to the problems that arise in historical accounts of film genres based on such criteria. Staiger argues that much of genre theory has created a "purity thesis," the assumption that classical Hollywood ("Fordian Hollywood," in Staiger's terminology) created generically pure films. Sampling critical methods often used by genre theorists, she demonstrates that these films "do not provide clean examples of the critically defined genre" and that "historically, no justification exists to assume producers, distributors, exhibitors, or audiences saw films as being 'purely' one type of film" (Staiger 2003, 194–95). Neale makes very similar claims, saying that genre theory has "constructed a series of misleading pictures of Hollywood's output," focusing on "exemplary films," however defined, and ignoring both the majority of Hollywood films and the way in which these films were produced, distributed, and consumed (Neale 2000, 251–55). Altman (1998) recognizes the kinds of problems identified by Staiger and Neale, but he approaches the issues differently. In discussions of film genres, critics and scholars tend to use generic terms as if they had fixed, ahistorical meanings, instead of recognizing that generic terms often had different meanings to filmmakers and audiences at different points in time. Altman's awareness of the multiple meanings and multiple users of genres and generic terms leads him to define genre as an ongoing discourse rather than a fixed category: critics and scholars participate equally with filmmakers, audiences, and others in the "genrification" process, by which genres become confirmed and defined. Despite the evident difficulties, Staiger, Neale, and Altman all encourage further work in genre studies—specifically, work that takes into account the historical and industrial realities of Hollywood films as well as the multiple uses and users of generic terms.

DEFINING THE FILM MUSICAL AS A GENRE: (1) DIFFERING VIEWS

Many scholars find definitive aesthetic characteristics of the musical by examining the genre's stage-bound historical influences. Raymond Knapp (2005, 19–63), for example, has mapped sources from mid-nineteenth-century European operetta to early twentieth-century American stage entertainments (vaudeville, burlesque, pantomime, among others).[3] Neale's brief survey of the film musical (2000) is divided into subgenres, many of which are based on these theatrical influences, and Jerome Delamater (1978) and Knapp (2005; 2006) incorporate discussions of the stylistic influences of these historical predecessors into their studies of dance and identity in the musical, respectively. Richard Traubner (1983), Gerald Mast (1987), James Collins (1988), and Sean Griffin (2002) all differentiate between narrative-focused musical dramas that find their roots in opera and operetta, on the one hand, and more episodic musical comedies that descend from burlesque, the variety show, and vaudeville, on the other. Traubner's thorough study of operetta points to the narrative-focused musical or the "musical play," which he says is "a euphemism for romantic operetta" (Traubner 1983, 377), as the primary heir of the operetta tradition in twentieth-century America, epitomized by the stage and film works of Jerome Kern, Oscar Hammerstein II, and Richard Rodgers. In his brief study, Griffin provides insight into the racial politics of the film musical by examining the episodic, variety show-influenced musical comedies of 20th Century Fox that continued to thrive in cinemas alongside the musical dramas of studios such as MGM.[4]

Other scholars focus more on the structure and narrative content of the film musical, defining it based largely on textual analyses of numerous films. Schatz (1981), Altman (1981, 1987), Jane Feuer (1993), and Richard Dyer (1981) all argue that the musical's narrative structure attempts to resolve two diametrically opposed poles. These poles may be represented by the male and female members of a romantic couple (Schatz; Altman), work and entertainment (Altman; Feuer; Dyer), narrative and number (Dyer), performers and spectators (Feuer), or fantasy and reality (Feuer; Dyer).

Altman's and Schatz's focus on the romantic couple works well for many musicals, but, as Altman admits, does exclude a substantial number of films, particularly child-focused titles such as *The Wizard of Oz* (1939), *Dumbo* (1941), and *Mary Poppins* (1964) (Altman 1987, 103–6). Neale questions the prevalence of Altman's genre-defining dual-focus romance narrative and observes that it is also a structural element of the nonmusical romantic comedy (Neale 2000, 112). Neale suggests that the romance-musical is not the only type, but rather just one place (or node) where the musical intersects with another genre. Knapp's discussion of the fairy-tale musical, one of Altman's three subgenres, shows that this type of genre intersection is not an isolated case (Knapp 2006, 121–63). Knapp argues that in their stage-bound forms operetta and fairy tale are two separate entities that can, but do not always, share generic characteristics. Not all operettas, with their penchant for "contrived happy endings" and "sexually charged intrigue," are fairy tales, and not all fairy tales, which often feature magical happenings and child protagonists, are operettas. Knapp asserts that Altman "simply conflates the two, thereby essentializing the 'happily ever after' component of operetta," while leaving out many of the child- and fantasy-oriented aspects of the fairy tale (Knapp 2006, 121). In Knapp's view, Altman's fairy tale musicals are more operetta than fairy tale, which "has almost no presence within the broader category that bears that name in Altman's typology" (Knapp 2006, 396). Altman himself observes that films such as *Pinocchio* (1940), *Dumbo* (1941), and *Alice in Wonderland* (1951) are indeed part of a group of films that "borrows heavily from a widely shared European fairy tale tradition" (Altman 1987, 105), yet he excludes them from the fairy tale musical subgenre and even from the musical genre writ large because they do not correspond with his romance-focused definition.

Dyer (1981) uses dualities effectively to argue that the musical promises utopian solutions to real-world problems. Feuer (1993), Schatz (1981), and Altman (1987) imply that the musical's utopianism is generally uncomplicated and usually fulfilled by the film's end, but Kenneth MacKinnon (2000) argues that what endures long after the film's finale is the sense of longing for utopia, rather than a sense of fulfillment. Dyer (2000), Griffin (2002), and Kelly Kessler (2010), among scholars who focus on the presentation and participation of race and gender in musicals, each take a more skeptical view, questioning not only the strength of the utopian fulfillment, but also the race and gender constitution of that utopia.[5]

The narrative/number duality is perhaps the most prevalent issue in scholarship on the musical. Although, as we shall see, the narrative side of the equation is the principal site for theoretical and critical discussion, the number (musical performances) has also garnered some analytical attention from scholars. Altman's development of the concept of the audio dissolve (fluid shift from the diegetic to a layering of diegetic and nondiegetic musical elements) does offer key insights into the way the soundtrack accomplishes the transition from narrative to number (Altman 1987, 62–74), but he limits his discussions of the musical numbers to general remarks about style and narrative content. Feuer offers a bit more insight insofar as she delineates a few techniques, such as bricolage, folk choreography, and the passed-along song, that are often used to make the performances seem more spontaneous and natural (Feuer 1993, 1–22). Richard

Barrios (1995), Mast (1987), Geoffrey Block (2002), and Timothy Scheurer (1974) discuss the general styles of the songwriters and lyricists responsible for the music in these films. Barrios, Schatz (1997, 2010), and Griffin all describe individual studios' and filmmakers' signature styles, with general remarks about musical and performance styles. Scheurer, Greg Faller (1987), Delamater, and John Mueller (1984, 1985) all examine the use and style of dance in musicals, though only Delamater and Mueller discuss music in conjunction with specific dance numbers. Knapp (2005, 2006) and Mast use analyses of specific songs to inform and add depth to their expansive studies. On a smaller scale, Heather Laing's work demonstrates how music analysis can form a strong basis for critical study as she argues that the structure of the musical number, relying heavily on the essential structural elements of the popular song, "[allows] a particular representation of emotional, physical, and formal excess," all of which is safely confined within the formal boundaries of the popular song so that the excess only temporarily disrupts the film's narrative (Laing 2000, 10).[6]

Defining the Film Musical as a Genre: (2) Privileging Integration

If only a relatively small number of scholars have examined the detailed makeup of the musical number, nearly everyone discusses how numbers are related to narrative. For most authors, integration refers to the relationship of the number to the development of plot and character. With this idea in mind, Mueller outlines six types of integration, ranging from "numbers which are completely irrelevant to the plot," through "numbers which enrich the plot, but do not advance it," to "numbers which advance the plot by their content" (Mueller 1984, 28–30). His list is comprehensive, but the wording, ordering, and ensuing discussion reveal his belief that the best performance numbers are those that are fully integrated, that "advance the plot by their content." Mueller uses his list to argue for a more sophisticated view of Fred Astaire's musicals—a sophistication born out of the highest level of integration. Schatz (1981), Collins, and Delamater all reinforce both the hierarchy of the narratively integrated musical and the idea of Fred Astaire as progenitor of this ideal, focusing on Astaire's innovative use of dance in his films with Ginger Rogers at RKO. Schatz, for example, has an entire section devoted to the topic of "Fred Astaire and the rise of the integrated musical" (Schatz 1981, 191–93), and Delamater argues for Astaire to be considered as an auteur performer (Delamater 1978, 51).

In a manner similar to histories of great men in politics, literature, and the arts, studies that champion the integrated musical have traced a history of the musical film that privileges star personae such as Judy Garland, Fred Astaire, and Gene Kelly; auteur filmmakers such as Busby Berkeley, Stanley Donen, and Vincent Minnelli; legendary composers and lyricists such as Rodgers and Hammerstein or Lerner and Loewe; and even "auteur" studios and production units (notably, RKO and the MGM Freed Unit).[7] After a nod to predecessors in stage-bound forms of entertainment, this historical narrative typically presents the Astaire/Rogers films of RKO as ushering in a new type of musical in the early1930s through performance numbers that arise from dramatic contexts—numbers usually designed and choreographed by Astaire himself. The prototype of these integrated numbers is "Night and Day" from *The Gay Divorcee* (1934), in which Astaire's character (Guy Holden) gradually wins Rogers's (Mimi Glossup's) affections. In this way narrative integration finds its way out of the old European stylings of operetta and into the distinctly American musical comedy.

Taking another place in this history during the 1930s are the Busby Berkeley productions, which are considered the quintessential backstage musicals. In the backstage musical the performances, which rarely have anything to do with the film's plot, are sufficiently motivated by the fact that the characters are all show people involved in putting on some kind of live entertainment. Though these films are not considered part of the evolution toward the fully integrated musical, they are included in the canon largely due to their innovative visual style and because Berkeley's name continues to pop up in subsequent decades, though few of his later films are discussed by scholars in any detail.

Judy Garland's star ascends in the 1940s at MGM, as does Gene Kelly's. They appear together in Kelly's first film, *For Me and My Gal* (1942), directed by Berkeley, and again in *The Pirate* (1948), directed by Vincent Minnelli. All of these films are discussed often in the literature, but the Garland/Minnelli production that is considered a cornerstone of the integrated musical is *Meet Me in St. Louis* (1944). Described by Altman as a folk musical (1987, 274), the film takes place in a comfortable neighborhood of family homes at the turn of the twentieth century—nowhere near a night club or professional theater. Thus, even the diegetic performances, such as Garland's "Skip to My Lou" and Garland and Margaret O'Brien's "Under the Bamboo Tree," are presented as somehow integrated into the dramatic narrative of a family facing a move to a distant large city and the threat of an end of their happy way of life.

Gene Kelly helps bring the integrated musical into the 1950s, starring in hits like *On the Town* (1949), which he codirected with Stanley Donen, Minnelli's *An American in Paris* (1951) and *Singin' in the Rain* (1952), again codirecting with Donen. Whereas Astaire usually portrays a seasoned professional in his films, Kelly tends to portray an amateur who makes music out of his expressive energy, as in *On the Town* and *An American in Paris*. Even *Singin' in the Rain* counteracts Kelly's role as a silent film star by presenting most of his musical performances not in a rehearsed professional setting, but in spontaneous moments of light-hearted fun ("Moses Supposes"), sudden joy ("Good Morning"), and romantic love ("You Were Meant for Me," "Singin' in the Rain," and the final reprise of "You Are My Lucky Star"). These MGM films of the early 1950s also represent attempts to move the musical toward the realm of high art. Both Astaire and Kelly partner with ballet-trained dancers such as Cyd Charisse and Leslie Caron. Astaire's graceful tap-dancing style remains the same with all his partners, but Kelly increasingly uses elements of ballet and modern dance in his film performances. If MGM's appeal to the realm of high art is not made clear enough by these elements, Minnelli also references stylistic highlights of French painting in *An American in Paris*.

The integrated musical continues to dominate the rest of the decade primarily through the film adaptations of Rodgers and Hammerstein's stage hits. *Oklahoma!*, staged in 1943 and adapted to film in 1955, is considered by many musical theater scholars as the apotheosis of the integrated stage musical. As a film adaptation it has its flaws, but it is still considered a highly integrated dramatic musical, due in large part to the use of folk stylings in many of the songs and dances. At the same time, Agnes de Mille's dream ballet, choreographed in the modern dance style, represents yet another attempt to push the musical genre toward high art.

The later Rodgers and Hammerstein film musicals reveal a shift, or possibly a division, in the priorities of the integrated musical, away from the abstract world of high art and toward the realism of dramatic narrative film. The team continued to have success with film adaptations such as *The King and I* (1956) and *South Pacific* (1958).[8] These films more overtly address social problems such as racism and sexism. It is *The Sound of Music* (1965), however, that is considered by many scholars to be the best and most dramatically integrated of their film adaptations, notably with more changes made to the musical score in the adaptation process than any previous Rodgers and Hammerstein production. The cinematic realism of the location sets (as opposed to the abstract sets of *An American in Paris* or the theatrical sets of *Oklahoma!*) provides one of this musical's strongest links to nonmusical dramatic narrative film. As in those two earlier adaptations, *The Sound of Music* also presents a potentially less idealistic plot, with the unhappy resolution of the secondary romance (Liesl and Rolfe) and the somewhat open ending as the Von Trapp family become refugees in a foreign country. These films are certainly still quite optimistic, but they do not follow the typical plot formulas of films such as the Astaire/Rogers/RKO cycle, nor do they offer the contrived happy endings of *Meet Me in St. Louis* or *An American in Paris*.

These are the highlights of the historical narrative of the integrated musical in the classical Hollywood era. *The Sound of Music* is generally considered to be the last, dying breath of the integrated musical as the genre either moves toward the darker, more pessimistic films of Bob Fosse and Robert Altman or is eclipsed by the teen-focused rock and roll films of Elvis Presley and other recording stars.

DECENTERING THE INTEGRATED MUSICAL

Although scholars' descriptions of the films mentioned above are generally accurate and often insightful, many of the conclusions drawn from studying this canon can be misleading, primarily because the sample is small and unrepresentative but also because ties to canons and model films remain mostly unexamined. In Neale's words, priority to integration "has tended to produce a canonic crest-line, a tradition of landmark films, shows and personnel" in the history of the development of the film musical (Neale

2000, 106–7). Altman dubs this the "proper noun history" of the American musical film, which, he says, "tends to exclude from consideration all those films not associated with a canonized proper noun" (Altman 1987, 111–12).[9] Those scholars who have resisted narrative integration as the determining aspect of the genre have usually done so by organizing their studies in terms of chronology, ideology, or subgenre—avoiding focus on names (directors, composers, actors) whenever possible. Though Barrios's introduction reiterates the traditional belief in the integrated musical, his comprehensive chronological study of pre-Depression musical films focuses primarily on film production, reception, and style rather than on a canon of names. Both Feuer and Knapp organize their studies by ideological concepts. Feuer does not stray outside the canon in her sample of films, but Knapp adds Disney fairy-tale musicals, a group of films routinely ignored in the academic literature, to his analytical repertoire, which includes a wide range of stage musicals with film adaptations. As mentioned above, Neale's brief survey of the genre is organized loosely by subgenres such as operetta, musical comedy, musical drama, and the rock musical. Bruce Babington and Peter Evans (1985) are haphazard in their approach to subgenres, identifying such content- and setting-defined groups as "the musical biopic" and "the pastoral musical" as well as traditional proper-noun groups such as "the Astaire-Rogers musical" and even mixed categories such as "Minnelli and the introspective musical."

Altman's expansive study (1987) is also organized by subgenres, but despite his insight into the historical problems of the focus on integration, he inadvertently reinforces this history. Though his subgenres (the fairy-tale musical, the show musical, and the folk musical) are useful, well-defined typological categories, they are essentially based on settings and plot formulas that, as discussed above, emphasize a particular set of oppositions that must be resolved through the workings of a dual-focus narrative. Not only does he eliminate from his corpus those films that do not revolve around a central romance, but his discussions assume that performances must be integrated since they help mediate essential plot conflicts.

Another way scholars resist privileging the integrated musical is by using film history rather than, or in conjunction with, theoretical models of genre. Faller (1987), Griffin (2002), and Shari Roberts (2002), grounding their work in film reception and star studies, argue that the nonintegrated Hollywood musical was important because it allowed star personae, especially those of minority performers, to take center stage. Even Delamater, a champion of the integrated musical, notes this phenomenon in connection with Eleanor Powell: "Few attempts were made to integrate her dances into the narrative, for the dances represented an aggressive individuality which was the Powell persona. The stylistic consistency of her work manifested that persona in all her roles" (Delamater 1978, 77–78).

Delamater's statement about the consistency of Powell's star persona could be said of many musical stars. Todd Decker uses archival evidence to argue that Astaire in fact considered himself a song-and-dance man first and foremost, and he presented that persona both on and off screen (Decker 2011). Decker argues that Astaire never worried about integrating his performances into the surrounding plot and focused exclusively on creating, performing, and filming his performance numbers. Any subsequent narrative integration was simply a matter of course (Decker 2011, 53–71). Steven Cohan also uses evidence of Astaire's star persona to argue that his performances were part of a uniquely gendered spectacle that often superseded and directed the narrative, challenging traditional notions of integration that place the musical number in subservience to the plot (Cohan 2002a). Evidence of a recognizable Astaire persona even shows up in studies that tend toward privileging integrated musicals. Both Feuer and Altman regularly refer to Astaire by his real name, rather than his character name, in their film analyses. They also note Astaire's trademark technique of moving seamlessly from non-dancing (usually walking) into dancing (Feuer 1981, 113–17; Altman 1987, 67). Delamater remarks that Astaire and Rogers's "foot-loose and easy-going personae" seemed to be the impetus behind every aspect of their films—so much so that, as noted earlier, he suggests the idea of "a possible theory of performer as auteur," with Astaire as author (Delamater 1978, 51–52).

Feuer's overview of the musical careers of Astaire and Garland strengthens the argument that their star personae often overshadowed any attempt at character portrayal in their films (Feuer 1981, 113–22). Deanna Durbin, Shirley Temple, Betty Grable, Mickey Rooney, Bing Crosby, and many other musical stars also had star personae that tended to overwhelm whatever fictional character they were playing in their films. One major reason for this is the prevalence of star-genre formulas in classical Hollywood. According to Schatz, "each studio's stable of contract stars and its repertoire of presold genre variations were its most visible and viable resources" (1997, 43). Studios operated under the belief that the presentation of stars was at least as important as any narrative formula in a genre film.

In addition to other signature star-genre cycles, most of the major and minor studios in Hollywood had a musical cycle whose star neared the top of the box office polls at some point during the studio era. In the 1930s Fox starred Shirley Temple in a series of musicals, many of which were based on classic children's stories (such as *Heidi* [1937] and *The Little Princess* [1939]). In 1933, Paramount signed Bing Crosby, by far the most bankable radio and film star from the 1930s through the mid-1950s. In addition to the occasional dramatic film, the studio starred him in dozens of musicals held together primarily by comic bits and Crosby's signature crooning. Also in 1933, RKO stumbled upon the fortuitous pairing of Astaire and Rogers in *Flying Down to Rio* and featured them in eight more films in the 1930s. Starting in the mid-1930s Universal starred Deanna Durbin in several films that featured the classical singing abilities of the teenaged ingenue (notably *One Hundred Men and a Girl* [1937], about the daughter of an orchestral musician). In a move similar to that of Paramount with Crosby, Republic capitalized on Gene Autry's radio popularity beginning in 1935 by creating a highly profitable series of singing cowboy films starring Autry as himself. These were some of the best-known, highest-grossing box office stars of the 1930s (to be discussed in detail in the next section below).

In the late 1930s and early 1940s MGM adapted some of the popular Hardy family films into musicals that featured established favorite Mickey Rooney and, in several, the ascending starlet Judy Garland (*Love Finds Andy Hardy* [1938] being the best known). The pair also starred in a cycle of kids-putting-on-a-show films during this time. One of the most prolific producers of musicals, MGM also developed a series of immensely popular operettas for established star Jeanette MacDonald and newcomer Nelson Eddy. In both pairings the settings and character names change from film to film, but the characterizations and general style of the films remain consistent throughout the cycle. At Fox in the 1940s, as Shirley Temple's box-office value faded, Betty Grable rose from popular costar and pin-up girl to full-fledged star. Her films, such as *Down Argentine Way* (1940) and *Mother Wore Tights* (1947), did not have the consistency of plot and character that marked many other musical star-genre formulas, but they provided Grable with ample opportunity to showcase her million-dollar legs and her song and dance skills in diegetic performances that usually took place in nightclubs or theatrical revues.

Along with Grable, Crosby continued to dominate the list of the top box office stars year after year. Beginning in 1940, Paramount teamed Crosby with comedian Bob Hope and the exotically beautiful Dorothy Lamour in the enormously successful Road movies, the first of which was *Road to Singapore*. The series ran to six entries, the last being *Road to Bali* in 1952. Just as Paramount capitalized on Crosby's already established radio career, Warner Bros. turned the up-and-coming recording artist Doris Day into the studio's new musical star in the late 1940s and early 1950s. Day often starred opposite Jack Carson or Gordon McRae and played irrepressible, unsophisticated young women with dreams of being a musical star.

The film cycles listed above were some of the most profitable, most widely disseminated musical films of the classical era, and the stars were among the most popular in Hollywood. One consequence of their weak representation in the canon, thus, is that significant industry trends and practices have been almost entirely overlooked, in particular the relations of radio, recording, and television to the feature film. Crosby, Autry, and Day, for example, all started in the radio and recording industries and then became film stars. Others, such as Astaire and Garland, developed radio and recording careers as an extension of their screen careers. Also, as the number of traditional musicals declined in the 1950s, many musical stars increasingly took advantage of variety shows and other opportunities afforded by television. Decker (2011), Stanfield (2002), and Grant (1986) have all examined aspects of the relationship between the musical and the popular music industry as regards specific stars and film cycles, but no scholar has yet undertaken a more comprehensive study of this relationship.

The traditional canon points to the films of Vincent Minnelli and Gene Kelly in the 1950s and high-profile Broadway adaptations in the 1950s and 1960s as the culmination of the integrated musical, but as Neale points out, films such as *An American in Paris, Singin' in the Rain, A Star is Born* (1954), and *The Sound of Music* were not typical of classical Hollywood's output (Neale 2000, 107). Despite their high artistic profile, these films do not represent the musical genre as a whole: the Freed unit at MGM did move in this direction, but other studios and even other MGM units continued to produce films according to earlier generic models and the new star-genre formulas. Joe Pasternak, also an MGM producer, even made several traditional operettas in the 1950s—many of them remakes—starring Kathryn Grayson, Howard Keel, and Jane Powell. Paramount continued to earn large profits from the Road films of Crosby, Hope, and Lamour in the early part of the decade and introduced the team of Dean Martin and Jerry Lewis in a new series of madcap musical comedies. Other new cycles appeared as well, such as Frankie Avalon and Annette Funicello's beach-blanket teen pics for American International and the Rat Pack films, most of which were released by Warner Bros. If these and other cycles are taken into account, the historical narrative does not take the form of an evolutionary model moving toward the fully integrated musical and then dying out. Rather, the musical remains heterogeneous throughout its history, with cycles and subgenres appearing, changing, and disappearing for a wide variety of reasons.

Expanding the Canon: Singing Cowboy Films

In order to demonstrate how the musical cycles and subgenres listed above might suggest paths to broader accounts of the film musical, I introduce here a brief case study. The repertoire is singing cowboy films, which enjoyed many years of production and exhibition success (from the mid-1930s through the 1950s). I will, however, focus my discussion on the earlier years and specifically on the Gene Autry films released beginning in 1934 and going into the early 1940s. Autry is widely recognized as the quintessential singing cowboy, and, if his were not the only films of their kind being released at the time, they were certainly the most successful. As such, his films provided a generic model that influenced both contemporaneous and later productions.

Singing cowboy films are intimately tied to the rise of country and western music in the 1930s. Don Cusic (2011, 11–17) argues that although cowboy songs themselves were not new, the singing cowboy during this time became the central figure in the development of music aimed specifically at rural radio audiences—this was, in Allen Lowe's words, the "mainstreaming of country music" (Lowe 1997, 155). Autry's own career path corroborates Cusic's and Lowe's claims. By the time Autry made his first film appearance in 1934, he was already a radio and recording star, with an established persona as a singing cowboy on the nation's most popular country music radio show at the time, WLS's National Barn Dance, broadcast from Chicago. He was a big enough star to sell records and personally endorse merchandise through Sears, Roebuck and Co., and he did this to such an extent that Stanfield describes Autry as "a singing merchandise store" (Stanfield 2001, 67). Enabled by Herbert Yates, who owned both the film studio and the recording company that held Autry's contracts in the 1930s, the singer's film stardom enhanced rather than eclipsed the other elements of his entertaining career, giving him a consistent star persona that was equally successful in the film, radio, recording, and television industries from the 1930s through the mid-1950s.

Stanfield attributes the singing cowboy's success in linking together the various media industries to his representation as an authentic and trustworthy member of a community (2002, 5). In order to accomplish such a representation, these films must come to grips with the singing cowboy's prominent position as a radio star with commercial endorsements (virtually every radio show in the mid-1930s was sponsored by corporations). Many of the films—Autry's in particular—do not attempt to hide the fact of the singing cowboy's simultaneous presence in the radio and recording industries but present him as himself, not as a fictional character, and often directly acknowledge his star status. In the final moments of *The Old Corral* (1936), for example, a close-up of a phonograph playing an Autry record fades into a two-shot of Autry singing to his female lead (Irene Manning). The sound quality remains unchanged during the transition, depicting in literal fashion how Autry the film character is synonymous with Autry the recording star (see Figures 9.1 a–c).

At the same time, however, the films find ways to legitimize (or else to efface) the singing cowboy's position as a commercial agent. Lynette Tan (2001) points out that in order to protect the integrity of radio in the public's mind, several of Autry's films, such as *Colorado Sunset* (1939), *The Old Barn Dance* (1938), and *Mexicali Rose* (1939), make an explicit point of punishing those who misuse the influential power of radio. Stanfield goes one step further, arguing that by bringing restitution and justice to the onscreen community in these films Autry "reconfirms the public's trust in radio and in Autry as agent of community values," despite his actual position as an agent of commercial industry (Stanfield 2002, 106).

These comments sound strikingly similar to Feuer's claim that, although the musical's status as mass entertainment produced by professionals for audience consumption effectively stifles any possible communal connection between the performers and the audience, the musical continually attempts to efface this condition by "[aspiring] to the condition of a folk art, produced and consumed by the same integrated community" (20). This practice is eminently clear in the singing cowboy films. Stanfield attributes Gene Autry's unparalleled popularity to "his ability through song and performance to credibly suggest that he was part of the community that constituted his core audience" (Stanfield 2002, 6) and argues that his amateurish acting and unpolished performance style allow him to negotiate the barrier between the media industries and his audience more successfully than any other singing cowboy. In these films the implication to the film audience is that Autry sings for his own enjoyment and the enjoyment of the community, rather than for money or personal acclaim.

Autry's amateur persona also falls perfectly in line with the musical, which, as Feuer says, displays "a remarkable emphasis on the joys of being an amateur" (Feuer 1993, 17). She argues that the amateur status of the performer is extremely important in diverting attention away from the commercial nature of the musical film because it assuages the audience's fear that they are being exploited (13). In many ways Autry's films accomplish this in an arguably more believable manner than any musical starring Judy Garland or Gene Kelly, who are often depicted as amateurs but whose talent and charisma clearly exceed those of any ordinary person, a point only emphasized further by the high production values of their films. Autry's musical performances, in contrast, are simply staged and shot, rarely emotionally charged, and are often cajoled out of him by members of

(a)

(b)

(c)

FIGURE **9.1** a–c: *The Old Corral (1936)*, ending: fade from close-up of phonograph to Gene Autry singing.

FIGURE **9.2** a–c: *Down Mexico Way* (1941), Gene Autry sings for a picnic gathering.

the community or the circumstances of the plot. His companions and even the entire cast frequently sing along with him and he often walks or rides among them as he sings, identifying himself with the community rather than as a performer on a stage in front of a formal audience. As one example among many, the opening sequence in *Down Mexico Way* (1941) shows Autry entertaining a community picnic, walking among the tables and encouraging the people to sing with him at times. See Figures 9.2 a–c.

Stanfield also notes that Autry's performances often take place in private or semi-public spaces, such as a private homes, bunkhouses, or sheriff's offices (Stanfield 2002, 107–9), further identifying him as an amateur rather than a professional. Such domestic, natural settings also appear in the musical, but the world of the singing cowboy does not become a stage, as Feuer says of the world of the musical (Feuer 1993, 23–26). Autry typically does not sing in makeshift prosceniums such as doorways or windows. *The Old Corral* has a revealing sequence in this regard. Autry is in a saloon and ends up being asked to sing a song. He grabs a guitar and stands beside the piano, on the floor, singing to the tavern's patrons, who are both sitting and standing. There is no stage, and although Autry is standing under a large archway, neither he nor the camera uses it as a makeshift proscenium—in fact, his body actually blocks our view of the base of the arch. See Figure 9.3. As also happens in instances where Autry does sing on a stage of some sort, the audience encroaches upon the space—here they literally surround him. In other films, the audience joins him in singing the chorus from their seats, another way of negating the separation between performer and audience. Thus, the singing cowboy film works with much of the same ideology as the musical, but with far fewer markers of professional entertainment.

The music in the singing cowboy film promotes another ideological aspect of the musical genre: utopianism. Dyer says that the musical offers "the image of 'something better' to escape into, or something we want deeply that our day-to-day lives don't provide" (Dyer 1981, 177). It does not offer a particular plan for achieving utopia, but rather offers a utopian "sensibility."[10] Dyer (1981), Feuer, and Altman (1987) agree that this utopianism is often promoted through a strong sense of nostalgia for a shared, mythicized American past. This can be achieved through setting, such as the turn-of-the century cities in *Meet Me in St. Louis* and *Coney Island* (1943), or through the use of old songs and past forms of entertainment, such as minstrelsy or vaudeville. In the singing cowboy films, nostalgia is often achieved through old songs and new songs that seem old, and similarly through old forms of entertainment and new forms that seem old.

FIGURE **9.3** *The Old Corral*, Gene Autry sings in a saloon.

Autry's films, and many other singing cowboy films, are set not in the mythicized Old West, but in the modern rural America of the 1930s. As a cowboy, however, he stands in the films as a link between the modern and the premodern, between past and present, for the rural community. The film settings are often a blend of nostalgic Old West icons such as the horse, the unfenced prairie, and the six-shooter, and images of contemporary society such as the car, the tractor, and the radio. A simple example in a sequence from *Down Mexico Way* has Autry traveling to that country, driving a car and hauling his horse in a trailer. When the car breaks down, the next shot shows Autry using his horse to tow the car (see Figures 9.4 a–b). Here, as in many of his films, the traditional ways of the rural community prove to be more reliable than so-called modern "conveniences."

The plots of Autry's films often revolve around his helping the community learn to cope with the problems of the Depression and increasing modernization (Tan 2001, 93), while the musical performances invoke a strong sense of nostalgia for the days and values of the frontier. Historical forms of entertainment such as minstrelsy and medicine shows appear from time to time, as do barn dances, which are presented as traditional communal events (although according to Stanfield they were actually an invention of

(a)

(b)

FIGURE **9.4** a–b: *Down Mexico Way*, mingling of past and present in horse and car.

1930s radio programs [Stanfield 2002, 68–70]). Thus the films blend new forms of commercial entertainment with venerated traditional forms, presenting both categories as integrated into community life.

The songs themselves are also often a mixture of the old, like "Oh! Susanna" and "Home on the Range," and the new passing as old, like "When the Bloom is on the Sage (Round-Up Time in Texas)" and "On the Sunset Trail." According to Stanfield and Tan, these new cowboy songs intentionally use folk-song stylings and lyrical content to invoke nostalgia, using "familiar names, events, and places help locate the songs in a recognizable historical (and firmly American) past" (Stanfield 2002, 55). This seamless blend of old and new, especially in the musical performances, firmly grounds nostalgia for the Old West as the utopian sensibility of the modern rural society depicted in the films. This utopianism is confirmed by the musical involvement of the entire community in many songs. Autry often extends this sensibility to the film audience through the typical musical device of direct address (see Feuer 1993, 35–42), looking straight into the camera as he sings. In *Git Along Little Dogies* (1937) he even leads both the onscreen audience and the theater audience in a community sing-along, complete with the words printed on the bottom of the screen.

If nostalgia for a shared but imagined utopian past is the driving force behind such musicals as *Meet Me in St. Louis* (1944) and *Oklahoma!* (1955), as Knapp (2005, 119–51) and Altman (1981, 272–327) both have it, then these films have a clear antecedent in the 1930s singing cowboy film. Knapp, however, primarily traces theatrical influences on musical films, rather than looking at influences from within the film industry. Altman's theory of genre, despite being able to take into account "the influence of one genre on another" (114), nevertheless limits the influence of the western film to the scenery of folk musicals with wilderness and western settings (182). It should be clear from the case study, however, that singing cowboy films do more than that: they act as a link between the genres of the non-singing western and the musical. Indeed, it is difficult to believe that the original stage production of *Oklahoma!* (1943) did not draw upon the persona of the singing cowboy, by then a well-established fixture in film, radio, and recorded music. Many of Gene Autry's films open as both the stage and film versions of *Oklahoma!* do, with the star cowboy singing for his own pleasure as he rides through the countryside. In fact, there are only three key differences between Autry's films and Altman's folk musical, as exemplified by *Oklahoma!*: first, Autry's films take place in the present time while the folk musical usually takes place in the past; second, Autry's films rarely center on romance, the linchpin for Altman's definition of the musical; and, finally, Autry's films rarely involve folk dancing of any kind. His films do often contain an emphasis on family relationships among the members of the community, and although the family home of Altman's folk musical does not have a strong presence in Autry's films, the two film groups nevertheless share the settings of small towns and rural areas, "where everyone is a neighbor, where each season's rituals bring the entire population together" (Altman 1981, 275). In both kinds of films, everyone in the community sings "because music is a natural means of expression" and "is as much a part of the life cycle as eating and sleeping" (287). Most importantly, both groups of films use a strong sense of nostalgia for a mythicized past, as presented primarily through musical performance, to establish a distinctly American, conservative community.

Prospects

Neale (2000), Staiger, Altman (1998, 1999), and Tudor all call for genre studies that do not simply organize films under a taxonomic rubric, but rather shed light on the various relationships that were (and are) an inextricable part of Hollywood filmmaking: relationships among filmmakers in various roles and at various studios, relationships between Hollywood studios and exhibitors, between studios and audiences, exhibitors and audiences, even audiences and the films themselves.[11]

The case study of singing cowboy films above has already suggested one way to put the call into action: by looking at the relationships between the musical genre and other media industries. Michele Hilmes (1990), for example, examines the relationship between Hollywood and radio. Her study, and the history of the American popular music industry by Russell and David Sanjek (1996), both point to large-scale interweavings between the film industry and other media industries. If musical films are placed in this kind of industrial context, they become part of a web of relationships among film, radio, recording, and music publishing. In this connection, Barry Grant goes so far as to claim that "any analysis of the film musical is necessarily incomplete without a consideration of the genre's relation to developments in popular music and the recording industry" (Grant 1986, 195). Despite the fact that his statement is now more than twenty-five years old, Grant's brief study of early rock'n'roll musicals remains the only work that directly examines this relationship. Decker, Stanfield, and John Mundy (2006) all offer key insights into the relationship between certain groups of films and the popular music industry, but the focus of their attention is not the musical genre.

The studies mentioned above all reveal various aspects of the relationship between the musical genre and the popular music industries. One way Hollywood assimilated rock 'n' roll music, for example, was by taming it to the conservative conventions of the musical (Grant 1986). Singing cowboy films are inextricably linked to the rise and consolidation of country and western music, primarily consumed via radio and recordings (Stanfield 2002). Astaire created his screen performances both in reaction to and as contributions to popular music trends, particularly those related to jazz (Decker 2011). Even the films in the traditional canon of musicals point to the relationships between musicals and other media. Composer biopics, such as MGM's *Till the Clouds Roll By* (1946), and songbook musicals, such as MGM's *An American in Paris* (1951) and *Singin' in the Rain* (1952), have obvious tie-ins with the music publishing industry, which would then use the film's success to revitalize sales of former hit songs. Many film studios held copyrights to the songs written for their films; some even owned record labels and publishing houses, further complicating the relationship between musicals and other media industries.

Stars also participated in these intermedia relationships. Autry, Crosby, Doris Day, Elvis Presley, and Annette Funicello, among others, all had a strong presence in other media before they became musical film stars, and they all continued to record and give live or televised performances while they made films. Other musical stars, such as Judy Garland, took the opposite path, becoming recording stars because of their film popularity. As with any prominent film actor, their onscreen characters had to contend or cooperate with their offscreen personae, largely defined by how they were presented in other media. Feuer's assertion that it is important for the star to be presented as an amateur, as someone who performs simply for the love of performing, in the musical genre because it effaces his or her role as a commercial agent could be equally applicable to the star's presentation in all media outlets. Autry's conservative, genuine persona was presented consistently in both film and radio, and Astaire's television performances were often constructed with the same spontaneous style and bricolage techniques that marked his film performances. Bing Crosby's and Bob Hope's appearances in USO and radio shows present their real-life relationship in a manner strikingly similar to their characters' relationship in Paramount's Road movies. For these and many other musical stars, their film performances must be placed in the context of their presence in other entertainment industries.

Studies of the classical Hollywood musical traditionally take into account what is present on screen but are less curious about how the films were produced and consumed. Many musicals were made as adaptations of a variety of presold properties, such as musical and nonmusical Broadway plays, biographies of well-known musical figures, and even other nonmusical films. Musicals, whether original or adapted, contain music, usually popular music, that was licensed by publishing houses and that was being sung by stars who in most cases had a simultaneous presence in other media industries. Musicals were made by popular-song composers and arrangers and by film studio executives who often had investments in other arms of the entertainment industry; indeed, even the stars, such as Crosby and Autry, often had financial investments in other media. Musicals were consumed by audiences who listened to the radio, watched television, and bought records and sheet music. Looking at these fundamental aspects of the genre, then, we can move outside the historical narrative of the canon. Indeed, we might be moved to ask, not whether a certain group of films are musicals—as with Elvis Presley's rock 'n' roll films, for example—but, as Grant does, why these films invoke the musical genre at all. Or we might ask, as Griffin does, why one studio (20th Century Fox, in that case) would make musicals that highlight the professional status of their musical stars and the performance status of the musical numbers, whereas another (MGM) worked hard to hide any aura of professionalism surrounding their stars and musical performances. Or we might ask whether the industrial practices surrounding the musical changed throughout the classical era in response to—or in sync with—changes in the popular music industry. By adding more of these kinds of studies to the existing work on the genre, we will be able to locate the musical in its historical and industrial contexts and add concrete knowledge to well-developed genre theories, resulting in a more complete picture of the musical film in classical Hollywood.

Notes

1. For another historical account of the critical literature on the musical, see Grant 2012, 37–54.
2. On early uses of the word "genre" and on different understandings of "genre" and "style" in English and in Latin languages (especially French and Italian), see Fabbri and Shepherd 2003.
3. On connections between nineteenth-century theatrical forms and later cinematic forms, see also Pisani Chapter 22 below.
4. For a survey and critique of racial politics in the musical theater, specifically with respect to miscegenation, see Riis 2111. See also the editor's introduction to the section "Racial Displacements" (155–56) and the section's essays in Cohan 2002.
5. My focus here is on historical narratives and genre models as they relate to the integrated musical, and therefore I have not addressed questions of gender and sexuality at a level that reflects their importance in the literature. For a succinct summary, see Wolf 2011; on camp with respect to film musicals, see Knapp and Morris 2011b, 146–50; on gay readings, see Feuer, 139–43; on gender and sexuality in post-classical film musicals, see Kessler 2010; on gender in music and film (not musicals), see Laing 2007, 9–24; on theories of gender and sexuality in film and film music, see Buhler Chapter 14 below.
6. On this see also Knapp and Morris 2011a, 81–96.
7. See Lovensheimer 2011 for an extended critique of the concepts of "author" and "text" in relation to the stage musical.
8. For a contrary view of *South Pacific*, in its original Broadway production, as a "jerrybuilt collage" rather than a fully integrated musical, see Savran 2011, 245–47.
9. See Morris 2011 for an extended critique of the construction of historical narratives, with reference to the stage musical, not the film musical.
10. For an account of the utopian in musicals, see Grant 2012, 41–45.
11. Obviously, still another way to extend the reach of historical and critical accounts of the film musical is to engage repertoires beyond Hollywood. To this, see especially chapters in Marshall and Stilwell 2000, Cohan 2002, and Conrich and Tincknell 2006.

Bibliography

Altman, Rick. 1981. "The American Film Musical: Paradigmatic Structure and Mediatory Function." In *Genre: The Musical*, edited by Rick Altman, 197–207. London: Routledge & Kegan Paul.

——, ed. 1981. *Genre: The Musical*. London: Routledge & Kegan Paul.

——. 1987. *The American Film Musical*. Bloomington: Indiana University Press.

——. 1998. "Reusable Packaging: Generic Products and the Recycling Process." In *Refiguring American Film Genres: Theory and History*, edited by Nick Browne, 1–41. Los Angeles/Berkeley: University of California Press.

——. 1999. *Film/Genre*. London: British Film Institute.

Babington, Bruce, and Peter Evans. 1985. *Blue Skies and Silver Linings: Aspects of the Hollywood Musical*. Manchester: Manchester University Press.

Balio, Tino. 1993. *Grand Design: Hollywood as a Modern Business Enterprise, 1930–1939*. Berkeley: University of California Press.

Barrios, Richard. 1995. *A Song in the Dark: The Birth of the Musical Film*. New York: Oxford University Press.

Block, Geoffrey. 2002. "The Melody (and the Words) Linger on: American Musical Comedies of the 1920s and 1930s." In *The Cambridge Companion to the Musical*, edited by William Everett and Paul Laird, 77–100. Cambridge: Cambridge University Press.

Browne, Nick, ed. 1998. *Refiguring American Film Genres: Theory and History*. Los Angeles/ Berkeley: University of California Press.

Chapman, James. 2006. "A Short History of the Big Band Musical." In *Film's Musical Moments*, edited by Ian Conrich and Estella Tincknell, 28–41. Edinburgh: Edinburgh University Press.

Cohan, Steven. 2002a. "'Feminizing' the Song-and-Dance Man: Fred Astaire and the Spectacle of Masculinity in the Hollywood Musical." In *Hollywood Musicals: The Film Reader*, edited by Steven Cohan, 87–101. London: Routledge.

——, ed. 2002b. *Hollywood Musicals: The Film Reader*. London: Routledge.

Collins, James. 1988. "The Musical." In *Handbook of American Film Genres*, edited by Wes Gehring, 269–284. New York: Greenwood.

Conrich, Ian, and Estella Tincknell. Eds. 2006. *Film's Musical Moments*. Edinburgh: Edinburgh University Press.

Culler, Jonathan. 1975. *Structuralist Poetics: Structuralism, Linguistics, and the Study of Literature*. Ithaca: Cornell University Press.

Cusic, Don. 2011. *The Cowboy in Country Music: An Historical Survey with Artist Profiles*. Jefferson, NC: McFarland.

de Bruyn, Frans. 1993. "Genre." In *Encyclopedia of Contemporary Literary Theory*, edited by Irena Makaryk, 79–85. Toronto: University of Toronto Press.

Decker, Todd. 2011. *Music Makes Me: Fred Astaire and Jazz*. Berkeley: University of California Press.

Delamater, Jerome. 1978. *Dance in the Hollywood Musical*. Ann Arbor, MI: UMI Research Press.

Dubrow, Heather. 1982. *Genre*. London and New York: Methuen.

Dyer, Richard. 1981. "Entertainment and Utopia." In *Genre: The Musical*, edited by Rick Altman, 175–189. London: Routledge & Kegan Paul.

——. 2000. "The Colour of Entertainment." In *Musicals: Hollywood & Beyond*, edited by Bill Marshall and Robynn Stilwell, 23–30. Portland, OR: Intellect.

Fabbri, Franco, and John Shepherd. 2003. "Genre." In John Shepherd, David Horn, Dave Laing, Paul Oliver, and Peter Wicke, eds. *Continuum Encyclopedia of Popular Music of the World. Vol. 1: Media, Industry and Society*, 401–404. New York and London: Continuum.

Faller, Greg. 1987. *The Function of Star-Image and Performance in the Hollywood Musical: Sonja Henie, Esther Williams, and Eleanor Powell*. PhD diss., Northwestern University.

Feuer, Jane. 1981. "The Self-reflective Musical and the Myth of Entertainment." In *Genre: The Musical*, edited by Rick Altman, 159–174. London: Routledge & Kegan Paul.

——. 1993. *The Hollywood Musical*. 2nd Edition. Bloomington: Indiana University Press.

Fischer, Lucy. 1981. "The Image of Woman as Image: The Optical Politics of *Dames*." In *Genre: The Musical*, edited by Rick Altman, 70–84. London: Routledge & Kegan Paul.

Fowler, Alistair. 1982. *Kinds of Literature: An Introduction to the Theory of Genres and Modes*. Cambridge, MA: Harvard University Press.

Gehring, Wes, ed. 1988. *Handbook of American Film Genres*. New York: Greenwood.

Geraghty, Lincoln, and Mark Jancovich, eds. 2008. *The Shifting Definitions of Genre: Essays on Labeling Films, Television Shows and Media*. Jefferson, NC: McFarland.

Grant, Barry K. 1986. "The Classic Hollywood Musical and the 'Problem' of Rock'n'Roll." *Journal of Popular Film & Television* 13, no. 4: 195–205.

——, ed. 2003. *Film Genre Reader III*. Austin: University of Texas Press.

——. 2012. *The Hollywood Film Musical*. 2d ed. Hoboken, NJ: John Wiley.

Green, Douglas. 2002. *Singing in the Saddle: The History of the Singing Cowboy*. Nashville, TN: The Country Music Foundation Press and Vanderbilt University Press.

Griffin, Sean. 2002. "The Gang's All Here: Generic versus Racial Integration in the 1940s Musical." *Cinema Journal* 48, no. 1: 21–45.

Hilmes, Michele. 1990. *Hollywood and Broadcasting: from Radio to Cable*. Chicago: University of Illinois Press.

Kessler, Kelly. 2010. *Destabilizing the Hollywood Musical: Music, Masculinity and Mayhem*. New York: Palgrave MacMillan.

Knapp, Raymond. 2005. *The American Musical and the Formation of National Identity*. Princeton, NJ: Princeton University Press.

——. 2006. *The American Musical and the Performance of Personal Identity*. Princeton, NJ: Princeton University Press.

——, and Mitchell Morris. 2011a. "Tin Pan Alley Songs on Stage and Screen before World War II." *The Oxford Handbook of the American Musical*, edited by Raymond Knapp, Mitchell Morris, and Stacy Wolf, 81–96. New York: Oxford University Press.

——, and Mitchell Morris. 2011b. "The Filmed Musical." In *The Oxford Handbook of the American Musical*, edited by Raymond Knapp, Mitchell Morris, and Stacy Wolf, 136–151. New York: Oxford University Press.

——, Mitchell Morris, and Stacy Wolf, eds. 2011. *The Oxford Handbook of the American Musical*. New York: Oxford University Press.

Laing, Heather. 2000. "Emotion by Numbers: Music, Song and the Musical." In *Musicals: Hollywood & Beyond*, edited by Bill Marshall and Robynn Stilwell, 5–13. Portland, OR: Intellect.

——. 2007. *The Gendered Score: Music in 1940s Melodrama and the Woman's Film*. Aldershot, UK, and Burlington, VT: Ashgate.

Lawson-Peebles, Robert, ed. 1996. *Approaches to the American Musical*. Exeter, UK: University of Exeter Press.

Lovensheimer, Jim. 2011. "Texts and Authors." In *The Oxford Handbook of the American Musical*, edited by Raymond Knapp, Mitchell Morris, and Stacy Wolf, 20–32. New York: Oxford University Press.

Lowe, Allen. 1997. *American Pop from Minstrel to Mojo: On Record 1893–1956*. Redwood, NY: Cadence Jazz Books.

MacKinnon, Kenneth. 2000. "'I Keep Wishing I Were Somewhere Else': Space and Fantasies of Freedom in the Hollywood Musical." In *Musicals: Hollywood and Beyond*, edited by Bill Marshall and Robynn Stilwell, 40–46. Portland, OR: Intellect.

Marshall, Bill, and Robynn Stilwell, eds. 2000. *Musicals: Hollywood and Beyond*. Portland, OR: Intellect.

Mast, Gerald. 1987. *Can't Help Singin': The American Musical on Stage and Screen*. Woodstock, NY: Overlook.

Morris, Mitchell. 2011. "Narratives and Values." In *The Oxford Handbook of the American Musical*, edited by Raymond Knapp, Mitchell Morris, and Stacy Wolf, 9–19. New York: Oxford University Press.

Mueller, John. 1984. "Fred Astaire and the Integrated Musical." *Cinema Journal* 24, no. 1: 28–40.

——. 1985. *Astaire Dancing*. New York: Wings.

Mundy, John. 2006. "Television, the Pop Industry and the Hollywood Musical." In *Film's Musical Moments*, edited by Ian Conrich and Estella Tincknell, 42–55. Edinburgh: Edinburgh University Press.

Neale, Steve. 2000. *Genre and Hollywood*. New York: Routledge.

——. 2003. "Questions of Genre." In *Film Genre Reader III*, edited by Barry Keith Grant, 160–184. Austin: University of Texas Press.

Riis, Thomas L. 2011. "Minstrelsy and Theatrical Miscegenation." In *The Oxford Handbook of the American Musical*, edited by Raymond Knapp, Mitchell Morris, and Stacy Wolf, 65–80. New York: Oxford University Press.

Roberts, Shari. 2002. "'The Lady in the Tutti-Frutti Hat': Carmen Miranda, A Spectacle of Ethnicity." In *Hollywood Musicals: The Film Reader*, edited by Steven Cohan, 143–153. London: Routledge.

Sanjek, Russell. 1996. *Pennies from Heaven: The American Popular Music Business in the Twentieth Century*. New York: Da Capo.

Savran, David. 2011. "Class and Culture." In *The Oxford Handbook of the American Musical*, edited by Raymond Knapp, Mitchell Morris, and Stacy Wolf, 239–50. New York: Oxford University Press.

Schatz, Thomas. 1981. *Hollywood Genres*. New York: McGraw Hill.

——. 1988. "The Western." In *Handbook of American Film Genres*, edited by Wes Gehring, 25–46. New York: Greenwood.

——. 1997. *Boom and Bust: American Cinema in the 1940s*. Berkeley: University of California Press.

——. 2010. *The Genius of the System: Hollywood Filmmaking in the Studio Era*. Minneapolis: University of Minnesota Press. Originally published in 1989 by Pantheon.

Scheurer, Timothy. 1974. "The Aesthetics of Form and Convention in the Movie Musical." *Journal of Popular Film* 3, no. 4: 307–324.

Staiger, Janet. 2003. "Hybrid or Inbred: The Purity Hypothesis and Hollywood Genre History." In *Film Genre Reader III*, edited by Barry Keith Grant, 185–199. Austin: University of Texas Press.

Stanfield, Peter. 2001. *Hollywood, Westerns and the 1930s: The Lost Trail*. Exeter, UK: University of Exeter Press.

——. 2002. *Horse Opera: The Strange History of the 1930s Singing Cowboy*. Chicago: University of Illinois Press.

Tan, Lynette. 2001. "The New Deal Cowboy: Gene Autry and the Antimodern Resolution." *Film History* 13, no. 1: 89–101.

Todorov, Tzvetan. 1990. *Genres in Discourse*. Translated by Catherine Porter. Cambridge: Cambridge University Press.

Traubner, Richard. 1983. *Operetta: A Theatrical History*. New York: Doubleday.

Tudor, Andrew. 1973. *Theories of Film*. New York: Viking.

Wolf, Stacy. 2011. "Gender and Sexuality." In *The Oxford Handbook of the American Musical*, edited by Raymond Knapp, Mitchell Morris, and Stacy Wolf, 210–224. New York: Oxford University Press.

CHAPTER 10

"THE TUNES THEY ARE A-CHANGING": MOMENTS OF HISTORICAL RUPTURE AND RECONFIGURATION IN THE PRODUCTION AND COMMERCE OF MUSIC IN FILM

JEFF SMITH

FROM the perspective of the director, Quentin Tarantino observed that the success-ful—and indeed, memorable—use of music in cinema confers ownership of a particu-lar song title to the film in which it appears: "If a song in a movie is used really well, as far as I'm concerned, that movie owns that song, it can never be used again" (Romney and Wootton 1995, 131). Although he treats this notion of ownership in a metaphori-cal sense, his comments offer an intriguing perspective on the historical interactions of Hollywood and Tin Pan Alley. Clearly, Tarantino's suggestion here is that each part of a film and music "partnership" derives a measure of enhanced cultural capital from their successful interaction. In relatively rare instances, this enhanced cultural capital is transformed into enhanced economic capital as films and songs both benefit financially from the industrial synergies that lie at the heart of effective cross-promotion. Viewed in more concrete economic terms, one might well wonder if Tarantino is more right than he knows. Perhaps the acquisition of mechanical rights, master licenses, and synchroni-zation rights does, in fact, provide filmmakers with a degree of proprietary interest.

Of course, the history of Hollywood's interactions with the music industry is nearly as old as cinema itself. Although the relationship between the two industries has under-gone many changes, Hollywood generally has utilized the markets for sheet music and records to fulfill several broad goals. Besides the cross-promotion of films, theme songs, and soundtrack albums mentioned above, Hollywood's investment in music offers additional, if less obvious, economic benefits. First, a successful soundtrack may minimize the economic risks of film production by offering an ancillary revenue stream that can defray costs. Secondly, within large but tightly diversified corporations, the presence of active film and music divisions helps to balance out the volatile shifts in market share that take place within both industries on an annual basis. For its part, the record industry has enjoyed certain economic benefits from its relationship with Hollywood. The soundtracks for *Saturday Night Fever* (1977), *The Bodyguard* (1992), and *Titanic* (1997) are among the best-selling albums of all time. Moreover, film soundtracks themselves have offered exposure to emerging artists, provided ancillary revenues through the negotiation of synchronization and master licensing fees, and enhanced the value of music publishing and record companies' back catalogs.

Yet if Hollywood and Tin Pan Alley are, indeed, the Hope and Crosby of the entertainment business, their journey together has not been without its bumps in the road. Surveying the history of interactions between the film and music industries, one discerns a pattern of several long-term business cycles. A film historian or musicologist might periodize these cycles in a number of different ways, but I propose four distinct phases in the history of film music's production and commerce. These phases are each initiated by major changes in film or music technologies, changes in each industry's structure, or, in some cases, a combination of both. In charting this history, I nominate four specific dates, each of which represents a moment of historical rupture and reconfiguration: 1927, which saw the innovation of synchronized sound technology for feature films; 1958, the year in which all of the major studios laid claim to a recorded music subsidiary; 1975, the year in which Dolby Stereo technology was introduced into movie theaters; and 1999, the year that Napster galvanized the music industry with its music file-sharing software.

1927: *The Jazz Singer* Marks Vitaphone's Feature Film Debut

Cinema's innovation of synchronized sound technology may be the single most important development in the history of film. In their efforts to bring synchronized sound technology to the marketplace, the major studios exercised caution, introducing sound production to short films that could be used to test a technology's commercial potential. In 1926, Warner Bros. used its Vitaphone technology, newly acquired from Western Electric, to record performances by musicians and comedians for sound shorts. Fox, on the other hand, used its Movietone technology in newsreels (that is, short films that encapsulated highlights of the latest national news). Both companies also experimented with synchronized sound technology for music scores for feature films before finally using these innovative techniques in "talkies."

The Jazz Singer debuted in 1927 and became an immediate hit. The film was produced for a half-million dollars—a substantial sum at the time—and went on to earn more than two million dollars at the box office for its studio, Warner Bros. (Crafton 1997, 110–11). Yet even as it remains film history's oft-cited landmark for its innovation of synchronized sound technology, the film itself displays several traits that mark it as a transitional production, bridging the silent-film and sound-film eras. *The Jazz Singer* was a part-talkie that combined dialogue scenes and musical numbers with scenes that were shot silent but then synchronized with musical accompaniment. The film's visual style also displays something of a hybrid character. The scenes with only musical accompaniment were shot with a single camera, adhering to the established norms for silent cinema. Dialogue scenes and musical numbers were shot using three cameras located in a soundproof booth to minimize the noise made by camera motors. The three cameras recorded each scene in long shots, medium shots, and close-ups respectively, allowing the picture editor to get coverage for the scene and to maintain some visual variety. Multicamera shooting was also needed because sound could not be edited without destroying continuity, meaning that sound elements had to be captured in a single take. This multicamera approach became the norm between 1927 and 1932; some studios used as many as five cameras in order to get shots with a variety of angles and scales, which later could be cut together in picture editing.

The development of Vitaphone technology, though, also had an impact on the music industry, as Western Electric quickly learned that the control of music copyrights could be a major hurdle blocking its successful innovation. Because Vitaphone employed large phonograph discs for its recording and playback of film sound, Warner Bros. initially claimed that the discs were covered by already existing agreements for mechanical reproduction licenses. Under this agreement, Warner Bros. would have to pay only a two-cent royalty on every disc they produced. The Music Publishers Protective Association (MPPA) objected, on the grounds that phonographs were produced for home use whereas Vitaphone discs were produced for profits gleaned through public performance (Spring 2007, 48). Warner Bros. attempted to bypass the MPPA, but its firms threatened to withdraw their music from the catalog overseen by the American Society of Composers, Authors and Publishers (ASCAP). Since thousands of theaters had already paid ASCAP for performance rights to its catalog, the withdrawal of MPPA music threatened to place any theater showing a Warners film in violation of those copyrights (Sanjek 1996, 54). Western Electric responded through its subsidiary, Electric Research Products, Inc. (ERPI), which signed a five-year agreement with MPPA president Edwin C. Mills. ERPI's contract with Mills granted the right to record and reproduce music from ASCAP to all Vitaphone licensees. In exchange for these rights, the MPPA received minimum payments of $100,000 in the first year and $125,000 in the second year of the contract's term (Spring 2007, 49). These ERPI licenses, as they came to be known, proved to be unpopular with music publishers in the short term as MPPA members gradually came to realize that Mills had grossly undervalued these copyrights (49), but ERPI's contract with the MPPA had a lasting impact on both the film and music industries in that it established *synchronization rights* as a major source of potential revenue for music publishers.

For their part, film producers also grew disenchanted with the "Mills Agreement" for the simple reason that it granted rights only for venues in the United States and Canada (Spring 2007, 50). Producers often had to obtain separate licenses from European protective rights organizations for music included in any film that was shown abroad. Making matters worse, a piece of music might be in public domain in the United States but have copyright protection in other countries. Studio employees seeking to clear particular pieces of music sometimes had to run a gauntlet of different publishers to make sure that rights were obtained for every territory in which the film was shown. On Paramount's *Dishonored* (1931), for example, internal studio correspondence indicates that the filmmakers had some concerns about one song featured in the film, entitled "I Should Worry." During the production, Paramount learned that "I Should Worry" might be a Russian translation of another song by Joseph Feldman entitled "Flow, Flow Dear Wine." Although neither song was registered under American copyrights, Paramount believed that "I Should Worry" was registered in France and "Flow, Flow Dear Wine" was protected under Russian copyright.[1] It took studio employees several weeks to sort out the provenance of "I Should Worry," a process that was further complicated by the fact that composer Karl Hajos had translated the title as "Pouring, Pouring Dear Wine," which meant that the music department's search for copyright clearance was initially undertaken with the wrong title.[2] Paramount ultimately paid ERPI rates for both pieces of music in order to assure that *Dishonored* had copyright clearance for both American and European exhibition.

As Katherine Spring points out, by the summer of 1928, both film producers and music publishers sought an alternative to the Mills Agreement, one that might enable studios to retain copyright control over the music that appeared in their films (Spring 2007, 57–61). Starting in October of 1928, several of the majors began either buying stock in existing music-publishing concerns or created their own subsidiary companies for the express purpose of publishing the songs featured in their films. Paramount joined with Harms, Inc. to create Famous Music, a publishing firm that would handle the rights to all new songs from Paramount films. MGM, on the other hand, purchased a 50 percent interest in Robbins Music Corp. Under the deal, all new songs featured in MGM films were added to the Robbins catalog. Fox negotiated an agreement with De Sylva, Brown, and Henderson that made the latter the exclusive publisher of all of Fox's new motion picture songs. Warner Bros. proved to be the most ambitious studio in its acquisition of music copyrights. The studio would build a music publishing empire by the end of the decade, but its efforts began modestly with a nonexclusive deal with Irving Berlin, Inc. for numbers featured in Al Jolson musicals. Warners followed this deal with a far bolder venture when it paid $900,000 to acquire the entire catalog of M. Witmark & Sons. Just a few months after the Witmark deal, Warner Bros. placed a $10,000,000 bid on Harms, Inc. Since Harms owned majority stock in several other publishing subsidiaries, including Famous Music, Warners gained access to a wide range of composers and music catalogs. The deal not only enabled Warner Bros. to sidestep provisions of the Mills Agreement, but it also gave the studio a hefty share of the million dollars in profits that Harms earned each year from sales of sheet music, phonograph records, and synchronization licenses.

RCA was initially shut out of the sound technology and music copyright wars, but it soon established itself as perhaps the entertainment business' first conglomerate, with ownership of a vertically integrated movie studio (RKO), motion picture sound technology (RCA Photophone Co.), a national radio broadcast company (NBC), and a manufacturer of home audio equipment (RCA Victor Corp.). The only piece missing from this puzzle was a music publishing interest, and RCA rectified that in November of 1929 with the creation of the Radio Music Corporation. The new company was created through the acquisition and merger of Leo Feist, Inc. and Carl Fischer, Inc. Feist had been an important Tin Pan Alley firm while Fischer was a major publisher of concert music (Spring 2007, 62).

Writing in 1964, music historian David Ewen summarized the effects of these business transactions on the music industry as a whole:

> In [New York's Tin Pan Alley], the publisher had been the central force around which everything connected with songs gravitated—the writers, performers, salesmen, pluggers. It was the publisher who selected what songs were printed, and he picked them because he liked them and felt that the public would like them. Then he set about the necessary business of getting songs performed and popularized. . . . But now, in the new scheme of things created by the movie industry, the publisher was dictated *to*. He resigned not only his basic function of selecting songs for publication but also of determining the best ways of making them popular. (Ewen 1964, 322–23; emphasis in original)

By 1930, the major studios had overcome the challenge of gaining access to music copyrights. Yet the studios still had not solved some of the obstacles posed by recording music for film. As James Buhler, David Neumeyer, and Rob Deemer point out, "Although it had been technically possible to dub soundtracks since at least 1927 (*The Jazz Singer* used some rerecording), the process was risky due to the significant loss of fidelity in the process. Consequently, rerecording did not become standard until after 1930" (2010, 299). Music was usually recorded live, along with the film's images and other elements of the soundtrack. Scenes with dialogue and music had to be recorded with the musicians congregated on the same soundstage; they would play for every take of the scene. The attendant difficulties in maintaining appropriate balance between the volume levels of music and dialogue meant that music appeared in scenes only where it was thought to be absolutely necessary (300–301).

Improvements in technology established the rerecording of sound as the norm for postproduction after 1932. The ability to rerecord and mix sounds had important consequences for music in film since it meant that it no longer had to be recorded live with picture. Source music—that is, music heard within the fictional world depicted onscreen—was prerecorded and played back on the set during filming. Background scores, on the other hand, were recorded during postproduction, a technique that assured dialogue would be clearly recorded during shooting (Buhler, Neumeyer, and Deemer 2010, 318–19). By recording each component of the soundtrack separately and mixing them during postproduction, studios gradually increased the amount of music that appeared in their films. At United Artists, for example, films averaged about thirty music cues per title during the middle of the 1930s. That number increased to forty-seven cues per film by the end of the decade. The increase at Republic Pictures was even more dramatic. In 1935, Republic's productions averaged twelve music cues per film. By 1940, that number more than doubled to about thirty cues per film.[3]

Hollywood's studio system was organized to rationalize film production and to take advantage of efficiencies and economies of scale that such a mode of production offered. Studio music departments adhered to this model with a clear division of labor in which every employee took his or her part in the process of composing and recording a film score. A studio music department was led by its director, who performed many central administrative tasks in terms of budgeting, scheduling, and assigning composers to particular projects. Every studio also employed a staff of composers and songwriters. During the 1930s, it was not uncommon to have several of the studio's staff composers collaborate in the composition of a film score, even when the screen credit went to a single individual. For Paramount's *Love Me Tonight* (1932), for example, Richard Rodgers received screen credit for "original music," but the studio's conductor's score indicates that two other staff composers worked alongside Rodgers and each contributed individual cues to the final product.

Orchestrators and copyists also played important roles in the production process, even though they occupied a lower place in the department hierarchy. As Buhler, Neumeyer, and Deemer point out, orchestrators took the composer's sketches and separated out the individual instrument parts onto a full score that might contain as many as thirty or forty staff lines, one for each instrument (2010, 328–29). Copyists, on the other hand, wrote out the parts for the orchestral musicians themselves, who would perform the music during the recording session on the studio soundstage. Music editors played a number of different roles during the composition and scoring process. Early on, the music editor compiled a cue sheet for each scene that contained music. These cue sheets included an exact timing for the music required, a detailed description of the film's action, a transcription of the film's dialogue, and a summary of the type of camera framing and angles used during shooting (329). Later, the music editor also aided in the preparation of the film for the score's recording session. The music editor was responsible for marking up the work print and preparing a click track, if such was needed (329). (A click track was made by punching holes in the soundtrack of blank leader. The holes in the leader made clicking sounds as they passed over the sound head. These clicks could then function as a metronomic pulse played back to the orchestral musicians through headphones during the recording session.)

The costs for composing, scoring, and recording a film score made up a modest part of a film's overall budget. The music budget for *Peter Ibbetson* (1935), for example, was approximately $25,000, or about 6 percent of the average cost of an A-film during the 1930s (Balio 1993, 29). The $25,000 cost included the composer's fees along with charges for the work of orchestrators, copyists, and musicians. Besides the costs of producing the film's score, studios also budgeted for licensing fees for any copyrighted music that appeared in the film. Synchronization fees ranged from as low as $100 to as high as $1000 depending on the way the music was used. Generally speaking, higher rates were charged for a piece of music performed vocally onscreen in its entirety. Lower fees were requested for partial uses of a piece or for music played in the background of a scene. In some cases, though, an excessively high quote for synchronization rights affected the choice of music that appeared onscreen. On Preston Sturges's *Christmas in July* (1940), Paramount sought to use a piece of "coffee"-themed music as a tag for the sponsors of the radio contest that initiates the film's plot. The studio requested quotes on two pieces of music that fit the bill: "A Cup of Coffee, a Sandwich, and You" and "Let's Have Another Cup of Coffee." The former was published by Harms, who requested a fee of $500 for each background instrumental use. The latter was controlled by Irving Berlin, who asked $1375 for each background instrumental use, or more than double the rate requested by Harms. Since the music was expected to appear in each of the radio broadcasts featured in the story, Paramount anticipated having to pay for multiple uses. The decision was an easy one: Paramount licensed "A Cup of Coffee, a Sandwich, and You" for *Christmas in July*.

Hollywood's acquisition of music publishing houses was undertaken to control the copyrights for the music in their films, but it also functioned as an added revenue stream for studios. In 1935, Warner Bros. anticipated more than a million dollars in revenue from their music publishing holdings (Sanjek and Sanjek 1991, 55). From 1937 to 1939, studio-owned or -affiliated publishers earned about two-thirds of the total income distributed by ASCAP. Moreover, in 1939, it was estimated that a successful theme song could add as much as a million dollars to a film's box office total through a combination of radio airplay, record purchases, and sheet music sales (Sanjek 1983, 19). Indeed, many of the most popular songs on *Variety*'s charts originated from the silver screen. According to a Peatman survey, Hollywood and Broadway accounted for more than 80 percent of the most performed songs of 1942 (Sanjek 1988, 317–18).

The late 1930s also saw the debut of "movie music" record albums. In 1938, Victor Records released the soundtrack from Walt Disney's *Snow White and the Seven Dwarfs* (1937) on three 78-rpm discs as a tie-in to the film's release (Burlingame 2000, 2). Later, in 1942, RCA Victor commissioned composer Miklós Rózsa to rework his score for *Jungle Book* (1942) into a twenty-eight-minute suite that featured narration by the film's putative star, Sabu (Burlingame 2000, 3–4). Marketed as a three-disc "recordrama," *Jungle Book* was the first original film score to be circulated in a recorded format (Karlin 1994, 227). The first record marketed using the term "original soundtrack" was Disney's album for *Pinocchio* (1940) released in February of 1940 (Burlingame 2000, 3). In the late 1940s, MGM followed Disney's lead by releasing a series of albums linked to the studio's musicals that all bore the label "Recorded Directly from the Sound Track of the M-G-M Production" (Burlingame 2000, 5).

1958: The Hollywood Majors Enter the Record Business

Between 1957 and 1958, United Artists, Paramount, Warner Bros., 20th Century Fox, and Columbia Pictures all either purchased or started up their own recorded music subsidiaries. In doing so, they joined MGM and Universal as studios with business interests in the record market. MGM had established its record subsidiary in 1945 and installed former RCA Victor executive Frank Walker as the chief of operations for the new company (Sanjek 1996, 222). Louis B. Mayer's decision to start up a label proved propitious as the company entered the market in the midst of a sales boom that saw revenues for recorded music grow exponentially throughout the 1940s. By 1952, MGM was established as one of the record business' major manufacturers, a six-company oligopoly that, like the Hollywood studios, divided the lion's share of the industry's revenues among themselves.

In contrast, the relationship between Universal Pictures and Decca Records was forged when budding media mogul, Milton Rackmill, purchased 43 percent of Universal to become the company's largest stockholder. Rackmill then installed himself as the president of both Decca Records and Universal Pictures, the high point of a period of aggressive expansion during which Rackmill sought to position his company as a leading producer of television programs (Sanjek 1996, 244–45). Both companies would ultimately find themselves swallowed up by MCA, then the world's biggest talent agency, in a 1962 merger that quickly attracted the attention of the US Justice Department for antitrust violations (392–93).

A number of different factors prompted the Hollywood majors to invest in the recorded music business. Chief among these was the trend toward diversification that followed the resolution of two major antitrust cases directed at the Hollywood majors. The first of these, the well-known Paramount decision in 1948, concluded a decade-long investigation of collusion and restraint of trade arising from studio ownership of movie theaters. As a result, the studios signed a series of consent degrees with the federal government under which they agreed to end block booking as a distribution practice and to sell their theater holdings as part of a larger program of divestiture. Although it is less well known than the case, the Hollywood majors were also plagued by a second antitrust suit filed by E. H. "Buddy" Morris in March of 1950. Morris alleged that the studios monopolized the publication of motion picture music and conspired to fix prices and limit competition. Morris named Warner Bros., Loew's, 20th Century Fox, Paramount, Universal, and fourteen other affiliated companies as defendants, and further complained that this group controlled "at least 60% of all compositions" used in motion pictures. The studios settled the lawsuit out of court, and agreed to a five-year moratorium on their usual practice for assigning publishing rights for the songs in their films. Instead, the studios established a new system under which any publisher had sixty days to offer a competitive bid on the rights to a particular song (Sanjek 1996, 317).

Both of these antitrust actions may well have enhanced the appeal of record subsidiaries as a particular avenue of corporate diversification. The fallout from the Paramount decision had blocked studio ownership of television networks, and further investment in music publishing arms seemed imprudent both legally and fiscally. Sheet music sales declined throughout the 1950s, causing music publishers to shift their interests toward royalties and licensing fees rather than outright sales. By 1952, only 15 percent of sheet music sales came from popular music titles. The remainder comprised sales of classical, religious, and educational music (Sanjek 1996, 325).

Besides these antitrust suits and the concomitant shift toward strategies of horizontal integration, the Hollywood majors' interest in record subsidiaries was spurred by enormous growth in this sector of the music industry. The family hi-fi was quickly replacing the family piano as the chief medium of music entertainment in the home. Between 1946 and 1951, consumers purchased more than 22 million record players. During that same period, according to the RIAA's first published report, record sales grew from 8 million in 1946 to 186 million in 1951 (Sanjek 1996, 245). Revenues from record sales showed similar growth throughout the 1950s. In 1951, retail sales of recorded music totaled $191,000,000; by 1959 that figure had grown to $514,000,000. When the bulk of Hollywood majors established their record subsidiaries in 1957 and 1958, they obviously saw this emerging market as an opportunity for film and music cross-promotions, but they also saw these new companies as ventures that might be profitable in their own right. As *Variety* noted in 1958, "The film companies want in to the record business for more than just pic tie-in reasons. They realize it's a booming business and they want their share" (Gross 1958, 215).

New technologies, of course, themselves played an important role in film studios' new-found interest in the record business. At least some of the growth in the record business derived from the innovations in microgroove recording technologies. Columbia Records introduced twelve-inch long-playing microgroove records in 1948. RCA Victor soon followed with their own 45-rpm microgroove discs (Millard 1995, 204–7). For its part, the film industry also contributed to the fervor for improved audio quality as part of the cinematic experience. The early 1950s saw the introduction of seven-track and four-track magnetic stereo soundtracks as a feature of Cinerama, CinemaScope, and Todd AO (Belton 1992). The introduction of stereo sound was part of the push toward widescreen exhibition that was associated with colorful spectacle, as the new technologies seemed to favor certain kinds of motion picture genres, such as the Biblical epic, the Western, and, of course, the musical.

With all of the major studios invested in recorded music subsidiaries, the cross-promotion of film and music products took on a new sophistication in the period between 1957 and 1975. Obviously, the previous era had seen its share of popular musical themes from motion pictures, as evidenced by such titles as "The Moons of Manikoora" from *The Hurricane* (1937), *Laura* (1944), *The Third Man* (1949), and *Love Is a Many-Splendored Thing* (1955). Yet the combination of Hollywood investment in record subsidiaries and a new generation of composers ready to supply much-needed commercial appeal to film scores pushed the "big theme" approach commonly associated with Hollywood classicism to new heights. In 1960 alone, popular musical themes from *Exodus*, *The Apartment*, *The Alamo*, and *Never on Sunday* dominated record charts. Ernest Gold's million-selling title theme from *Exodus* placed four different albums in *Variety*'s Top Ten: the *Exodus* original soundtrack album, a recording of Gold's score by "elevator music" maven Mantovani, UA's collection *Great Motion Picture Themes*, and saxophonist Eddie Harris' genre-busting *Exodus to Jazz*. If anything, *Never on Sunday* proved even more successful. The UA soundtrack album from the Melina Mercouri film sold a very respectable 500,000 copies, but the title theme spawned more than thirty versions of the song in the United States and more than a hundred versions worldwide. These recordings, which were all released within a year of *Never on Sunday*'s premiere, accounted for an estimated total sale of between 14 million and 16 million units worldwide ("'Never' Racks up" 1961, 1; "'Sunday' Disks Hypo" 1962, 12).

The vogue for "big themes" also proved to be a defining characteristic of certain composers and even film franchises. During the 1960s, for example, Henry Mancini composed a half-dozen successful motion picture themes, including "Moon River" from *Breakfast at Tiffany's* (1961), the "Baby Elephant Walk" from *Hatari!* (1962), "The Days of Wine and Roses," "Charade," and the "Pink Panther Theme." Working with a number of other composers and lyricists, John Barry served up a string of successful title themes for the James Bond series, beginning with *From Russia with Love* in 1964. Bond's production team of Harry Saltzman and Albert Broccoli were acutely aware of the promotional value that a successful theme song provided. In a particularly telling anecdote, Saltzman and Broccoli rejected Bill Conti's initial submission of the theme for *For Your Eyes Only* (1981). When Conti inquired about the reason for the rejection, Satzman and Broccoli replied that they liked the theme very much. It simply had one problem; the first four words of the song needed to be "for your eyes only," thereby making it easier for Maurice Binder, who had designed Bond's credit sequences since *Dr. No* (1962), to match the lyrics to the film's title.

Many of the new film-owned record labels also experimented with innovative promotional gimmicks and campaigns. Not surprisingly, most of these efforts targeted disc jockeys, who proved to be the key node in efforts to gain exposure for theme songs on radio. On *Zorba the Greek* (1964), for example, 20th Century Fox Records sent disc jockeys free copies of the film's soundtrack album along with free bottles of Greek cognac ("'Zorba' Gets Full Drive" 1965, 6). For *Lawrence of Arabia* (1962), Colpix Records hired "harem girls" to deliver copies of the soundtrack featuring Maurice Jarre's famous score to disc jockeys in key cities ("Colpix Pushes" 1963, 6). UA Records offered free preview screenings of films to disc jockeys, station personnel, and key retailers. Disc jockeys received free promotional copies of the film's accompanying soundtrack album and single. Area retailers were given the opportunity to place advance orders for the soundtrack with UA distributors ("UA Previews" 1962, 5).

UA also experimented with rack sales in movie theater lobbies. Borrowing a strategy from the "rack jobbers" commonly found at the major labels, UA installed a compact, collapsible display rack in Brooklyn's Loew's Metropolitan Theater in October of 1960, and used it to display the soundtrack from Billy Wilder's film *The Apartment*. The LPs were encased in a special polyethylene sleeve, and were hung from the display rack by small holes at the top of the album's cover. After this pilot project proved successful, UA expanded the use of lobby displays to additional theaters, and even gave exhibitors a cut of the album's sales ("UA to Test" 1960, 18).

By the end of the decade, the compilation score of the late 1960s and early 1970s emerged as a profitable rival to the "big theme" approach. The reemergence of the compilation score in the late 1960s reflected the gradual incorporation of rock, funk, soul, and country and western styles into film composition. The soundtracks for *The Graduate* (1967), *Easy Rider* (1969), and *Super Fly* (1972) each sold more than a half million units between 1967 and 1973. Moreover, as evidence of the "long tail" potential of a successful soundtrack, the album for *The Graduate* sold more than a million additional copies on the occasion of the film's thirtieth-anniversary reissue. More importantly perhaps, each of these soundtracks also provides evidence of film and music's cross-promotional potential. The box office returns for these films range from modestly successful in the case of *Super Fly*, a low-budget blaxploitation film, to box-office smash in the case of *The Graduate*. The latter earned approximately $105,000,000 in its initial run and rereleases, a sum equivalent to more than a half billion in today's dollars.

1975: THE DOLBY ERA

Although the Dolby Labs began work on adapting their signature noise-reduction technologies to cinema in the late 1960s, Dolby Stereo did not make its debut as an exhibition technology until the 1975 release of *Tommy* and *Lisztomania*, two camp classics directed by the British music auteur Ken Russell. At the time, Dolby's interest in enhancing the cinematic experience of music in films may have been partially driven by the sales slump for soundtracks albums that Hollywood experienced in the mid-1970s. The sales of *The Sting* (1973) and *American Graffiti* (1973) notwithstanding, some industry analysts believed that the fad for rock soundtracks had run its course. *Tommy* itself proved to be a case in point. The film adaptation of the Who's rock opera was the first of several music-oriented projects developed by the Robert Stigwood Organization. Despite the fact that the film boasted memorable musical performances by Eric Clapton, Tina Turner, and Elton John, sales of *Tommy*'s soundtrack albums stagnated during the film's theatrical run. *Tommy* did achieve a gold record certification on March 18, 1975, a day before the film's New York premiere, but it never reached platinum status. More tellingly, it was the only soundtrack album to achieve gold record certification that year. This was followed by an even bigger sales slump as no soundtrack album would achieve even gold record status in 1976.

Most historians note that Dolby placed its early emphasis on music-oriented projects, ostensibly in an effort to bring the kind of sonic experience associated with rock concerts to movie theaters. Michel Chion describes the phenomenon:

For musical films in multitrack (Dolby Stereo), particularly rock films where musical sound explodes throughout the space, this presence of sound only amplifies something already perceptible in older musicals: the power and definition of the musical sounds, along with their quality of overflowing the boundaries of the screen, tends to displace the "place" of the film from the screen to the movie theater itself or, more precisely, to situate the music in the large auditory space defined by the loudspeakers. (Chion 2009, 219)

Vincent Canby's review of *Tommy* underscores Chion's point about the physical presence of the film's music:

Ken Russell makes movies the way another man might design a ride through a funhouse. He deals in headlong but harmless plunges from giddy heights, abrupt changes of pace, joke turns, anachronistic visual effects, ghouls that pop out of the dark, all accompanied by sound of a force to loosen one's most firmly rooted back teeth. (Canby 1975, 48)

But a funny thing happened on the way to the concert. As historians from Gianluca Sergi (2004, 11–35) to William Whittington (2007, 115–26) and the team of Buhler, Neumeyer, and Deemer (2010, 366–391) all note, Dolby seemed to find its true métier in the innovative sound designs for films like *Star Wars* and *Close Encounters of the Third Kind*, both released in 1977. According to Buhler, Neumeyer, and Deemer, the emphasis on special effects in films of the late 1970s proved to be an important factor in the relatively rapid diffusion of Dolby Stereo technologies: "These effects were aural as well as visual, and theaters that had invested in better sound systems found that their revenues were significantly outpacing those that had not" (Buhler, Neumeyer, and Deemer 2010, 374). Spurred by the enormous success of Dolby Stereo and 70mm six-track sound for *Star Wars*, the total number of movie theaters wired for Dolby stereo topped 200 by the end of 1977. That number rose to more than 1200 theaters by 1980 and soared above 6000 approximately a decade after *Star Wars'* debut (Buhler, Neumeyer, and Deemer 2010, 374; Block and Wilson 2010, 525–26).

Yet, while much of Dolby's burgeoning popularity in the late 1970s derives from its enhanced frequency range and dynamic response of sound effects, one should not overlook its equal impact on the audience's experience of music. As Stephen Handzo points out, "In some stereo films only the music is mixed stereophonically, with dialogue and sound effects still coming from the center channel alone" (1985, 423). Of course, both *Star Wars* and *Close Encounters* also featured memorable scores by composer John Williams, and the increased attention to sound in each film may have helped to drive sales of their accompanying soundtrack albums. The album for Steven Spielberg's film sold more than 500,000 units while the album for Lucas's was certified platinum just three months after *Star Wars'* premiere.

This combination of "cutting edge" sound design and booming symphonic music proved to be an important model throughout the 1980s for production teams working in the genres of both science fiction cinema and the newly designated "action" film. Steven Spielberg, for example, mined this combination in films like *E.T.: The Extra-Terrestrial*

(1982) and his Indiana Jones series. Others followed Spielberg's lead with a string of box office smashes that include director James Cameron's *The Terminator* (1984), *Aliens* (1986), and *The Abyss* (1989) and producer Joel Silver's *Predator* (1987) and *Die Hard* (1988). Silver is often pitted against the team of Don Simpson and Jerry Bruckheimer as action auteurs of the 1980s, but it is worth noting that all of them showed interest in the commercial potential of film and music synergies throughout their careers. Although the efforts of Simpson and Bruckheimer are well documented, Silver's activities should not go unnoticed. Silver served as coproducer of the Olivia Newton-John vehicle *Xanadu* (1980) and later employed such notable pop and jazz musicians as Eric Clapton and Herbie Hancock as film composers. Silver's productions of *Weird Science* (1985) and *Jumpin' Jack Flash* (1986) also feature scintillating title songs recorded by Oingo Boingo and Aretha Franklin respectively.

The enlarged frequency range, increased dynamic contrasts, and multitrack sounds afforded by Dolby Stereo proved to be an engine for sound design innovations through-out the late 1970s and early 1980s, but one should not lose sight of the fact that it also proved to be a key component of the soundtrack album's revival during this same time period. Robert Stigwood took another bite at the apple with *Saturday Night Fever*, and this time the end result was the best-selling soundtrack album of all time. The soundtrack was certified platinum less than three weeks after the film's premiere, but unlike *Tommy*, it went on to sell an additional 10 million copies over the course of the next seven years. There seems little doubt that at least part of the music's appeal derived from Dolby's fuller bass response and the "walls of sound" that Michel Chion notes was part of the initial impetus to use the technology for "pop films" of the mid-1970s. A. D. Murphy underscored this point in his initial review of the film in *Variety*, noting that the sheer amount of music in *Fever* meant that it frequently plays in the background of scenes: "With Dolby sound and modern recording techniques, the music can be played at mercifully high noise levels" (Murphy 1977, 12). More importantly, perhaps, *Saturday Night Fever*'s success was duplicated by other nonsinging musicals, such as *Flashdance* (1983) and *Footloose* (1984), which sold six million and nine million units respectively.

These two forces unleashed by the development of noise reduction and multitrack sound systems—that is, advances in sound design and the "wall" of popular music—existed more or less in tension with one another during the first decade of the Dolby era. This tension was finally resolved in a very successful string of action films mounted by the production team of Don Simpson and Jerry Bruckheimer. This cycle, which included *Beverly Hills Cop* (1984) and its sequel, *Top Gun* (1986), and *Days of Thunder* (1990), achieved industry recognition for a potent combination of pop music and action film sound aesthetics. Taken together, these four titles brought Simpson and Bruckheimer more than $1.1 billion in global box office revenues and soundtrack album sales of more than 12.5 million units.

If one accepts this historical overview of film production and commerce circa 1975, then Dolby Stereo emerges as a hidden mainspring for the soundtrack album's ascendance as a particular type of music commodity and ancillary revenue stream for cinema. The period between 1977 and 1999 appears now as a kind of "golden age" of film and music synergies. The Dolby era bore witness to several of the biggest selling soundtrack albums of all-time, including *Purple Rain* (1984), *Dirty Dancing* (1987), *The Bodyguard* (1992), *Forrest Gump* (1994), and *The Lion King* (1994). Each of these titles enjoyed sales of at least 10 million units and are also among the Top 100 best-selling albums of all time. They also serve as exemplars of a formula for successful film and music cross-promotions that was already established in industry trade press as early as 1979. As Susan Peterson noted in *Billboard*, this formula included "commercially viable music. Timing. Film cooperation on advanced planning and tie-ins. Music that's integral to the movie. A hit movie. A hit single. A big-name recording star. A big-name composer" (1979, ST–2).

Besides providing ancillary revenues and cross-promotional opportunities, soundtrack albums and theme songs offered an additional economic benefit during this period, namely minimizing risks. For example, when Thom Mount, Universal's head of film production, agreed to greenlight *The Wiz* (1978), he did so only after consulting the record sales of the film's star, Diana Ross. According to Mount, the thinking was that, with a $13,000,000 budget for *The Wiz*, Universal would break even on sales of the film's soundtrack regardless of whether or not it succeeded at the box office. When *The Wiz*'s budget swelled to approximately $37,000,000, though, the cost overruns negated the studio's efforts to minimize financial risks, and the film went down in history as one of the biggest flops of its time. Viewed in retrospect, Mount's business philosophy was sound, even if his ability to handle Ross and director Sidney Lumet was not.[4] A similar pattern appeared in the mid-1990s in low-budget films, whose soundtracks enjoyed exceptional sales apart from the films they accompanied. For example, the albums for *Above the Rim* (1994) and *Set It Off* (1996) enjoyed long stretches in *Billboard*'s Top Ten that extended well beyond their films' theatrical runs. The tepid box office figures for these films suggested that many of those who bought the albums never bothered to see the films that they accompanied. Thus, although the *Above the Rim* and *Set it Off* themselves were flops, their costs of production were nonetheless counterbalanced by the strong sales of their respective soundtrack albums.

With the debut of MTV in 1981, film producers and record labels soon added music video to this already established formula. It is tempting to argue that MTV exposure simply offered " wine in old wineskins," but that description overlooks the extent to which a music video was able to communicate information about a film in a more complete and efficient fashion. A music video for a film functioned essentially as an elongated trailer that, if successful, aired for free up to eight times a day on a channel that was often popular with the film's target demographic. More than that, however, since a "music trailer" also included actual or additional footage from a film, it gave its audience a better idea of the film's stars, genre, story, and visual style than an accompanying album or single would. By circulating imagery from the film itself, a music video established a natural connection to the film that, for the most part, could have been realized previously only through a title song.

The sales patterns for soundtrack albums also reveal the kind of "long tail" economic activity that is the hallmark of the industry's biggest hits. Between 1984 and 1999, for example, the *Saturday Night Fever* soundtrack sold more than four million copies, bringing the album's final total to some 15 million units. Similarly, nearly half of the 9 million in sales enjoyed by the *Top Gun* soundtrack occurred between 1989 and 2000, a period at least three years after the film's initial release. These strong catalog sales, attained sometimes several years after the film's initial box office run, attest to the value of synergies within a diversified entertainment conglomerate. As evidence of a film's continued popularity, these sales not only add to a film's revenue streams, but they also enhance the value of a film on video platforms, in cable television markets, and in advertising revenues on broadcast television.

1999: The Downward Spiral

The year 1998 represented perhaps the peak year for soundtrack sales and for the film and music industry synergies that supported them. *Titanic* was the year's best-selling album overall, bringing its total to over 10 million units sold. *City of Angels* (1998), buoyed by the massive popularity of the Goo Goo Dolls' "Iris," also sold well and was certified quadruple platinum by the RIAA by the end of the year. Overall, some thirty-eight soundtrack albums were certified either gold or platinum in 1998, a total that amounted to about 11 percent of the overall number to achieve that distinction.

Since then, however, soundtrack sales have begun a slow downward slide. In 1999, some twenty-seven soundtrack albums were certified either gold or platinum. By 2004, that number shrunk to nine motion picture soundtrack albums. By 2007, the number of gold or platinum movie soundtracks had shrunk to two.

There are a host of factors that contributed to the decline in soundtrack album sales over the past decade, but chief among them was the growing popularity of digital file-sharing services. The prototype for MP3 technology debuted in 1991, but most industry analysts suggest that the rapid spread of digital file-sharing services was roughly coincident with the soundtrack album's commercial ascendance in the late 1990s. In 1997, Michael Robertson established MP3.com as a hub for internet users seeking free music, and as Steve Knopper notes, "'MP3' displaced 'sex' as the most-searched-for term through internet search engines, such as Yahoo and Alta Vista" (Knopper 2009, 119). This was followed by the introduction of Napster in 1999. Within a few months of its debut, Napster claimed approximately 150,000 registered users. By July of 2000, that total topped 20 million (130–35).

The RIAA attempted to stem the tide through targeted litigation, but the industry's legal strategy backfired, at least partly because it ended up criminalizing the very same music fans that record companies hoped would salvage the marketplace. Efforts to contain the effects of downloading undertaken in other countries have not fared much better. A 2009 article in *The Economist* reported an estimate by International Federation of Phonographic Industry that 95 percent of all downloads are illegal ("Singing a Different Tune," 73).

Album sales have declined steadily throughout the decade, largely as a result of downloading, both legal and illegal. The industry reported sales of almost 755 million units in 1999. By 2009, that number dropped to 374 million units, a little more than half the total sales of ten years earlier (Jurgensen 2010, W12). Long before the financial crisis of 2008, the music business was already hemorrhaging jobs as a result of this sales decline. From 2000 to 2007, record companies laid off more than 5,000 employees as Internet distribution rendered record manufacturers and warehouses anachronistic almost overnight. A more recent report places the total job loss at about 60 percent of the work force employed at major record companies (W12).

While the outlook is bleak for the music industry as a whole, the sales of soundtrack albums were affected even more than other kinds of products. Sales of soundtracks dropped some 34 percent between 1999 and 2004 compared to only a 12 percent drop in overall sales of recorded music during that same period. Much of this drop resulted from the fact that the soundtrack album became increasingly outmoded by a business model that favored the sales of individual tracks. During the 1990s, many soundtrack albums functioned as music samplers that bundled together a package of songs from different artists. In many instances, these soundtrack samplers offered consumers an overview of a particular musical style. *The Crow* (1994), for example, featured several goth and heavy metal bands while *200 Cigarettes* (1999) included several songs by classic punk and New Wave artists. Yet, in the era of iTunes and iPods, consumers no longer need to rely on film producers or soundtrack division executives to create a sampler of music from a particular film. With vast libraries of music available through the click of a mouse, fans of a film can create their own "samplers" for a film at a fraction of the soundtrack album's list price.

More importantly perhaps, the widespread popularity of illegal downloads has forced the industry to shift its demographic for soundtrack album sales. During the 1990s, soundtrack albums could serve as a marketing tool for just about any film or music genre. In 1999, for example, soundtrack sales certified gold or platinum were culled from romantic comedies (*You've Got Mail* [1998], *Notting Hill* [1999], *The Runaway Bride* [1999], *My Best Friend's Wedding* [1997]), comedian comedies (*Austin Powers: The Spy Who Shagged Me* [1999], *Life* [1999], *Blue Streak* [1999]), science fiction (*Armageddon* [1998], *The Matrix* [1999], *Star Wars Episode 1: The Phantom Menace* [1999], *End of Days* [1999]), animated films (*The Rugrats Movie* [1998], *Tarzan* [1999], *Pokemon: The First Movie* [1999]), and even some oddball generic hybrids (*Wild Wild West* [1999], *The Full Monty* [1997], *Bulworth* [1998]). By contrast, in 2006 and 2007, soundtrack albums were effective in targeting a single demographic: preteen girls. Among the top sellers of that two-year period were *High School Musical* (2006) and its sequel (2007), *Hannah Montana* (2006–), *Hairspray* (2007; starring heartthrob Zac Efron), *The Cheetah Girls 2* (2008), *Cars* (2006), and *Curious George* (2006; featuring Jack Johnson and friends).

This sales pattern is almost directly attributable to consumer habits related to illegal downloading. According to Mitchell Leib, the vice president and general manager of music and soundtracks at Buena Vista Music Group, "consumers younger than 13 and older than 30 do not download as much music as consumers between those ages"

(Conniff 2004, 24). "Tween" girls account for the lion's share of current soundtrack sales, but music-oriented films aimed at an older demographic have spun off several successful soundtracks over the past decade. This group of titles includes *O Brother, Where Art Thou?* (2000), *Walk the Line* (2005), *Chicago* (2002), and *Dreamgirls* (2006). In addition to those two groups we might include a third whose sales record is even spottier: quirky indie films, such as *Garden State* (2004), *Once* (2006), and *Juno* (2007). Evidence suggests that taste-making websites—notably, Pitchfork—have played an important role in promoting some of these quirky indie soundtracks (Barker 2010, 40). According to Pitchfork founder Ryan Schreiber, "There's definitely been a lot of overlap in the last few years between the music that we cover and music that's been used in film and TV soundtracks. Some of it is the result of people who grew up with independent and alternative music like we did...moving into those worlds, although I've also been told by people working in film and TV that they read Pitchfork" (Barker, 2010, 40).

Despite the decline in album sales, though, the amount of licensed music in films does not appear to have diminished. Since revenues for record companies have shrunk across the board, artists and labels have increasingly looked at licensing fees as an important source of income to offset the decline in album sales. Television shows, advertisements, video games, and of course, films all continue to provide exposure to new artists and opportunities to exploit the back catalogs of older artists. Moreover, when an artist's licensing activities are coordinated with release dates, the increased visibility garnered by advertisements and movie trailers can enhance actual sales, albeit usually in the form of digital downloads. Consider the Volkswagen campaign that featured five different tracks from Wilco's *Sky Blue Sky* album. More recently, Phoenix's song "1901" cracked *Billboard*'s "Hot 100" chart more than six months after the album's initial release, largely due to its appearance in a series of Cadillac ads.

The increased interest in licensing opportunities has been good news for film companies as the competition for placement has driven down costs. More than a decade ago, the licensing fees for an established artist ranged between $500,000 and $1,000,000. Today, the average licensing fee for a film tops out around $100,000. High price tags, of course, are still attached to the work of big-name artists. In a widely reported example, Conan O'Brien forced NBC to cough up $500,000 for the rights to the Beatles' "Lovely Rita." The song was used as "walk out" music for Tom Hanks, who appeared as a guest on the last show of O'Brien's tenure as the host of *The Tonight Show* (2009–2010). Earlier that same week, Conan O'Brien used the Rolling Stones' "Satisfaction" as walk-out music for guest Adam Sandler. For most music supervisors on films, however, these licensing costs are simply beyond the amount allocated for most music budgets and are likely to remain rarities, given that a smart music supervisor can license tracks from lesser-known artists for the bargain basement price of $2500.

With a decline in soundtrack sales and lower average licensing costs, film companies were encouraged to retrench throughout the 2000s. Studios are tightening their budgets in order to scale production costs for soundtrack albums to the current market. For example, by keeping the budget for the soundtrack of *The Wedding Crashers*

(2005) under six figures, it needed to sell only 100,000 copies in order to turn a profit (Fiore 2005, 15). Additionally, producers are spreading their financial risks by encouraging composers to accept a package or "all in" deal, "which require that the talent pay for the production costs out of their own pocket, including the hiring of musicians, studio time, engineers, orchestration, music editing and mixing" (Chagollan 2009, 20).

These "all in" deals can be traced to the early 2000s. Several music production houses tried to appeal to film and television producers by marketing a "one-stop shopping" concept that provided music composition, arranging, recording, and mixing all under one roof (McDonald 2002, A54). In 2002, *Variety* cited Hans Zimmer's Media Ventures and Jonathan Wolff's Music Consultants Group as leading innovators of this "one-stop" concept. Wolff himself noted that this growing trend was supported by technological advances in digital audio technology and by a turn away from orchestral scores toward electronic cues in television music. Yet the trend was also driven by the desire to cut music costs discussed earlier. As Kathy McDonald noted, "These days, film and TV producers expect music to include creative and production costs..." (2002, A54).

This strategy has helped producers keep their music budgets to about 1 percent of the overall total negative cost by making composers themselves responsible for any cost overruns. As a direct result, morale among Hollywood composers has slumped. According to former Society of Composers & Lyricists president James DiPasquale, "There has been a tremendous devaluation of music. Respect for composers has diminished. Technology has marched forward, and our income has plummeted. At the rank-and-file level, it's very hard for anyone to make a living" (Chagollan 2009, 20).

CONCLUSION

Looking at the current media landscape, it is hard not to conclude that the partnership between the film and music industries has reverted to the kind of relationship that prevailed in a previous era. Sales of compact discs continue their race to the bottom, and it seems unlikely that digital downloads of single songs will ever make up for the revenue lost. Filmmakers have retrenched in response by shrinking their music budgets. In 1973, director George Lucas spent about 10 percent of his overall budget getting the mechanical and synchronization rights to the forty-one songs that appeared in *American Graffiti* (Smith 1998, 172–73). That may not sound like much, but it is absolutely spendthrift when compared with current music budgets, which account for only about 1 percent of a film's total negative costs (the industry term for everything needed to create the film negative, or all of the planned expenses of the production—but not marketing—budget).

More importantly, perhaps, as soundtrack album sales have tanked, so have film producers' abilities to use film and music cross-promotions as a means of spreading risks.

It is unlikely that any producer will say, "The film may bomb, but we can still get over on sales of the soundtrack." This was a useful strategy during the 1990s when a commercially viable soundtrack album helped to defray the risks of a low-budget genre film, but it is now simply a way for film companies to throw good money after bad. And even the biggest box office smashes cannot carry their soundtrack albums to chart success the way *Titanic* did in 1999. In a telling comparison, James Cameron's *Avatar* (2009) earned more than a billion dollars in global box office by January 18, 2010. Yet the *Avatar* album could not even top *Billboard*'s soundtrack chart, much less its Top 200: its peak position was number 31, and after only five weeks in release, it had slipped down to number 91. As corroborative evidence of the pre-thirteen and after-thirty consumption patterns, *Avatar* trailed albums from *Alvin and the Chipmunks: The Squeakquel* (2009), *Glee* (2009–), and *Michael Jackson's This Is It* (2009).

Still, despite the forecasts of doom for both the film and music industries, there is a lot of popular music in films, and this simple fact alone may have strengthened their partnership for the long term. Even if consumers seem unwilling to pay for the music they enjoy, filmmakers can and do pay their "freight charges." Consequently, publishing revenues and performance fees remain important revenue streams for companies like Paramount or Fox, who do not have recorded music subsidiaries, but still see some economic benefits from a well-placed song.

Hollywood is also determined not to make the same mistakes as the music industry in managing the inevitable transition to some form of digital distribution. IMAX and 3-D both have been very effective in targeting high-value consumers for the film industry, and have even extracted additional dollars from filmgoers in the form of demonstrably higher ticket prices. Yet, just when it seems that stereoscopic, large-gauge films are the key to product differentiation, Sony and other electronic manufacturers seem to close that gap with 3-D television sets that can provide a similar experience without the viewers ever leaving home. Perhaps André Bazin and Aldous Huxley were both right in predicting more than a half century ago that cinema's teleology involves an inexorable march toward a fully sensory motion picture experience. But if the music industry's experience of the last ten years offers any lessons, it is that consumers may not pay for the "feelies" the way they once did for the movies.

NOTES

1. Studio Memo dated February 18, 1931. Music Department correspondence, *Dishonored*, Paramount Motion Pictures.
2. Studio Memo dated February 9, 1931. Music Department correspondence, *Dishonored*, Paramount Motion Pictures.
3. These figures are based on a sample of cue sheets from two archival collections of studio documents. The figures for United Artists films are based on cue sheets held in the United Artists Corporation Records, Series 2H (Mss 99An) at the Wisconsin Center for Film and Theatre Research, State Historical Society Library, Madison, Wisconsin. The figures for

Republic Pictures are based on cue sheets held in the Jack Mathis Collection (Mss 2389), Harold B. Lee Library, Brigham Young University.

4. Thom Mount offered these recollections at a workshop entitled "Film: Craft and Commerce" held at the Stern School of Business, New York University, May 8, 1998.

BIBLIOGRAPHY

Balio, Tino. 1993. *Grand Design: Hollywood as a Modern Business Enterprise, 1930–1939.* Berkeley: University of California Press.

Barker, Andrew. 2010. "A Prickly 'Fork in the Road.'" *Variety*, September 26, 40.

Belton, John. 1992. "1950s Magnetic Sound: The Frozen Revolution." In *Sound Theory/Sound Practice*, edited by Rick Altman, 154–167. New York: Routledge.

Block, Alex Ben, and Lucy Autrey Wilson, eds. 2010. *George Lucas' Blockbusting: A Decade-by-Decade Survey of Timeless Movies Including Untold Secrets of Their Financial and Cultural Success.* New York: Itbooks.

Buhler, James, David Neumeyer, and Rob Deemer. 2010. *Hearing the Movies: Music and Sound in Film History.* New York: Oxford University Press.

Burlingame, Jon. 2000. *Sound and Vision: 60 Years of Motion Picture Soundtracks.* New York: Billboard.

Canby, Vincent. 1975. "Film: 'Tommy', The Who's Rock Saga; Ken Russell's Method Finds Perfect Topic: Excess and Excitement and Many Decibels." *New York Times*, March 20, 48.

Chagollan, Steve. 2009. "Do Pix Value Noteworthy Work?" *Variety*, November 2, 20.

Chion, Michel. 2009. *Film, a Sound Art.* Translated by Claudia Gorbman. New York: Columbia University Press.

"Colpix Pushes Movie Track." 1963. *Billboard*, February 2, 6.

Conniff, Tamara. 2004. "Off Track: Soundtracks Continue to Fall Victim to the Overall Record-Sales Decline, But Musicals and Branded Releases Show Signs of Life." *Hollywood Reporter*, January 1, 24–25.

Crafton, Donald. 1997. *The Talkies: American Cinema's Transition to Sound, 1926–1931.* Berkeley: University of California Press.

Ewen, David. 1964. *The Life and Death of Tin Pan Alley: The Golden Age of American Popular Music.* New York: Funk and Wagnalls.

Fiore, Raymond. 2005. "Sound Waves: Battling a Slump, Movie Soundtracks Get Remixed." *Entertainment Weekly*, August 12, 14–15.

Gross, Mike. 1958. "Indies' Inroads on Major Diskeries' Pop Singles; $400,000,000 Record Mark." *Variety*, January 8, 215.

Handzo, Stephen. 1985. "Appendix: A Narrative Glossary of Film Sound Technology." In *Film Sound: Theory and Practice*, edited by Elisabeth Weis and John Belton, 383–426. New York: Columbia University Press.

Jurgensen, John. 2010. "The Lessons of Lady Gaga." *Wall Street Journal*, January 29, W12.

Karlin, Fred. 1994. *Listening to Movies: The Film Lover's Guide to Film Music.* New York: Schirmer.

Knopper, Steve. 2009. *Appetite for Self-Destruction: The Spectacular Crash of the Record Industry in the Digital Age.* New York: Free Press.

McDonald, Kathy A. 2002. "Technology Turns Composers Into One-Stop Music Shops." *Daily Variety*, July 29, A54.

Millard, Andre. 1995. *America on Record: A History of Recorded Sound*. Cambridge: Cambridge University Press.

Murphy, A. D. 1977. Review of *Saturday Night Fever*. *Variety*, December 14, 12.

"'Never on Sunday' Racks up Over 10-Mil Worldwide in Over 30 Disk Versions." 1961. *Variety*, August 9, 1.

Peterson, Susan. 1979. "Selling a Hit Soundtrack." *Billboard*, October 6, ST–2.

Romney, Jonathan, and Adrian Wootton, eds. 1995. *The Celluloid Jukebox: Popular Music and the Movies Since the 50s*. London: British Film Institute.

Sanjek, Russell. 1983. *From Print to Plastic: Publishing and Promoting America's Popular Music (1900–1980)*. Brooklyn, NY: Institute for Studies in American Music.

——. 1988. *American Popular Music and Its Business: The First Four Hundred Years*, volume 3, from 1900–1984. New York: Oxford University Press.

——. 1996. *Pennies from Heaven: The American Popular Music Business in the Twentieth Century*. Updated by David Sanjek. New York: Da Capo Press.

——, and David Sanjek. 1991. *American Popular Music Business in the 20th Century*. New York: Oxford University Press.

Sergi, Gianluca. 2004. *The Dolby Era: Film Sound in Contemporary Hollywood*. Manchester: Manchester University Press.

"Singing a Different Tune: Music Piracy." 2009. *The Economist*, November 14, 73–74.

Smith, Jeff. 1998. *The Sounds of Commerce: Marketing Popular Film Music*. New York: Columbia University Press.

Spring, Katherine. 2007. *"Say It With Songs: Popular Music in Hollywood Cinema During the Transition to Sound, 1927–1931."* PhD diss., University of Wisconsin Madison.

"'Sunday' Disks UA Hypo Plus." 1962. *Billboard*, March 24, 12.

"UA Previews 'Jessica' Film, Disk for Dealers & Deejays." 1962. *Billboard*, March 24, 5.

"UA to Test New LP Rack for Theaters." 1960. *Billboard*, September 19, 18.

Whittington, William. 2007. *Sound Design & Science Fiction*. Austin: University of Texas Press.

"'Zorba' Gets 20th-Fox's Full Drive." 1965. *Billboard*, March 27, 6.

CHAPTER 11

THE COMPILATION SOUNDTRACK FROM THE 1960S TO THE PRESENT

JULIE HUBBERT

In histories of American and Hollywood film music, the lion's share of attention has generally been given to the study of newly composed orchestral scores. Many histories (among them, Prendergast [1977] 1992, Palmer 1990, Marmorstein 1997, MacDonald 1998, Timm 2003, and Hickman 2006) present film music history as a parade of great composers, from Max Steiner and Erich Wolfgang Korngold to John Williams and Howard Shore. Important as these individuals were to the practice and development of music in Hollywood cinema, a full account must also include what was arguably the most substantial and long-standing method of musical accompaniment used in film: the compilation score. Although some have called the selecting and compiling of an accompaniment from preexisting sources a "second" practice, it was in fact among the first and is still today one of the most popular methods of film accompaniment (Rodman 2006, 120). Apart from obvious advantages in production efficiency and cost, its popularity as an aesthetic choice no doubt stems from the fact that it is quite separate and distinct from newly composed scores, which—orchestral ones especially—might be flexible and precise but have limited referential range. Compiled soundtracks, on the other hand, with their use of preexisting musical selections that hold a host of extrafilmic associations, have broad allusive powers that can easily and instantly add to a film's narrative power.[1]

The history of the compilation soundtrack begins with the beginning of the cinema itself. Sources tell us that improvisation was used in the early days, but musical accompaniments were also commonly constructed from preexisting sources, conglomerations of bits and pieces from different compositions often literally cut and pasted together (Hubbert 2011, 1–108). These rudimentary compilations varied in content and size depending on the length and genre of the film. Shorter, informative genres—sreels, travelogues, scenics, educational films, and comedies—were typically treated with popular music. Longer and more serious film dramas were treated with semiclassical or classical musical selections. Until music could be recorded directly onto the imagetrack, the technology used to articulate these compiled accompaniments were the instruments of live performance—piano, organ, and orchestra. There was some experimentation with the use of recorded music in silent-era accompaniment, but because phonograph records were difficult to edit or to manipulate in order to synchronize with the picture, live performance was the preferred method.[2]

When film production and exhibition converted to sound film in the late 1920s, compilation practice fell largely out of use. Sound film solved the perceived ills of live accompaniment, in particular, the lack of consistency and uniformity in exhibition. Now that music could be inscribed on the filmstrip itself, the soundtrack, and the film experience in general, no longer varied with each performance but was suddenly and uniquely uniform. As music became part of the production and postproduction process, the desire for it to be original and unique to each film, a feat first attempted in the silent period but abandoned as unfeasible, was also realized. Between roughly 1930 and 1965, composers were integrated into the industrial process to give each film a newly composed score, a musical accompaniment unencumbered by extrafilmic associations. Composers, especially well-known ones, were also incorporated into the process to give films prestige (Sklar 1994, 190–91; Balio 1993, 179–80). As sound film flourished, the practice of compilation quickly faded, being largely confined to low-budget pictures, including serials, and avant-garde and experimental films.

Thirty years later, however, the practice was revived, but now with important modifications. Most significantly, the medium of the music being manipulated was different. In the silent era, compilations were made by quilting together a variety of written scores, but in the postclassical period compilations were constructed from recorded music, in the same manner as stock or library music in the 1930s. The new compilation practice, however, repurposed music from readily available commercial recordings. With the element of live performance gone, the authorship of the compilation also shifted dramatically. Because the musical accompaniment was no longer controlled at the site of exhibition, authorship of the compilation passed from theater conductors to the film's director (in most instances). Composers were no longer needed. The popularity of the new compilation practice, in fact, is documented clearly in the complaints of composers being displaced and replaced by a new reliance on recorded music, or as one composer called it, "Griffithitis" (Raksin 1974, 26).

This resurfacing of compilation practice in the 1960s has not gone unnoticed by film or film music scholars, but the conditions of its return have been only partially accounted for. Some have tied its reemergence to the deep economic recession the film industry was experiencing at the time. The studios were revising their hierarchical structures to accommodate what they hoped would be a more lucrative, auteur form of filmmaking, one that allowed young, "second-generation" directors to control all aspects of the film including the musical soundtrack.[3] Others have argued that the compilation formula returned to accommodate new styles of popular music, rock music in particular.

Soundtracks turned to recorded music so that they would be fitted with healthy amounts of rock music that was proving to be very lucrative for the music industry.[4]

These events certainly influenced the return of compilation practice, but other considerations were equally significant, notably including changes in sound recording technology. Several scholars have theorized that the way we listen to and use music has been fundamentally shaped by the ways in which we store, disseminate, and access music. In his study of early analog sound reproduction technologies, Jonathan Sterne finds a direct correlation between technology and listening practices: "The very shape and function in technologies of sound reproduction reflect, in part, changing understandings of and relations to the nature and function of hearing" (Sterne 2003, 12). To some extent, he concludes, sound reproduction technologies, including radios, phonographs, records, and hi-fi stereos, have facilitated not only what we hear but how we hear it. Tim Taylor argues that the recent emergence of digital technologies has likewise changed our concepts of sound and music: "The increasingly personalized nature of music consumption," he observes, "made possible with digital modes of distribution, whether Internet or kiosk…means that listeners will be able to avoid buying a prepackaged bunch of songs on CDs or cassettes and instead put together whatever combination they want" (Taylor 2001, 19). Although digital technologies have allowed listeners to reconstruct the listening process in radically new ways, to some degree all sound recording technologies in this century, digital and analog, have done so. They have all altered the way we consume and consider music. As historian Mark Katz concludes, "Recorded sound is *mediated* sound. It is sound mediated through a technology that requires its users to adapt their musical practices and habits in a variety of ways" (2004, 2).

Certainly it is overly deterministic to claim that sound reproduction technology alone has changed musical practice. Katz, Taylor, and Sterne all argue that changes in listening practices have come from a fluid dynamic between technology and users, institutions, and personal agency; but at the same time they all conclude that to underestimate the importance of technology, or to overlook it, is equally dangerous. It is the "relationship between technology and its users that determines the impact of recording," notes Katz (2004, 4). "It is an influence [that] does not flow in one direction only, from technology to user,…users themselves transform recording to meet their needs, desires and goals and in doing so continually influence the technology that influences them." For Sterne, technology and cultural are not so much intertwined as they are manifestations of the same thing: "Technologies are repeatable social, cultural, and material processes crystallized into mechanisms…. Their mechanical character, the ways in which they commingle physics and culture, can tell us a great deal about the people who build and deploy them" (Sterne 2003, 8). Although there are dangers in this kind of "top down" model, Taylor warns, there are equal dangers in the opposite. "Bottom up" theories that deemphasize technology in favor of personal agency and cultural conditions are likewise limited. Social class, age, race, gender, and ethnicity are certainly involved in the making of artistic practice and conceptualizations of hearing and listening. The truth, he concludes, lies somewhere in between. Technology should be viewed "as neither voluntaristic nor deterministic but as caught up in a complex, fluid, variable dynamic of each" (Taylor 2001, 30).

In describing this deep connection between technology and the conceptualization of sound and music, scholars have focused on the effect technology has had on the production or composition of certain styles of popular music, in particular how technology has encouraged and facilitated the compositional phenomena of sampling and DJ-ing (Taylor 2001, 41–71; Katz 2004, 114–57; Théberge 1997, 186–213). Similar work, however, might well be undertaken to show how those same technologies have affected the mediation of music in visual or multimedia art forms such as film. Because film is not a purely musical art, because it is conventionally considered as primarily a mode of viewing rather than listening, the impact that sound recording technologies have had on the use of recorded music in film is easily overlooked, yet changes in the ability not just to record but to rerecord and manipulate music have in fact played a significant a role in the evolution of film music since the 1960s. Because of its reliance on preexisting recorded music, compilation practice in particular changed and adapted in direct response to innovations in recorded sound and music. The practice of compiling was shaped by economic conditions and marketing pressures within the film industry and by changing musical styles, but it also reemerged because of technical innovations in the way we construct, listen to, and access recorded music.

With an emphasis on these technological considerations, I will outline compilation practice in the postclassical period by describing the large-scale changes compilation practices have witnessed in the last several decades and by tying those changes to important advances in sound reproduction technology. Since the 1960s, at least three discernible and separate practices of compiling film soundtracks have emerged, practices that have been shaped by emerging analog, video, and digital sound reproduction technologies. The overarching goal is to contribute to a more detailed and nuanced account of the use of music in contemporary filmmaking over the last fifty years.

1960S: THE COMPILATION SCORE REEMERGES

For most scholars, compilation practice emerged with a group of films in the late 1960s that made significant, if not exclusive, use of preexisting or recorded work for their musical scores. *The Graduate* (1967) signaled this departure from traditional scoring practices: although the film made use of some underscoring—jazz-inflected cues composed by Dave Grusin—it prominently featured recordings of several preexisting popular songs. Selections from the Simon and Garfunkel album *Sounds of Silence* (1966) play over the opening credits and during three montage sequences. The film's director, Mike Nichols, had been listening to this album while shooting and editing the film, and he chose to insert songs from it because the text and style of the music accurately captured the mood of the film (Kashner 2008). On Nichols's request, Simon and Garfunkel even wrote a new song, *Mrs. Robinson*, for a montage sequence in the film. Technically speaking, the score for *The Graduate* is only a partial compilation, an amalgam of preexisting and newly composed music, but the striking use of contemporary pop music functioning as underscore (and thereby displacing orchestral music) began the process of revitalizing compilation practices.

Shortly thereafter, another critically acclaimed film, *2001: A Space Odyssey* (1968), featured a soundtrack similarly compiled from preexisting recorded music. Director Stanley Kubrick famously commissioned but then rejected a newly composed orchestral score by Alex North in favor of musical selections culled from recordings of nineteenth- and twentieth-century concert music. Stylistically, this compilation resembled a traditional orchestral underscore: easily identifiable classical selections such as Johann Strauss's *The Blue Danube Waltz* were mixed with the works of lesser-known composers, Dmitri Kabalevsky and Richard Strauss, and the then little-known avant-garde composer György Ligeti (Merkley 2007; Heimerdinger, 2011; McQuiston 2011). Nichols's compilation had been only partial, but Kubrick's was complete: the music consisted entirely of these preexisting and prerecorded works. Kubrick had made no accommodation at all for newly composed underscoring.

A year later, *Easy Rider* (1969) also challenged the conventional division of labor in the filmmaking process and altered the primary responsibilities of the director. Like Nichols and Kubrick, director Dennis Hopper seized control of the score and used recorded music. Where Nichols's film featured a mix of jazz underscoring and pop songs and Kubrick used only concert music, Hopper constructed an entire score from preexisting pop songs. To suit the contemporary themes and topics of his film, Hopper created a stylistically distinctive sound by repurposing songs from a variety of rock groups and artists including Steppenwolf, Jimi Hendrix, the Byrds, the Band, Fraternity of Men, the Electric Prunes, and Roger McGuinn (Smith 1998, 168–72).

The compilation format was pursued with increasing frequency throughout the 1970s, but sound and content varied widely. By the middle to end of the decade the practice of using preexisting music and preexisting recordings had not only become a legitimate scoring alternative but also one that seriously threatened the practice of the original orchestral score. Many films still used newly composed music or a mix of recorded music or songs and newly composed underscoring, but just as many of the most popular or critically acclaimed films of the decade used compilations of recorded music. *The Last Picture Show* (1971), *A Clockwork Orange* (1971), *American Graffiti* (1973), *Mean Streets* (1973), *Alice's Restaurant* (1969), *The Exorcist* (1973), *Rollerball* (1975), *Barry Lyndon* (1975), *The Shining* (1980), and *Raging Bull* (1980) all repurposed existing or recorded music exclusively. By the end of the decade, then, a new and definable practice had emerged, one with general characteristics that significantly challenged the sound, purpose, and authorial control of a conventional orchestral score.

These early compilations have a number of distinctive characteristics. Altogether they reveal a remarkable stylistic diversity, and they make use of a broad range of both popular and classical genres. Within individual films, however, stylistic restrictions apply. Each film for the most part adheres to a single style and often, especially when popular music is being used, to a stylistic time period. *The Last Picture Show*, for instance, features a nostalgic array of popular music from the 1950s, including songs by Hank Williams, Tony Bennett, Lefty Frizell, Pee Wee King, Frankie Laine, and others.[5] In *American Graffiti*, the nostalgia is for early rock 'n' roll, with songs by performers including the Big Bopper, Chuck Berry, Flash and the Cadillacs, the Flamingos, the Platters, the Diamonds, and the Monotones.[6] *Zabriskie Point* (1970) showcases music from a variety of contemporary psychedelic rock artists including the Grateful Dead, Pink Floyd, the Rolling Stones, Patti Page, and the Youngbloods. In *Alice's Restaurant*, a folk-rock soundtrack consists primarily of songs by Arlo Guthrie, with additional tracks by Joni Mitchell and Tigger Outlaw.

In other films from the period, compilations are patched together from excerpts of classical music. Kubrick's film *Barry Lyndon* features a few selections of Irish folk music, but also works by Schubert, Bach, Vivaldi, Handel, Mozart, and Paisello. The soundtrack for *The Shining*, likewise, includes a few pieces of popular music but consists primarily of classical music, including Bartók and avant-garde composers Ligeti and Penderecki.[7] Much of what William Friedkin uses in *The Exorcist* is equally contemporary, including recordings of works by Penderecki, Anton Webern, Hans Werner Henze, and George Crumb. Norman Jewison's sci-fi classic *Rollerball* also uses classical concert-hall music from multiple time periods—eighteenth century (Bach and Albinoni), nineteenth (Tchaikovsky), and twentieth (Shostakovich).[8] *The Sting* (1973), a nostalgia picture set in the "Roaring Twenties," repurposes turn-of-the-century piano rags by African American composer Scott Joplin. Only Scorsese's compilation for *Raging Bull* (1980) offers a range of musical styles, including jazz (Gene Krupa, Harry James, Ella Fitzgerald, Count Basie, Benny Goodman, Artie Shaw), popular song (Frank Sinatra, Nat King Cole, Louis Prima, Perry Como, Frankie Laine, Ray Charles), and opera (Mascagni).

If individual compilations were, in general, confined to a single style (that is, to either classical or popular music), the choice of style was determined primarily by filmic genre. Comedies or dramas with contemporary settings were given popular music; a classical or concert-music style was tapped for sci-fi, horror, or historical dramas. The size of the compilation also varied from film to film. Some, like *Easy Rider* and *The Exorcist*, used a modest number of works in their compilations, ten to twelve selections in all. Others were more expansive: *Mean Streets* cites twenty-three songs and *American Graffiti* forty-four.

The function of the music also varies widely. Those with large pop song collections, often employ music for *verité* purposes, to authenticate the film's temporal location and setting. In these films, the music is typically fragmented and distorted, sputtering and spilling out of car radios and jukeboxes. Other compilations foreground the music, using whole songs in extended montage sequences, letting the lyrics speak for characters, or commenting on screen action. In those films with classical compilations, the music also often follows scoring conventions by being placed "under" action or dialogue to set a mood or tone for a scene.

A key reason for the reemergence of the practice of compilation was the deep economic recession in which the film industry found itself by the late 1960s. With film attendance and revenue at record lows, film executives began to look for new sources of income. A key decision was to pursue the lucrative but underdeveloped youth market. To this end, studio executives began to recruit young filmmakers, many of whom were getting their training not in the industry but in newly formed university-based cinema school programs.[9] This new "film school generation" was given an unprecedented amount of artistic license by the studios, a change that produced an "auteur" style of filmmaking: these young directors assumed greater creative control over all aspects of production. As Claudia Gorbman notes, however, one of the elements they were most interested in controlling was music: "Significant changes in the post-studio era such as shifts in industry economics resulted in an influx of new musical idioms on one hand, and a vastly more flexible range of ideas concerning the nature, placements, and effects of music in movies on the other" (Gorbman 2007, 151). For some directors, music was a crucial aspect of their personal cinematic style. These "melomanes," as Gorbman calls them, treated music "as a key thematic element and a marker of authorial style" and thus placed "a premium on asserting control of the texture, rhythm, and tonality of [their] work, and of the social identifications made available through music choices" (149).

The industry recession in the 1960s also encouraged studios executives to form closer ties and in some cases new alliances with the music industry. As Jeff Smith notes, the reemergence of the compilation format in film music coincided with the expansion of the "theme song" model, but also with significant stylistic changes in the music itself (Smith 1998, 154–55). Rock music had been used in film throughout the 1950s in so-called "teen pics," or low-budget youth films, but in the 1960s it began to appear in more mainstream studio films.[10] Additionally, these films displayed not just a single style of popular music, but a growing diversity of rock 'n' roll styles. "Such diversity was especially important in the late sixties," Smith observes, "when the audience was increasingly fragmented into discrete demographic groups, and the charts were splintered by rock's growth into a number if distinct styles. Rock was no longer one entity but encompassed such varied forms as British pop, folk-rock, psychedelia, blues-rock, heavy metal, and even country-rock" (158). In order to produce film music that would have broad appeal, studio executives allowed their directors to embrace a scoring model with the potential to be lucrative, by capitalizing on this stylistic diversity of the marketplace. Compilation practice reemerged in part so that the film industry could share in the large profits the music industry was enjoying with rock music, but it also resurfaced in response to a fragmented marketplace. A miscellany of music was more appealing than a single theme-song approach, Smith notes, because it "spread the risk" and "would give the score and soundtrack album broader appeal by reaching a number of different segments of the music marketplace" (158).

Although these factors were certainly influential, they were not the only ones responsible for the reemergence of the compilation method. New sound recording technologies were making it possible for recorded music to be easily rerecorded and placed. Throughout the 1950s, many of the technical changes made to the recording of sound and music stemmed from a general interest in improving sound quality. Under the umbrella term "high fidelity," the goal was recording technology that could capture and reproduce a live performance as closely as possible.[11] Better equipment was seen as the key. By the mid to late 1960s, however, the discussion formed around the development of the new "stereophonic" or "stereo" sound. As major music serials and journals like *Billboard*, *Variety*, *High Fidelity*, and the newly established *Rolling Stone* magazine reveal, the music recording industry was making a large-scale conversion from monaural to stereo sound. "The real intent of stereo," sound historian Lawrence Morton observes, "was to add a sense of three-dimensionality to recordings of music. Consumers were told that stereophonic recordings sounded better because the sound was more 'realistic'. That is, stereo was marketed to consumers as an innovation in high fidelity, another step toward a system that could reproduce in the home the sound of the concert hall" (Morton 2004, 147).

The conversion to stereo addressed problems of sound quality, but it offered economic benefits as well, first of all to consumers: "What had started as a luxury good for the technically minded elite in the 1960s became a mass-produced consumer good in the 1970s. High-fidelity sound was now within the reach of college students and apartment dwellers" (Millard 2005, 222). The phasing out of monaural recordings forced listeners to buy new releases in the new format, but it also encouraged them to repurchase their old favorites. The conversion appears to have begun in earnest in early 1968 and was in full swing by July of that year. Although there was some resistance, including discussion about whether both platforms could be maintained, the conversion to stereo was largely complete by the end of the year (Fox 1968; "Col. Keys" 1968; McClay 1968).[12] Much of the unprecedented $1 billion in profits the music industry enjoyed in 1968 came from listeners seeking not only to expand their collections but also to convert them to the new stereo format.

The conversion to stereo also temporarily widened musical tastes. Because fidelity was a more pressing issue for classical music producers, especially the producers of avant-garde music, classical releases initially dominated the marketplace for stereo recordings: "Sales of highbrow music were...the core of the record business....Many in the record companies were high culture aficionados who used their positions to further the cause of technological development geared toward 'good' music listening and sincerely hoped that the public would respond" (Morton 2000, 45). The conversion to stereo encouraged listeners to be nostalgic, to replace old favorites with new stereo versions of them, but also to be adventurous, to buy newly recorded avant-garde music on the new format as well, an impetus that allowed niche companies such as Nonesuch Records to flourish.

Another dramatic technical change in the 1960s was the adoption of magnetic tape. In the 1950s, this had become the medium of choice in studio recording because it allowed musical performances to be "constructed" instead of simply captured. Tape could be physically altered, cut, and spliced, which meant that a musical performance could be easily edited, manipulated, assembled from parts. As a result, sound recording became more properly a process of rerecording, of mixing and layering or overdubbing of two or more recorded parts, of playing with speed and "punching in" corrections.[13] These innovations obviously encouraged and facilitated experimentation, but they also dramatically altered the relationship between recording and live performance. As historian Lawrence Morton observes, "Tape destroyed the already tenuous concept of an 'original' performance and made the performance a source of content to be refined rather than something to be preserved" (2000, 46).

In the mid-1960s, this process was modified with the introduction of the multitrack tape. The expansion from two to four channels dramatically expanded the ability to create a more complex sound landscape. The wave of experimentation that multitrack tape unleashed in pop music circles has been well documented. Recording artists like the Beach Boys, the Beatles, Frank Zappa, and Simon and Garfunkel developed new sounds from the methods of manipulation that multitrack tape permitted.[14] In the late 1960s, eight-track machines were introduced into studio recording; by the early 1970s, sixteen- and twenty-four-track recorders were common. With each expansion, sound recording became more complex and nuanced, but the new technology also shifted authorial control away from the musicians performing the music to producers and recording engineers who were doing the sound manipulation (Jones 1992, 173–77). As Chanan puts it, by the late 1960s recorded music, pop especially, was not only "a form based on fragmentation and distortion" but a form of music composed in the studio. It was "a unique artistic act whose artistry was produced through technology" (Chanan 1995, 147). By the late 1960s, recording had irreversibly become a process of ever-increasingly complex assemblage and collage. "The use of multitrack recorders," Morton observes, "transformed the recording process. It became routine for performers recording a song to make not one recording of a complete song but many partial recordings. The resulting recordings ... were constructed or synthesized from a collection of components, assembled from pieces like any other complex technological product" (Morton 2004, 150).

Magnetic tape also had a dramatic effect on the consumption of music. Some attempts were made to introduce tape recorders and players in the1950s, but because those options were more expensive, the phonograph continued to dominate the marketplace. The situation was reversed in the 1960s and early1970s, however, as the desire for portability grew. The market for car stereos allowed magnetic tape (eight-track, later the cassette) to challenge the LP record as the dominant sound recording format, so that, by the early 1970s, having already revolutionized studio recording, magnetic tape revolutionized personal listening as well. By 1975, over 12 million tape recorders were being sold every year in the United States, in comparison to a little over 1.3 million record players. The consumption of music on vinyl records still outpaced magnetic tape, but the boom in sales of tape recorders and the parallel boom in consumption of blank magnetic tape—in 1975, a startling 162 million blank cassettes were sold—indicated that consumers had found a new use for tape technology (Morton 2004, 164).[15] When paired with a tape recorder, which had now become portable and affordable, the blank tape offered consumers the ability to become recording engineers, selecting, rerecording, mixing, and editing music on their own. Tape technology had facilitated mobility, but now it also introduced a strong element of personal choice.

SCORE BY TOWER RECORDS

It was no accident that the compilation score based on recordings should emerge at this same time. The film score was reacting to the dramatic changes affecting the medium in which music was being recorded but equally to dramatic changes affecting *access* to recorded music. Up until the mid-1960s, most purchases were made at small record shops (which often doubled as camera and audio equipment shops) or at department stores. The situation changed around the middle of the decade when a new retail phenomenon emerged—the music "supermarket" or "megastore." By incorporating merchandising strategies borrowed from large grocery stores, the megastore offered consumers recorded music at heavily discounted prices. The strategy is a familiar one for big box stores: selling a vast number of items could generate just as much if not more revenue than selling fewer items with higher markups per item. Because the megastores purchased and sold huge numbers of record albums, the record companies also gave them lower wholesale prices. Floor space was, on average, triple the size of previous record stores. When the second Tower Records store opened in San Francisco store in 1967, for example, it had an unheard-of 5,000 square feet of retail space. By 1987, Tower Record's new Boston store was a staggering 39,000 square feet (Fabrikant 1987).

The new record stores flourished, and of course they also contributed to unprecedented growth and profits for the music industry. In the mid-1970s, music became the most lucrative entertainment medium, generating more profits than film, radio, or books (Millard 2005, 315). The large discounters all practiced variations on the basic marketing strategy, and by the mid-1970s, certain megastores dominated the marketplace in different regions of the country: Sam Goody in New York, Peaches in the South, Strawberry in New England, and Tower Records in the West (Levy 1976; see also "Record Industry" 1969). The last was one of the earliest and most influential. Founded by Russ Solomon in 1960, Tower Records opened its first store in Sacramento in 1960. By the end of the decade the megastore had seven locations, including San Francisco, which opened in 1967, and the Sunset Strip in Los Angeles (1969). As Solomon was one of the first to pursue the supermarket discount strategies, his stores created many of the other practices that defined the music megastore experience. Most carried a variety of styles beyond hit albums at discount prices, but Tower Records pursued this model of "deep cataloguing" more aggressively than others, carrying not only a large variety of musical styles but also a large number of niche or obscure recordings in each style (Welles 1984). Just as the conversion to stereo was encouraging consumers to have wider appetites, so was the music megastore. Solomon's stores also stayed open late and prided themselves on highly informed salespeople. Tower Records was also one of the first chains to have live in-store performances. Throughout the1960s and 1970s, many of the biggest acts in popular music, including the Rolling Stones, the Righteous Brothers, Arlo Guthrie, and the Dave Clark Five, all performed at Tower Records stores (Silberman 2000).

These technological and physical changes to the production and marketing of music in the late 1960s and early 1970s were dramatically changing the consumption of recorded music, and, inevitably perhaps, they also had a measurable effect on film music. Although few of the early practitioners of the post-classical compilation comment directly on the technical roots of compilation practice, on the influence of sound recording technologies and consumption patterns on their compiling or scoring activities, their actions and statements on selected occasions suggest just such a connection. For some directors, it was simply the new mode of access to music—the megastore with its unprecedented stylistic variety and nearly twenty-four-hour availability—that was responsible for the new, postclassical compilation. When William Friedkin, for example, jettisoned the score he had commissioned Lalo Shifrin to write for *The Exorcist*, he did so because he had a clear and easy alternative: recorded music. As he put it, "I went out and got the music off the records that I wanted, Penderecki and Henze and Anton Webern and I found a few little other things along the way and it really is Music Score by Tower Records." Friedkin also turned the knife a bit: as he put it, "I'd rather have the original Penderecki than bad Penderecki or rip-off Stravinsky" (Bernstein 1974–1975).

Mike Nichols had originally planned for Simon and Garfunkel to "do the music for the film" by providing *The Graduate* with a score of newly composed songs, but when they showed a lack of interest in doing so, Nichols worked instead with the film's editor to use excerpts from their latest recording (Kashner 2008). This easy substitution of pre-existing music for newly composed music, the easy transfer of music from one recorded format (record) to another (soundtrack), and the ease of editing the music to fit into certain spaces in the film, all reflect the new personal and portable status that recorded music was enjoying in the late 1960s.

For other directors, rerecording technology itself was very obviously atomizing and making mobile not only the music soundtrack but also all sound-related aspects of filmmaking, from dialogue and script writing to dubbing and creating voiceovers. As scriptwriter Jeremy Bernstein reveals, while making *2001: A Space Odyssey*, Kubrick's auteurism—his ability to personally choose and assemble parts of the film—was facilitated by a host of new technologies. "When we reached [his] trailer," Bernstein writes of Kubrick's production habits during the making of the film,

> I could see that it was used as much for listening as for writing, for in addition to the usual battery of tape recorders (Kubrick writes rough first drafts of his dialogue by dictating into a recorder, since he finds that this gives it a more natural flow) there was a phonograph and an enormous collection of records. (quoted in Agel 1970, 65)

Both dialogue and music for the film thus were enabled by technology that allowed them to be not only portable and fragmented, but also reassembled and compiled. The director's musical style choices also reflect the music marketplace. Bernstein continues from the quote above to say that "practically all of [the recordings] were of contemporary music," including not only for traditionally scored ensembles but also "*musique concrète* and electronic music in general" (quoted in Agel 1970, 63).

Bernstein's description clearly reflects the significant impact the new stereo technology was having on musical style, the increased availability of avant-garde classical music in particular.

Although Kubrick himself rarely spoke about his compiling aesthetic, the few remarks he did make suggest that his interest in the practice stemmed from a perceived gap in compositional skill between film composers and concert-hall composers but was greatly facilitated by the easy availability of the music of great composers, classical and avant garde, through high-quality, high-fidelity, stereo recordings.

> However good our best film composers may be, they are not a Beethoven, a Mozart or Brahms. Why use music which is less good when there is such a multitude of great [recorded] orchestral music available from the past and from our own time? When you're editing a film, it's very helpful to be able to try out different pieces of music to see how they work with the scene...with a little more care and thought, these temporary music tracks can become the final score. (quoted in Ciment 1983, 177)

THE MUSIC VIDEO COMPILATION

As we have seen, new sound reproduction technologies and marketing strategies helped the music industry produce a more varied, accessible, and precisely edited product, at the same time they were helping the film industry create a new, more varied, and personal soundtrack. Compilation practice resurfaced in the 1960s, but once it was reintroduced, it continued in play with increasing frequency throughout the 1970s. By the mid-1980s, however, the conditions of the compiling process had changed and were discernibly different: compilation scores became strikingly more uniform. The use of preexisting or recorded music was still central, but the size of the compilations, their stylistic content, and the music placement had all become less varied and idiosyncratic. This new uniformity was expressed in a number of characteristics, the most noticeable being musical style. Classical concert music was seldom heard, avant-garde classical selections even less so. Compilations now consisted primarily of contemporary popular music, rock music especially, and they now typically had a uniform length of ten to fourteen songs. The vast and varied collections heard earlier in films like *American Graffiti* and *Raging Bull*, unwieldy compilations that had been difficult to package, had been replaced by compilations that were easily transferable to a commercial soundtrack format.

As the recession of the early 1980s eased and the lucrative youth market was accessed by the use of a new "blockbuster" formula that replaced the auteur model, authorship also shifted. Directors were still often involved in the compiling process, at times in complete control of it as before, but with increasing frequency the selection of material was constrained by production company administrators. A new supernumerary in the process, the "music supervisor," oversaw licensing arrangements and other practical considerations necessary for the use of preexisting or recorded music (Smith 1998, 209–14). As before, directors and supervisors were often restricted in their musical choices by copyright permission and licensing fees, but now they were also confined by financial arrangements made between film and music executives. Since they continued to view the film soundtrack as a source of significant ancillary profits—and continued to own or forge alliances with record companies and music publishers—studios made more intense and direct efforts to cross-promote both products, film and music. Executives often restricted a director's or supervisor's compiling choices to music they owned or to music from groups with which their subsidiary record company had contracts (Romney and Wooten 1995, 133–34).[16]

What changed even more dramatically than the content of the compilation, however, was the film itself, specifically the visual style the film adopted when the compilation selections were heard in the soundtrack. This music was typically isolated within montage sequences, and directors pursued a new visual style that featured a distinctly faster editing pace. The editing style became not only faster but also more abrupt, and the imagery was often more abstract and at times only tangentially related to the narrative content of the film. These new characteristics are evident in a majority of studio films throughout the 1980s, but the conditions for them were articulated by a group of highly profitable films from the mid-1980s including *Flashdance* (1983), *Footloose* (1984), *Ghostbusters* (1984), *Purple Rain* (1984), *Beverly Hills Cop* (1984), *Top Gun* (1986), and *Dirty Dancing* (1987). Showcasing the soundtrack's pop music selections in a contemporary "music video" style and cross-promoting the selections with film-related imagery on MTV generated not only record ticket sales but record soundtrack sales for the studios.

At the heart of this new style was a host of new economic, aesthetic, and technical concerns. As Smith observes, the compilation persisted into the 1980s because of the studio's continued economic interests in using popular music to increase revenues from both ticket and soundtrack sales (Smith 1998, 196–208), but other factors were also constraining soundtrack compilations. A new "high concept" style of filmmaking was partially responsible, a change that consolidated many aspects of production to a stylized "look" or concept that could be easily marketed and merchandized to a large audience (Wyatt 1994, 20–22). Established or rising movie stars were tied to simple plots, and films had a modular structure that allowed for easy manipulation of the narrative. In this formula, several modules in each film were typically given over to the promotion of popular music, typically fast-paced montages set apart from the rest of the film by their lack of diegetic sound and noise and by their editing tempo which changed temporarily to articulate the rhythm and meter of the song (Wyatt 1994, 36–44). The changes were also being driven by a new generation of directors with different musical allegiances: as director Allison Anders put it, popular music is preferable to classical or newly composed orchestral music because it has greater extrafilmic referential capabilities. "Popular music is the only cultural reference we hold in common any more," she observes (Romney and Wootton 1995, 119). Economics, tastes, and new structures thus were all informing the change, but, as we shall now see, the formation of this new or "second" compilation practice was also being significantly influenced by the rise of the music video and cable television.

Although music videos had a unique and innovative style, they were far from the first attempt the recording industry had made at combining the visual aspects of a music performance along with the sonic. As historian John Mundy points out, the "visual economy" of popular music stretches back to the advent of sound film when the first Vitaphone shorts and early film musicals captured the sound and image of live musical performances. The first noncinematic visualization of pop music, however, came in the 1940s, with the advent of the "soundie." This short-lived phenomenon filmed the live performances of an array of popular musicians and displayed them by way of a special visual jukebox. This new technology allowed viewers not only to hear but also to see their favorite musicians and groups perform. Although prolific in production—between 1941 and 1947, the Panaram Company made over 2000 "soundies" (Mundy 1999, 93–95)—the format failed to catch on commercially. Nevertheless, record producers and music industry executives continued to look for noncinematic ways to capture and disseminate both audio and visual aspects of musical performances, such as "promotional clips," performances of single songs taped for use in TV variety shows, and "concert" films and full-length documentaries from the 1960s and 1970s that featured pop musicians and groups performing on screen. For the most part, however, until the 1980s, popular music was an audio experience accessible only through recordings or radio (Mundy 1999, 206–10).[17]

The new visual style of the music video was facilitated by a change of media. Before this, performances had been captured on film, but now the preferred format was half-inch videotape, which was not only cheaper than celluloid but, like magnetic tape for audio recordings, also easier to manipulate and edit. As a result, directors were inclined to do greater manipulation of the visual imagery and, significantly, to detach that imagery from live performance altogether in some cases. Older-style static, concert-like performances of pop songs thus were replaced by visually constructed montages that borrowed heavily from the vocabulary of avant-garde and experimental film.[18]

The editing pace of the visual material in music videos was also new and distinctive: intentionally abrupt and disjunct. If the aim of the music video was to use imagery to capture something other than a live music performance, then it was also to create something other than a conventional cinematic narrative. As Robert Pittman, who was the executive vice-president of MTV at the time, explained it, "What we've introduced with [music videos] is a non-narrative form. As opposed to conventional television where you rely on plot and continuity, we rely on mood and emotion." Music videos, he continues, "make you feel a certain way as opposed to you walking away with any particular knowledge" (quoted in Denisoff and Romanowski 1991, 346). The editing tempo of music videos was without precedent in either cinema or television, its much faster pace aimed specifically at young viewers. "If older viewers find the quick-edit communication motif disjointed and disorienting," the same executive observed, "the TV babies find it exciting and even stimulating" (346).

The music video had a strong effect on the mode of dissemination of recorded music: rather than LP records and radio, music video privileged—and required—an audiovisual mode of dissemination. Although television had become a very successful alternate medium for film—and continued to serve that role in cable television—in the early 1980s TV also became an important access point for the distribution of recorded music, thanks to the advent of a single network devoted to the display of music videos. When MTV—short for "Music Television"—began broadcasting in 1981, it was built around the novel idea of reconceptualizing television as a "visual radio." Exhibiting a continuous, twenty-four-hour stream of popular music, MTV pioneered a presentation format that specialized in audiovisual or music video performances. With little serious competition, MTV quickly became one of the most subscribed networks on cable, establishing itself in 22 million homes by 1984 and growing steadily to well over 30 million by the end of the decade.[19]

MTV and the Movies

The success of MTV and the music video had a profound effect on film marketing and production. Because videos targeted the same demographic that the studios had long identified as being most profitable—twelve to twenty-five year olds—MTV quickly replaced radio as the essential tool for advertising and promoting film soundtracks. Music videos of songs featured in films often incorporated footage from those films, and as a result they succeeded in promoting not just the film's soundtrack, but the film itself. Where radio airplay aimed primarily at selling soundtracks, music videos and MTV were used to sell both soundtracks and films. "With the introduction of music videos," one studio executive noted, "it was clear nothing sells films better than films" (Meyer 1985, 168).

The music videos' double promotional value altered the industrial model of both soundtrack and film promotion by consolidating the promotion of both to a single site. With minimal financial investment, a music video could turn a soundtrack into a hit record and, in certain cases, even help create a blockbuster film. Where radio had once reigned supreme, using saturation airplay to promote songs associated with movies, music videos and MTV facilitated a new "synergy" between film production and cable television. Videos were so successful at increasing box office as well as soundtrack profits, in fact, that studios began to invest directly in music video production, especially of songs featured on soundtrack compilations.[20]

Music videos also affected film structure and cinematic style. The idea of interrupting the narrative to feature a musical performance was hardly new, but what made these musical insertions different was the way in which they shifted into a dramatically different visual style and rhythm featuring disparate imagery, unstable camera movements, and quickly shifting perspectives. The visual tempo noticeably quickened at the beginning and slowed again at the end of the song, and even the length of the montages reflected music video practice, typically conforming to song lengths, which radio had for some time dictated be roughly three minutes (Dickinson 2001).[21] As the practice became more established, however, these "videoized" montage sections became shorter to conform to marketing research, which had established an alternative length, a minimum amount of time needed to catch the viewer's attention. "[You have] to go through the chorus twice or else [the audience] won't notice it," one music supervisor observes, "and presumably won't buy the soundtrack album" (Bob Last, quoted in Romney and Wootton 1995, 139). *Flashdance*, an early example of this "videoized" compilation practice, makes repeated use of "MTV moments." With the introduction of every song on the soundtrack, the film adopts a visible "MTV style." These inserts of "moments" are defined by "quick-cut montages of film imagery set to [the] driving beat [of the song]" (Meyer 1985, 168). The film visibly changes, the tempo suddenly quickens to fit the rhythm and structure of a pop song, and the "paper-thin story" easily accommodates the necessary modular structure.

Music videos thus altered the content of the compilation score not only by making it feature the styles and genres of music being heard on MTV but also by making films as a whole visualize music in the same fast-paced, disjunct, hyperstylized manner. Music videos forced films to develop a new structure, the modular design that alternated back and forth between cinematic style and music video style. As one music supervisor observes, the accompanying visual structure it demanded was one of the defining characteristic of the new compilation practice:

> There are a lot of mainstream movies where you can see the MTV moment coming up. . . . How do you tell it's coming up? There are subtle cues in the pacing of a movie. . . . There's a change in the tempo [pace,] it adjusts itself, sometimes very subtly [as if to say]. "OK, this is our MTV moment." . . . An audience can spot it a mile off. (Last, quoted in Romney and Wootton 1995, 139)

Such "moments" were noticeable not just because of their dramatic change in tempo, but because of their ubiquity: throughout the 1980s and 1990s, they were an expected part of most studio films.

The transfer of music video techniques to narrative filmmaking and to compilation practice was no accident. Many esteemed film directors such as John Landis, Brian de Palma, and Martin Scorsese made music videos, and many young directors, including David Fincher and Michel Gondry, got their start directing music videos. This exchange of talent between the two media directly facilitated the videoization of the compiled soundtrack and remade the filmmaking process. When *Flashdance* became one of the most popular films in 1983, many saw the influence of MTV and music videos in its structure and simplistic plot. It was like "looking at MTV for 96 minutes," claimed one critic ("Flashdance" 1983). This conclusion was confirmed by the film's producer who acknowledged that in the film's structure, "the modules were interchangeable—they were even moved around in the editing—and that's what made the movie adaptable to MTV" (Sragow 1983, quoted in Denisoff and Romanowski 1991, 359). *Risky Business* featured a compilation of classic pop songs, but as one critic described it, the film was "the

Easy Rider of the MTV generation" (Connelly 1986, quoted in Denisoff and Romanowski 1991, 368). All the dance sequences in the film *Footloose* (1984) were directly modeled after the music videos being shown on MTV, which the director Herbert Ross confessed to "watching religiously throughout production on the film" (Meyer 1985, 168).

By the mid-1990s, the "videoization" of the compilation soundtrack was so ubiquitous that directors no longer felt compelled to mention the influence of MTV, which points not only to the fact that the station's popularity was waning but also to the complete saturation the practice of videoizing music had achieved in studio filmmaking. But by then it had also become stereotypical and stale, as directors like Tarantino noted. Although the use of popular music, he argues, is still valid, abruptly inserting the shorthand language of the music videos was becoming the hallmark of a fading or obsolete practice. "It's like, 'Let's put a familiar song in—let's put "Pretty Woman" on the soundtrack or some old ditty that everyone knows and then build a little montage around that song.'" That's "lazy film-making," he argues (Romney and Wootton 1995, 139).

THE DIGITAL SCORE

By the late 1990s, films no longer systematically featured popular music in MTV-inspired modules. The interest in using preexisting, recorded music to score a film, on the other hand, has persisted into the present and in fact is as prevalent as ever, but the format for compiling it and placing it in a film has changed once again as still another practice of compilation has begun to emerge. The most interesting compilations in recent years reveal significant changes in size and content. Most are remarkably large, well beyond the typical length of a pop album of ten to fourteen songs. Many are so large, in fact, that, as in the late 1970s, it is difficult to extract all the music and contain it on commercial soundtrack recordings. In order to accommodate these large compilations, record companies have resorted to using a double-disc format, for example, with *He Got Game* (1998), *Casino* (1995), *Rushmore* (1998), and *Marie Antoinette* (2006). This is not to be confused with another double-album phenomenon used to accommodate films with both newly composed and preexisting music. For the films *Batman* (1989), *Dick Tracy* (1990), and *American Beauty* (1999), for instance, the studios released two albums, one of orchestral scoring and one of pop songs. Another strategy has been to reduce the compilation to a single disc by selecting from the compilation those songs and pieces producers think are most thematic or marketable. Both single- and double-disc schemes are widely practiced and strongly indicative of the distinctively large size of recent compilations.

Another characteristic of the new, third practice is stylistic variety. Instead of incorporating only popular music, many now feature a broad range of musical styles and genres. Although reminiscent of the 1960s and 1970s, there is one crucial difference. In the earlier period, compilation scores limited themselves primarily to one musical style, broadly speaking, either classical or popular. In recent compilations, the stylistic diversity occurs *within* individual films: a single compilation might feature not just several but a diverse range of musical styles, genres, and subgenres, from pop songs and opera selections, to television themes and rhythm and blues standards. The length of individual selections is also noticeably altered in the new practice. Preserving aspects of song structure and cadence points are no longer a priority. With large compilations especially, songs and individual pieces of music are often given only brief or fragmented presentation. Although this was also a characteristic of "Tower Records" compilations in the late 1960s and 1970s, what distinguishes recent practice is a difference in placement and function. In recent films, filmic space is not so rigidly reinforced by the soundtrack. The musical selections instead often move fluidly between diegetic, nondiegetic, and extradiegetic space, generating a host of narrative effects.

Anticipations of this trend surfaced in the late 1990s, as for example in *Casino* (1995), the last installment of Scorsese's trilogy of films that center on mob culture, where he crafts a large, stylistically diverse compilation that encompasses pop music from Louis Prima and Hoagy Carmichael to the Rolling Stones and Devo, theme songs and selections from previous films scores by Elmer Bernstein and George Delerue, and classical music. The film begins and ends with long excerpts from the opening movements of Bach's St. Matthew Passion. Another prominent example is Spike Lee's *He Got Game* (1998). In a film about basketball culture in urban inner-city life, Lee mixes a number of different orchestral selections by Aaron Copland from the 1930s and 1940s with rap songs from the 1990s by the controversial and politically charged group Public Enemy. Lee uses both genres of music to speak for the contemporary black urban experience (Gabbard 2004, 251–74).

Since 2000, stylistic diversity and stark juxtapositions of popular and classical music have become defining features of the compilation practice of a new generation of auteurs like Wes Anderson, Sofia Coppola, and Paul Thomas Anderson. In *The Royal Tenenbaums* (2001), Anderson serves up a soup of different pop, rock, and classical music from Bob Dylan, the Rolling Stones, Paul Simon, the Clash, and the Ramones to Erik Satie, Antonio Vivaldi, and Maurice Ravel. Although the range is somewhat less eclectic in *The Life Aquatic with Steve Zissou* (2004), the selections of preexisting music Anderson uses are nonetheless varied, ranging from J. S. Bach to David Bowie, Iggy Pop, Joan Baez, the Brazilian songwriter Jorge Seu, and the contemporary Icelandic rock group Sigur Rós. In his epic film about American oil prospecting at the turn of the century, *There Will Be Blood* (2007), Anderson alternately underscores and interrupts the film with dissonant orchestral and chamber works by contemporary Estonian composer Arvo Pärt and by Johnny Greenwood, bassist for the rock group Radiohead, bits of the Brahms Violin Concerto, and American hymn tunes.

If the idea of segregating compilations by musical style has been abandoned, so has the practice of confining certain styles of music to certain film genres.[22] As another period film, Sofia Coppola's *Marie Antoinette* (2006), proves, popular music is no longer reserved for films with contemporary themes and settings—even historical biographies can be made to accommodate an eclectic array of music. In Coppola's film, instrumental works by Vivaldi and Couperin and operas by Rameau share space with classic pop songs from the 1980s by Adam Ant, the Cure, Siouxsie and the Banshees, Bow Wow Wow, contemporary electronica by Aphex Twin, Squarepusher, Dustin O'Halloran, and recent rock hits by the Strokes, Radio Dept., and Windsor of the Derby.

Older auteurs have also adjusted to the new stylistic eclecticism. Kubrick's previous compilations did offer isolated instances of stylistic variety (in one notable instance, the song "Singin' in the Rain" interrupts Rossini and Beethoven excerpts in *A Clockwork Orange*), but in his last film, *Eyes Wide Shut* (1999), snippets of "Midnight, the Stars and You" and other popular songs play quietly in the background of a score dominated by Bartók, Penderecki, and Ligeti. His method here is related but clearly different from his earlier compilations. In what Gorbman terms a case of "systematic heterogeneity," Kubrick mixes jazz standards from the 1920s, 1930s, and 1940s with contemporary pop songs by Chris Isaak, orchestral music by Shostakovich, avant-garde piano music by György Ligeti, and newly composed music by Jocelyn Pook (Gorbman 2006, 18). Spike Lee's film *Inside Man* (2006) has an extensive jazz score by Terrance Blanchard that is reminiscent of 1950s scoring practices, but Lee also bookends the film with highly contrasting selections of preexisting music: at the opening, a hip-hop cover (by Panjabi MC) of a Bollywood tune, "Chaiya Chaiya," from the classic Indian film *Dil Se* (1998), and at the end, a Bruce Springsteen song, "The Fuse," from his 2002 album *The Rising*. Even directors like Quentin Tarantino, notoriously devoted to popular music, has succumbed to the trend: in *Kill Bill: Vol. 1* (2003), Tarantino mixes 1970s funk by Isaac Hayes and Ike Turner with television themes (Quincy Jones's theme for *Ironsides*) and orchestral music from preexisting cinema scores by Ennio Morricone, Riz Ortolani, and Bernard Herrmann.[23]

If recent compilations liberate directors from the unarticulated stylistic and genre prejudices of the past, that stylistic diversity has been accompanied by a similar liberation in terms of filmic placement. Directors have been using preexisting, recorded music for an array of purposes within a single film, shifting quickly from background to foreground and employing music both diegetically and nondiegetically. Although pioneers like Kubrick experimented with some of this, recent compilations have more consistently used a variety of filmic placements to generate a dense and allusive range of meanings.

This shift towards stylistic eclecticism may yet again be tied to profound technological shifts in the consumption of, and access to, recorded music. In the mid-1990s, that shift centered on the digitization of recorded music and the new modes of access and consumption patterns it required. Although the effects were nothing short of a revolution, on par with Edison's invention of the phonograph, the process unfolded slowly with a series of innovations running over the course of a decade. The digitization of music effectively began in the mid-1990s when researchers at a lab in Erlanger, Germany, sought to compress the data stream of audio recordings. The technology already existed to convert it to a digital format, but the information was so massive and unwieldy it was largely useless. By removing redundant and irrelevant parts of the code, the lab researchers discovered they could compress the stream to a useful and portable size that they called an MPEG (Morton 2004, 189–91). The group's third algorithm, known first as MPEG-3 and later as simply MP3, soon became the industry standard. Although the technology was first used by record companies to record more information on existing technologies like compact discs, it soon became available to the public, via the personal computer, for the purposes of copying and distributing music. Software programs and CD burners soon proliferated to help consumers render audio material from traditional formats like CDs into digital MP3s which could be easily stored on computers. As Millard notes, the writable CD player helped introduce the words "rip" and "burn" into the lexicon, as consumers could take a commercial CD and convert it, or "rip" it, to MP3 and store it on their computer, as well as export it by "burning" the information onto a blank CD (Millard 2005, 389).

COMPUTERS, PEER-TO-PEER SHARING, AND THE CINEMA

Once recorded sound was digital and compressed enough to be easily portable and transferrable, the distribution and consumption of music changed dramatically. Consumers were still articulating conventional consumption patterns using existing storage formats, like CDs, and access points, like record stores, until the late 1990s, when the advent of powerful software programs like Napster introduced the idea of "peer-to-peer" sharing.

Now that music could be easily rendered as a computer "file," music could be "shared" quickly and easily through the Internet. Napster facilitated the transfer by allowing users to access each other's music collections via their home computers. Between 1999 and 2001, and through websites like Napster and Gnutella, the concept of "file sharing" completely revolutionized the dissemination of recorded music (Coleman 2003, 182–204). In the first few months of operation, for instance, Napster alone had a half million users. Two short years later, it had 70 million users (Millard 2005, 394). Napster also became powerful because it kept the access to music free, to which the record industry of course objected vociferously. In 2001, the record industry's trade organization, the Recording Industry Association of America (RIAA), was successful in shutting down the site and others like it, but not before access to recorded music had been permanently altered (Coleman 2003, 177–200). As Millard notes, "Peer-to-peer exchange of music was a simple idea with enormous consequences. It did more than create a massive public library of sound recordings; it forged a global community of listeners" (2005, 392).

In the wake of the disintegration of Napster, the concepts of "file sharing" and "swapping" were replaced with the phenomenon of "downloading." Monthly online subscription services, such as Musicnet and Press Play soon sprang up. These were controlled primarily by record companies and media corporations; they offered listeners music digitally but at a price, typically through a monthly fee of $10. Rhapsody's service distinguished itself by allowing subscribers to purchase song "singles" instead of whole albums, a feature that allowed it to grab a larger share of the market as it gave customers greater choice and flexibility in personalizing their music libraries. But it was Apple Computer's digital store, iTunes, that standardized the purchase and consumption of digital music. Opened in 2003, iTunes had no subscription fee and charged users a flat rate of 99 cents for every song and piece of music in its inventory (Coleman 2003, 204–7). Making downloading easy and affordable has had an enormous effect on the consumption of music. Most noticeably it has succeeded in rendering traditional brick and mortar music stores obsolete. The bankruptcy of Tower Records in 2006 was perhaps the most visible evidence not just of the digital revolution and the substitution of the home computer for the megastore, but more specifically, of the success of iTunes (Noguchi 2006; Laurson and Pieler 2006).

Consumers' ability to control individual songs or tracks instead of whole albums has also had significant consequences for the production of recorded music. Over the previous fifty years, sound historian Mark Coleman observes, "music [had] come prepackaged in collections of ten or fifteen or so songs. From the LP era through the CD regime, the album ruled as a creative format. The rise of digital music threw the individual song back into high relief" (2003, 207–8). In addition to forcing the music industry to rethink production and promotion, the focus on the individual song track has also dramatically transformed the listening experience by expanding the range of musical styles available to listeners. The megastore started this project of expanding listener's tastes by expanding the physical space of the record store. Because the digital store has made the marketing of individual songs profitable, an even greater range of styles has become available. As recorded music has thus been fractured into smaller parts, listeners have responded by becoming more global in their tastes (Chanan 1995, 151–78).

Just as transformative, however, has been the introduction of technology that has made digital listening portable, that has liberated it from the home computer. The first devices playing MP3 files surfaced in the late 1990s. Diamond's MP3 player called the Rio, launched in 1998, was one of the first and most successful, but it was the Apple iPod, introduced in 2001, that standardized and popularized the digital listening experience. Recorded music had already been made portable via the cassette tape in the 1970s and early 1980s. What the iPod and other MP3 players improved on was storage capacity and in the process they helped make the listening experience more eclectic and personal than ever before. As tools of fracture and disruption, these devices allow listeners to consume individual songs or parts of songs and to manipulate their ordering at will. The "iPod culture," as Michael Bull terms it, has radically altered experience by allowing individuals to privatize their audio environment: it is "a world in which we all possess mobile phones, iPods, or automobiles—it is a culture which universalizes the privatization of public space, and it is a largely auditory privatization" (Bull 2007, 4). Digital listening devices allow listeners to mask or drown out the sonic aspects of the world around them to replace ambient sound with music, and thus they stand "as both example and metaphor for a culture in which any of us increasingly close our ears to the multi-faceted world through which we daily move" (4).

Because these changes have been so far reaching, it is all the more difficult to gauge the effect that portable digital technologies have had on the cinematic experience. Several contemporary directors, however, help draw the connection for us, as some fingerprints of a digital listening process are available in their eccentric and idiosyncratic listening patterns, patterns that then inform a compilation practice that has become particularly dense, expansive, and stylistically diverse. Sofia Coppola's music supervisor Brian Reitzell, for example, emphasizes the need for compilations with these characteristics. In his comments on the music for *Marie Antoinette*, he reveals Coppola's interest in using music to make the film's eighteenth-century subject matter current and contemporary through music. A stylistically authentic and uniform compilation—a "score by Tower Records"—with its careful placement of whole pieces of music, would not work. A contemporary reading of the historical figure needed a more "digital" approach, a compilation that was large, fragmented, and stylistically eclectic. As Reitzell observes, "it would have been a lot harder to get across [Marie's] *teen angst* with a Masterpiece Theater type of soundtrack" (Sony Pictures, "Production Notes: Musical Inspiration"). Coppola herself says that "I wanted to use a mixture of eighteenth-century and contemporary music, to use music that had the emotional quality that the scene should have." For example, "when [Marie goes] to the ball, she was excited and I picked the music that gives that feeling the most." The end result is "a collage of different kinds of music . . . a post-punk-pre-new-romantic-rock-opera-odyssey with some eighteenth century music and some very new contemporary music."

In his observations on the music for the film *There Will Be Blood*, which mixes preexisting music with some newly composed cues by Johnny Greenwood, Paul Thomas Anderson emphasizes a kind of "sensory gating" in his compilation practice. In a statement redolent of Bull's observations about "iPod culture," Anderson advocates the erasure of ambient sound in favor of music. Although most montage sequences suppress diegetic sound, the length and volume of the music in Anderson's is extreme, an attempt to "top" Kubrick with a new practice rooted in digital culture. "It's so hard to do anything that doesn't owe some kind of debt to what Stanley Kubrick did with music in movies. . . . The whole opening 20 minutes [of *There Will Be Blood*] was meant to be silent. I always had a dream about trying to make a movie that had no dialogue in it, that was just music and pictures. I still haven't done it yet but I tried to get close in the beginning [of *this film*]" (Willman 2007).

Perhaps the most convincing evidence that iPod culture has influenced contemporary compilation practices comes not from directors, however, but from listeners. As some describe it, the relationship between film soundtracks and digital listening is not one of influence but of overlap. The listening experience itself has become an act of compilation. With iPods, playlists have become soundtracks, compilations of preexisting recorded music with the potential to give narrative function and meaning to the activities they accompany. As one user in Bull's anthropological study observes,

> I now listen to music any time I can. Walking to and from work, at work, on vacation, on a train or airplane, even at home when I don't want to disturb my partner. I have

any song I want to listen to at my fingertips at any particular moment. It truly is my own personal jukebox, and puts the soundtrack to my life in my pocket and at my fingertips. (Bull 2007, 3)

CONCLUSION

The evolution of the compilation soundtrack has been affected by a host of circumstances, economic and aesthetic, but it has also been deeply and directly affected by a parallel evolution in the technology of recorded music. Over the last half century, the way in which we store, access, and consume music has changed dramatically. These technical innovations have had a profound effect on we listen to music, how we value it, and on how we repurpose it, including on mixed-media platforms. Although the film soundtrack has been influenced by a number of new technologies, only a few have succeeded in altering the landscape and galvanizing certain conditions into practice. The historical narrative I have outlined it here shows that the compilation score since the 1960s has seen three separate incarnations, separate and observable practices. Magnetic tape, videotape, and the iPod have each had a measurable effect on the use of preexisting music in film. Each has been responsible not only for making the act of repurposing possible, but for making it possible in a new way. Each has facilitated or conditioned differently the ways in which directors have appropriated recorded music cinematically.

NOTES

1. This chapter surveys the history of the compilation score in relation to changes in sound technology and music commerce. Since the compilation score is defined by its basis in available musics (rather than original composition designed for a specific film), the topic intersects with related but distinct treatments of historical musics and sound recording. See, among others, the case studies in Powrie and Stilwell 2006.
2. For a more detailed discussion of compilation practice in the silent film era, see Marks 1997; Altman 2004. On recorded music to accompany silent-era films, see Altman 2004, 321–30; Buhler, Neumeyer, and Deemer 2010, 278–82.
3. See especially Gorbman 2006 and 2007.
4. On the reinvigoration of the compilation model and ties to contemporary pop music in film, see Smith 1998, 154–85; Denisoff and Romanowski 1991, 129–200.
5. For a discussion of the music in *The Last Picture Show*, see Harris 1990, 98–99; Atkins 1983, 51–54; Hubbert 2003 195–98.
6. See Hubbert 2003, 198–210; Smith 1998, 176–84.
7. Kubrick briefly discusses the music in *A Clockwork Orange*, *Barry Lyndon*, and *The Shining* in Ciment 1983, 152–53,174–77, and 192. See also Kate McQuiston 2014. With *Barry Lyndon*, Kubrick had the Schubert and Paisello selections rearranged, somewhat recomposed and

rerecorded by the executive producer Jan Harlan and by the composer Leonard Rosenman for inclusion on the film's soundtrack.

8. As Kubrick did with *Barry Lyndon*, director Norman Jewison, in consultation with composer André Previn, temp-tracked rough cuts of *Rollerball* with existing recordings. For the final cut of the film, however, Jewison selected excerpts which were rerecorded by the London Symphony Orchestra. See Hubbert, "Records, Repertoire, and *Rollerball* (1975): Early Compilation Practice," (conference "Music and the Moving Image," New York University, June 8, 2012).

9. For more on this phenomenon, see Monaco 2001, 44–46; Cook 2000, 14–19; Baxter 1972, 7–13; Sklar 1994, 269–285.

10. On rock music in film in this period, see Doherty 2002, 58; Lev 2003, 244–46; Denisoff and Romanowski 1991, 1–71.

11. The "Hi-Fidelity" movement is discussed in a number of sources including Morton 2004, 129–40; Millard 2005, 189–222. For discussions of the postwar consumer electronics boom and how it affected music recording technology, see Morton 2004, 103–16; Millard 2005, 195–201; Chanan 1995, 96–98.

12. For a general overview of "stereophonic" sound and the effect it had on the recording industry, see Morton 2000, 39–44; Millard 2005, 208–22).

13. On the impact of tape recording, see Brainard 1968; Chanan 1995, 142–44.

14. For an overview of the introduction of multitracking to sound recording see Morton 2004, 148–51; Millard 2005, 295–312; Chanan 1995, 147–50.

15. For discussion of the impact tape and cassette technologies had on the aesthetic appreciation of music and the consumption of music, see also Millard 2005, 313–27; Chanan 1995, 146–50.

16. For accounts of individuals involved in or affected by these conditions, see the roundtable discussion of directors, producers, music supervisors and musicians featured in Romney and Wootton (1995, 119–21, 126–28, 130–39).

17. For an overview of concert films and music documentaries of the 1960s especially, see Barsam 1992, 330–33; Barnouw 1993, 240–45.

18. Several scholars have placed the "music video" in a longer history of visualized musical performances: Goodwin 1992; Denisoff and Romanowski 1991; Berg 1987. The unique visual style of the music video has also been heavily analyzed: see, for instance, Goodwin 1987, Kinder 1984, Straw 1988, Vernallis 2004, Björnberg 1994.

19. On MTV's early history see Viera 1987; Denisoff 1988, "Foreword," 2; Kaplan 1987, 1–2; Denisoff and Romanowski 1991, 345–57.

20. For further discussion of the impact music videos and cable television had on the promotion and marketing of films, see Denisoff and Plasketes 1990, 257–76; Smith 1998, 200–1; Denisoff and Romanowski 1991, 399–468.

21. Other scholars of 1980s and 1990s filmmaking have also observed to varying degrees the effect music videos had on film structure and style: see Denisoff and Romanowski 1991, 399–468; Smith 1998, 196–209; Wyatt 1994, 36–44; Prince 2000, 132–41; Mundy 1999, 221–47.

22. Smith 2001, 423–27, is a good analysis of another of Paul Thomas Anderson's films, *Boogie Nights* (1997), that is also instructive about the director's compiling methods as a whole.

23. For a good discussion of Tarantino's musical aesthetic, see Garner 2001.

BIBLIOGRAPHY

Agel, Jerome, ed. 1970. *Making of Kubrick's 2001*. New York: Signet.

Ahern, Eugene A. 1913. *What and How to Play for Pictures*. Boise, ID: privately printed.

Altman, Rick. 2004. *Silent Film Sound*. New York: Columbia University Press.

Antheil, George. 1935. "Composers in Movieland." *Modern Music* 12, no. 2 (January/February): 62–68.

Atkins, Irene Kahn. 1983. *Source Music in Motion Pictures*. Rutherford, NJ: Fairleigh Dickinson University Press.

Balio, Tino. 1993. *Grand Design: Hollywood as a Modern Business Enterprise, 1930–1939*. Berkeley: University of California Press.

Barlow, Priscilla. 2001. "Surreal Symphonies: *L'Age d'or* and the Discreet Charms of Classical Music." In *Soundtrack Available: Essays in Film and Popular Music*, edited by Pamela Robertson Wojcik and Arthur Knight, 31–52. Durham: Duke University Press.

Barnouw, Erik. 1993. *Documentary: A History of Non-Fiction Film*. 2nd rev. ed. New York: Oxford University Press.

Barsam, Richard M. 1992. *Nonfiction Film: A Critical History*. Bloomington: Indiana University Press.

Baxter, John. 1972. *Hollywood in the Sixties*. New York: A. S. Barnes.

Berg, Charles M. 1987. "Visualizing Music: The Archaeology of the Music Video." *One Two Three Four: A Rock 'n' Roll Quarterly* no. 5 (Spring): 94–103.

Bernstein, Elmer. 1974–1975. "The Annotated Friedkin," *Film Music Notebook* 1, no. 2: 10–16.

Beynon, George W. 1921. *Musical Presentation of Motion Pictures*. New York: Schirmer.

Björnberg, Alf. 1994. "Structural Relationships of Music and Image in Music Video." *Popular Music* 13, no. 1: 51–74.

Brainard, Tory. 1968. "The Making of a Record—1968." *Billboard*, February 24, B-10.

Brunette, Peter, ed. 1999. *Martin Scorsese: Interviews*. Jackson: University of Mississippi Press.

Buhler, James, David Neumeyer, and Rob Deemer. 2010. *Hearing the Movies: Music and Sound in Film History*. New York: Oxford University Press.

Bull, Michael. 2007. *Sound Moves: iPod Culture and Urban Experience*. London: Routledge.

Chanan, Michael. 1995. *Repeated Takes: A Short History of Recording and Its Effects on Music*. London: Verso.

Ciment, Michael. 1983. *Kubrick*. Translated by Gilbert Adair. New York: Holt, Rinehart, and Winston.

"Col. Keys Monaural Output to Stereo Usage Campaign." 1968. *Billboard*, January 27, 3.

Coleman, Mark. 2003. *Playback: From the Victrola to MP3, 100 Years of Music, Machines, and Money*. New York: Da Capo.

Connelly, Christopher. 1986. *Rolling Stone*, June 19, 38.

Cook, David A. 2000. *Lost Illusions: American Cinema in the Shadow of Watergate and Vietnam, 1970–1979*. Berkeley: University of California Press.

Davison, Annette. 2004. *Hollywood Theory, Non-Hollywood Practice: Cinema Soundtracks in the 1980s and 1990s*. Aldershot, UK, and Burlington, VT: Ashgate.

Denisoff, R. Serge. 1988. *Inside MTV*. New Brunswick, NJ: Transaction.

Denisoff, R. Serge, and George Plasketes. 1990. "Synergy in 1980s film and Music: Formula for Success or Industry Mythology?" *Film History* 4, no. 3: 257–276.

Denisoff, R. Serge, and William D. Romanowski. 1991. *Risky Business: Rock in Film*. New Brunswick, NJ: Transaction.

Dickinson, Kay. 2001. "Pop, Speed and the 'MTV Aesthetic' in Recent Teen Films." *Scope: An Online Journal of Film & TV Studies.* June. http://www.scope.nottingham.ac.uk/article.php ?issue=jun2001&id=275&section=article. Partially Reprinted in *Movie Music: The Film Reader*, edited by Kay Dickinson, 143–152. London: Routledge, 2003.

Doherty, Thomas. 2002. *Teenagers and Teenpics: The Juvenilization of American Movies in the 1950s.* Revised and expanded edition. Philadelphia: Temple University Press.

Fabrikant, Geraldine. 1987. "Tower Records' Giant Steps." *New York Times*, April 25, 137.

"Flashdance." 1983. *Variety*, April 20, 12.

Fox, Hank. 1968. "Stereo Rattles Stations—Mfrs. Strangle Monoral; Phasing Out to Choke Supply." *Billboard*, January 6, 1, 8.

Gabbard, Krin. 2004. *Black Magic: White Hollywood and African American Culture.* New Brunswick, NJ: Rutgers University Press.

Garner, Ken. 2001. "'Would You Like to Hear Some Music?': Music in-and-out-of-control in the Films of Quentin Tarantino." In *Film Music: Critical Approaches*, edited by K. J. Donnelly, 188–205. New York: Continuum.

Goodwin, Andrew. 1987. "From Anarchy to Chromakey: Music, Video and Media." *One Two Three Four: A Rock 'n' Roll Quarterly* no. 5 (Spring): 17–32.

——. 1992. *Dancing in the Distraction Factory: Music Television and Popular Culture.* Minneapolis: University of Minnesota Press.

Gorbman, Claudia. 2006. "Ears Wide Open: Kubrick's Music." In *Changing Tunes: The Use of Pre-existing Music in Film*, edited by Phil Powrie and Robynn Stilwell, 3–18. Aldershot, UK, and Burlington, VT: Ashgate.

——. 2007. "Auteur Music." In *Beyond the Soundtrack: Representing Music in Cinema*, edited by Daniel Goldmark, Lawrence Kramer, and Richard Leppert, 149–162. Berkeley: University of California Press.

Harris, Thomas. 1990. *Bogdanovich's Picture Shows.* Metuchen, NJ: Scarecrow.

Heimerdinger, Julia. 2011. "'I have been compromised. I am now fighting against it': Ligeti vs. Kubrick and the music for 2001: *A Space Odyssey*." *Journal of Film Music* 3, no. 2: 127–143.

Hickman, Roger. 2006. *Reel Music: Exploring 100 Years of Film Music.* New York: W. W. Norton.

Hubbert, Julie. 2003. "'Whatever Happened to Great Movie Music'?: Cinéma Vérité and Hollywood Film Music of the Early 1970s." *American Music* 21, no. 2: 180–213.

——. 2011. *Celluloid Symphonies: Text and Context in Film Music History.* Berkeley: University of California Press.

——. 2012. "Records, Repertoire, and *Rollerball* (1975): Early Compilation Practice." Conference paper, *Music and the Moving Image*, New York University.

Jones, Steve. 1992. *Rock Formation—Music, Technology and Mass Communication.* London: Sage.

Kalinak, Kathryn. 1992. *Settling the Score: Music and the Classical Hollywood Film.* Madison: University of Wisconsin Press.

Kaplan, E. Ann. 1987. *Rocking around the Clock: Music Television, Postmodernism, and Consumer Culture.* New York: Methuen.

Kashner, Sam. 2008. "Here's to You Mr. Nichols: The Making of the Graduate." *Vanity Fair*, March, 418–432.

Katz, Mark. 2004. *Capturing Sound: How Technology Has Changed Music.* Berkeley: University of California Press.

Kelly, Maura. 2005. "Mark Mothersbaugh: Interview." *The Believer*, September.

Kinder, Marsha. 1984. "Music Video and the Spectator: Television, Ideology and Dream." *Film Quarterly* 38, no. 1: 2–15.

Kolker, Robert. 1980. *A Cinema of Loneliness: Penn, Kubrick, Coppola, Scorsese, Altman*. New York: Oxford University Press.

Laurson, Jens F. and George A. Pieler. 2006. "The Tower That Fell." *Forbes*, November 15. http://www.forbes.com/2006/11/15/tower-music-bankruptcy-oped-cx_jfl_1115tower.html.

Lev, Peter. 2003. *The Fifties: Transforming the Screen, 1950–1959*. Berkeley, University of California Press.

Levy, Lawrence C. 1976. "A Long-Playing Price War." *New York Times*, November 21, 126.

MacDonald, Laurence E. 1998. *The Invisible Art of Film Music: A Comprehensive History*. New York: Ardsley House.

Marks, Martin Miller. 1997. *Music and the Silent Film: Contexts and Case Studies, 1895–1924*. New York: Oxford University Press.

Marmorstein, Gary. 1997. *Hollywood Rhapsody: Movie Music and Its Makers, 1900-1975*. New York: Schirmer.

McClay, Bob. 1968. "Industry's All-Stereo Push Puts the Needle in Consumer Instead of In Between the Grooves," *Rolling Stone*, July 6, 1, 4.

McQuiston, Kate. 2011. "'An effort to decide': More Research into Kubrick's Music Choices for *2001: A Space Odyssey.*" *Journal of Film Music* 3, no. 2 (2011), 145–154

——. 2014. *"We'll Meet Again": Musical Design in the Films of Stanley Kubrick*. New York: Oxford University Press.

Meyer, Marianne. 1985. "Rockmovideo." In *The Rolling Stone Review*, edited by Ira A. Robbins, 168–171. New York: Scribner.

Merkley, Paul, A. 2007. "'Stanley Hates This But I Like It'!: North vs. Kubrick on the Music for *2001: A Space Odyssey.*" *Journal of Film Music* 2, no. 1, 1–34.

Millard, Andre. 2005. *America on Record: A History of Recorded Sound*. 2nd ed. Cambridge: Cambridge University Press.

Miller, Mark Crispin. 1990. "Hollywood: the Ad." *Atlantic Monthly*, April, 41–62.

Monaco, Paul. 2001. *The Sixties, 1960–1969*. Berkeley: University of California Press.

Morton, David. 2000. *Off the Record: The Technology and Culture of Sound Recording in America*. New Brunswick, NJ: Rutgers University Press.

——. 2004. *Sound Recording: The Life Story of a Technology*. Westport, CT: Greenwood.

Mundy, John. 1999. *Popular Music on Screen: From Hollywood Musical to Music Video*. Manchester: Manchester University Press.

Noguchi, Yuki. 2006. "A Broken Record Store." *Washington Post*, August 23, sec. D.

Palmer, Christopher. 1990. *The Composer in Hollywood*. London: Marion Boyars.

Patterson, David W. "Music, Structure and Metaphor in Stanley Kubrick's *2001: A Space Odyssey*," *American Music* 22, no. 3: 444–474.

Powrie, Phil, and Robynn Stilwell. 2006. *Changing Tunes: The Use of Pre-existing Music in Film*. Aldershot, UK, and Burlington, VT: Ashgate.

Prendergast, Roy. (1977) 1992. *Film Music: A Neglected Art*. 2nd ed. New York: Norton.

Prince, Stephen. 2000. *A New Pot of Gold: Hollywood under the Electronic Rainbow, 1980–1989*. New York: Scribner.

Raksin, David. 1974. "Raksin Raps State of Art." *Variety*, May 15. Reprinted as "Whatever Became of Movie Music," *Film Music Notebook* 1, no. 1. 24–30.

"Record Industry Hits Stride of Billion Dollars." 1968. *Rolling Stone*, September 28, 4.

"Record Industry Ups LP and Single Prices." 1969. *Rolling Stone*, February 15, 6.

"Record Sales Over One Billion in 1967." 1968. *Rolling Stone*, August 24, 6.

Rodman, Ronald. 2006. "The Popular Song as Leitmotiv in 1990s Film." In *Changing Tunes: The Use of Pre-existing Music in Film*, edited by Phil Powrie and Robynn Stillwell, 119–136. Aldershot, UK, and Burlington, VT: Ashgate.

Romney, Jonathan and Adrian Wootton, eds. 1995. *The Celluloid Jukebox: Popular Music and the Movies Since the 50s*. London: BFI Publishing.

Silberman, Jeff. 2000. "30 Days Celebrate 30 Years; Tower Sunset Hosts In-stores and Giveaways to Mark the Occasion." *Billboard*, October 14, 60, 62.

Sklar, Robert. 1994. *Movie-Made America: A Cultural History of American Movies*. New York: Vintage.

Smith, Jeff. 1998. *The Sounds of Commerce: Marketing Popular Film Music*. New York: Columbia University Press.

——. 2001. "Popular Songs and Comic Allusion in Contemporary Cinema." In *Soundtrack Available: Essays on Film and Popular Music*, edited by Pamela Robertson Wojcik and Arthur Knight, 407–430. Durham: Duke University Press.

Sony Pictures. "Production Notes: Musical Inspiration." *Marie Antoinette Film Site*. http://www.sonypictures.com/movies/marieantoinette/site/ (accessed June 23, 2011).

Sragow, Michael. 1983. "Flashdance: Last Go-Go in Pittsburgh." *Rolling Stone*, May 26, 64.

Sterne, Jonathan. 2003. *The Audible Past: Cultural Origins of Sound Reproduction*. Durham, NC: Duke University Press.

Straw, Will. 1988. "Music Video in Its Contexts: Popular Music and Post-Modernism in the 1980s." *Popular Music* 7, no. 3: 247–266.

Taylor, Timothy D. 2001. *Strange Sounds: Music, Technology and Culture*. New York: Routledge.

Théberge, Paul. 1997. *Any Sound You Can Imagine: Making Music/Consuming Technology*. Hanover, NH: Wesleyan University Press.

Timm, Larry M. 2003. *The Soul of Cinema: An Appreciation of Film Music*. Upper Saddle River, NJ: Prentice Hall.

Viera, Maira. 1987. "The Institutionalization of the Music Video." *One Two Three Four: A Rock 'n' Roll Quarterly* no. 5 (Spring): 80–93.

Vernallis, Carol. 2004. *Experiencing Music Video: Aesthetics and Cultural Context*. New York: Columbia University Press.

Welles, Merida. 1984. "Tower's Costly Gamble." *New York Times*, August 5, F6.

Willman, Chris. 2007. "There Will Be Music." *Entertainment Weekly*, November 8.

Wyatt, Justin. 1994. *High Concept: Movies and Marketing in Hollywood*. Austin: University of Texas Press.

CHAPTER 12

THE ORIGINS OF MUSICAL STYLE IN VIDEO GAMES, 1977–1983

NEIL LERNER

In his 2004 monograph *Videogames*, James Newman suggests several possible reasons why academics to date had ignored video games as an area of serious study. The most important among these reasons are, first, that video games were seen as a children's medium, as something trivial and cartoonish, and, second, that since the games are part of mass culture, they must necessarily lack sophistication, gravitas, and intellectual legitimacy.[1]

Surely scholars of popular music, and film music, can recognize some of these objections as being similar to the ones that must have played a role in why, for instance, the study of music in animation has taken so long to join the study of music in other media genres like the science fiction film, documentary film of persuasion, or horror film, to name but a few of the types of motion picture whose music has been treated with scholarly rigor in recent decades. Unsurprisingly, however, given the ubiquity of video games, a robust scholarly discussion has recently begun to coalesce around the question of their particular strategies of rhetoric and representation. For some scholars, such as Gonzalo Frasca, the save/die/restart element of video games (in which a player figures out how to succeed in a video game by repeatedly failing and retrying a section of the game) may be another trivializing factor. Other scholars (like Newman and Ian Bogost), however, have recognized in the save/die/restart model a powerful new rhetorical mode that allows what some regard as the exploration of regret.[2]

In the time since Newman's book appeared, the reality of video game study within the academy may no longer be viewed with such a raised eyebrow. Certainly the field that has emerged around video game studies has made tremendous strides, even as a growing (and much discussed) rift appears to have formed between the narratologists, who tend to borrow more liberally from the theories of film and narrative studies, and the ludologists, who seek to foreground the activity of play in their analyses. For such a young field of study, it is gratifying and perhaps telling of the state of sound and media studies that several significant works of scholarship—in particular the writings of Karen

Collins, Axel Stockburger, and Kiri Miller—have already appeared that address the way sound and music work in video games.[3]

Collins's writings have done the field an especially huge service in her wide-ranging research on the techniques and technologies behind the music throughout the history of video games (see in particular her 2008 monograph, *Game Sound: An Introduction to the History, Theory, and Practice of Video Game Music and Sound Design*, as well as the 2008 essay collection she edited, *From Pac-Man to Pop Music: Interactive Audio in Games and New Media*). Among other things, Collins's *Game Sound* offers a much-needed survey of music throughout the history of video games, and she takes great care to explain many of the technological particularities that have played such a key role in what has been possible in video game music.

Yet with such a massive topic, one that encompasses such a wide range of issues as well as a large and growing number of texts, much work remains to be done, not the least being closer investigation of the stylistic distinctiveness that occurs in the history of video game music. Indeed, a specter haunts early video games—the specter of early film music conventions, as filtered through the practices of some cartoon music. In particular, the stylistic development of music in video games from the late 1970s and early 1980s loosely paralleled the growth of music in early cinema, adopting many of the same strategies for fitting music to screen action.[4]

Factors Affecting Early Video Game Music

This chapter will consider games principally from 1977 through 1983, the year regarded by most video game enthusiasts and historians as the year of a great crash in the video game market, and it will dwell principally on coin-operated (coin-op) arcade games because these games had the most complex graphics and gameplay reaching the widest market. Key triggers to this crash included a disastrous home release of the highly popular game *Pac-Man* for the Atari 2600 home unit, followed a few months later with another disappointing Atari game, this time one based on the film *E.T.: The Extra-Terrestrial* (1982); it is widely believed that Atari buried piles and piles of unsold *E.T.* game cartridges in a New Mexico landfill (Kent 2000, chap. 14).

Understanding that some uncertainty exists regarding just what might be the first video game, and also being aware that the first coin-operated game to be commercially released appeared in 1971—*Computer Space* (Nutting), a flop that nonetheless makes a brief cameo in the 1973 dystopic film *Soylent Green*—I will begin my discussion of video game music six years after *Computer Space*, in 1977, with the appearance of a game called *Circus* (Exidy).[5] One of the very first games to incorporate recognizable melodies into its accompanying sounds, *Circus* requires the player to move a springboard back and forth as clowns bounce off it and up into three rows of balloons (see Figure 12.1).

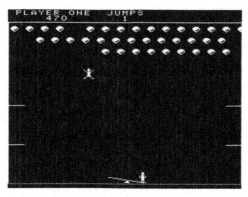

FIGURE 12.1 *Circus* (Exidy, 1977).

A falling clown must be greeted with an empty springboard spot or else have a harsh encounter with the ground. *Circus* was promoted in part on the distinctiveness of its music: a flyer advertising the game to arcade operators touted the fact that "when the clown bursts the last balloon in a row, he hangs there momentarily as appropriate 'award music' is played." The same advertisement explains that "if the clown misses the board, he tumbles and falls, and appropriate music is played." The "award music" is a monophonic version of the popular and peppy late nineteenth-century music hall song "Ta-ra-ra Boom-de-ay" (1891), while the "appropriate music" for the dead—or at least temporarily flattened—clown is the opening melody of the third movement of Chopin's Second Piano Sonata, the familiar funeral march of early film music. Why these particular melodies were chosen raises several questions whose answers start to come into sharper focus as more games began to incorporate music in their soundtracks.

The earliest coin-op video games employed sounds, but only at a basic level of white noise (for an explosion) or the strident bleeps and blurts that easily drew the kind of casual dismissal one can sense in the *Time* cover story of January 18, 1982, "Gronk! Flash! Zap! Video Games Are Blitzing the World." *Computer Space*'s soundtrack did not even have "gronks" or "flashes," or at least not melodic ones, for all of its sounds were sound effects attempting to bring a sense of realism to this descendent of the *Spacewar!* game (Steve Russell, 1962) where one controlled a spaceship maneuvering around a two-dimensional plane while attempting to shoot the other player's spaceship. Promotional flyers for *Computer Space* explain how "the thrust motors from your rocket ship, the rocket turning signals, the firing of your missiles and explosions fill the air with the sights and sounds of combat," while another advertisement (for the second-generation version of the game that featured a two-player option) boldly trumpets its "SPACE BATTLE SOUNDS— Rocket and thruster engines, missiles firing, explosions" as a selling point.

Pong (Atari, 1972), the coin-op much more successful and famous than *Computer Space* and thus incorrectly thought by many to be the first arcade video game, produced two simple electronic tones (heard by some to be an appropriate "ponging" sound): a B♭ each time the paddle (represented on screen with a rectangle) hits the ball (a small square), a B♭

an octave lower each time the ball strikes the wall, and a B a half step higher each time the ball makes it past a paddle and scores a point. A computer designer who worked on *Pong*, Al Alcorn, has explained how he had been asked to create the sounds of a roaring crowd when a point was scored, but because of the severe technical limitations, he gave up on that idea and instead "poked around the sync generator to find an appropriate frequency or tone. So these sounds were done in a half a day. They were the sounds that were already in the machine" (Kent 2000, 34). As with many of these 1970s video game soundscapes, there is an aleatoric and minimalistic quality to the rhythmic surprises of *Pong*'s severely limited pitch collection.

With roots in pinball machines, slot machines, and other arcade machines, arcade video games are the inheritors of a rich sonic tradition that dates back well into the nineteenth century. The sounds and ballyhoo music of these machines form an important part of the foundation for the soundworld of the video game arcade between 1977 and 1983, and this point brings attention to the function of music and sound in attracting and retaining players to play a particular game. If music were to be deployed for this function, it would need first of all to be loud to be effective, for it would often be but one machine among many competing for players' quarters. When the sounds contained melodies, more often than not they were familiar melodies; when music was used in early video games to express information about play or about story, it needed to communicate quickly and to as wide an audience as possible. Because the programmers of these early games were often the sound designers as well as the composers, they may have been more inclined to use preexisting melodies because of an inability to write their own. While some video game designers appear not to have considered the possible copyright infringement that could happen in a game's soundtrack—see for instance the game *Vanguard* (TOSE, 1981), which opens with Jerry Goldsmith's main theme from *Star Trek: The Motion Picture* (1979) and whose power-ups are accompanied by Vultan's theme from *Flash Gordon* (1980), all without any apparent acknowledgement of an existing copyright on those melodic themes—there must have still been a practicality to using musical works whose age would put them in the public domain and thus render them inexpensive to employ.

Zach Whalen's useful 2004 effort at developing a theory of videogame music ("Play Along: An Approach to Videogame Music," Whalen 2004) asserts that "early cartoon music and horror films established certain tropes that videogames rely on today." Whalen draws attention to the close correspondence in some games between player control and musical gestures, finding a correlate of "mickey-mousing" in something like the ascending octave leap that accompanies any of Mario's visual leaps in the highly popular and influential game, *Super Mario Brothers* (Nintendo, 1985), initially released in the United States on the Nintendo Entertainment System. Similar mickey-mousing had appeared earlier, however, with Mario's first appearance in *Donkey Kong* (1981), as each of Mario's jumps over a barrel results in a short melodic phrase that moves quickly from lower to higher to lower pitches. Although Whalen's examples (*Super Mario Brothers*, *Legend of Zelda: Ocarina of Time* [Nintendo, 1998], and *Silent Hill* [Konami, 1999]) support his argument, the number of what he calls "ancestral forms" extends beyond just two: musical accompanying practices for films from the 1910s—musical practices that would also have led into Whalen's two primary genres of cartoon and horror—appear in some of the earliest video games with music.

Although it appears that most of the programmers may not have been terribly creative or innovative composers, that they were able to include any sound and music at all is nothing short of a small miracle given the primitive computing technologies of the 1970s. Memory was severely limited and, as with early cinema, sound and music were often treated as secondary in importance after the visual elements. When the Atari 2600 Video Computer System (VCS) was released in October 1977, it brought into millions of homes joysticks and an MOS Technology 6532 chip that contained the machine's memory of 128 bytes of RAM.[6] *Combat* (Atari, 1977), a game included with every VCS unit and based on an earlier arcade game called *Tank* (Kee Games, 1974), contained no music per se but only rudimentary sound effects created with white noise: low rumbles for the tank; higher rumbles when the tank moved; a firing burst; and an explosion upon a successful hit (see Figure 12.2). Other home systems, such as the Bally Astrocade, had more powerful computing capabilities, and they also had relatively more sophisticated sound and music as a result. In 1978's *Gun Fight* (Bally Astrovision)—the video game equivalent of *The Great Train Robbery* (1903) and its significant place in film history?—the two players in the shoot-out receive a melodic signal whenever one of their gun-toting avatars takes a bullet: the Chopin funeral march sounds for one player's demise, while "Taps" plays for the other (see Figure 12.3). Both melodies come from the tradition of film accompanying that scholars can document to the 1910s and 1920s, as a number of film accompanying manuals and mood books have both the Chopin funeral march and also "Taps" among their offerings for funereal scenes. By 1977, *Circus* was appearing in arcades and presenting its two simple, and highly touted, melodies, one of them the Chopin funeral march.

It would not be long before programmers of the Atari VCS also began to introduce musical gestures into their games for their home systems. Atari's 1979 version of *Adventure*—a game that had emerged from Will Crowther's 1975 interactive fiction (or text adventure) also titled *Adventure*[7]—has been discussed by scholars like Mark J. P. Wolf (2001) in connection with its remarkably innovative reconceiving of space, in the way that it allows the character (represented by an avatar of a simple square) to move

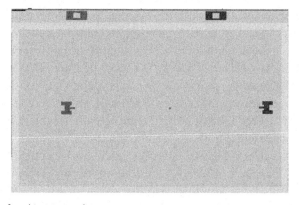

FIGURE 12.2 *Combat* (Atari, 1977).

FIGURE 12.3 *Gun Fight* (Bally Astrovision, 1978).

FIGURE 12.4 A. Picking up an object in *Adventure* (transcribed).

FIGURE 12.4 B. Putting down an object in *Adventure* (transcribed).

to the end of one screen and then appear at the other end of the next screen, creating an illusion of continuous space (and in this game, even some non-Euclidean spaces). Musically, however, this game also looked ahead to the kinds of mickey-mousing present in *Super Mario Brothers*, for whenever the character avatar picked up or dropped an object, a quick ascending or descending melody sounded (see Figures 12.4a, 12.4b, and 12.5). A similar use of music as a signal to a player's action occurs in Atari's 1981 *Haunted House*, an ancestor to later survival horror games, in which an avatar consisting of a synecdochic pair of eyes (Figure 12.6) navigates an unlit space and where every ascent up a staircase gets coupled with a three-note pitch collection whose acrid chromatic sound is similar to that of the well-known Viennese trichord of atonality: in the labeling method of pitch-class set theory, it is [0, 3, 4], and the Viennese trichord is [0, 1, 6]. Descending the staircase brings the same three pitches with a more hesitant rhythm (see Figures 12.7a and 7b). Traditions of using dissonance and disjunct melodies as a way of creating feelings of fear and unease reappear here, although they are offset by the whimsical character of the game's visual iconography. In these early examples of home games, the player may be positioned in a kind of unconscious fantasy role as musical accompanist, performing avatarial actions that yield changes in the game world and contributing to the elements of immersion, agency, and transformation that narratologist Janet

FIGURE 12.5 *Adventure* for the Atari 2600.

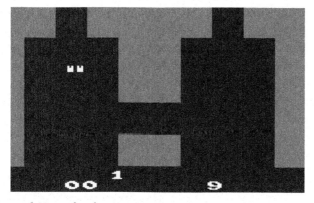

FIGURE 12.6 *Haunted House* for the Atari 2600.

FIGURE 12.7 A. Ascending a staircase in *Haunted House* (transcribed).

FIGURE 12.7 B. Descending a staircase in *Haunted House* (transcribed).

H. Murray set forth in *Hamlet on the Holodeck: The Future of Narrative in Cyberspace* (1997). (Murray is quoted among game scholars with a frequency similar to Claudia Corbman's *Unheard Melodies: Narrative Film Music* among film music scholars.)

Collins points to *Frogger* (Konami, 1981) as "one of the first games to incorporate dynamic music," (2008b, 19); by this term she seems to mean music that changes according to particular game actions initiated by the player. In *Frogger*, the object of which is to guide a frog avatar across a busy highway and then over a river, Collins counts "at least eleven different gameplay songs" (2008b, 20), and she notes how the music will change abruptly at a point in the game when the player successfully maneuvers a frog into one of its five "safe houses." Within a year, even closer connections between player movements and musical accompaniment would be programmed into *Dig Dug* (Namco, 1982), a game in which the music occurs only when the player keeps the avatar moving; bringing the avatar to a stop results in a cessation of the music, no matter where it is in the phrase (see Figures 12.8 and 12.9). A different melodic figure sounds to indicate that the end of a level is drawing near, after which point the main accompanying music returns but in double time, creating an effect of urgency reminiscent of the stock musical mood of the "hurry" in early film accompaniment, wherein tempo generates additional suspense. The completion of a level of *Dig Dug* triggers a cadential melodic phrase, always to be followed by the beginning of the main accompanying music at the start of the next level. The game has two other musical ideas that appear only for the introduction (see measures 2–4 of Figure 12.8) and conclusion of the entire game. Interestingly, the bassline for the music that accompanies the gameplay descends chromatically from a C to a G, and while the key signature of C major may not align the example too closely with a lament tetrachord like the famous one in Purcell's "When I Am Laid in Earth" from *Dido and*

FIGURE 12.8 The opening musical accompaniment of *Dig Dug* (transcribed).

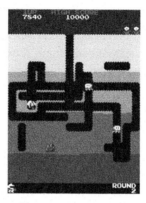

FIGURE 12.9 *Dig Dug* (Namco, 1982).

Aeneas, the *Dig Dug* tetrachord nonetheless accompanies another narrative situation involving a descent into the ground.

The music in *Dig Dug* brings attention to a not uncommon situation where the logic of the gameplay takes precedence over the purely musical considerations: the jarring starts and stops anywhere within the musical phrase disrupt the melodic line even if the cause of the starting and stopping—a player making particular movement decisions in the game—may make sense from the ludological perspective. Live performers of music for early film were faced with similar situations when it came to matching the length of a film scene with the length of a musical cue. Ernö Rapée, in his 1925 *Encyclopedia of Music for Pictures*, describes these issues as problematic. When explaining how to use a march as an accompaniment for a newsreel, he states that "the procedure of coming to a satisfactory end of a march is a very important one" (Rapée 1925, 10). He also writes of the "trouble" with the "making of musical endings. The brutal procedure of breaking your music no matter where you are just because the cue for the next number is flashed on the screen is an antiquated procedure not in use any more in first-class theatres" (14). A few years later, in the early sound-film era, the ability to synchronize music more closely quickly removed such discontinuities from film scoring. In video games, on the other hand, synchronization presents greater challenges due to the dynamic nature of the gameplay itself.

CONTINUOUS MUSIC

One of the principal assumptions about music in silent cinema exhibition practice has been that it would have sounded continuously throughout a film; although later examples of film accompaniments from the 1910s and 1920s may indeed have featured constant musical underscoring, scholars such as Rick Altman have helped us to understand these examples as only one possibility for the way music was used in connection with film presentations.[8] Still, there were instances where music was heard from start to finish in early cinema, and that assumption lives on today. Comparing early video games with regard to whether or not the music was continuous provides another point of similarity with early film practice, for just as cinema sometimes found it useful to have wall-to-wall music, so too did some early video games, although the music in these early games may be rather primitive and even boring in its construction. *Pong* had continuous if arrhythmic tones, and the nature of these tones—one pitch signaling when the ball is hit, another for when it hits the wall, and a third one for when it is missed—is such that they are easily understood as having a function that supports the gameplay rather than having a musical function. In later games music can become an important game element for creating the effect of immersion discussed by Murray, but it seems not to carry that function in *Pong*. Rather, a player immersed in *Pong* may discern important information about the game play by noting which tone sounds, thus hearing whether the ball will be volleyed back or not, but the simple, irregular, and unpredictable alternation of tones makes for a musically unsatisfying experience. Not quite sound effects—a missed ball in the real world creates almost no sound at all, not the similar but higher-pitched tone found in the game—the musical tones here provide much more value as attempts at realism within the abstractions forced by the technological limitations than as musically compelling structures.

The boundary between sound effect and musical underscore becomes even trickier to assess in later games. Collins describes the tones used in the highly successful video game *Space Invaders* (Midway, 1978) as "nondiegetic," writing that that the game "set an important precedent for continuous music, with a descending four-tone loop of marching alien feet that sped up as the game progressed" (Collins 2008b, 12). If the four-tone loop is heard as the "marching alien feet," their representation of something from the world of the game's story would enable the loop to be understood as a diegetic sound, but the short motivic loop is constructed in such a way that it functions at least equally well as a nondiegetic sound, four notes that form what can be seen as the most musically complete video game score up to its time. Collins, on the other hand, is rather quick to dismiss any games before 1980 as having anything of musical interest, writing that "by 1980, arcade manufacturers included dedicated sound chips known as *programmable sound generators*, or PSGs . . . into their circuit boards, and more tonal background music and elaborate sound effects developed" (Collins 2008b, 12; emphasis in original).

In *Space Invaders*, sounds built from white noise emanate when the player fires a missile as well as when the player's missile hits an invader; synthesized tones happen when the UFO speeds across the top of the screen, and then another sound if the player successfully hits it (see Figures 12.10 and 12.11). Most important, however, is that four-note loop associated with the advancing invaders. The attackers can be shot and destroyed one at a time, but the game possesses a strikingly bleak procedural rhetoric, to borrow Ian Bogost's phrase, which he defines as "the practice of authoring arguments through processes" (Bogost 2007, 28). Much of Bogost's scholarship to date has dwelt on the ways that video games can make persuasive arguments about culture, economics, and politics.[9] In *Space Invaders*, as with nearly all other games from this period, there is no way

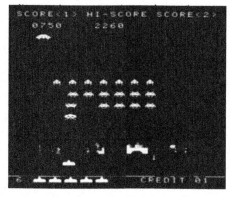

FIGURE 12.10 *Space Invaders* (Midway, 1978).

(gradually faster upon repetition)

FIGURE 12.11 The ostinato accompanying play in *Space Invaders* (Midway, 1978) (transcribed).

to win the game on its own terms: here, the invaders will always eventually outshoot or overrun the human player. (*Missile Command* [Atari, 1980] featured another unwinnable scenario with a depressing procedural rhetoric, one where the player must attempt to shoot down nuclear warheads before they reach the cities, but the player will always lose to the computer's ever-quickening rain of missiles; unless the player has achieved a high score, the game then concludes with a morbid taunt by flashing "The End" on the screen instead of the more familiar "Game Over.")

As the player shoots missiles and the number of descending invaders decreases, their speed increases, something that was actually a feature resulting from the limitations of the early computer processor. The game's programmer, Tomohiro Nishikado, noticed that the invaders could be drawn more quickly by the processor as fewer appeared on screen, and he decided to keep that as an element of gameplay:

> Originally I wanted to move 55 Invaders at the same time, but the hardware only let me move one Invader every 1/60 second. As a result, Invaders began to move faster as they decreased in number. But in the end, this actually added more thrills to the game. ("Nishikado-san," n.d.)

The accelerating advance of the invaders gets accompanied by a four-note descending melody that spans the interval of a perfect fourth and which gradually increases in speed, eventually becoming indistinguishable as a multinote melody. The increase in musical tempo as the level reaches its end marks another descendant of the "hurry"

trope from early cinema. This diatonic descending tetrachord, like the chromatic tetrachord appearing later in *Dig Dug*, falls within that long history of the descending
fourth as an emblem of lament, a not inappropriate register to signal given the devas-
tating failure that must accompany every playing of the game.[10] Considering what the
game's music presents for us from the historical moment of the late 1970s, and a further
way to understand this sound emerges. The game employs a four-note motive with fixed
pitches, a fixed timbre, and fixed rhythms; all that changes is tempo, which goes through
a simple procedure of gradually increasing. This loop thus belongs to the culture of repetition that Robert Fink describes in *Repeating Ourselves: American Minimal Music as
Cultural Practice*; whether death-driven libido or capitalism-driven advertising, the
strategy of the sound fits with composer Steve Reich's concept of "Music as a Gradual
Process" (1968).[11]

Other games quickly began to imitate *Space Invaders'* continuous yet repetitive
music. A steadily pulsating rising half-step between E and F accompanies the action
of shooting asteroids in *Asteroids* (Atari, 1979); again, as the number of targets dwin-
dles, the pace of the loop (in this case, a two-pitch loop) increases (see Figure 12.12).
Montfort and Bogost recount Sherry Turkle's interview with a twelve-year-old
Asteroids player who stated that the musical pulse of the game was "its heartbeat"
(Montfort and Bogost 2009, 85–86). Another of the most popular games from that
era, *Centipede* (Atari, 1980), also underscored its gameplay with a driving ostinato
pulse, here, an even more heartbeat-like single pitch (B). As other insects appear on
the screen—the player's goal is to shoot as many as possible before being ultimately
overrun—they are each accompanied by their own distinctive musical marker.
When the spider appears and starts bouncing up and down, a rapid five-beat melody mickey-mouses the action with a contour that similarly moves up and down (see
Figures 12.13 and 12.14), while the intermittent dropping of a flea down the screen
brings with it another musical gesture that attempts to illustrate the visual action: a
quick portamento from high to low.

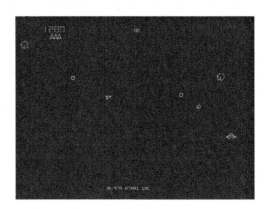

FIGURE **12.12** *Asteroids* (Atari, 1979).

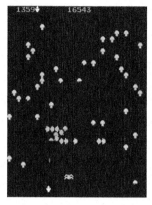

FIGURE **12.13** *Centipede* (Atari, 1980).

FIGURE **12.14** The music for the spider in *Centipede* (Atari, 1980) (transcribed).

PLAYING THE PICTURE, SCORING THE GAME

The continuous ostinati found in these early games were soon accompanied by, or replaced with, more elaborate and often familiar melodies, such as 1980's *Carnival* (Sega), which contains continuous music during gameplay ("Over the Waves," also known as "The Loveliest Night of the Year," sounds progressively higher and faster as the player fires a gun at various targets; see Figure 12.15).[12] As we saw with 1977's *Circus*, early game melodies not only were familiar, but they possessed narrative functions similar to those same melodies as they had been used in early cinema accompaniment. By the later part of the silent era, pianists, organists, and musical directors performing music during a film were usually expected to make the music support that film's narrative. Essentially the same practices—that is, the ways the music was used to undergird a film—transferred to video games beginning in the late 1970s. We know that early accompaniments for film frequently turned to preexisting musical works ranging from works of concert-hall and chamber-music composers to popular songs of the nineteenth and early twentieth centuries. Similar repertoire sometimes appears in the soundtracks for early coin-op video games. It is important to keep in mind that for coin-op games in an arcade, music had to fill at least two important roles. Besides attempting to add to the immersive experience for the player, this music would also often have to compete with music from surrounding coin-op machines, and so the music also fulfilled a function as ballyhoo, inviting arcade visitors to play the game or watch as others played.

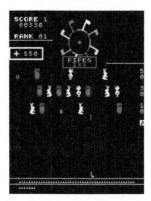

FIGURE 12.15 *Carnival* (Sega, 1980).

Advances in programmable sound chips in 1980 (Collins 2008b, 12) ushered in more elaborate music, at both the start of the game as well as throughout it. In his seminal study of the *Kojak* (1973–1978) theme, Philip Tagg ([1979] 2000) writes of the "reveille function" and "preparatory function" of title themes in relation to television music. The reveille function "attract(s) the attention of potential listeners to the fact that something (undefined) new is going to be presented" while the preparatory function "prepare(s) listeners or viewers emotionally with an affective musical description of the kind of general mood found in the subsequent presentation" (93). Music performing these two functions begins to appear in video games with some regularity in 1980, although an important pioneer in this regard would be *Galaxian* (Midway, 1979), a *Space Invaders* derivative that opens with a brisk fanfare whose blistering pace and chromaticism issue an attention-grabbing call to (virtual) arms, while preparing the player for the subsequent challenge of reflexes the game is about to offer. One of the most familiar of all arcade-game melodies first appeared in 1980: the bouncy two-voice arpeggiated passage that signals the start of every game of *Pac-Man* (Midway, 1980), announcing not only the beginning of something, but also a promise of something whimsical (see Figure 12.16). These brief musical introductions could sometimes become quite elaborate, as in the complicated three-voice nonimitative polyphony present in the opening to *Galaga* (Midway, 1981), a sequel to *Galaxian* (see Figure 12.17). In addition to the polyphony, *Galaga* displays surprising harmonic shifts: C to A♭, moving briefly to B♭, then settling, though still somewhat ambiguously, on the sonority of A–D–E, suggesting something of the unpredictability that one may expect from the gameplay.

Some introductory fanfares borrowed from existing pieces of music that by the early 1980s already carried decades of cultural associations from their use in screen media. Some of these borrowings have obvious connections to the story of the game about to begin, while others lack such cohesiveness. *Scramble* (Stern, 1981), one of the first sideways scrolling shooters, starts with a fanfare highly reminiscent of the famous cavalry charge in Rossini's *Guillaume Tell* Overture, the part made famous by its use in film and television, in particular through its connection with the Lone Ranger radio

FIGURE 12.16. Opening music from *Pac-Man* (Midway, 1980) (transcribed).

FIGURE 12.17 Opening fanfare from *Galaga* (transcribed).

and television series (see Figures 12.18 and 12.19). The *Scramble* fanfare triggers associations with narratives of heroism, of charging in to the rescue; it is an obvious affective button to push at the start of this game. Music less connected to the game narrative could be found in something like the introductory music for the space shooter *Gyruss* (Konami, 1983), which breathed new life (along with a backbeat) into an electronic version of J. S. Bach's Toccata and Fugue in D Minor, a work that had appeared with some regularity in films, especially in horror films (see Figure 12.20). Stripped here of its accumulated cultural resonances with the gothic and the horrific, the Bach Toccata might seem to be a surprising eccentricity of early video game music, just an example of randomness, but again, a comparison with early film practices might help to explain its presence here.[13]

We know that early accompaniments for film frequently turned to preexisting musical works ranging from works of concert-hall and opera composers to popular songs of the nineteenth and early twentieth centuries. Similar repertoire sometimes appears in the soundtracks for early coin-op video games. In *Phoenix* (Amstar, 1980), another *Space Invaders* derivative, the game opens with a two-voice reduction of the anonymous Spanish guitar piece "Romance d'Amour," a melancholic, minor mode work that does little, in accordance with Tagg's preparatory function, to alert a player to the outer space battles about to begin (see Figures 12.21 and 12.22). Perhaps the music's sad register foreshadows the player's ultimate and inevitable loss in the game, but that the music was preexisting and in the public domain provide an easier explanation. Still, it can be strangely troubling to discover that upon completing the final level in *Phoenix*, the player is rewarded with a bit of Beethoven's *Für Elise* (see Figure 12.23); note that the barring of

FIGURE 12.18 Opening fanfare from *Scramble* (Stern, 1981) (transcribed).

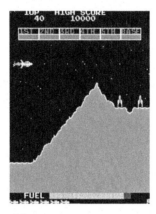

FIGURE 12.19 *Scramble* (Stern, 1981).

FIGURE 12.20 *Gyruss* (Konami, 1983).

this transcription follows the game's pulseless version of *Für Elise* instead of its usual anacrusis.

The graphics limitations of the early video games encouraged a remarkably abstract and at times surreal array of narrative situations and characters (*Donkey Kong* [Nintendo, 1981], *Pac-Man*, *Centipede* [Atari, 1980], and *Burger Time* [Bally Midway, 1982] are but a few of the many that could fit this description).[14] Such a rhetoric of randomness and imagination may serve as one explanation for why a game like *Kangaroo* (Sun Electronics, 1982) would contain snippets of Beethoven, Stephen Foster, and a nineteenth-century march, yet another and perhaps more probable reason may be

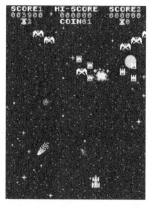

FIGURE 12.21 *Phoenix* (Amstar, 1980).

FIGURE 12.22 The "Romance d'Amour" from the opening of *Phoenix* (transcribed).

the extension of the tradition of early film accompaniment. In the first level of *Kangaroo*, a mother kangaroo gets separated from her baby kangaroo and must traverse up and through a simple maze while dodging apples hurled by monkeys (see Figure 12.24). The music introducing the level presents a part of Beethoven's *Marcia alla turca* before turning to F. W. Meacham's "American Patrol" March (1885) as continuous accompaniment for the level. As the kangaroo avatar jumps, climbs up a ladder, punches monkeys, and acquires fruit, corresponding musical gestures create several instances of mickey-mousing (for instance, climbing upwards triggers a rising melody). Ringing a bell hanging in the maze causes the Westminster Chimes to sound forth (another early film accompanying possibility: using a piano to simulate bell sounds). When the mother

FIGURE 12.23 *Für Elise* as reward for completing the final level of *Phoenix* (transcribed).

kangaroo successfully rescues her baby, a fast snippet of Stephen Foster's "Oh! Susanna" emerges to mark the victory. Such blending of concert hall (Beethoven) and popular (Foster and Meacham) was common in early film accompaniment, and the connection to the early twentieth century becomes even stronger when considering that the music I have labeled here as "popular"—the Foster and Meacham pieces—would most likely not have been what a typical young person in a 1982 video game arcade would have thought of as "popular."

A composite score like the one accompanying *Kangaroo* derives in part from the tradition of Carl Stalling's cartoon music, which Daniel Goldmark has traced back to Stalling's early training as a cinema musician in the early years of the twentieth century.[15] Stalling's pastiche scores for Warner Bros. cartoons are famous for their rapacious use of existing songs and concert-hall and operatic music, and because of Stalling's background as a cinema pianist and conductor he was a primary conduit for bringing those earlier traditions into mass media of the mid-twentieth century. By the early 1980s, it was common to find video-game music quoting liberally from a similar range of popular and concert-hall and operatic works. *Frogger* occasionally sounds a melodic phrase from "Camptown Races" (see Figure 12.25), whose unsung words—"Goin' to run all night / Goin' to run all day"—are surprisingly apt for this game about a frog trying to dart through a crowded highway and over a treacherously crowded river. Besides *Kangaroo*, Stephen Foster's music shows up again in *Tapper* (Bally Midway, 1983). *Crazy Climber* (Taito, 1980) opens with a bit of Henry Mancini's "Baby Elephant Walk" before later presenting some of Pachelbel's Canon in D, Scott Joplin's *The Entertainer*, and Mancini's theme from *The Pink Panther*. Gameplay in *Pengo* (Sega, 1982) is accompanied by Gershon Kingsley's synthpop instrumental "Popcorn," while the cinematic scenes between every other level employ the "Ode to Joy" from Beethoven's Ninth Symphony (see Figure 12.26). *Crystal Castles* (Atari, 1983) takes a more Russian turn, turning to Tchaikovsky ("Marche" from the "Danses Caractéristiques" from the *Nutcracker* Suite, and the march melody from the third movement of his Sixth Symphony; plus a quick eight-note motive of chromatically ascending perfect fourths that originates

FIGURE **12.24** *Kangaroo* (Atari, 1982).

FIGURE **12.25** *Frogger's* phrase from "Campton Races" (transcribed).

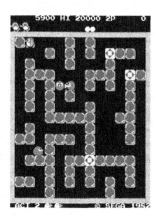

FIGURE **12.26** *Pengo* (Sega, 1982).

in Moussorgsky's "The Hut on Chicken Legs" from *Pictures at an Exhibition*) (see Figure 12.27). Bits of Rimsky-Korsakov's "Flight of the Bumblebee" underscore a level with a beehive in *Donkey Kong 3* (Nintendo, 1983).

Rick Altman has drawn attention to early film composer J. S. Zamecnik's functionally clever habit of constructing his various photoplay cues—his generalized situational and mood pieces, like "Funeral March," "Plaintive Music," or "Death Scene"—in related keys. While such a practice made it easier for a film accompanist to shift from scene to scene, this kind of tonal coherence also allowed the music to unify the film in subtle but important ways.[16] Similar practices begin to appear in video game music in the early 1980s.

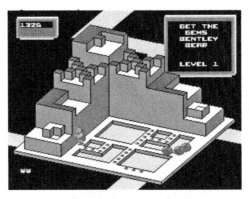

FIGURE **12.27** *Crystal Castles* (Atari, 1983).

FIGURE **12.28** The intermission music from *Pac-Man* (transcribed).

Pac-Man contained only two musical cues: the opening fanfare and the music accompanying the intermissions that occurred after every few levels. Spectral analysis of samples
from the original arcade soundtrack reveal that the pitches fall squarely between C and
C♯ major, just as the intermission falls in between F major and F♯ major; for consistency
here I am notating both in the lower keys. The intermission establishes F major as its key
(compare Figures 12.16 and 12.28). The opening section occurs only once in a game, but
the intermissions could happen as often as a player continued to advance through the
levels. Still, the amount of time between levels and the repetition of the same intermission music each time work against the establishment of a compelling key relationship.

More elaborate tonal design exists in the sequel to *Pac-Man*, *Ms. Pac-Man* (Midway,
1981). Like its original, *Ms. Pac-Man* features introductory music, this time with a
greater sense of independence between the two voices (see Figure 12.29), and again,
intermissions break up gameplay every few levels. But here, the intermissions take on a
more overtly cinematic quality by featuring the icon of a clapperboard (declaring it to be
"Act I") with the words "They Meet" before illustrating how Pac-Man and Ms. Pac-Man

FIGURE 12.29 The introductory music for *Ms. Pac-Man* (Midway, 1981) (transcribed).

collided into each other while avoiding their respective monsters (see Figure 12.31). The music for Act I moves from the F major of the opening theme to a more ominous F minor (see Figure 12.30). This is a simple musical maneuver for signaling a sinister turn in the story but one that makes more sense when situating it against the framework of the early silent-film world that the intermission evokes. The second intermission, or

FIGURE 12.30 Act I music from *Ms. Pac-Man* (transcribed).

FIGURE 12.31 Act I from *Ms. Pac-Man*.

Act II, presents Pac-Man and Ms. Pac-Man chasing each other across the screen with increasing speed, and here the music assumes the character of a ragtime piano piece whose syncopations and momentary chromaticisms evoke Scott Joplin's mature style (see Figure 12.32).

The music in *Donkey Kong* also contains stylistic allusions to early twentieth-century ragtime and Tin Pan Alley gestures; furthermore, the various musical cues are constructed in a way that they establish a tonal center (B♭ major) that provides an important unifying function to the game and its narrative. Besides containing several important innovations in game design and introducing Mario, who would become a franchise character for their company, *Donkey Kong* also stands apart from its fellow arcade video games for the relative complexity of its musical accompaniment. The game centered on a carpenter (who would later be identified as a plumber) with a large nose and bushy moustache, a character all the more remarkable for its lack of any special abilities: Mario could run, jump, climb, and occasionally wield a hammer, but without any superhuman powers. The efforts at story-telling were groundbreaking for the time. The game uses introductory and interlevel animated sequences to reveal a story where a giant ape has taken a woman (Mario's girlfriend) up a ladder and then jumps with such force that it causes the girders to bend. Accompanying the opening sequence is, in parallel fifths, the melodic phrase from the *Dragnet* (1951–1959) television series that Jon Burlingame describes as "the decisive and melodramatic four-note phrase [that] became a kind of American musical code for 'you're in trouble now'" (1996, 15) (see Figures 12.33 and 12.34). Although the *Dragnet* phrase has not yet surfaced in any of the early

FIGURE 12.32 Act II music from *Ms. Pac-Man* (transcribed).

FIGURE 12.33 Opening *Dragnet* theme as used in *Donkey Kong* (Nintendo, 1981) (transcribed).

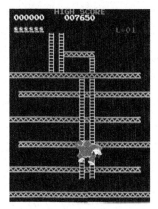

FIGURE 12.34 Opening sequence from *Donkey Kong*.

FIGURE 12.35 *Dragnet* theme as used in *Wizard of Wor* (Midway, 1980) (transcribed).

twentieth-century photoplay books, its diminished harmonic structure and exaggerated character nonetheless tie it to that musical world. (*Wizard of Wor* [Midway, 1980] had earlier used this *Dragnet* melody to good effect, opening each level with the first four notes of the phrase and withholding the final chord until a successful completion of a level; see Figures 12.35 and 12.36.)

Each level of *Donkey Kong* begins with an identical cue that playfully establishes B♭ major as the home key (Figures 12.37 and 12.38). The first level has a constant syncopated bassline (Figure 12.39) that spells out a B♭ triad, while each time Mario successfully jumps over one of the barrels thrown at him by the ape, it is accompanied by a rapid five-note melody (Figure 12.40) that momentarily introduces an E♭ chord into the mix.

FIGURE 12.36 *Wizard of Wor.*

FIGURE 12.37 Level introduction music from *Donkey Kong* (transcribed).

FIGURE 12.38 Level introduction from *Donkey Kong.*

FIGURE 12.39 First level ostinato bass line from *Donkey Kong* (transcribed).

FIGURE 12.40 Melody accompanying a successful jump over a barrel in *Donkey Kong* (transcribed).

That melody's rapidly rising and falling contour matches Mario's physical movements as he rapidly jumps up and down over a barrel. Each of Mario's deaths unleashes a torrent of chromatically related sixths and fifths before delivering a return to the stability of the B♭ major tonic (Figure 12.41). If the player has remaining lives, the death music is then followed by the level introductory music (see again Figure 12.37). Completing each level brings a musical reward, although each respite from the ape's assaults linger for only a moment. Successfully completing the first ramp level elicits a short, happy moment in the music before three ominous low F♯s sound, which accompany the ape again stealing Mario's girlfriend and causing the heart above them to break, only then to be followed again by the introductory level music (of Figure 12.37) (see Figures 12.42 and 12.43). Three of *Donkey Kong*'s four levels have continuous musical accompaniments; the basslines of the rivet level (Figure 12.44) and the conveyor belt level (Figure 12.45) also support the B♭ tonality. Defeating the rivet level on the first stage, which causes the ape to fall, allowing Mario and his girlfriend a brief moment together, triggers another ragtime-flavored cue that ends with a B♭ seventh chord. With the start of the next level, B♭ major returns as the primary tonality. The entire game then uses a single key area to unify the various levels and actions, using the brief disruption of the chromatic death music as contrast and to add momentum back into the home key.

Besides having no precedent in any video game soundtrack, this remarkable tonal coherence operates in interesting ways next to game theorist Jesper Juul's categories of incomplete *versus* incoherent story worlds.[17] Incomplete worlds leave out

FIGURE 12.41 Mario's death music from *Donkey Kong* (transcribed).

FIGURE 12.42 Completion of level one in *Donkey Kong* (transcribed).

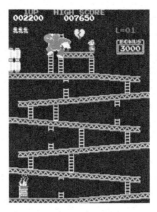

FIGURE 12.43 Completion of level one in *Donkey Kong*.

FIGURE 12.44 Rivet level ostinato bass line from *Donkey Kong* (transcribed).

FIGURE 12.45 Conveyor belt level ostinato bass line from *Donkey Kong* (transcribed).

information about the fiction; Juul gives as an example the way that the Super Mario Brothers games tell us the names of the brothers Mario and Luigi but do not name their parents. Incoherent worlds present inexplicable contradictions, such as in a game like *Donkey Kong*, where Mario's girlfriend finds herself repeatedly kidnapped, no matter what else happens in the game; even if a player, as Mario, successfully saves the girlfriend in levels 1 and 2, by level 3, she has been kidnapped again and apparently returned to the original hideout. To further flesh out the idea of incoherent worlds, Juul asks the question, "Why does Mario have three lives?" Mario's ability to die and then be reborn three times (in most settings of the game), or to earn an extra "life" after achieving a certain number of points, are two more examples of incoherence in the world of *Donkey Kong*. Juul proposes "that we call this type of fictional world an *incoherent world*, meaning that there are many events in the fictional world that we cannot explain without discussing the game rules" (2005, 130). Apart from the opening C minor cue—perhaps a musical example of incoherence following Juul's categories for story worlds—the *Donkey Kong* underscore actually creates a powerful thread unifying the game from start to finish, thereby defying its narrative incoherence. The contradiction of tonal coherence and narrative incoherence points to the need for further work bridging the fields of video game and music scholarship.

FIGURE 12.46 Bonus level music from *Mappy* (Namco, 1983) (transcribed).

CONCLUSION

The early phase of video-game history discussed in this chapter reveals several examples where the incorporation of music mirrors several of the characteristic functions of early film music, even sometimes borrowing the harmonic and melodic vocabularies of the music associated with that era. The technology behind the sounds made important advances between 1977 and 1983, allowing for a relatively quick shift from monophony to homophony to polyphony, rapidly ushering video games from a medieval era to one in comparison more floridly renaissance in style. By 1983, some game scores began to take advantage of the multiple voices now available; the platform game *Mappy* (Namco, 1983) has a musical underscore that employs four-voice nonimitative polyphony (see Figure 12.46). But the ability to program more than one line of melody at once is only one element tied in with the way music works in video games; at least as important are the increasingly sophisticated ways that the music and the game action begin to interact. After the crash of 1983, video-game arcades began to decline as they faced competition from increasingly advanced home units as well as the suddenly unfolding market for personal computers. Collins posits 1984 as the important moment in video game music when "looping…began to gain real prominence" (2008b, 19), and although the simple ostinati of soundtracks like those of *Space Invaders* and even *Donkey Kong* appear before 1984, her point stands because of the much greater ability of video games to offer music that can react in dynamic ways with the player's actions in the games. The emphasis on repetition found within the early video-game scores remains, but with far greater possibilities for variation. Scholars studying music and media interactions have only begun to scratch the surface of this rich new field of video games and the cultural resonances of their musical strategies.

NOTES

1. I am grateful for the crucial feedback and help of Rick Altman, Daniel Goldmark, Michael Pisani, Mauro Botelho, Dan Boye, Bill Lawing, Jim Buhler, Kevin Donnelly, and Thomas Lodato.

2. See the work of Kahneman and Tversky 1982, cited by Newman 2004, 86 for more on the exploration of regret.

3. See in particular: Collins 2008a and 2008b; Stockburger 2006, chap. 4 ("The Game Space from an Auditive Perspective"); Miller 2007, 2008, 2009.

4. Important discussions of early film music and sound can be found in: Altman 2004, Abel and Altman 2001, Lastra 2000, Marks 1997.

5. Clips of *Computer Space* may be seen here: http://www.computerspacefan.com/Videos. htm.

6. See Montfort and Bogost 2009, especially pages 19–30, for a helpful explanation of how the Atari VCS worked.

7. See Montfort 2003.

8. See Altman 1996.

9. See Bogost 2007, 28–40.

10. See Williams 1997.

11. In Reich 2002, 34–36.

12. Van Burnham hears the music in *Carnival* as "mind-numbing." See Burnham 2003, 219.

13. William Gibbons discusses later video game uses of Bach's Toccata and Fugue in D Minor, along with other works, in Gibbons 2009.

14. See Lamoureux 2004, 78–91.

15. See Goldmark 2005, 12–16.

16. See Altman 2004, 261–263. David Neumeyer and James Buhler address the question of large-scale tonal design in film music in Neumeyer and Buhler 2001, 26–28.

17. See chapter 4 of Juul 2005.

Bibliography

Abel, Richard, and Rick Altman, eds. 2001. *The Sounds of Early Cinema*. Bloomington: Indiana University Press.

Altman, Rick. 1996. "The Silence of the Silents." *Musical Quarterly* 80, no. 4: 648–718.

——. 2004. *Silent Film Sound*. New York: Columbia University Press.

Bogost, Ian. 2007. *Persuasive Games: The Expressive Power of Videogames*. Cambridge, MA: MIT Press.

Burlingame, Jon. 1996. *TV's Biggest Hits: The Story of Television Themes from "Dragnet" to "Friends."* New York: Schirmer.

Burnham, Van. 2003. *Supercade: A Visual History of the Videogame Age, 1971–1984*. Cambridge, MA: MIT Press.

Collins, Karen, ed. 2008a. *From Pac-Man to Pop Music: Interactive Audio in Games and New Media*. Aldershot, UK, and Burlington, VT: Ashgate.

——. 2008b. *Game Sound: An Introduction to the History, Theory, and Practice of Video Game Music and Sound Design*. Cambridge, MA: MIT Press.

Fink, Robert. 2005. *Repeating Ourselves: American Minimal Music as Cultural Practice*. Berkeley: University of California Press.

Gibbons, William. 2009. "Blip, Bloop, Bach? Some Uses of Classical Music on the Nintendo Entertainment System." *Music and the Moving Image* 2, no. 1: 40–52.

Goldmark, Daniel. 2005. *Tunes for 'Toons: Music and the Hollywood Cartoon*. Berkeley: University of California Press.

Gorbman, Claudia. 1987. *Unheard Melodies: Narrative Film Music*. Bloomington: Indiana University Press.

Juul, Jasper. 2005. *Half-Real: Video Games between Real Rules and Fictional Worlds*. Cambridge, MA: MIT Press.

Kahneman, Daniel, and Amos Tversky. 1982. "The Psychology of Preferences." *Scientific American* 246, no. 1: 160–173.

Kent, Steven L. 2000. *The First Quarter: A 25-Year History of Video Games*. Bothell, WA: BWD.

Lamoureux, Mark. 2004. "8-Bit Primitive: Homage to the Atari 2600." In *Gamers: Writers, Artists & Programmers on the Pleasures of Pixels*, edited by Shanna Compton, 78–91. Brooklyn, NY: Soft Skull.

Lastra, James. 2000. *Sound Technology and the American Cinema: Perception, Representation, Modernity*. New York: Columbia University Press.

Marks, Martin Miller. 1997. *Music and the Silent Film: Contexts and Case Studies, 1895–1924*. New York: Oxford University Press.

Miller, Kiri. 2007. "Jacking the Dial: Radio, Race, and Place in *Grand Theft Auto*." *Ethnomusicology* 51, no. 3: 402–438.

——. 2008. "The Accidental Carjack: Ethnography, Gameworld Tourism, and *Grand Theft Auto*." *Game Studies* 8, no. 1. http://gamestudies.org/0801/articles/miller.

——. 2009. "Schizophrenic Performance: *Guitar Hero*, *Rock Band*, and Virtual Virtuosity." *Journal of the Society for American Music* 3, no. 4: 395–429.

Montfort, Nick. 2003. *Twisty Little Passages: An Approach to Interactive Fiction*. Cambridge, MA: MIT Press.

——, and Ian Bogost. 2009. *Racing the Beam: The Atari Video Computer System*. Cambridge, MA: MIT Press.

Murray, Janet H. 1997. *Hamlet on the Holodeck: The Future of Narrative in Cyberspace*. Cambridge, MA: MIT Press.

Neumeyer, David, and James Buhler. 2001. "Analytical and Interpretive Approaches (I): Analysing the Music," in *Film Music: Critical Approaches*, edited by K. J. Donnelly, 16–38. Edinburgh: Edinburgh University Press.

Newman, James. 2004. *Videogames*. London: Routledge.

"Nishikado-san Speaks." n.d. *Retro Gamer* 3: 35.

Rapée, Ernö. 1925. *Encyclopedia of Music for Pictures*. New York: Belwin. Reprint, New York: Arno, 1970.

Reich, Steve. 2002. *Writings on Music, 1965–2000*. Edited with an introduction by Paul Hillier. New York: Oxford University Press.

Stockburger, Axel. 2006. "The Rendered Arena: Modalities of Space in Video and Computer Games." PhD diss., University of the Arts, London.

Tagg, Philip. (1979) 2000. *Kojak: Fifty Seconds of Television Music: Toward the Analysis of Affect in Popular Music*. New York: Mass Media Music Scholars' Press.

Whalen, Zach. 2004. "Play Along: An Approach to Videogame Music." *Game Studies* 4, no. 1. http://www.gamestudies.org/0401/whalen.

Williams, Peter. 1997. *The Chromatic Fourth during Four Centuries of Music*. Oxford and New York: Oxford University Press.

Wolf, Mark J. P. 2001. "Space in the Video Game." In *The Medium of the Video Game*, edited by Mark J. P. Wolf, 51–75. Austin: University of Texas Press.

PART 3

··

INTERPRETATIVE THEORY
AND PRACTICE

··

CHAPTER 13

CLASSICAL MUSIC, VIRTUAL BODIES, NARRATIVE FILM

LAWRENCE KRAMER

A kiss makes a good beginning. Two kisses, actually, separated by exactly one century. The first is the kiss impending in Antonio Canova's sculpture of 1796, "Eros and Psyche," long a favorite of visitors to the Louvre. The wings of Eros aside, the figures prefigure the romantic rapture of the classic Hollywood clinch, including the use of the climactic kiss as a substitute for a climax that cannot be shown. How odd, then, that the first cinematic kiss was anything but romantic or rapturous. It was the subject of an 1896 Edison short—very short: fifteen seconds—with the then provocative title *The Kiss*. Linda Williams describes the film's subject as a "theatrical smooch" between "two plump middle-age actors mugging for the camera," but she goes on, against the odds, to nudge this primitive screen kiss towards the visual rhetoric of Eros and Psyche. The conventions governing kissing (and what follows it) at any historical moment are most likely to be learned from representational media: stories, images, and later the cinema. In that context, "Edison's *The Kiss* is emblematic of a new kind of sexual voyeurism unleashed by moving pictures. Screening sex, learning how to do it through repeated and magnified anatomization, would henceforth be a major function of the movies" (Williams 2006, 295).[1]

For that function to flourish, however, something else was required that both the film and the sculpture lack but that only the film needs: music. "Screening sex" is virtually never a simply visual process. The classic screen kiss of narrative cinema would not be possible, perhaps not even thinkable, without music. The music involved, moreover, not only carries the erotic charge of a scene but also extends it throughout the experience of cinema spectatorship. The eroticism "unleashed" by the combination of music with the cinematic image cannot be confined to "sex" in any literal sense—which means at the same time that literal sex in cinema becomes emblematic of something foundational about cinema itself. The character of that something is the subject of this chapter. And for guides to it we could not do better than the two characters with which we began.

Projection, Love, and Music

The legend of Eros and Psyche was an allegory of cinema long before such a thing as cinema could be conceived. Psyche, whose name identifies her with mind or soul, was allowed to receive the divine Eros as her lover only if she would receive him in the dark. He was to remain unknown because unseen. But the stipulation left Psyche's desire prey to anxiety. Eventually the darkness of her obscure chamber drove her to light a lamp to see the lover who, in truth, was never really there until he became visible. A later age might say that Psyche had read the book but wanted to see the movie. Eros, whom she both gains and for a long time loses with her desiring gaze, assumes his true identity as an image projected in light across the darkness. He emerges as the primary moving target of visual pleasure: the first movie star. The only thing missing from this scene— an absence no less severe than its visual double—is the music to go with the kiss or the clinch or, in this case, their interdiction.

In a short philosophical text that reads like a prose poem, Jean-Luc Nancy remedies the lack. He rewrites the visual economy of the legend by dwelling on an earlier moment that ends, as he evokes it, by letting the music in along with the light. This time it is Eros who gazes at the sleeping Psyche, as if, one might speculate, he were her dream. But her sleep is so deep that she herself is nothing but a pure dispersion, a body cast outside of itself and outside of its every outside, "a dispersion of indefinitely parceled-out locations in places that divide themselves and never interpenetrate" (Nancy 1993, 393).[2] The only thing that holds this Psyche together is the dream-gaze of Eros, the cinematic image, which/who concentrates her dispersion. But not just visually: the concentration is also musical, enacted in Nancy's text by a change of language: "Everything thus ends with this brief tune: 'Psyche ist ausgedehnt, weiss nichts davon'" (Psyche is extended, knows nothing of it). The German phrase is a cryptic note scribbled by Freud, who will turn up again at the close of the remarks to follow.

The key to this allegory is the double principle that the embodied psyche is incomplete without projection and that its projection—always a love story—is incomplete without music. This, I want to propose, is the originary condition of music in narrative film. It can be satisfied by any kind of music but its model, both historical and phenomenological, is classical music. The music's kind is more important in this usage than its location, live or recorded, diegetic or extradiegetic. What counts most is the music's disposition to concentrate, like Eros, the body of the Psyche who/that hears it out of the dark.

Four Theses

To explicate these proposals requires four theses, which I will state bluntly and apo-dictically to establish a point of departure. Departure in every sense: my expectation is that the theses will prove true up to a point and that their interest lies partly in just where that point is located. The inevitable breakdown of these ideas, beyond the bounds of this chapter, is meant to be as revealing as their construction. What the theses describe is not a social, aesthetic, or institutional norm but something else entirely. It is a perceptual event: an event that individual projections of bodies on screen may or may not, may *and* may not, incarnate, but never without significance. This event is one of a series in the early history of modern media (the photograph, the phonograph, the telephone, the radio) by which the human subject becomes the subject of perception at the very moment when perception, illusion, and mechanism begin to become indistinguishable.

My theses are extended, but we need to know something about them. They all make a significant omission. One fleeting reference aside, they address the significance of musical embodiment in film without reference to its technical means. That those means make a difference is obvious, but that is just the point: they make a difference in how we perceive the things they render, but to do that they must have something to render in the first place. Not even cinematic forms free of indexicality escape this condition. Animation tells stories; computer-generated imagery mimics events and spectacles. Media cannot escape mediation (no matter how hard they may try). Our friends Psyche and Eros can help illuminate this dual identity. Their liaison has two phases, one marked by her contemplation of his image, the other by the material effect of her lamp, from which a drop of oil falls on his body and startles him awake. The imaginary form of cinematic embodiment needs to be thought through independent of the supplement of its material realization. That is the project of these theses, which deal, to steal a phrase, with the imaginary signifier.[3]

First thesis: Cinema is above all a matter of moving bodies, or rather of moving images of bodies, and the cinematic body requires music to constitute it. The transition from still to moving images entailed a loss of corporeality. The moving image cannot be handled, as a photograph can, and it has no material composition, as a painting does. Especially before the standardization of projection speed and the replacement of orthochromatic by panchromatic film stock (both accomplished during the 1920s), the cinematic image of the body is spectral, and its spectrality persists even once the primitive state of the medium has been left behind. Gilles Deleuze's argument that primitive media have to be understood for what they become, not what they are—"things are never defined by their primitive state, but by the tendencies concealed in that state" (Deleuze 1986, 25)—has an inverse that is perhaps even more compelling: that media never wholly escape their primitive conditions.

In order to flesh out the spectral image, the image must be joined to a vibratory depth, and to do that the cinematic image must be combined with music. The reason for this is less historical than it is phenomenological. The body *is* a vibratory depth; its depth is where music vibrates, to add music to the primitive cinematic image is literally, not metaphorically but literally, to give the image a body. Psyche is extended; in Eros she re-envelops herself. As a sounding chamber, a vibratory interior, music is the medium without which what Deleuze calls the time-image of cinema, its modeling of a continuous temporality similar to the Bergsonian *durée*, would not be possible.[4]

This relationship of music and image has a positional counterpart in the subject's address to/by the soundtrack as the medium of ambient sound other than music or voice. The sonic environment provides the image with a sense of location, that is, of being in a place—a condition that, phenomenologically speaking, is as much auditory (lived space) as it is visual (mapped space). Or, to draw the full triangle, voice occupies the site of immediacy, environmental sound the span of world-space, and music the space of subjectivity, resonant and/or interior—the housing of self.

Second thesis. The cinematic body is primarily or originally erotic. This is again a phenomenological truth: the cinematic look is structurally voyeuristic, especially in the classic situation of peering through the dark; the cinematic image is sexualized by the condition for its perception. This is the kernel of truth in Laura Mulvey's much-debated essay on narrative pleasure and the gaze (Mulvey 1975). Virtually as soon as there are movies there are pornographic movies; the movie industry from the outset, even at its most respectable, has been an explicit factory for the production of desire.

We can take two emblematic or allegorical instances of this in a recent film and an art-film classic: not for nothing is David Fincher's *The Curious Case of Benjamin Button* (2008) structured around opposed narrative arcs that meet in the middle when its reverse-aging protagonist is young enough and its heroine old enough to create a classic Hollywood romance. And not for nothing does Dziga Vertov's *Man with a Movie Camera* (1929) open with the performance of a symphony and proceed quickly to a gaze through a window at a half-naked young woman slowly putting on her clothes. Here again the entry of Eros has to end in a tune. Insofar as the audience receives music as a direct address to sensation and affect—and that of course is the default mode of the reception of virtually all music—the music reveals that the cinematic body belongs to Eros.

To say this is not, of course, to make the absurd claim that all film music is erotic or eroticized in the everyday sense of the term. The claim rather is that the corporeality of the cinematic body is defined by the erotic potential of the marriage of music and gaze. The cinematic look is structured by the degree to which the bodies that attract its primary concern are both seen and heard as objects of desire or repulsion. In turn the cinematic world is structured by the degree to which these bodies subject to music become focal points / listening posts for a more general sense of world embodiment or, on the contrary, present themselves as exceptional, the primary carriers of the sense of the real.

Third thesis: Classical music is the paradigm of cinematic embodiment. Its place in cinema history is of course well known, from silent film accompaniment to symphonic film scoring to a long line of diegetic appearances. The basis of these usages is the tendency of classical music to define the cinematic body. To understand the role of music in movies is to ask what kind of body or bodies classical music tends to address and, in addressing, to construct.

Fourth thesis: The answer to this question turns on a contradiction that classical music cultivates without having either the capacity or, for the most part, the intent to resolve. Roughly speaking, this is a contradiction between the body as sensorial and the body as form or figure. This contradiction most often plays itself out in erotic terms, in the sounding chamber where Eros and Psyche are locked in each other's gaze.

MUSIC AND THE PRIMITIVE CONDITION OF CINEMA

It does so in part because the contradiction itself is one of the primitive conditions of cinema. In the previous section I proposed reversing Deleuze's claim that, in effect, media should be understood from back to front: by what they become rather than by what they have come from. The question needs some further consideration before we can go any further.

The concept of the primitive condition is basic to understanding the relationship between music and the cinematic image, and I would suggest that it needs to be taken more fully on board in theorizing media in general. As Walter Benjamin famously observed, media as technological forms typically give a belated realization of perceptual phenomena envisioned, but only envisioned, in earlier media (Benjamin [1939] 2003, 4: 266). The primitive condition defines this crossing point and builds an irreducible historicity into the form of media as such. It does so under the principle that, in media, phenomenology equals ontology: what a medium makes appear is what *is* within the frame of that medium.

With film above all, perhaps: no medium has been more decisive in the history of perception. To watch a film originally meant to see a photographic image come to life. As time passed, the photographic image faded (as such images do): to watch a film then meant to see an image that has come to life long since, to see a bodiless form act as—or better, be, become—an embodied one. Image and body are inseparable forms that can neither be opposed nor assimilated to each other. At a certain moment, in response to the persistence of the primitive conditions of cinema, classical or classically inspired film music emerged as a principal mechanism for the working out of their reciprocal address.

What is at stake in these transformations? How do they change perception and the perceiver? These questions are best answered by thinking—heuristically, not literally—of the primitive condition as the original condition of passage from the imaginary to the virtual. This passage is the hypothetical moment of remediation (the reinscription of one medium in second, successor medium): the moment, say, that pictorial portraiture becomes photographic, that is, an indexical trace rather than an imaginary reconstruction, or the moment that the still image of photography becomes animate—the moment it comes to life by moving. My use of a mythic narrative to guide the discussion of this problem is itself a recourse to a primitive condition, that of projection itself. Projection is an imaginary form long before it is a mechanical one and it never loses its imaginary identity.

At this point it is important to acknowledge that technical developments that post-date the primitive condition have always proceeded to a point after which the media they nominally support have irrevocably changed, even to the point of becoming something else. This change has now, of course, overtaken cinema, which no longer necessarily has much, or anything, to do with photographic images, their supposed indexicality, or analog reproduction. We are currently on the threshold of a new primitive condition for which a new vocabulary and a new theory will be needed. Likewise the saturation of everyday life by audiovisual simulacra creates a situation of near-continuous virtuality which differs from cinema in ways yet to be described. Cinema, "the movies," lies outside the ordinary. Movies were historically promoted that way and they still are. The medium assumes a certain intermittency, a certain firm division between the virtual and the real, the initial or classical site of which is the movie theater—increasingly an anachronistic locale. It might even be said that there no longer *is* an "outside the ordinary"—not when you can download a cinematic spectacle onto a handheld device. In terms of our guiding myth, the digital or posthuman condition may involve an extension of Psyche lacking the concentration of Eros, who keeps moving away at twice the speed of her approach. My concern in this chapter, however, is specifically with the "classical" mode of cinema from its inception in the 1890s to its residual, not to say spectral, existence as of this writing in 2010.

One witness to the primitive condition of cinema, Maxim Gorky, wrote after seeing films by the Lumières in 1896 that

> everything takes place without your hearing the noise of the wheels, the sound of the footsteps, or of speech. Not a sound, not a single note of the complex symphony which always accompanies the movement of a crowd. Without noise, the foliage, gray as cinder, is agitated by the wind and the gray silhouettes—of people condemned to perpetual silence, cruelly punished by the privation of all the colors of life—these silhouettes glide [over the gray ground] in silence. (quoted in Wierzbicki 2009, 21)[5]

Gorky's description embraces what might plausibly be regarded as the full spectrum of sound forms addressing the image: voice, environmental sound, and, figuratively at least, music. And music, precisely because it is missing except in Gorky's metaphors, is the apex of this triangulation. The lack of an acoustic envelope, represented in and as a lack of music, means that the images, though animate, impress at least one astute contemporary observer as already post-mortem. They are ashen silhouettes.

To make them *living* images, as opposed to the disturbingly undead, music must supply its sensorial dimension to the bodily image as form or figure. It must do so as both supplement and contradiction, something that has typically proved most seductive, in every sense, when rooted in the erotics of spectatorship. (As noted earlier, this recourse does not necessarily involve romance, though it very often has; nor, Eros and Psyche notwithstanding, are the erotics of cinema by any means necessarily heterosexual. In cinema as elsewhere, moreover, the erotic is, almost in an instant, transmutable into violent antagonism—the erotics of combat, be it verbal, mental, or physical, much as the sufferings in the myth would suggest.) The sensorial dimension arises because music in performance is always music incarnate. It has body, has a body, because it always lodges in the listener's body and usually—even in the digital age—issues from the performer's body. The ears, Hegel tells us, serve the most intellectual of the senses, but someone should have told Hegel: when we listen to music, we may be deeply attentive, but we are not all ears.

The pulse-pounding subwoofers at the latter-day Cineplex make that obvious enough. But what about the primitive condition, and the force of classical music as the model of cinematic embodiment?

Classical music is what it is—is, at any rate, what it increasingly became between the Enlightenment and the close of modernity—because it cultivates an identity beyond embodiment. Although the story involved is complex, classical music in general, music notated in detail and published in scores and/or parts for intact but interpretive reproduction, has historically imagined itself as an ideal form that performance can represent or approximate but never capture. The music may be embodied but it is itself bodiless. Classical music so conceived has a tangible, recognizable consistency, but no material quality, a living presence but no life. That is one reason why we talk—or used to—about the music itself. The music itself is an essence, perhaps the only thing in our worldly experience that corresponds to what we imagine an essence to be. We idealize the music "itself" in order to hold on to the incarnate music that we actually experience and enjoy but lose in the act of doing so. That is one reason why the use of classical music in film has tended to migrate over time from extradiegetic commentary to diegetic encounter. The music's discrete identity, even when fragmented by extracts, abbreviations, and alterations, tends increasingly to act as a spirit for which the characters as well as the audience provide the body.

Of course only a small fraction of narrative films actually enact this process of onscreen embodiment, but the paradigm is always latent, even in films that recycle the annoying convention that real vitality requires a switch from classical to popular genres. The cinematic body in this context is a figure both in the sense of a metaphor and in the literal sense of a personification, an allegorical image or statue, one of the numberless progeny of Eros and Psyche.

The results make no sense. Perhaps they're not supposed to.

Music draws the body away from social constraint and into the dense sphere of material being and physical urgency, the free and even reckless overflow of energy and desire, up to and including gross carnality and the flouting of social order. Bodily movements, gestures, and gesticulations that would be absurd or frightening in their own right become plausible, appealing, charismatic when done to music.

But classical music reinscribes this bodily whirligig within the ideal frame of form, rhythm, structure, logos, all the synonyms of the figure of harmony. It enrolls the heightened corporeality addressed and released by music in general within the sheltering span of culture, truth, and reason. When music is treated as art and held up for contemplation, its corporeal force does not disappear, but is displaced both *onto* the body of the performer and *into* the music as sounding presence, which becomes a historically specific model of bodily habitation—a model that can be ignored or ascetically denied, and often has been, but never entirely escaped.

These tendencies are simultaneous, confused, irreducible.

Music envelops and penetrates the body of the listener or performer but it has no bodily shape or form. Music can be embodied, and must be if it is to be heard, but in itself it embodies nothing.

But classical music as composition, as notated work, imagines the body it seeks; it defines the bodily conformation by which alone it can be heard properly. This act of imagination is performative; it is efficacious. Classical music does not seek out preconfigured bodies that it twists topologically into new shapes, or it does not do that alone. In part the bodies in which we embody ourselves are formed by our experiences of listening to, moving to, the music that surrounds us or the music we produce. Music has no body but it teaches embodiment.

These tensions create through music an impossible body, both more and less definite than what we call "the" body, denser than counterpoint and lighter than air: an angel's body (but angel bodies, we remember from Milton, are even more erotic than their human counterparts).

Music and Sexuality: *Impromptu*

One the most familiar and also most derided of music's uses is as a sexual lure, a kind of acoustic pheromone. The musical body is always keyed up; what Oliver Sacks would identify as the body's innately musical sense of its own aliveness is returned to it many fold in the experience of actual music. But some music is not content with the vitality of one body; it seems to demand the ecstatic meeting of two. In its break with singularity, such music often seeks or foments an anamorphosis, a spur—the word is chosen carefully—to the sexuality of the music itself.

In *Impromptu*, James Lapine's 1991 film about their romance, Chopin and George Sand meet to the accompaniment of a climactic moment in Chopin's G minor Ballade, Op. 23. Or, better, their meeting is the accompaniment to the music. (An entertaining farce, the film pales by comparison with its witting or unwitting model, Jean Renoir's 1939 *Rules of the Game*. I have dealt with *Impromptu* before [Kramer 2009, 92, 93–97], and do so again here, not because it is great cinema but because its treatment of classical music is remarkably symptomatic as well as sympathetic.)

Sand (Judy Davis) has been locked in her bedroom by a pathologically jealous lover. Hearing the sounds of the Ballade drift in through her window, she determines to follow them. She has heard fragments of this music twice before, also from behind closed doors, but each time its source, Chopin, has left the room before she could enter, leaving her only the music, afloat in disembodied form.

The film makes explicit that what Sand seeks in Chopin is precisely the embodiment of this music, which presents itself to her as an antidote to the snobbery and fatuous art-worship that rule her social world. The open window gives her the chance she has been waiting for. Sand climbs out of the window into the night (see Figure 13.1a), crosses the balcony to Chopin's window like a second-story man—she's wearing men's clothes—and steals inside.

The audience does not know quite where she has gone; Chopin (Hugh Grant) does not notice her entrance except for a rattling at the windowpane. At this point he is about to make the transition between a restatement of the Ballade's brooding first theme and a lavish transformation of the lyrical second theme (Figure 13.1b), but he interrupts himself to shut the window. Returning to the piano, he picks up where he has left off, only to be interrupted again as the lyrical theme is about to reach its climax. The interruption this time is the sound of a vase being smashed by Sand's frustrated lover; as the music breaks off, we hear Sand herself cry out "Oh don't *stop!*" as she thrusts herself out of her hiding place under Chopin's piano (Figure 13.1c).

The *double entendre* in this outburst is not lost on either party, nor is its relationship to the music. Sand, in fact, bargains for more—"Play me one more piece and I'll go" (see Figure 13.1d)—but the unnerved Chopin throws her out. For Sand this doesn't matter. In the next scene she declares herself "redeemed" as she sits down on the bed in her maid's room, crosses her leg over her knee, and pulls off her boot. This homely detail is a little at odds with the soundtrack, which now chimes in with a treacly orchestration of the Ballade's lyrical theme. Still, even though Sand has her foot in the viewer's face, the boot doesn't really stick out yet. But it will.

Once Sand and Chopin have become better acquainted, a new scene spells out the implications of their meeting. Chopin is heard, not seen, playing the turbulent beginning of the coda to his Fantaisie-Impromptu in C♯ minor; the music coincides with a close-up of George Sand's boot as she wiggles her foot in time with the music (Figure 13.2a). Sand is lying full-length under the piano, her body absorbing the music from the body of the instrument (Figure 13.2b). The camera pans slowly from her foot to her head, then goes on to Chopin's foot on the pedal (Figure 13.2c), which is reached at just the moment that the coda dissolves into the closing reminiscence of the work's lyrical middle section. As the music dies away to the cadence, the camera gently swerves upward, tracing the line of sublimation from Chopin's foot to his hands, torso, and head (Figure 13.2d). The reaching of the cadence here suggests the consummation curtailed in the earlier scene, and once again the suggestion is not lost on anyone. After the music ends, Sand emits a satisfied moan from her place under the piano (Figure 13.2e), then a fuller sigh as she pulls herself to her feet on the ledge of the instrument (Figure 13.2f).

The piano in these scenes is an acoustic camera; its sound pictures the body as an image of things heard. It shows us that there is nothing between Sand and Chopin but the body of the music, housed in the sounding chamber of the instrument under which Sand, like Psyche, is extended. Her extension is above all vibratory, like that of the strings left to shimmer when the pedal is down. Underlying the Ballade's transfigured lyrical theme is a wavelike series of sonorous washes created by the pedal. First every measure, then every half-measure, the space between the widely separated hands becomes replete with blended chords. Lying under the piano, one would literally feel this music. One

(a)

(b)

(c)

(d)

FIGURE 13.1 a–d: *Impromptu* (1980), George Sand enters Chopin's room.

would resound with it, as one would also with the ending of the Fantaisie-Impromptu, which states its slow lyrical melody in, or more exactly as, a low-slung bassline.

In both passages, too, the pedal's holds and releases sustain an unstable harmony under a limpid melody, a diffuse longing under the promise of pleasurable release. Both the texture and the form of the music conduce to a movement from the upper to the lower body, and from a body above to a body below. As the camera recognizes, the vibratory presence of the sound literally tends downward, communicating itself to a body supine on the floor, even as its lyrical aspirations figuratively soar upward. The music sexualizes itself from head to foot. And regardless of the sublimating tendency that runs in the opposite direction, the expressivity of the music, the music itself, cannot disengage from the anamorphotic visual excess that literally gives these scenes their pediment. The beauty and romance of the pieces, the glamour of the narrative, are intimately connected with that lowest, dirtiest, and smelliest of body parts and object of fetishistic desire par excellence, the foot.

The foot—and what it can step in, too. It is worth noting that in the balcony scene, Sand momentarily loses her footing and almost falls, a slip to which she responds with a heartfelt, if whispered, "Oh, shit!" The film presents her earthiness as the very means of authenticating her higher longings as embodied in Chopin and his music. Narratively, this relationship takes the form of Sand's successful effort to draw Chopin into a sexual relationship, that is, to reconcile his musical gifts with the bodily pleasure that is part of their meaning and medium.

CONCLUSION

These two scenes from *Impromptu* hear the musical body as an erotic body and hear the erotic body as a musical body—all before any of these bodies can be seen: for in each case the body of the other, player and listener, is out of sight until the moment of consummation or frustration, the moment the legend of Eros and Psyche comes to a cinematic happy ending or its prognosticating deferral. At its most invested, the cinematic body is visible music. And the music thus concentrated makes sure that Psyche, extended, knows at least a little of it.

But musical embodiment in cinema has a wider scope than that. It goes beyond the framing of erotic energy to the energy of Eros in the larger sense of the Freudian life drive, "the Eros of the poets and philosophers which holds all living things together" (Freud [1919] 1961, 60–61)—a concept that has had so much less theoretical play than the more dramatic death drive. Eros sets civilization the task of "uniting separate individuals into a community bound together by libidinal ties" (Freud [1930] 1961, 86). Or, if you prefer a nonpsychoanalytic formulation, the primitive condition of film music, never discarded, never evaded, is surplus animation. The music is heir to the artificial voices so often built into the automata of the eighteenth and nineteenth centuries to prove their virtual life, as well as to the free-floating subjectivity that the composers of the same

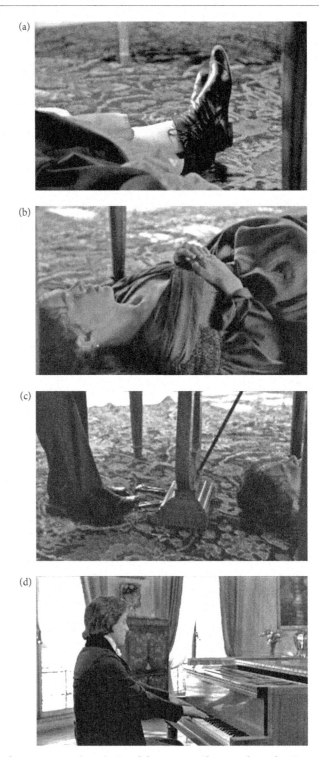

FIGURE 13.2 a–f: *Impromptu* (1980), Sand listens as Chopin plays the Fantaisie-Impromptu in C#-minor.

(e)

(f)

FIGURE 13.2   (*Continued*)

era had learned to release through the movement of sound. Music in cinema projects embodiment onto the moving image as (and while) the cinematic apparatus projects the moving image onto the screen. The music is the animate substance that completes the transformation of the image from the mimetic to the virtual. This is not a metaphor, not any more; it is a historical condition of perception. In the original legend, Psyche is forced to wander for years before she can be reunited with Eros. We know now where she finds him again, like an old tune—these days almost anywhere: it's right on screen.

NOTES

1. Williams's article reproduces several stills from *The Kiss* and credits Adam Phillips for the point about conventions of kissing.
2. Jacques Derrida (2005, 11–19) devotes a chapter to Nancy's "Psyche" and also (2007, I:1–47) reinvents the legend of Eros and Psyche independently as a figure for the self-reflexivity by which language removes itself from the other it seeks to address. My own usage is neither inconsistent with Derrida's figure nor a reproduction of it; my cinematic Eros and Psyche form a figure for the relationship between the image and the body.
3. The reference is to the title of an influential book in which Christian Metz makes a turn from a structuralist semiotics grounded in linguistics to one strongly informed by psychoanalysis

It has been generally assumed that this shift was inspired by the work of Julia Kristeva, a critic, philosopher, and trained psychoanalyst who was also responsible for sharp changes of direction by Roland Barthes and Raymond Bellour, among others, in the early 1970s. For Metz, cinematic signifiers are not only effects of a "technique of the imaginary," that is, of "photography and phonography," but also extensions of the imaginary in the Lacanian sense of "the basic lure of the ego... [including] desire as the effect of pure lack and endless pursuit" (Metz [1977] 1982, 3).

4. The relation of music to cinematic time has commonly been neglected by film theorists preoccupied with the visuality of the medium. For example, Mary Anne Doane makes only one point about music—and makes it only in passing: "Before the invention of phonography and cinema, written texts and musical scores were the only means of preserving time" (Doane 2002, 34; the comment subsequently receives a glancing allusion on 63). This neglect is a symptom of a broader one that is widespread outside the film music community. In her essay on the kiss, for example, Williams observes the role of music only in one film, *Casablanca* (1943), of which she says that "As Time Goes By" swells up on the soundtrack for the kisses between Rick and Ilse. And there she stops; the music is no more than a conventional signifier that lacks any significant dimension of its own.

5. Wierzbicki rather oddly cites this passage shortly after expressing skepticism about the spectrality of the unvarnished cinematic image—precisely the phenomenon that Gorky was observing.

BIBLIOGRAPHY

Benjamin, Walter. (1939) 2003. "The Work of Art in the Age of its Mechanical Reproducibility, Third Version." Translated by Edmund Jephcott and Harry Zohn. In *Selected Writings*. 4 vols. Edited by Howard Eiland and Michael W. Jennings, 4: 251–283. Cambridge, MA: Harvard University Press.

Bergson, Henri. (1896) 2007. *Matter and Memory*. Translated by N. M. Paul and W. S. Palmer. New York: Cosimo Classics.

Buhler, James, Caryl Flynn, and David Neumeyer, eds. 2000. *Music and Cinema*. Hanover, NH: University Press of New England.

Cavell, Stanley. 1996. *Contesting Tears: The Hollywood Melodrama of the Unknown Woman*. Chicago: University of Chicago Press.

Chapin, Keith, and Lawrence Kramer, eds. 2009. *Musical Meaning and Human Values*. New York: Fordham University Press.

Deleuze, Gilles. 1986. *Cinema 1: The Movement-Image*. Translated by Hugh Tomlinson and Barbara Habberjam. Minneapolis: University of Minnesota Press.

——. 1989. *Cinema 2: The Time-Image*. Translated by Hugh Tomlinson and Robert Galeta. Minneapolis: University of Minnesota Press.

Derrida, Jacques. 2005. *On Touching—Jean-Luc Nancy*. Translated by Christine Irizarry. Stanford: Stanford University Press.

——. (1987) 2007. *Psyche: Inventions of the Other*. 2 Vols. Edited by Peggy Kamuf and Elizabeth Rottenberg. Stanford: Stanford University Press.

Doane, Mary Anne. 2002. *The Emergence of Cinematic Time: Modernity, Contingency, the Archive*. Cambridge, MA: Harvard University Press.

Franklin, Peter. 2011. *Seeing through Music: Gender and Modernism in Classic Hollywood Film Scores*. Oxford: Oxford University Press.

Freud, Sigmund. (1919) 1961. *Beyond the Pleasure Principle*. Edited and translated by James Strachey. New York: Norton.

——. (1930) 1961. *Civilization and its Discontents*. Edited and translated by James Strachey. New York: Norton.

Goldmark, Daniel, Lawrence Kramer, and Richard Leppert, eds. 2007. *Beyond the Soundtrack: Representing Music in Cinema*. Berkeley: University of California Press.

Gorbman, Claudia. 1987. *Unheard Melodies: Narrative Film Music*. Bloomington: Indiana University Press.

Kassabian, Anahid. 2001. *Hearing Film: Tracking Identifications in Contemporary Hollywood Film Music*. New York and London: Routledge.

Kramer, Lawrence. 2002. *Musical Meaning: Toward a Critical History*. Berkeley: University of California Press.

——. 2009. *Why Classical Music Still Matters*. Berkeley: University of California Press.

Laing, Heather. 2007. *The Gendered Score: Music in 1940s Melodrama and the Woman's Film*. Aldershot, UK, and Burlington, VT: Ashgate.

Metz, Christian. [1977] 1982. *The Imaginary Signifier: Psychoanalysis and the Cinema*. Translated by Celia Britton, Annwyl Williams, Ben Brewster, and Alfred Guzzetti. Bloomington: Indiana University Press.

Mulvey, Laura. 1975. "Visual Pleasure and Narrative Cinema." *Screen* 16/3: 6–18.

Nancy, Jean-Luc. 1993. "Psyche." Translated by Emily McVarish. In *The Birth to Presence*, translated by Brian Holmes and others, 393–394. Stanford: Stanford University Press.

Powrie, Phil, and Robynn Stilwell, eds. 2006. *Changing Tunes: The Use of Pre-existing Music in Film*. Aldershot, UK, and Burlington, VT: Ashgate.

Wierzbicki, James. 2009. *Film Music: A History*. New York: Routledge.

Williams, Alastair. 2001. "Voices." Chapter 3 in *Constructing Musicology*. Aldershot, UK, and Burlington, VT: Ashgate.

Williams, Linda. 2006. "Of Kisses and Ellipses: The Long Adolescence of American Movies." *Critical Inquiry* 32, no. 2: 288–340.

CHAPTER 14

....

GENDER, SEXUALITY, AND THE SOUNDTRACK

....

JAMES BUHLER

PHOTOGRAPHY, painting, and similar forms of visual art invite the gaze, contemplatively, at our leisure, or more: they invite staring—in some instances to see the human body. The cinema, likewise, frames an image and invites us to look at it. Narrative cinema, because it requires agency, almost always invites the viewer to look at a human body (and anthropomorphizes bodies in general). It is therefore not surprising that the gaze—and its effects on all concerned, from actors to production personnel to viewers—has been a central issue for a critical theory of the cinema from early on. As Lawrence Kramer puts it, "the cinematic look is structurally voyeuristic, especially in the classic situation of peering through the dark" (Chapter 13, above). He goes a step further to assert that "the cinematic image is sexualized by the condition for its perception." This is the starting point for that important segment of critical theory that is based in gender and sexuality and whose overriding aim has been to reveal the systemic oppression that flows from the social structures of power. In this chapter, I discuss two main lines of work as they relate to film: feminist theory and queer theory. I also consider the adjustments necessary to these two theoretical positions when attention is brought to bear on the soundtrack. In Chapter 15, I examine how psychoanalysis provides a theoretical grounding.

SOUNDTRACK THEORY AND FEMINIST THEORY

....

The supplemental status of the soundtrack (and especially music) in much film theory has made it particularly susceptible to analysis based on gender. As Amy Lawrence bluntly puts it, "in classical film, sound is conflated with the feminine" (1991, 111). Mary

Ann Doane notes that sound technicians from early on used the metaphor of "marrying" the sound to the image to conceptualize the task of sound editing, and the soundtrack was understood as a promiscuous, unruly force that needed to be carefully controlled (Doane 1980, 50). Caryl Flinn adds that sound is cast in "the role of an irrational, emotional 'other' to the rational and epistemologically treasured visual term" (Flinn 1992, 6). The "marriage" therefore ensures a "proper"—that is, culturally sanctioned—relationship between image and sound. If sound supplements the image, its "marriage" to the image "domesticates" any threat that sound might pose as it extends the image (43).

Despite this opening for a strong feminist critique of film sound, feminist film criticism has focused primarily on the image. (For a succinct, early overview of feminist film theory's concern for image, see Kaplan 1983, 23–35.) An especially influential article in this tradition is Laura Mulvey's "Visual Pleasure and Narrative Cinema," which argues that the image of women is structured as a spectacle that rewards a tacitly masculine "gaze." This gaze objectifies the image (of woman) in order to integrate it into narrative and assert (masculine) control over it at both the level of story and spectator (Mulvey 1975, 12). Kaja Silverman takes issue with this exclusive focus on the image, arguing that, in classic Hollywood, the soundtrack also delimits the representation of women. Silverman claims that a "woman's words are...even less her own than are her 'looks'. They are scripted for her, extracted from her by an external agency, or uttered by her in a trancelike state. Her voice also reveals a remarkable facility for self-disparagement and self-incrimination" (Silverman 1988, 31). Indeed, "Hollywood's soundtrack is engendered through a complex system of displacements which locate the male voice at the point of apparent textual origin, while establishing the diegetic containment of the female voice" (45). Silverman's analysis of the voiceover, which she notes is rarely female in classic Hollywood, underscores the stakes of the gendered voice. The male voiceover is, she argues, the prototype of the masculine screen voice in general, because it is granted discursive authority and proximity to the apparatus, whereas the female voice's prototype lies in the embodied voice as an object of spectacle and display (39). "To the degree the voice-over preserves its integrity, it also becomes an exclusively male voice" (48).

The situation with music has been even more explicitly gendered than sound in general, due to the long cultural tradition of coding music as feminine and the tradition in silent film of associating the primary recurring theme of a film with the heroine (Rapée 1925, 14). This treatment continued in the sound era, most rudimentarily in the typical doubling of the love theme with the theme for the heroine, suggesting that the heroine existed in the film primarily to be the love object of the hero: "The fact that the love theme doubles the signification in this way reinforces the male-dominated point of view that characterizes most narrative film—at least in classical Hollywood" (Buhler, Neumeyer, and Deemer 2010, 198). In those instances "where the male character has a well-defined theme, [the love theme] suggests that she *is* essentially identical to [her] relationship [with him], whereas the theme for the hero establishes a musical identity for him that cannot be reduced in the same way."

Such difference in treatment between male and female characters was pervasive. As Claudia Gorbman notes, music in the studio era rarely failed to register "the presence of Woman on screen. It is as if the emotional excess of this presence must find its outlet in the euphony of a string orchestra" (Gorbman 1987, 80). If film theory equates vision with knowledge and rational control, Doane argues that the very presence of music in film is an acute source of anxiety, since it "marks a deficiency in the axis of vision. Because emotion is the realm in which the visible is insufficient as a guarantee, the supplementary meaning proffered by music is absolutely necessary" to any film genre, such as melodrama or the love story, that depends on the representation of character emotion (Doane 1987, 85). "Music takes up where the image leaves off—what is in excess in relation to the image is equivalent to what is in excess of the rational. Music has an anaphoric function, consistently pointing out that there is more than meaning, there is desire. To music is always delegated the task of pinpointing, isolating the moments of greatest significance, telling us where to look despite the fact that the look is inevitably lacking" (97). In Doane's analysis music gains this function, however, only by relinquishing all claims to meaning, which needless to say makes music's place in film exceedingly ambivalent. "There is always something horrifying about pure affect seemingly unanchored by signification. The heightening effect of music, its straining to direct the reading of the image, is paradoxically highly visible and risks spectatorial repudiation. It is as though music continually announces its own deficiency in relation to meaning" (97). Music is therefore a burden; and it is a burden because it underscores and asks us to look at what cannot be seen and what the film itself cannot show; that is, it is the positive manifestation of a central lack, a concern that will prove integral to the psychoanalytic accounts of the soundtrack that I will consider in Chapter 15. In this respect music doubles and is allied with film's other gendered, supplemental, and generally excessive modes of representation.

This burden is not spread equally across film, but falls more heavily on certain characters who are marked out for excessive musical attention much as the camera marks them for gazing upon. Heather Laing, in her excellent study of music in 1940s melodramas, carefully traces the differential musical treatment on the basis of gender. Music, she argues, is not simply a "signifier of emotion" but "a central element of the way in which we actually understand emotion within the construction of gender" (Laing 2007, 7). This construction and its binding with music was established in the nineteenth century, and the style of Hollywood film music is therefore not accidental, and it comes with real consequences.

> The film scoring style of the 1940s in fact burdens female characters with a Romantic relationship to music that carries with it both psychological and physical implications.... The musical representation of their emotions suggests the transcendent nature of women's interiority. At the same time, however, it also demonstrates the inevitable frustration of destructive power of this interiority in the context of contemporaneous—or historical—social mores and/or nineteenth-century ideas of the female constitution. (Laing 2007, 10)

The pure, unanchored affect to which Doane draws attention is, Laing argues, bound specifically to studio-era cinema's strongly gendered constructions of interiority, and the horrifying aspect of the one seems to mirror the horrifying aspect of the other. Film thus often presses music into an excessively close relationship with the heroine, as Laing notes:

> The sense of interiority usually associated with the female character comes from her specific connection with a theme that can vary to her emotional states with some degree of intimacy, and the frequent combination of statements of this theme with extended, often close-up, shots of her face. It seems that the increasingly familiar and developing music, in a concentrated convergence with her facial expression, allows us to believe that we understand the woman's thoughts and emotions to an intimate degree. (Laing 2007, 141)

From Doane's perspective, we might take issue with Laing's formulation that audiences come to "understand" to the extent that understanding is generally linked to mastery in rational thought. It is more that music allows audiences to believe that they experience moment to moment something like the feel of a character's fluctuating emotions, emotions that are beyond the mastery of rational thought, not to mention language. Doane's formulation has the advantages of mapping the terms more strictly in the gendered categories of classic cinema, but it has the disadvantages of accepting the excluded middle, which simply equates understanding with reason and conceives any emotion unmediated by reason as the expression of irrationality, a configuration that has many negative representational consequences for women. Laing's perhaps less careful formulation is also somewhat more flexible, and it permits conceiving emotion as something other than the opposite of reason.

We can recognize the theoretical stakes and see the extent to which music specifically underscores female interiority by comparing, as Laing does, the musical treatment of male characters. "Men are rarely associated with such intimate themes or shot in close-up to their accompaniment. Although, therefore, isolated emotional moments may be recorded through the combination of a close-up and sentimental music, its lack of thematic relevance seems to register the emotion at a rather more general level than tends to be the case with female characters" (Laing 2007, 141). When it comes to men, music does not, in fact, tend to underscore the image as particularly lacking and so in need of supplementation. Instead, men say what they think, and there is rarely an issue of emotion overrunning the word. When it does, emotion tends to spill over into rash action, that is, exteriorization, rather than remaining in the unfathomable depths of interiority, enclosed within the spectacular but static close-up, typical of female representation. The musical score follows suit: it allows that male emotion is fundamentally comprehensible, however moved he may be, his emotion remains contained and mastered and so the music need only express the presence of emotion rather than probing the image to reveal signs of the unmastered interiority that are projected as signs of an irrational interior life. On this point, Laing draws close to Doane's formulation: "in very general terms, we are asked to witness and sympathize with male emotion, whereas our drawing into the woman's musical-emotional trajectory offers the sense of experiencing female emotion" (Laing 2007, 141). Our inability to say specifically what the music means, the fact that it remains at the level of connotation, reflects the inability to master in words that underlying emotional experience, which is felt rather than understood.

SOUNDTRACK THEORY AND QUEER THEORY

If feminist studies of the soundtrack are concerned primarily with exposing and critiquing the ways Hollywood represents and reinforces existing cultural hierarchies of gender, queer studies—a critical study of sexuality focused primarily in gay, lesbian, and transsexual perspectives—calls into question the very opposition of the sexes that grounds the hierarchy (Butler 1990; Sedgwick 1990). Like feminist and postcolonial theory, it seeks not only to unmask stereotypes but to analyze their discursive functions in order to displace and destabilize the social structures and power relations that support them. According to Ellis Hanson's concise definition of the practice,

> queer theory submits the various social codes and rhetorics of sexuality to a close up reading and rigorous analysis that reveal their incoherence, instability, and artificiality, such that sexual pleasure or desire, popularly conceived as a force of nature that transcends any cultural framework, becomes instead a performative effect of language, politics, and the endless perversity and paradox of symbolic (which is also to say historical and cultural) meaning. The very word queer invites an impassioned, even an angry response to normalization. (Hanson 1999, 4)

Focused on revealing the cultural processes and mechanisms of normalization, queer theory is more concerned with transgressing boundaries and/or drawing attention to the arbitrary nature of cultural constructions than it is with establishing, defining, and defending the identities that culture proffers or withholds in either positive (subject) or negative (abject) aspects. For Annamarie Jagose, this means that queer theory "marks a suspension of identity as something fixed, coherent and natural" (1996, 98), and Alexander Doty adds that "ultimately, queerness should challenge and confuse our understanding and uses of sexual and gender categories" (1993, xvii). If queer theory thereby positions itself against the norm, whether as antithesis, opposite, or contrary, it does so to unsettle the norm, to call into question its status as something natural. In this respect it is perfectly possible to produce a queer reading of a film without "obvious...non-straight elements" (Doty 1998, 150), the point being to look for figures that destabilize and denaturalize (or can be used to destabilize and denaturalize) the cultural norms of straightness, what is more militantly called "compulsory heterosexuality" (Rich 1980).

A critical theory of the soundtrack informed by gender and queer theory would be concerned with the "articulation of power and sexuality" on the soundtrack, how desire is made audible on it, for whom, by whom, and to what purpose (Hanson 1999,

1). It might ask whether and to what extent the soundtrack enforces a compulsory heterosexual code, examining, for instance, how the soundtrack imposes normative gender roles and lines of sexual desire on the film's characters and our apprehension of them. (These are general concerns that Hanson outlines for critical queer studies rather than for the soundtrack per se.) According to Scott Paulin, "music often participates directly in constructing on-screen representations of desire and sexuality, usually encouraging the audience to identify with a (hetero)sexual relationship and to desire its consummation" (1997, 37). Catherine Haworth adds that "correspondence with prescriptive and patriarchal gender norms signifies not just sexual conformity, but also that this in turn becomes a marker of a more generalized acceptable morality.... The relative homogeneity of sonic and visual codes signaling positive or negative constructions of gendered and sexual identity across [various] media (as well as other categories of difference) demonstrates both their interconnectedness and the deeply engrained nature of these representational archetypes" (2012, 124). One can certainly imagine, at a first stage, analytical studies of how, say, gay or lesbian characters are scored, the way the soundtrack reinforces or resists engaging cultural stereotypes, whether it chooses to demonize, complicate, or valorize the character types the film presents, and so forth (Kassabian 2001, 72–76; Farmer 2005; LeBlanc 2006). Glyn Davis, for instance, provides a brief account of stereotyping of the gay, lesbian, and transsexual voices (Davis 2008, 179–81). This sort of analysis is similar to the identification of stereotypes in musical topics or examining positive or negative portrayals of women and race on the soundtrack. But queer theory as a field stands in a similar relation to such analysis as postcolonial theory does to the analysis of the cultural field of stereotypes (see Chapter 7, above), and as such it is oriented around identifying and analyzing the processes of subjectification embedded within the representations of sexuality proffered by film, around looking at those representations less as reflecting power relations of the society than of signifying them.

QUEERING ASYNCHRONOUS SOUND

Many have argued for treating asynchronous sound—or at least sound that does not settle easily into the body with which it is synchronized—as part of a queer aesthetic. Lucretia Knapp, for instance, offers the example of Marnie from Hitchcock's eponymously titled film. "There are many incongruencies between the film's visuals and its soundtrack, and they create a space for Marnie outside the dualistic economies of patriarchy" (Knapp 1993, 16). Such incongruities, Knapp says, give Marnie a queer voice. Thomas Waugh likewise notes that more overt deployment of asynchronous sound, especially the offscreen voice and voiceover, is common in homoerotic cinema as a figure of gay desire and that its use is an aesthetic strategy that "reflects more than its logistic and economic suitability for artisanal and underfinanced industrial cinema" (Waugh 1996, 57). Instead, "image-sound separation...[is] at the center of the erotic give-and-take: ... [it] cements the irreconcilability of subject and object, exacerbates the tension of the teasing relationship of look-but-don't-touch, touch-but-don't-possess, appear-but-don't-speak, speak-but-don't-appear, and so forth" (57).

Glyn Davis, writing specifically about television sound, likewise suggests that queer disruptions of normal modes of viewing "frequently operate via the aural channel, or, more accurately, bring the aural and visual streams into a dissonant—and dissident— relationship to each other" (Davis 2008, 173). This formulation, reminiscent of the call by Eisenstein, Pudovkin, and Alexandrov for audiovisual counterpoint at the dawn of the commercial sound film (Eisenstein 1949, 257–60), aligns the queer aesthetic fairly closely with the aims of the old avant garde, a sort of Brechtian alienation effect, which is perhaps not surprising given that both aim to disrupt a normative social order. Davis explicitly disavows a connection, however, arguing that unlike Brecht, who sought to distance his audience from the drama that they might recognize the mechanisms of social power operating in the drama, the disruptive effects in television often "enhance the relationship with television, producing a purposefully heightened level of attention to the qualities of the text. They may, however, be correctly described as perplexing, destabilizing, perhaps even disorienting" (Davis 2008, 185). Whatever its relation to Brecht, its similarity to Russian montage theory is striking, except that the unexpected "jolts" of television are, unlike edits in film, often unscripted. More to the point is the interpretive strategy: a queer reading understands such disruption not simply as an attack on the social order but as an opening for a desire not sanctioned by that order to appear.

Queerness and Spectacle

As with postcolonial theory (see Chapter 7, above), queer theory often employs an interpretive strategy that reads against the grain. In the case of queer theory this strategy seeks out figures of camp, "an oppositional reading of popular culture which offers identifications and pleasures that dominant culture denies to homosexuals" (Smelik 1998, 141). Jane Feuer advocates such a camp approach when she suggests that " 'queer' readings of musicals would shift the emphasis from narrative resolution as heterosexual coupling (an emphasis on the comic plot) and toward readings based on non-narrative, performative and spectacular elements (and emphasis on numbers)" (Feuer 1993, 141). Camp readings seize on elements of textual spectacle or excess to bifurcate the film into competing structural levels, one that carries a dominant meaning, the other a secret, subversive or at least nonnormative one. Figures of spectacle and narrative excess are also sites of filmic artifice, points at which the film acknowledges its peculiar status as a cultural construction. "Mainstream Hollywood images," Lloyd Whitesell writes, "freely invite queer consumption. Of course, nominal narrative safeguards are in place to maintain the appearance of alignment with prevailing concepts of gender. But the storylines are hardly strong enough to contain all that is going on in the affective and aesthetic realms" (Whitesell 2006, 273). Mitchell Morris argues in similar fashion that the performative artifice common to the musical is especially conducive to queer reading because "artifice is a way of indicating that there is a secret; in the past century's prime cultural texts, if there is a secret, how could it not be that secret?" (Morris 2004, 152).

The situation is in fact characteristic of much classic Hollywood cinema, since the male hero is always in danger of being treated as a spectacle, as an object to be looked at rather than narratively identified with (Miller 1997, 46–47). The result, Anneke Smelik writes, is that "male homosexuality is always present as an undercurrent; it is Hollywood's symptom. The denial of the homoeroticism of looking at images of men constantly involves sado-masochistic themes, scenes, and fantasies; hence the highly ritualized scenes of male struggle which deflect the look away from the male body to the scene of the spectacular fight" (Smelik 1998, 140).

D. A. Miller brilliantly analyzes *Rope* (1948) and *Suddenly, Last Summer* (1959) along these lines (Miller 1990;,1997). These two films, each featuring a prominent and needless to say problematic level of homosexual thematics, bracket a decade when the Hollywood production code, which had prohibited overt mention of homosexuality, was eroding. Miller's analysis reveals a regime of representation that requires and so produces symptoms of pathology even as the film must attempt (and fail) to contain them. Drawing on Roland Barthes, Miller says that homosexuality in *Rope* remains at the level of connotation, where the prohibition against allowing it to pass into denotation has its own perverse effect: "if connotation, as the dominant signifying practice of homophobia, has the advantage of constructing an essentially insubstantial homosexuality, it has the corresponding inconvenience of tending to raise this ghost all over the place" (Miller 1990, 119). What this structure produces, Miller says, is the desire for homosexuality—"the spectacle of 'gay sex'"—to appear as denotation, precisely what the production code forbids. The perversity lies not in "gay sex" or this desire to see it but in the "structure of occultation"—what Eve Sedgwick describes as "the epistemology of the closet" (1990)—that would raise and even require this desire only to proscribe its actual appearance. In this way, the desire to see transmutes into a desire not to see, and the closet becomes the acceptable cultural structure for this "homophobic, heterosexual desire for homosexuality" (Miller 1990, 125), a desire that culture cannot acknowledge as its own. As Scott Paulin notes in his critique of Miller, this structure of occultation becomes considerably less "tidy" in *Rope* once the soundtrack is taken into account since music does not fit neatly under the binary of connotation and denotation that Miller instrumentalizes in his analysis (Paulin 1997, 37-40).

SUDDENLY, LAST SUMMER (1959) AND THE ECONOMY OF SACRIFICE

Similar issues come into play in Miller's provocative analysis of *Suddenly, Last Summer.* Based on a play by Tennessee Williams and directed by Joseph L. Mankiewicz, this film is the story of a psychologically traumatized young woman, Catherine Holly (Elizabeth

Taylor), and a doctor's attempt to help her. As the film opens, Catherine's rich, domineering aunt, Violet Venable (Katharine Hepburn), has had Catherine institutionalized for telling scandalous stories about her cousin Sebastian's death, and Violet has offered to build a new wing of a run-down New Orleans' psychiatric hospital if Dr. Cucrowicz (Montgomery Clift) agrees to perform a lobotomy on Catherine. The doctor is reluctant to do so unless he is convinced that Catherine's issues cannot be addressed through traditional psychiatric means, and he places her on a rushed course of psychoanalytic diagnosis and treatment. The outcome ostensibly hinges on getting Catherine to recount the gruesome tale of Sebastian's death, which she finally does near the end of the film, where an elaborate flashback reveals that Sebastian was killed in Cabeza de Lobo by a band of local boys from whom he had been procuring sex.

If *Suddenly, Last Summer* was able to obtain official permission to denote homosexuality explicitly, if not by name, it approaches the representation of gay sex, indeed the homosexual body, coyly, by displacement. Sebastian is only ever seen partially, primarily from the rear, and close-ups of Catherine routinely substitute, Miller notes, "whenever such possibility [of representing gay sex] would be on the verge of realization" (1997, 36). The result is "*a homosexual closet constructed for general heterosexual use,* for the indulgence, in other words, of a homosexual fantasy that we must mainly understand as not the peculiar coinage of the gay male brain but the common, even central daydream of the normal world" (37; emphasis in original). The operation of the closet, which is here seemingly underwritten by a desire for literal transparency, is particularly evident in Catherine's final narration, where her voice recounts the story of Sebastian's death but the image, in flashback, never manages to dissolve Catherine's body. Yet if the film effects another displacement here, it does so by seeming to desynchronize the image to Catherine's narration: on her mention of the "indecent" white bathing suit Sebastian had made her wear, the image shows instead a man in a white bathing suit, and although Catherine does soon appear, "in a crucial respect, she has arrived too late" (41). In this way, "Cathy's body is implicated in male homosexuality not merely as its sign, or even its analogy, but as its very evidence" (42). Writing about the stage play rather than the film, Robert F. Gross makes a similar point about Catherine, who "comes to embody a desire as much her cousin's as her own, combining female heterosexuality and male homosexuality in a single vector. Hence, her profoundly threatening advances to Doctor Cucrowicz erase any difference between gay and straight *eros*; a seemingly heterosexual action is permeated with gay desire" (Gross 1995, 240).

Although persuasive, Miller's interpretation in particular shows an undeniable visual bias—"the level that, in every film, counts most" (Miller 1997, 50)—which precisely because he recognizes and so adeptly diagnoses the pervasive blindness at the heart of Mulvey's influential analysis of the look, is most curious. For it simply reproduces the hegemonic status of the image, as though this status were some self-evident property of the medium. Miller does, however, closely attend to Catherine's narration in *Suddenly, Last Summer* and implicitly recognizes the important and complex work that the play of synchronization and desynchronization performs within it; both her lack of visual transparency and the unruly appearance of the man in the bathing suit are, however, irreducibly audiovisual figures whose appearance of uncanniness requires not just a particular joining of sound and image but also the assumption of a representational regime of compulsory synchronization that owns the distinctions by which those particular joins can appear especially uncanny.

Miller also mentions, in passing, the musical score's alignment with a normative heterosexuality, as it celebrates, in a way that otherwise seems outrageously excessive, Catherine's ability to stand up just prior to delivering the full story of Sebastian's death: "If the musical track salutes her achievement with sonorities befitting the most wondrous miracle, or the most heroic triumph, this is implicitly because, in managing to get upright, Cathy has simultaneously become straight as well. She is hardly on her feet for a second before, throwing her arms about her doctor's shoulders, she begins to cover his face with passionate kisses" (Miller 1997, 57). Although the orchestral score here is typical in asserting access to Catherine's interiority and follows the so-called "talking cure" film in working to express the properly gendered female subject as an object of heterosexual desire, Miller notes that the doctor does not reciprocate. Before she had found the strength to stand, however, the doctor had pricked Catherine with the truth serum, and it is striking that her reaction to being thus penetrated by the shot is an ecstatic embrace of the role as object of heterosexual desire. If this is indeed music that expresses Catherine's emotions and desire, if the doctor's reluctance indicates that she is "peculiarly unlucky in love" as Miller suggests (58), she also gains in her loss of sex appeal a measure of autonomy that allows her to appear as something other than the role offered by compulsory heterosexuality as romantic object.

Surprisingly, Miller does not mention the other music of the film—the boys' band of home-made instruments—that serves as both the most prominent sign of Catherine's psychological blockage and as the accompaniment for the climactic portion of the flashback, which is otherwise uncannily without diegetic sound aside for her scream that concludes it. In fact, the first time she tries to recount the story for the doctor, she falters when "that awful noise…, that awful music" rises up on the soundtrack to overwhelm her voice. When under the truth serum she recounts the story the second time, it is clear why she had earlier failed: not only had the music served to drive Sebastian through the streets of the city to ceremonial slaughter but the instruments were apparently also used as ritual tools in his dismemberment. Literalizing Jacques Attali's insight that noise is a simulacrum of essential violence and music its channelization into ritual sacrifice (Attali [1977] 1985, 21–31), this unruly sound positioned between noise and music is no simulacrum here but the actual instrument of ritual murder. Catherine has witnessed a primal scene of essential violence, with Sebastian as sacrificial victim.

According to René Girard (1977), the basic social function of sacrifice is to break cycles of violent retribution. Consequently, if sacrifice meets violence with violence, it must do so in a form that avoids provoking a new cycle of retribution, which is why the scapegoat is usually an outsider and if not an outsider, an innocent. Designed to end retribution, the ritual must avoid signs of retribution (vengeance is reserved for the divine), which carries the taint of impurity. That Catherine's flashback nevertheless represents Sebastian's ritual murder as a form of retribution suggests that we might take her narrative as a misreading serving her own psychic ends. That misreading would also raise questions as to whether Catherine has in fact misconstrued her role as bait, which, however overdetermined, would therefore be a red herring in interpreting the film.

If the function of this sacrificial rite remains obscure within the social context of Cabeza de Lobo, amnesia of the sort Catherine experiences is usually understood psychoanalytically as a traumatic sign of unconscious recognition and psychic censorship rather than as unintelligibility. Catherine can't remember not because she doesn't understand what she has seen, but because she is terrified by what it reveals about herself: she recognizes in its displaced form the traumatic violence of her own primal scene, which twines a compulsory heterosexuality that uses the fantasy of "perverse" homosexuality to police and uphold its boundaries with a revenge fantasy against a perverse patriarchal privilege that blames her,[1] rather than her rapist—"a very ordinary married man," Violet assures—for her "loss of honor." Catherine's narrative thus makes the scene into an allegory whereby she merges with Sebastian and assumes his face and he her anus, as in Miller's reading, but now this fusion is understood as instrumentalized to surmount the shame of the original sexual trauma she experienced at the Dueling Oaks. In that respect, Violet is not so far off the mark when she claims that Catherine killed Sebastian: Catherine's narrative begins to offer Sebastian as her substitute, as a ritual sacrifice for her sins (or to be more precise the sins that society has pinned on her), just as at the social level the homosexual functions in the "economy of sacrifice" as the scapegoat for the regime of compulsory heterosexuality. But if sacrifice demands separation and establishment (or reestablishment) of social marks of distinction as the price of that separation, Catherine's separation from Sebastian is especially violent, traumatic, and laden with guilt sufficient to trigger extreme psychological defenses. Symptoms of this trauma appear not only in the amnesia but also in Catherine's demonization of exploitation as (ab)use, as a perversion of social order: her commitment to the idea that Sebastian used people only for his pleasure and in particular that he used Catherine as bait; that she had been used by her rapist, who warned that saying anything about it would disrupt the social order (as it did); and that Violet used Sebastian as an outlet to live a more interesting life than her husband was willing to provide for her. In negative form, demonization of exploitation also prompts Catherine's suicide attempt by conforming to the brutal cultural logic: because she was of no use other than as the bearer of a social trauma that society could not acknowledge, she was "in the way," expendable, and so also herself a potential scapegoat. What this symptom disguises, however, is Catherine's own need to exploit Sebastian as a sacrifice in order to find her place again in the social order.

The band of Cabeza de Lobo rewrites this psychic dynamic into a social framework along the lines of social power that Attali outlines: the band's noise announces the threat to social order; the band's music channels that threat into acceptable social form. Janice Siegel traces the numerous parallels between Sebastian and Pentheus from Euripides' *The Bacchae* and notes that ways in which the film strengthens these parallels compared to the stage play. She also reads the instruments, which she sees as guitar-like, and other aspects of the costumes as invocations of Orpheus and notes the ambiguity that the boys' call for "pan" is not only Spanish for bread, as the doctor notes, but also the name of a central figure in the Dionysus myth (Siegel 2005, 556). The word "panic," which Siegel (and also Catherine in her narration) uses to describe Sebastian's flight and many use to describe the film's engagement with its homosexual thematics, also has its roots in this Greek figure. Albert Johnson, in his contemporaneous review of the film for *Film Quarterly*, suggests as well the resemblance of the stringed instrument to "a primitive-looking banjo" (Johnson 1960, 42). If this invocation of the banjo allows the band at Cabeza de Lobo to sound like a distant echo of a New Orleans string band and the costumes of its members resembles a mardi gras parade where the mummers' costumes have been plucked—Catherine herself describes the band as looking "like a flock of plucked birds"—we should recall that Catherine's rape takes place after a mardi gras ball. This uncanny resemblance relocates the central trauma to the Dueling Oaks, as does her scream, the only synchronized diegetic sound of the flashback and one that has the power both to silence this music—it is not heard again—and to burst across the narrative frame, collapsing past and present, her roles as narrator and narratee; but the scream—a prime example of what Michel Chion calls a "screaming point" ([1982] 1999, 75–79)—also has the power to cross another narrative line and to deliver the call for help that she had earlier placed, mysteriously dislodged from herself, at the site of the rape. She can evidently separate the two traumatic events only by renouncing Sebastian, but the music—"if you can call it that," she says—does not offer to her a convincing social order where she can locate herself, since its categories remain indistinct, "a music made out of noise."

In refusing the music and choosing to silence it, she ruins the ritual. Where there is no music, there is no society, no distinction, no social support. As she continues her narration after the scream and recounts the depths of her horror, the lack of music does not so much express a collapse into stark realism as it underscores a final realization that society is not possible under the conditions being proffered. Strikingly, music returns only after Catherine has completed the story, on a shot of Violet closing the empty book that was to contain Sebastian's summer poem. The music continues as Violet, mistaking the doctor for her son, begins speaking as though she were on a voyage with Sebastian. If, as Attali says, music is "an affirmation that society is possible" ([1977] 1985, 29), music's appearance here in association with madness suggests that society itself exists in a deluded state. "All great music," Adorno writes, "is snatched from madness" ([1960] 1996, 71). This is not great music to be sure, but it is music, brilliantly deployed, to sound as serenely mad as the society that it underwrites and that underwrites it. The music continues through to the final shot, where Catherine gently offers the doctor her hand, he takes it, and they both walk to the door. Especially after the attempted kiss before the narration, nothing about the gesture except the overenthusiastic music suggests further romantic entanglement, and the music, we now understand, is party to delusion and not to be trusted, most particularly when it beckons with apparently comforting social roles that refuse to acknowledge the sacrifice they require to occupy and uphold.

It is quite possible to read Catherine's attraction to the doctor prior to her narrative as a defense against Violet, whom Catherine knows is pressuring the doctor to give her a lobotomy. In that respect, Catherine's attempts to encourage Dr. Cucrowicz to take her as a heterosexual object of desire may have more to do with self-preservation than with actual desire to assume that normative social role. Kevin Ohi argues that Catherine's status as Sebastian's bait and Violet's insistence that the doctor's devotion to his medicine reminds her of Sebastian place the doctor (but also the film) in a "double bind" to the extent that he (but also the film) insists on a "curative heterosexual gaze" (Ohi 1999, 37). Ohi, perhaps persuaded by the deluded music, misses Cucrowicz's coolness toward romance that Miller points out. The doctor most certainly does not treat Catherine "as the saving heterosexual object of desire." Aside from the music, the film does not either.

The Hours (2002) and Sacrificial Inversion

The economy of sacrifice that proved so traumatic in *Suddenly, Last Summer* also plays a significant if highly ambivalent role in *The Hours*, a film that entwines three loosely linked stories from disparate time periods around the themes of sacrifice and suicide. The contemporary story involves a lesbian couple, Clarissa (Meryl Streep) and Sally (Allison Janney), and Clarissa's relationship with her former lover, Richard (Ed Harris), a gay writer who has grown embittered as he has been ravaged by AIDS.

Michael LeBlanc (2006) discusses how Philip Glass's music for the film works within and against the economy of sacrifice to support Richard's suicide as an inverted form of sacrifice. Glass's score captures the melancholic repetition that structures and haunts heterosexual romance in all three stories, but that of Clarissa and Richard, LeBlanc says, is particularly fraught because the melancholic attachment to Richard is presented as a block to Clarissa's happiness. The final moments between Clarissa and Richard are "steeped in melancholia, those drawn-out piano notes hanging on a given pitch, clinging tightly to the loss of heterosexual romance. Clarissa, also, is trapped in this place with Richard" (LeBlanc 2006, 135). The music here then emphasizes the heterosexual ideal as something lost, unobtainable and so also as a bad object that traps Richard and Clarissa in a cycle of unending melancholic repetition.

> By embodying the heterosexual ideal in these last moments, Richard bears the burden of that ideal, volunteering to take it off Clarissa's shoulders. What is compelling here is thus how Richard inverts the conventional logic of sacrifice. If sacrifice is typically performed as a method of abjecting the nonnormative term, so that those bodies that signify otherness are repetitively ejected from the symbolic order, Richard performs the opposite move by embodying heteronormative romance in his final moments, thereby ejecting that very norm. In other words, if the visionary is typically a form of otherness, Richard becomes a sort of antivisionary, carrying the burden of conventionality so that Clarissa does not have to. By sacrificing himself, he carries with him the ideal of heterosexual romance; he becomes a martyr so that Clarissa might move on from that stifling and melancholic fantasy. (LeBlanc 2006, 135)

Richard's suicide, then, becomes a way of ending the cycle and the music traces a similar process. Susan McClary notes that Glass's "music acknowledges [Richard's] emotional contradictions, but withholds the catharsis both we and the characters so deeply crave." At the same time, in contrast to melancholic repetition of the rest of the score, Glass affirms, by suspending after Richard's death "his own stylistic rules," the relationship between Clarissa and Sally, which McClary finds "remarkable" since it endows their embrace with the musical cinematic signs of normal romantic feeling (McClary 2007, 61–62).

Even so, if Richard's sacrifice is thus novel in terms of the social forms and distinctions it is meant to uphold, LeBlanc cautions that it remains caught within "an economy of sacrifice that demands that abjected individuals carry the burden of melancholic loss so the rest of us don't have to" (LeBlanc 2006, 136). The comparison with *Suddenly, Last Summer* on this point is instructive. Sebastian's sacrifice obviously conforms to the conventional logic; but Catherine's resolutely melancholic response to the trauma destabilizes the economy by refusing the exchange.

CONCLUSION

As the analyses of *Suddenly, Last Summer* and *The Hours* demonstrate, it is often difficult to neatly separate feminist and queer readings because both bear on sexuality as it relates to power. This does not mean, however, that feminist and queer theory can be reduced to one or the other nor that they will necessarily yield similar or even consistent critical evaluations. Within critical practice, feminist and queer theories carry quite distinct emphases. Attending to Sebastian's representation in *Suddenly, Last Summer*, for instance, we note that Sebastian is not only shown primarily from the rear; he is also only allowed to speak through Catherine (and to a lesser extent Violet), exhibiting the split between image and voice—albeit in negative form—that Waugh (1996, 55–58) sees as one attribute of representing queer desire, here almost infinitely displaced and deferred. Attending to Catherine, however, we note the extent to which even in the flashback her voice is only ever momentarily allowed to leave her body; her narration is anchored to the physical presence of her body, which, in various degrees of close-up, floats along the right edge of the frame as the events she recounts play out in the rest of the frame, exhibiting the unity of image and voice, the compulsory synchronization, that Silverman (1988, 42–71) sees as the primary disciplining function of Hollywood sound practice. The treatment of Sebastian and Catherine in the flashback is in marked contrast to Dr. Cucrowicz, whose voice passes fluidly from offscreen to onscreen and back again and so serves as the authoritative norm against which the representations of Catherine and Sebastian are each understood as somehow deficient.

Although feminist and queer theory both confront the cultural norm of compulsory heterosexuality, they are each concerned with analyzing, unveiling and dismantling different aspects of power configured under the norm. It is occasionally the case that a figure, say the spectacular image of a woman, may open to the liberatory potential of a camp reading from a queer perspective, but also appear exceptionally regressive from a feminist perspective. Such cases are highly ambivalent, not just in the weak sense that the critical reception is mixed, but in the strong sense that there can be no real deciding between the alternatives without positing gender or sexuality as the essential category for understanding. Unexamined, this ambivalence therefore easily devolves into exchanging competing charges of misogyny and homophobia. What is missed is that the forced choice between alternatives serves primarily to enforce the power of the norm, which gains in virtue of dividing resistance and creating the impression that any gain on one front must be paid for by a more or less equivalent loss on another.

Notes

1. Siegel (2005) notes that Violet's account of the sea turtles on the Galapagos Islands draws explicitly on Melville's story "The Encantadas or The Enchanted Isles." Melville's story, she says, reads the scene as a revenge fantasy, claiming that most sailors "earnestly believe that all wicked sea-officers, more especially commodores and captains, are at death (and in some cases before death) transformed into tortoises" (quoted 558).

Bibliography

Adorno, Theodor W. (1960) 1996. *Mahler: A Musical Physiognomy.* Translated by Edmund Jephcott. Chicago: University of Chicago Press.

Attali, Jacques. (1977) 1985. *Noise: The Political Economy of Music.* Translated by Brian Massumi. Minneapolis: University of Minnesota Press.

Buhler, James, David Neumeyer, and Rob Deemer. 2010. *Hearing the Movies: Music and Sound in Film History.* New York: Oxford University Press.

Butler, Judith. 1990. *Gender Trouble: Feminism and the Subversion of Identity.* New York: Routledge.

Chion, Michel. (1982) 1999. *The Voice in the Cinema.* Translated by Claudia Gorbman. New York: Columbia University Press.

Davis, Glyn. 2008. "Hearing Queerly: Television's Dissident Sonics." In *Queer TV: Theories, Histories, Politics,* edited by Glyn Davis and Gary Needham, 172–187. Hoboken, NJ: Routledge.

Doane, Mary Ann. 1980. "Ideology and the Practice of Sound Editing and Mixing." In *The Cinematic Apparatus,* edited by Teresa de Lauretis and Stephen Heath, 47–56. Milwaukee: MacMillan.

——. 1987. *The Desire to Desire: The Woman's Film of the 1940s.* Bloomington: Indiana University Press.

Doty, Alexander. 1993. *Making Things Perfectly Queer: Interpreting Mass Culture.* Minneapolis: University of Minnesota Press.

——. 1998. "Queer Theory." In *Oxford Guide to Film Studies,* edited by John Hill and Pamela Church Gibson, 148–152. New York: Oxford University Press.

Eisenstein, Sergei. 1949. *Film Form: Essays in Film Theory.* Translated by Jay Leyda. New York: Harcourt Brace.

Farmer, Brett. 2005. "The Fabulous Sublimity of Gay Diva Worship." *Camera Obscura* 20, no. 2: 165–195.

Feuer, Jane. 1993. *The Hollywood Musical.* 2nd ed. Bloomington: Indiana University Press.

Flinn, Caryl. 1992. *Strains of Utopia: Gender, Nostalgia, and Hollywood Film Music.* Princeton, NJ: Princeton University Press.

Girard, René. (1972) 1977. *Violence and the Sacred.* Translated by Patrick Gregory. Baltimore: Johns Hopkins University Press.

Gorbman, Claudia. 1987. *Unheard Melodies: Narrative Film Music.* Bloomington: Indiana University Press.

Gross, Robert F. 1995. "Consuming Hart: Sublimity and Gay Poetics in *Suddenly, Last Summer.*" *Theatre Journal* 47, no. 2: 229–251.

Hanson, Ellis. 1999. "Introduction." In *Out Takes: Essays in Queer Theory and Film*, edited by Ellis Hanson, 1–19. Durham: Duke University Press.

Haworth, Catherine. 2012. "Introduction: Gender, Sexuality, and the Soundtrack." *Music, Sound and the Moving Image* 6, no. 2: 113–135.

Hill, John, and Pamela Church Gibson, eds. 1998. *Oxford Guide to Film Studies.* New York: Oxford University Press.

Jagose, Annamarie. 1996. *Queer Theory: An Introduction.* New York: New York University Press.

Johnson, Albert. 1960. "[Review of] *Suddenly, Last Summer.*" *Film Quarterly* 13, no. 3: 40–42.

Kaplan, E. Ann. 1983. *Women and Film: Both Sides of the Camera.* New York: Methuen.

Kassabian, Annahid. 2001. *Hearing Film: Tracking Identifications in Hollywood Film Music.* New York: Routledge.

Knapp, Lucretia. 1993. "The Queer Voice in 'Marnie.'" *Cinema Journal* 32, no. 4: 6–23.

Laing, Heather. 2007. *The Gendered Score: Music in 1940s Melodrama and the Woman's Film.* Aldershot, UK, and Burlington, VT: Ashgate.

Lawrence, Amy. 1991. *Echo and Narcissus: Women's Voices in Classical Hollywood Cinema.* Berkeley: University of California Press.

LeBlanc, Michael. 2006. "Melancholic Arrangements: Music, Queer Melodrama, and the Seeds of Transformation in *The Hours.*" *Camera Obscura* 21, no. 1: 105–145.

McClary, Susan. 2007. "Minima Romantica." In *Beyond the Soundtrack: Representing Music in Cinema*, edited by Daniel Goldmark, Lawrence Kramer, and Richard Leppert, 48–65. Berkeley: University of California Press.

Miller, D. A. 1990. "Anal Rope." *Representations* 32: 114–133.

——. 1997. "Visual Pleasure in 1959." *October* 81: 34–58.

Morris, Mitchell. 2004. "Cabaret, America's Weimar, and Mythologies of the Gay Subject." *American Music* 22, no. 1: 145–157.

Mulvey, Laura. 1975. "Visual Pleasure and Narrative Cinema." *Screen* 16, no. 3: 6–18.

Ohi, Kevin. 1999. "Devouring Creation: Cannibalism, Sodomy, and the Scene of Analysis in *Suddenly, Last Summer.*" *Cinema Journal* 38, no. 3: 27–49.

Paulin, Scott. 1997. "Unheard Sexualities?: Queer Theory and the Soundtrack." *Spectator* 17, no. 2: 37–49.

Rapée, Ernö. 1925. *Encyclopedia of Music for Pictures.* New York: Belwin.

Rich, Adrienne. 1980. "Compulsory Heterosexuality and the Lesbian Experience." *Signs* 5, no. 4: 631–660.

Sedgwick, Eve. 1990. *The Epistemology of the Closet.* Berkeley: University of California Press.

Siegel, Janice. 2005. "Tennessee Williams' *Suddenly Last Summer* and Euripides' *Bacchae.*" *International Journal of the Classical Tradition* 11, no. 4: 538–570.

Silverman, Kaja.1988. *The Acoustic Mirror: The Female Voice in Psychoanalysis and Cinema*. Bloomington: Indiana University Press.

Smelik, Anneke. 1998. "Gay and Lesbian Criticism." In *Oxford Guide to Film Studies*, edited by John Hill and Pamela Church Gibson, 135–147. New York: Oxford University Press.

Waugh, Thomas. 1996. "Cockteaser," in *Pop Out: Queer Warhol*, edited by Jennifer Doyle, Jonathan Flatley, and José Estaban Muñoz, 51–77. Durham, NC: Duke University Press.

Whitesell, Lloyd. 2006. "Trans Glam: Gender Magic in the Film Musical." In *Queering the Popular Pitch*, edited by Sheila Whiteley and Jennifer Rycenga, 263–277. New York: Routledge.

CHAPTER 15

PSYCHOANALYSIS, APPARATUS THEORY, AND SUBJECTIVITY

JAMES BUHLER

As I noted in Chapter 14, one of the aims of critical theory based in gender and sexuality has been to reveal the systemic oppression that flows from the social structures of power, and it has most typically turned to psychoanalysis to provide the theory for how these social structures work and reproduce themselves through the formation of their social subjects. Psychoanalysis, whether derived from Freud or Lacan (and psychoanalysis in film studies and musicology rarely ventures beyond Freud and Lacan), provides this theory of subjectivity, of the formation of social subjects. As such, critical theory generally understands psychoanalysis not as providing a true account of innate psychological drives and forces per se but rather as providing an accurate model for how culture shapes, channels, and deforms those psychological drives and forces to produce the norms that society requires to reproduce itself. In psychoanalytic terms, "normal" individuals are therefore those who fit within the variance that the norm tolerates (or, to frame it from the other side, those who can effectively manage the pressure the norm brings to bear on them); because of its history in the clinical practice of diagnosing and treating mental illness, psychoanalysis has been quite interested in classifying deviance from the norm, which psychoanalysis, at least in its humanistic mode (as in ego psychology), generally sees as pathologies to be treated in order to bring the patient back to mental "health," that is, back within the norm.[1]

Critical use of psychoanalysis, by contrast, is unconcerned with clinical treatment and is interested in turning psychoanalysis back on itself in order to examine how it formulates the norm, what the social norms that it posits reveal about the society, and how the pathologies that psychoanalysis identifies are in most cases best considered symptoms of contradictions in the social structure. The pathological in such cases "is the symptom of the normal, an indicator of what is wrong in the very structure that is threatened with 'pathological' outbursts" (Žižek 2006, 555–56). Thus, feminists show that the psychoanalytic model relies on a systematic reduction of gender to sex that allows it to naturalize the social hierarchy on the basis of sexual difference, and queer theorists show that the model deploys homosexuality as a privileged fantasy that serves to domesticate desire to the heterosexual form society apparently requires to reproduce itself. As a theory of patriarchal, heteronormative perversion, of how society produces and manages its distinctive pathologies and regime of damaged subjectivity, psycho-analysis therefore provides real insight into the use of gender and sexuality as levers of power, but psychoanalysis also remains caught within the closure of that society. Ellis Hanson notes with respect to homosexuality:

> the exclusively psychoanalytic framework also poses a problem, not the least since the definition of homosexuality in these theories almost always relies on dubious Freudian conceptions of same-sex desire as a narcissistic crisis in gender identification. Homosexuality becomes the return, or perhaps merely the persistence, of the repressed in an otherwise anxious and heterosexual narrative. This theory does much to explain the paranoid aspect of homoeroticism in classic cinema, queerness as the monster who threatens the heteronormative coherence of the narrative. (Hanson 1999, 14)

The result, however, is that from within the psychoanalytic theory nonheteronormative desire can only appear only as something perverse. The same applies to the analysis of gender, where, as E. Ann Kaplan notes, psychoanalysis requires women to "accept a posi-tioning that is inherently antithetical to subjectivity and autonomy" (2000, 125). From within psychoanalytic theory, the proper place for woman, as a psychical structure, is as the object of desire of the male subject and so she is denied access to the position of full social subject and to autonomous desire (Mulvey 1975; Doane 1987). Although subject, object, male, and female are socially constructed fantasy positions that actual empirical individuals can never fully—that is, properly—assume (hence the symptoms of homo-sexuality and, in Lacan, of woman), these positions and the particularity of their het-eronormative alignment in the social structure reflect the reality of a social demand, its internalization by those who live within the society and who experience it as power.

> The panoptic gaze defines, then, the perfect, i.e., the total, visibility of the woman under patriarchy, of any subject under any social order, which is to say, of any subject at all. For the very condition and substance of the subject's subjectivity is his or her subjectivization by the law of the society which produces that subject. One only becomes visible—not only to others, but also to oneself—through (by seeing through) the categories constructed by a specific, historically defined society. These categories of visibility are categories of knowledge. (Copjec 1989, 55)

In this respect, psychoanalysis seems to reveal the psychic mechanism of ideology, not so much as false consciousness—though inasmuch as it is founded on mis-recognition it is that too—but rather as the means by which the social imaginary works to encourage individuals to accept the symbolic code of society, its regime of truth, as the representation of reality. The terms "imaginary" and "symbolic" in this formulation have a technical meaning in the Lacanian version of psychoanalysis that has served as the basis of the dominant appropriation of psychoanalysis in film theory. In film theory, these terms have also been inflected by Louis Althusser's theory of ideology (itself explicitly modeled on the psychoanalytic theory of the unconscious), in particular his explication of the concept of the Ideological State Apparatus (1995, 100–140). The so-called "apparatus theory" was inaugurated with a suggestion from Marcelin Pleynet, at the time managing editor of the influential journal *Tel Quel*, that the cinematic technology had been treated as a neutral ground instead of as a profoundly ideological instrument.[2] "The cinematographic apparatus is a strictly ideological apparatus; it disseminates bourgeois ideology before anything else. Before a film is produced, the technical construction of the camera already produces bourgeois ideology" (Pleynet and Thibaudeau 1978, 155). Jean-Louis Baudry developed this idea in a pair of influential articles on the cinematic apparatus (1974–1975 and 1976). The titles of the English translations of Baudry's articles both contain "apparatus," but the word actually serves to translate two different French terms, *appareil* and *dispositif*, and so an operative distinction is being missed. Both terms in fact derive from Althusser (1995), where *appareil* designates the institutional structure, its support, and techniques and *dispositif*, much less thoroughly worked out, designates in contrast "the absolutely ideological 'conceptual' device" that hails and interpellates the subject, that is, produces or prepares in advance a place for "a subject endowed with consciousness in which he freely forms or freely recognizes ideas in which he believes" (Althusser 1995, 126). (To add to the confusion, *dispositif* is also picked up by Michel Foucault to extend his concept of "discursive formation" to nonlinguistic cultural formations (Bryukhovetska 2010, Žižek 2010, 416–18, Agamben 2009, 1–24).) Each of Baudry's essays therefore focuses on a different aspect of the Ideological State Apparatus, with the "basic cinematographic apparatus" (*appareil*) concerning the technology and its general institutional support and "the apparatus" (*dispositif*) concerning the specific processes of interpellation and subject construction. Apparatus theory has generally followed Baudry's lead here, with scholarship divided between uncovering the ideological implications of the basic equipment and institutional technical practices on the one hand and revealing how institutional imperatives construct and interpellate the cinematic subject on the other.

APPAREIL: BAUDRY, COMOLLI

In "Ideological Effects of the Basic Cinematographic Apparatus," Baudry (1974–1975) hews closely to Pleynet's suggestion, arguing that cinema technology, even its construction of a camera that adopts a mode of representation as ubiquitous as perspective, is not ideologically neutral in virtue of its scientific basis. Like Pleynet, Baudrey therefore also distinguishes between two levels of ideological work: the familiar ideology of the content, that is, the film as a representational text and its attendant features; and the ideology inscribed in the technology, which anyone deploying it can accept or resist depending on the individual case but which in any case confronts the filmmaker as a basic determinant of the media. The camera "lays out the space of an ideal vision and in this way assures the necessity of transcendence—metaphorically (by the unknown to which it appeals—here we must recall the structural place occupied by the vanishing point) and metonymically (by the displacement that it seems to carry out: a subject is both 'in place of' and 'a part of the whole')" (Baudry 1974–1975, 41–42). Baudry then extends the analysis of the camera to the mechanism that allows the illusion of motion. Projected, film creates the impression of reproducing an intentional continuous movement at the expense of effacing the actual differences that obtain between the individual frames. This effacement is symptomatic rather than simply academic in the sense that the impression of continuity depends on the forgetting of the fact of the technology, so that the technology comes to serve as a kind of unconscious of film. He then extends this analysis to the cut, arguing that the drive to develop principles of continuity editing derived from the same impulse to forget the technology. Baudry concludes the article by drawing an analogy between the screen and Lacan's mirror phase (Lacan 1968). Just as the young child recognizes a more unified image of him- or herself in the mirror and so begins to construct the function of the ego on the basis of that imaginary identification, so too the spectator in the cinema recognizes the screen as the source of a unified meaning. Unlike the mirror, where the imaginary unity is located in the image, the screen encourages an imaginary identification with the look itself, that is, with the camera, which the spectator takes as a substitute for his or her own defective organ but which maintains its superiority only to the extent that awareness of the technology that makes it possible is repressed. Here, again, the technological base of the cinema functions as the unconscious of the film, and the ideological work of the apparatus—its superego function, as it were—consists in preserving the imaginary identification from recognizing the repression of just that technological base.

In his work toward constructing the terms of a materialist history of cinema, which was published in a series of articles in *Cahiers du cinéma*, Jean-Louis Comolli provides a historical account of the transformations of basic apparatus. For Comolli the unconscious that migrates into technology is that of economic relations. Comolli pays particular attention to perspective, especially as it figures as a celebration of deep-focus cinematography in the then still dominant realist theories of cinema. For Comolli, authors such as Andre Bazin (2005) perpetrate an idealist philosophy to the extent that they mistake the symbolic code and conventions of perspective for the natural world, which is a way of naturalizing and so repressing awareness of the economic relations that support it. The move toward an image with a greater depth of field is not a natural tendency of the technology but rather a symptom of ideological deception that extends across filmmaking, film criticism, and film scholarship. "What we intend therefore is a rereading of the idealist discourse from the standpoint of the main area it represses— that complex of economic, political, and ideological determinants which shatter any notion of 'the aesthetic evolution of the cinema' (any claim for complete autonomy for the aesthetic process)" (Comolli 1986, 423). Like Pleynet and Baudry, Comolli also distinguishes between the ideology of the individual films and that of the basic technology. But Comolli makes the additional point that the overt ideology of the individual films and, even more so, critics' attempts to sort the films on the basis of quality serve primarily to disguise the basic ideological unity of the institutional apparatus. These films "are the innumerable realizations of the cinema as an ideological instrument, a vector and disseminator of ideological representations where the subject of ideology (the spectator of the spectacle) cannot fail to identify himself since what is involved is always the communication of 'A meaning ever present to itself in the presence of the Subject'" (423). Comolli here is drawing on a long article (printed in two parts but translated in three) that he wrote with Paul Narboni in 1969 announcing the change in editorial position of *Cahiers du cinéma* to an explicitly Marxist one (Comolli and Narboni 1971a, 1971b, 1972). This earlier article included a more detailed typology of a film's possible relationship to the underlying ideology of the institution and outlined a series of strategies for criticizing a film's particular relation to that ideology on the basis of type, but it agreed with the basic claim in "Technique and Ideology" that the vast majority of films, whatever their explicit ideological position, remained committed to communicating a univocal meaning rather than revealing cinema as a site for the production of (multivocal) meaning.

Comolli also opposes the fetish that idealist histories make of tracking the appearance of various techniques (such as the close-up) because they presume that the technique can be isolated from the discourse or signifying chain from which it receives its identity and meaning. (Jean Mitry is his particular target here.) In order to understand a technique, one has to understand the historical state of the discourse in which it is embedded and the material factors, not all of which are technical, that determine that discourse, as a close-up only means in virtue of what it does because of the discourse, and the discourse is something other than a list of transhistorical conventions, of technical devices without concrete historical determinants (1986, 429–30). Comolli also notes that we must be careful not to let those technologies that are most evident substitute for the whole, in the way that the ideological distortions of the camera can seem to serve metonymically for the whole of the cinematic apparatus. That path is also marked by distortions of its own, in particular the effacement and erasure of all work not directly attributable to the camera (such as lab work or the soundtrack) and so also raises the visible to the seat of knowledge but at the expense of allowing the invisible to remain the natural ground of film's unconscious and so also its largest ideological threat.

Comolli devotes much of the final two parts of his technology and ideology series to the issue of the soundtrack, examining in particular how the introduction of synchronized speech interacted with an attenuation of deep-focus photography on the one hand and how speech assumed the indispensable ideological role of figuring subjective depth on the other (Comolli 1971–1972, 1972).

APPAREIL: DOANE, ALTMAN

The most thorough English-language account of the soundtrack in terms of apparatus theory is found in the early work of Mary Ann Doane and Rick Altman. In 1980, Mary Ann Doane published two articles on the topic, one devoted to technology and institutional discourse and the other to the processes by which the soundtrack participates in the construction of the cinematic subject (Doane 1980a, 1980b). That is, the respective concerns of these articles divide along the break between *appareil* and *dispositif*. In "Ideology and the Practice of Sound Editing and Mixing" (Doane 1980b), the article devoted to technology and technique, Doane investigates both the soundtrack practices and the language that technicians working on the soundtrack use in discussing their work. "Not only techniques of sound-track construction but the language of technicians and the discourses on technique are symptomatic of particular ideological aims" (47). The most characteristic aspect of this ideology is the "effacement of work," the development of a sound-editing and mixing practice whose labor is inaudible. If sound is positioned by the industry as a supplement to the image, that is, as something added, the split between image and sound ends up having wider consequences as it "is supported by the establishment and maintenance of ideological oppositions between the intelligible and the sensible, intellect and emotion, fact and value, reason and intuition" (48). Effective sound work is precisely that which coordinates the sound to the image so that the split can signify these distinct but entwined spheres of being. But the split is fraught and liable to dissolve the imaginary unity of sound "properly" synchronized to image back into the "material heterogeneity" of the various sounds and images. The imaginary unity thus conceals "the highly specialized and fragmented process, the bulk and expense of the machinery essential to the production of a sound-track which meets industry standards" (51).

The mixing also gives precedence to the voice, which, unlike background sounds, is not generally faded in or out and which travels with the picture throughout the editing process. This practice allows film "to preserve the status of speech as an individual property right—subject only to a manipulation which is not discernible" (Doane 1980b, 52). Yet here the code of intelligibility comes into conflict with the code of mimetic realism that allows us to recognize the actual ideological priorities and commitments of the institution whatever its statements: moments where realistic sound would obscure the intelligibility of the dialogue are decided in favor of intelligibility unless the situation is to be read as a threat to the speaking character. Speech, in other words, "*belongs to the individual, defines and expresses his or her individuality, and distinguishes the individual from the world*" (52). The emphasis on intelligible speech indicates a privileging of interiority over exteriority, of the world of intention over actuality—ultimately of what is not depicted over the visible—as the site and guarantee of individual definition. "The truth of the individual, of the *interior* realm of the individual (a truth which is most readily spoken and heard), is the truth validated by the coming of sound" (60). Yet the speaking film character is not a subject of pure interiority but rather one who needs to bear the marks of place, the marks of belonging to just this body depicted in just this way, so that its voice can be converted into a measure of depth while also remaining precisely invisible, and so out of conceptual view. The appearance of a body synchronized to a voice recorded to match thus disguises the profound ideological work not only of the voice but also of sound in general, as sound constructed—edited and mixed—to be "the bearer of a meaning," one "not subsumed by the ideology of the visible" (56). Sound in a sense gains ideological potency the more it figures within the representational system of sound film as a site of repression; but the fact that it must serve as a site of repression means that its power is always going to be, like the unconscious, many of whose processes it models, an uncertain ally. "The ideological truth of the sound-track covers that excess which escapes the eye. For the ear is precisely that organ which opens onto the interior reality of the individual—not exactly un-seeable, but unknowable within the guarantee of the purely visible" (56).

Rick Altman's work on the soundtrack begins from a similar place. In his introduction to the 1980 special issue of *Yale French Studies*, a publication that launched the contemporary phase of soundtrack studies in English, Altman notes the strongly visual emphasis that Baudry and Comolli place on the apparatus. "According to this approach the spectator is placed, within the film as well as within the world at large, primarily by visual markers; even within the limits of this method of handling spectator placement, however, it is surprising that more emphasis has not been placed on the sound track's role in splitting and complicating the spectator, in contesting as well as reinforcing the lessons of the image tract" (Altman 1980a, 4). The omission undoubtedly lies in the fact that apparatus theory was initially designed less to tease out the complexities of film spectatorship, even if half of the theory was devoted to the interpellation of the *dispositif*, than to show the certainty of a particular ideological inscription in the basic equipment and formal techniques of the cinema. In this respect, it is perhaps not surprising that soundtrack studies begin to gain traction around 1980: at this point concern for the *appareil*, which had initially received more emphasis, passes, as we will see, to a far more complicated if also highly problematic consideration for the *dispositif*. It is in this context of working out a theory of the cinematic subject, a subject situated between the ideological imperatives of the institution and the particular desires of empirical spectators, that "the sound track's role in splitting and complicating the spectator," of offering resistance to ideological determination by opening up a site of contradiction and contestation, of offering an opening for a deconstruction of the cinematic subject, becomes an advantage.

It is interesting in this respect that Altman seeks to inaugurate critical soundtrack studies with a consideration of the *appareil*, focusing particularly on the representational qualities of the microphone technology in his introduction (parallel to perspective in the camera) and the formal device of synchronization (parallel to continuity editing) in his larger contribution to the volume. In Chapter 7, I previously noted Altman's analysis of synchronization as a profoundly ideological figure, and we are now in a better position to appreciate his conclusion that "the sound track is a ventriloquist who, by moving his dummy (the image) in time with the words he secretly speaks, creates the illusion that the words are produced by the dummy/image whereas in fact the dummy/image is actually created in order to disguise the source of the sound" (Altman 1980b, 67). The very visibility of the image perpetrates the deception, as it serves to distract from the actual mechanism of auditory production, the loudspeakers, and so also diverts attention from the ventriloquist—now understood as the institution itself—who is controlling the words. Altman assigns the words in the first instance to the screenwriter and notes how auteur theory has served to "repress" the work of scripting (70). Yet it was not the director who "repressed" the screenwriter but the institution; these figures of director and screenwriter are ultimately actors the institution mobilizes in a drama to obscure the economic base of synchronized sound. Onscreen, the character seems to speak and own the words, the divided apparatus of synchronized sound simply being the "neutral" technology that makes this possible, just as individuals seem to speak and own their words outside any determination by language aside from the fact that it exists as (again) a "neutral" technology of communication. Synchronization therefore is a mythic figure, one that forges "a new myth of origins" for the soundtrack (the image rather than the loudspeaker, the character rather than the script) but so also indoctrinates spectators into a belief about their own autonomy. Altman recalls Baudry's discussion of the mirror phase but now takes account of sound. What is mirrored is precisely an impression of sensory unity: "If the human audience accepts the cinema's unity, it is because it cannot affirm its own without admitting the cinema's; conversely, the cinema appears to assent to the unity of the human subject only in order to establish its own unity" (71).

Rather than pursuing this analysis into the apparatus as *dispositif*, as a "machine" for the interpellation of subjects through suture, as much film theory at the time would (see below), Altman's later work on the soundtrack continues with a strong emphasis on the *appareil*, with detailed historical studies of the technologies of production and reproduction (Altman 1985, 1986), of sites and technologies of exhibition, usually coupled with careful and insightful analysis of the industry discourse on sound as promulgated through the trade papers and technical journals. Throughout, he remains committed to a concept of cinema always already divided by a representation organized to extract profit from "the material resources that it engages" (1992, 6). The commercial pressures of cinema mean that homogeneity (standardization) is always driving out heterogeneity wherever it finds it (1999, passim); but heterogeneity, the "noise" in the system, is also irreducible because any substantive change in the apparatus brings with it enough heterogeneity that the basic apparatus is not self-identical as an historical object whether or not it undergoes a name change (1984); because sound film is a dual system that means a relationship between its parts will always have to be constructed (1980b, passim); because sound recording always bears the imprint of its original space of recording and is reproduced in another (1992, 5); because sound recording is always a representation rather than a simple reproduction (1984, 121); because theaters vary the conditions of presentation as a means of product differentiation (1992, 8); and because heterogeneity is an important source of innovation (it allows the appearance of alternatives) and often a location of pleasure and identification for audiences, who are frequently also its source. Thus in a quintessential demonstration, Altman traces the way in which those sound practices in the nickelodeon that specifically addressed the audience, especially the popular illustrated songs and musical accompaniments that parody the film, are replaced by a musical practice addressed to the drama of the film (2004, 231–85). But he also notes that theater technology such as soundproofing likewise evolved towards eliminating extraneous sound (1999, 33); that codes of conduct were created to quiet the patrons and keep them focused on the screen (1999, 38–43; 2004); that the technology of synchronized sound was developed to standardize exhibition; that booms and microphones were designed to standardize the clarity of dialogue (1992, 58ff.): the whole institutional apparatus has been designed to use representation to reduce material heterogeneity and make profits more predictable (1999, passim). Film scholarship has, he thinks, been complicit as well: scholars opt to distill neat linear narratives rather than acknowledge the complicated, uneven quality of actual historical development; they use the concept of the text to occlude the rich, contradictory context of its production and reception; they focus on the artistic conception and occasionally finance, rarely on the technical workers who execute the needed tasks (1992, 6–7); in terms of the soundtrack they borrow musical terminology that has the effect of abstracting an idealized musical conception from the particularity of sound (1992, 16). While Altman's radical nominalism treats each of these approaches as reductively and ungenerously as he accuses them of treating cinema, his aim is to show that processes of representation, homogenization, narrative, meaning and ideology are at a fundamental semiotic level all of a piece (1999, passim); although they operate on different cultural levels, they are all means of structuring and ordering difference hierarchically, of transforming the actual complexity of the world into something simpler, more efficient and more manageable but without fully acknowledging the loss of doing so—or worse yet they naturalize away the actual arbitrary quality of the differences by reifying them within an oppositional hierarchy of essential and inessential.[3]

The strength of Altman's focus on heterogeneity is the way it allows him to track and give an account of the particularity of the sound and of the context of production and exhibition and reception without the normal hierarchies culture imposes on it. Its weakness largely derives from the same source: since the abstraction required of theoretical discourse demands a movement from the particular to the general, a theory centered directly on heterogeneity will always be fraught and constantly threatened by incoherence. This threat comes out most strikingly in his otherwise reasonable insistence that "there is no such thing as representation of the real; there is only representation of representation. For anything that we would represent is already constructed as a representation. The structure of representation is thus that of an infinite mise-en-abyme, with the new apparatus having to represent the old, itself representing the previous one, and so on" (Altman 1984, 121). Under this formulation, the appearance of the real is an illusion; the real, assuming it exists, is of an entirely different and incommensurate order than representation. Representation does not concern it. Where then is heterogeneity to be located in this scenario? Heterogeneity cannot be something excluded from representation; it cannot be located in the real, because then neither he nor anyone else could discuss it, as it would fall outside representation. But heterogeneity is also not represen-tation because that is the very figure of hierarchical sense that has excluded the hetero-geneous. That leaves the mirroring: heterogeneity evidently appears in the process of representational reflection as nonidentity, as that which falls out of the series. Yet even here, although it is perfectly clear that we can recognize what gets left out of the series, it is not at all evident how any representation along the series can add anything besides another reflection to representation, since what is new could only be something that was not contained in a previous representation. Either the series degrades or the represen-tation is somehow replenishing itself along the way, but neither provides a consistent account. The incoherence suggests that there is something amiss in, or at least some-thing missing from, the model.

CRITIQUE OF *APPAREIL*: LASTRA

Although James Lastra appropriates Altman's concept of "representational technology" and shares an interest in producing rich empirical history of the sound technology *appa-reil*, he is concerned more with discourse analysis and identifying broad cultural cur-rents than is Altman. Lastra takes device, discourse, practice, and institution as the four "defining parameters" of his work and produces a "thick epistemology" of sound film technology that offers a self-conscious correction of the *appareil* in the work of Baudry and Comolli (Lastra 2000, 4, 13). Both Baudry and Comolli have a strong current of technological determinism in their understanding of the *appareil*. In order to disqualify any move that would exempt technology from the point of ideological critique, Baudry and Comolli both insist on locating ideology in the "technology itself." But Lastra notes that this formulation, which insists on a grand continuity from the introduction of lin-ear perspective in Renaissance painting to the grinding of lenses to record perspective in cameras, dehistoricizes the technology, obscures the difference between technological inscription and sensory experience, and so also ignores actual changes in the technol-ogy as well as the ways in which technological change is driven by the representational needs of the institution regulating the technology. "Our specific standards and prac-tices of listening are always a function of particular contextual and often institutional demands and often appropriate only to those demands, hence no *single* context or set of evaluative criteria can—without elaborate justification—provide a reference point for theorizing all others" (132). Thus attempts to locate the essence of ideological transfor-mation in the device are problematic as they reduce out the necessary mediations of the institution. Ideological effects, in other words, are not uniform and are therefore not stabilized by the device.

With respect to sound technology, Lastra takes issue not only with those who would locate ideology in the device but also with those who champion heterogeneity as well. Indeed, Lastra sees critics like Altman, Alan Williams (1980), and Tom Levin (1984), who insist on the heterogeneity of sound, as radicalizing the ideological critique of the technology itself: for such critics, every representation is an abstraction or sample from some original full phenomenological reality, and so any technology, like sound recording, that presents itself as an undistorted reproduction of that reality harbors a pernicious ideological deception. Lastra counters that this radically nominalist formulation carries its own ideological deception: the concept of the original itself: "Contrary to the claims of theory, which locates all the significant ideological work in what the device does to the original event, the primary ideological effect of sound recording might rather be in creating the *effect* that there is a single and fully present 'original' independent of its representation at all" (Lastra 2000, 134).

Instead of tracing that heterogeneity resists representation, Lastra focuses instead on strategies of hierarchization that organize representation. What tends to fall away in Lastra's approach is the figure of ideology itself; ultimately institutionally mediated perspectives determine the significance and adequacy of the representation from the details that it preserves and to which it gives emphasis. Yet these representations are not understood as distortions; that is, it is precisely this sense of representation as distortion that the concept of the original—Platonic or not and however imaginary or unobtainable in itself—preserves.

MUSIC AND THE *APPAREIL*

Music has received little attention under the rubric of the *appareil*, at least with respect to technology. Aside from studies of the early days of sound film, when recording often required special musical instruments (Sabaneev 1935, 56–90; London 1936, 163–210), and technical handbooks and recording manuals (for example, Karlin and Wright 1990, 103–24, 332–421), little research has addressed in a critical and systematic way the mediations of music and the basic technical apparatus as it applies in film. (The relationship between the phonograph and the recording industry, by contrast, has been extensively studied.) The most thorough work has been done on the use of electronic instruments, such as the theremin and synthesizer (Hayward 1997; Wierzbicki 2002; Leydon 2004). But even such basic music production technologies as streamers, click tracks, cue sheets, and temp tracks, though mentioned often in passing, have not received sustained scholarly attention. (The grab-bag approach of the final chapter of Burt 1994, 217–47, is typical).

The situation with respect to the institutional aspects of the musical *appareil* is somewhat better. Sociological studies by Robert Faulkner (1971, 1983) and James P. Kraft (1996), discussed in Chapter 7, have examined the institutional organization of musical labor for both Hollywood musicians and composers. Claudia Gorbman (1987) demonstrates how the institution of classic Hollywood has determined the music for its films. She is particularly interested in the conventions and other habits of thought, conscious or not, that the musical practice of Hollywood presupposes. If "classical Hollywood film works toward the goal of a transparent or invisible discourse, and promoting fullest involvement in the story" (Gorbman 1987, 72), Hollywood film music, she says, follows guidelines similar to those that govern the rest of the filmic system. She identifies seven basic "principles of composition, mixing, and editing" that underlay classical film music practice. These well-known principles are: (1) invisibility; (2) inaudibility; (3) signifier of emotion; (4) narrative cueing; (5) continuity; (6) unity; (7) escape clause (73). The first two principles point to the transparency of classic narrative and the effacement of work as a mark of professional competence and skill. As with the ideology of mixing in Doane's analysis, the work of film music does not generally draw attention to itself or its conditions of production. Principles 3 and 4 concern the semiotic capabilities of music and its ability to clarify the narrative, especially in representing the emotional tenor of character, mood and setting that are difficult to convey through action or mise-en-scène. Principles 5 and 6 indicate music's ability to provide coherence, by providing either acoustical "connective tissue" that ties together disparate shots, sounds and events or a musical thematic structure that reinforces narrative structure. The final principle is perhaps the most important of all, though Gorbman comments on it least. It permits any principle to be suspended "at the service of the other principles" (73), which ensures that the musical subsystem remains flexible and pragmatic in orientation. In this way, all the principles (and so also the musical subsystem) are evaluated in terms of and so also subordinated to the requirements of the overriding narrative system. We can therefore abstract from these principles a basic set of ideological values that are reproduced in and transmitted by the institutional practice of Hollywood film music: transparency, clarity, coherence, and subordination.

Caryl Flinn (1992) takes as her starting point the stability of the musical subsystem in the studio era and looks at how this stability was created and sustained. "The classical conception of film music," she writes, "maintains that the score supports the development of the film's story line, that it exists to reinforce the narrational information already provided by the image" (14). Subordination serves to regulate the musical subsystem according to narrative, and it is this regulative function of subordination that accounts for the appearance of stability. The justification for subordination was not stability, however, but aesthetic legitimization. The institutional discourse on music in the studio era drew extensively on Wagnerian tropes. Wagner's insistence that drama required music to serve the word in the production of meaning ensured that music could be subservient even as it provided a rationale for music's presence in supporting the drama. The invocation of Wagner also redounded to film, which in virtue of its music could be said to resemble the idea of *Gesamtkunstwerk*, which fit neatly with "Hollywood's own investment in unified, coherent texts, since both maintain that textual components should work toward the same dramatic ends" (34). If in the classic Hollywood system Wagnerian synthesis was reduced to redundancy and overdetermination, as Flinn claims (34), music nevertheless gained by its subordination a relatively secure place within the filmic system that would allow it to codify its practice, stabilize its position, and reproduce its values in the institution.

Both Gorbman and Flinn point out that the institutional discourse on music and Hollywood has tended to discount the role of technology, since one of the traditional functions of music has been to mask the presence of technology (London 1936, 27–28). In this respect, music is itself a particularly efficient technology for effacing the work of the soundtrack and therefore also the labor that goes into constructing it.

DISPOSITIF: BAUDRY, COMOLLI, METZ

Whereas, in "Ideological Effects of the Basic Cinematographic Apparatus" (1974–1975), Baudry considers the way in which ideology is inscribed into the basic machinery of cinema, especially the camera, in "The Apparatus" (1976) he examines the way in which the cinema, by structuring a viewing situation reminiscent of a dream, proffers a representational regime that constructs and interpellates a certain kind of cinematic subject. The concern here is not apparatus as *appareil*, that is, as institutionally mediated and ideologically determined technology, but as *dispositif*, that is, as the general set of institutional devices aimed at preparing in advance the place of the cinematic subject. For Baudry, the cinema presupposes a transcendental subject, which the totality of the cinematic situation, the *dispositif*, uses all its power to encourage us to identify with. In developing the concept of the *dispositif*, Baudry draws on the frequently invoked analogy of the cinema to the scenario of Plato's cave but offers the twist of comparing Plato to Freud: what for Plato is metaphysical delusion, for Freud becomes fantasy, dream. The cinema, Baudry thinks, follows the psychoanalytic account of the dream in constructing its subject. "The cinematographic *dispositif* reproduces the *dispositif* of the psychic apparatus [appareil] during sleep" (1976, 122; translation modified). Like the dream, the cinema offers the subject a dark place of immobility and passivity, a situation that encourages regression to a state where perception and representation coincide. "Taking into account the darkness of the movie theater, the relative passivity of the situation, the forced immobility of the cine-subject, and the effects which result from the projection of images, moving images, the cinematographic apparatus [*dispositif*] brings about a state of artificial regression" (119). In the dream, the sleep of the subject serves as defense against the impression of reality so that the dream state regression is clearly marked as fantasy. In the cinema, on the contrary, the subject is awake, so that, even though perception and representation coincide, the cinematic *dispositif* is "capable of precisely fabricating an impression of reality" (111). The impression of reality is therefore a subject effect prepared by cinema, one that follows a path of regression in the psychoanalytical sense.

This subject effect remains somewhat amorphous in Baudry's account, as it is focused on immobility and a generalized impression of reality rather than on a specific cinematic figure, but it is given better definition by several other writers of the time. Comolli, for instance, notes the way that the impression of reality on the one hand is undermined during the 1920s by increased technical facility with montage, which underscored the constructed quality of the image sequence, but then on the other hand is restored by the introduction of the talking film. This marked shift suggests, he says, that the impression of reality is tied not so much to a technical measure, such as depth of field, as to the ability of spectators to extract meaning from the film. With sound film, the figure of the synchronized word, especially, allows the film to speak the subject. "For with the Hollywood talking picture, not only sound and noises are synchronized to the image, an image that invests in those sounds and noises and draws toward them: but also and above all the word, that is to say the interiority, the discourse of the subject, this lack, this hollow space that the word identifies as a full presence and in fact does not cease to fill out the ideological statements [énoncé] that speaks this subject" (Comolli 1971–1972, 100).[4] The *dispositif*, then, is "cinema as an ideological instrument, a vector and disseminator of ideological representations where the subject of ideology (the spectator of the spectacle) cannot fail to identify himself since what is involved is always the communication of 'A Meaning ever present to itself in the presence of the Subject'" (1986, 423). It is therefore also a "social machine,... the arrangement of demands, desires, fantasies, speculations (in the two senses of commerce and the imaginary): an arrangement which give[s] apparatus and techniques a social status and function" (1980, 122). The *dispositif* does not concern the particulars of ideological statements, then, but the structure of singular meaning that makes such statements possible. In this way, it prepares a place in the discourse for the subject, hails this subject with the call of meaning.

Christian Metz agrees that cinema is "one vast socio-psychical machinery" (1982, 80). Metz, who did much to develop the semiological paradigm in film studies, worked to synthesize his structuralist film semiotics with insights drawn from the psychoanalytically inflected apparatus theory, especially the work of Baudry. For Metz, psychoanalysis offered a theory of the cinematic subject that had been lacking in structural semiotics, whereas a semiotic orientation offered a way of systematizing psychoanalytic insights to the workings of all facets of the cinematic institution, that is, to the *dispositif*. As befits the application of psychoanalysis to the cinema, Metz emphasized the imaginary and understands film theory as reproducing the tensions of psychoanalytic practice. He opens *The Imaginary Signifier* thus:

> Reduced to its most fundamental procedures, any psychoanalytic reflection on the cinema might be defined in Lacanian terms as an attempt to disengage the cinema-object from the imaginary and to win it for the symbolic, in the hope of extending the latter by a new province: an enterprise of displacement, a territorial enterprise, a symbolising advance; that is to say, in the field of films as in other films, the psychoanalytic itinerary is from the outset a semiological one, even (above all) if in comparison with the discourse of a more classical semiology it shifts its point of focus from the statement [énoncé] to the enunciation [énonciation]. (Metz 1982, 3)

This shift to enunciation is similar to the shift, discussed in Chapter 7 and Chapter 14, in postcolonial, feminist, and queer theory, from identification to subjectification, that is, a displacement from an analysis of the statement as an ideological form to a consideration of the social structure that makes the ideological form possible. As

Harvey R. Greenberg and Krin Gabbard note in their assessment of psychoanalytic film theory: "Research has been deflected away from the meaning of the text, toward the processes through which any assumed meaning is generated. Cinema semioticians focus on how the audience experiences a movie. Rather than psychoanalyzing characters or filmmakers, students of Lacan explore the complex fashion in which the cinematic apparatus invokes the Imaginary and Symbolic orders of the viewer" (1990, 101). The resemblance of enunciation to subjectification should not be not surprising, given that postcolonial, feminist, and queer theory have all been greatly influenced not only by the same Lacanian psychoanalytic theory that underwrites apparatus theory but also by apparatus theory itself, especially in those aspects of the theory, gathered under the term suture, that have been concerned with the construction of the cinematic subject.

DISPOSITIF AND SUTURE

Derived from Lacan's rewriting of classical Freudian psychoanalysis, suture is an account of how filmic discourse renders the subjectivity it constructs as natural, as an "imaginary unity" (Johnston 1976; quoted in Silverman 1983, 222). According to Jean-Pierre Oudart, "suture represents the closure of the cinematic *énoncé* in line with its relationship with its subject (the film subject or rather the cinematic subject), which is recognized, and then put in its place as the spectator" (1977–1978, 35). In particular, suture concerns the construction of the cinematic subject through the relation to a constitutive absence, that which is excluded in a shot, which gives rise in turn to what Oudart calls "the Absent One." The shot/reverse-shot combination so integral to the syntax of classic Hollywood, for instance, gains its efficacy because the first shot presents not only a field of vision but also asserts a position from which that field is seen. But that position, the place of the camera, is itself not seen. The reverse shot, by contrast, seems to reveal the excluded field, what was lacking in the original shot (Dayan 1974; Oudart 1977–78; Heath 1977–78; Silverman 1983; Bonitzer 1990). The shots together thus "seem to constitute a perfect whole," which helps "assure" the viewer that "his or her gaze suffers under no constraints" (Silverman 1988, 12). But although the field of the second shot seems to contain the position of the first, the means of that vision—the camera on the one hand, but the subject-who-knows on the other—remains absent from the image, is indeed displaced to the character whose partial body (over the shoulder) intervenes to stand in for the Absent One, to allow a particular meaning to fill the absence even as the Absent One seems to migrate again out of field. In this way, the Absent One always leaves an empty space that it bids the spectator to occupy as subject and to insert a particular meaning. The obliquity of the representation—the presence of the partial body that displaces the subject—divides the absence into lack and meaning, or rather maps meaning into the empty space of the signifying chain. Through the intervention of the figure of representation, the shot succession becomes interpretable. "This necessary obliquity of the camera," Daniel Dayan says, "has the function of transforming a vision or seeing of the film into a reading of it. It introduces the film (irreducible to its frames) into the realm of signification" (1974, 29).

Dayan also claims that "the system of suture is to classical cinema what verbal language is to literature" (1974, 22), and he therefore understands cinematic suture as a subset of the general suturing effects of language. Nevertheless a basic difference between language and the semiotic system of cinema makes the comparison problematic. Whereas Dayan admits that language is not reducible to ideology, he insists that because the historical origins of cinema are recoverable that ideology therefore must play a much more constitutive role in cinema. Although this seems to extend the critique of the ideological determinations of the *appareil* to the *dispositif*, the result is not simply to insist on cinema's ideological substrate and to recognize that its fiction is "a mythical organization through which ideology is produced and expressed" (22). Instead, Dayan uses suture to reduce cinema to ideology in a rather unidimensional way. Because suture is the device that allows film to deny its origin as something made, as a construction, it is also the source of film's primary ideological deception, which constructs the cinematic subject only to deny it. "By means of suture, the film-discourse presents itself as a product without producer, a discourse without an origin. It speaks. Who speaks? Things speak for themselves and of course, they tell the truth. Classical cinema establishes itself as the ventriloquist of ideology" (31).

Dayan's conception of suture, though influential, has also been much criticized. William Rothman, for instance, follows critics of Baudry, such as Jean-Patrick Lebel (1971), who argued that the camera is a scientific instrument and so ideological neutral. Rothman likewise insists on the basic ideological neutrality of cinematic technique, in this case the point-of-view cutting that is central to suture theory, on the basis of content. According to Rothman, such cutting can carry no inherent ideological content because "the point-of-view sequence in itself makes no statement about reality—that is, makes no statement—at all" (1975, 48). Although neither Rothman's claim that technique makes no statements itself nor the idea that technique can be used to express a range of ideological statements in fact bears on the ideological level that the theory of suture addresses, Rothman's critique does reveal the profoundly reductive quality to Dayan's conception, one that does not adequately account for the play between subject formation under interpellation and psychoanalytic identification.

Responding to charges that suture is overly reductive and empirically suspect, Stephen Heath offers a more subtle account that attempts to avoid simplistic reduction:

(1) the ideological is not reducible to the imaginary...; the ideological always involves a relation of symbolic and imaginary (the imaginary is a specific fiction of the subject in the symbolic);

(2) the symbolic is not reducible to the ideological; there is no ideological operation which does not involve symbolic construction, a production of the subject in meaning, but the symbolic is always more than the effect of such operations (language is not exhausted by the ideological);

(3) the symbolic is never simply not ideological; psychoanalysis, and this is its force, has never encountered some pure symbolic, is always engaged with a specific history of the subject (language is not exhausted by the ideological but is never met other than as discourse, within a discursive formation productive of subject relations in ideology);

(4) the unconscious is not reducible to the ideological; it is a division of the subject with the Other, a history of the subject on which the ideological constantly turns but which it in no way resumes. (Heath 1977–78, 73)

Suture remains in this formulation, however, a way of binding ideology and the construction of the cinematic subject to the Lacanian registers of the symbolic and the imaginary. If Heath avoids the reductions and determinations of the early versions of suture in particular and apparatus theory in general, the most pressing issue nevertheless devolves on the hermeneutic imperative, ideological at base, that drives the *dispositif*, the social machine of the cinema: the self-forgetting of the subject in the pursuit of meaning. Heath may admit that it is a mistake to locate ideology in the social forms of direct psychic processes. The social basis of ideology is such that it cannot be reduced to the psychoanalytic concepts of symbolic, imaginary and unconscious, however necessary it might be for ideology to work on the subject through such psychic processes. Like language, empirical individuals are not exhausted by the ideological. Nevertheless, Heath still presses the cinematic system, the *dispositif*, to reveal the way that it produces an underlying homogeneity, an economy of identity, that is a mark of its ideological project. The lure of the statement, of a particular meaning (or set of meanings) that a film intends to communicate, allows film to appear differentiated, whereas its structure as meaning commits any subject who would understand it to accept the identity proffered by the terms of the discourse. Ideology works on and through the subject in order that society might reproduce itself, and, in these terms, psychoanalysis provides a theory of the subject and its construction. Ideology and psychoanalysis thus intersect in the cinematic subject, the imaginary form of the subject presupposed by and constructed in *dispositif*, that is, the cinematic system. Psychoanalysis opens this form and its constitutive figures (suture) to a particular ideological critique focused not on the filmic statement (*énoncé*) but on the system, on the point of systemic articulation of the subject (*énonciation*); and this analysis and critique reveal something of how ideology works through the general psychic economy of drives, desires, repressions, and other processes to interpellate cultural subjects.

As the term "suture" suggests, this place of the subject is conceived as the site of a wound. It is here that the individual acquiesces to its own abstraction in order to gain coherence as a social subject but with the loss of all particularity that goes along with abstraction. Suture is an act of binding, of tying up, of closing the wound in the name of meaning; but it is also an act of closing off that particularity in the face of the demand to be meaningful. In that sense suture is a process of homogenization aimed at creating the image of a unified subject. In this way industrial standardization of production runs hand in hand with the suturing process of discourse formation that speaks the subject into being. By contrast, heterogeneity becomes what is incoherent, extraneous, accidental, contingent—everything that cannot be made meaningful to the empirical individual as subject. Suture demands that the individual as subject work on film in terms of meaning—learn to distinguish the meaningful detail from that which is merely contingent— so that film can reproduce the subject as just that place in meaning. But the empirical spectator's identification with the subject must remain effaced or that spectator will come to recognize that the unified subject belongs to the imaginary at the expense of the real.

SUTURE AND THE SOUNDTRACK

Although suture has been applied primarily to shot transitions, with the shot/reverse-shot syntax as its most exemplary figure, the basic notion also extends readily to the soundtrack, or rather image-sound relations in the classical Hollywood regime of compulsory synchronization (Chapter 14), what Heath aptly terms "the law of the speaking subject" that grounds the practice of commercial film in a particular conception of language and a particular order of sound as a property of bodies (Heath 1981, 178, 201). Indeed, Doane understands synchronization, rather than the shot/reverse-shot editing, as a key figure to the imaginary identification of the cinematic subject: "The body reconstituted by the technology and practices of the cinema is a *fantasmatic* body, which offers support as well as a point of identification for the subject addressed by the film" (Doane 1980a, 33–34). This fantasmatic body is, as Doane points out, a figure of unity and subjective coherence, and it responds, she says, to a threat; or, since it is a product of suture, it might be better to say that the filmic system creates the threat in order to offer the fantasmatic body as a response. "Sound carries with it the potential risk of exposing the material heterogeneity of the medium" (35). Altman's account of "moving lips" discussed above, which he attributes to this "ideology of synchronized sound," also presupposes this fantasmatic body, as does, in a slightly different way, the use of offscreen sound to motivate what Heath describes as "a kind of metonymic lock in which off-screen space becomes on-screen space" (Heath 1981, 45). If the moving lips of synchronized dialogue serve as the privileged figure of sound film, offscreen sound functions much like the eyeline match that leads to out-of-field space and it serves an analogous suturing purpose: the offscreen sound momentarily suspends synchronization, a filmic emblem of subjective coherence, but the following shot restores synchronization, allowing the viewing subject to claim the prior offscreen space as its own (Silverman 1988, 48). If "there is always something uncanny about a voice which emanates from a source outside the frame," such sound, Doane says, "deepens the diegesis, gives it an extent which exceeds that of the image, and thus supports the claim that there is a space in the fictional world which the camera does not register. In its own way, it *accounts for* lost space. The voice-off is a sound which is first and foremost in the service of the film's construction of space and only indirectly in the service of the image.

It validates both what the screen reveals of the diegesis and what it conceals" (Doane 1980a, 40; emphasis in the original). The risk entailed in offscreen sound is recovered in the continual confirmation of a wider reality. As is the case with the shot/reverse-shot syntax, offscreen sound calls into question the adequacy of any particular shot and the movement among shots then opens out into an economy of desire that the term suture both names and regulates.

Pascal Bonitzer has given detailed consideration to the signification of both onscreen and offscreen sound. Bonitzer notes that synchronization seems to fix the meaning of every voice, to belittle it by placing a check on the voice's power. Any asynchronous voice, by contrast, retains a certain power over the image. "So instead of looking, it is necessary to think" (1986, 322). Bonitzer notes that sound film divides the asynchronous voice into two different registers (322–23), a distinction that is now usually called nondiegetic (voiceover) and diegetic (voice-off), and that both obtain a power over the image in virtue of the lack of synchronization. The power of the voiceover, he thinks, lies in twining its "absolutely other," that is, its transcendent position, where it "is presumed to know," with an address to someone "who will not speak," namely the spectator (324). "The voice speaks *from the place of the Other*, and this must also be understood in a double sense. It is not charged with manifesting in its radical heterogeneity, but on the contrary with controlling it, with recording it (that is, with suppressing and conserving it), with fixing it by means of knowledge. The power of the voice is a stolen power, stolen from the Other; it is a usurpation" (324). It silences the Other that it might speak for them. Voiceover does not, therefore, present point of view. "Its problem is precisely how to silence a point of view" (331). One of the ways it does this is through mythologization, using the captioning capacity of the voice to extract univocal meaning from the image. "To do violence to the image and to impel its referential reality is to extort a surplus meaning from it, to interdict its ambiguity, to congeal it into a type, symbol, metaphor ... This is what makes for propaganda" (326–27). The voiceover in this respect works similarly to montage.

The voice-off, by contrast, is both more mundane and potentially more disruptive insofar as it does not mark itself as coming from a radically other space. This is the uncanny quality that Doane mentioned above. Normally, the offscreen sound serves to signify the extension of onscreen space and so also to motivate cuts, but the longer the synchronization of the offscreen sound is delayed, the more uncanny it becomes. Occasionally, the exclusion can become systemic, in which case a peculiar power accrues to the voice. That the villain in Kiss Me Deadly (1955), for instance, only ever appears in partial shots for most of the film and so is known visually by his shoes rather than by his face "gives his sententious voice, inflated by mythological comparison, a much greater disquieting power, the scope of an oracle—somber prophet of the end of the world" (Bonitzer 1986, 323). Michel Chion develops Bonitzer's description here into the figure of the *acousmêtre*, or acoustical being. Chion defines the figure thus: "a kind of voice-character specific to cinema that in most instances of cinematic narratives derives mysterious powers from being heard and not seen" (1994, 221). The powers derive principally from an apparent camera awareness: only a character who recognizes the place of the camera could avoid it so thoroughly.

Consequently, the *acousmêtre* is presented as one-who-knows, appropriating the power of the Absent One so long as the character remains without visualization. Conversely, when the character becomes visible, the power dissipates. "It suffices for the subject of this voice to appear in the image...for it to be no longer anything but the voice of a man....A gunshot, he falls—and with him, but in ridicule, his discourse with its prophetic overtones" (Bonitzer 1986, 323). This process of de-acousmatization dramatizes suture; it presents dispossession through unveiling: once the monster can be shown, it can be killed. "The acousmêtre has only to show itself—for the person speaking to inscribe his or her body inside the frame, in the visual field—for it to lose its power, omniscience, and (obviously) ubiquity...*Embodying the voice* is a sort of symbolic act, dooming the acousmêtre to the fate of ordinary mortals" (Chion 1999, 27–28). Here, then, through the *acousmêtre* we understand the suturing effect of synchronization as controlling the imaginary—or rather its threat—by binding it to the symbolic.

Suture does not require this binding off of the imaginary in order to ensure identification with the cinematic subject. Indeed, the unity of Doane's "fantasmatic body" is typically obtained through an imaginary (rather than symbolic) identification, and film music likewise generally works through—or is at least theorized as—an imaginary identification. Indeed, Claudia Gorbman argues that film music is a suturing device that "immerses the spectator" in a "bath of affect." It serves the suturing effects of editing by helping "to ward off...the spectator's potential recognition of the technological basis of filmic articulation. Gaps, cuts, the frame itself, silences in the soundtrack—any reminders of cinema's materiality which jeopardize the formation of subjectivity—the process whereby the viewer identifies as subject of filmic discourse—are smoothed over, or 'spirited away'...by the carefully regulated operations of film music" (1987, 58). In this way, film music facilitates absorption and identification with the narrative by "draw[ing] the spectator further into the diegetic illusion" (59). Because of the investment in the imaginary, the suturing effects of film music also entail regression in the psychoanalytic meaning of the term. "The classic narrative film encourages the film subject's return to a primitive narcissism, in which there are no boundaries between active and passive, body and environment, self and other. The cinema simulates not reality but *a condition of the subject*" (63), the goal of which is to create "an untroublesome social subject" who will more easily accept the filmic fiction and so also, one presumes, the illusion of social harmony proffered by the *dispositif* (57).

Doane similarly notes that the soundtrack as a whole, not just music, places the listener in a psychologically regressive scenario. "Space, for the child, is defined initially in terms of the audible, not the visible....The first differences are traced along the axis of sound: the voice of the mother, the voice of the father" (1980a, 44). Sound, moreover, "is not framed" but rather "envelops the spectator" (39). The "sonorous envelope" in the cinema thus promotes an infantile, narcissistic fantasy of unity, usually associated in Lacanian psychoanalysis with the maternal voice. According to Kaja Silverman, this fantasy of unity can be presented either positively (Kristeva, Rosolato) or negatively (Chion), but either way Silverman finds a gendered relation to the body and the voice structured around "the loss of imaginary plenitude" through which the subject emerges as a recognition that the self is not one with the mother's voice. She explains: "In its guise as 'pure' sonorousness, the maternal voice oscillates between two poles; it is either cherished as an *objet (a)*—as what can make good all lacks—or despised and jettisoned as what is most abject, most culturally intolerable—as the forced representative of everything within male subjectivity which is incompatible with the phallic function, and which threatens to expose discursive mastery as an impossible ideal" (Silverman 1988, 86). Silverman is particularly critical of Chion, who, she argues, aligns the maternal voice with sound but the paternal voice (tacitly and through displacement) with meaning, so that the conception of the maternal voice comes to dominate and demonize representations of interiority (49). Within this formulation, the representation of subjectivity is obtained by containing that interiority, synchronizing that voice to the female body, the body of the other (74–77). Chion's formulation, she thinks, lies perilously close to that of classic Hollywood film because in both "sexual difference almost invariably functions as a major point of reference" so that "the female body [becomes] the site not only of anatomical but of discursive lack" (49, 50). Silverman's critique of Chion basically follows the lines of the feminist critique of the discursive construction of female as the other of reason discussed in Chapter 14. Silverman ignores two points, however: first, that Chion's account presumes apparatus theory, and within the context of the *dispositif,* the place of discursive authority and sense is always already an ideological one, a point that Silverman herself will press in her detailed analysis of classic Hollywood's asymmetrical treatment of the voice along the lines of gender; second, Chion's account is shaped by his understanding of Lacan; and though Lacan has also been criticized on his theory of sexuality, there are good reasons to think that this critique misses its mark (see below).

Along with apparatus theory in general, the theorization of film music along psychoanalytic lines has come under attack. As noted above, proponents of feminist and queer theory have long expressed dissatisfaction with psychoanalytic theory because it seems to presume a patriarchal heteronormative subject. Others have found it by turns incoherent, reductive, totalizing, ahistorical, dogmatic, and lacking in empirical support.[5] With respect to the soundtrack, Jeff Smith takes issue with psychoanalytic theories of film music. He notes that film music assumes "a privileged position within a suture model. Because of its tendencies toward both inaudibility and abstraction, film music is thought to be especially well suited to the process of binding the spectator into the world of the fiction" (Smith 1996, 233). Yet Smith also points out that a psychoanalytic model that presumes the suturing effect of music through its inaudibility cannot provide a coherent account of how we also come to attend to the supposedly unheard music—to recognize a leitmotif, say, when it recurs within a film, or even more significantly outside the film (236). Whatever unconscious (or more likely preconscious) apprehension of music occurs in the theater, it is clear that we as spectators are not barred from attending to music per se in the manner psychoanalysis presumes that the psychological structure prevents subjects from directly accessing their unconscious drives. In this respect, music is at best a signifier of these unconscious drives, a way of granting us imaginary access to them by representing their force on, their knowledge of, and determination of the diegetic action. The suturing effect of music resides not so much in its inaudibility, then, as in its ability to clarify meaning for us without quite letting on as to how it is accomplishing its work. Like the unobtrusive cut, which may pass noticed or unnoticed but whose presence seems supplemental to the basic meaning of the sequence, the figure of inaudibility points not to the fact that music is never consciously heard or attended to but only to the fact that it need not be consciously attended to in order to produce its distinctive effect of clarifying meaning. That is, nothing essential seems to depend on us listening consciously to it (though nothing bars us from doing so either). The point is that the music, when we consciously attend to it, still seems, like the observed unobtrusive cut, merely supplemental, nothing more than a fine artistic touch, a formal mark of stylization. For the psychoanalytic theorist, then, it is this appearance of supplementarity that grounds ideology and serves as the basis for musical suture because its status as supplement both neutralizes the otherwise disruptive presence of music and effaces its work in producing meaning.

Neo-Lacanian Theory

The most cogent critique of apparatus theory has come not from those opposed to a psychoanalytic film theory but rather from those committed to a strong interpretation of Lacanian psychoanalysis. Philosopher and cultural critic Slavoj Žižek is the best known and most prolific of the so-called neo-Lacanians, but he tends either to interpret films through a Lacanian lens or, more commonly, to use films to illustrate Lacanian concepts rather than to engage specifically at the level of film theory. The same cannot be said of Joan Copjec, who has taken direct aim at apparatus theory, accusing it of using a Foucauldian misreading of Lacan in a way that empties it of psychoanalytic content.[6] "The relation between apparatus and gaze creates only the mirage of psychoanalysis. There is, in fact, no psychoanalytic subject in sight" (Copjec 1994, 26). According to Copjec, apparatus theory radically misconstrues Lacan's mirror phase: where it understands the screen as a mirror, Lacan understands exactly the reverse: the mirror is a screen (15–16). Todd McGowan likewise argues that "at its most basic level, [apparatus theory] understands the cinema as a machine for the perpetuation of ideology" (McGowan 2007, 2). Apparatus theory, he claims, urges "critical distance from the scene of cinematic manipulation" in order obviate its ideological inscriptions. Neo-Lacanian theory, on the contrary, understands such critical distance as "another way of avoiding the real of the gaze" (14). Instead, neo-Lacanian theory recognizes cinema as a machine for encountering the real.

This revival of psychoanalytic film theory has been concerned especially with reappraising the gaze, which apparatus theory construes as a mastering perspective that delivers meaning. Copjec explains the difference in how apparatus theory and Lacanian psychoanalysis conceptualize the gaze this way:

> In [apparatus] theory the gaze is located "in front of" the image, as its signified, the point of maximal meaning or sum of all that appears in the image and the point that "gives" meaning. The subject is, then, thought to identify with and thus, in a

sense, to coincide with the gaze. In Lacan, on the other hand, the gaze is located "behind" the image, as that which fails to appear in it and thus as that which makes all its meaning suspect. And the subject, instead of coinciding with or identifying with the gaze, is rather cut off from it. Lacan does not ask you to think of the gaze as belonging to an Other who cares about that or where you are, who pries, keeps tabs on your whereabouts, and takes note of all your steps and missteps, as the panoptic gaze is said to do. When you encounter the gaze of the Other, you meet not a seeing eye but a blind one. The gaze is not clear or penetrating, not filled with knowledge or recognition; it is clouded over and turned back on itself, absorbed in its own enjoyment. The horrible truth … is that the gaze does not see you. So, if you are looking for confirmation of the truth of your being or the clarity of your vision, you are on your own; the gaze of the Other is not confirming; it will not validate you. (Copjec 1994, 36)

McGowan likewise argues against an analysis based on uncovering the ideological investment in an imaginary identification with the gaze of the camera, an identification that serves to occlude and naturalize the functioning of the symbolic order, and instead focuses on the gaze as "the site of a traumatic encounter with the Real, with the utter failure of the spectator's seemingly safe distance and assumed mastery. The crucial point is that not only is this failure of mastery possible in the cinema, but it is what spectators desire when they go to the movies" (McGowan 2003, 29). Although problematizing the way apparatus theory discounts the real, McGowan makes the gaze its privileged site and thereby reproduces film theory's long investment in the visual at the expense of the aural. We need not abandon his analysis, however, so long as we continue to recognize its incompleteness and understand this incompleteness as systemic and recognized as such within the theory. If the gaze marks a limit of filmic representation, the point at which the film looks blindly back at us, it also approaches the real, this limit, from only one side, that of the image. The reason we cannot simply dismiss this analysis as inadequate despite its manifest incompleteness is because approaching the real from the side of the soundtrack—here, the voice will serve as the equivalent term to the gaze— would not in any respect complement or complete the analysis. Although Lacan himself includes both gaze and voice as instances of *objet (a)* and though both reveal the real as a failure of the symbolic, they are not fully reciprocal. As Žižek writes:

Voice and gaze relate to each other as life and death: voice vivifies, whereas gaze mortifies. For that reason, "hearing oneself speak" [s'entendre-parler] as Derrida has demonstrated, is the very kernel, the fundamental matrix, of experiencing oneself as a living being, while its counterpart at the level of gaze, "seeing oneself looking" [se voir voyant] unmistakably stands for death: when the gaze qua object is no longer the elusive blind spot in the field of the visible but is included in this field, one meets one's own death. (Žižek 1996, 94)

The terms voice and gaze are not symmetrical in the sense that hearing and speaking map a different order of distinction than do seeing and looking. (The equivalent distinction to seeing and looking would be closer to hearing and listening.) Žižek's analysis, however, performs something of a short circuit by not fully recognizing the disanalogy that obtains, and so obscuring rather than illuminating the relation between them. Like McGowan, he privileges the gaze both by making it the ground that legitimates the voice (we hear because we cannot see) as well as by placing it in the position of an agent of sublime terror (seeing what we cannot hear). The voice also relates directly to the symbolic—it is a medium of the production of meaning—in the way that the gaze does not, so that the voice reaches the limit of the real in sense, or rather, in its dissolution. Gaze and voice therefore mark two distinct ways that the subject encounters its internal limit, two distinct ways that its symbolic construction of the world can fail, and these follow in turn the contours of sexual difference as theorized by Lacan.

For Lacan, sexual difference is located in the phallic function.[7] But it is not the absence or presence of the phallic function that determines sexuation—the production of sexual differentiation—but the way a subject positions itself with respect to a set of antinomic statements that relates to the order of meaning and expresses an impasse, the failure of meaning. On the masculine side, this relation is through exclusion and prohibition. On the feminine side, the relation is through nonexistence and impossibility. Thus, with respect to the image, we might formulate the antinomies of filmic representation according to the masculine principle of the relation: (1) at least one image is not an object of diegetic representation; (2) all images are possible objects of diegetic representation. The imagetrack constitutes a universe of diegetic representation, but at least one image cannot be reconciled with that world. Formally, this excluded image serves to mark a limit that makes the field of diegetic representation possible. The frame, for instance, imposes a formal limit; it is, Chion says, "the place of not seeing all" (1999, 121), and creates a place for images, though it is not itself a formal part of the diegesis. In this way, the limit of the frame allows the imagetrack to appear coherent. A similar analysis applies to the shot, whose beginning and end are usually marked by a cut that determines its extent. The gaze is another, more radical type of excluded image, a blank spot that refuses to disclose itself within the visual field. Yet to return to Copjec's description of the gaze above, we find that the blankness and blindness of the gaze likewise serve to impose a limit: "The subject, instead of coinciding with or identifying with the gaze, is rather *cut off from it.*" The excluded image is also the reason that the theory of the gaze can only ever yield an incomplete rather than mastering account of filmic representation.

NEO-LACANIAN THEORY AND THE SOUNDTRACK

What then might a neo-Lacanian account of the soundtrack look like? Here we return to Chion and his perplexing claim that "there is no soundtrack" (1999, 1–6; 1994, 39–40; and 2009, 226–30). Read through the lens of Lacan, this statement now evokes Lacan's notorious statement that "woman does not exist." Because no empirical woman can complete the concept of man, Lacan says, woman is a symptom of that concept. If we extend this idea to the soundtrack, we arrive at the idea that no sound—or set of sounds—can adequately complete the image. The soundtrack is, in other words, the symptom of the image. This conception, however, runs the risk of simply privileging the image, granting it priority. In this case, the soundtrack would register the lack of the image but nothing more. What, then, might the soundtrack be or consist in beyond the registering of this lack?

Here, the concept of the voice becomes important. If the gaze is the blank spot in the imagetrack that looks blindly back at us, then on first approximation the voice might be taken as the silence of the soundtrack that speaks to us mutely. "The voice is precisely that which cannot be said" (Dolar 2006, 15). It is that which is in sound that does not communicate, that resist meaning; put more traumatically, it is the sound of the world's deafness, its indifference to us. This formulation, though one suggested by Žižek, is however perhaps too symmetrical (Žižek 1991b, 49; 1996, 92–93),[8] since it presumes that the soundtrack, like the imagetrack, is governed by castration, by the limit of the symbolic. Just as the figure of woman appears in Lacanian psychoanalysis and approaches the limit of sense in a different manner than does the figure of man, so too the soundtrack does not find its limit as prohibition but as impossibility, the impossibility of film as a consistent symbolic endeavor.

Chion does indeed align the soundtrack with the Lacanian conception of woman. According to Chion, the soundtrack is an incoherent construction that does not produce a consistent universe. "A film's aural elements are not received as an autonomous unit" (1999, 3). The soundtrack is also unruly, overrunning boundaries—sound editing, he says, does not yield "a neutral, universally recognizable unit" like the shot (1994, 41)— and allowing the appearance of "sounds and voices that are neither clearly inside nor clearly outside" the image or narrative (1999, 4). Essentially, the soundtrack is incoherent because it does not encounter a limit. "Sound is first of all *content* or 'containable', with no actual frame" (2009, 226). If Chion acknowledges that the imagetrack is "no less fictive," he nevertheless grants it priority—sound is interpreted or "triaged," he says, through the image—and coherence that aligns it, analogously, with the Lacanian conception of man. By contrast, the imagetrack, Chion says, remains "a valid concept. The image track owes its being and its unity to the presence of a frame, a space of the images in which the spectator is invested" (1994, 39). The appearance of the frame, then, is crucial for the existence of the imagetrack: "The absence of a frame for sounds inevitably creates a dissymmetry between what we see and what we hear" (2009, 227). The frame gives form to the image; the soundtrack has no equivalent form. Consequently, the phallic function of diegetic representation operates on it in a different fashion.

With respect to the soundtrack, we can formulate the antinomies of filmic representation according to the feminine principle of the relation: (1) there is no sound that is not an object of possible diegetic representation; (2) not every sound is a possible object of diegetic representation.[9] The soundtrack confronts no limit since it includes nothing that cannot be made part of the diegetic representation, but the sounds themselves are individually delimited and so constitute an indefinite rather than infinite set; each sound can be individually paired with an image source; but not all sounds will constitute the world of diegetic representation. Sound encounters no formal limit—it has neither frame nor shot to delimit it. Instead sound is subject to the contingencies of filmic unfolding, that is, temporality. If sound's "temporalizing power greatly exceeds the image" (Chion 2009, 266), so that sound can seem to insist upon a vectorized temporal flow, upon the appearance of a temporality not reducible to that captured in the movement of the image, music by contrast is, Chion says, "first and foremost a machine for manipulating space and time, which it helps to expand, contract, freeze, and thaw at will" (409). Music therefore ordinarily serves to veil "the palpability of time" (274), the real of temporality, which emerges, Chion says, at "the decisive moment, the climax, the *alea jacta est* or point of no return, the moment of truth and of real time" (272), where music (but also speech) recedes and allows the sounds of the world to reverberate and form the ground of the real of temporality that renders the figure of silence, the "fundamental noise," audible (453–58; see also, Žižek 1996, 93). The conception of the soundtrack cannot therefore be extracted from the representation of temporality, which means that we cannot construct a general concept of the soundtrack.

What binds the masculine and feminine principles together in Lacanian theory is the appearance of the sexual relation. The analogous figure in sound film would be synchronization, the joining of image and sound, which is why, from a neo-Lacanian perspective, the metaphor of "marrying" sound to image is no more innocent or coincidental than it is from a feminist perspective. For this "marriage" follows the cultural myth of unity wherein two become one to produce the imaginary diegetic world. According to the Lacanian account of the sexual relation, this joining yields two principles, based on the pleasure and reality principles of Freud. Translated into the terms of sound film, the pleasure principle consists in an immediate satisfaction of the apparatus: sound and image appear synchronized, they follow a coordinated path through the apparatus, and they are bound to one another in the play of an imaginary world. Traditional sound film is constructed along the lines of the pleasure principle: a diegesis appears to exist, it is not troubled by an antagonism between sound- and imagetracks, and it therefore seems to promise a "natural" synchronization between image and sound. The pleasure principle also lies behind the traditional "rules" of proper synchronization—something along the lines of Gorbman's seven rules—that govern the exchange of sound based on an order or set of common values that have already been laid out in advance. Under this scenario, image can relate to sound only insofar as sound enters the frame of the image and becomes "diegeticized." Jacques Aumont, summarizing this situation, writes: "all the work of classical cinema and its contemporary by-products has aimed to *spatialize sound elements*, by offering them points of correspondence in the image, and therefore assure a bi-univocal bonding between image and sound, what we might call 'redundant'" (Aumont, Bergala, Marie, and Vernet 1992, 35, quoted in Chion 2009, 228). Although image relates to sound through this redundant effect of spatialization and diegetization, sound is not exhausted in this correspondence. Even in the classical cinema, sound is split because it is what the lack in the image signifies, and that lack is itself divided: both what the image does not contain, which spatializes sound and binds it to the diegesis as a property of the image; and what lies beyond the image, which opens up the nondiegetic, the absolutely out of field, where sound—especially music and voiceover—stands in the place of the Absent One, the other who knows and, because outside the diegesis, can serve to guarantee its existence. Under the pleasure principle, sound complements the image, even as it completes it in the imaginary.

The reality principle, by contrast, consists in the reality of the apparatus: sound and image are separate, they follow different paths through the apparatus, they are materially alienated from one another, and the desire for synchronization appears only in virtue of this original alienation. The reality principle points to the fact that in Lacan's theory the sexual relation is always a failed relation—the satisfaction of the pleasure principle is always a hallucination—and so long as synchronization is theorized along analogous lines, it should suffer the same fate in sound film. Indeed, under this description there would be two ways for the sound film to fail: through the image and through the sound. As noted above, the image fails through exclusion; it is defined by a prohibition, a lack: it cannot show everything. Sound, on the contrary, fails because it has no limit. The soundtrack promises what the imagetrack lacks, what the image cannot show: everything, the continuity of a world that lies beyond the frame line. But the soundtrack pays for this everything with an indefinite formlessness, a lack of boundary, a lack of containment. Because it has no limit, it is not all, not whole. Conceived in these terms, the question is not how to produce complementary accounts of image and sound, where the lack of the one is compensated for by the other and vice versa, but rather to reveal the fantasy on which such complementarity rests. This shifts the issue from explaining the rules of synchronization to what it means, given the fact of the division that underlies the construction of the apparatus, to speak of the soundtrack at all. Chion writes:

> There are many consequences of this negative claim I have been making that "there is no soundtrack." First, it necessarily explodes any pretense of establishing an overall theory of film composed of two complementary elements, image and sound, and instead leads us to an incomplete and fluctuating model of cinema that does not allow for simply transposing the technical model (one channel for images and one channel for sounds, distinct yet parallel) and where a radical break is produced between the technical level and the levels of perception, discourse, effects, and theory. (Chion 2009, 229–30)

If sound serves as the support for the concept of synchronization, it also makes evident the impossibility of actually establishing synchronization as a consistent system that would uphold the diegesis. Without a frame to contain it, the soundtrack both simultaneously embodies the diegesis in its entirety and denies the possibility of its appearing. The soundtrack is the point at which the impossibility of sound film's diegesis assumes positive form. Because sound is thus simply a fantasy screen of the image—the image in its ideal completeness—the soundtrack does not exist. This does not mean that sounds, music, and voices do not exist, of course; rather it is that the soundtrack cannot serve to guarantee the image's fantasy of completion.

The relation between imagetrack and soundtrack is therefore better conceived in terms of antagonism rather than complementation. If sound film fails because image and sound do not come together to produce a world, then sound cannot be added to the image; it can only be differentiated from it. The diegesis is the site, not of unity, but of this differentiation, and the claim that the soundtrack does not exist does not so much deny existence as it asserts that the category of synchronized fantasy is false. The claim that there is no soundtrack therefore carries a perhaps surprising corollary: there is no diegesis. The diegesis is not simply a fiction, but sound film's primal myth, an imaginary projection that uses synchronization as a barrier against reality, against the recognition of the division into image and sound, projecting a unity through which the actual split is continually denied. Two do not make one, and yet the sound film exists on the assumption of this one; but this unity suppresses not just the heterogeneity so beloved by the first generation of Lacanian film theorists, but also for the neo-Lacanians the gap of human desire. This gap is made manifest in the figure of asynchronous sound and the uneasy feeling that there is something awry whenever we encounter it. The effects are felt as a hole in the fabric of the diegetic representation. We can perhaps now understand why the *acousmêtre* is such an important figure for Chion: It marks precisely this hole in the diegetic, the opening of desire at the point where the pleasure principle fails. Sound is rendered in sound film to satisfy desire, to signify what sound is not, not to be what it is. "The whole enterprise of sound effects in film," Chion writes, "consists of hijacking some sounds to express others" (2009, 239). The signifier of this desire resides not in the sound but in the way the image signifies its own lack. For it is here, where the image delimits the depiction of the diegesis that sound addresses itself, locates itself as a property that the image desires. Synchronization fuses a representation that deprives sound a place in the image with a desire that the image cannot contain. Because it is rendered to satisfy a desire that does not belong to itself and that it does not signify, sound can often be cold, indifferent to the demands of the image so long as it fulfills the basic requirements of synchronization.

As opposed to this frigidity of sound, which points to difficulties inherent in the relation of synchronization that requires sound to be both inside and outside the image, pure asynchronous sound, or sound undetermined by its relation to the image, would be psychotic sound, sound that has excepted itself from the symbolic order—the signifying network—of narrative. Sound completely unbound from the image in this way would mean the end of the symbolic universe, a sound lost to meaning. Such sound would in fact also presume a place of perfect objectivity with respect to sound choice: that it is possible to get outside the signifying network and make an entirely free choice with respect to sound. As Chion notes, this is virtually impossible to accomplish: "If the image had a resistance to being layered with nonsynchronous sounds not anchored spatially or diegetically in the image, this resistance ... would communicate to us something powerful in its very violence. The real problem is that everything 'works'; there never is any resistance, only a sort of laissez-faire abandonment of sounds and images to this passive superimposing that generates effects erratically, zinging us here and there with momentary pleasures" (2009, 230).

RENDERING

If asynchronous sound has proven too capricious to reliably tap its traumatic kernel, it has provided something of a map for locating that kernel in the contemporary practice of rendering. A profound uncertainty follows from the attempt to substitute the continuity of the soundtrack, which has no formal limit, for the image as the ground of diegetic representation. In many films today, sound takes the place of the establishing shot, and it loses the promise of plenitude that had always been the opening of desire marked by the frame edge. This loss is compensated for by rendering of sound.

> In fist- or sword-fight scenes, the sound does not attempt to reproduce the real noises of the situation, but to render the physical impact of the blow or the speed of the movement.... The rendering is naturally linked to the texture of the auditory and visual material of the film, to their definition, but not necessarily in the sense in which a sharper and more "faithful" image (a more accurate replication) would ipso facto give a better rendering. (Chion 1990, 71)[10]

Žižek notes how Chion's formulation of rendering, especially the way it supports a shift from the image- to the soundtrack as the basic field of orientation, leads to a psychotic conception of the relation of sound and image:

> The soundtrack gives us the basic perspective, the "map" of the situation, and guarantees its continuity, while the images are reduced to isolated fragments that float freely in the universal medium of the sound aquarium. It would be difficult to invent a better metaphor for psychosis: in contrast to the "normal" state of things in which the real is a lack, a hole in the midst of the symbolic order (like the central black spot in Rothko's paintings), we have here the "aquarium" of the real surrounding isolated islands of the symbolic. In other words, it is no longer enjoyment that "drives" the proliferation of the signifier by functioning as a central "black hole" around which the signifying network is interlaced; it is, on the contrary, the symbolic order itself that is reduced to the status of floating islands of the signifier, white *îles flottantes* in a sea of yolky enjoyment. (Žižek 1991a, 40)

Žižek's description of rendering resembles in many respects Chion's description of asynchronous sound, where "laissez-faire abandonment of sounds and images" is analogous to the "sea of yolky enjoyment" and the "momentary pleasures" of accidental sync points fill the place of the "white *îles flottantes*." Yet the points of disanalogy are worth noting as well: however much the real has intruded upon the scenario of asynchronous sound, however much asynchronous sound asserts the reality principle and opens a gap of desire that it threatens to ignore, the overall structure nevertheless respects the drive of enjoyment. The persistence of the drive of enjoyment—gratification in this case as merely arbitrarily deferred—is why it necessarily lacks resistance.

Rendering, however, is of a different order, and its situation is closer to nondiegetic music inasmuch as it retains a fundamental relation to fantasy. Both present a certain stylized excess over the real. "Rendering," Chion suggests, falls "somewhere between a code and a simulacrum. And between code, rendering, and simulacrum there may be a certain continuity—one might slip from one into another without necessarily being aware of it" (2009, 238). In Lacanian terms, code belongs to the symbolic, and simulacrum belongs to the imaginary (Žižek 1991a, 40). The continuity—the slippage—dislocates rendering from the image, which the sound no longer accompanies, and so the imagetrack and the diegesis built upon it threaten to dissolve. Rendering attacks the power of the diegesis, its myth of unity, from within. Nondiegetic music, by contrast, is doubled, serving on the one hand as the sublime extradiegetic counterpart to rendering but on the other hand as an external guarantee of the diegesis. By retaining the anachronistic term "pit music," which is otherwise somewhat inexplicable, Chion is able to emphasize a displacement of music that will anticipate the very dislocations taking place within rendering. Music's passage from the theatrical pit to the apparatus had the effect of obliterating all sense of place and labor of production. Absorbed into the apparatus, music loses all specificity:

> From the beginning to the end (or periodically if it's not continuous), the music is emitted from the orchestra pit, the grandstand, from a place beyond all places, that contains all times and all spaces, and leads everywhere: to the past as well as the future, to the sea and the city, to depths as well as to the heavens, a place that has no here or there, neither once upon a time nor now. The place is both a pit, where the elementary principles of these mean streets called life muck around, and a balcony in the sky, from where we can view as detached observers—out of time, through instantaneous cuts—past, present, and future. (Chion 2009, 412)

But music does not become universal in virtue of this loss of specificity. In that respect, at least, music in film is an allegorical figure. Doubled, it is also divided: pit and sky. Rendering ("life mucking around") is already its lower element. As the movement and logic of rendering raise the pit to the sky, the stars go out, music loses its special fascination—is it anything more than a mode of acoustical stylization? (Buhler and Neumeyer 2005, 283–86)—and the view from heaven now reveals an abyss: "the hole in the Other (the symbolic order), concealed by the fascinating presence of the fantasy object" (Žižek 1991a, 86). Music convinces us that the image on the screen is the screen of fantasy; and rendering proves a means of traversing this particular fantasy.

NOTES

1. Lacan and to a lesser extent Freud understand psychoanalysis antihumanistically, in the sense that it does not presume a stable ego. As Juliet Mitchell notes, "Humanism believes that man is at the centre of his own history and of himself; he is a subject more or less in control of his own actions, exercising choice. Humanistic psychoanalytic practice is in danger of seeing the patient as someone who has lost control and a sense of real or true (identity) and it aims to help regain these. The matter and manner of all Lacan's work challenges this notion of the human subject: there is none such" (Mitchell 1982, 4).

2. The original publication of the discussion between Pleynet and Thibaudeau prompted a sharp response from Jean-Patrick Lebel, who argued in a series of articles published in *La Nouvelle Critique* and collected in Lebel 1971 that because the camera was a scientific instrument it produced and was the product of knowledge not ideology, that ideology could come only from the use to which the neutral instrument was put. On this discussion between Pleynet and Thibaudeau as the origin of apparatus theory, see Comolli 1990.

3. Responding to criticism from James Lastra, Altman admits that his defense of heterogeneity leads him to hold a problematically nominalist account of sound. See Lastra 1992, 65–86; and Altman 1992, 40–42.

4. "Car avec le parlant hollywoodien, non seulement le son, le bruit, rentrent synchroniquement dans l'image, l'investissent et la tirent à eux: la parole aussi, surtout, c'est-à-dire l'intériorité, le discours du sujet, ce vide, ce creux que la parole cerne comme une présence pleine et qu'en effet ne cessant pas de remplir le énoncé Newsidéologiques qui parlent ce sujet."

5. See particularly Carroll 1988; Bordwell 1989; and the essays in Bordwell and Carroll 1996, especially those by Bordwell, Carroll, and Prince.

6. Bordwell is extremely critical of both Žižek and Copjec, although Bordwell 1996 glosses over important distinctions between early Lacanian film theory and the neo-Lacanians (23–24). The first chapter of Žižek 2001, 1–30, takes Bordwell to task for this conflation. Bordwell responds twice: 2005a, 260–64, and more thoroughly and more testily 2005b, in an essay published on his website. For another cogent critique of Žižek's work, see Harpham 2003.

7. The following paragraph is based on Copjec's discussion of sexual difference (1994, 212–36). See also Lacan 1998, 78–89.

8. Cf. Buhler 2001, 53–55, where, *contra* Chion, I proposed a symmetrical reading of sound- and imagetrack in order to locate the audiovisual as the product of a dialectical tension.

9. The first part of this paragraph again follows Copjec's discussion of sexual difference (1994, 212–36).

10. See also Chion 2009, 237–45.

BIBLIOGRAPHY

Agamben, Georgio. 2009. *What is an Apparatus and Other Essays*. Translated by David Kishik and Stefan Pedatella. Stanford: Stanford University Press.

Althusser, Louis. 1995. "Ideology and Ideological State Apparatuses (Notes towards an Investigation)." In *Mapping Ideology*, edited by Slavoj Žižek, 100–140. New York: Verso. Originally published in La Pensée 151 (1970): 3–38.

Altman, Rick. 1980a. "Introduction: Cinema/Sound." *Yale French Studies* 60: 3–15.

——. 1980b. "Moving Lips: Cinema as Ventriloquism." *Yale French Studies* 60: 67–79.

——. 1984. "Toward a Theory of the History of Representational Technologies." *Iris* 2, no. 2: 111–125.

——. 1985. "The Technology of the Voice [Part I]." *Iris* 3, no. 1: 3–20.

——. 1986. "The Technology of the Voice, Part II." *Iris* 4, no. 1: 107–119.

——, ed. 1992. *Sound Theory/Sound Practice*. New York: Routledge.

——. 1999. "Film Sound—All of It." *Iris* 27: 31–48.

——. 2004. *Silent Film Sound*. New York: Columbia University Press.

Aumont, Jacques, Alain Bergala, Michel Marie, and Marc Vernet. 1992. *Aesthetics of Film*. Translated by Richard Neupert. Austin: University of Texas Press. Originally published in 1983 as *L'esthétique du film*. Paris: Nathan.

Baudry, Jean-Louis. 1974–1975. "Ideological Effects of the Basic Cinematographic Apparatus." *Film Quarterly* 28, no. 2: 39–47. Originally published in *Cinéthique* 7–8 (1970): 1–8.

——.1976. "The Apparatus." *Camera Obscura* 1, no. 1: 104–126. Originally published in *Communications* 23 (1975): 56–72.

Bazin, André. 2005. *What is Cinema?* Translated by Hugh Grey. 2 vols. Berkeley: University of California Press.

Bonitzer, Pascal. 1986. "The Silences of the Voice (*A propos of Mai 68* by GudieLawaetz)." In *Narrative, Technology, Ideology*, edited by Philip Rosen, 319–334. New York: Columbia University Press. Originally published in *Cahiers du cinéma* 256 (1975): 22–33.

——.1990. "Off-Screen Space." Translated by Lindley Hanlon. In *Cahiers du Cinéma, 1969–1972: The Politics of Representation*, edited by Nick Browne, 291–305. Cambridge, MA: Harvard University Press. Originally published in *Cahiers du cinéma* 234–35 (1971–1972): 15–26.

Bordwell, David. 1989. *Making Meaning: Inference and Rhetoric in the Interpretation of Cinema*. Cambridge, MA: Harvard University Press.

——. 1996. "Contemporary Film Studies and the Vicissitudes of Grand Theory." In *Post-Theory: Reconstructing Film Studies*, edited by David Bordwell and Noël Carroll, 3–36. Madison: University of Wisconsin Press.

——. 2005a. *Figures Traced in Light: On Cinematic Staging*. Berkeley: University of California Press.

——. 2005b. "Slavoj Žižek: Say Anything." *David Bordwell's Website on Cinema*. http://www.davidbordwell.net/essays/zizek.php (accessed May 20, 2012).

Bordwell, David, and Noël Carroll, eds. 1996. *Post-Theory: Reconstructing Film Studies*. Madison: University of Wisconsin Press.

Browne, Nick, ed. 1990. *Cahiers du Cinéma, 1969–1972: The Politics of Representation*. Cambridge, MA: Harvard University Press.

Bryukhovetska, Olga. 2010. "'Dispositif' Theory: Returning to the Movie Theater." *ArtItMagazine*. August 10. http://www.art-it.asia/u/admin_ed_columns_e/apskOCMPV5ZwoJrGnvxf/.

Buhler, James. 2001. "Analytical and Interpretive Approaches to Film Music (II): Analysing Interactions of Music and Film." In *Film Music: Critical Approaches*, edited by Kevin J. Donnelly, 39–61. Edinburgh: Edinburgh University Press,

——, and David Neumeyer. 2005. "Music—Sound—Narrative: Analyzing *Casablanca*." In *Interdisciplinary Studies in Musicology* 5, edited by Maciej Jablonski and Michael Klein, 279–293. Poznań, Poland: Rhytmos.

Burt, George. 1994. *The Art of Film Music: Special Emphasis on Hugo Friedhofer, Alex North, David Raksin, Leonard Rosenman*. Boston: Northeastern University Press.

Carroll, Noël. 1988. *Mystifying Movies: Fads and Fallacies in Contemporary Film Theory*. New York: Columbia University Press.

——. 1996. "Prospects for Film Theory: A Personal Assessment." In *Post-Theory: Reconstructing Film Studies*, edited by David Bordwell and Noël Carroll, 37–68. Madison: University of Wisconsin Press.

Chion, Michel. 1990. Translated by Ben Brewster. "Quiet Revolution . . . or Rigid Stagnation." *October* 58: 69–80.

——.1994. *Audio-Vision: Sound on Film*. Translated by Claudia Gorbman. New York: Columbia University Press. Originally published in 1990 as *L'audio-vision*. Paris: Nathan.

——.1999. *The Voice in the Cinema*. Translated by Claudia Gorbman. New York: Columbia University Press. Originally published in 1982 as *La voix au cinéma*. Paris: Editions de l'Etoile.

——. 2009. *Film, a Sound Art*. Translated by Claudia Gorbman. New York: Columbia University Press..

Comolli, Jean-Louis. 1971–1972. "Technique et idéologie (5): Caméra, perspective, perfondeur de champ." *Cahiers du cinéma* 234–235: 94–100.

——. 1972. "Technique et idéologie, 6: Quelle parole?" *Cahiers du cinéma* 241: 20–24.

——. 1980. "Machines of the Visible." In *The Cinematic Apparatus*, edited by Teresa de Lauretis and Stephen Heath, 121–142. Milwaukee: MacMillan Press.

——.1986. "Technique and Ideology: Camera, Perspective, Depth of View [Parts 3 and 4]." In *Narrative, Technology, Ideology*, edited by Philip Rosen, 421–443. New York: Columbia University Press. Originally published in 1971: Part III, *Cahiers du cinéma* 231: 42–50; Part IV, *Cahiers du cinéma* 233 : 39–45.

——. 1990. "Technique and Ideology [Parts 1 and 2]: Camera. Perspective, Depth of Field." Translated by Diana Matias. In *Cahiers du Cinéma, 1969–1972: The Politics of Representation*, edited by Nick Browne, 213–247. Cambridge, MA: Harvard University Press. Originally published in 1971: Part I, *Cahiers du cinéma* 229: 4–21; Part II, *Cahiers du cinéma* 230: 51–57.

Comolli, Jean-Louis, and Jean Narboni. 1971a. "Cinema/Ideology/Criticism." *Screen* 12, no. 1: 27–36. Originally published in *Cahiers du cinéma* 216 (1969): 11–15.

——. 1971b. "Cinema/Ideology/Criticism (2)." *Screen* 12, no. 2: 145–155. Originally published in *Cahiers du cinéma* 217 (1969): 7–13.

——. 1972. "Cinema/Ideology/Criticism 2 Continued." *Screen* 13, no. 1: 120–131. Originally published in *Cahiers du cinéma* 217 (1969): 7–13.

Copjec, Joan. 1989. "The Orthopsychic Subject: Film Theory and the Reception of Lacan." *October* 49: 53–71.

——. 1994. *Read My Desire: Lacan against the Historicists*. Cambridge, MA: MIT Press.

Dayan, Daniel. 1974. "The Tutor-Code of Classical Cinema." *Film Quarterly* 28, no. 1: 22–31.

Doane, Mary Ann. 1980a. "The Voice in the Cinema: The Articulation of Body and Space." *Yale French Studies* 60: 33–50.

——.1980b. "Ideology and the Practice of Sound Editing and Mixing." In *The Cinematic Apparatus*, edited by Teresa de Lauretis and Stephen Heath, 47–56. Milwaukee: MacMillan Press.

——. 1987. *The Desire to Desire: The Woman's Film of the 1940s*. Bloomington: Indiana University Press.

Dolar, Mladen. 2006. *A Voice and Nothing More*. Cambridge, MA: MIT Press.

Faulkner Robert R. 1971. *Hollywood Studio Musicians: Their Work and Careers in the Recording Industry*. Chicago: Aldine-Atherton.

——. 1983. *Music on Demand: Composers and Careers in the Hollywood Film Industry*. New Brunswick, NJ: Transaction.

Flinn, Caryl. 1992. *Strains of Utopia: Gender, Nostalgia, and Hollywood Film Music*. Princeton, NJ: Princeton University Press.

Gorbman, Claudia. 1987. *Unheard Melodies: Narrative Film Music*. Bloomington: Indiana University Press.

Greenberg, Harvey R., and Krin Gabbard. 1990. "Reel Significations: An Anatomy of Psychoanalytic Film Criticism." *Psychoanalytic Review* 77, no. 1: 89–110.

Hanson, Ellis. "Introduction." In *Out Takes: Essays in Queer Theory and Film*, edited by Ellis Hanson, 1–20. Durham: Duke University Press, 1999.

Harpham, Geoffrey Galt. 2003. "Doing the Impossible: Slavoj Žižek and the End of Knowledge." *Critical Inquiry* 29, no. 3: 453–485.

Hayward, Philip. 1997. "Danger Retro-Affectivity! The Cultural Career of the Theremin." *Convergence* 3, no. 4: 28–53.

Heath, Stephen. 1977–1978. "Notes on Suture." *Screen* 18, no. 4: 48–76.

——. 1981. *Questions of Cinema*. Bloomington: Indiana University Press.

Johnston, Claire. 1976. "Towards a Feminist Film Practice: Some Theses." *Edinburgh Magazine* 1: 50–59.

Kaplan, E. Ann. 2000. "Is the Gaze Male?" In *Feminism and Film*, edited by E. Ann Kaplan, 119–138. New York: Oxford University Press. Originally published in 1983 in *Powers of Desire: The Politics of Sexuality*, edited by Ann Snitow, Christine Stansell and Sharon Thompson, 309–327. New York: Monthly Review Press.

Karlin, Fred, and Rayburn Wright. 1990. *On the Track: A Guide to Contemporary Film Scoring*. New York: Schirmer.

Kraft, James P. 1996. *Stage to Studio: Musicians and the Sound Revolution, 1890–1950*. Baltimore: Johns Hopkins University Press.

Lacan, Jacques. 1968. "The Mirror-Phase as Formative of the Function of the I." *New Left Review* 51: 71–77. Originally published in *Revue française de psychanalyse* 13, no. 4 (1949): 449–455.

——. 1998. *On Feminine Sexuality: The Limits of Love and Knowledge. Encore: the Seminar of Jacques Lacan, Book XX*. Translated by Bruce Fink. New York: W. W. Norton. Originally published in 1975 as *Le seminaire, livre XX, encore, 1972–1973*. Paris: Editions du Seuil.

Lastra, James. 1992. "Reading, Writing, and Representing Sound." In *Sound Theory/Sound Practice*, edited by Rick Altman, 65–86. New York: Routledge.

——. 2000. *Sound Technology and the American Cinema: Perception, Representation, Modernity*. New York: Columbia University Press.

Lauretis, Teresa de, and Stephen Heath, eds. 1980. *The Cinematic Apparatus*. Milwaukee: MacMillan Press.

Lebel, Jean-Patrick. 1971. *Cinéma et idéologie*. Paris: Editions Sociales.

Levin, Tom. 1984. "The Acoustic Dimension: Notes on Cinema Sound." *Screen* 25, no. 3: 55–68.

Leydon, Rebecca. 2004. "*Forbidden Planet*: Effects and Affects in the Electro Avant-garde." In *Off the Planet: Music, Sound and Science Fiction Cinema*, edited by Philip Hayward, 61–76. Eastleigh: John Libbey.

London, Kurt. 1936. *Film Music: A Summary of the Characteristic Features of its History, Aesthetics, Technique, and Possible Developments*. Translated by Eric S. Bensinger. London: Faber and Faber.

McGowan, Todd. 2003. "Looking for the Gaze: Lacanian Film Theory and Its Vicissitudes." *Cinema Journal* 42, no. 3: 27–47.

——. 2007. *The Real Gaze: Film Theory after Lacan*. Albany: SUNY Press.

Metz, Christian. 1982. *The Imaginary Signifier: Psychoanalysis and the Cinema*. Bloomington: Indiana University Press. Originally published in 1977 as *Le Signifiant imaginaire : psychanalyse et cinéma*. Paris: Union générale d'éditions.

Mitchell, Juliet. 1982. "Introduction—I." Translated by Celia Britton, Annwyl Williams, Ben Brewster, and Alfred Guzzetti. In *Feminine Sexuality: Jacques Lacan and the école freudienne*, edited by Juliet Mitchell and Jacqueline Rose, 1–26. New York: W. W. Norton.

——, and Jacqueline Rose, eds. 1982. *Feminine Sexuality: Jacques Lacan and the école freudienne*. New York: W. W. Norton.

Mulvey, Laura. 1975. "Visual Pleasure and Narrative Cinema." *Screen* 16, no. 3: 6–18.

Oudart, Jean-Pierre. 1977–1978. "Cinema and Suture." *Screen* 18, no. 4: 35–47. Originally published in *Cahiers du cinéma* 211 (1969): 35–39 and 212 (1969): 50–55.

Pleynet, Marcelin, and Jean Thibaudeau. 1978. "Economic—Ideological—Formal." In *May '68 and Film Culture*, edited by Sylvia Harvey, 149–164. London: British Film Institute. Originally published in *Cinéthique* 3 (1969): 7–14.

Prince, Stephen. 1996. "Psychoanalytic Film Theory and the Problem of the Missing Spectator." In *Post-Theory:Reconstructing Film Studies*, edited by David Bordwell and Noël Carroll, 71–86. Madison: University of Wisconsin Press.

Rosen, Philip, ed. 1986. *Narrative, Technology, Ideology*. New York: Columbia University Press.

Rothman, William. 1975. "Controversy and Correspondence: Against 'The System of the Suture.'" *Film Quarterly* 29, no. 1: 45–50.

Sabaneev, Leonid. 1935. *Music for the Films*. Translated by S. W. Pring. London: Pitman.

Salecl, Renata, and Slavoj Žižek, eds. 1996. *Gaze and Voice as Love Objects*. Durham: Duke University Press.

Silverman, Kaja. 1983. *The Subject of Semiotics*. New York: Oxford University Press.

——. 1988. *The Acoustic Mirror: The Female Voice in Psychoanalysis and Cinema*. Bloomington: Indiana University Press.

Smith, Jeff. 1996. "Unheard Melodies? A Critique of Psychoanalytic Theories of Film Music." In *Post-Theory:Reconstructing Film Studies*, edited by David Bordwell and Noël Carroll, 230–247. Madison: University of Wisconsin Press.

Wierzbicki, James. 2002. "Weird Vibrations: How the Theremin Gave Musical Voice to Hollywood's Extraterrestrial 'Others.'" *Journal of Popular Film and Television* 30, no. 3: 125–135.

Williams, Alan. 1980. "Is Sound Recording Like a Language?" *Yale French Studies* 60: 51–66.

Žižek, Slavoj. 1991a. *Looking Awry: An Introduction to Jacques Lacan through Popular Culture*. Cambridge, MA: MIT Press.

——. 1991b. "Grimaces of the Real, or When the Phallus Appears." *October* 58: 44–68.

——. 1996. "'I Hear You with My Eyes'; or, the Invisible Master." In *Gaze and Voice as Love Objects*, edited by Renata Saleci and Slavoj Žižek, 90–126. Durham: Duke University Press.

——. 2001. *The Fright of Real Tears: Krzystof Kieślowski between Theory and Post-Theory*. London: BFI.

——. 2006. "Against the Popular Temptation." *Critical Inquiry* 32, no. 3: 551–574.

——. 2010. *Living in the End Times*. London: Verso.

CHAPTER 16

....

CASE
STUDIES: INTRODUCTION

....

ROBYNN STILWELL

THE *Oxford English Dictionary* defines a case study as "the attempt to understand a particular person, institution, society, etc., by assembling information about his or its development; the record of such an attempt." The term has its roots in the studies of psychology and law. In the present, case studies provide the research methodology for a great deal of the social and life sciences, but the practice is also common in the humanities, where a case study is an in-depth examination of a single text: a book, a painting, a piece of music, a film. The part about "assembling information about...its development," however, means that a case study must encompass more than the single text, recognizing its sources as well as how the text channels its influences.

Case studies are thus the building blocks of a discipline. They lay the foundation for our understanding of how the field operates.

The analysis that grounds case studies can also be intellectually engaging. Like a gardener digging into the soil or a sculptor or dressmaker feeling out materials, sinking one's analytical fingers into a film or other text can be deeply rewarding. And there is no doubt that there is a certain amount of performance in any case study: some can be dutiful recitations, but others are analytical fantasias, rooted in the material of the subject text, but also bearing the distinct fingerprints of the interpreter.

Case studies are also teaching tools, often the best. Students are generally drawn to study film because they like movies. The case study (for the most seasoned scholar, as well as the neophyte student) recapitulates the experience of encountering a film, understanding how we react to it, why we like what we do, why we dislike what we do, even why we may come to love something that initially strikes us as overly conventional or wrong or just awkward. The puzzle-solving can be pleasurable in itself.

Doing case studies would thus seem to be a patently fundamental project, but, nevertheless, the need for and value of case studies in the humanities does occasionally come into question. The reasons can range from the idea that any one text does not really tell us anything about the field in isolation, to the faintly puritanical suspicion that doing case studies is somehow self-indulgent on the part of the analyst (or, to round back to the first objection, too trivial).

The objection that doing a case study somehow isolates and abstracts the object of study is negated by most case studies, and especially by the good ones: whether one is looking at an illness, a criminal case, or a creative text like a film, it is only in the individual instance that we gather the information we need to understand both the instance and its context. The diagnosis of an illness demands a medical history; the legal process demands motive, evidence, and a framework of legal precedent; a creative text's meanings emerge in the nexus of an almost infinite number of texts already created, performed, and recalled. A case study can be an anchor, a starting point from which to explore issues that are particularly well represented in a single text. At the same time, a case study can also be a window, a way of looking out on a field, letting us frame a circumscribed but meaningful cross-section of information. And, too, it is no more partial to study a single text with many aspects than to study a single aspect across many texts— we need both, even if the latter may seem somehow more theoretically and analytically elevated.

Without case studies, expansive theorizing can be a little like putting on the roof before the foundation is laid. The best theory is based on a solid foundation of repertoire, built up with a framework of analytical modes. Some of these theories are vertical, rooted firmly in the foundation of individual case studies; some of them are horizontal, like auteur theory or genre study that cut across a number of films. The best can do both: for example, Peter Franklin's analysis of Ann Darrow's voice in *King Kong* not only illuminates the workings of that specific film, but also opens out to the horror genre; eventually, her voice becomes a metaphor for the place of film music in classical Hollywood film (Franklin 2001).

In one of the most influential essays on film (if not *the* most influential), Laura Mulvey famously put into words the common feeling that analyzing an artwork—like dissecting a living creature—destroys its beauty (Mulvey 1975). I remember hearing this assertion when I was a very green freshman at a university School of Music, encountering the academic study of music for the first time. It seemed plausible, until I took my first music history course and discovered that—for me, at least—this was the furthest thing from the truth. Understanding how musical grammar and syntax could create affect provoked more wonder than deflation. When, for example, in the final movement of the Ninth Symphony, Beethoven sets "vor Gott" to a move from tonic to ♭VI, the description by itself seems so dry and mathematical; but that progression will never not raise the hairs on the back of my neck, never not make me feel as if the floor were dropping out from under me—never not give me, as an atheist-leaning agnostic, a sense of what it might feel like to stand "before God." And that sensation was all the more amazing because it was such a simple thing to do, not at all outside the realm of traditional major-minor harmony.

Mulvey set out to analyze the place of women in classical Hollywood cinema precisely because she wanted to destroy those films' ability to generate pleasure at the expense of women's agency and even bodily integrity. However genuinely revolutionary and even necessary her desire to tear down the Hollywood process as an independent feminist filmmaker in the 1970s, Mulvey's own work since her seminal article demonstrates the pull of the case study. Her concentration on performance in the Douglas Sirk remake of *Imitation of Life* is multilayered, interleaving class and race and motherhood: Hollywood star Lana Turner's performance as actress Lora is placed in a matrix with the performance of white actress Susan Kohner as the young African American Sarah Jane passing as white, where Sarah Jane's black mother, Annie, allows Lora to pursue her career as an actress by relieving her of the labor of housekeeping and child-rearing. The juxtaposition to the 1934 film version of the same novel highlights changes in the place of women and of race in the intervening quarter-century: in the earlier version, the white woman literally uses the image and labor of the black woman to succeed (she markets the woman's pancake recipe with an image strongly reminiscent of "Aunt Jemima"); in 1959, this exploitative relationship is transformed into something more covert and complex, a masquerade, or performance, on the original, more overt exploitation (Mulvey 1996). A frame-by-frame viewing of the opening moments of the film reveals a young black woman, lost in the flash of a camera aimed at white-clad, bleached-blonde Lana Turner. Turner's Lora bumps into the photographer, initiating what becomes a romantic relationship, but at the same time preventing him from repeating the photograph with the second subject. That moment of eclipse/occlusion encapsulates the theme of the film in a moment that most will never see except subliminally, yet it is the sort of detail that one would never find in anything *but* a close reading—indeed, as Mulvey points out, it is only available to audiences since the advent of home video, a new form of spectatorship (Mulvey 2006). This intimate relationship with the text is what the case study not only demands but also offers.

Music often plays a pivotal role in our experience of a film, and the explosion of the field of film music studies in the past couple of decades, both in publication and education, is proof of the interest in and power of music in film. It is more obvious than ever that a film score is not just music that happens to go along with a film. Even if it does not seem to "fit," that "mismatch" is something to explore. How does the music relate to the images, narrative, even color schemes and set design? Does the score try to draw us in with emotive leitmotifs, or is it a comment on the film itself, standing slightly aloof and encouraging us to do the same? Are the conditions of the production (Hollywood studio product, low-budget independent, polemical documentary) relevant? Of course they are. So, how? Here is a simple, but potent example: John Carpenter's driving 5/4 motif played on a relatively cheap synthesizer for the low-budget horror film *Halloween* (1978) is a classic example of music created in extremely restrictive circumstances that fulfilled its function of obsessive tension-building in large part *because* of the limitations. Industrial history is a constant, if at times submerged, element of film history. This shift in industrial structure coincided with the emerging music-video aesthetic from popular music and television (*Miami Vice, Moonlighting*, for instance) and created a productive resonance.

The two case studies presented in Chapter 17 and Chapter 18 below are exemplary not just in the superlative sense, but also in the literal sense. They are examples of "how to," models of not only going deep into but widely out from a film text, even though they are quite different in both subject matter and approach.

Mitchell Morris's study of Cecil B. DeMille's *The Ten Commandments* takes us back over half a century to the Biblical epic of the end of the Hollywood studio system and a shift in the place of religion in postwar American culture. DeMille's monumental style had been established already in the silent era (during which he had directed an earlier version of *The Ten Commandments* [1923]) and was derived from the popular art of Maxfield Parrish and the theatrical productions of David Belasco, who was known for marshaling technology in aid of "naturalism," or at least the representation of naturalism. As Morris's essay traces, DeMille's style had gone from representing "naturalism," to seeming old-fashioned, to acquiring a patina of authenticity through its familiarity. Elmer Bernstein's music, both the source music for which he was originally hired, and the underscore, is the frame for a naturalistic representation that the audience will accept as real because of its recognizability.

The careful, painterly constructions of *The Ten Commandments* contrast sharply with the vertiginous fragmentations of time and space in *12 Monkeys*. Julie McQuinn explores the ways in which Terry Gilliam's film questions and collapses the borders between madness and sanity, the real and the artificial, truth and fantasy. Unlike Bernstein's architectural frame, over which DeMille's cinematic canvas is stretched, the compilation score of *Twelve Monkeys*—composed of quotation, recomposition, and disintegrating loops—opens up spaces in which timelines converge and collapse: the atrium of a department store echoes with Christmas music, a relic of the past and/or an underscore to a memory; a movie theater foyer is the setting for an awkward recreation of an iconic movie scene, its awkwardness not only apparent in comparison to the "original," but drawing out the awkwardness in the original. Music, one of the most potent cues for memory, is a pivot point for recollection, nostalgia, and delusion.

Although the two authors were working independently, the richness of their work also brought up similarities that probably never would have emerged had the films been approached from a "theory first" perspective: for instance, both *The Ten Commandments* and *12 Monkeys* play heavily on conventions of previous media—Belasco theaters for the former, a welter of mid-century forms like cartoons, television commercials, and Hollywood movies for the latter. In both cases, the directors have distinct authorial fingerprints—a tactile metaphor for the stylistic traits of these auteurs who are both known for the epic sweep of their cinematic eyes and ears. Both DeMille and Gilliam, in these films in particular, intentionally use rich fields of sound and vision to overwhelm the audience, to create a sense of wonder and/or disorientation. Tellingly, in *The Ten Commandments*, this overwhelming of the audience is to foster the sense that what they are seeing is "the truth"; in *12 Monkeys*, it is to make them question what "the truth" is.

One of the satisfyingly productive characteristics of case studies is that no one analysis will do everything. Some, if not most, texts will bear revisiting on multiple occasions, so no film has ever really been "done." One analyst's work might well open up a gap that another analyst had not noticed was there, leading to further study, and one analysis will build on another—Mulvey's work on the 1959 *Imitation of Life*, for instance, draws on Lauren Berlant's study of the 1934 version (Berlant 1991), and that is only one, simple example among many. Every analyst is different, but so is every film, and it is often exciting to let the film lead us, letting us respond to the themes, ellipses, and juxtapositions that each will offer. And if we are to proceed to more abstract theory, we really need to lay the foundation, brick by case-study brick. In order to understand how film works, we first have to understand how films work.

BIBLIOGRAPHY (1): WORKS CITED

Berlant, Lauren. 1991. "National Brands/National Body: Imitation of Life." In *Comparative American Identities: Race, Sex, and Nationality in the Modern Text*, edited by Hortense J. Spillings, 110–140. New York: Routledge.

Franklin, Peter. 2001. "*King Kong* and Film on Music: Out of the Fog." In *Film Music: Critical Approaches*, edited by Kevin J. Donnelly, 88–102. Edinburgh: Edinburgh University Press.

Mulvey, Laura. 1975. "Visual Pleasure and Narrative Cinema." *Screen* 16, no. 3: 6–18.

——. 1996. "Chapter 2, Social Hieroglyphics: Reflections on Two Films by Douglas Sirk." In *Fetishism and Curiosity*, 29–39. Bloomington: Indiana University Press.

——. 1996. "Chapter 8: Delaying Cinema". In *Death 24x a Second: Stillness and the Moving Image*, 144-60. London: Reaktion Books.

BIBLIOGRAPHY (2): SELECTED CASE STUDY EXEMPLARS

Brown-Montesano, Kristi A. 2003. "*Pathétique* Noir: Beethoven and *The Man Who Wasn't There*." *Beethoven Forum* 10, no. 2: 139–161.

Buhler, James. 2000. "Star Wars, Music, and Myth." In *Music and Cinema*, edited by James Buhler, Caryl Flinn, and David Neumeyer, 33–57. Hanover, NH: University Press of New England.

Citron, Marcia J. 2004. "Operatic Style and Structure in Coppola's '*Godfather* Trilogy'." *Musical Quarterly* 87, no. 3: 423–467.

Citron, Marcia J. 2008. " 'An Honest Contrivance': Opera and Desire in *Moonstruck*." *Music & Letters* 89, no. 1: 56–83.

Fisher, Alexander. 2009. "Med Hondo's *Sarraounia*: The Musical Articulation of Cultural Transformation." *Music, Sound, and the Moving Image* 3, no. 2: 195–213.

Franke, Lars. 2006. "*The Godfather Part III*: Film, Opera, and the Generation of Meaning." In *Changing Tunes: The Use of Pre-existing Music in Film*, edited by Phil Powrie and Robynn Stilwell, 31–45. Aldershot, UK, and Burlington, VT: Ashgate.

Franklin, Peter. 2001. "*Deception*'s Great Music: A Cultural Analysis." In *Film Music II*, edited by Claudia Gorbman and Warren Sherk, 169–198. Sherman Oaks, CA: Film Music Society.

Gabbard, Krin. 2001. "Borrowing Black Masculinity: The Role of Johnny Hartman in *The Bridges of Madison County*." In *Soundtrack Available: Essays on Film and Popular Music*, edited by Pamela Robertson Wojcik and Arthur Knight, 295–318. Durham, NC: Duke University Press.

Jenkins, Jennifer R. 2011. " 'You want a love that's truly true'? Looking Back at Orpheus in *A Star Is Born*." *Music and the Moving Image* 4, no. 1: 1–8.

Joe, Jeongwon. 2006. "Reconsidering *Amadeus*: Mozart as Film Music." In *Changing Tunes: Issues in Music and Film*, edited by Phil Powrie and Robynn Stilwell, 57–73. Aldershot, UK, and Burlington, VT: Ashgate.

Knee, Adam. 2001. "Class Swings: Music, Race, and Social Mobility in *Broken Strings*." In *Soundtrack Available: Essays on Film and Popular Music*, edited by Pamela Robertson Wojcik and Arthur Knight, 269–294. Durham, NC: Duke University Press.

Kramer, Lawrence. 2007. "Melodic Trains: Music in Polanski's *The Pianist*." In *Beyond the Soundtrack: Representing Music in Cinema*, edited by Daniel Goldmark, Lawrence Kramer, and Richard Leppert, 66–85. Berkeley: University of California Press.

Leppert, Richard. 2007. "Opera, Aesthetic Violence, and the Imposition of Modernity: *Fitzcarraldo*." In *Beyond the Soundtrack: Representing Music in Cinema*, edited by Daniel Goldmark, Lawrence Kramer, and Richard Leppert, 99–119. Berkeley: University of California Press.

Lerner, Neil. 2005. " 'Look at that Big Hand Move Along': Clocks, Containment, and Music in *High Noon*." *South Atlantic Quarterly* 104, no. 1: 151–173.

Liang, Dong. 2007. "Marguerite Duras's Aural World: A Study of the *Mise-en-son* of *India Song*." *Music, Sound, and the Moving Image* 1, no. 2: 123–139.

Magee, Gayle Sherwood. 2008. "Song, Genre, and Transatlantic Dialogue in *Gosford Park*." *Journal of the Society for American Music* 2, no. 4: 477–505.

Martin, Ruth Lee. 2011. "Framing Ambiguity and Desire through Musical Means in Sally Potter's Film *Orlando*." *Music, Sound, and the Moving Image* 5, no. 1: 25–37.

Morris, Mitchell. 2007a. "In Marginal Fashion: Sex, Drugs, Russian Modernism, and New Wave Music in *Liquid Sky*." In *Composing for the Screen in the USSR and Germany*, edited by Robynn J. Stilwell and Phil Powrie, 161–177. Bloomington: Indiana University Press.

Pekkilä, Erkki. 2007. "Stardom, Genre, and Myth: Music in Aki Kaurismäki's Film *The Man Without a Past*." In *Essays on Sound and Vision*, edited by John Richardson and Stan Hawkins, 155–174. Helsinki: Helsinki University Press.

Radigales, Jaume. 2010. "Music and European Identity: Notes on Pere Portabella's *The Silence Before Bach*." *Music, Sound, and the Moving Image* 4, no. 2: 213–224.

Ramaeker, Paul B. 2001. " 'You Think They Call Us Plastic Now...': The Monkees and *Head*." In *Soundtrack Available: Essays on Film and Popular Music*, edited by Pamela Robertson Wojcik and Arthur Knight, 74–104. Durham, NC: Duke University Press.

Stilwell, Robynn J. 1997. " 'I just put a drone under him...': Collage and Subversion in the Score of *Die Hard*." *Music & Letters* 78, no. 4: 551–574.

——. 1997. "Symbol, Narrative, and the Musics of *Truly, Madly, Deeply*." *Screen* 38, no. 1: 60–75.

——. 2000. "*Sense & Sensibility*: Form, Function, and Genre in the Film Score." *Acta Musicologica* 72, no. 2: 219–240. A version (2004) of this article for non-music specialists was published as "*Sense & Sensibility*: Musical Form and Drama in the Film Adaptation." In *Film Music II*, edited by Claudia Gorbman and Warren Sherk, 169–198. Sherman Oaks, CA: Film Music Society.

Van der Merwe, Ann. 2010. "Music, the Musical, and Postmodernism in Baz Luhrmann's *Moulin Rouge*." *Music and the Moving Image* 3, no. 3: 31–38.

Volker, Reimar. 2007. "Herbert Windt's Film Music to *Triumph of the Will*: Ersatz-Wagner or Incidental Music to the Ultimate Nazi-*Gesamtkunsterk*?" In *Composing for the Screen in the USSR and Germany*, edited by Robynn J. Stilwell and Phil Powrie, 39–53. Bloomington: Indiana University Press.

Wierzbicki, James. 2003. "Grand Illusion: The 'Storm Cloud' Music in Hitchcock's *The Man Who Knew Too Much*." *Journal of Film Music* 1, nos. 2/3: 217–238.

CHAPTER 17

....

THE ORDER OF
SANCTITY: SOUND, SIGHT,
AND SUASION IN *THE TEN*
COMMANDMENTS

....

MITCHELL MORRIS

Is Cecil B. DeMille's 1956 epic *The Ten Commandments* actually still a film? More than fifty years have passed since its release, and in that time it has become less a film than an institution. For many years, small-scale screenings were a centerpiece of Protestant fund-raising alongside bake sales, car washes, and chicken dinners. Beginning in 1973, the film became a notable feature of ABC's Easter/Passover programming, and the seasonal viewing has almost seemed in some parts of the United States to be like a religious rite in itself. A number of the most vivid moments and characters in *The Ten Commandments* have also led a richly varied parodic life in later films and TV programming, not to mention the more casual parodies that seem to have proliferated in everyday life—notably, of Charlton Heston's Moses, Yul Brynner's Rameses, and of course, Anne Baxter's gloriously stylized Nefretiri—a sure testimony to the original's effectiveness.

Moreover, the devotional appeal of DeMille's film was always explicitly melded with an intensely conservative political worldview that has provided a moderate but persistent amount of emotional energy to the ongoing debates about the role of religion in American civic life. The Supreme Court case *Van Orden v. Perry* (2005) concerned the public display of a Ten Commandments momument donated to the State of Texas by the Fraternal Order of Eagles with the support of Cecil B. DeMille. There had been in fact a substantial number of such monuments created as high-profile donations, perhaps the most grandiose part of Paramount's huge publicity campaign for the picture. The display of the monument on the state capitol grounds in Austin, Texas (the object of this specific case), was held constitutional by a vote of 5 to 4.[1] *The Ten Commandments* continues to resonate in contemporary culture, whether its presence is recognized or not.

Outlining the history of this kind of cultural influence, however, offers no immediate answer to the opening question. Again, does (or can) DeMille's final work actually matter nowadays as a film? Is it not possible that its devotional and political elements, so ostentatiously foregrounded in sight, word, and deed, simply overwhelm its aesthetic qualities? Is it not possible that the continuing presence of *The Ten Commandments* in twenty-first-century America comes from its usefulness as advertising—or propaganda, whichever term you prefer—rather than from the more abstract pleasures of viewing and hearing the film in itself? I think this is not true; at least, it need not be true, but the film's religious and social impact and its formal design—most saliently including its expertly crafted music—are inextricable, and they raise enduring questions about how the sundry worlds of art and life collide, overlap, and intertwine.

Let the dance around the Golden Calf, the final crisis of the picture's narrative, serve as an exemplary case. DeMille had declared that he wanted this film to be something that could be shown in a parish hall, but even so, he was extremely partial to dramatic moments of lewdness. In this matter he was at one with his presumed audience; as the history of the moral panics surrounding Hollywood reveals, what was most intolerable to would-be censors was not unacceptable conduct in itself, but the possibility that it would be shown without sufficiently vigorous condemnation. Although DeMille had long been criticized for filming scenes suggesting all kinds of sexual mischief, but then always framing them with pompous moralizing that never quite covered a prurient core, this was not as great a concern among general audiences as it was among professional critics and other urbanites. Probably most viewers, pro or con, realized that DeMille's disapproval was mostly an alibi, allowing them to enjoy the spread of succulent flesh without feeling personally contaminated by the richly depicted sin.

In the filming of this dance, however, the challenge of creating the effect of depravity without actually showing any of it was simply too much for DeMille to manage; he had enormous trouble getting what he wanted. Filming of the riot around the Golden Calf ran on and on. DeMille's temper finally broke, and he lambasted his cast one day, concluding: "Moses bringing the tablets down at the end of this orgy is the climax of our picture—and everyone looks like they're going on a Sunday school social!" In exasperation, he turned back to his older manner and brought in a set of exotic dancers (that is, strippers) to heat up the crowd's blocking, filming the whole thing as if it were a silent movie, with music played on the set to coordinate the action.[2] It was at that point that crowd sounds could be reintroduced, DeMille's grandiose voiceover could be folded in, and Elmer Bernstein could intervene with a boisterous number chock-full of orientalist decorations, familiar Hollywood musical material largely drawn out of the Ballets russes stylebook, thus enabling them to be immediately legible to the audience as markers of old-fashioned sexual excess. Together with the silent film histrionics, the score created the necessary orgiastic impression and DeMille's narration created the distance that freed the scene from any risk of censorly reproach. If it seems harmless enough to present-day eyes, our representational customs have admittedly shifted vastly since DeMille's time.

The account of DeMille's painstaking work on this scene is one of a huge array of anecdotes documenting his ambitions surrounding the production of *The Ten Commandments*. DeMille quite clearly meant his film to be much more than a financially successful Hollywood epic. To begin with, it was in part a remake of his celebrated silent film of 1923, which, in a manner reminiscent of films like Griffith's *Intolerance*, cut between ancient history and modern times, contrasting the sublime spectacle of Moses's lawgiving (plus an eventual New Testament supplement) with a contemporary good son/bad son tale, in the sentimental style that both Griffith and DeMille favored. The 1956 version certainly courted public recollections of the old silent film, but it was planned to be a much bigger production, and the details of its planning as well as its execution illuminate many of the crucial cultural issues at stake.

DeMille's Agenda

The film's political and religious work is foregrounded by DeMille himself. After the brief overture—a lush, late-Romantic potpourri sounding from behind the jewel-colored simulacrum of an embossed leather book cover—the film cuts to a stage whose silver and gold traveler curtain is drawn. Mr. DeMille emerges from behind this curtain, dapper, balding, bespectacled, the possessor of a voice that had become instantly recognizable thanks to years of radio broadcasts; he steps up to the microphone awaiting him, then begins to orate, adroitly presenting the crucial points of his film (transcription is mine):

> Ladies and Gentlemen, young and old—This may seem an unusual procedure, speaking to you before the picture begins. But we have an unusual subject: the story of the Birth of Freedom, the story of Moses. As many of you know, the Holy Bible omits some thirty years of Moses' life: from the time he was a three-month old baby, and was found in the bulrushes by Bithiah, the daughter of Pharaoh, and adopted into the court of Egypt, until he learned that he was Hebrew, and killed the Egyptian. To fill in those missing years, we turn to ancient historians such as Philo and Josephus. Philo wrote at the time that Jesus of Nazareth walked the earth; and Josephus wrote some fifty years later, and watched the destruction of Jerusalem by the Romans. These historians had access to documents long-since destroyed, or perhaps lost, like the Dead Sea Scrolls.
> The theme of this picture is whether men are to be ruled by God's Law, or whether they are to be ruled by the whims of a dictator like Rameses. Are men the property of the State, or are they free souls under God? This same battle continues throughout the world today. Our intention was not to create a story, but to be worthy of the divinely-inspired story created three thousand years ago in the Five Books of Moses. The story takes 3 hours and 39 minutes to unfold. There will be an intermission. Thank you for your attention.

The political message might seem to take almost no unpacking at all: this is an obvious Cold War narrative, with Moses and the recalcitrant Children of Israel standing in for the "free world," especially the United States, and Rameses occupying the unfortunate position of Stalin (who was only three years' dead at the time of the film's release). In characteristic fashion for the period, "the State" is carefully opposed to "God's Law" (the capitalization is mine, but it follows DeMille's delivery).[3]

The anticommunism in the film's message was all the more upfront because of DeMille's long-standing, vehemently public dedication to reactionary politics, most infamously in his outspoken support of McCarthy, his reports on suspected communists to the FBI, and his high-profile struggles to require film directors to take the loyalty oaths instituted in the Taft-Hartley Act of 1947. But in fact, DeMille's political program, as significant as its influence has turned out to be, is a subordinate aspect of his film's preface: the evocation of the Cold War occurs near the end of the oration, and then almost as a passing thought. The majority of DeMille's speech demonstrates that the principal anxieties of this film are centrally religious, and at the core, conservative Protestant—deeply anti-Communist and pro-business, to be sure, but nevertheless preoccupied with characteristically turn of the century Protestant concerns.

HISTORY AND THE BIBLE

Chief among those concerns was the historical specificity and plain-text accuracy of the Bible—not the entire Bible in this case, but specifically the origin-stories found in Genesis and Exodus. Since the late seventeenth century, a number of scholars and philosophers had begun to question the ancient traditions shared by all three of the Abrahamic religions attributing the Torah to Moses himself. Using the scholarly tools developed earlier for the interpretation and emendation of Greek and Latin texts, a group of Biblical researchers came to argue that the extant texts of the Pentateuch (as Christians had traditionally called the Torah) were not single-authored, but rather a conflation of texts brought together by redactors. The attempt to distinguish between the Torah's various authors became known as "Higher Criticism," with the term "Lower Criticism" referring to the practice of recognizing and emending textual corruptions as well as commenting on obscure details of historical reference.

The classic formulation of the Higher Criticism was created by the German scholar Julius Wellhausen (1844–1918), who synthesized the existing scholarship in what is now known as the Documentary Hypothesis.[4] Wellhausen attempted to sort out the strands of writing that were compiled to create the Torah through a careful philologically based reading of the biblical texts. The characteristic diction of the various strands, their varying assumptions about such matters as the proper locations and personnel of ceremonies and sacrificial offerings, the timing and ritual conduct of seasonal feasts, the constitution and prerogatives of the priesthood, and a host of divergent details in their narratives—all were assembled to support the argument that the Torah had at least four authors or sources. The complex multiwriter textual history of the Torah was also said to be characteristic of the rest of the Hebrew Bible. In New Testament scholarship, the application of methods from the Higher Criticism yielded a complicated set of possible sources, traditions, and authors—and provoked vigorous disputes about them. Further muddying the waters were a variety of apocryphal and variant texts that were increasingly difficult for philologically minded scholars to ignore.

None of this was good news from the point of view of traditionalist Jews or Christians. The accretionary process described by scholars such as Wellhausen, by rejecting the tradition of Moses's single authorship, also seemed to diminish the divine authority of the text. The histories of creation seemed questionably authored in many situations; the histories of canonization seemed equally dubious at times. Where, in such a hotchpotch of authors and points of view, was there room for unambiguous Divine Truth? For Protestants, in particular, this was a terrible problem, since the sixteenth-century reformers had dismissed as unnecessary (when not positively harmful) the layers of commentary and tradition that characterized Catholicism and Orthodoxy, and for that matter, Rabbinic Judaism and most schools of Islam. *Sola scriptura* had been a powerful rallying cry for Protestants. But what happens when that very scripture solely to be depended upon comes into question?

The Higher Criticism also raised difficult questions about translation *versus* tradition. The year 1881 saw the release of the Revised Version of the New Testament, the work of an Anglo-American interdenominational panel of scholars and theologians that used recent discoveries and advances in textual criticism to correct numerous errors found in the Authorized or King James Version (KJV). The New Testament was followed in 1885 by the Old Testament and in 1895 by the Apocrypha. This edition came to be known as the English Revised Version; the American Standard Version appeared in 1901. Together, the new translations marked the first time that the authority of the KJV had been challenged.[5] In the United States, the American Standard Version was worrisome to conservatives, but the challenge to the KJV became much more serious with the publication of the Revised Standard Version (RSV) in the late 1940s and early 1950s. Although these extended projects of revision had taken place in a hopeful atmosphere of ecumenical outreach, intellectual seriousness, and evangelical optimism, the reception of the English and American Standards proved otherwise: they set the tone for increasing resistance to an increasing array of versions.[6]

The difficulties fell into two main spheres, aesthetics and dogma, but it is arguable that aesthetic concerns were much more important to everyday readers. Few partisans of the RSV, for instance, could deny that its flat-footed style compared unfavorably with the elegant prose of the KJV, whose stylistic beauty was amplified by its ever-deepening patina of archaism. The devout and less devout alike had deeply internalized the cadences and diction of the KJV, and some advocates of the new translation saw the choice between versions as a distressing contest between Beauty and Truth. As the Anglican divine F. W. Farrar wrote: "Do we desire the *plain bare facts* of that which we call the Word of God, or do we desire *melodious glosses* and mistaken interpretations?" (quoted in Thuesen 1996, 614; my emphasis).

The expansion of the Higher Criticism alongside the newly released Bible translations was only one part of a larger set of disturbances within late nineteenth-century Protestantism. The anxieties posed by scientific advances—particularly Darwin's theory of natural selection, which was increasingly supported by fossil data—began to seem of a piece with the Wellhausenesque approach to Biblical authorship. "Liberal theology," which sought to modernize traditional Protestant practices and beliefs to meet contemporary culture, and the Social Gospel, with its emphasis on the improvement of everyday common life, were folded into the intellectual challenges presented by science and scholarship. In the wider social context of large-scale immigration to the United States, the depredations of unrestricted major capitalism, rapid population growth, the increasing public visibility and activity of women, and the disruptions of the Spanish-American War as well as the First World War, conservatively minded Protestants began to organize around what would soon be given the name Fundamentalism.

This movement took its name from *The Fundamentals*, a series of pamphlets, published between 1910 and 1915, outlining what conservative Protestants took to be the central points endangered by modernist Christianity: among these were the Virgin Birth and the orthodox interpretations of the Personhood of Christ and the nature of the Trinity, but increasingly the historical accuracy of the Bible as it relates to the "inerrancy" of Scripture became a much more fraught issue. Additional support for defenders of literal inerrancy came from the publication of the *Scofield Reference Bible* in 1909: this work comprised the text of the KJV with copious marginal annotations (including speculative dates for past and future Biblical events) and cross-references added by the American Bible student Cyrus I. Scofield, an ardent disciple of the premillennial dispensationalist John Nelson Darby. (Premillennial dispensationalism asserts that historical time can be divided by shifts in the mode of relationship between God and the human race. A carefully prepared and attentive reader can sift through the scriptural texts not only to analyze the past but also to prepare for the incipient apocalypse.)[7] The density of such writings at the beginning of the twentieth century constitute the framework around which Fundamentalist Protestantism began to organize itself.

In addition to defending traditional articles of faith, *The Fundamentals* took pains to scour contemporary life to find support for its views. Essays with titles such as "The Testimony of the Monuments to the Truth of the Scriptures" and "The Recent Testimony of Archaeology to the Scriptures" point to a final important development: the rise of Biblical archaeology. Most closely associated with the influential American scholar William F. Albright, this school of archaeology sought material evidence to support various historical accounts in the Bible. In Albright's terms, this was not a matter of denying Higher Criticism: instead, he assumed that the broadest historical outlines of the narratives in the Old Testament were correct, and he believed that excavations could offer valuable contexts for their understanding. Albright's scrupulous treatment of the Bible texts, however, was not usually transmitted to popular religious literature, where the tiniest material detail could be seized upon as proof of the Bible's accuracy. And the successes of archaeology in uncovering new information could at times be sensational indeed. The discovery of a stockpile of scrolls in caves near the ruins of Qumran in the late 1940s caused tremendous excitement, not only among archaeologists, religious historians, and textual critics, but also among the general public. Scholars were most interested in disentangling the complex world of the communities that produced these scrolls and in documenting the fascinating variants of scripture that they contained, but accounts for the general public tended to stress the tantalizing possibility that more "proof" of scriptural accuracy would be forthcoming. The unearthing of the Nag Hammadi library took place at roughly the same time, and although the texts were more relevant to the early history of Christianity, their description also amplified hopes of future revelatory Biblical documents to be uncovered.

The Bible and *The Ten Commandments*

The literal historical veracity of Scripture—"the divinely inspired story created three thousand years ago in the Five Books of Moses"—is precisely what DeMille's address is meant to affirm, melding Biblical archaeology to Biblical literalism in an ornate KJV ambience congruent with the tone and intent of *The Fundamentals*. When DeMille offers up the names of Philo and Josephus, he invokes the non-Scriptural writers most likely to be familiar to his audiences; his mention of the Dead Sea Scrolls is a reference to something likely to be even more present in the minds of an audience in 1956, since popularizing accounts of that find were abundant.

This defense of Scripture is merged with DeMille's spectacular ballyhoo in the opening credits, which I reproduce here in the approximate form they appear onscreen after the main credits.

Those who see this motion picture—

Produced and Directed

By

CECIL B. DEMILLE

—will make a pilgrimage over the very ground

that Moses trod more than 3,000 years ago—

* * * * *

In accordance with the ancient texts of—
    Philo
        Josephus
            Eusebius
                The Midrash
                    and—

* * * * *

THE HOLY SCRIPTURES

Sensationalist, unquestionably. If the context were less determinedly reverential, this might seem so grandiose as to be parody. But no parody is intended, and in fact the film's loud claims to scholarship are not entirely wrong. Every plot point in the dramatic action can be defended by reference to one or another of the texts cited in the credits, as well as a few that do not appear there. Although three pious novels—*Prince of Egypt* by Dorothy Clarke Wilson, *Pillar of Fire* by the Reverend J. H. Ingraham, and *On Eagle's Wings* by the Reverend A. E. Southron—were also included in the credits, they seem to have served as imaginative springboards, to be supplemented by scholarly work. And DeMille was scrupulous in the breadth of his background research, which extended even to the Qur'an. An additional support for the research aspect of the film came with the publication of a book by Henry Noerdlinger titled *Moses and Egypt: The Documentation to the Motion Picture "The Ten Commandments"* (Noerdlinger 1956). This was not history in its usual sense—critics frowned upon Noerdlinger's indiscriminate and uncritical use of everything that could be found, reliable or not—but the capacious array of materials was great enough to overwhelm most general readers.

Even though the details of the plot clearly cost DeMille and his researchers the greatest anxiety, the film's serious antiquarian program is most heavily present in the film's extraordinary visual display. DeMille had after all apprenticed in the theater of David Belasco himself, and many of the tastes and values formed in those years remained with him throughout his life. He continued and in this case, amplified Belasco's interest in obsessively documented visual detailism as integral to his "stage" pictures. Such pictorial realism in the theater, commonly dated to Planché's historically researched costuming in the 1820s, had reached a sumptuous climax in the stage of Belasco's time, which saw an astonishing range of techniques used to create effects meant to be true as well as pleasing to the eye. As stylized as they may have been, they were used as a token of theatrical honesty, a promise of accurate representation, made from producer to audience. The suasive force of realness in this aesthetic contract depended upon the careful historical grounding of the specifics of costumes and props, with such research carefully balanced against the needs of stage pictures and the producer's sense of what was plausible for modern expectations.[8]

Likewise, DeMille's production of *The Ten Commandments* entailed a vast amount of painstaking work in getting the materials and their designs historically correct. Moses's emblematic robe, for instance, was dyed and hand-woven—at UCLA, moreover—to duplicate as closely as possible the most likely methods used in the time of Rameses the Great, whom DeMille's researchers had settled on as the Pharaoh of the historical Exodus. The multitudinous personal ornaments and architectural details were crafted after extensive research and consultation with authorities (hence the parade of museum professionals included in the credits). The concern with visual accuracy extended down to actorly bodies, so that it shaped casting decisions. Several accounts of the production have mentioned that Audrey Hepburn, who was DeMille's first choice as Nefretiri, was eventually surrendered because the necessary costumes simply looked wrong on her slight frame. In similar fashion, DeMille insisted on brown contact lenses for blue-eyed actors; his most notable exception to this was in the case of Yvonne De Carlo, whose eyes he thought so lovely that he would forgo the lenses. And with respect to crowd scenes, too, no detail was unattended; DeMille took pains to make sure that the extras were in some degree individualized, as if he were constructing a gigantic history painting in motion.

Such exquisite attention to authentic visual detail is central to what Belasco, and DeMille after him, meant by realism. When attention turned from the concrete particulars of an object to its impact on audiences, this interest in authenticity was always trumped in favor of emotional immediacy, but such flexibility did not destroy the continuing value of the aim. Audiences would prefer a degree of stylization. Belasco himself seems to have conceded that his brand of historicism had limits, that "the true realism . . . is to produce the realities of heart and mind," and observation of his practice indicates that such realities of interior experience were taken to be universals. Costumes were history; feelings were timeless. This dual focus also mattered in characterization: concerns with precise social description and dialogue were not of this stage—rather the opposite. Belasco had repeatedly expressed himself on these matters in typically vigorous terms. As late as 1917, he was still reciting his creed in newspaper interviews: "The American people as a race are melodramatic. . . . We feel love, hate, jealousy and revenge with an intensity so great that when these passions are expressed to us through any form of art they at once quicken our understanding and awaken our sympathy." Only one genre could be expected to reach an appropriate level of clarity and grandeur: "It is because melodrama handles the emotions without gloves that it stirs the latent bigness in each of us, grips our heartstrings and absorbs our interest as does no other form of play" (quoted in Bergman 1953, 111–12). DeMille himself seems never to have departed from Belasco's view. Within its intricate research-laden frame and its careful reference to ancient textual authorities, *The Ten Commandments* is a direct descendent of Belasco's theater. But this inheritance carries through into the film's larger sensibilities as well.

Visual Style

At the same time that the film wallows in gorgeous (but historically precise) material profusion, that profusion is stylized by the color and overall design of the stage pictures in which it appears. DeMille was enormously fond of late nineteenth-century artists whom we might regard as popular Pre-Raphaelites or Symbolists. That is, in his visual art he liked idealized figures, most often with mythical or legendary associations or foregrounded symbolic resonance, drawn with almost photographic exactitude, and painted in a luminous, vibrant style. The work of Maxfield Parrish, in particular, seemed to appeal to him, and DeMille was known for bringing in posters and reproductions to his art department, in particular to designer Arnold Friberg, to show them the kind of effects he wanted in the film. Friberg was a skilled commercial artist whom DeMille had found after an extended search; his training and experience as an illustrator suited DeMille's tastes perfectly (in addition to his formal study at the Art Institute of Chicago, Friberg had a brief set of lessons with Norman Rockwell in New York). In preparation for the filming, DeMille commissioned a suite of illustrative paintings. Thanks to widescreen Technicolor, the qualities that DeMille sought and Friberg assisted in realizing proved to be feasible: Parrish's intensely saturated, lush colors, achieved in painting by a technically dazzling virtuosity with transparent colored glazes, could be matched in nearly every frame of the film.

The connection to Parrish matters not least because at the beginning of the twentieth century, he was the most popular artist to be found in America. His posters and especially his book illustrations were pervasive.[9] By the middle of the twentieth century, however, Parrish's work had been relegated to the historical thrift store. Dated in style, sentimental in content, illustrations such as his were part of the undifferentiated wash of popular art: their descendants were showing up in Illustrated Bibles and record jackets. That is, they had rapidly achieved the sort of ubiquity that gave them an increasingly denatured, abstract visual tone suitable for framing DeMille's researched objects.

Likewise, the early film studios had striven to resemble the theater of their time, hoping to borrow from the older art's ability to marry glamour and elevation. Belasco's style had been imitated with particular intensity, and thus DeMille's predilections were directly in line with the hopes of studios as well as the expectations of their eager audiences.[10] Film aesthetics changed over the decades, of course—but DeMille's, in some central ways, did not. Already a bit fusty by the appearance of sound films, the older taste DeMille stood for remained so long as he continued to produce films, and his style eventually passed through obsolescence to acquire an aura of the legendary. This aura is crucial to the effect of the Golden Calf scene: the combination of sensation and sanctimony resonated with the manner and content of the Bible's disapproving descriptions—and exactly suited DeMille's literalist archaizing approach to the Biblical story of Moses.

Being just passé enough was an advantage in almost every aspect of the film's production. With the presumed factual accuracy of the story anchored in its scholarly seeming approach to ornament and decor as well as to historically plausible plot construction, other aspects of production could create its more universal or archetypal qualities. This sense of timeless truth depends on the curious way that the film's dated conventions, precisely because they *are* dated, point to the higher reality that they are held to embody through such obvious fictions. This is an old technique, not surprisingly. It was, for example, fundamental to pageants, which in the late nineteenth century often were grand ceremonial reenactments of historical events that incorporated part or all of their audiences. In their attempt to recreate historical memory in the service of a renewed common identity, pageants were in some sense allegorical. The present-day fiction by its very artifice pointed to a past reality that reciprocally underwrote the fiction.[11] Pageants were enormously popular in the period immediately before the First World War, and their notable success in drawing general audiences offered an obvious parallel to the new art of film. As one advocate of pageants pointed out, "it is not presuming on the relationship to say that the pageant is the cousin of the cinema,—an in-law cousin perhaps, but still a cousin. It shows action mainly and calls for a body of proletariat appreciators. It was this wide appeal that proved the pageant's main efficacy as a medium for community amusement and instruction" (Wright 1919, 163). The elevation of action over dialogue, not to mention the function of community amusement (in this case, edification) and instruction are good descriptions of dramaturgy and its aims in *The Ten Commandments*.

The film's heavy artifice, unquestionably within the range of the pageant style, is also apparent in the ways that the film's characters are realized. The antediluvian qualities of the script and blocking, for instance, are shaped by many of the actors in ways that foreground their actorly personae. Surely DeMille had an ear for dialogue that was truly awful, clunk and hysteria in alternation, resembling nothing so much as overwrought silent film title cards. The most floridly implausible lines in the screenplay tend to fall to Nefretiri and Dathan, that is, the femme fatale and the assistant villain in DeMille's melodramatic plot, and it matters that both roles are inhabited by performers who are gifted at playing *themselves* playing their roles. Anne Baxter's brilliant, tumultuously heaving Nefretiri is always "Anne Baxter as Nefretiri," exactly as her card in the credits says. Edward G. Robinson's Dathan is always "Edward G. [Little Caesar] Robinson as Dathan." Although Charlton Heston's Moses and Yul Brynner's Rameses do not effuse or scheme to the same degree, they too have plenty of doubtful lines, and once again it is their actor's persona that helps them manage the stagey dialogue. The foregrounded presence of recognizable actors in their roles carries down even into many minor parts, and DeMille's frequent recycling of his favorite performers gave those little cameos special appeal to the audiences who had seen his many films. The weight of these associations lie heavy on the film's characterization and dialogue, tending to slow the sense of the story's progress, and risking the possibility that an already long film (3 hours 39 minutes, as DeMille noted) would feel even longer.

MUSIC'S TASKS

The primary means of balancing all this weight of signification is the film's music, which received the same kind of attention DeMille lavished on the rest of the film. Originally, Victor Young had agreed to write the underscore and the young Elmer Bernstein was brought on to write the diegetic numbers, but Young, who was in declining health and unenthusiastic about working for DeMille again in any case, withdrew from the project, suggesting Bernstein be hired for the whole. This meant that DeMille spent large amounts of time in close discussion with Bernstein at all stages of the production. This relationship became Bernstein's model for collaboration, as he later stated:

> Ideally, the composer should be in on the filming from the start of production and be able to develop his concepts along with the director and the others, but this seldom happens. It did happen early in my film career with *The Ten Commandments* because DeMille liked to have his composers with him through the production. He had a solid sense of music and regarded it as a story-telling device, and he would discuss scenes in detail, seeking my advice on whether music was needed or not. (quoted in Thomas 1979, 159–60)

Bernstein's praise of DeMille is particularly worth remembering, coming as it does from a composer who had a most distinguished career: his later work included such important scores as *The Magnificent Seven* (1960) and *Thoroughly Modern Millie* (1967), down to *The Age of Innocence* (1993) and *Far From Heaven* (2002). But in the early 1950s, Bernstein's career was only beginning, and *The Ten Commandments* was just his fourth film score. DeMille heard Bernstein's first prepared number, the dance of Jethro's daughters, and liked it well enough to agree to take him on for the entire work; but he specifically requested a Wagnerian manner in the score. And so it was.

DeMille, when he invoked Wagner, meant the most obvious things. He expected that there would be leitmotifs and that Bernstein would range through various lofty musical states, from *religioso* through *nobilmente* to *grandioso* and back. Bernstein could easily oblige, and did so at several levels. At a few moments, for instance, he was apparently relaxed enough to give an overt Wagnerian wink: the infant Moses, first placed on the waters, drifts into the Nile with a tiny flourish from the primal Rhine; God's pillar of fire manifests in the sly form of a Valkyrie's whirring trill. More seriously, Bernstein's instances of musical reverence can take the form of sweet high strings with descending Parsifalian lines-with-suspensions. With respect to the character or situation themes DeMille ordered, Bernstein crafts motives that fall into three large categories: a complex of largely diatonic, martial melodies associated with Moses, the "God of Abraham" (the film's standard term), and the Exodus itself, with attendant Children of Israel; darker, often more chromatically inflected figures and Borodin-style orientalisms that accompany Rameses and the Egyptians, as well as Dathan; and voluptuous swoony chromatic lines that appear alongside Nefretiri. Figure 17.1 gives a representative sample of these leitmotifs.

As in most of Hollywood's derived Wagnerian practice, these motives slip usefully and interestingly around one another, acquiring additional connotations as the drama progresses by the way they are combined and the way their settings are transformed.[12] But the function of Bernstein's leitmotifs is primarily exterior: they do not offer themselves as revelations of interior states, but instead as part of the dramatic-affective action, especially as it fits into the flow of subjective time.

It is worth remembering that before Bernstein took on the task of the underscore, he had been hired to write the diegetic music, and that music also shows an interesting relationship with the rest of the production. There is in fact a substantial amount of it, but it appears mostly as backdrop. Almost every scene of Egyptian royal life has instrumentalists playing in the background, using archaeologically inspired models for lyres, harps, zithers, pipes, and percussion. Most of this music is extremely discreet, held in the background of the mise-en-bande; it is present not to perform any story-telling function, but to assist the construction of the scenic reality. (This is especially clear on the occasions when the musicians are dismissed onscreen.) In the same way, moments such as the song sung by Jethro's daughters at the well, or Lilia's private lament on Passover night serve as an index of their scenes' reality. More significant in the film's musical structure are the plethora of diegetic fanfares that punctuate the action by marking out ceremonial actions and speeches as well as, in the case of Joshua's horn, by interrupting an

FIGURE 17.1 a-f: *The Ten Commandments* (1956), leitmotifs (music transcribed from the soundtrack): (a) Exodus/Liberation/God; (b) Moses; (c) Egyptian oppression; (d) Dathan; (e) The Nile; (f) Nefretiri/Love.

ongoing frenzy. Their formal functions are nevertheless built on their identity as part of the film's historical realism: the visible appearance and use of shofars is only the most direct example of this.

Most interesting diegetically are the two dances that act as set-pieces. The first of these takes place at Sethi's court, just before Moses is revealed as a Hebrew and the prophesied Liberator. It is a general rule of *The Ten Commandments* (and many other films besides) that oriental musical motifs tend to be undifferentiated from archaic ones, and the court dance cue is marked by this coincidence. It is slightly heterophonic, limited in compass, and simple but spritely in its rhythmic motion. Here again, there is something resolutely archaeological about this moment: the music closely matches the dance, which in turn incorporates gestures modeled directly on the positions of dancers from tomb paintings. In this case, the authenticating function of the music moves further into the middleground of the filmic space, creating a pleasant, mildly erotic diversion that speaks to the gracefully un-Abrahamic moral atmosphere of Sethi's pagan court. (The dancers are presumably sexually available slave girls.)

The contrasting erotic display of the second dance is strongly foregrounded. A full-blooded archaic orientalism characterizes the dance of Jethro's six daughters, who appear before the sheiks of Midian in hopes that Moses will choose one of them as a wife—a monogamous wife, as the accompanying dialogue makes clear. This dance is the only point in the film where the performance is commanded: Jethro calls his men to "strike the bow," and they launch in quasi-unison into a sinuous tune featuring "un-Western," rather Locrian contours. A recollection of the barbaric splendors in Borodin's Polovetsian tents is not far off. (It is to be regretted that the music is imperfectly synced with the performers, and begins before the instruments are actually played onscreen, but the diegetic point is clear enough.) Again, the instruments are antiquarian renderings. The music, however, is much closer to the performers—we notice it much more—because it is part of the main action. Jethro's daughters, other than Sephora, have been portrayed as man-crazy, silly in the style familiar from turn-of-the-century popular-culture stereotypes of the old maid or the farmer's daughter; by the 1930s, Al Capp's Sadie Hawkins, from the popular comic strip *Lil' Abner*, would be the most immediate reference. Their dance is a giddy exhibition, safely chaste but more or less a belly dance, and Sephora's refusal to be "displayed like a caravan's wares" demonstrates the seriousness and self-respect that makes her convincing as Moses's eventual wife. No one in the audience is surprised when Moses balks at the choice he is offered in the tent and wanders off into the night to brood—where he will find Sephora against the backdrop of God's glowering Mount Sinai.

In addition to the dances, moments of protoliturgy occur diegetically. The various chants of the Egyptian priests are used like the background instrumental music to support the effect of authenticity. Chants by the Children of Israel, however, have a more important function: they are meant to foreshadow modern religious practice. During the tense Passover sequence, fragments of the Psalms appear as simple chants—they do not form part of a formal liturgy, but they seem to be tending in that direction. Indeed, the whole scene is constructed to give the effect of what will be the Pesach liturgy already coming into being. In the Exodus proper, the elders who carry the embalmed body of Joseph to be buried in Canaan sing what is to all intents and purposes a spiritual. The presence of an orientalizing augmented second in the melodies last phrase does nothing to conceal its close resemblance to "Go Down, Moses."

In keeping with his fundamentalist position on Scripture, DeMille presents later historical religious practice as an unfolding of what was present at the moment of origin, and the music, in both these cases, helps to foretell that present. The continuity denies the possibility that history—in the sense of particular, contingent changes over time— has any real bearing on the inner meaning of the story.

The film's underscore is not shaped by archaeological concerns. Indeed, its function is to confirm that continuity established more subtly in the diegetic chants. Wagnerian manner and all, the underscore aims for a kind of immediacy, a present-tense quality, that bridges the antiquarian gap to make the past into a (religious) modern-day experience. We might say that DeMille looked to "the Wagnerian" because he thought of it as a musical commonplace—a style that was elevated enough to establish the film's high seriousness but accessible enough to provide the equally necessary melodramatic power. If DeMille followed Belasco—as he surely did—in counting on the American taste for big feelings, a popular Wagnerism was the most plausible choice. Like Parrish and DeMille himself, Wagner was just passé enough to to have acquired a slight, usefully antique glaze.[13]

MUSIC AND THE TEMPORAL

Music's function of onscreen time management is almost as important as its rhetoric of immediacy in *The Ten Commandments*. This temporal role contrasts with its avoidance in situations of intense interpersonal engagement, for instance. When characters have very serious direct things to say to one another, they do it in musical silence. Awful moments, such as the massacre of the male infants of Israel, or Rameses's putting Nefretiri in her place, tend to be without music. If music does enter, it typically does so only after the crisis, the dramatic stroke. Yochabel, Moses's birth mother, acquires music only at the moment her belt becomes caught under the moving stone that is about to crush her. Lilia, whose major plot purpose is to represent perpetually besieged virginity, finds underscore support whenever her virtue is about to be imperiled. Moses predicts the death of Nefretiri's son in bare words, but musical trouble comes close behind. This practice of delay parallels an important feature of DeMille's directorial style—he preferred to avoid showing actual violent moments, cutting instead to the reactions immediately after. In a similar way, Bernstein's underscore tends to appear after a particular emotional tone has been established, confirming and amplifying the affective color and carrying the sense of the scene on into the next one.

Music's most powerful management of the audience's sense of temporal flow, however, comes in the vast crowd scenes that DeMille was famously expert at crafting. Although the special effects scenes, like the parting of the Red Sea or that oddly staid orgy around the Golden Calf, depend on music to modulate their pace, the most interesting case is the beginning of the Exodus. I have already suggested that it might be thought of as a history painting set in motion: let me elaborate with special attention to the music.

First, the scene involved a staggering number of elements. Filmed in Egypt, it employed somewhere between 8000 and 14,000 extras (the numbers were never exact), not to mention a huge number of animals. Most of the extras were Egyptians, who were grouped into clusters of fifty and moved by nonverbal signals as well as a few memorized Arabic phrases. A set of four cameras, all mobile, ensured a variety of shots. After detailed arranging of the crowd, DeMille made three takes of the procession away from the specially constructed set. (It was during the third of these that DeMille suffered a heart attack, which he concealed from everyone he could so that he could maintain control of the shooting.) These massive takes formed the basis for the procession into the desert that is one of the great spectacles of the film.

But the broad shots of ponderously moving crowds are only one element in the construction of the sequence. In later nineteenth-century history paintings and realist scenes of public life, the people in the crowds tend to be given individualizing features, and just such vignette treatment is a crucial part of DeMille's design. Compare, for instance, *Religious Procession in Kursk Province*, a famous work by the Russian realist painter Ilya Repin, with a characteristic frame from DeMille's Exodus: the approach to individualizing the crowd is extremely close (see Figure 17.2).

The roughly nine minutes of the Exodus contain over eighty shots, and many of these are tiny type-sketches of this sort: a little girl searches for her doll Rebecca; other children herd sheep, geese (in the desert?), and water buffalo; a greedy camel steals dates from a cluster carried in front of him; a father exults in a new son. Individualization comes not only from the particulars of costume, dialogue, and manner, but also from DeMille's variations in the type of shot. These miniatures are scattered throughout a larger-scale structure that divides the slowly moving crowd's action into three segments. The initial gathering is broken by a turn to a brief scene at Dathan's house; although Dathan refused to have blood painted on his doorposts, Joshua did so anyway to save Lilia's life, and so the entire household is ejected from Egypt. The middle segment of the crowd's action ends with a turn to Moses, apprehensively waiting to give the final signal, the marshaling of his forces to lead the throng eastward (the final segment).

In each case, Bernstein's score attends to the film's formal divisions and holds the disparate vignettes together. The diegetic fanfares that launch the sequence merge into a march that first appeared in the film's entr'acte (placed between the Burning Bush and the onset of the Plagues); it grows out of the theme previously associated with Moses, and in effect aligns the prophet's identity with that of his people (see Figure 17.3).

This march is wonderfully varied in orchestration, accompanimental figures, key, and mode, and acts as a substratum for most of the crowd's activity. In general, its tempo is lively: according to Bernstein, he had first planned slow music to match the actual tempo of the crowd's music, but DeMille insisted on a faster pace, which he declared would make the onscreen motion subjectively faster. The march vanishes during the

(a)

(b)

FIGURE 17.2 a, b: (a) Ilya Repin, *Religious Procession in Kursk Province* (Tretyakov Gallery, Moscow); (b) *The Ten Commandments* (1956), Exodus.

FIGURE 17.3 *The Ten Commandments* (1956), The Children of Israel Depart/Moses (music transcribed from the soundtrack).

large structural articulations of the sequence, replaced in the first instance by a variation on Dathan's villainous theme, and in the second by a reverent string moment for Moses. Crucially, however, Moses's reverential music comes to an end as he gathers himself to proclaim the Exodus. After a swirling fanfare, he announces the Exodus, and the Children of Israel respond with the *Sh'ma Israel* (the central creedal statement in Judaism; this is its third occurence in the film). Only then does the music return.

When the march begins again, with a full frontal shot of Moses heading toward the camera, a massive crowd flowing behind him, it might seem as if the sequence were ready to come to an inspiring close. But DeMille, ready to milk the extravaganza for all it is worth, throws in one last assortment of vignettes. This is pageantry at its effective peak: the individualized figures range through a host of types, as if to attempt to include one of every type that might be in the audience. In a startling move, Bernstein's march suddenly introduces a quick string-with-xylophone figure that sounds almost Copland-like in its wide leaps and folkish ornaments—the venerable story of the Exodus now seems to contain the seeds of American history within it, in a way that corresponds to the parallels DeMille had drawn in his initial speech. (Not for nothing had Bernstein studied with Copland!) The score's adroit connection to the genre of the Western, with all its nationalist overtones of Manifest Destiny, was once again perfectly suited to DeMille's ideology—although best known for ancient world costume dramas and sentimental tales, DeMille had directed several important early Westerns as well. And with that shift into American musical territory, the primary work of the underscore is finished in this scene. As the imagetrack cuts to a sublimely high long shot—figuratively, under the eye of eternity—the crowd slowly pours out onto the desert, and the music fades towards its cadence under one of DeMille's authoritative voiceovers (see Figure 17.4).

Looked at as a real-life event, the Exodus as DeMille plays it is physically impossible. The unruly, messy forces assembled for the scene would get less than a day's march before animals would be dying, much equipment would have failed, and people would begin to perish of thirst and exhaustion. But that's not the point. DeMille's notion of reality was highly poetic. What mattered was that it *feel* true, and for this the factual had to be surpassed. Not entirely, of course: the anxieties of early twentieth-century Protestantism combined with DeMille's inexhaustible taste for period detail meant that the film never completely forsook its luxuriant version of historical truth. But that truth was carefully limited. And what mattered most, in the end, was what he would have considered the timeless truth of feeling. For this purpose, the stagey fabrications of the old melodrama offered a better avenue to the latent bigness that would give his tale of Moses—no, THE tale of Moses, as he thought of it—the suasive force that it must have to succeed. And in its multifaceted ways, the score he got from Elmer Bernstein cinched DeMille's sprawling project together, as the example of the Exodus demonstrates.

FIGURE 17.4 *The Ten Commandments* (1956), Bernstein's "Copland" (music transcribed from the soundtrack).

CONCLUSION

To equate the dense historical complexity acquired by sacred texts like the Bible with the much briefer layers created by a short time's style shift is unquestionably problematic and probably irreverent, but the cultural space offered in film was accommodating. And by the 1950s, as film underwent its serious contest with television, that cultural space suddenly seemed much less frivolous, much less subject to the Devil's use, than it had a few decades earlier. *The Ten Commandments*, with all its old-fashioned ways, was already aging fast at its premiere. If the film had tried to convince its audiences of truth by its richly seamed artifice, its appearance on television added yet another layer of antiquity. The television rite of passage I mentioned at the beginning of my discussion even made its way, in turn, back to film: in the 1977 film *Close Encounters of the Third Kind*, a brief discussion of watching *The Ten Commandments* on TV is part of the furniture of everyday life, a sign of the ordinariness of a family about to be undone by the fall of another kind of fire from heaven. So let it be rewritten, so let it be redone.... In all forms of culture, art that becomes dated will eventually move past decay into fossilization. Their contexts fade, their structure somehow hardens. They become another thing entirely from what they once were. They become something strangely new.

And they give us as viewers a new set of problems—historical problems—to deal with. If I have spent such a great extent of this space on contexts that now seem arcane, it is for two reasons. First, a great deal of cultural history in general, and perhaps the history of the arts in particular, requires not only saying many things that once were said but also those that went without saying. Thus, we must say all of them. But what, once we have these old-said things combined with the unsaid things newly said, are we to do with them? We all differ on this question. I would suggest that one useful approach sees those reconstituted sayings as a pole against which we pose our own experiences of a newly reconstituted past. And so, I wonder if it is only now that *The Ten Commandments* CAN be considered a film. Maybe before now, it has simply been too much—too charged with desire and dread, at once too prim and too prurient, too creaky in its style to be believed anymore. And in that lack of belief is our new regard founded.

NOTES

1. For an interesting survey of the public use of the Ten Commandments, see Watts 2004. An overview of key cases in recent disputes over the Establishment Clause can be found in Maier and Mull 2005–2006. Citations from Hall 2002, 174.
2. This tale has a wide circulation; my account follows Eyman 2010, 456–457.
3. For this context, see Shaw 2002; and in particular, Nadel 1993.
4. Wellhausen's first statement of this position came in *Geschichte Israels* (1878), republished in 1882 as *Prolegomena zur Geschichte Israels*. It is difficult to overstate the importance of this work in shaping a huge number of religious disputes that continue into the present.

5. Thuesen 1996, 609.

6. Thuesen 1996, 610–613.

7. Premillennial dispensationalism clearly requires a highly concrete approach to the Biblical text. For more on this rendition of the Bible, overwhelmingly important in the history of conservative Evangelical Protestantism, see Sandeen 1967; Mangum and Sweetnam 2009.

8. For useful accounts of this history, see Murphy 1987; Vardac 2005, 27–36.

9. See the overview by Ludwig 1965–1966, 143–146.

10. See Higashi 1990, 1994.

11. For more on this point, and including a useful discussion of audience involvement, see Halloran 2001.

12. An overview of this general process is found in Darby and Du Bois 1990, 430–436.

13. This point, and many others in my discussion of the film's retrospectivity, is indebted to Flinn 1992.

Bibliography

Bergman, Herbert. 1953. *David Belasco's Dramatic Theory.* University of Texas Studies in English, vol. 32. Austin: University Press.

Darby, William, and Jack Du Bois. 1990. *American Film Music: Major Composers, Techniques, Trends, 1915–1990.* Jefferson NC: McFarland.

Eyman, Scott. 2010. *Empire of Dreams: The Epic Life of Cecil B. DeMille.* New York: Simon & Schuster.

Flinn, Caryl. 1992. *Strains of Utopia: Gender, Nostalgia, and Hollywood Film Music.* Princeton, NJ: Princeton University Press.

Hall, Sheldon. 2002. "Selling Religion: How to Market a Biblical Epic." *Film History* 14, no. 2: 174.

Halloran, S. Michael. 2001. "Text and Experience in a Historical Pageant: Toward a Rhetoric of Spectacle." *Rhetoric Society Quarterly* 31, no. 4: 5–17.

Higashi, Sumiko. 1990. "Cecil B. DeMille and the Lasky Company: Legitimating Feature Film as an Art." *Film History* 4, no. 3: 181–197.

——. 1994. *Cecil B. DeMille and American Culture: The Silent Era.* Berkeley: University of California Press.

Ludwig, Coy L. 1965–1966. "From Parlour Print to Museum: The Art of Maxfield Parrish." *Art Journal* 25, no. 2: 143–146.

Maier, Haynes, and Eric R. Mull. 2005–2006. "Holy Moses: What Do We Do with the Ten Commandments?" *Mercer Law Review* 57: 645–671.

Mangum, R. Todd, and Mark S. Sweetnam. 2009. *The Scofield Bible: Its History and Impact on the Evangelical Church.* Colorado Springs: Paternoster.

Murphy, Brenda. 1987. *American Realism and American Drama, 1880–1940.* Cambridge: Cambridge University Press.

Nadel, Alan. 1993. "God's Law and the Wide Screen: *The Ten Commandments* as Cold War 'Epic.'" *PMLA* 108, no. 3: 425–430.

Noerdlinger, Henry S. 1956. *Moses and Egypt: The Documentation to the Motion Picture "The Ten Commandments."* With an introduction by Cecil B. DeMille. Los Angeles: University of Southern California Press.

Orrison, Katherine. 1999. *Written in Stone: Making Cecil B. DeMille's Epic "The Ten Commandments."* Vestal, NY: Vestal Press.

Sandeen, Ernest R. 1967. "Toward a Historical Interpretation of the Origins of Fundamentalism." *Church History* 36, no. 1: 66–83.

Shaw, Tony. 2002. "Martyrs, Miracles, and Martians: Religion and Cold War Cinematic Propaganda in the 1950s." *Journal of Cold War Studies* 4, no. 2: 3–22.

The Ten Commandments. 2004. Commentary. DVD, Special Collector's Edition. Paramount.

Thomas, Tony. 1979. "Elmer Bernstein on Film Music." In *Film Score: The View from the Podium*, edited by Tony Thomas, 154–163. South Brunswick, NJ: A. S. Barnes.

Thuesen, Peter J. 1996. "Some Scripture Is Inspired by God: Late-nineteenth-century Protestants and the Demise of a Common Bible." *Church History* 65, no. 4: 609–623.

Vardac, A. Nicholas. 2005. "Realism, Romance, and the Development of the Motion Picture." In *Theater and Film: A Comparative Anthology*, edited by Robert Knopf, 27–36. New Haven: Yale University Press.

Watts, James W. 2004. "Ten Commandments Monuments and the Rivalry of Iconic Texts." *Journal of Religion & Society* 6: 1–12.

Wellhausen, Julius. 1878. *Geschichte Israels. In zwei Banden. Erster Band*. Berlin: G. Reimer. Republished in 1882 as *Prolegomena zur Geschichte Israels*. Berlin: G. Reimer.

Wright, Richardson. 1919. "The School of the Pageant." *Art & Life* 11, no. 3: 162–167.

CHAPTER 18

STRANGE RECOGNITIONS AND ENDLESS LOOPS: MUSIC, MEDIA, AND MEMORY IN TERRY GILLIAM'S *12 MONKEYS*

JULIE MCQUINN[1]

(1) James Cole has been sent from the future to obtain information about a deadly virus that destroyed most of the world's population. What he learns will enable the scientists of the future to defeat that virus and move the underground survivors of this apocalypse back to the surface of the planet. (2) James Cole is insane.

Terry Gilliam's *12 Monkeys* (1995) continually asks its audience to choose between these statements while continually undermining their ability to do so. If Cole is from the future, then there is a mystery to be solved, clues to be processed and analyzed as he searches for the origin of the virus. But his mental state is also a mystery, forcing the audience to reprocess and manage still more information. As these two investigations begin to merge and expand, as a dizzying array of bits of information and experiences starts to loop, it becomes impossible to tell the difference between information that matters and information that does not. Our search for knowledge, for truth, for the real, becomes entangled with the elusive processes of memory, nostalgia, and déjà vu. Like Cole, our memories become unreliable, even as they are invoked.

This is a film of strange recognitions, as the main characters and the audience are confronted with ideas, situations, people, places, objects, and experiences that are not new to them and yet are new. Music plays a prominent role in these moments of recognition, these cyclings, these touchpoints that realign time, creating suspended spaces of the uncanny in which binary divisions can collapse, in which we can rethink what we thought we knew, in which codes and clichés can be invoked, unveiled, disabled, or given new power. Many of these moments involve what I will call "musical recognitions": music is yet another form of information to be processed. Whether it is repetitions within the film itself, quotations from other media sources, composer Paul Buckmaster's use of musical codes and clichés, or circular aspects of the musics themselves, musical refrains define and defy boundaries of space and time, merging diegetic and audience space, interweaving the tangible with the intangible, creating and revealing connections, tensions, and contradictions. In the process, music is inextricably linked with media and technology and is thus placed in a position of power but simultaneously subjected to a harsh interrogation as part of a critique of society's relationship with that media and technology. Even though music is exposed as part of a media culture that dangerously substitutes the artificial for the real, it can also dissolve these boundaries—it can create memories, realities. Gilliam asks his audience to make a decision about the value of these realities.

The beginning of the film sets the stage for these issues. The opening credits effect a squashing of time and space. The sound of swirling winds evokes a vast and empty landscape. Green words emerge out of the blackness, letter by letter, the images suggesting a computer screen, but the sounds, a typewriter. These words warning of an apocalypse by deadly virus are dated from 1990 through a caption that also attributes them to a "clinically diagnosed paranoid schizophrenic"; the apocalypse is foretold to take place in 1997; and the wind sounds seem to suggest that the surface of the planet may have already been abandoned. Multiple times seem to coexist.

A percussion roll shimmers and surges to an image of circles within circles of red monkeys moving round and round, creating a tunnel into infinity, the opening credits moving across it in a gradual shifting from blurriness to clarity and back to blurriness. Gilliam calls this main title graphic a mandala (Gilliam 2005). The mandala is a symbol of the infinity and unity of the universe and a meditative tool for communing with that infinity and achieving that unity. It has a long history as an object of ritual (Adamenko 2006, 207). Carl Jung connected the mandala to the human psyche, claiming it "can lead to . . . a liberation of the inner personality from its emotional and intellectual involvements and entanglements, so producing a unity that can rightly be called a 'rebirth of man on a transcendental plane'" (Jacobi 1973, 141). Victoria Adamenko calls the mandala a "traditional tool for ordering chaos" (2006, 209) and explores its connection to music, including the ways in which the use of circular forms and notation in some music of the twentieth century transforms time into space and relates to myths of timelessness and even to myth itself (201–40). The mandala is a spiritual gateway that defies linear notions of time.

These mystical and musical resonances connect to the film in ambivalent ways. Through its very juxtaposition with the opening texts, this monkey mandala is already linked to madness, and Gilliam makes it clear that he takes a cynical view of its endless cycling. He describes the monkeys as "each dutifully following one ass after the other" (Fulton and Pepe 2005) and the hypnotic "wheel" as "going round and round and round; the characters never get off it; they die and are reborn" (Gilliam 2005). For Gilliam, this circling is a cage, a trap, and there is no peace in this universe. He has stated, "This is humanity, except for one that breaks loose" (Fulton and Pepe 2005), and "The film is about a nostalgic sense of loss, a doomed civilization" (Gilliam 1999, 227). What if the very aspects of humanity that repeat, that are "eternal," are the elements that cause us to destroy ourselves?

The music that emerges out of the initial percussive surge to accompany those cycling monkeys is Buckmaster's arrangement of the "Introducción" of Astor Piazzolla's *Suite Punta del Este*. Gilliam calls this music "the theme for the movie," describing it as "mad and passionate and dangerous" and asserting that there is "something existential about it" (Gilliam 2005). Piazzolla's music resides in a space between, a mix of the tango of Buenos Aires, jazz, and classical music, especially of the twentieth century. The distinctive sound of the solo bandoneon, with its airy yet driving tone, has come to define "the iconic sound of the tango" (Corrado 2003, 297). Here the melody jerks downward in two small spurts and then spasms upward, each gesture erupting from a single motion of the bellow, always starting on the upbeat, creating a sense of urgency. Under the bandoneon line, the downbeats explode with power, the repeated notes in the strings added by Buckmaster like extended reverberations of the energy of that downbeat, the harsh downbow articulation and the low register generating a violently percussive sound, driving relentlessly forward.

Yet this music goes nowhere. The rhythmic pattern in the bandoneon, disjunct as it is, is relentlessly repetitive. Phrase length is always consistent, but there is no balance, no coherent trajectory. And each line is punctuated by percussive cranks, plocks, grinds, and rattles (added by Buckmaster), always with an eerie rhythmic precision, evoking the sounds of moving machinery, parts and gears. Melodic repetition soon gives way to more erratic motion. The rhythm becomes a bit muddier, the bandoneon's line veering further and further from E minor, the clarinet a bumbling shadow, trying to follow the bandoneon's unpredictable lead. Taken in succession, the final, high, held notes of each phrase meander, evoking a kind of wild abandon or uncertainty, creating the impression of an unraveling, a disintegration, and yet a persistence. In conjunction with the sounds of airplanes taking off, an announcement of a flight, and finally, chaotic yells and cries, this music creates a soundscape that disallows any positive notion of infinity.

Déjà vu or "Real" Memory?

The chilling cyclings of the film's opening moments mirror a world in which violence, decay, and scientific control are unnervingly similar before and after the apocalypse. The prisoners of the future in their layers of endless cages resemble the animals in the animal experimentation video and the rowdy prisoners in the jail of the present. In both worlds, Cole is inhumanly disinfected, scrubbed like an old tool, and violence is a constant presence. Drugs are used as chemical restraints, treatment equally useful for criminals and the "mentally divergent." Science has power to define the real and the unreal, the insane and the sane, and those people in white jackets interrogate and control Cole, denying him basic human agency based on behavior that does not fit their constructed definition of normal. And of course it is a scientist who is responsible for the release of the virus as punishment for a selfish, consumerist society.

According to production designer Jeffrey Beecroft, "the central image of 12 Monkeys is a mouse in a maze": Cole "never gets to the end of that maze." Beecroft explains that the production team aimed "to repeat images consistently throughout, so that you keep wondering, 'Did I see that before'? You have pieces of the past and the future and the present in all scenes, whether it's a vent or a fan or a drinking glass" (quoted in Calhoun 1996, 36). Or, as Gilliam (2005) put it, "Everything is a reference to something else." The torrent of information is overwhelming, tangled, and often contradictory; it is impossible to process every detail, every connection. The first time we see the scientists of the future, for example, the wide-angle lens captures a setup so filled with unidentifiable bits and pieces that it is impossible to take it all in, and the scientists, in their strange, plastic jackets, seem to be part of this unwieldy roomscape. Cogs, clocks, books, metal, pipes, a clothesline with clips and white pieces of paper like orders in a diner—it looks like a scientific thrift shop, simultaneously ridiculous and terrifying. We look and listen for connections, for clues, but those clues give and take, push and pull. Logic must be set aside as linear notions of cause and effect break down, replaced by confusion and disorientation.

The nameless voice that Cole hears—the voice that calls him a palindromic name (Bob)—might come from within his mind, but in 1996 that voice claims the body of a homeless man who warns Cole that the scientists are tracking him through a device in his teeth. When Railly, his psychiatrist, sees the man later, he speaks with that same voice and even says similar things, but he does not remember her and does not know anything about the future. His words may trigger our memories of his earlier words—*has* he said these things before? Did we imagine it?

The authoritative voiceover is a consistent and eerily familiar presence in both worlds. Emanating from hidden speakers, these disembodied voices, with the same calm inflection and clear, careful diction, provide order, information, warnings, and threats. In the future as Cole prepares for his surface exploration duty, the voice warns, "If the integrity of the suit is compromised in any way...readmittance will be denied"; in the bathroom at the airport in the present he hears "Any luggage found unattended... will be removed and destroyed."

Music contributes significantly to the confusion of memory. In one striking example, "Silent Night" seems to echo through the cavernous, chaotic, cobweb-filled ruins of a large department store in the postvirus universe that Cole is sent to explore. There is no clear source for this music—because of the remains of holiday decorations that eerily adorn glass towers of dress shoes covered in a thick layer of grime, it *sounds* as though it might be coming through the store speakers. After the dissonant chords and angular lines of the previous scene, these a cappella voices of a boys choir are otherworldly, sounding in a space where there is not a human soul to be seen except Cole in his protective suit. Layered against the sounds of Cole's movement through broken glass and unidentifiable rumblings, this impossible music emphasizes the devastation of the planet's surface; it is a sonic residue, a sounding lack, a sign of a humanness that no longer exists.

Later in the film, back in 1996, "Silent Night" sounds again in that same store as Railly and Cole purchase disguises in order to escape from the police. Here the music is linked to a very different kind of humanness: it is holiday Muzak, devoid of deep meaning, meant to entertain and lull shoppers. A sudden eruption of sound causes Cole to turn his head and look upward as the ceiling dissolves into its future decrepit state; the source of the sound is the startled, fluttering birds from the future store that shoot upward in a replay of a moment from the beginning of the film—but that same sound now seems to glide through the boundaries of time or memory as we hear the voice of the store clerk. Cole was the only one to hear the sounds of the birds, and because he turns his head to follow the sound, he clearly hears it as outside of his own mind. Is this his memory of the future? Is this an illusion, a sign of his insanity? Or is there a split-second rip in time? Perhaps the "Silent Night" voices in the future also came from Cole's mind, or perhaps these sounds are floating around in the space, waiting to be heard. These possibilities blur boundaries between experiences we remember and experiences we dream, imagine, or construct, between an actual jump in time and a memory.

REFRAIN TRAJECTORIES

When music repeats, as in the case of "Silent Night," connections are made, our memories triggered, flags created in our subconscious or conscious minds. Some of the film's musical refrains create or lose momentum as the film progresses. The power of the Piazzolla "Introducción" eventually fades and disappears, but the repetitions of Cole's dream music build to a climax at the end of the film.

PIAZZOLLA PETERS OUT

The "Introducción" sounds again when Cole finds a sign with the 12 Monkeys logo on the planet's future surface and thus reasserts the connection made in the opening of the film. At the end of the fourth repetition of the opening phrase, the strings' rising arpeggio matches the motion of his glance upward, where a lion roars atop a building. The music is thus linked to the real quest of the Army of the 12 Monkeys and the final result of the virus—the freeing of the animals. Fragments of this music emerge when the scientists show Cole slides of the logo and the Army. The music reappears when Cole's fellow psychiatric patient, Jeffrey Goines, acts out in the hospital dormitory, leaping from bed to bed, the beds arranged in a circle just like the monkey mandala, making each patient ("Nutcase, lunatic, maniac devils," as Jeffrey calls them) one of those monkeys. His unruly behavior seems more comical than dangerous: he moons the guards, rips a pillow apart, and yells, "Colonics for everyone!" In a re-creation of a clichéd movie prison break, he raises his hands as if caught by the police when the flashlight is first shone on him; a driving percussion line simulates what could be either the sound of a firing squad or a riff accentuating a stage-comedian's joke.[2] As Jeffrey addresses the guards directly, the music drops to the background, the bandoneon playing fragments of its previous lines, with a bassline that bounces instead of drives, mimicking the rocking inflection of Jeffrey's line—"My father's going to be really upset." The scene ends with a quick, ornamental, scalar flourish, as though this were all a performance. The image that follows is a monkey in a cage, part of a videotape displaying animal experimentation on the television in the hospital's dayroom. All comedy vanishes as a now drugged Jeffrey states, "We're all monkeys."

The suggestion that Jeffrey's madness is a performance is reinforced when he stages an acting-out session to distract the guards so that Cole can escape. The "Introducción" sounds again, seemingly prompted by the downbeat created when Jeffrey bangs a game board on the table, his wildly inflected soliloquy of clichés in chaotic counterpoint with the bandoneon's tune. This time, as the melody fades, the heavy downbeats and rocking bassline tread a fine line between comedy and tension; Jeffrey's outbursts align closely to the music, as though he were performing an accompanied recitative. As he later explains, he had not conceived of the Army of the 12 Monkeys when he was in the hospital. The music, however, links him to the Army in advance, as it were, even as it connects to Jeffrey's performative behavior, thereby foreshadowing the red herring that the Army will become. Like the opening music itself, in the end, the music that was so powerful at the beginning slowly fizzles out, these refrains, these recognitions, leading nowhere. We hear the "Introducción" only twice more, each time associated directly with the Army: when they kidnap Jeffrey's father, and the next morning when we see the results—the animals freed from the zoo.

DREAM MUSIC

Piazzola's "Introducción" is set against Buckmaster's musical "soundalike" for the dream sequences based on the second movement of Jacques Loussier's Concerto for Violin and Percussion ("L'Homme nu," 1988). Loussier's composition was used as the temp track for the dream sequences, and following a familiar pattern, the director became fond of it: "The music's so simple. It's not cheap sentiment. It's real beautiful and tragic" (Fulton and Pepe 2005).

In the first scene, an exploding sound disrupts the "Introducción," lurching us straight into the eyes of a child (Figure 18.1a), which move left and right as the explosion reverberates, a beeping sound emerges, and a woman screams. The reverberating echoes of these sounds add depth to this space; a cut to a long corridor with a blinding light at its end makes it seem surreal (Figure 18.1b). The boy is a witness—a woman runs to a fallen man, she lifts his bloody hand to caress her face; we cannot see their faces.

A solo violin plays a monophonic line in C minor (see Figure 18.2)—it could not be more different from the "Introducción." The tempo is slow and the rhythm is played quite freely. The melody moves upward from the tonic to the dominant, only to fall down an octave. The phrase

(a)

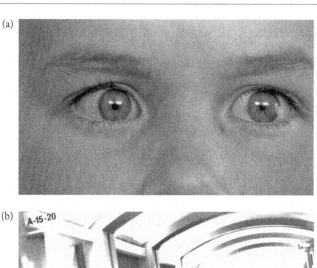

(b)

(c)

FIGURE 18.1 a–c: *12 Monkeys* (Gilliam 1995), opening scene.

FIGURE 18.2 *12 Monkeys* (Gilliam 1995), violin solo in opening scene (music transcribed from the soundtrack).

begins again, this time jumping up an octave to the tonic, then landing down a step on the sub-tonic and dropping down another fourth. Whereas each of the two phrases begins on the first beat of the measure, the final, falling note sounds on the last beat, held over the bar line, thus disabling a sense of pulse. This reaching upward only to fall, this cycling back to the tonic, and this lack of a strong rhythmic and harmonic drive generate a melancholy feel along with a sense of floating and incompleteness. The first note glides into the soundscape, and the first held note seems to follow or even carry the woman running across the screen. The cuts do not coincide with the downbeats, nor with the attacks of the violin's notes; rather they come just after, on, or near the upbeats, but never at regular intervals, seeming to pull the slow motion of the images toward total stasis. The cut to a sleeping Cole (Figure 18.1c) places the sequence in his dreaming mind, in his subconscious; yet the final note of the violin rings on after he wakes, like the remnant of a dream, lurking in the space between waking and sleeping.

Cole's dreams occur multiple times, each instance providing a bit more information, but it is never enough. Cole himself says that he always has the same dream, but if we experience what he experiences, the dream is never *exactly* the same, nor is the music. In the second dream, for example, the first phrase of the previously heard music is played just a bit differently: more time is taken between the subdominant and dominant pitches. In the fourth dream, only the second phrase is played, much more slowly than in the first dream. These alterations—music rerecorded rather than simply reused—amount to views from different sonic angles, reexperiencing and reacting to the dream images anew. In the third dream, the electronic beeping sound serves as a metronome, parsing or breaking the violin's held note into fragments, but again the violin voice comes to the forefront, as if a refocusing were required. This memory-dream is a fluid, ever-changing entity. The fact that the violin music does not sound in slow motion indicates a separation of some kind, of space or time or perspective. This is music of knowledge, of emotion; it lies both within and outside the dreamspace.

These sequences remind us, in retrospect, of the malleable nature of dreams and memories. Memories are colored by feelings and desires of both past and present. We never simply remember; we engage with the past. Cole's memory-dreams not only repeat but also reconstruct. The overlapping sounds between dream space and waking space hint at the existence of parallel worlds, of spaces beyond what we can see, of competing realities. The dream becomes a nexus, a space of convergence for time, spaces, consciousnesses, but the variations and the slow motion also create the effect of getting inside time, turning these moments inside out. Claude Lévi-Strauss has asserted that "ritual gives the impression of 'slow-motion' camera-work marking time to the point of stagnation" (quoted in Adamenko 2006, 239). The dream becomes an involuntary ritual for Cole and for the audience, its relationship to the real a mystery that grows with every refrain.

MEDIA MUSIC

The ambivalence present in *12 Monkeys* regarding the power of media still resonates today, as researchers investigate the effects of our technology-dominated lives on the ways we learn, behave, and think. A *New York Times* article cites concerns that "exposure to technology may be slowly reshaping your personality," that excessive use of technologies "can cause us to become more impatient, impulsive, forgetful and even more narcissistic" (Parker-Pope 2010). It is telling in this regard that when a video becomes popular via the Internet, it is called "viral."

Through the media, through technology, characters and audience alike receive information in *12 Monkeys*, and just like the characters, the audience must decide what to do with that information. We are often forced to rely on these voices of authority even when we have seen evidence of misinformation. Television, which Gilliam has described as "almost like another character in the film" (Gilliam 2005), is a constant sonic presence, issuing a steady stream of cartoons, news, movies, documentaries, and commercials, each with a different relationship to truth. This truth hierarchy soon breaks down, however, as all genres are shown to relate to and interact with those in the spaces they share.

The viewer is often faced with media doublings, as we hear about or see backgrounded images of the characters on a radio or television while seeing and hearing them in front of us. Cole and Railly, in particular, are often doubled in this way. In the future, Cole and the scientists are also doubled, as they interact in the same room via a video ball with an array of monitors that project images of the scientists. We sometimes even hear a character's voice and its technified double overlapping. These doublings expose technology as a tool for separation and domination, and question its authority as a conveyer of truth, identifying a possible split between the real and the media.

Music becomes entangled with these issues as a media voice that also conveys information with dubious connections to the real while carrying an authority that stems from its very recognizability and its capacity to become loosened from its source. In the three sections below, I discuss extended examples of musical quotation of and intertextual reference to cartoons, radio oldies and commercials, and Hitchcock's *Vertigo*, which trigger and play on our memories, our familiarity with media culture, our common experiences, real or perceived, simultaneously drawing us into and pushing us out of the diegesis, connecting diegetic space with audience space, prompting us to recognize this world as uncomfortably like our own.

Cartoon Music and the Mentally Divergent

In the psychiatric ward, Cole is told by an orderly to relax, his head jerked violently into submission. A cartoon (Tex Avery's *Swing Shift Cinderella*, 1945) on a television in a padlocked cage responds to the command via a shock cut with the hardly relaxed, hysterical yell of the wolf displaying his ardor for the sexy Cinderella he has just encountered, accompanied by a jazzy brass lick and swirl figures in the winds matching the motion of his body speeding around the trunk of a tree as only a cartoon character's body can.

This lively music continues as Cole is brought through a locked cage-like door into the crowded dayroom where the television is always on. Jeffrey Goines, dressed in a wacky combination of pajamas, dress shoes, and a velour pullover, has lifted his shirts to cover his head, but he is called out of his clothing cave by the orderly. His head pops out of his shirts with a dazed look to the sound of a cartoon "boing." Though we have already seen the plausible source of the music, the music/action match makes Jeffrey appear to be a cartoon figure, and by extension, this world a cartoon world.

Jeffrey then gives Cole a manic tour of madness, accompanied by cartoon sounds, music, and images. Wide-angle lenses and deep focus keep the television visible in the background, serving as prop and accompaniment for Jeffrey's rant against consumerism. He tells Cole that he is not here because he is mentally ill—"You're here because of the system." The cartoon's soundtrack (now *Little Tinker*, 1948) prompts him and eggs him on, at one point causing his head to jerk cartoon-style toward the television. As he lists consumer products, all linked to technology, Jeffrey works himself into a frenzy in direct parallel to a rabbit on the television doing multiple body flips to a drum roll. The chemically restrained Cole watches the cartoon intently after Jeffrey is ordered to calm down—a bunny bangs her head on a wooden fence in response to the crooning of a Frank Sinatrified skunk. These cartoon sounds and images simultaneously affirm and undermine his message in a loop of reflexive referentiality.

Even the serious, logical words of patient L. J. Washington, who explains his "mental divergence" to Cole, are ultimately undermined as Cole looks down and his bunny slippers are revealed, clashing with his black suit and bow tie, and the children's song "Here we go round the mulberry bush" comes forward. Throughout this dayroom scene, cartoon music has sounded, in varying degrees of prominence, linking itself with hospitalized psychiatric patients, with madness. Cartoon characters do often act in "mad" ways, but unlike the patients, this music is not confined there: it oozes through space via technology, accompanying and interacting with the spaces and actions of everyday life in revealing ways that are not so different from the proceedings in that hospital dayroom.

Radio Oldies and the Commodification of Nostalgia: "Sleepwalk" and "Blueberry Hill"

In the same dayroom, the television displays a beach at sunset, a couple kissing in the sparkling water accompanied by sounds of a pedal steel guitar, a slow drum beat, and faint cries of seagulls. The voiceover urges, "Take a chance. Live the moment. Sunshine. Gorgeous beaches. The Florida Keys." This music recurs in a radio ad for the Florida

Keys that plays just after Cole has kidnapped Railly: "This is a personal message to you. Are you at the end of your rope? Are you dying to get away? The Florida Keys are waiting for you. Ocean waves...". The sliding tones of the pedal steel sound mellow and relaxed, a perfect match for what these commercials are selling.

Even if the viewer does not recognize the song, it is sure to sound familiar, perhaps nostalgic, and even clichéd. The song is "Sleep Walk" by Johnny and Santo Farina, their *Billboard* number one hit from 1959, played here by B. J. Cole. This piece has been covered by many artists and heard in film, television shows, and commercials. The creators of *12 Monkeys* made their own commercial for the Florida Keys, with text from the screenplay added to the music of "Sleep Walk."

In his memoir, the poet Christopher Buckley gushes nostalgically about "Sleep Walk," which he describes as "the anthem of our adolescence, of the end of an age" (Buckley 2006, 75). He recalls, "All through the early '60s it was played at sock-hops, on hi-fis at parties, with live bands echoing that drawn-out melody near the end of school dances in the gym.... 'Sleep Walk' translated and transported a good deal of our locked-down and inarticulate teenage emotions." (64). Thus there is no room in his reading of the song in *12 Monkeys* for a possible critique of superficiality or commercialism: the music is too embedded in his idealized memories of adolescence and his feelings about those memories to be tampered with. For Buckley, this music in the film acts as "a perfect coefficient for that dream light coming out of the past" (75).

Buckley's nostalgic reading resonates with David Shumway's description of the exploitation of oldies in film: "If hearing an old song on the radio invites us to remember our own past, movies use the same technique to evoke the fiction of a common past" (Shumway 1999, 40). In other words, popular music has the ability to create prosthetic memories: "Commodified nostalgia evokes the affect of nostalgia even among those who do not have actual memory of the period being revived." Shumway asserts the power of the "false" to create real desires and experiences, as does Alison Landsberg, who argues that such prosthetic memory—especially as produced and spread by the mass media—has material significance: we use it to construct our identities, validate our experiences, organize our presents, and think about our futures (Landsberg 2000, 190–91).

12 Monkeys self-consciously brings this media-constructed power to the fore. Key West is Cole's and Railly's escape destination, because Cole has never seen the ocean, because Railly tells him he needs to "stop and smell the flowers." But even this desire to give him something he has never had—to help him relax, just like the commercial says—is discomfiting, because Railly's actions seem to be in direct response to those commercials, to that music, to the psychiatric patient who told the escaping Cole, "The best place to go would be Florida—the Keys are lovely this time of year." Railly may have chosen the Keys precisely because she knew Cole had responded to the commercial, or she may have been subconsciously influenced by the commercials herself. This ambivalent situation resonates deeply with Gilliam's 1986 description of his experience living in America: "A simple thing like walking down the beach—sun setting, birds flying, waves lapping, the sand beneath your feet: was I enjoying it because it was genuinely enjoyable

to walk along the beach with the sun setting, or because I'd seen it in ten hundred commercials telling me, '*This* is what life is all about'? And I couldn't tell. I had to get out"
(Gilliam 2004, 34; emphasis in original).

Cole is more like Buckley, adoring the oldies he hears on the car radio as symbols
for what he lacks, signs of a more ideal past. Amy Herzog describes "the actual experience of listening to pop music" as "the strange confluence of drama and spectacle with
the banality of the everyday. Music transports and extends us, yet always within the
same walls that remain oblivious to our transformation" (Herzog 2010, 194). This power
seems out of place in the world of *12 Monkeys*, even as we see it affect Cole while he listens to the radio. When he hears "Comanche" (1959), he declares, "I love this music; we
don't have this; we don't have anything like this." And he smiles as if comforted by Louis
Armstrong's 1968 performance of "What a Wonderful World," which became widely
known in large part because of its use in *Good Morning Vietnam* (1987). These are not
just random songs—they are iconic, easily recognized, suggesting Shumway's "fiction of
a common past," a past that we share with Cole.

Cole's most intense reaction is to "Blueberry Hill," as performed by Fats Domino in
1956. Our ability to be fully drawn into this moment, however, is undermined, inviting
an interrogation of the very processes that Shumway identifies.

Buckmaster's music for Cole's assault and kidnapping of Railly is violent and chaotic.
It punctuates his actions and amplifies his distorted, gravelly voice with angular brass,
scurrying strings and brass, and fierce, percussive string hits. Overlapping held notes
in the brass create dissonant sonorities, and percussive ostinato patterns layer atop one
another. Canted extreme close-ups of Railly's fear-filled face make that fear more pal-
pable and Cole more dangerous. When Railly recognizes Cole, muted trumpets play an
unstable fanfare that drives into a dissonant point of arrival. His voice returns to its normal, more gentle inflections, and the music halts. Yet the violence communicated by that
music lingers. With every sudden motion, Railly jerks in fear. During the Florida Keys
commercial, Cole's face shows rapt attention, while Railly's face experiences spasms,
tears in her eyes. Cole speaks directly to the radio: "I've never seen the ocean," causing
the psychiatrist to quip, "It's not a personal message to you." His naïveté about the commercial makes his actions no less unstable, the line between inexperience and insanity
thinning. With this lingering threat of violence and unpredictability in the air, we experience the "Blueberry Hill" moment.

The introduction of the song excites Cole, causing him to lurch forward. As he listens, he does not just become nostalgic; he is overcome. He cries and whines; he sticks
his head out the window and laughs and moans and sort of sings, his behavior strongly
paralleling that of the patients in the psychiatric ward, his tears of joy a stark contrast
to Railly's tears of fear. He cries, "I love the music of the twentieth century!" Music that
is empty to Railly means everything to Cole. Their responses interact with and mediate our own, the music a sonic point of convergence. We cannot lose ourselves in the
music the way Cole does; instead we are asked to think critically about Cole's reaction
and about the music itself: these sonic symbols of an ideal past and an ideal present ring
hollow. The fact that this music is delivered by a form of mass media complicates matters

further. The commercial and radio songs are too closely linked to the media as manipulative commercial products. Media itself has agency in this film; can its products ever be pure or meaningful in the way that Buckley describes his experience of "Sleep Walk"?

Both "Sleep Walk" and "Blueberry Hill" return later in the film, dislodged from their original media sources. There is no clear diegetic source when "Sleep Walk" sounds again in conjunction with the television news announcement that little Ricky Newman, thought to have fallen down a well, was in fact hiding in a barn. The media had been tracking the story throughout the film, Cole asserting that it was merely a prank. The music enters just before the declaration is made and little Ricky himself is shown. For the first time in the film, the introduction is heard, highlighting the familiar four-chord progression that cycles throughout most of the song: I–vi–iv–V⁷. The camera tracks in on a quiet and disturbed Railly as we hear the rest of the story via the television voiceover.

At this moment, Railly's world is turned upside down; here is "evidence" of the truth of Cole's knowledge of the future, evidence of his "sanity," evidence of time travel. Cole knew it was a prank because he had already experienced it. This music, with its multitude of previous associations, turns this epiphany into a cliché, a commercial even, perhaps evoking a nostalgia for a more simple, idealized time when relaxation and escape were possible, a time without time travel, a time when she could be sure of herself. Now the music mocks, creating a moment of irony, its unanchored presence a symbol of a breakdown of hierarchies and clear meanings.

As the pedal steel guitar enters, there is a cut to a beautiful landscape that fills the entire screen, but the view seems not quite real. It takes a second or two to realize that it is a painting. The camera tracks left across it and then tilts slightly; a close-up of Cole's profile emerges from the left, in opposition to that tracking motion, a bright yet warm light shining on him, as though emanating from that landscape; yet his head is too big, its three-dimensionality placing the flatness of the painting in relief, exposing the artificiality of the landscape and creating a surreal image. The sounds of seagulls and a gentle surf confirm that this music comes from the Florida Keys commercials. The voiceover, however, is not that of the commercial announcer, but inelegant voices singing "I found my thrill" in a less-than-appealing chorus of "Blueberry Hill." These two familiar musics do not mesh: they are in different keys, with different rhythms and different feels, perhaps even sounding in different spaces, dissonantly juxtaposing past and present, reality and artificiality, reality and dream, commercialized cliché and iconic oldie. "Sleep Walk" begins to recede and the singing comes to the fore. The heads of the scientists pop up, at odd angles, followed by a jump cut to an extreme close-up of Cole's confused eyes. The scientists finish the chorus and clap, one scientist blowing a party favor horn. "Sleep Walk" returns and the harmonic changes are somewhat awkwardly paralleled in the editing, rocking unevenly between shots of Cole in a hospital bed and the scientists, from diverse positions and angles. The quick dialogue interspersed among the scientists makes them appear to be a multi-headed octopus.

Gilliam calls this scene "[Monty] Pythonesque," "nightmarish," and a "Mad Hatter's tea party" (Gilliam 2005). The setting is revealed gradually, putting the audience in Cole's surreal position and provoking the inevitable question: Is it real or a creation of

Cole's deranged mind? The fact that "Sleep Walk" recedes as "Blueberry Hill" comes forward might indicate that "Sleep Walk" *is* located within Cole's mind, another effect of advertising, the "jingle" still playing in his subconscious, a signifier of his desire to escape. The music returns after the scientists's song, however, while they are clapping and during the subsequent dialogue, highlighting the chasm between what that commercial and its music promised and this frightening reality of absurdities: his pardon document like a grammar school certificate of merit in a yellowed, dirty, crinkled, burnt plastic folder; the painting suspended creakily from the wall; the plastic sheathing that the scientists wear, perhaps for protection, perhaps for fashion; and the immediate violent force that counters his outburst. The music cadences in alignment with the female scientist's verbal cadence—"and you will be well James, soon," as she tucks him in, raising a teddy-bear sheet to his neck in a gesture of maternal care. There is no music at all when he laughs unnervingly, hysterically, telling them that they are his insanity, rejecting the music and the false message of the "commercial" that the scientists have put together. The song could also simply correspond to their optimism. The meaning of this music floats precariously between nostalgia, idealism, authenticity, cliché, and artificiality, and this scene critiques the very commercial culture that the music has come to represent. This future is far, far away from the Florida Keys; these gorgeous beaches no longer exist. Yet, perhaps the Keys as they were advertised never did exist. So where is the world that the music represents? Perhaps it is in the space where memory and desire meet.

VERTIGO: A MOVIE MOMENT AND THE POWER OF MUSICAL CLICHÉ

Hitchcock's *Vertigo* plays in the movie theater where Cole and Railly apply their disguises and plan their escape. As they talk, music and dialogue sound under and in interaction with them, highlighting eerie points of connection, especially for those who, like Cole, have seen this film before. The screenwriters, David and Janet Peoples, were not referring simply to Hitchcock, but to another film that makes use of the same scene, Chris Marker's *La Jetée* (1962), which they used as inspiration for their own work on *12 Monkeys*. The layers of intertextuality, however, extend far beyond the screenplay authors' original intentions in a strange moment in the theater lobby.

When Cole wakes up in that movie theater from yet another dream, Hitchcock's *The Birds* is playing, the sound of the attacking, fluttering birds acting as dream soundtrack. He rushes out to find Railly. New music sounds in the distance with a long shot outside the theater. With the cut back to the lobby, as Cole bursts through the door, the music becomes louder, seeming to come from within the lobby space. This music, however, comes from *Vertigo*, from what composer Bernard Herrmann labeled the recognition scene. Jack Sullivan describes this scene as "one of the most sustained and passionate interactions between music and imagery in any movie" (Sullivan 2006, 228), but the interactions between the two main characters, Judy and Scottie, are tangled up with deception and obsession: Judy was pretending to be Madeleine, to be possessed by a distant past not her own, to commit suicide; Scottie, on the other hand does not want Judy—he wants Madeleine—yet while Judy was pretending to be Madeleine, she fell in love with Scottie. In this scene, Scottie attempts to transform Judy into Madeleine, his fetishistic desire actualized as Judy emerges from the bathroom and an otherworldly haze as Madeleine. Sullivan describes Herrmann's music for this scene as "ten minutes of trembling lyricism rising in a crescendo of longing" (228). With this music, Scottie loses himself in his obsession, his fantasy. There is no dialogue, only the music and a swirling kiss, the power of desire to overcome the real.

Cole enters his own recognition scene when he crosses the lobby threshold, in the middle of a winding line of tremolos that soon rise chromatically to a climactic presentation of the *Vertigo* love theme as Railly turns from the phone to say, "We have 9:30 reservations for Key West." Her disguise has transformed her, without a doubt, into the woman in Cole's dream. The parallels abound. Railly approaches Cole like Judy (as Madeleine) approaches Scottie; like Scottie, Cole is visibly overcome. The red light, presumably from the neon-lit marquee, creates a warm but artificial glow that mirrors the green neon glow in *Vertigo*.

And there is the music, which John Antony compares to "the sequences of *Tristan*": "Herrmann's seemingly endless sequences act as a signifier of the erotic.... The striving for a registrally higher melodic goal relentlessly increases tension, inverting the vertiginous descent, yet conveying the same feeling of a total loss of control" (Antony 2001, 532).[3] Against this erotic tension, this loss of control, this relentless striving in the music, the disguised Railly and Cole speak quietly and breathlessly.

COLE: I...just didn't recognize you.
RAILLY: Well you look pretty different yourself. |
 [He touches her hair and she brings his hand to her face.]
COLE: It was always you...in my dream...it was... [He is too overcome to finish.]
RAILLY: I remember you like this. I felt I've known you before.
 I feel like...I've always known you.
COLE: I'm so scared. [Railly has to draw his hands around her body, her trenchcoat.]

This moment is uncanny, clichéd romantic lines whispered by people in disguises in a movie theater lobby to clichéd movie music. The audience is set up to feel a moment of déjà vu, if not outright recognition, even if they are unfamiliar with *Vertigo*, as the love theme was heard earlier (as part of a different scene) inside the theater. The tinny sound of this highly acclaimed music, seemingly filtered through the low-quality lobby speakers, creates a sonic distance and an aura of artificiality, working against complete immersion in the music's erotic writhing. This is a movie moment, perhaps critiquing the artificially constructed and powerful nature of film itself as another technological medium that impedes, substitutes for, or defines real human relationships. H. Marshall Leicester has identified similar moments in Jean-Luc Godard's *Prénom Carmen*: "[The] use of other movies to make the movie in front of us is…a way of exploring the extent to which movies themselves have come to form a vernacular imaginary" (Leicester 1994, 252).

Godard's characters use this imaginary to build their own movie moments, "which function for them…as signifiers and bearers of passion, intensity, *jouissance*," in order to suture together a desired identity, to pursue "the elusive feeling of selfhood" (Leicester 1994, 252, 253). Cole seems to construct his own recognition scene, made with his memories of *Vertigo*, its music forming his constructed soundtrack. This reading makes sense, given that it was *The Birds*, and not *Vertigo*, that was playing when he left the theater: the disjuncture potentially takes this moment out of the flow of linear time.

This awkward, artificial movie moment at least partially informs reviewer Philip Strick's criticism of "the underwritten romance [between Railly and Cole] which, despite the simmering beauty of Madeleine Stowe, refuses to raise much of a temperature" (Strick 1996, 56). The relationship between these two characters does not, in fact, adhere to conventional Hollywood romance standards. Every moment of potential intimacy they share is undermined or interrupted, often violently. And their "theme," insofar as they have one, is nothing like the *Vertigo* music; instead, it is a stark, solemn, two-part, wandering counterpoint in the strings, where the parts often meet on empty open fifths, tritones, and major sevenths. This is the music of their connection, recurring many times, almost always varied, as their feelings toward each other shift and reshift amidst the chaos of his quest and their shifting conceptions of the real.

We hear the "theme," for example, when Railly removes a bullet from Cole's leg in the forest: see Figure 18.3. He looks around, saying, "I love seeing the sun," and his emotion turns a stark fifth into an *almost* lush passage as a low bassline rises expansively through the texture. When he falls and she catches him, they linger in the moment as another open fifth sounds. He tells her, "You smell so good," and a long chain of reverse suspensions responds, thirds resolving to tritones. This moment of strange intimacy fades, however, as she tells him that he has to turn himself in: the soaring bassline returns in a much more dissonant context, chromatic oscillations forming augmented sonorities, as though he is reminded of reality. Dissonance and volume increase as he violently grabs her shoulder and then her wrists. Given his past actions, we have no idea what he is going to do. Later, in that warped hospital of the future, the music from the forest scene returns, all of it, like a memory, as Cole converses with that disembodied voice about his desire to be back with Railly. Again, the soaring bassline amidst dissonance affirms both Cole's longing and the seeming impossibility of its fulfillment; this music teeters on the brink between hope and hopelessness. At best, all that Cole and Railly's "theme" can manage is to strive unsuccessfully to become the *Vertigo* music.

When the *Vertigo* moment does occur, it is an uneasy musical point of arrival. On one level, it gives audiences and characters alike the music for "real" movie romance (albeit one immersed in deception and fantasy), but Cole and Railly cannot live up to their movie moment, not even with the *Vertigo* music as their soundtrack. In fact, the music stops in the middle of its second rising sequence, waiting only for the nonchord tone of the melody to resolve down, cutting it off from further ascension. There is no

FIGURE 18.3 *12 Monkeys* (Gilliam 1995), Cole and Railly's "theme" (music transcribed from the soundtrack).

reiteration of the love theme and no "majestic C-major close... musically reinforcing the triumph of illusion over reality, of the irrational over the rational" (Antony 2001, 532). Cole is denied Scottie's momentary illusionary triumph. This is the erotic from the outside looking in, a transparent wall revealing a view of a possibility that will always be on the other side.

But maybe Cole gets something else, something real. As with Jeffrey's chain of clichés from television shows, movies, commercials, typing tests, and ancient quotes, which serve to help Cole to escape the hospital dayroom, more literal readings of this cliché-filled dialogue are possible here. Railly could be referring to the recurrent, strange feeling of having met Cole before. Her words could also imply that they *have* experienced this moment before, as part of the endless loop of human existence. And Railly is *literally* the woman of Cole's dreams—it really was always her.

While Scottie and Judy kiss onscreen, Cole and Railly embrace awkwardly, the camera denying us a final glimpse of their faces. We see only Railly's back and Cole's hands; he whispers, not about his love, but his fear. For even as the scene exudes artificiality, this faltering intimacy, these two people connecting, however inadequately, seems much more "real" than Scottie's constructed moment. One can argue that this scene is moving precisely because of its ultimate failure as a movie moment, because in this moment of definitive recognition (which is also our moment of recognition), dream, reality, memory, desire, past, present, and future converge; it trembles with eruptive possibilities. Cole is brought to the brink of transfiguration, the brink of passion, where reality and artificiality, cliché and depth of feeling, become inextricably linked. Amy Herzog, informed by the ideas of Deleuze, defines the "musical moment," which occurs when music carries "dramatic presence," "draws attention to itself in some way," and can create "a point of rupture" (Herzog 2010, 6, 7), thus carrying the potential to reveal, provoke, resist, and create, even as the moment reinforces and reproduces the status quo. This is a "musical moment" on Herzog's terms: false and not false, empty and not empty, a moment in which limits and unlimited possibilities coexist.[4] It pulls us in and pushes us away, and we are left dangling in an ambivalent space between, where anything can happen. It is also through this lens that we should consider Buckmaster's dream music, which is film music too, and another of the film's musical refrains.

"This is my dream."

When Cole enters the airport with Railly, he recognizes it immediately, saying, "This is my dream." The dream violin takes up the note of the double bass, an octave higher, then plays the first phrase of the dream music and passes the line back to the bass, which repeats the final note down an octave, creating an ominous pedal tone (a characteristic sound in Buckmaster's score). The fluid way these musics connect foreshadows the final collapse of the boundary between dream space and real space.

Much later, we see everything, we recognize everyone, and we can now place all the previous dream images in a context and measure them against this reality. After Cole punches the police officer and breaks through the security gate, the beeping starts, beckoning in the dreamscape, and the slow motion begins, setting this space apart and further blurring the line between dream, memory, and reality, past, present, and future. There is no music as Railly screams and the gun explodes deafeningly. After Cole is shot, however, the violin line emerges, and the music is suddenly our only sonic guide: all other sounds are barred from our ears, and we are drawn into this intimate convergence space. Railly's mouth opens but we hear only the music. She reaches Cole as the penultimate note of the first phrase falls down an octave (see Figure 18.4, m. 2), but this note becomes a new beginning, the pickup to a new melody (mm. 3ff.), and for the first time in the dream music, the sound of a string orchestra emerges. This textural and harmonic expansion of the music gives an emotional and tangible weight to the scene, marking this moment as a point of arrival, one that Buckmaster bathes in sounds that are simultaneously lush and desolate—pedal tones, anticipations, neighbor and passing tones generating a gentle dissonance. This music is so slow and played with so much *rubato* that it is difficult to find a consistent beat, and the meter seems to shift at the whim of the solo line. This is real time, dream time, out of time.

The editing and cinematography highlight an intimate connection between the music and the characters. The split second before the orchestra enters, there is a cut to the boy, who we now know is young Cole. This chord (downbeat of m. 3) holds through a cut to an extreme close-up of Railly's hand over Cole's wound, the added-tone dissonance giving the spurting blood a visceral presence. The strings move in parallel first-inversion chords around an F pedal just as Cole's and Railly's hands move to join together over his wound, the inner parallel fifths adding an element of starkness (mm. 3–4).

When the violin line jumps an octave to form a striking B♭ major chord (downbeat of m. 5), the camera follows Cole's hand in close-up as it moves up Railly's arm to her face. A melodic sequence begins, the gentle motions of the violin's line matching the gentleness of their movements, their touching; it caresses each slow-motion gesture, as if this melody knows this scene so well (mm. 5–7).

The move to the dominant, the preparation for Cole's death, spans three shots connecting young Cole, Railly, and Cole. The V⁷/V at the end of m. 7 sounds with a shot of young Cole, moving to the dominant with a 4–3 suspension that resolves with a cut to Railly (m. 8). The final shot on Cole occurs outside the confines of metered time (as notated, beginning of m. 9), prolonging that dominant even further, a suspension of time before death. As the lower line falls by step from G to C, paralleling Cole's falling hand and fading life, the solo violin soars up an octave—the distance between these parts creating a vast space of emptiness (mm. 9–10). Cole's death, thus, occurs on a striking deceptive cadence, the major chord highlighting the simultaneous strangeness and inevitability of this moment; there is a cut on the beat (insofar as there is one) to a long shot and Cole's arm falls to the ground. The cut to young Cole while that A♭ chord rings on is like the death of Cole passing to the life of his younger self, a connection strengthened by the camera movement and editing. When Cole's hand falls, it falls toward young Cole, setting up a trajectory of motion. The cut to a slow tracking shot moving in to a close-up of young Cole is followed by a close-up of Railly as she takes Cole's dead hand from her right and puts it back on her face, picking up where the motion of the camera toward Cole left off, as though the hand could be young Cole's (latter half of m. 10). Thus young Cole is musically and visually drawn into a circle with Cole and Railly, a circle we trace with our eyes and our ears. And unlike the earlier dream sequences, there is a *merging* of music and motion and image here that makes tangible the time-loop paradox of these moments.

After Cole's death, Railly looks for young Cole, a repeated-note pattern providing a new rhythmic intensity (Figure 18.5, mm. 1–2). Now the violin's motion clearly corresponds to Railly and her gaze, her head turning on points of arrival. When she finds him (see m. 3), the music conveys the intensity of this meeting of eyes, the energy flowing between them, with increasingly complex pre-dominant harmonies (mm. 3–5). The violin's move to D♭ calls in tremolos in the other strings to form an iridescent Neapolitan chord to accompany a faint smile of recognition on Railly's face (m. 5). As the violin continues to arpeggiate this triad, young Cole's facial motions occur in uncanny alignment with the motion of the violin's line. The D♭ slides up to D with a cut to Railly (mm. 5–6); she is pulled out of the frame by the police to this shimmering dominant, which continues to resonate into the next scene. This half-step shift in the violin line, this irregular resolution from scale degree ♭2 to ♮2, creates an unusual, outright saccharine effect. Buckmaster clearly chose to emphasize this shift, at the expense of regular voice-leading, in order to impart a sense of unearthliness and perhaps even hope to this moment of recognition.

FIGURE 18.4 *12 Monkeys* (Gilliam 1995), final dream sequence, first part, music collated with action (music transcribed from the soundtrack).

FIGURE 18.5 *12 Monkeys* (Gilliam 1995), final dream sequence, second part, music collated with action (music transcribed from the soundtrack).

CONCLUSION

The director has asserted that his intention in *12 Monkeys* was "to let the audience maintain a total uncertainty about his mental state, whether the future was in [Cole's] mind or was real. And I think the music is gonna help that" (Fulton and Pepe 2005). Both the uncertainty and the role of music are sustained to the end of the film, which offers no definitive narrative closure. For it is at this point that all tensions come to the interpretive fore—between a pull toward human connections and a desire to solve the mysteries this film has presented, between the individual and society, between logic and feeling, and even between musics. And yet, the power of the music to influence our reading of this ending and of the film as a whole depends on our own relationship to media culture, including what we want from our filmic experiences, and on our reaction to all the information we have received, musical and non-musical, out of which we must *choose* what matters and what's real.

Although Gilliam initially resisted including them, the final scenes take place in the airplane and outside the airport, in which the future scientist sits next to Dr. Peters on the plane and young Cole watches the plane fly over, respectively. As Dr. Peters moves toward his seat in the plane, the violin line drops down to a G, under which a C minor chord eventually sounds, with nothing like the drama of the move to the preceding dominant. The music of the last two scenes reads as a sonic resonance of what has come before more than a resolution, an extension, leading to the final slow arpeggio in C minor and the extreme close-up on young Cole's eyes, closing and beginning yet another circle.

I lose myself in this dream music—like Scottie loses himself in his fantasy in *Vertigo*— even though I have been taught by this film not to trust the media, even though I have been shown the "falsity" of film music, even though musical clichés abound. Once again, the real and the unreal converge, as do cliché and heartfelt feeling. Buckmaster's music seems to be not merely a lament for a death that will keep repeating into infinity, but a testament to the power and value of human connections. And it does not matter whether or not the scientist will get the virus, it does not matter if Cole was mad; even the imminent destruction of the world fades to the background in these moments. It is the very questioning that both Cole and Railly participate in and their willingness to reach out to one another that emanates from the final minor arpeggio.

NOTES

1. I would like to thank Robynn Stilwell, David Helvering, and Stephen McCardell for their invaluable help with this project.
2. I thank Robynn Stilwell for pointing out the prison break parallel. Here and in so many scenes, the audience is rewarded for their movie knowledge.
3. Antony cites a reduced musical score for this scene. Measures 57–88 are used in *12 Monkeys*.
4. Del Rio has described the "creative and affective possibilities spun by the intensely disorienting powers of the false" related to music performances in David Lynch's films (Del Rio 2008, 196). Berthold Hoeckner has also identified the power of musical cliché to simultaneously limit and spur the imagination (Hoeckner 2007, see esp. 167–68).

BIBLIOGRAPHY

Adamenko, Victoria. 2006. *Neo-Mythologism in Music: From Scriabin and Schoenberg to Schnittke and Crumb*. Hillsdale, NY: Pendragon.

Alaimo, Stacy. 1997. "Endangered Humans?: Wired Bodies and the Human Wilds in *Carnosaur, Carnosaur 2*, and *12 Monkeys*." *Camera Obscura* 40–41: 227–244.

Antony, John. 2001. "'The Moment That I Dreaded and Hoped For': Ambivalence and Order in Bernard Herrmann's Score for *Vertigo*." *Musical Quarterly* 85, no. 3: 516–544.

Azzi, María Susana, and Simon Collier. 2000. *Le Grand Tango: The Life and Music of Astor Piazzolla*. New York: Oxford University Press.

Bellin, Joshua David. 2005. *Framing Monsters: Fantasy Film and Social Alienation*. Carbondale: Southern Illinois University Press.

Buckley, Christopher. 2006. *Sleepwalk: California Dreamin' and a Last Dance with the '60s.* Spokane: Eastern Washington University Press.

Calhoun, John. 1996. "*12 Monkeys*: Jeffrey Beecroft Builds a Maze Through Time for Terry Gilliam's Bizarre New Film." *TCI: Theatre Crafts International* 30, no. 3: 34–37.

Corrado, Omar. 2003. "Bandoneón." In *Continuum Encyclopedia of Popular Music of the World.* Vol. 2. *Performance and Production,* edited by John Shepherd, 296–298. New York: Continuum.

Del Rio, Elena. 2001. "The Remaking of *La Jetée*'s Time-Travel Narrative: *Twelve Monkeys* and the Rheotric of Absolute Visibility." *Science Fiction Studies* 28, no. 3: 383–398.

———. 2008. *Deleuze and the Cinemas of Performance.* Edinburgh: Edinburgh University Press.

Düblin, Christian. 2009. "Special Interview Music: Paul Buckmaster." Xecutives.net, http://www.xecutives.net/index.php?option=com_content&task=view&id=224&Itemid=80 (accessed August 9, 2010).

Fulton. Keith, and Louis Pepe, directors. 2005. *The Hamster Factor and Other Tales of Twelve Monkeys.* In Gilliam, *12 Monkeys* special ed. DVD. Universal City, CA: Universal.

Gilliam, Terry. 1999. *Gilliam on Gilliam.* Edited by Ian Christie. London: Faber and Faber.

———. 2004. *Terry Gilliam Interviews.* Edited by David Sterritt and Lucille Rhodes. Jackson: University Press of Mississippi.

———. 2005. "Director's Commentary." In *12 Monkeys,* special ed. DVD. Universal City, CA: Universal.

Herzog, Amy. 2010. *Dreams of Difference, Songs of the Same: The Musical Moment in Film.* Minneapolis: University of Minnesota Press.

Hoeckner, Berthold. 2007. "Transport and Transportation in Audiovisual Memory." In *Beyond the Soundtrack: Representing Music in Cinema,* edited by Daniel Goldmark, Lawrence Kramer, and Richard Leppert, 163–83. Berkeley: University of California Press.

Jacobi, Jolanda Székács. 1973. *The Psychology of C. G. Jung: An Introduction with Illustrations.* New Haven: Yale University Press.

Lashmet, David. 2000. "'The Future is History': *12 Monkeys* and the Origin of AIDS." *Mosaic* 33, no. 4: 55–72.

Landsberg, Alison. 2000. "Prosthetic Memory: *Total Recall* and *Blade Runner*." In *The Cybercultures Reader,* edited by David Bell and Barbara M. Kelly, 190–201. London: Routledge.

Leicester, Jr., H. Marshall. 1994. "Discourse and the Film Text: Four Readings of *Carmen*." *Cambridge Opera Journal* 6, no. 3: 245–282.

Parker-Pope, Tara. 2010. "An Ugly Toll of Technology: Impatience and Forgetfulness." *New York Times,* June 6.

Shumway, David R. 1999. "Rock 'n' Roll Soundtracks and the Production of Nostalgia." *Cinema Journal* 38, no. 2: 36–51.

Strick, Philip. 1996. "*12 Monkeys*." *Sight and Sound* 6, no. 4: 56–57.

Sullivan, Jack. 2006. *Hitchcock's Music.* New Haven: Yale University Press.

PART 4

CONTEMPORARY APPROACHES TO ANALYSIS

CHAPTER 19

....

TRANSFORMATIONAL THEORY AND THE ANALYSIS OF FILM MUSIC

....

SCOTT MURPHY

PATRICK McCreless's article "Contemporary Music Theory and the New Musicology" (McCreless 1996) suggests a disciplinary relationship between the two subject areas that amounts to a Foucauldian turf war at the end of the twentieth century. The similar construction of the title for the present chapter, however, refers—with meager exceptions—to mutually foreign realms of knowledge and research largely oblivious of one another at the beginning of the twenty-first.[1]

This estrangement is no great surprise. The modern version of transformational theory combines a branch of mathematics that falls outside the usual preuniversity curriculum with fervent neologistic tendencies into a rarefied analytical method used almost exclusively by, and for, academic music theorists. Current practitioners of film music analysis, in contrast, come just as often from professional fields outside of music as from within, and tend to prefer discourse that is as accessible to the general reader as the subject of their study.

Bringing these two fields into disciplinarily close quarters has all the makings of, if not a turf war, at least an "Odd Couple" scenario. Film theorist K. J. Donnelly, using an argument not dissimilar to one recounted in McCreless's article, contends that music theory's penchants for formalism and abstraction "neglect the materiality of music— its particular context of appearance, its individual instrumental (or vocal) sounds, the ethos of rhythm as pulse and the cumulative effect of repetition; and the relation of music to other things, such as history, society or film" (Donnelly 2001, 2). He criticizes such musical formalism for "apprehend[ing] the object in a void, losing the sense of living relationship that music has with its surroundings." His caution and underlying advice are well taken. Music theory's inherent tendency toward recondite abstraction and the occasional mathematical formalism doubtlessly exemplifies the objects of Donnelly's criticism, and will doubtlessly be approached by those outside of academia's music-theory enclave with caution and even suspicion. However, film music study has already shown a willingness to assimilate concepts and their related terminology from other enclaves. For example, the contributors to a special issue of *Yale French Studies* devoted to "Cinema/Sound" (introduced by Altman 1980) tapped into not only current film theory but also the ideas and terminology from semiotics, psychoanalysis, Marxist theories, and literary and narrative theories. In reviewing this issue, Martin Marks recognized that, "to uninitiated readers, this language, now common currency in academia, may seem either frustratingly opaque or unnecessarily complex for the material at hand; yet for all its difficulties it is worth the trouble. It compels us to rethink assumptions and contexts, leading us to a point where films can be seen, and their music heard, anew" (1997, 24). One purpose of this chapter is to demonstrate that the adoption of, and adaptation to, ideas and terminology from transformational theory, now common currency in music academia, into the analysis of film music is likewise worth the trouble.

I also bring together film music studies and transformational theory because it appears that each is at a point in its growth where one of the important next steps would be significantly facilitated by a recognition and an incorporation of one form of the other. To make this argument, the chapter begins by selectively outlining the histories and methodologies for each area, followed by the presentation of a new approach that lies at their intersection. I conclude with an analytical application that engages most of the features of music's materiality that Donnelly lists.

ANALYSIS OF FILM MUSIC: PERSPECTIVES ON ITS PAST, PRESENT, AND FUTURE

Claudia Gorbman (1995) proposed a division of traditional and contemporary film music studies into five categories: study of film music *qua* music, a fan-based guide to the market for commercial recordings of film music, an academic examination of how a score relates to and illuminates other elements in a particular film, a survey of trends in film scoring and how they reflect their socioeconomic or cultural contexts, and the incorporation of musical observations as one element of mainstream film criticism. This classification covers considerable ground and indeed accounts for many of the varied activities and ventures that would partially, if not fully, fit under the umbrella of film music studies. Like many other disciplines, however, the very definition of film music studies is continuously in flux. One potential first step in anticipating novel trends or developments in some fields of knowledge can be to classify the variety of things or activities that are already known using a taxonomy based on features instead of partitions. One example of this is Dmitri Mendeleev's discovery of chemistry's two-dimensional periodic table: rather than inventing categories that would divide all known substances into separate categories, Mendeleev used certain properties of the elements to arrange them into overlapping groups. This created the possibility of undiscovered combinations of features, which, as it turned out, accurately predicted the existence of new elements.

A consideration of the future prospects of film music studies may benefit from a similar feature-based taxonomy that borrows from both Gorbman's fivefold division and musicology's distinctions among the activities of theory, analysis, and criticism (Cone 1967; Lewin 1969; Morgan 1982). This taxonomy takes the form of three continua or dimensions.

First, there is the *scope* of a film music study, which may range from the focus on a single film to the consideration of an entire repertoire. The continuum between theory and analysis as these terms are used in music scholarship runs roughly parallel with scope: analysis focuses more on the idiosyncratic aspects of an individual artwork, whereas theory, in line with scientific parlance, aims instead to codify generalities observed among a large set of individual artworks.

Second, there is the *object* of the film music study, which may range from primarily examining the music's relationship with the other aspects of the film to its consideration solely as music: basically, the third and first of Gorbman's five categories, respectively. In the extreme case of the latter, the fact that some music was incorporated into, or specially written for, the soundtrack of a film matters for only one purpose: to qualify it as an object for film music study.

Third, there is the *approach* of a film music study, which may range from utilizing perspectives both subjective and, using New Musicology's locution, critical—"the way of looking at art that tries to take into account the meaning it conveys, the pleasure it initiates, and the value it assumes, for us today" (Kerman 1965, 63)—to objective and often exacting and technical descriptions of "the music itself." Certainly a film music study does not have to exemplify an absolute end of one of these continua; in fact, one might argue that, for one or more of these dimensions, such limits exist only hypothetically, and some blend of the two extremes, however uneven, is not only unavoidable but also desirable.

The resulting three-dimensional categorical space yields eight possible combinations of the three pairs of contraries as shown in Figure 19.1. This visualization of the discipline of film music studies—or of studies of musical multimedia in general—brings into relief its historical trajectories and its inevitable biases and interdependencies. Consider first the half of the space occupied by those studies that concentrate on technical and formalist musical description, represented by the top half of Figure 19.1. These studies historically stretch from the earliest cue-by-cue exegeses—for Martin Marks (1997, 17), it is Lawrence Morton's (1946) probe into Franz Waxman's music for *Objective, Burma!* (1945); for William Rosar (2009, 119), it is Frederick Sternfeld's (1947) examination of Hugo Friedhofer's music for *The Best Years of Our Lives* (1946)—up to the articles, dissertations, monographs, and books of the early twenty-first century. A relatively small number of these studies import contemporary music-analytical techniques of varying degrees of sophistication and specialization from the discipline of music theory. Beyond concepts and vocabulary that would be familiar to undergraduate students of music, these techniques include reductive graphs of tonal harmonic-contrapuntal behavior modeled after those of the music theorist Heinrich Schenker (Cochran 1986; Burt 1994; Neumeyer 1998; Davison 2004; Watson and Burns 2010); measures notated into

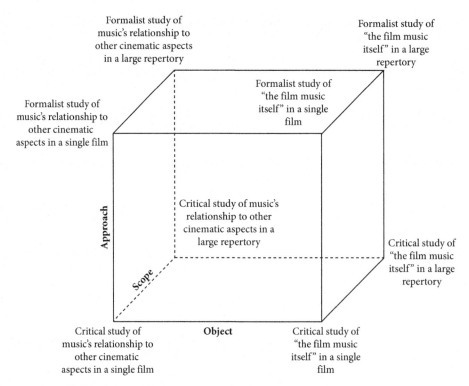

FIGURE 19.1 Film music studies space.

groupings of longer, "hypermetric" periodicities (Cooper 2001, Davison 2009); considerations (or refutations) of chords that put a key's leading tone in an unusual harmonic context as "chromatic dominants" (Buhler 2000; Cooper 2001); balanced pairings of keys into a "double-tonic" complex (Neumeyer 1998; Rodman 2000; Cooper 2005); and arrangements of notes around "axcs of symmetry" (Cooper 2005; Code 2010; Murphy 2012). These studies fluctuate between—and even foster a dialogue among—the analytical objects of "the music itself" and their interaction with other elements of the film. Nevertheless, one evident characteristic that these and many other music-technical studies share, as well demonstrated by current publication preferences, is a delimiting of scope to the analysis of a single film or perhaps a small set of films. On the space of Figure 19.1, this means that the more a study is toward the top, the more it tends toward the front. This delimitation—what music theorist David Neumeyer (1990, 25) has called "work-analyses" and to what Lawrence Morton's (1953, xi) description of film music scholarship's "ant's-eye view" still pertains—contrasts with the use of music-technical apparatuses to seek commonalities among a relatively large set of film scores; that is, to theorize.

In contrast, when film music scholars (such as Gallez 1970; Kalinak 1992; Lexmann 2006) propose a so-called "theory of film music" that is intended for such broad applications, the object of their study is typically the relationship between music and the other components of the cinematic product (or, a theory of "music *with* film"), rather than "the film music itself" in relative isolation from these components (or, a theory of "music *for* film"). On the space of Figure 19.1, this means that the more a study is toward the back, the more it tends toward the left. This characterization also holds for other studies that nominally may not be labeled "theory" but whose chief concern is to put forward widely applicable methodologies, which are typically for examining music-image or music-narrative interfaces (Cook 1998). Such studies would also include those that scrutinize of the inner workings of the cinematic leitmotif (London 2000) and those that, as latter-day scholarly counterparts of silent-film cue compilers, catalog intertextually consistent associations between musical gestures and extramusical objects or states (Tagg 1979; Tagg and Clarida 2003). Lastly, film music compositional manuals (Karlin and Wright 2004) understandably offer considerably more insight into the craft of creating effective interactions between music and film than into the strictly musical elements that set film music apart from other kinds of music.

Is it even possible or desirable to study film music as a *bona fide* musical object unto itself, or is film music instead, in Christopher Palmer's words, "not quite film and not quite music" (1990, 9)? While this type of isolation is atypical in, and perhaps even antithetical to, most academic studies, it occurs rather often in the domain of soundtrack recording reviews in trade magazines, blogs, and the customer comments on the websites of online retailers. Not all critics cordon off a film's music from its cinematic context: when Royal S. Brown began his "Film Musings" column for *Fanfare* magazine, for example, he promised to "continue to make ample reference to films as well as to their music, as I simply do not see the domains as separable, at least as far as critical approach is concerned" (Brown 1983, 144). This focus set Brown apart from some of his fellow critics at *Fanfare*, who did not necessarily treat a viewing of the film as a prerequisite to reviewing its soundtrack recording. A similar situation holds for the three oldest websites offering soundtrack reviews—http://www.filmtracks.com, http://www.moviemusicuk.us, and http://www.movie-wave.net. The first of these sometimes explicitly opts for a distinction between "Music as Written for the Film" and "Music as Heard on Album" before providing an overall score, whereas the other two sites also make this distinction, only less explicitly. Studies that treat the "film music itself" as an object of study would also include manifestos that either praise the merits of a general type of film scoring or bemoan its overall decadence or banality. What all of these studies generally have in common is an eschewal of technical, and thus parochial, descriptions of structure in favor of personal, but more accessible, judgments of aesthetic value. On the space of Figure 19.1, this means that the more a study is toward the right, the more it tends toward the bottom.

Returning to the dimension of approach brings this survey of film music studies back full circle. Although it was admittedly selective, this survey neglected one corner of the proposed three-dimensional disciplinary space precisely because it has no significant representation within film music studies: a technical-formalist study of the music of a large film repertoire with more concern for the "music itself" than for how it interacts with the film, represented by the upper right back corner of Figure 19.1. My survey's tangential sweeps past this corner suggest that each of its three defining aspects—a wide scope, "the film music itself" as object, and a technical approach—have, individually, already played a significant role in film music studies, but they simply have not been bundled together into a significant subtype of film music studies, arguably serving as one example of Alexander Binns's observation that "the broadening of film musicology's ambit has also drawn attention to its selective fields of coverage" (2009, 726).

What good could any studies in this corner of the disciplinary space provide? Ultimately, any results could, at least, shed light on idiolectical components of film music's sound and structure, and, more ambitiously, shape an understanding of a "film music style." They can help to answer questions like "In what ways does this music sound like film music?" or "Knowing that this music is film music, how does this change one's expectations for its behavior?" I acknowledge the widely held views that "there is no single style of music that can be defined as 'film music'" (Rona 2009, 17) and that it is a mélange of various preexisting styles instead. But William Rosar contends that "despite all its stylistic variability throughout the decades—whether the often cited 'late Romantic' style or passing trends in musical fashion—there was and remains a film music sound, elusive though it may be to define" (2009, 115). And if "sounding like film music" should be one of the criteria for a film music ontology, as suggested by Jeff Smith (2009, 190), then it behooves film music scholarship to be able to state with as much precision and empirical validity as possible what "sounding like film music" actually entails. In the third part of this chapter ("Toward a Syntax and Semantics of Recent Popular Music and Related Visual Media"), I will propose one of what might be many possible responses to this challenge. To prepare that discussion, the section below provides an overview of the history and prospects for transformational theory.

TRANSFORMATIONAL THEORY: PERSPECTIVES ON ITS PAST, PRESENT, AND FUTURE

The timeline for studies in transformational theory parallels that of film music studies in multiple ways: both involve a new extramusical "technology" (either mechanical or mathematical) standardized toward the end of the nineteenth century; sporadic examples of what later would become more commonplace for both begin to appear in the years immediately following the Second World War; and landmark books published in the 1980s and 1990s authoritatively staked out disciplinary ground for both. In the twentieth century, after Schenker's theory of hierarchical tonality (1935) and set theory as applied to atonal music most noticeably by Allen Forte (1973), transformational theory is the third important and far-reaching branch of structure-centered English-language music theory.

At the heart of transformational theory is mathematical group theory, a significant subject within abstract algebra that, in the latter half of the nineteenth century, subsumed earlier observations concerning certain symmetrical patterns within the relatively distinct fields of geometry, permutations, polynomials, and modular arithmetic. A group is the merger of two components: a set of some elements, and a manner of combining two of these elements to produce a third element. This manner of combining two elements is called a binary operation. To be a group, its binary operation needs to follow four rules, which, since they are far from common mathematical knowledge, are spelled out anew nearly every time a music scholar invokes group theory:

- the third element must always be a member of the set ("closure");
- when three elements in a row are combined into one element, it does not matter if the first and second are combined first, or the second and third are combined first ("associativity");
- there should be an "identity" element in the set such that any element when combined with the identity produces itself;
- for each element, the set should contain an "inverse" element, such that the combination of an element with its inverse produces the identity element.

For example, the set of whole numbers, or integers, together with the binary operation of addition, is a group, since (1) adding together two integers gives you a third; (2) the order in which adjacent integers in a string of three integers are added does not change the sum; (3) any integer added to the identity element of 0 leaves the original integer unchanged; and (4) every integer's negative (or positive) partner is its inverse. The set of integers together with the binary operation of multiplication, however, is not a group; although it abides by the first three rules—in this case, the identity element is 1—only 1 and –1 have an integer for a multiplicative inverse.

The elements in the set do not have to be—for lack of a better word—"objects" such as integers, but rather "actions," or what music scholars may label "transformations," such as rotations and reflections of a geometric figure or reorderings of items in a series. Gerald Balzano (1980) referred to these two classifications of a group as "static" and "dynamic," respectively. The binary operation for dynamic groups is direct succession: one transformation follows another. To be a group, it still needs to follow the rules: for example, the sequential execution of two transformations from the set of transformations must be replaceable by a single transformation in the set, the set must contain a transformation that does nothing, and every transformation must be reversible. Static groups resonate little with everyday musical cognitions—what pitch is middle C plus the E♭ a third higher?—but dynamic groups make more intuitive sense to musicians, for at least two reasons. First, so much musical description—and, by extension, experience and understanding—is couched in metaphorical terms of spatiotemporal motion and change: a melody rises or falls, a tempo accelerates or decelerates, a theme is transposed or inverted, a pivot chord enables a change of key, and so forth. Second, two or more of these musical transformations can follow one another in time, producing a cumulative transformation: the succession of the binary operation can be readily grasped as chronological succession and accretion, although not necessarily so.

Thus, one advantage of particularly the first and fourth rules of a group is that a smaller set of more salient and familiar musical transformations can—through concatenation, inversion, and ultimately closure and symmetry of the group—give rise to novel musical transformations that can feed back into our characterization and experience of music; one "pursu[es] algebraic aspects of the model in order to identify possible broader families of musical phenomena to which the transformations in the model might belong." (Cook 2005, 122).

Milton Babbitt; Allen Forte

One of the earliest studies of music that was informed by group-theoretic principles is a Princeton dissertation by the composer and music theorist Milton Babbitt (1992), which was completed in 1946 but not accepted until forty-six years later upon his retirement from the same institution's faculty. Babbitt examined various properties of the twelve-tone system, a system of composition promulgated foremost by composer Arnold Schoenberg and his pupils, in which a row—a particular ordering of the twelve notes of the chromatic scale—serves as the kernel of a composition's melodic and harmonic materials. Among other observations, Babbitt noticed that the four Schoenbergian transformations of transposition, inversion, retrograde, and retrograde plus inversion form a group under the binary operation of succession. Retrograde plus inversion, by some accounts the most abstruse of the four transformations, comes in last during Babbitt's exposition, achieving group closure among the other three. During the next four decades, musicians applied group theory intermittently either as a precompositional construct—such as Iannis Xenakis's *Nomos Alpha* of 1965 for solo cello, which uses the group of twenty-four possible rotations of a cube (DeLio 1980)—or as a tool to support theoretical claims—such as Balzano's aforementioned article, which uses group theory to highlight a serendipitous feature of the twelve-tone chromatic scale.

Allen Forte's musical set theory (1973) explicitly uses the concepts and language of its mathematical counterpart, but implicitly relies upon the closure of group theory, in that two unordered collections of octave-undifferentiated notes—what he named "pitch-class sets"—are considered equivalent and given the same set-class label if one can be transformed into the other by a transformation from a group of canonic transformations. For Forte, this group was the set of twenty-four possible transpositions and inversions, such that not only would all major triads be assigned one label, but also all minor triads, as inversions of major triads, would be given the same "set-class" label as their inversional partners: 3–11 or (037). The inclusion of inversional equivalence, obviously derived from the twelve-tone tradition, perturbed some (Browne 1974) but nonetheless availed to others a potential for analytical insight, as two chords perhaps heard as distinct could still be understood as having something in common. Nonetheless, the canonic group that stipulates equivalency among pitch-class sets can be one of several other groups of transformations, such as the smaller group of twelve transpositions, where major and minor triads receive different designations (Rahn 1980), or larger groups that add other sets of transformations to Forte's twenty-four (Morris 1987).

David Lewin; Hugo Riemann

Forte's set theory provided for analysts a multitude of new labels for musical objects such as chords, motives, scales, and collections, while the transformations that subsidize the labeling of the objects served a less prominent, supporting role. One view of the innovations of David Lewin, the music theorist and composer who is justly considered the founder of "transformational theory," essentially reverses the terms of this summary of Forte's project: Lewin provided for analysts a multitude of new transformations, while the musical objects that subsidize the labeling of the transformations served a less prominent, supporting role, particularly with the promotion of "transformational networks" (Lewin 1987, 1993). In short, whereas Forte's new labels befit musical objects, Lewin's new labels befit the relationships between musical objects. These relationships took on different conceptual and metaphorical guises for Lewin: they could be "intervals" that measure a precise span between musical objects in various broadly construed kinds of musical "space," or they could be the aforementioned "transformations" that breathe animated life into these and other intervals, chronicling the motion or mutation experienced not only by musical objects, but also by the performers and listeners of such objects. Underlying Lewin's new approach are the strictures of group theory, which regulate the uniformity of the intervallic spaces and the transformational actions.

Also underlying Lewin's new approach was a historically informed awareness that his approach was not entirely new, or at least not without some precedent. Hugo Riemann, the most influential music scholar in Europe in the decades surrounding 1900, developed some ideas regarding what I will describe as "paradigmatic" (this-for-that) and "syntagmatic" (this-with-that) relationships of major and minor triads that, when looked at from a certain angle, resemble nascent transformational concepts. Riemann's paradigmatic type of triadic relationship is encapsulated in his enduring notion of *function* (Riemann 1893): that a normative tonal harmonic progression of I–IV–V–I or T(onic)–S(ubdominant)–D(ominant)–T(onic) would remain normative even if one (or more) of these primary triads were changed into another triad such that the new triad preserved two of the original notes and, hence, preserved the primary triad's syntactical function. For example, in the key of C major, the progression C–F–G–C (the case of the letter-as-triadic-root represents the triad's mode: upper case for major, lower case for minor) could be transformed to C–d–G–C without altering the grammaticality of the harmonic progression: the d still carries subdominant function, or, to use more modern terminology, predominant function. Lewin's English-language label for Riemann's transformation of F to d was REL (RELative), which applies to any transformation that changes a triad's mode while maintaining two common tones separated by a major third. Lewin's labels for the other two possible function-preserving transformations were PAR (PARallel), which preserves two common tones separated by a perfect fifth (for example, C to c), and LT, which preserves two common tones separated by a minor third (for example, C to e).

Riemann's (1880, 1887) syntagmatic type of triadic relationship is codified in his catalog of *Schritte* (steps) and *Wechseln* (changes), which offers a sometimes unwieldy, but nonetheless systematically derived name for every possible ordered pair of triads. This perspective was particularly suitable for much nineteenth-century music that was still triadic but relied considerably less on an overarching tonic to impart meaning to each triad. Each *Schritt* describes an ordered pair of like-moded triads; for example, *Terzschritt* labels a progression of C→E or G♭→B♭. Hence, just as both C and G receive the same Forte set-class label of 3–11, since one triad is a transposition of the other, C→E and G♭→B♭ receive the same Riemann "progression-class" label of *Terzschritt*, since one progression is a transposition of the other. *Terz* in this case is short for "major third," the directed interval from the first triadic root up to the next. A *Gegenterzschritt* inverts this directed interval in pitch-class space or, equally, reverses the progression in time: it would describe a progression of E→C or any of its transpositions, putting them in the same *Gegenterzschritt* "progression-class." This kind of class describes "partially ordered" pitch phenomena, for while the chords are in an order, the notes within each chord are not; thus, it lies between the kind of class for Schoenberg's rows, which require a total ordering of the notes, and Forte's kind of class, which requires no ordering.

Each *Wechsel* describes an ordered pair of opposite-moded triads. For example, *Terzwechsel* labels a progression of G→e or F→d. In fact, *Terzwechsel* is equivalent to Lewin's REL; moreover, all three of the function-preserving transformations presented earlier are *Wechseln*. In labeling these three transformations, Lewin uses the familiar names of REL and PAR that are derived from key relationships, but the third enjoys no such easy translation, so LT is a reference to the Riemann's original name of *Leittonwechsel*. Notice that the interval of a third from the first root to the second in the *Terzwechsel* progression (G→e, F→d, etc.) is minor, not major, and goes down instead of up. Rather than an inconsistency with the ascending major third of *Terzschritt*, this apparent difference is instead one manifestation of Riemann's "dualism." Riemann, like Forte nearly a century after him, calibrated his labeling system by the conception that major and minor triads are inversions of one another. For Riemann and other nineteenth-century dualists, a major triad results when adding a perfect fifth and a major third above a root, but a minor triad results when adding a perfect fifth and major third *below* what musicians generally describe as the fifth of the minor triad, but what dualists deemed the minor triad's root. For instance, dualists call the root of e the note B, the fifth of e. Hence, a *Terzwechsel* of G→e is consistent with *Terzschritt*, since the ordered interval from the first root to the second root, considered dualistically, is the ascending major third from the note G to the note B. Another related manifestation of Riemann's dualism surfaces when *Schritte* and *Wechseln* act upon minor triads, whereupon the interval of the label is inverted. For example, a *Terzschritt* that acts upon g♯ produces e—*down* a major third—instead of b♯ (enharmonically, c). Likewise, a *Terzwechsel* that acts upon e produces G—*down* a major third from the dual root B to the root G.

As with Forte's inversional equivalence of pitch-class sets, Riemann's inversional equivalence of pitch-class progressions, particularly the *Schritte*, may rankle some as a defiance of intuition. But, as with Forte's inversional equivalence, this conflation bestows some benefits. Riemann used the inversional equivalence of progression classes to efficiently address possible pitfalls in part writing: for example, the potential for writing parallel perfect fifths between two voices or an augmented second in one voice remains even if the progression is flipped over. Tymoczko also found value in this voice-leading consistency, "because it identifies pairs of chords which can be linked by structurally analogous voice leadings that are of exactly the same size" (Tymoczko 2008, 11). Lewin (1987, 1992) used the inversional equivalence of progression classes to deepen analytical and hermeneutic understanding: for example, the fact that G♭→B♭ and g♯→e are both *Terzschritte* helped him to demonstrate that the harmonic progressions of two leitmotifs from Wagner's *Das Rheingold*, associated with regal Valhalla and the sinister Tarnhelm respectively, share more than an initial hearing might suggest. Furthermore, when Riemann's *Schritte* and *Wechseln* are considered as a collection of transformations, they can also follow the rules and thus achieve the symmetry of a group. A succession of two *Wechseln*, such as the more intuitive function-preserving transformations, produces single transformations between like-moded triads that must behave like Riemann's less intuitive *Schritte* to achieve group closure. For example, a *Terzschritt* is the succession of LT then PAR, which is how Lewin (1992, 52) originally presented his *Rheingold* analysis: LT of G♭ is b♭, and PAR of b♭ is B♭ (overall, G♭→B♭); LT of g♯ is E, and PAR of E is e (overall, g♯→e). (See Figure 19.2, reproduced from Lewin 1992.)

Neo-Riemannian Theory

Exploration of the group-theoretical prospects of Riemannian transformations has been one of the many preoccupations of the research following from this aspect of Lewin's work, and a number of these pursuits fall under the subdisciplinary heading of "neo-Riemannian theory." Brian Hyer (1989, 1995) abbreviated LT, PAR, and REL to L, P, and R, and he investigated the ways these three transformations generate groups by themselves or in conjunction with pitch-class transformations. Richard Cohn (1996, 1997) initially focused on L, P, and R's exceptional potential for voice-leading smoothness or "parsimony," and inventoried the assorted triadic progressions one obtains through patterned alterations of these three transformations. In 1998, the *Journal of Music Theory* dedicated an entire issue (vol. 42, no. 2; introduced by Cohn) to neo-Riemannian theory. One article in this issue by Adrian Childs opens with the following: "Initial work applying the theories of neo-Riemannian triadic transformations has focused primarily on late nineteenth-century chromatic repertoire, particularly

(a)

(b)

FIGURE 19.2 a, b: (a) Wagner, *Das Rheingold*, "Tarnhelm" theme, sc. 3, mm. 37ff.; (b) Wagner, *Das Rheingold*, modulating section of "Valhalla" theme, sc. 2, mm. 5ff. Examples from Lewin 1992, 50.

the operas of Richard Wagner. While the analytical insights provided have proven rich and stimulating, a fundamental problem has also arisen: the composers whose works seem best suited for neo-Riemannian analysis rarely limited their harmonic vocabulary to simple triads" (1998, 181). He then laid out a group of transformations that act upon certain seventh chords; these transformations are then applied to an analysis of excerpts from various nineteenth-century works.

The first decade of the twenty-first century has witnessed, alongside an abundance of scholarly analyses using preexisting transformations, additions of new groups of transformations—notably, Julian Hook (2007a) proposed transformations between triads and certain seventh chords—and a mainstreaming of these ideas through their inclusion in academic curricula and textbooks. Among both present applications and future predictions (Hook 2007b), however, one object of research remains largely neglected: the use of transformational theory in general, or neo-Riemannian theory in particular, to make new and meaningful observations regarding one or more stylistic practices; that is, to truly be a "theory" in the manner that this word was used earlier. Thomas Christensen has observed that the goal of the practitioners of neo-Riemannian theory "is not so much to deduce insight analytically from musical practice, or to regulate music pedagogically. Rather, they aim for a more traditional goal: to explore the universe of tonal material in order to understand its boundless properties and potential" (Christensen 2002, 12–13). This is particularly evident in Cohn's aforementioned inventory, for, although he cites one or two examples of each transformational pattern from nineteenth-century art music, his aim appears to be a demonstration of the manifold ways a composer *could* write extended parsimonious progressions with major and minor triads, rather than to claim that composers of a certain era *did* make such progressions a significant part of their output.

Toward a Syntax and Semantics of Recent Popular Film Music and Related Visual Media

The intersection between the two potential future research avenues proposed in the previous two sections should be clear by now: my basic objective for the remainder of this chapter is to use neo-Riemannian theory to draw stylistic generalizations about a broad repertoire of film music. Before plunging in, however, it is incumbent to ask what aspects of neo-Riemannian theory are, or are not, particularly well suited to theorizing about film music and what repertoires of film music are, or are not, particularly well suited as subjects of a neo-Riemannian inquiry. Addressing the latter might begin with a look at the handful of existing examples of neo-Riemannian perspectives on film music, which include a brief postscript to an article by Guy Capuzzo (2004) that brings up the "Council of Elrond" cue from *The Lord of the Rings: The Fellowship of the Ring* (2001), Frank Lehman's (2013) analysis of some of James Horner's music for *A Beautiful Mind* (2001), and Jamie Webster's (2009) dissertation on the music for the first five Harry Potter films, which includes a neo-Riemannian examination of John Williams's music for "Buckbeak's Flight" in *Harry Potter and the Prisoner of Azkaban* (2004) (Webster 2009, 774–78). With respect to harmony, what the musical cues analyzed in these studies have in common with each other—and in common with much newly composed, typically orchestral, musical cues for mainstream, typically Hollywood, motion picture productions especially from the mid-1970s to the 2000s—is a pronounced tendency toward using only major and minor triads. This means that not only *can* the triad-transforming *Schritte* and *Wechseln* be applied to this kind of music written for those kinds of films, but that they are even *more* relevant to this brand of popular film music than its nineteenth-century art-music antecedent. Childs's observation that "the composers whose works seem best suited for neo-Riemannian analysis rarely limited their harmonic vocabulary to simple triads" is accurate for Wagner, Franck, Richard Strauss, and their contemporaries, but it is much less accurate for Horner, Williams,

James Newton Howard, and their contemporaries, who *often* limit their harmonic vocabulary to simple triads for recent popular movies. (By "popular" movies here and subsequently, I refer to those mainstream and primarily Hollywood studio products of motion picture entertainment that primarily employ A-list actors and directors, mostly incorporate traditional plot techniques and visual styles that are familiar and appealing to a broad consumer base, and are widely marketed and distributed, but are not necessarily box office successes. By "recent," I refer to films released roughly between 1975 and 2010.)

A transformational explication for the succession of these simple triads, *versus* a traditional tonal analysis, is particularly germane for recent popular film music. Composer Irwin Bazelon wrote that "film music is impatient. It has a function to perform and must make its presence felt without procrastination" (1975, 51). The immediate juxtaposition of two major or minor triads can fit this bill well, particularly when the juxtaposition is atypical—for example, the two triads cannot fit within a diatonic collection—or when the juxtaposition avoids participating in a larger harmonic trajectory but instead self-encapsulates somehow, often through undulation, pointing toward itself, creating what the early twentieth-century music theorist Ernst Kurth called an "absolute progression" (discussed in Rothfarb 1988, 158–63). Like distinctive timbres, the distinctive triadic successions that pervade this style of music can serve as a medium for communication even more expeditious than an associative theme. As musicologist Carl Dahlhaus has observed regarding Romantic-era music, "unusual progressions may even acquire a characteristic identity comparable to that of a *Leitmotiv*" (paraphrased in Smith 2009, 63).

As for which transformations best support theorizing about this repertoire of film music, some *Wechseln* in particular already provide sufficient specificity to permit one to make meaningful correspondences within this repertoire. For example, in his analysis of Howard's music for *The Sixth Sense* (1999), musicologist Lloyd Whitesell describes the undulation between g♯ and G in the main title—the harmonic backbone of what he calls the score's "motto"—as "harmonically ambivalent, slipping chromatically back and forth between a minor chord and a major chord" (Whitesell 2010, 208). This language might plausibly characterize a number of *Wechseln*; a more precise labeling of the triadic progression as a *Gegenterzwechsel*, or what Lewin (1987, 178) mercifully called a SLIDE (compare to Whitesell's "slipping"), could facilitate the progression's incorporation into networks of intertextual associativity within either art music or film music. Whitesell does not appear to have this as his primary aim, yet he notices that, of all the distinctive elements in Howard's score, the motto is "the most elusive in terms of its narrative associations" (Whitesell 2010, 210). For some viewers and listeners who have heard SLIDEs before in multimedia contexts, intertextual associations might fill, or be pulled into, this associative vacuum. For example, four years earlier, Howard also used an undulating SLIDE (this time, between e and E♭) at nearly the same moment in his exposition of main-title music for *Outbreak* (1995) and throughout the film seemed to associate the SLIDE with the liminal space between life and death.

Other conventions are better observed by refashioning neo-Riemannian labels in two specific ways. First, a distinction between *Schritte* involving major triads and *Schritte* involving minor triads, while depriving one of the opportunity to making analytical insights like those of Lewin regarding Wagner, sensibly teases apart progressions that, in practice, are treated quite differently. This distinction is the "progression-class" analogue to removing inversion transformations as one means to create Fortean set-class equivalence. The result is that the number of "progression-classes" doubles, from the twenty-four *Schritte* and *Wechseln* to forty-eight. Second, as demonstrated below, a progression's identification of one of its triads as tonic, or at least as "more tonic" than the other, is far more definitional in this style of film music than the order of the triads, as well elucidated in undulatory situations that abound in this style. Although this changes the means of triadic ordering from chronological to hierarchical—in other words, the two triads in the progression are distinguished from one another not as "first" and "second," but as "tonicized" and "not tonicized"—the number of "progression-classes" does not change. The tonic bias required to define one of these forty-eight "tonal-triadic progression classes"—which I will abbreviate to TTPCs—could occur with a clear tonicization before or after the progression or, through an imbalance in the presentation of the triads themselves, commonly through an initial flanking of one triad by the other (I–X–I...) or, less often, through an emphasis of one triad over the other through metrical placement, duration, or volume.

As with the set-class names of "diminished triad" and (036), one could either assign to each TTPC an *ad hoc* moniker or devise a consistent but drier numerical label. I have opted for the latter and so will use the nomenclature "MnM," where the case of the first "M" reflects the mode of the tonicized triad, the case of the second "M" reflects the mode of the other triad, and "n" the number of semitones from the root of the former up to the root of the latter in between. For example, a SLIDE where the major triad is tonicized is an M1m (read "major-one-minor"), whereas a SLIDE where the minor triad is tonicized is an m11M (read "minor-eleven-major"). Two options of mode for each of the two triads, times twelve possibilities for "n," produce forty-eight ($2 \times 2 \times 12$) possible TTPCs. However, MoM and mom label triad repetitions—or, to put it in transformational terms, they name the result of the identity transformation—so the number of nontrivial TTPCs drops to forty-six. In the case of Mom and moM, the case of the first "M" reflects the prevailing mode; for example, Richard Strauss's *Also Sprach Zarathustra* opens with two triadic progressions (C→c, c→C) that, in retrospect, are both labeled Mom. See Figure 19.3 for a table of all forty-eight TTPCs in music notation, using a C major or C minor triad as the tonic; the order of the triads in each pair as presented in the figure does not necessarily correlate with their order as presented in time in a musical cue. It is important to recognize at this juncture the concerted move away from an overt transformational theory, since any nontrivial MnM is not a kind of musical transformation, but a class of musical objects: while the SLIDE transformation acts on all twenty-four major and minor triads in a uniform manner, m11M, if construed as a transformation, does not.

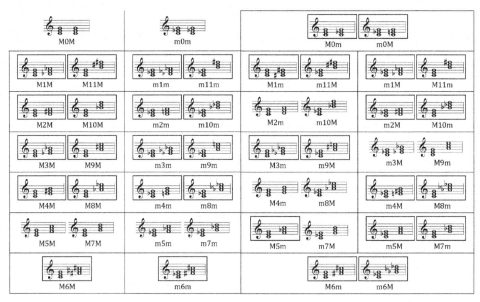

FIGURE 19.3 The 48 TTPCs in music notation, using C as the tonic pitch. The twenty-four TTPCs that correspond to the twelve *Schritte* appear in the fourteen cells on the left half of the table. The twenty-four TTPCs that correspond to the twelve *Wechseln* appear in the thirteen cells on the right half of the table. Tonal inverses are within the same cell; a TTPC that is alone in a cell is its own tonal inverse. A TTPC within its own enclosure is considered to be "chromatic" (for example, M1M is chromatic but M5M is not).

A SEMANTICS OF TRIADIC PROGRESSION

The following stylistic generalizations are drawn both from written notes on the harmonic language of the scores for over three hundred recent popular movies and from the tacit experience accumulated through many years of listening to, composing, researching, and teaching this kind of music. Although the number of films that belong to the genre under consideration well exceeds the number of films for which I have written and mental records, I believe my sample is large enough to yield an adequate representation of the repertoire as a whole.

The observations will come in two successive batches. The first will report on recurrent associations between certain TTPCs and narrative states: a semantics of triadic progression for recent popular film music. The second will aim more squarely at the challenge raised at the end of the first section (and obliquely at a challenge raised not once but twice by David Neumeyer [1990, 1998] that "it is nearly impossible to study a film score purely in terms of the structuralist/formalist descriptions of design that most of us are used to as the primary activity of music analysis" [1990, 16]) by using TTPCs to characterize the syntax of recent popular film music in and of itself as a distinct musical language. Rather than use transcriptions, the description of musical content in the following text deliberately focuses only on triadic modes and roots. This choice is a notational manifestation of a theory that controls for harmonic relationships amidst all of the other musical parameters—melody, bass line, rhythm, timbre, texture, and so forth—that may influence a film score's semantics and syntax. The only other musical parameter that might play a supporting role in the theorizing to follow is form, in that the two triads of a TTPC generally do not cross over a formal seam, the division between the end of a phrase or section to the beginning of the next.

Of the forty-eight TTPCs, m8m enjoys perhaps the most consistent and pointed narrative association in this style: antagonism, with offshoots of the eerie and sinister. This association's *locus classicus* is John Williams's "Imperial March" from *Star Wars: Episode V—The Empire Strikes Back* (1980) and subsequent films in the Star Wars saga, which links the theme's g–e♭–g to Darth Vader, but it can also be found in dozens of other scores. Matthew Bribitzer-Stull (2007) has traced this association back to Wagner's union of the same "Tarnhelm" progression (g♯→e) that Lewin deciphered and the dark magic Alberich wields to advance his nefarious plot in *Das Rheingold*. But the "Tarnhelm" progression—both Wagner's original and its countless uses in recent popular film music—is certainly more than a *Terzschritt* and even more than a *Terzschritt* between minor triads: it is an m8m. The tonicization is crucial to the precision of the association because, associativity aside, m4m seldom occurs in this style, let alone is it set aside as a marker with consistent extramusical associations. Note that m4m is m8m's "tonal inverse," the TTPC obtained when the two triads maintain their roots and modes but swap the roles of tonic and nontonic. In Figure 19.3, tonal-inverse pairs are placed in the same cell.

Two studies of mine bring to the fore other significant associations involving TTPCs in recent popular film music. The first (Murphy 2006) showed that M6M—what I christened the "major tritone progression"—is associated in fourteen movies, plus four others identified since, with images and narratives that refer to outer space. The second is a current study (forthcoming) that indicates an association between M4m, often the undulatory type, and sorrow, particularly in the contemplation of some kind of considerable loss, commonly the death of a loved one, in twenty-nine films released between 1985 and 2012, and throughout Michael Giacchino's patently cinematic music for the television program *Lost* (2004–2010). Tonicization is moot regarding M6M, which is its own tonal inverse, but it is key to recognizing the latter association, for while the L transformation undergirds both M4m and its tonal inverse of m8M (what Charles Smith [2001] has called "L major" and "L minor," respectively), any association between m8M and sorrow is nowhere near as frequent and pointed in this delimited repertoire, which is quite remarkable given m8M's minor-mode tonicization.

Other consistent associations, although still statistically significant, occur less often or involve more diffuse narrative correlations. Composers of this kind of film music, for example, have used M5m as a musical symbol for Middle Eastern locales, but this TTPC has also been associated with another subject equally exotic for the young male demographic: romantic heterosexual encounters with a female character. The less frequent m6m shares with the more frequent m8m an exclusive employment of minor triads and the inability to fit in a diatonic collection, and, indeed, it is also quite at home accompanying antagonism. At the same time, I have observed that, more often than m8m, m6m accompanies mortal threats and dangers issued less from adversarial characters, and more from situations, objects, or natural phenomena. Both M7m and its tonal inverse of m5M seem to be associated with experiences of wonderment, optimism, success, or transcendence; nevertheless, I have recognized in this repertoire neither a tonal bias nor an associative distinction between these two TTPCs overall. The TTPC m2M is extremely common in mainstream film music and tends to match up with a general experience of suspense or mystery, or perhaps dark humor. The TTPC M2M, one of recent popular film music's most recurrent and distinguishing harmonic figures, commonly accompanies narrative functions such as protagonism and heroism or, less melodramatically, light-hearted enjoyment and fun; at the same time, M2M's connection to the Lydian mode—film music's signature mode that enjoys similar narrative associations—creates an explanatory overlap. Lastly, M8M shares with M2M a sound immediately identifiable both with recent popular film music in general and with the aforementioned positive narrative associations but, perhaps owing to its chromaticism, typically blends such associations with ample references to the fantastical.

I recommend against making too much—if also, too little—of these findings. On the one hand, even if they collectively are construed as a semiotic system, that system is far from complete and hardly compulsory. A film composer certainly may use one of many stylistically appropriate musical accompaniments for antagonism that does not involve m8m, or, conversely, may use m8m to accompany a scene that has little or nothing to do with antagonism. On the other hand, both film composers and moviegoers, whether consciously or not, are undoubtedly acquainted with many, if not all, of these associations through repeated exposure. Depending upon your viewpoint, to reuse these associations as a composer or to experience them again as a moviegoer becomes either a moment of perpetuated cliché or a moment of clear communication, stylistic consistency, and continuity of tradition—to co-opt both the title and the premise of a book by film scholar David Bordwell (2006), this is simply "the way Hollywood music tells it." If a composer for popular film avoids using these associations directly, they can still exert an influence when using only one half of the associational pair—that is, the TTPC or its narrative correlate. As one example of the former, an M6M accompanying something not associated with outer space can still import traces of its narrative affiliate. This occurs in both *Toy Story 2* (1999) and *Monsters Inc.* (2001), in which Randy Newman synchronizes multiple M6Ms with the protagonists' eye-opening entrance into a cavernous indoor space—Al's Toy Barn (E♭–A–G♭–C–A♭–D) and the door-storage area (E–B♭–E–B♭–G–D♭), respectively. As one example of the latter, a TTPC other than M6M accompanying something belonging to outer space in a recent popular movie can be heard as "not-M6M" in a musically significant way that a composer can exploit, as I hypothesized in my 2006 analysis of Howard's score to *Treasure Planet* (2002).

A SYNTAX OF TRIADIC PROGRESSION

Narrative associations aside, a TTPC perspective also provides a sharper picture of recent popular film music's general harmonic behavior, that is, of one element of what this "music itself" sounds like. To simplify matters, the TTPCs to be considered as most distinguishing should include only the thirty-five "chromatic" ones, those in which the nontonic triad, spelled diatonically, cannot fit within the scale—the major and either the natural or harmonic minor—appropriate to the key and mode of the tonic triad. These "chromatic" TTPCs are enclosed in boxes in Figure 19.3. Of these thirty-five TTPCs, some have occurred in popular film music more frequently than others, with varying degrees of discrepancy, and are thus more characteristic of the style. This approach refines the point of view that, for example, all chromatic mediant progressions are equally clichéd, as implied in a lecture by film composer Ira Newborn (2008). As one case in point, for every M3M used in this repertoire between 1975 and 2000, I estimate that there were at least twenty M8Ms to match it. Newborn cites *The Lord of the Rings* series (2001–3) as an example of the type of movie where mediant clichés run rampant. Regardless of how true this may be, Howard Shore's "Fellowship" theme—one of the most immediately recognizable themes in the entire trilogy—is perhaps so recognizable and fresh, at least in part, because it opens with a little-used M3M, and yet this M3M, as a chromatic TTPC, nonetheless suits a blockbuster movie.

A composer's goal of striking a balance between conforming with the style, as reflected by using any one of the chromatic TTPCs, and finding a less conventional sound, as reflected by choosing a less frequently used TTPC, could also explain fluctuations of TTPC usage over time. For example, a randomly chosen SLIDE—either M1m or m11M—from a score for a popular film between 1975 and 2010 is much more likely to come from a film in the second half of that time period than the first. I suspect that, perhaps in conjunction with a consideration of SLIDE's structural features that befitted the accompanied narratives, composers starting in the mid-1990s were simply looking for relatively unused TTPCs to include in their scores. The conspicuous SLIDEs in Hans Zimmer's scores for Christopher Nolan's *The Dark Knight* (2008) and *Inception* (2010) testify against any current obsolescence. Another common way film composers have struck a balance between the conventional and the new is to link together a relatively novel sequence of well-worn TTPCs: not unlike how Galant composers of the eighteenth century strung together familiar schemata to form original musical utterances (Gjerdingen 2007). Elliot Goldenthal's "Fanfare" music that opened both *Batman Forever* (1995) and *Batman & Robin* (1997) exemplifies this "recombinant" approach, as m8m, m9M, M6M, and m2M are stitched together into a tonally roving theme that is both tellingly cinematic and undeniably new.

Lastly, a certain kind of discrepancy among the frequencies of TTPC occurrences has potent ramifications for the perceptions of tonal centricity and syntax peculiar to this style. Recall that the tonal inverse of a tonal-triadic progression comes about by toggling the roles of tonic (or more tonic) and nontonic (or less tonic).

With regard to the TTPC label, this swaps the case of the two Ms (if they are different), and it inverts the pitch-class interval in between: for example, m8M is the tonal inverse of M4m. Some TTPC tonal-inverse pairs appear to have similar frequencies in this repertoire, such as the aforementioned M7m and m5M pair, and the m1M and M11m pair. Other pairs seem to be less balanced. For example, m11m has a fair showing, while m1m is considerably less frequent; M2M is quite common, but M10M is not quite as common. However, the two pairs M8M/M4M and m8m/m4m have an immense discrepancy in their frequencies—perhaps more so before 2000, but nonetheless they are still the two pairs with the highest discrepancy throughout the time period under scrutiny—in that the first member of the pair pervades this repertoire, and the second member almost never occurs. This style-specific discrepancy confidently points an acculturated listener toward a provisional tonic based on the hearing of a single *Terzschritt* in this music, particularly a *Terzschritt* within a formal unit instead of one spanning formal units. I will refer to the kind of "tonic finding" that originates from a significant asymmetry between the frequencies of tonal inverses as "TTPC tonicization." The effect is akin to how statistical disparities in tonal harmonic progressions for a certain kind of music can generate expectations as to what will follow certain tonal harmonies heard within the style (Huron 2006), but it comes closer to Hyer's acknowledgement "that certain harmonic configurations do seem to insist on an intrinsic relation or affiliation with a referential tonic, even if that affiliation is of our own imaginative making" (1995, 128).

TTPC TONICIZATION: IMPACT ON HEARING MUSIC IN RECENT FILMS

This style-specific TTPC tonicization impacts my experience of this repertoire in at least five ways. Four of these will be discussed here; the last will be reserved for the next section and discussed in the context of a more extended analysis.

First, it impacts the degree to which certain kinds of chromaticism and tonicization can be heard to coexist. Harald Krebs has suggested that a progression such as I-♭VI-I (M8M) in nineteenth-century art music may confound the tonal ear and weaken a listener's sense of tonic (Krebs 1980, 104). Yet M8M's pervasiveness, coupled with M4M's extreme scarcity, in recent popular film music arguably compensates for this disorientation, creating what Joseph Swain called a "trading relationship": "When an evolutionary trend within a language threatens its ability to communicate, the language corrects itself by making adjustments elsewhere. The same kind of adjustment can take place within a musical language" (Swain 1997, 152).

Second, style-specific TTPC tonicization impacts the beginnings of formal units, such as the d→f♯ progression that opens Jerry Goldsmith's main theme for *Basic Instinct* (1992) and which also opens the film. With no music before the solitary d, its primacy makes it the tonic triad by fiat, and yet when f♯ follows, d immediately passes to f♯ the title of tonic triad for listeners familiar with the m8m/m4m disparity. Although the chromatically creeping parallel thirds over d stop moving once f♯ enters, this cessation is more confirmation than authorization of the new tonic and the "off-tonic" beginning. Anticipating the subject material of the movie makes the m8m evocation even more germane, and even seems to make the tonicization of f♯ all the more discernible. Goldsmith's music subsequently cadences on neither triad, but I submit that, in general, an off-tonic beginning is not only a way of hearing but also a reliable form of prediction in this repertoire, in that, if either of the two triads involved in an opening *Terzschritt* is simultaneously, or soon thereafter, promoted by other tonic-finding or tonic-asserting measures, one can safely predict that it will be the tonic of the opening M8M or m8m, even if it is an off-tonic opening.

Third, style-specific TTPC tonicization impacts the ends of formal units, such as the second phrase of the main theme for Horner's score to *Star Trek II: The Wrath of Khan* (1982), heard first during the opening credits. Its harmonic progression, which comes on the heels of a first phrase solidly in C major, is C–A♭–C–A–C–G♭–C–E. A more "common practice" hearing of this phrase might interpret the concluding E as more active within the asserted key of C, and anticipate F or a to come next, or, at the least, perceive the phrase's ending as a harmonically odd cadence, since it ends neither on tonic or dominant in C major nor with a common cadential progression in another key. A hearing that acknowledges the M8M/M4M disparity, however, has little trouble interpreting E as a stable tonic, for that is its customary role when E and C, or their transpositions, occur adjacently in this kind of music. The fact that a undulatory, tonally transparent M8M sounds right before this cadence (the C–A♭–C) makes the interpretation of the concluding C–E *Terzschritt* as an M8M all the more relevant. I submit that, in general, when a phrase in this style ends with a *Terzschritt*, the root motion—speaking nondualistically—will usually be an ascending major third and will bear the stamp of an authentic "film music" cadence.

Fourth, style-specific TTPC tonicization impacts the interpretation of multiple TTPCs within a phrase. John Williams's "Ark" theme from the *Indiana Jones* tetralogy (1981–2008) employs a progression of c–f♯–c–f♯–c–a♭–e♭–g–b♭–d♭. The opening m6m undulation between c and g♭ comports well with the Ark of the Covenant as a dangerous object but is inherently unbiased toward which triad is tonic. I tentatively read the conclusion of the progression as containing two instances of m3m, since, although m3m is not that common, m9m is far less common; this intimates a rather weak but cumulative shift toward nontonic in the theme's conclusion. A more convincing style-specific TTPC tonicization occurs in the progression's middle: c→a♭ is an m8m that departs from its tonic and thus generates tension, and e♭→g is an m8m that returns to its tonic and thus releases tension. Even though these two motions do not overlap and involve different tonic triads, they may still be heard to reciprocate one another in the manner of what Daniel Harrison has called "accumulative analysis," which is the "eventual resolution" of "the accumulation of unpaid [tonal] charges," even if the music changes key (1994, 155).

Another example of this reciprocity comes from the final measures of end credits music for *Star Trek II*. Horner's basic harmonic progression is B–G–E–B♭–E–D–F♯, and the opening two harmonies are elaborated with an "open" undulation of B–C♯–B–C♯ and "closed" undulation of G–A–G; the prolonged roots of the two embellished triads, sustained underneath as bass pedals, clearly mark these triadic embellishments as M2Ms. The basic progression may be interpreted as beginning with a "departure" M8M progression of B→G, continuing to a "neutral" M6M undulation between E and B♭, and finishing with a "return" M8M cadence of D→F♯ that answers the earlier departure. Moreover, although the frequencies of M2M and M10M do not approach the disparity of those of M8M and M4M in the general repertoire, the embellishing M2Ms that open Horner's perorative progression augment the modest intertextual bias with a temporary intratextual bias that designates the E→D progression as a "return" progression that answers the M2M left "open" earlier, and anticipates the D→F♯ cadence. Horner takes advantage of the potential for E→D to be a cadence on its own when, in one instance of his self-borrowing, he reuses the same progression to conclude the end credits music for both *The Rocketeer* (1991) and *Bicentennial Man* (1999), but he leaves off the final F♯ from the *Star Trek II* progression which, after all, accompanied a final statement of Alexander Courage's signature eight-note motive from the original *Star Trek* (1966–1969) television series. This change converts the E→D M2M penultimate resolution into an E→D M2M ultimate cadence.

THE IMPACT OF TTPC SYNTAX ON THE NARRATIVE: AN ANALYSIS

The fifth, and final, style-specific TTPC tonicization impacts how TTPCs interact with the narrative. The aforementioned perceptions of departure and return, of activity and stability, of tension and release as informed by TTPC disparities can shape an interpretation of the rest of the filmic content. When the title character in Roland Emmerich's *Godzilla* (1998) smashes through a Manhattan city street from underneath and finally emerges into the camera's full view for the first time in the movie (45:30), composer David Arnold sensibly begins his underscore of the scary moment with a danger-associated m6m undulation between e and b♭ in blaring brass, a TTPC Arnold also used for earlier, preliminary appearances of the monster. But then the music changes course, introducing a soaring, long-breathed melody for high strings and French horns over broad, consonant harmonies in the rest of the orchestra—the venerated sound of an uplifting Hollywood theme. This shift in tone initially appears to capture the reaction of biologist Dr. Nick Tatopolous (Matthew Broderick) who, although just as frightened as the soldiers around him, cannot help but admire the towering creature. Astonishment spreads through the heavily armed soldiers turned helpless onlookers as Godzilla makes his way down the street and helps himself to a huge mound of fish; all the while, the soundtrack presents slightly modified versions of the inspiriting theme three more times in various keys. To listen only to this theme's expansive melody, rich timbres, and sonorous harmonies not once but four times is to hear the music archetypically declare Godzilla as the eponymous protagonist upon its grand stage entrance, spotlights and all. And, in some respects, the monster is the hero, as it outsmarts, outmuscles, and outruns its human enemies during the course of the film and as it is inwardly mourned by Tatopolous at film's end.

But, in many other respects, Godzilla defies this role, and this characterization is well captured by Arnold's harmonic choices for this theme. The harmonic progression of A♭–C–A♭–E♭–b♭–G♭–f–E♭ undergirds the first appearance of the theme, and the concluding E♭ resolves as dominant to the A♭ tonic that begins the theme's second statement. Despite its rarity in this repertoire, the theme unmistakably begins with an M4M by virtue of a closed undulation and A♭'s primacy. We might speculate that Arnold chose a relatively untapped member of the TTPC universe to give the start of his theme a fresh sound. Yet this particular untapped member is very special in that its tonal inverse of M8M is one of the most tapped members of all of the chromatic TTPCs. (Arnold uses M8M for a heroic moment earlier in *Godzilla* at 29:43, and this TTPC also figures prominently in *Stargate* (1994) and *Independence Day* (1996), his two previous collaborations with Emmerich.) This brings to my ears a mix of tonal signals: with the first chord, A♭ is presumed as tonic; with the second, the strong tonal bias of the opening *Terzschritt* suggests a tonicization of C and an off-tonic beginning; on the third and subsequent triads, C is abruptly demoted and A♭ is reaffirmed as tonic. For one whose key-finding sense is modified by TTPC disparities, this tonal volatility comes across as palpably disconcerting, which is, at the least, how a giant aggressive lizard lumbering through New York City should come across.

The second and third statements curiously play down this tonal volatility: the second statement in A♭ begins with A♭–C–f, changing the TTPC into a functional progression; and the third in D♭ adds a minor seventh to the second chord (D♭–F♭^{7}–D♭...), disqualifying it as a stable tonic. The fourth statement in C, which accompanies Godzilla's arrival at the fish, is preceded by music that clearly establishes its opening chord of C as tonic. Once again, the C–E–C opening invokes tonal disquiet inherent in any M4M due to the ubiquity of its tonal inverse, but, rather than continue as before, the undulation between C and E continues, during which each triad, heard thrice, lasts an average of three seconds. The initial sense of C as tonic ebbs as the TTPC tonicization of M8M gains a foothold, gradually promoting E as tonic through the musical equivalent of an Escher-like reversal of figure and ground. And, as Tatopolous's character smiles and takes pictures, and as a sergeant realizes that "we need bigger guns," the cue's final and protracted E glimmers and trails off. Thus, although the music begins by placing the stereotypical heroic M8M into a tonal context that undercuts and overturns the stereotype, thus initially intensifying the tonal tension and depicting Godzilla as antihero, the scene's gradual and eventual restoration of M8M's proper tonal environment reverses these experiences. But Godzilla's reception as heroic, and the theme's conformity to M8M's tonicization, are both short lived: never again will Arnold's resplendent theme cadence on the triad to which its opening *Terzschritt* points. Instead, the theme brings back the antiheroic M4M for the celebration of Godzilla's death and, although E and G♯ undulate during the final minute of the film proper, Arnold's score finishes in the key of E (the triad to which the antiheroic M4M points), instead of the key of G♯ (the triad to which the heroic M8M points). Arnold's theme provides a fine example of film music that, from one particular perspective, does not exactly sound like film music, and the syntactical and semantic ramifications of this difference, plus the affective potential of these ramifications, are only revealed by a theory of musical structure designed especially for the repertoire to which the subject of the analysis most clearly belongs.

A HISTORIOGRAPHIC POSTSCRIPT

One primary purpose of this chapter has been to present a pitch-based theory of what recent popular film music sounds like beyond the customary invocation of the style of nineteenth-century art music; for example, in applying his aforementioned "sounding like film music" criterion for film music's ontology, Jeff Smith equated it "with the romantic idiom of Wagner, Strauss, and Mahler" (2009, 190). To be sure, some scholarly observations of distinguishing characteristics of nineteenth-century music anticipate components of this TTPC-based theory. Joseph Kerman has described as "fully Romantic" certain undulatory harmonic fixations in some music of Schubert, where the tonic triad (T) alternates with a coloristic chord (X) to create patterns such as T–X–T and T–X–T–X–T (Kerman 1962, 38). Bribitzer-Stull, in describing triadic progressions, proposes that "perhaps more than any other development in compositional technique, the increased application of chromatic third relations distinguished the harmonic practice of the nineteenth century from that of the eighteenth. Even a cursory survey of the literature strongly suggests that nineteenth-century composers favored progressions featuring major triads whose roots were a major third apart" (Bribitzer-Stull 2006, 169). Bribitzer-Stull does not speak to any bias between M8M and M4M, but David Kopp partially addresses it regarding nineteenth-century composers' direct harmonic connections to a major tonic triad: "The lower flat mediant [♭VI] is perhaps the most frequently employed of the four chromatic mediants [♭VI, VI♯, ♭III, III♯]" (Kopp 2002, 15). Kopp further suggests that, starting with the music of Schubert, the progression I–♭VI–I (M8M) "may sound perfectly natural, meaningful, and functional" (29), *pace* Krebs's impression of the progression stated earlier.

But theorizing about any nineteenth-century tonal-harmonic bias, especially a bias between a TTPC and its tonal inverse, generally goes no further than this; for example, Kopp neither claims that I–III♯–I (M4M) sounds unnatural and without function nor stipulates that, for the progression A♭→C to sound perfectly natural, meaningful, and functional, C should be heard as tonic. Rather, contemporary theorizing about nineteenth-century harmonic progression prefers a more inclusive approach, as particularly evidenced by scale-degree function theory (Smith 1986; Harrison 1994). Within this approach, III♯ may function as a "chromatic dominant," since it contains the leading tone, thus bestowing a kind of logic to its otherwise atypical resolution to tonic. Harrison further calls this resolution a "double-barreled discharge" (Harrison 1994, 105) since it permits both the leading tone to resolve to tonic and the "dual leading tone" of the enharmonic flatted sixth scale degree to resolve to the fifth scale degree. Yet the implications from scale-degree function theory of the logic and (ballistic) strength of a harmonic resolution to tonic poorly correlate with the film-music biases proposed here: while the common m8m is double-barreled, so is the rare M4M; while the rare m4m is a chromatic dominant, the common M8M is not.

Scale-degree theories are at least in touch with the Romantic times: they accommodate the maxims that: (1) a variety of chords can each resolve, in its own way, to tonic, and (2) the individualized rhetoric of tonic assertion generally trumps the conventionalized logic of tonic finding whenever the music grows chromatic. In a review of a series of essays called *The Second Practice of Nineteenth-Century Tonality* (Kinderman and Krebs 1996), whose ambitious title seemingly claimed that the techniques explored therein reified the understanding of a distinct Romantic musical style, Robert Morgan argued that this particular repertoire "cannot be pinned down to a single practice" and "is thus stubbornly resistant to any single analytical bias" (Morgan 1999, 137). He suggested that any such theorizing would be paddling against certain nineteenth-century currents:

> communality in music unquestionably begins to decline during the nineteenth century; and this is nowhere more evident than in the way tonal relationships are configured in the music forming the subject of this book. This reconfiguration did not lead to a new set of stable tonal conventions, however, but on the contrary was associated with a growing distrust of the very idea of a conventional tonal system. Compositions became increasingly more individual, requiring the underlying pitch grammar to be contextually defined. (Morgan 1999, 160)

But imagine what composers would write if, during the nineteenth century, communality in art music did not decline but instead increased to the levels found in art music of the late eighteenth century or popular music of the twentieth. What then would become of the harmonic innovations of Schubert and Liszt? Hollywood, with its emphasis on a consistent, popular appeal and its initial embrace of European émigré composers whose post-Romantic musical language has been revisited and reshaped with each passing generation of film composers, has essentially enabled history to play out this alternate-universe timeline in a manner worthy of a Hollywood science-fiction script. One can detect the seed of some of recent popular film music's stylistic traits lying dormant in the "long nineteenth century": for example, of 102 *Terzschritt* undulations between major triads that I know of in music from Schubert and Meyerbeer to Dvořák and Mahler, from chamber works and solo piano pieces to symphonies and operas, 74 percent are M8Ms and 26 percent are M4Ms. This seed may have been too small to sprout into a "stable tonal convention," especially in European post-Romantic soil that was, per Morgan's view, predisposed against nourishing such growth. But when planted in the soil of American popular motion picture production, with its broad aims of stylistic uniformity and tonal accessibility, this seed, packed with undulating chromatic triadic progressions among other musical materials, grew into a fairly reliable tonal norm by the end of the twentieth century.

NOTES

1. I am indebted to Frank Lehman for closely reading this chapter, making many insightful suggestions, and helping me avoid some embarrassing gaffes, although I am obviously responsible for any that remain. Exchanges with Daniel Harrison, Julian Hook, William Rothstein, Charles J. Smith, and David Temperley early on also helped to focus my ideas.

BIBLIOGRAPHY

Altman, Rick. 1980. "Introduction: Cinema/Sound." *Yale French Studies* 60: 3–15.

Babbitt, Milton. 1992. "The Function of Set Structure in the Twelve-Tone System." PhD diss., Princeton University.

Balzano, Gerald J. 1980. "The Group-Theoretic Description of 12-Fold and Microtonal Pitch Systems." *Computer Music Journal* 4, no. 4: 66–84.

Bazelon, Irwin. 1975. *Knowing the Score: Notes on Film Music.* New York: Van Nostrand Reinhold Co.

Binns, Alexander. 2009. "The Development of Film Musicology: An Overview." In *Sound and Music in Film and Visual Media: An Overview,* edited by Graeme Harper, Ruth Doughty, and Jochen Eisentraut, 725–738. New York: Continuum.

Bordwell, David. 2006. *The Way Hollywood Tells It: Story and Style in Modern Movies.* Berkeley: University of California Press.

Bribitzer-Stull, Matthew. 2006. "The A♭–C–E Complex: The Origin and Function of Chromatic Major Third Collections in Nineteenth-Century Music." *Music Theory Spectrum* 28, no. 2: 167–190.

——. 2007. "From 'Nibelheim' to Hollywood: The Associativity of Harmonic Progression." Paper presented at the annual meeting of the Society for Music Theory, Baltimore, Maryland.

Brown, Royal S. 1983. "Film Musings." *Fanfare* 7, no. 2: 144–147.

Browne, Richmond. 1974. Review of *The Structure of Atonal Music,* by Allen Forte. *Journal of Music Theory* 18, no. 2: 390–415.

Buhler, James. 2000. "*Star Wars,* Music and Myth." In *Music and Cinema,* edited by James Buhler, Caryl Flinn, and David Neumeyer, 33–57. Hanover, NH: University Press of New England.

Burt, George. 1994. *The Art of Film Music.* Boston: Northeastern University Press.

Capuzzo, Guy. 2004. "Neo-Riemannian Theory and the Analysis of Pop-Rock Music." *Music Theory Spectrum* 26, no. 2: 177–200.

Childs, Adrian. 1998. "Moving Beyond Neo-Riemannian Triads: Exploring a Transformational Model for Seventh Chords." *Journal of Music Theory* 42, no. 2: 181–193.

Christensen, Thomas. 2002. "Introduction." In *The Cambridge History of Western Music Theory*, edited by Thomas Christensen, 1–23. Cambridge: Cambridge University Press.

Cochran, Alfred W. 1986. "Style, Structure, and Tonal Organization in the Early Film Scores of Aaron Copland." PhD diss., The Catholic University of America.

Code, David J. 2010. "Rehearing *The Shining*: Musical Undercurrents in the Overlook Hotel." In *Music in the Horror Film: Listening to Fear*, edited by Neil Lerner, 133–151. New York: Routledge.

Cohn, Richard. 1996. "Maximally Smooth Cycles, Hexatonic Systems, and the Analysis of Late-Romantic Triadic Progressions." *Music Analysis* 15, no. 1: 9–40.

——. 1997. "Neo-Riemannian Operations, Parsimonious Trichords, and Their 'Tonnetz' Representations." *Journal of Music Theory* 41, no. 1: 1–66.

——. 1998. "An Introduction to Neo-Riemannian Theory: A Survey and Historical Perspective." *Journal of Music Theory* 42, no. 2: 167–180.

Cone, Edward T. 1967. "Beyond Analysis." *Perspectives of New Music* 6, no. 1: 33–51.

Cook, Nicholas. 1998. *Analysing Musical Multimedia*. New York and Oxford: Oxford University Press.

Cook, Robert C. 2005. "Parsimony and Extravagance." *Journal of Music Theory* 49, no. 1: 109–140.

Cooper, David. 2001. *Bernard Herrmann's Vertigo: A Film Score Handbook*. Westport, CT: Greenwood Press.

——. 2005. *Bernard Herrmann's The Ghost and Mrs. Muir: A Film Score Guide*. Lanham, MD: Scarecrow Press.

Davison, Annette. 2004. *Hollywood Theory, Non-Hollywood Practice: Cinema Soundtracks in the 1980s and 1990s*. Aldershot, UK, and Burlington, VT: Ashgate.

——. 2009. *Alex North's "A Streetcar Named Desire": A Film Score Guide*. Lanham, MD: Scarecrow Press.

DeLio, Thomas. 1980. "Iannis Xenakis' *Nomos Alpha*: The Dialectics of Structure and Materials." *Journal of Music Theory* 24, no. 1: 63–95.

Donnelly, K. J. [Kevin]. 2001. "Introduction: The Hidden Heritage of Film Music: History and Scholarship." In *Film Music: Critical Approaches*, edited by K. J. Donnelly, 1–15. New York: Continuum.

Forte, Allen. 1973. *The Structure of Atonal Music*. New Haven: Yale University Press.

Gallez, Douglas W. 1970. "Theories of Film Music." *Cinema Journal* 9, no. 2: 40–47.

Gjerdingen, Robert O. 2007. *Music in the Galant Style*. New York: Oxford University Press.

Gorbman, Claudia. 1995. "The State of Film Music Criticism." *Cineaste* 21, nos. 1–2: 72–75.

Harrison, Daniel. 1994. *Harmonic Function in Chromatic Music: A Renewed Dualist Theory and an Account of Its Precedents*. Chicago: University of Chicago Press.

Hook, Julian. 2007a. "Cross-Type Transformations and the Path Consistency Condition." *Music Theory Spectrum* 29, no. 1: 1–40.

——. 2007b. "David Lewin and the Complexity of the Beautiful." *Intégral* 21: 155–190.

Huron, David. 2006. *Sweet Anticipation: Music and the Psychology of Expectation*. Cambridge, MA: MIT Press.

Hyer, Brian. 1989. "Tonal Intuitions in *Tristan und Isolde*." PhD diss., Yale University.

——. 1995. "Reimag(in)ing Riemann." *Journal of Music Theory* 39, no. 1: 101–138.

Kalinak, Kathryn. 1992. *Settling the Score: Music and the Classical Hollywood Film*. Madison: University of Wisconsin Press.

Karlin, Fred and Rayburn Wright. 2004. *On the Track: A Guide to Contemporary Film Scoring*. Revised Edition. New York: Routledge.

Kerman, Joseph. 1962. "A Romantic Detail in Schubert's *Schwanengesang*." *Musical Quarterly* 48, no. 1: 36–49.

——. 1965. "A Profile for American Musicology." *Journal of the American Musicological Society* 18, no. 1: 61–69.

Kinderman, William, and Harald Krebs, eds. 1996. *The Second Practice of Nineteenth-Century Tonality*. Lincoln: University of Nebraska Press.

Kopp, David. 2002. *Chromatic Transformations in Nineteenth-Century Music*. Cambridge: Cambridge University Press.

Krebs, Harald. 1980. "Third Relation and Dominant in Late 18th- and Early 19th-Century Music." PhD diss., Yale University.

Lehman, Frank. 2013. "Transformational Analysis and the Representation of Genius in Film Music." *Music Theory Spectrum* 35, no. 1: 1–22.

Lewin, David. 1969. "Behind the Beyond: A Response to Edward T. Cone." *Perspectives of New Music* 7, no. 2: 59–72.

——. 1987. *Generalized Musical Intervals and Transformations*. New Haven: Yale University Press.

——. 1992. "Some Notes on Analyzing Wagner: *The Ring and Parsifal*." *19th-Century Music* 16, no. 1: 49–58.

——. 1993. *Musical Form and Transformation: Four Analytical Essays*. New Haven: Yale University Press.

Lexmann, Juraj. 2006. *Theory of Film Music*. Frankfurt am Main; New York: Lang.

London, Justin. 2000. "Musical Leitmotivs in Cinema and Proper Names in Language: Structural and Functional Parallels." In *Music and Cinema*, edited by James Buhler, Caryl Flinn, and David Neumeyer, 85–96. Hanover, NH: University Press of New England.

Marks, Martin Miller. 1997. *Music and the Silent Film: Contexts and Case Studies, 1895–1924*. New York: Oxford University Press.

McCreless, Patrick. 1996. "Contemporary Music Theory and the New Musicology: An Introduction." *Music Theory Online* 2, no. 2. http://www.mtosmt.org/issues/mto.96.2.2/mto.96.2.2.mccreless.html.

Morgan, Robert P. 1982. "Theory, Analysis, and Criticism." *Journal of Musicology* 1, no. 1: 15–18.

——. 1999. "Are There Two Tonal Practices in Nineteenth-Century Music?" Review of *The Second Practice of Nineteenth-Century Tonality*, edited by William Kinderman and Harald Krebs. *Journal of Music Theory* 43, no. 1: 135–63.

Morris, Robert. 1987. *Composition with Pitch Classes: A Theory of Compositional Design*. New Haven: Yale University Press.

Morton, Lawrence. 1946. "The Music of Objective: Burma" *Hollywood Quarterly* 1, no. 4: 378–395.

——. 1953. Foreword to *Film Composers in America: A Checklist of Their Works*, by Clifford McCarty. Glendale, CA: J. Valentine.

Murphy, Scott. 2006. "The Major Tritone Progression in Recent Hollywood Science Fiction Films." *Music Theory Online* 12, no. 2. http://www.mtosmt.org/issues/mto.06.12.2/mto.06.12.2.murphy.html.

——. 2012. "The Tritone Within: Interpreting Harmony in Elliot Goldenthal's Score for *Final Fantasy: The Spirits Within*." In *Music in Fantasy Cinema*, edited by Janet Halfyard, 148–74. London: Equinox.

——. forthcoming (2014). "Scoring Loss in Recent Popular Film and Television." *Music Theory Spectrum* 36, no. 2.

Neumeyer, David. 1990. "Film Music Analysis and Pedagogy." *Indiana Theory Review* 11: 1–27.

——. 1998. "Tonal Design and Narrative in Film Music: Bernard Herrmann's *A Portrait of Hitch* and *The Trouble With Harry*." *Indiana Theory Review* 19: 87–123.

Newborn, Ira, Gillian B. Anderson, and Ronald H. Sadoff. 2008. "Convention or Cliché: How Original Can You Be?" *Music and the Moving Image* 1, no. 3: 35–41.

Palmer, Christopher. 1990. *The Composer in Hollywood*. London and New York: Marion Boyars.

Rahn, John. 1980. *Basic Atonal Theory*. New York: Schirmer.

Riemann, Hugo. 1880. *Skizzeeinerneuen Methode der Harmonielehre*. Leipzig: Breitkopf and Härtel. Second edition in 1887 as *Handbuch die Harmonielehre*.

——. 1893. *VereinfachteHarmonielehreoder die Lehre von den tonalenFunktionen der Akkorde*. Leipzig: Breitkopf and Härtel.

Rodman, Ronald. 2000. "Tonal Design and the Aesthetics of Pastiche in Herbert Stothart's*Maytime*." In *Music and Cinema*, edited by James Buhler, Caryl Flinn, and David Neumeyer, 187–206. Hanover, NH: University Press of New England.

Rona, Jeffrey C. 2009. *The Reel World: Scoring for Pictures*. 2nd edn. Milwaukee, WI: Hal Leonard Corporation.

Rosar, William. 2009. "Film Studies in Musicology: Disciplinarity vs. Interdisciplinarity." *Journal of Film Music* 2, nos. 2–4: 99–125.

Rothfarb, Lee. 1988. *Ernst Kurth as Theorist and Analyst*. Philadelphia: University of Pennsylvania Press.

Schenker, Heinrich. 1935. *Der freie Satz*. Vienna: Universal Edition.

Smith, Charles J. 1986. "Functional Extravagance in Chromatic Music." *Music Theory Spectrum* 8: 94–139.

——. 2001. "Functional Fishing with Tonnetz: Toward a Grammar of Transformations and Progressions." Paper presented at the Third Symposium on Neo-Riemannian Theory, Buffalo, New York.

Smith, Jeff. 2009. "Music." In *The Routledge Companion to Philosophy and Film*, edited by Paisley Livingston and Carl Plantinga, 184–195. London: Routledge.

Smith, Peter H. 2009. "Brahms's Motivic Harmonies and Contemporary Tonal Theory: Three Case Studies from the Chamber Music." *Music Analysis* 28, no. 1: 63–110.

Sternfeld, Frederick W. 1947. "Music and the Feature Films." *Musical Quarterly* 33, no. 4: 517–532.

Swain, Joseph P. 1997. *Musical Languages*. New York: W.W. Norton.

Tagg, Philip. 1979. *Kojak: 50 Seconds of Television Music. Towards the Analysis of Affect in Popular Music*. Göteborg: Musikvetenskapligainstitutionen vid Göteborgsuniversitet.

——, and Bob Clarida. 2003. *Ten Little Title Tunes: Towards a Musicology of the Mass Media*. New York: Mass Media Music Scholars' Press.

Tymoczko, Dmitri. 2008. "Scale Theory, Serial Theory and Voice Leading." *Music Analysis* 27, no. 1: 1–49.

Watson, Jada and Lori Burns. 2010. "Resisting Exile and Asserting Musical Voice: the Dixie Chicks Are 'Not Ready to Make Nice.'" *Popular Music* 29, no. 3: 325–350.

Webster, Jamie Lynn. 2009. "The Music of Harry Potter: Continuity and Change in the First Five Films." PhD diss., University of Oregon.

Whitesell, Lloyd. 2010. "Quieting the Ghosts in *The Sixth Sense* and *The Others*." In *Music in the Horror Film: Listening to Fear*, edited by Neil Lerner, 206–223. New York: Routledge.

....

CHAPTER 20

LISTENING IN FILM: MUSIC/ FILM TEMPORALITY, MATERIALITY, AND MEMORY

....

MARIANNE KIELIAN-GILBERT

(RE)CONTEXTUALIZING MUSIC LISTENING— MULTISENSORY, MULTIDIMENSIONAL, MULTIMEDIA MUSICAL INTERACTIONS

"TRUCK STOP" is a scene in *Thirty-Two Short Films about Glenn Gould* (Francois Girard, USA 1993). In it, the protagonist (played by Colm Feore), shown while driving his car, hears the sounds of Petula Clark's tune "Downtown." Although the sounds come from the car radio, they become an element of musical-dramatic underscoring.

The film's imagetrack then shifts, showing the car approaching a café, where Gould stops to have breakfast. While awaiting his food, the famous but eccentric pianist's ears adapt to the café environment of overlapping conversations: in his perception, those sounds become musical. Through his discerning and filtering, shading and shaping, multiple contrapuntal strands form different vocal lines and intensities; the polyphonic and fugal-like exchanges of conversations become rhythmic in varying intensities. Clark's doo-wop tune returns at the end of the scene, now as a sonic marker articulating the conclusion of this "performance" and Gould's intensely focused listening.

This music to Gould's ears inhabits a listening environment framed via material sounds (vocal media) and sound contexts (café conversations, attributes of performance). As the environment becomes musically more vivid for Gould, he begins subtly to trace the interrelationships of the lines, physically performing and miming the temporal units separating the subsequent entries. The camera shot visually highlights the minute gestures and inflections of the fingers on his hand rendering his aural attention, focused listening, and thus his hearing the relational/contrapuntal play of conversational lines "as music."

An alternative analysis of this scene might follow from Kathryn Kalinak's observation that music in film "functions as part of an interdependent and complicated process of narrative construction in film by controlling connotation and positioning the audience to respond" (Kalinak 2010, 20). In this reading, we can hear (listen to) Clark's tune as a performing metaphor—that is, telling Gould to "go downtown" (to the diner as a public space) to "get rid of your worries." Gould's skill in perceiving music "absolutely" suggests his "control" and construction of the experience. His skill in being able to take in three threads of conversation simultaneously sets him apart from the other people in the diner. His construction of the conversations "as music" implies that the "content" of their conversations is unimportant. How might interventions of content become performative for another listener? Does his moving finger register a seismographic profile of sonic or social intensity as music? Is he intervening in the conversations as a conductor or responding to their modulations in the complex interactions of a listener, or somewhere in between? Can the "watched" or "heard" act back? How might they have the power to intervene in the unseen and unheard "screens" that include the camera and "ear" as elements of control?

Such musical landscapes and "spaces" of listening interact and change with the people who occupy and bring them to life. Sonic-musical expressions in different physical/material and historical contexts bring about, interact with, and change the terms of music perception and understanding. They call attention to the multidimensionality of music and music experience in different registers of address and evocation. The study of music-sound in film thus sheds light on music and practices of music listening and analysis more generally. How might such study contribute to an analytical-theoretical experiencing and reading of music-sound through a filmic text—or vice versa? Experiencing music in film and film in music offers windows to practices in which interactions of content, orientation, and relational context become critical to practices of music theory and analysis.[1]

Cinematic contexts of film/music thus present a kind of "anthology" or "perceptual laboratory" for music analysis that incorporates music's multiple media orientations, modes of temporal interaction, life situations and receptions, in the potential of "vivid listening" for music's temporal figurations in and of material contexts (music/film, audio/visual). This chapter explores some of these issues and questions with respect to the interactions of music, medium/media, memory, and temporality, and with particular emphasis on listening in film. I am interested in how listening in film becomes a problem for analysis, and how recontextualizing music in cinematic settings (moving images) interacts with experiences of their (music/filmic) temporal unfolding. Since music events both mark and inhabit time, how do their temporal unfoldings interact with the "rhythms" of different media settings?

The work proceeds in two stages, each of which involves discussion of two films. The first stage focuses on listening and the affects of directional forces of medium/media/materiality. In particular, I consider directional tendencies or forces toward cross-modal engagement (modal redundancy) or toward modality-specific discernment and differentiation, remembering W. J. T. Mitchell's famous dictum, "There are no visual media. All media are mixed media, with varying ratios of senses and sign-types" (Mitchell 2002, 170). The case studies are Jirí Kylián's choreography of Stravinsky's *Symphony of Psalms* (Amsterdam 1991) and Cocteau/Petit and Twyla Tharp's choreography in *White Nights* (Taylor Hackford, USA 1985). My discussion of these texts pursues ways of construing temporality from within (inside) affective experiences of cinema (audiovisual settings of music and moving images) and investigates how temporally changing orientations/movements between "inside" and "outside" can shape music/film listening. This listening involves the interplay and interactions of listening/reading "into" and listening/reading "off of"—"against," or "in relation to" a music-cinematic "text."

The second stage investigates music listening, memory, and temporal (re)contextualization in films directed by Agnès Varda (*Les plages d'Agnès* [The Beaches of Agnès], 2008) and Federico Fellini (*La Strada* [The Road], 1954) and the potential of embodying "listening" as performative awareness. I use the term "recontextualization" to capture the shifting odd senses of identity between musical contexts that involve repetition and to construe processes whereby one repetition or context interacts with, reflects back on (infolds), and/or transforms another. Beginning as repetition, the recombinations become and perform temporal difference, doubly articulated—singing a song in double address—telling the story of the song while being a character in it. This vertical (conceptual) and linear (temporally presentational) interaction projects particular expressive affects. Jeff Smith (2001) calls attention to humor and comic allusion in contemporary cinema created through incongruent frames of reference, for example, recognizing the discrepancies of the original scenario of a song in contrast to its ironic potential in a cinematic narrative. Anahid Kassabian (2001) contrasts music practices that produce assimilating (narrow limited positions) or affiliating identifications (multiple mobile positions), linking these types of identification with stylistic aspects of composed or compilation scores, respectively.

The approach to repetition and recontextualization I will develop centers on temporal difference in perceptions of repetition, considering and adapting orientations of Gilles Deleuze (*Difference and Repetition*, 1994) and Deleuze and Guattari (*A Thousand Plateaus*, 1987). Context interacts with experiential qualities of music (and vice versa) rendering hierarchical or rule-based formulations of musical structure mobile and multiple. I explore these interactions of music/filmic contexts in which musical or visual processes transform an earlier event or "memory," such that that "memory" or particular earlier contextual event also changes and interacts with the transformation. One can extend analytical/theoretical work dealing with repetition and recontextualization to capture some of the multidimensionality of music experience.[2] According to Dora Hanninen, the phenomenal transformation of repetition in recontextualization "signals perception not of repetition but of change" (Hanninen 2003, 64) in ways different from situations of varied repetition and quotation; her theory of music analysis helps to explain "why some changes of context sound transformative" (64).

Moments of difference in repetition work as impulses for transforming context, jostling with those of identification and recognition. This is suggestive of a listening experience in which one hears and absorbs something that changes sonic orientations and performance toward the future. One listens for difference that has the potential to reshape what one hears. This differentiation infolds and/or extends outward to transform the context in which it occurs. By "infolding" I mean the redoubling or folding back of experience in a self-referencing exchange that preserves difference. The interactive processes of intercontextualization, embodiment/infolding, and/or materializing/outfolding may be suggestively "musical," that is, performative in their character, temporal orientation and expressive/rhetorical effects. I call these "listening moments."

For Roland Barthes, "[h]earing is a physiological phenomenon; listening is a psychological act." (1985a, 245). He describes listening in terms of three "objects" of attention: alert—listening for indices, traces of sound source and location (what/where); deciphering—listening in relation to signs (secrets), codes (deciphering, enciphering); and listening for "the grain of the voice"—material/unconscious; who speaks, who emits; history, intersubjective space and "dispersion" of signifiers [signifiance] (1985a; 1985b). Michel Chion parallels Barthes's outline with his three listening modes that "overlap and combine in the complex and varied context of the film soundtrack" (Chion 1994, 33): causal listening (for information about source), semantic listening (for a code or language needed to interpret a message), and reduced listening (for material traces and traits of the sound itself, independent of its cause and semantic meaning, from Pierre Schaeffer) (see Chion 1994, 25–34). Associated both with causal and reduced listening, acousmatic listening, hearing the sound without seeing its cause, "intensifies causal listening in taking away the aid of sight" (32).

In my account, listening becomes an act of attention, of an effort to hear toward affect. Sensory listening tunes to visual, pictorial, tactile, aural, balance-kinesthetic and/or, discernment (taste, smell) affects, sensations, or orientations. Metamorphic listening tracks experience in which one hears as one also listens for cues or changes with potential to reshape what one hears. Vivid listening for music's temporal figurations in film activates nonautomatic perceptions attending to awareness or implications of subjectivity, context (medium/media/materiality) and reception.

My strategy in the ensuing discussion is to augment analytical and descriptive entry points to music (as multidimensional, and therefore temporal) in particular by opening to the ways music re-links (and recontextualizes) different artistic processes and values in multisensory, multimodal, multimedia, and multidimensional audiovisual settings. An underlying goal of this work is to emphasize the affect, sensation/intensity, and temporal experience of music-sound in film/music study in contrast to, or in interaction with, approaches that emphasize music's correspondence, representation, and relationship to the visual image.

MUSICAL/CINEMATIC EXPERIENCING OF STRAVINSKY'S *SYMPHONY OF PSALMS* AND JIRÍ KYLIÁN'S CHOREOGRAPHY

As a listener, I thought I "knew" Stravinsky's *Symphony of Psalms*. Nonetheless, experiencing this music choreographed by Jirí Kylián was thrilling, not only to have a physical real-time enactment of the work before my eyes and ears, but also to see-hear a physical modeling of this work as a visual/material analysis-interpretation of musical thought.[3] The moving images (us "moving" to them; they moving to us) of Kylián's balletic reading materialized particular dimensions of metamorphic listening.

How are the orientations of listeners toward music-sound in audiovisual settings related to orientations of music in contexts of contemplation/reflection or as performed/real-time performance? Are these pairings as separable as spheres of activity as we tend to think?

In *Theorizing the Moving Image*, Noël Carroll devotes the first part of his discussion toward a critique of theories of media specificity (of media essentialism) in film—and the negative implications of a range of presuppositions tied to this essentialism: "that each art form has a distinctive medium, that the material cause, so to speak, of an art form—its medium—is also its essence (in the sense of its telos); that the essence of an art form—its medium—indicates, limits or dictates the style and/or content of the art form; and, finally that film possesses such an essence." (Carroll 1996, 50). Somewhat paradoxically, in a later passage he highlights music's "modifying function" in cinema: "The [modifying music] possesses certain expressive qualities which are introduced to modify or to characterize onscreen persons and objects, actions and events, scenes and sequences" (141).

How might one think outside of a "container" approach to medium and media essentialism, as Carroll does in the first statement, though he nevertheless stresses music's modifying functions in the second? Varying responses to the problem acknowledge media interactions, permeability, and combinatorial potential (multiplicity). Gilles Deleuze wrote, "In fact, all the sound elements, including music, including silence, form a continuum as something which belongs to the visual image" (1989, 241). Michel Chion asked, "What do I see of what I hear? What do I hear of what I see?" (1994, 192). I would similarly phrase these ideas, "How do I see what I am (musically) listening to? How do I listen to what I see?"

When multidimensional "analytical" or "compositional" characterizations respond to particular music by Stravinsky, their singular analytical "voices" do not simply substitute less formidable meanings for formidable/technical ones. They suspend power hierarchies between dominant and subordinate (compositional, performative, analytical) narratives and alter perceptions of Schoenberg or Stravinsky's music as self-contained, change the topography of music perception and experience, and open the authorial music text to the suggestions of additional/simultaneous texts and the discourse of others. Although associative connections entail logical operations (mappings between apparently "analogous" situations), their expressive impact draws also from "difference" and material dimensions outside those operations.[4]

Image and music interact and intersect similarly in Kylián's choreography of Stravinsky's *Symphony of Psalms*, where balletic performance gestures articulate experiential complexes of sonic materials in material patterns of thought (qualia in bottom-up and top-down comprehensions). The dancers' movements materialize flesh in sounds—sound in dance; dance in sound—in a multiplicity of relational/temporal interactions that resist discursive appropriation.

The first movement begins with gestures of the men sitting down and the women bowing down (in slow motion). This silent physical gesture of genuflection later materializes sonically-musically at the opening and conclusion of the third movement. Here (in the first movement) the four intercut articulations of the famous and timbrally distinctive "Psalms chord" (first heard at the very outset) span the choreographic genuflection prior to the musical/textural "downbeat" of the white-note (Phrygian) music at rehearsal number 2 (Piano: E pedal with right-hand arpeggios). Subsequently the moving and bobbing of heads align to coordinate and track the pitch patterns as comparable neighboring patterns: B3-C4-C4-B3 in cello and horns at rehearsal number 2; E4-F4-F4-E3 in the altos at rehearsal number 4 (repeated at number 7); and D5-F5-F5-D5 in the full choir at rehearsal number 5.

The visual/physical movements allow one to take in the temporal successions of melodic "neighbor-note patterns" as comparable, yet varied, and interestingly, to hear the choir's (SATB) D5–F5 vocal oscillation at rehearsal number 5 as a response and "inner" component of a larger/longer neighbor-note "phrase" from rehearsal numbers 4 to 7 (the music and choreography at rehearsal number 7 both end the melodic "neighbor" patterns and initiate new material) prior to the larger textural "downbeat" of Phrygian music interjected at rehearsal number 9 (reminiscent of that at rehearsal number 2).[5]

Musical/visual/movement interactions also embody—give physical form to—related temporal visualizations of music-spatial patterns of the fugal entries in the second movement as each pair of dancers presents fugal subject and countersubject, respectively. Notably these interactions incorporate cinematic, visual, and physical affects (unfolding, momentum, resistance, volume and "attitude"—character) to the tensional profile, pacing, and energy of the musical line (composed into music, composed into dance). The physical/bodily dynamics of sound becomes the cinematic-physicality-materiality of temporal experience, that is itself musically, visually, and materially interactive.

When I analyze music, I am presented with a dilemma: I may choose to regard a musical structure as "fixed" or "stable" across different contexts, for example, as based on relations evident in a score, or to regard that music and its structures materialized—angled, nuanced, or changing in response to the material/conceptual pressures of particular contexts. Alternatively, the musical values may present such riches that call for selectivity, facilitated in response to shaping pressures of related sensory, dimensional, or mediumed modalities of experience. Or these values may elicit the perceiver's projection and filling in of ambiguities, silences, and/or ambiguities of presentation. In the discussion that follows, I contrast the interplay and interaction of listening/differentiating "from" and listening/reading "into,"—modes of experience and analysis that appear motivated "from the outside in," with modes of experience/affect and analysis that appear motivated "from the inside out."

Changing relationships between performance and experience/understanding modulate the apparent fixity of musical structure. Consider the familiar music-analysis situation of guiding perception in terms of or in relation to the framework of a formal-structural reading, for example, a Schenkerian voice-leading graph that models an abstract structure not evident directly on or at the surface of the musical form, in contrast to a reading that meshes with or models the immediacy of that surface directly. In the second situation one might listen to the surface details of the music as a realization of the conventions of Schenkerian voice-leading ("outside in"); in the first, one might shift attention to ways in which the conventions require adjustment to fit the musical situation ("inside out"). Alternatively, these directions can interact with expressive affect.

Music in film exists as part of the soundtrack along with spoken dialogue and sonic/sound effects. Gilles Deleuze has called attention to the relational dimensions and interactions between these elements:

> Perhaps an even greater number of sound components should be distinguished: noises (which isolate an object and are isolated from each other), sounds (which indicate relationships and are themselves in mutual relation), phonations (which cut into these relations, which can be shouts, but also genuine "jargons," as in the talking burlesque of Chaplin or Jerry Lewis), words, music. It is clear that these different elements can enter into a rivalry, fight each other, supplement each other, overlap, transform each other. (Deleuze 1989, 234)

In Hans Richter's *Vormittagsspuk* (Ghosts before Breakfast) (1927–1928), a bowtie unravels and begins to dance. Propelled by the music, it resists the owner's efforts to corral it to order. In this film, the music of the dance enacts "the rebellion of the objects."[6] Their willed actions take on a resistance and life of their own, apart from their owners. As music-bowtie dances, its performative elements convey intentional movement with a certain theatricality. In contrast, the "dancing hippo" of Walt Disney's 1940 *Fantasia* ("Dance of the Hours," from *La Gioconda* by Amilcare Ponchielli) creates a music-visual disjunction of phantom aspects of weight, depth, force and spirit. The "sensory dissonance" between the social expectations and conventions of weight and the hippo's apparent lightness accentuates the humor: the relational mix of the hippo's appearance/size, its visual music-dancing-movement "en pointe," the music's careful metric patterning and textural lightness, and the social (and potential racial) connotations of this cartoon. This performative setting obscures ever-present material problems: is it less strange when lighter people become heavy (perform heaviness), as in Marcel Marceau's Bip's wings of a butterfly, than for those heavy to become light (perform lightness)? Notice the subtle play or tension that arises between the experience of saying something in a different way so as to understand it better (modify it?) and/or of encountering the form/content of a particular expression in a unique expressive way (or sense)—in the fullness of the particularity of an expressive modality.

Claudia Gorbman describes music's flexibility and variety of functions with respect to the film's diegesis (narrative world) as "temporal, spatial, dramatic, structural, denotative, connotative—both in the diachronic flow of a film and at various interpretive levels simultaneously" (Gorbman 1987, 22). David Neumeyer has argued for the utility of oppositional functions that accrue to distinctions of diegesis and underscored the importance of processive/transitional processes that Robynn Stilwell and James Buhler attributed to the malleable "fantastical gap" between diegetic and nondiegetic music (Neumeyer 2009; Buhler 2000, 2001; Stilwell 2007).

Music "in experience" may articulate "narrative"/formal functions related to those in cinematic settings. The following examples from film, from music, are suggestive for multidimensional approaches to music analysis. For example, film music can function outside narrative (Buhler 2000), develop its own intertextual references to other music, or in turn provide an associative function analogous to that of quotation (Duncan 2003; Powrie and Stilwell 2006). Image can appear to enact music; music may appear to suspend action or narrative. Music may sound connections that can cut across or within a film. Musical "ciphers" can problematize the order or hierarchy of seeing and hearing. The semiotic reference of a leitmotif can suggest a particular connection that can become undone as it takes on a specifically musical function or operates within a musical summary (Buhler 2000). In these crossings of function, music can create or erase distinctions between symbolic and literal meanings, cinema and performance, fixed, double, and multiple meanings, and traverse the gap or the illusion between reality and fiction, ironic displacement or authorial commentary.

Ben Winters has argued for regarding music in film not so much as presenting a "narrating" voice as an "indicator of narrative space" and of the "fictional state of the world created on screen," that is, as "belonging to the same narrative space as the characters and their world" (Winters 2010, 227–29). Annabel Cohen (1993, 2000) has identified eight functions of music in film as seen from a cognitive perspective: to mask noise and distractions, provide continuity between shots, direct attention to important features, induce mode and changes in feeling, communicate meaning, cue memory, heighten arousal and facilitate belief, and add an aesthetic dimension. Finally, Jeff Smith has proposed treating film music as a "cluster concept," one employing "disjunctively necessary conditions, some of which must be instantiated if the object under investigation is to fall under the concept [for example, of film music]" (Smith 2009b, 189), and including "film music audition as a type of subliminal perception" (193). In the next sections I link such indexical (Winters), cognitive (Cohen), and categorical (Smith) functions to experiencing film/music's temporality and feeling affects.

SYNCHRONIZATION AND DIFFERENCE—
WHITE NIGHTS, COCTEAU, AND
BARYSHNIKOV/HINES

> In the transsensorial or even metasensorial model, which I am distinguishing from
> the Baudelarian one [of synaesthetic correspondences], there is no sensory given
> that is demarcated and isolated from the outset. Rather, the senses are channels,
> highways more than territories or domains. If there exists a dimension in vision that
> is specifically visual, and if hearing includes dimensions that are exclusively auditive,
> these dimensions are in a minority, particularized, even as they are central. (Chion
> 1994, 137).
>   In this vast sonic aquarium the image is sometimes found swimming just like
> another fish. (Chion 2009, 119).

One of the interesting aspects of materiality/medium/media is its participation and
role in creating aspects of illusion—of undoing itself and hiding its presence through
the play of perceptual absorption and identification. Its function as nonreflective material channel provides a direction toward an "inside" "content"; embodying/infold-
ing itself, medium provides a vehicle, yet an illusion, toward an "outside," a movement
toward the immateriality of analogy and synonymy with other media. The particular
content, for example the content of a letter, may blind us to the formative expressive
character of the "medium," by making the channel appear to have no role, no "content."
Marshall McLuhan offers an instructive example: "The electric light escapes attention as
a communicative medium just because it has 'no content.' And this makes it an invaluable instance of how people fail to study media at all" (McLuhan 1964, 24). How might
aspects of one medium/material provide a frame for, or help shape the multisensory
experience of another? How do we yield or succumb to, or alternately resist and refigure
music's media-specific aspects?

Descriptions of "the sound of painting" (an image evoked by Karin von Maur [1999]),
the painterly aspects of music, the music in poetry, the movement of images/shots in
film, or the specifics of a particular media/medium, call attention to the sensory integration, interference, and incompleteness of cross-modal exchanges and the tension or gap
between what is evoked experientially and what is imagined. Relatedly, the "effect" of
suture produces the spectator as a subject even as it naturalizes the artificiality of a cinematic shot.[7] One function of "suture" is to engage the viewer with onscreen narrative
events in order to hold the viewer's attention. For Slavoj Žižek, as a spectator confronts
the shot, deriving pleasure and becoming absorbed, that pleasure/absorption does not
result in complete immersion. The potential of a "delicate fiction" and "interface" lingers
in awareness; thus the "suture" becomes evident and undermined by spectators' degree
of awareness of the frame as such. Krzysztof Kieślowski, in particular among film directors, engages the spectator while showing the illusory or constructed/artificial nature of
truth and reality (Žižek 2001).

How are psychological images given presence even in the face of perceptual absences? A commutation test involves substituting, transposing (reordering), adding, deleting different audio materials for the visual image (or vice versa) to highlight the import and implications of one setting as a way of studying the demands and implications of a particular combination. Chion's ideas of negative space or phantom, ghostly projections have comparable implications: "The image calls for them but the music does not produce them for us to hear" (Chion 1994, 192). He asks: What phantom sounds inhabit the image, and what phantom (negative) images do we construct or "look" for in the sound? Because of these "phantom-like" qualities, we tend to think they do no aesthetic or cultural work. Despite their functioning on the level of expectation or implication, such constructions keep open and call attention to a gap or space between experience and conceptual understanding. In this gap reside the discrepancies and discontinuities associated with the presentational-experiential and material specifics/specificity of cinematic work.

The opening scene of *White Nights* sets the ballet by Jean Cocteau *Le Jeune homme et la mort* (*The Young Man and Death*, 1946), with Mikhail Baryshnikov and Florence Faure as the two title characters. The music for this ballet is Ottorino Respighi's orchestral arrangement of the Passacaglia from J. S. Bach's Passacaglia and Fugue in C Minor for Organ, BWV 582. The volume and intensity of the music grow with each succeeding variation of the Passacaglia bass as Cocteau's choreographic tale of love, desire, and death plays out the inescapable doom surrounding the young man. Notably, impressions of a close correlation between the drama of dance and music can materialize through other, related musical environments, as the perceiver soon realizes that this ballet opens up narratives (balletic, musical, dramatic) within the cinematic narrative.

Cocteau was interested in a principle that he called "the mystery of accidental synchronization"—the idea in film "in which any music of quality integrates the gestures and emotions of the characters" (Ries 1986, 112). He wanted to "prove that a dance, set to rhythms suiting the choreographer, could do without them and gain strength in a new musical climate" (112). Cocteau would gear the choreography to specific jazz rhythms and deliberately apply a classical composition to the rehearsed choreography at the final dress rehearsal. In 1946 the choreography was rehearsed for fifteen days before the performance with a percussion jazz band accompanying the movements to a set of rhythms chosen by Cocteau along with choreographer/dancer Roland Petit. At the last general rehearsal the music was changed: "the dance piece and the music had never been practiced together, and one could not be sure of the timing of music and dance" (119). Underlying the illusion of this "synchronization," the "integrity and structural differentiation" of an art form created a force toward material specificity through "a delicate arrangement of unbalance" (112). This differentiation requires sensory incompleteness (openness), "interference," or intersensory bias—Cocteau's experimentation of different modes of experience conflicting yet interacting with one another as when viewing one's hand through a prism.

Though never realized in an actual performance, Cocteau intended to replace the sonic narrative of "continuous" variation in the Bach passacaglia with one of "sonata design" of Mozart's overture from the *Magic Flute* for the later American performances (Ries 1986, 221 n. 14). Both works present comparable literal timings and narrative trajectories toward a highpoint. The idea was to stimulate new levels and types of synchronization of potential values in the material from the interrelation created by the succession or combination of disparate/contrasting materials. The perception of correspondence, synchronicity, or parallels, also underlies montage theory, an artistic analogue of collage technique practiced by artists from William Burroughs to John Cage.

Thus synchronicity—the apparently acausal or nonintentional connection, yet perturbation of events that renders them meaningful to a listener—is a function of contextual pairing by which perceivers construe parallel corresponding accent-structural relationships or semantic pairing through common structural tropes (a term used by Lawrence Kramer to refer to common/comparable cultural strategies) (Kramer 1990, 10). Perceptions of synchronicity can also apply to intentional artistic and media pairing and thus are not functionally limited to apparently "nonintentional" simultaneous combinations or "nonreferential" arts such as music.

In the following example from later in the film, I consider the interaction of music-media combinations as much from the "inside out," in contrast to the "outside in" of media pairings: that is, interactions directed as much from the overall "content" of the shot and musical passage as from the function of its contextual position or the similarity/dissimilarity between shots or a series of shots. Later in *White Nights* the Russian ballet dancer Nikolai Rodchenko (Baryshnikov) and an American defector, dancer Raymond Greenwood (Hines), dance the David Pack song "Prove Me Wrong," Twyla Tharp's choreographic counterpart to the earlier Cocteau ballet. Each choreography (by Cocteau/Petit and Tharp, and performances by Baryshnikov and Hines) emanates a different aesthetic affect and shapes interactions both musical and dramatic within the filmic narrative that gradually shift in focus from the aesthetic of the male ballerino (Baryshnikov) to the interactive and often asymmetrical understanding between Baryshnikov and Hines materialized in their double enactment of the Pack song. Though Baryshnikov "moves with fluency in other dance genres... there is a difference in the virtuosity of execution between Baryshnikov and Hines in this passage with Hines clearly the tap virtuoso" (Royce 2004, 32). Hines has "integrated the tap rhythm" (33) into his body in a way that Baryshnikov has not—compare Figures 20.1 and 20.2, from the opening ballet

FIGURE 20.1 *White Nights* (Hackford 1985), Baryshnikov–Faure duo.

FIGURE 20.2 *White Nights*, Baryshnikov–Hines duo.

and the Baryshnikov–Hines duo, respectively. With the shift in musical genre, these differences "between a virtuoso trained in the technique and extra-technical elements of a dance genre and a great dancer of another tradition adapting to a different genre" (33) affect the temporal/narrative pacing and experiential understanding of the film.

Questions of accidental, random, or intentional parallels or synchronizations thus also point to a significant relation and interconnection between perceptions of *similarity* (whether contiguous or formal) and *difference*, a nonadditive relationship. Affective forces work to naturalize or hide as well as to call attention to the arbitrariness of convention in experiencing music in and through cross-sensory transfer and/or difference.

One of the functions of multisensory exchange is to provide an antidote to the apparent arbitrariness of a sign. Inter- and multisensory relationships suggest forces that work to naturalize or hide the arbitrariness of convention; they are the "multimedia" dimensions of a music setting. Cultural anthropologist Bradd Shore has observed that synaesthetic or cross-sensory analogical transfers are "good candidates for elementary forms of meaning construction by which the mind constructs nodes of resistance to the arbitrariness of signs and provides a sensory basis for their psychogenic motivation" (Shore 1996, 359). Relatedly, differing interpretive contexts, combinations of media, and/or receptions (past and present), also simulate and enact intelligible, integral holistic experience that both colors and is shaped by its own performance.

Both types of interactions—unifying or naturalizing inter- and trans-sensory orientations and those calling attention to the discrepancies and defamiliarizing forces of media specificity—figure the "mark" of media/materiality in rhythmic movements toward, or away from, modally redundant or modality-specific discernment and differentiation.

Redundant modal features are notably rhythmic, and involve synchrony, movement, tempo, rhythm, narrative and intensity—aspects that link strongly with music's aspects of changing temporal experience. Noël Carroll has observed, "Features like line, color, volume, shape, and motion are fundamental across various art forms and are unique to none" (1996, 51). In contrast, nonredundant or modally specific dimensions emphasize the expressive uniqueness, specificity and discrepancy of material content. Always present, "forces" of modal redundancy and specificity act and interact, undoing "container-like" theories of media/medium that regard medium/media as a vessel or receptacle or as self-enclosed and contained. In the next set of examples, performative awareness emerges in interventions between music, imagetrack, and aesthetic constructions that expose or alter prevailing experiential frames.

MUSIC/FILM TEMPORALITY—MEMORY AND MATERIALITY, BERGSON AND DELEUZE

> This membrane which makes the outside and the inside present to each other is called memory...the membrane which, in the most varied ways (continuity, but also discontinuity, envelopment, etc.), makes sheets of past and layers of reality correspond, the first emanating from an inside which is always already there, the second arriving from an outside always to come, the two gnawing at the present which is now only their encounter. (Deleuze 1989, 207)

Henri Bergson was an influential French philosopher whose ideas about memory and duration in *Memory and Matter* (1896) were revitalized in the work of Gilles Deleuze, beginning with *Bergsonism* (1966). Deleuze was drawn to Bergson's concept of multiplicity as differentiation within mixture.[8] Deleuze has written two volumes on cinema as philosophy: *Cinema 1: The Movement-Image* (1986) and *Cinema 2: The Time-Image* (1989). Provisional and selective, key philosophical ideas in his texts are expressivity and processes of becoming that incorporate experiential affects, sensations, and actions. Ronald Bogue emphasizes that Deleuze's theory of cinema "is not 'about' cinema, but about the concepts that cinema gives rise to...yet they are cinema's concepts, not theories about cinema." (Bogue 2009, 368, quoting Deleuze 1989, 280). Deleuze's ideas emphasize changes in the temporal experience of the shot.

In *Matter and Memory* Bergson distinguished between habitual and recollective memory, "habitual" memory referring to learned (expected) patterns and "recollective memory" to an inner/felt connection and qualitative extension of past events in the present. Learned/habitual memory responds to a present that invites a turn from the immediate to the useful: "[S]eek experience at its source, or rather above that decisive *turn* where, taking a bias in the direction of our utility, it becomes properly *human* experience.... The *turn* of experience...illuminat[es] the passage from the *immediate* to the *useful*" (Bergson [1896] 1988, 184–185; emphasis in original). Thus recollective memory becomes "a memory profoundly different from the first [habitual], always bent upon action, seated in the present...it no longer represents our past to us, it acts it;...it prolongs their useful effect into the present moment" (82).

In Bergson's account, memory departs from perception. Closer to intuition, through discernment and differentiation, memory constitutes an "integral experience" made up of an indefinite series of acts, which correspond to degrees of duration of images (*la durée*). The duration is a qualitative multiplicity that extends or prolongs the past into the present, or vice versa: "Every perception fills a certain depth of duration, prolongs the past into the present, and thereby partakes of memory" (Bergson [1896] 1988, 244).

In contrast to the flattening of temporal difference in associationism, Bergson highlighted the multiplicity of temporal difference and degrees of movement between action and representation in memory: "the ever-varying degree of the *tension* of memory" is its "tendency to insert itself in the present act or to withdraw from it" (Bergson [1896] 1988, 243). The double movement of remembering (the inward and outward stroke of memory, extending into or out of the present) is what distinguishes memory from representation "in a certain activity of the mind, in a *movement* between action and representation" (243): "Every perception fills a certain depth of duration, prolongs the past into the present, and thereby partakes of memory" (244).

In *Cinema 2: The Time-Image*, Deleuze describes the turn or difference between "classical and modern cinema" in terms of the temporal experience of the shot. The so-called "classical" cinema dealt with the succession of movement-images, such that the cut is subordinate to image. Cinematic images link by association and constitute a "direct presentation" of time ("reality in the process of unrolling" [Deleuze 1989, 211]):

> The so-called classical cinema works above all through linkage of images, and subordinates cuts to this linkage.... Time here is, therefore, essentially the object of an indirect representation, according to the commensurable relations and rational cuts which organize the sequence or linkage of movement-images. (Deleuze 1989, 213)

In montage theories of "classical cinema," the side-by-side juxtaposition of images creates meaning, in contrast to the content from within the images themselves.[9] For example, David Cook (1996) describes the Kuleshov effect in film theory as recounted by V. I. Pudovkin in his 1929 *Film Technique and Film Acting*:

> [Kuleshov] took unedited footage of a completely expressionless face...and intercut it with shots of three highly motivated objects: a bowl of hot soup, a dead woman lying in a coffin, and a little girl playing with a teddy bear. When the film strips were shown to randomly selected audiences, they invariably responded as though the actor's face [that of prerevolutionary matinee idol Ivan Mozhukhin, who had emigrated to Paris after the Revolution] had accurately portrayed the emotion appropriate to the intercut object. As Pudovkin recalled: "The public raved about the acting of the artist. They pointed out the heavy pensiveness of his mood over the forgotten soup, were touched and moved by the deep sorrow with which he looked on the dead woman, and admired the light, happy smile with which he surveyed the girl at play." (Cook 1996, 137)

The "intellectual montage" of Eisenstein in which juxtapositions multiply became the "apogee" of this "grandiose conception" (Deleuze 1989, 210).

In contrast, for Deleuze, the effects of "modern cinema" lie within the shot such that the interstice or cut has replaced association. Relinkages are now "subject to the cut," instead of the cut "subject to the linkage." For "modern cinema" can communicate with the old, and the distinction between the two can be very relative. However, it [modern cinema] will be defined ideally by a reversal where the image is unlinked and the cut begins to have an importance in itself.... [T]he images are certainly not abandoned to chance, but there are only re-linkages subject to the cut, instead of cuts subject to the linkage. (Deleuze 1989, 213–14)

This experience of the cut, and of the image or shot as idea/concept, has implications for the nature of a perceiver's temporal experience:

In the first place [classical cinema], the cinematographic image becomes a direct presentation of time, according to non-commensurable relations and irrational cuts. In the second place [modern cinema], this time-image puts thought into contact with an unthought, the unsummonable, the inexplicable, the undecidable, the incommensurable. The outside or the obverse of the images has replaced the whole, at the same time as the interstice or the cut has replaced association. (Deleuze 1989, 214)

Working with the temporal formations of the cut as a memory slice, Deleuze extended Bergson's ideas, describing how memory takes form in cinematic (and musical) processes:

For memory is clearly no longer the faculty of having recollections: ... But, if memory makes relative insides and outsides communicate like interiors and exteriors, an absolute outside and inside must confront each other and be co-present. (Deleuze 1989, 207)

Agnès Varda's *The Beaches of Agnès* is emblematic of Deleuze's "cinematic philosophy" that changes the temporal experience of "the shot" and opens up and multiplies avenues for cinematic experience and study in "vertical" or "simultaneous" dimensions, as well as "linear" or "narrative" dimensions. In this film Varda combines the pictorial, the documentary, with film movement and narrative progression. Without discounting Carroll's remarks on film and media discussed earlier or Duncan's cautionary remarks that "film and music are different media, and they play by substantially different rules" (Duncan 2003, 77), I will stress the idea that presenting ways of listening in and apprehending Varda's films in part "as music" provides a concrete illustration of the "relinkages" described by Deleuze as aspects of a philosophy of modern cinema.

FILM/MUSIC TEMPORALITY—FROM INSIDE OUT AND OUTSIDE IN—*LES PLAGES D'AGNÈS* (THE BEACHES OF AGNÈS) "AS MUSIC"

In the seventh of the nine sections in *Les plages d'Agnès* (The Beaches of Agnès), 2008, Agnès Varda remarks on memory during a conversation with English actress Jane Birkin: "I've said it before, memories are like flies swarming through the air, bits of

(a)

(b)

FIGURE 20.3 a: Titian, *Venus of Urbino*.
b: corresponding image from *Les Plages d'Agnès* (Varda 2008).

memory jumbled up" (at 1:33:22). In the course of this, Birkin herself embodies onscreen an arresting shot as a live model who poses as the nude woman in Titian's oil painting *Venus of Urbino* (Figure 20.3a). Calling attention to the "fourth wall" of the camera lens, hundreds of tiny black flies impose themselves against the "invisible screen" between the viewer and the fleshy surface of her skin (Figure 20.3b).

As the audio track sounds the low buzzing of flies, memories (cultural and individual) materialize residues unforeseen (as audio sound) and tangible (as images, dispersed flies clinging to a surface). This multidimensional configuration is evoked by David Schwarz in his notion of the "listening plane" in music, "an impression of a threshold at the surface of a speaker that divides our listening space from a fantasy of performance space" (Schwarz 1997, 95). Sonic events that "[breach] the listening plane ... [can impede] identification with the narrator's fantasy of intrusion" (95).

Preceding the staged pose of "Venus," the younger and older maids that figure in the background of the Titian painting enact an imaginary exchange in the film: the younger maid (Birkin again?) slaps the hand of the older maid and we are left to wonder what they argued about. Was the younger maid perhaps defying the order of the older woman to retrieve clothes for the nude "Venus?" After the "silent" slap, the younger maid bends down to search out something from the chest (an image shown in the background of the Titian painting). The temporal casting of the cinematic shot thus temporally stretches, reinvents, and perhaps recontextualizes the historical image and its relational and pictorial potential.

Writing about *The Beaches of Agnès*, Cynthia Fuchs notes: "Each of the memories she conjures leads to another, sometimes sequential and sometimes not, the movement back and forth in time showing that they are not linear but cumulative and perpetual (swarming)" (Fuchs 2010). Scenes of women protesters in an abortion rights demonstration[10] mix with a series of photos and video clips of friends as different characters of Agnès Varda's, Jacques Demy's, or French New Wave films. These include character roles played by French actresses such as Delphine Seyrig (as different filmic characters, for example, Joan of Arc), Catherine Deneuve (Jacques Demy, *Peau d'âne* [Donkey Skin], 1970), Sandrine Bonnaire (Agnès Varda, *Sans toit ni loi* [Vagabond], 1985), and English actress Jane Birkin (Serge Gainsbourg, *Je t'aime moi non plus* [I Love You, I Don't], 1976).

This textured "memory" play precedes and follows the enactment/staging of the Titian painting. In answer to Birkin's question about filmmaking, Varda responds: "It's like doing a puzzle. You place the pieces here and there until it comes together but there's a hole in the center. It happens at dinner parties. Suddenly it goes quiet and someone says, 'Sing us a song!'" (Figure 20.4a). To this last Birkin responds "A song? Gainsbourg…," and then follows a clip of her with Joe Dallesandro singing their duet "Je t'aime…moi non plus" (I love you…nor do I) featured in the movie of the same name (Figure 20.4b). The song was released in 1969; Birkin and Gainsbourg were lovers at the time. The film directed by Gainsbourg appeared in 1976 to scandalous reception: Birkin starred (as Johnny) in an affair with Dallesandro (as Krassky, a homosexual man). The film dealt with themes of death, decay, the taboo of anal sex, and painful sexual encounters with a woman first thought to be a boy. In Varda's film the shot location changes abruptly as Jane Birkin continues to speak: she dumps out the contents of her purse onto a set of stairs as the Eiffel Tower shows in the background (Figure 20.4c), and she says "Even when we dump it all out, we reveal little."

At this point Varda interjects another ironic switch, now commenting on herself and her cinematic legacy: "The Eiffel Tower by day, The Eiffel Tower by night. I created an ephemeral monument to the glory of cinema" (Figure 20.4d).

Responding to interviewer Liza Béar's question about whether some moments of her life were hard to revisit in the film, Agnès Varda offered another cinematic remembering from the film, "As I walk backward on the Santa Monica pier I say, 'Memories are like flies swarming around me and I'm not sure I want to remember'" (Béar 2009). Moments of memory carry unpredictable triggers of emotion and feeling, moving constantly yet playfully with unforeseen directions and emotional dispersal (several of the shots suggested emotions that led Varda back to the death of her husband, filmmaker Jacques Demy).

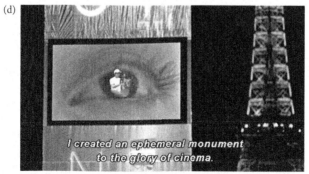

FIGURE 20.4 a–d: *Les Plages d'Agnès*, screen stills.

For Yvette Bíró, "time itself is the main protagonist of Varda's films—not just its passage, its fertile construction-destruction, but its many facets, its metamorphoses and burdens." In Varda's first film, *La Pointe-Courte* (1955), for example, narratives of landscape (a documentary of the struggles of a fisherman) and personal drama (the changing relationship of a married couple) figure different temporal experiences ("The simple events of this fishing village are more than merely a backdrop to the story of a couple in the grip of their emotions: rather, they become a strange sort of dramatic adversary" [Bíró 1997, 2]). Both segments (documentary/landscape and interpersonal relationship) convey the passage of time but in different rhythms, suggesting the combinational richness of temporal simultaneity—of simultaneous events ("the simultaneity of many millions of events" [3] "...the dizzying heterogeneity of things" [2]).

Michel Chion characterizes the post-Hollywood sound possibilities as permitting "several layers of sound to work on the moviegoer's attention at different rates of speed," that is, negotiating layers of sound as multiple centers of attention without "imposing a rhythm that dominated all" (Chion 2009, 122). Agnès Varda's "moving" images in *The Beaches of Agnès* present layers of image movement that work at different rates of speed and slowness in temporally staging and spatializing the effects of memory and experience. "There is no line of demarcation between crude reality, carefully composed image, and fiction.... This constant flow between the objective world and its subjectivity, the permeability between external and internal are the basic features of Varda's *cine-criture* [cinematic writing]" (Bíró 1997, 8). Experiencing Varda's *Beaches*—"as music"—brings attention to the potential of perceiver's engagement with a "vertical" or "simultaneous" realm of perception in film/music listening that is ever in flux. Composing with and into cinematic forms, Varda's "listening in film"—filming Birkin as both "Venus" and "maid" in the Titian sequence and side by side with the emotional intervention of her singing "Je t'aime"—layers film/music simultaneity and narrative succession as compositional (musical) play. This cinematic multiplicity "as music" in turn illuminates music's multidimensionality in potential horizontal, vertical, and circular modes of engagement.

> As I see it, to use a cinematic approach or framework means finding a form for each idea you have. The chronology's there, but an emotion will throw it off.... So there's an emotional fluidity to the film, several points of access. (Agnès Varda, Béar 2009)

FEDERICO FELLINI, *LA STRADA*: GELSOMINA LISTENS

> [Fellini] began with films of wandering, which relaxed the sensory-motor connections, and made pure sound-and-optical images rise up.... He became increasingly concerned with entering into a new element, and multiplying the entrances.... Two things happen at once. On the one hand, purely optical and sound-images crystallize: they attract their contents, make them crystallize and

compose them from an actual image and its virtual image, its mirror-image. (Deleuze 1989, 88, 89)

Gelsomina (Giulietta Masina, Fellini's wife), the itinerant female circus character in *La Strada*, listens. In listening, she hears something that changes (moves, transforms) its sonic orientations and performance toward the future, toward the unknown. In listening, one is open to cues and transformations that reshape what one hears. The temporal transforming and (re)hearing changes these "crystal-images" through impulses that fold in and/or extend out from a virtual context to transform that relationship to the actual contexts in which they occur (and vice versa).

Ronald Bogue captures Deleuze's idea of the crystal-image as an interaction between the present actuality and virtual potential: "It is on the basis of this doubling of each moment as an actual present and virtual past that Deleuze delineates 'crystals of time', or *hyalosigns*: 'an actual image *and* its own virtual image, to the extent that there is no longer any linkage of the real with the imaginary, but *indiscernibility of the two*, a perpetual exchange'" (Bogue 2009, 372; citation is from Deleuze 1989, 273).[11] A second time-image of Deleuze is that of a "forking labyrinth of coexisting possible worlds" (Bogue 2003, 373; Deleuze 1989, 131). "What Deleuze finds in modern cinema is a similar coexistence of compossible [mutually harmonious] and incompossible worlds, not as a reflection of the divine mind, but as an image of time as a branching labyrinth of possible realities" (Bogue 2003, 373).

The following reading gives priority to interventions of both Gelsomina's character and musical themes.[12] She *becomes* childlike in opening to and creating relational connections, in contrast to being childish, ignorant, or essentialized in and by music—in particular by the music of what I refer to as Gelsomina's "name" (which has two motivic components, a circus-music-style pointed dotted-quarter-plus-eighth figure, opposed to a slower moving chromatic descent) and her forming of a trumpet "tune."

Gelsomina listens and hears in and through different modalities and social registers, as do her themes. Sold to an uncouth and callous man, Zampanò (Anthony Quinn), in the place of her dead sister, Rosa, Gelsomina goes "on the road" as his "assistant" in an itinerant circus-like show as a body-builder strong man. I have chosen several encounters in which she and/or other characters (including *Il Mato*, "The Fool" [Richard Basehart]) respond by listening and performing, metamorphically becoming other, temporally oscillating between and partaking of virtual and actual (multiple) conditions and identities in music-sound.

"*They call me Gelsomina*"—Gelsomina listening in and muttering to other frequencies, becoming "bird," flapping her cape, tuning the worldly to the psychic:

Gelsomina (gradually becoming audible/intelligible): "Sparks fly up and vanish from sight... oo, oo, oo, said the sky of the night."...

Zampanò (observing). "Hey, what're you doing?"

Gelsomina: "It will rain day after tomorrow"

Zampanò: "How do ya know?..."

Gelsomina: "hm, hm, it will rain."

Zampanò: "Come here... get in" [begin underscore/fade in of full music-cue, beginning with the slow chromatic figure]

Gelsomina: "I will sleep outside...."

Zampanò: "What's your name?"

Gelsomina: "They call me Gelsomina...."

In the setting of the silence that follows the musical pause, Zampanò forcibly again commands her to "Get in!" The violin concludes the cue with a portentous tritone, A5-Eb, further marked by an exclamation, a sonic omen both commanding the listener's attention and forcibly ending the "music" of Gelsomina's name.

"Make him laugh, Gelsomina"—listening to and with others; listening to and from particular positions of subjectivity; listening/hearing where phantom silences persist. The children bring Gelsomina to see the child Oswaldo:

Children: "Oswaldo—they never let him out of this room."..."Make him laugh, Gelsomina!" [begin underscore/fade in of music cue: again the chromatic part of the "name" theme]

After attempting to make Oswaldo laugh by mimicking/becoming a chicken-bird, Gelsomina stops, listens, and hears in the ensuing silence. Rota's uncanny woodwind music, wavering *pianissimo* neighbor-note trills with a staccato release (for example, E5-D♯5; F5-E5), registers "in secret" and from somewhere else, accenting the visual-sonic encounter between the two, as if outside or suspending the linear narrative. An extended but ultimately broken-off triadic A minor ascent, A4-C5-E5, lights the close-up of Gelsomina's face, a pattern that replaces the ending tritone as a moment subject to a loss of breath. Metamorphically "becoming Oswaldo," Gelsomina registers him and his world in the "silence" of an encounter that honors, registers without negating or substituting, their differences. An older nun abruptly interrupts this "listening moment": "What are you doing here you little monster? (to one of the children) Get out immediately before I throw you out!" (a retort undermined, however, by the children's taunting).

Gelsomina singing—She sings the first five notes *"Dee-De-De-De-Dee"* (measures 1-2) and then continues with "Gelsomina's tune" using these syllables (see Figure 20.5a): "That song, do you remember it Zampanò?" She half-sings/hums the tune, not yet played on the trumpet—a forming listening in which a relived memory becomes musical ("that day it rained and we didn't work, do you remember how nice it was?") into the unknown and uncertain future (stops singing tune before its conclusion), "Why don't you teach me how to play the trumpet, Zampanò? I would learn very quick...."

Circus sounds and circus calls—listening to let music touch and captivate, listening, submitting to music's desire. Gelsomina, despondent and abandoned by heartless Zampanò, sits by the side of the road. When an itinerant group of musicians from the traveling circus passes her, she listens to their music and submits to its call. The "march" acts upon her in a linear pull of desire: she moves with its repetitions materializing a tension between its musical affective force/effect and her gradual transformation, becoming and internalizing its energy.

FIGURE 20.5 a: *La Strada* (The Road) (Fellini 1954), music by Nino Rota, "Gelsomina's name" as "performed" on trumpet by Gelsomina (after she teaches herself to play "music," in contrast to the comic effects for Zampanò's act) (transcription from the soundtrack).

b: version of "Gelsomina's tune" as first played on a miniature violin by Il Matto (a step higher than Gelsomina's later performance), with first and second ending (transcription from the soundtrack).

Gelsomina (trumpet) *and Il Matto ("The Fool")* (violin) (*Richard Basehart*)—plays "Gelsomina's tune" on a miniature violin (see Figure 20.5b). Intersubjective listening: incongruities, discrepancies, contradictions that turn toward or portend the future; his performance of her tune is tonally circular, cycling without conclusion.

Gelsomina plays the trumpet—performing "Gelsomina's tune" (as in Figure 20.5a) for the sister/nun who has taken them in and Zampanò; listening with care, discernment, detail, materializing-imagining music-sound and one's transforming involvement with it. In this "crystalline" time-image, playing a waltz-like tune on her trumpet first performed by the "clown" Il Matto on a miniature violin. This is the tune she has struggled to sing and play for most of the film—her music-sound-listening becomes both an extension and a process, now becoming song, a musical intentionality and expressivity to be reckoned with. Her performance (is it hers?) breaks uncomfortably through the cinematic texture of the film: she travels to a new place, concludes the tune, and returns. She, and we, are aware of the discrepancies between these places, of a "crystalline" moment where the virtual potential of the sound image makes its presence known by concluding with the minor mode (lowered scale-degree 3, G♭5): at that "moment," Gelsomina realizes that she and trumpet do not sound "beauty" in the present moment—as her playing and "performance" breaks off, the sound becomes independent (unanchored, free from source) for a moment, making evident its otherworldly quality and potential.

Zampanò listens: Gelsomina's tune (a woman sings in the distance)—Zampanò's hearing and listening for the consciousness (presence, intentionality) of and in the music; listening to the performative. The woman's memory of Gelsomina "No one around here knew her...she seemed a little bit crazy...."

Zampanò's future—listening (memory, tune now silent) as possibility for transformation in tension with sound as the force/weight of the past (fragment of tune as underscore with chromatic conclusion; end of film).

Gelsomina's "listening in film" portrays and performs multiple dimensions ("crystals") of musical time ("presents which are passing" and "the raising or falling back of pasts which are preserved" [Deleuze 1989, 93]), opening cinematic potential to a future unknown.

CONCLUSION

In this essay, I have highlighted aspects/components of listening in film in music: temporal unfolding as vertical/linear (spatial/temporal) play, relational character and metamorphic transformation, the roles of intersensory/intermodal redundancy and difference, and the pull of materiality (performance in the drama and soundtrack). By opening to the interactions and discrepancies (incompleteness) of multiple sensory and contextual combinations, we can effect a critical reorientation of music theory's projects in a way that allows for music's more mobile dispositions of exchange and interchange, for its material transgressions, as well as for its individual particularities and possibilities.

"Listening" in/to music and listening to/in film differs from, though is interactive with, processing and figuring a score/scenario—multidimensional, performative, and experiential, temporally changing in ways that analysis can address only indirectly. From and in experiential encounters—listening (differentiating and discerning)—emerge subtle play and interactions between left-to-right and back-to-front experience-interpretation. More than "adding depth," similarity and analogy metamorphize as difference enters with profound affect. Propelled by and in affective encounters, forged through and in temporal pressures of affect and sensation interacting contingently with ideas, audio/visual differentiation and dimensionality becomes musically-cinematically experiential, ever interrelating and transforming outside in and inside out.

NOTES

1. See also Kielian-Gilbert 2004 in this regard.
2. For additional discussion, see Kielian-Gilbert 2010.
3. The choreography was originally presented as a production of the Nederlands Dans Theater in November 1978.

4. See composer-theorist Elaine Barkin's poetic rendering of visual images in and through music sound that portrays ways in which music (such as Schoenberg's Little Piano Pieces, Op. 19, nos. 2 and 6, or passages from Stravinsky's *Rite of Spring*) extends into different modalities and dimensions of experience (Barkin 1997).

5. Kylián's visual/filmic choreography enacts the musical intuitions of Figure 20(a-c). Its cross-modal, experiential and perceptual dramatization actualizes a sense of presence, affect, and temporal engagement. Though I did not have access to her work in writing this essay, Erin Brannigan's *Dancefilm: Choreography and the Moving Image* (Oxford University Press, 2011, see page 11 and passim) highlights ways in which cinema has become a cultural, structural, and aesthetic influence and reference point for dance practitioners. My thanks to Michael Long, Indiana University, for this reference.

6. This phrasing is taken from "Richter on Film" (short film; Cecile Starr 1972). In the English version, *Ghosts Before Breakfast*, the second title card declares: "The Nazis destroyed the sound version of this film as 'degenerate art.' It shows that even objects revolt against regimentation."

7. See the discussion of suture and Jacques Lacan's account of subject formation in Žižek 2001, and also the controversy articulated by Bordwell 2005.

8. Ronald Bogue has stressed Deleuze's connections to Bergson's ideas: "Deleuze's approach to cinema is predominantly Bergsonian, rather than Peircean" (Bogue 2009, 362); also Bogue 2003 and Kielian-Gilbert 2010.

9. Also see Duncan 2003, 75–76.

10. These scenes reference the *Manifesto of the 343 Bitches*, a document named by the press that Varda and other feminists signed to protest class inequities pertaining to women's reproductive rights.

11. Bogue misquotes the final words as "and perpetual exchange." I have corrected it to "a perpetual exchange."

12. Thomas Van Order (2009) offers a valuable discussion of the differences between the 1954 Italian version of the film and the 1956 English-language version, noting that Fellini had no control over the English audio track. According to Van Order, the English-language version departs from Fellini's intent to push "the envelope much further than other Italian directors in separating voice from image" (62).

BIBLIOGRAPHY

Barthes, Roland. 1985a. "Listening." In *The Responsibility of Forms: Critical Essays on Music, Art, and Representation*, translated by Richard Howard, 245–260. New York: Hill & Wang.

Barthes, Roland. 1985b. "The Grain of the Voice." In *The Responsibility of Forms: Critical Essays on Music, Art, and Representation*, translated by Richard Howard, 267–277. New York: Hill & Wang.

Barkin, Elaine. 1997. *e: an anthology. music, text, and graphics*. Red Hook, NY: Open Space.

Béar, Liza. 2009. Interview with Agnès Varda, March 9, 2009. http://www.interviewmagazine.com/film/agnis-varda/ (accessed August 15, 2010).

Bergson, Henri. (1896) 1988. *Matter and Memory*. Translated by Nancy Margaret Paul and W. Scott Palmer. New York: Zone.

Bíró, Yvette. 1997. "Caryatids of Time: Temporality in the Cinema of Agnès Varda." Translated by Catherine Portuges. *Performing Arts Journal* 19, no. 3: 1–10.

Bogue, Ronald. 2003. *Deleuze on Cinema*. New York: Routledge.

——. 2009. "Gilles Deleuze." In *The Routledge Companion to Philosophy and Film*, edited by Paisley Livingston and Carl Plantinga, 368–377. London: Routledge.

Bordwell, David. 2005. "Slavoj Žižek: Say Anything." http://www.davidbordwell.net/essays/zizek.php#_ednref11 (accessed August 15, 2010).

Brannigan, Erin. 2011. *Dancefilm: Choreography and the Moving Image*. New York: Oxford University Press.

Buhler, James. 2000. "*Star* Wars, Music and Myth." In *Music and Cinema*, edited by James Buhler, Caryl Flinn, and David Neumeyer, 33–57. Hanover, NH: University Press of New England.

——. 2001. "Analytical and Interpretive Approaches to Film Music (II): Interpreting Interactions of Music and Film." In *Film Music: Critical Approaches*, edited by K. J. Donnelly, 39–61. Edinburgh: Edinburgh University Press.

Buhler, James, Caryl Flinn, and David Neumeyer, eds. 2000. *Music and Cinema*. Hanover, NH: University Press of New England.

Carroll, Noël. 1996. *Theorizing the Moving Image*. Cambridge Studies in Film. Cambridge: Cambridge University Press.

Chion, Michel. 1994. *Audio-Vision: Sound on Screen*. Edited and translated by Claudia Gorbman. New York: Columbia University Press.

——. 2009. *Film, a Sound Art*. Translated by Claudia Gorbman. New York: Columbia University Press.

Cohen, Annabel J. 1993. "Associationism and Musical Soundtrack Phenomena." *Contemporary Music Review* 9, nos. 1–2: 163–178.

——. 2000. "Film Music: Perspectives from Cognitive Psychology." In *Music and Cinema*, edited by James Buhler, Caryl Flinn, and David Neumeyer, 360–377. Hanover, NH: University Press of New England.

Cook, David A. 1996. *A History of Narrative Film*. 3rd ed. New York: W. W. Norton.

Deleuze, Gilles. 1989. *Cinema 2: The Time-Image*. Translated by Hugh Tomlinson and Robert Galeta. Minneapolis: University of Minnesota Press.

——. 1994. *Difference and Repetition*. Translated by Paul Patton. New York: Columbia University Press.

Deleuze, Gilles, and Félix Guattari. 1987. *A Thousand Plateaus: Capitalism and Schizophrenia*. Translated by Brian Massumi. Minneapolis: University of Minnesota Press.

Dell'Antonio, Andrew, ed. 2004. *Beyond Structural Listening? Postmodern Modes of Hearing*. Berkeley: University of California Press.

Duncan, Dean. 2003. *Charms that Soothe: Classical Music and the Narrative Film*. New York: Fordham University Press.

Fuchs, Cynthia. 2010. Reviews: POV: *The Beaches of Agnès* (*Les plages d'Agnès*) by Cynthia Fuchs. In *Pop Matters* (Popular Voices, Cultural Matters), June 29, 2010. http://www.popmatters.com/pm/review/127634-pov-the-beaches-of-agnes-les-plages-dagnes (accessed August 2010). The film was broadcast on PBS stations on June 29, 2010 for the program *Point of View*. http://www.pbs.org/pov/beachesofagnes (accessed June 30, 2010).

Goldmark, Daniel, Lawrence Kramer, and Richard Leppert, eds. 2007. *Beyond the Soundtrack: Representing Music in Cinema*. Berkeley: University of California Press.

Gorbman, Claudia. 1987. *Unheard Melodies: Narrative Film Music*. Bloomington: Indiana University Press.

Hanninen, Dora A. 2003. "A Theory of Recontextualization in Music: Analyzing Phenomenal Transformations of Repetition." *Music Theory Spectrum* 25, no. 1: 59–97.

Kalinak, Kathryn. *Film Music: A Very Short Introduction*. NewYork: Oxford University Press, 2010.

Kassabian, Anahid. 2001. *Hearing Film: Tracking Identifications in Contemporary Hollywood Film Music*. New York: Routledge.

Kielian-Gilbert, Marianne. 2004. "*Chopiniana* and Music's Contextual Allusions." In *The Age of Chopin: Interdisciplinary Inquiries*, edited by Halina Goldberg, 162–200. Bloomington: Indiana University Press.

——. 2010. "Music and the Difference in Becoming." In *Sounding the Virtual: Gilles Deleuze and the Theory and Philosophy of Music*, edited by Brian Hulse and Nick Nesbitt, 199–225. Aldershot, UK, and Burlington, VT: Ashgate.

Kramer, Lawrence. 1990. *Music as Cultural Practice, 1800–1900*. Berkeley: University of California Press.

Kuleshov, Lev V. 1974. *Kuleshov on Film: Writings*. Edited and translated by Ronald Levaco. Berkeley: University of California Press.

Maur, Karin von. 1999. *The Sound of Painting: Music in Modern Art*. Translated by John W. Gabriel. Munich: Prestel Verlag.

McLuhan, Marshall. 1964. *Understanding Media: The Extensions of Man*. New York: McGraw-Hill.

Mitchell, W. J. T. 2002. "Showing Seeing: A Critique of Visual Culture." *Journal of Visual Culture* 1, no. 2: 165–181.

Neumeyer, David. 2009. "Diegetic/Nondiegetic: A Theoretical Model." *Music and the Moving Image* 2, no. 1: 26–39.

Powrie, Phil, and Robynn Stilwell, eds. 2006. *Changing Tunes: The Use of Pre-existing Music in Film*. Aldershot, UK, and Burlington, VT: Ashgate.

Pudovkin, V. I. 1929. *Film Technique and Film Acting*. Translated by Ivor Montagu. London: Gollancz; Reprint, New York: Grove, 1970.

Ries, Frank W. D. 1986. *The Dance Theatre of Jean Cocteau*. Ann Arbor, MI: UMI Research Press.

Royce, Anya Peterson. 2004. *Anthropology of the Performing Arts: Artistry, Virtuosity, and Interpretation in a Cross-Cultural Perspective*. Walnut Creek, CA: Alta Mira Press.

Schwarz, David. 1997. *Listening Subjects: Music, Psychoanalysis, Culture*. Durham: Duke University Press.

Shore, Bradd. 1996. *Culture in Mind: Cognition, Culture, and the Problem of Meaning*. New York: Oxford University Press.

Smith, Jeff. 2001. "Popular Songs and Comic Allusion in Contemporary Cinema." In *Soundtrack Available: Essays on Film and Popular Music*, edited by Pamela Robertson Wojcik and Arthur Knight, 407–430. Durham, NC: Duke University Press.

——. 2009a. "Bridging the Gap: Reconsidering the Border between Diegetic and Nondiegetic Music." *Music and the Moving Image* 2, no. 1: 1–25.

Stilwell, Robynn. 2007. "The Fantastical Gap between Diegetic and Nondiegetic." In *Beyond the Soundtrack: Representing Music in Cinema*, edited by Daniel Goldmark, Lawrence Kramer, and Richard Leppert, 184–202. Berkeley: University of California Press.

Van Order, Thomas. 2009. *Listening to Fellini: Music and Meaning in Black and White*. Madison, NJ: Fairleigh Dickinson University Press.

Winters, Ben. 2010. "The Non-diegetic Fallacy: Film, Music, and Narrative Space." *Music and Letters* 91, no. 2: 224–244.

Žižek, Slavoj. 2001. *The Fright of Real Tears: Kieslowski and the Future*. Bloomington: Indiana University Press.

....

CHAPTER 21

AUTEURSHIP AND AGENCY IN TELEVISION MUSIC

....

RONALD RODMAN

TELEVISION is often linked to film, both being understood in public discourse as belonging to the visual and sound media. The two are often linked in the scholarly community as well, from the evidence of journals and bibliographies that append the word "television" onto the title, as, for example, *The Journal of Film and Television*, *Film and Television Index*, and the *New Review of Film and Television Studies*. The Society for Cinema Studies (SCS), founded in 1959 as the Society of Cinematologists, changed its name to Society for Cinema and Media Studies (SCMS) in 2002, in recognition not only of the increasing importance of television but also of the growth of audiovisual content on the Internet.

Although it is true that film and television share the traits of presenting images, dialogue, sound effects, and music simultaneously to a viewing audience, research in the two areas traditionally has come from different scholarly communities, film being the property of film studies scholars—many of whom have ties to literary studies or history—and television being in the bailiwick of the communications or media studies community. This bifurcation is significant, in that film is now generally regarded as a narrative art form, whereas television is usually still considered a communications medium and—perhaps more prominently—a commodity exchange medium, whose primary purpose is to disseminate information and entertainment to a mass audience while simultaneously selling goods and services to that same audience. This distinction creates a discourse on television that is often distinctively postmodern: TV is said to deal with intertextual *bricolage* that includes real-life events, fictional narratives, and a bartering system of commercials in an electronic marketplace (at least in almost all areas of American TV). Film—by which we mean primarily the vast repertoire of feature films—is studied for its artistic originality in displaying moving images and sounds on a large screen, and for its depth in bringing expression to social issues. Television, on the other hand, is often relegated to the study of audience demographics or the economics of commercial sponsorship; when the subject of sound and image comes up, it is usually in the context of how these sounds and images generate a liminal or subliminal message. The study of film, thus, has tended to be aestheticist (formalist) or ideological (critical), whereas work on television has tended to the sociological or to marketing research.

Like film studies, television studies have tended to focus on the visual aspects of the medium. Sound has been an area of interest by many, but until recently, music has been a relatively neglected area. As Claudia Gorbman notes in her foreword to a recent book on TV music:

> like film studies twenty years ago, television studies ignores music. How can it be that so few commentators on popular culture recognize the role of television music in reflecting and cultivating popular tastes and understanding of nationhood, race, class, and other socially crucial factors—not just in the USA but worldwide? (Gorbman 2011, ix)

While it is true that "television studies" have said relatively little about music in television to date, writing about music in television began with the advent of television. Articles and books by journalists in the popular press, television enthusiasts, and in-house professionals have contributed to a literature in this field. Now, as in film studies, a musicology of television music is emerging, with research drawing from film studies, television studies, and historical musicology. Steven Westcott's (1985) pioneering research guide to film *and* television music, which has been supplemented by two recently published research guides for music that include both film and television in their purview (Pool and Wright 2011; Sherk 2011). The history of television music is also being chronicled through the Internet with websites from the Museum of Broadcast Communications, and the Internet Movie Database (which includes television), and others.

One path for studying music in television has been to use methods of historical musicology, focusing on the TV composer, production practices, and the score as historical artifact. In this camp, much writing on television music to date has produced nostalgic overviews of TV theme music, collections of composer interviews, and "how to write a TV score" manuals. Early writings on television scoring by Sosnik (1949) and later, Marlin Skiles (1976) contained mostly professional advice on how to "break into the business," but also contained tips on composing for the medium, as well as some material on concepts of meaning and affect in television music. Technical manuals aside, the musicological approach imitates the "auteurist" approach of film studies, where the TV composer is studied in much the same manner as a famous director, usually regarded as the primary creative force in a media text. Literature in this auteurist approach ranges from Rose Heylbut's (1945) interview of NBC radio-TV composer Thomas Belviso, up through the many composer studies, such as Jack Sullivan's (2006) coverage of Bernard Herrmann's Hitchcock TV scores.

Other avenues of research in TV music have been taken to apply traditional methods of television studies, notably semiotics (Cook 1998, Donnelly 2005, Rodman 2010, among others) and culture theory (Deaville 2006, 2007; Meizel 2011; among others), and even traditional music theory (Stilwell 2011), to search out the essence of television music. This approach tends to deal more with "agency," that is, what music *does* on television, that is, how television music conveys stories, narratives, or conveys a sense of time and place to its audience.

In this chapter, I shall survey literature and approaches in the field, beginning with the composer-based "auteurist" model (Section 1), and moving on to "agency"-oriented models (Section 2), television as commodity (especially music in TV commercials; Section 3), the distinctive character of music video (Section 4), and concluding with discussion of the current state and prospects for television music research (Section 5).

1 A MUSICOLOGY OF TELEVISION SOUND: THE TV COMPOSER AS AUTEUR

The link between film and television music observed by some scholars is no accident, for, historically, many of the professionals who worked with music in television also had experience in film music (see Royal Brown's [1994, 294–304] interview of Henry Mancini, and Jack Sullivan [2006], whose work on Hitchcock's film music includes a chapter on the Hitchcock TV series, with much of the music composed by Bernard Herrmann). Many television music composers moved over in the 1950s from composing for films, and their transition from the one to the other was not onerous, as early scoring practices not only mimicked film scoring, but also operated within what was essentially still a studio-based soundtrack post-production process. Among the familiar names that had prior film music credentials are William Lava, Dominic Frontiere, Leith Stevens, Henry Mancini, Bernard Herrmann, and Hershel Burke Gilbert, among others. Nevertheless, in the very early years of television (c.1949–1956), composers actually were drawn more from radio than the cinema. This link has been largely overlooked in the current scholarly literature (for exceptions, see Burlingame 1996 and Rodman 2010) but was a big issue for practitioners of TV music in its early days (see Sosnik 1982, 1986; Heylbut 1945). In its early years, before the era of television filming production, television dramas were produced live on stage with a live musical ensemble accompanying the actors, as was the practice with radio drama.

The auteurist approach was evident as early as the mid-1940s. As in film music, musicians were also concerned about the general quality of music in early television. And as in film, one issue for TV music soundtracks was the tension between the use of stock or library music—that is, prerecorded tracks—and music that was newly composed. This tension led some music critics to call for more original TV scores, a viewpoint that was often in direct contrast to network producers, who sought to save money by using library music. While library music was used extensively in some TV productions, music by composers well known for their concert music did find its way into television. In 1956, Albert Elias cited the many musical contributions of such high-caliber contemporary composers as Norman Dello Joio, Paul Creston, George Antheil, William Schuman, and Henry Cowell, all of whom had either created original scores for television documentaries or had bits of their preexisting music used as theme music for other programs (Elias 1956). One notable program, *The Twentieth Century* (1957–1966), was critically acclaimed for its excellent music, which featured a theme by George Antheil and scores in many episodes by such renowned composers as Creston, Franz Waxman, Alan Hovhaness, Gail Kubik, and Darius Milhaud.

By the mid-1950s, some television composers had come to grips with the problem of limited budgets in producing high(er)-quality scores. Tom Scott (himself a TV composer) claimed in 1956 that low-budget shows had in fact produced the most daring and successful original scores on television to date. He cited *Camera Three*, a long-running anthology series on CBS, as having broadcast several teleplays using a minimal score to great effect. In Scott's view, such minimal scoring for television was a strength, not a weakness, as it differentiated television from film and created a new form of dramatic expression. Scott's account reflects the development of television music as it moved away from massive film scores and toward the creation of its own language. In effect, Scott's view paved the way for a new television music aesthetic (Scott 1956, 19–23).

The early writing on television music arose from the effort of some critics and composers to maintain what they believed to be a high standard of music, that is, the use of original music by high-caliber composers. This trend has led TV music scholars to imitate film musicologists, who in turn have found it easy to imitate their colleagues in cinema studies, who regard film directors as auteurs, the primary creative forces of films—analogous to authors of poems or novels. Of course, the auteur model is essentially the same model that venerates the composer in the masterwork tradition in nineteenth- and twentieth-century studies of concert music and opera. As Claudia Gorbman points out, however, this auteur study of film music composers actually trails behind the auteur school of cinema:

> First of all, its [film music studies] parent discipline was not psychoanalysis, or literary criticism, or political science, but musicology, which lagged a generation behind literary and film studies' embrace of psychoanalysis, Marxism, feminism, queer studies, and other culturally politicized approaches. When musicologists turned to film music as a genre worthy of study, they were obliged to treat it as high art in order to maintain credibility in their institutional milieu, just as twenty years before film studies latched on to auteurism, considering the director as autonomous artist, as a crucial step in establishing film studies itself as a worthy pursuit in the academy. (Gorbman 2004, 15)

This auteurist approach to film music as it has been applied to television music was, and remains, one component of television music studies. Much of the current scholarship has yielded an archive of composers who work in television—composers who otherwise would have remained in obscurity, especially in early television, as many were not credited on the small screen.

1.1 Two Takes on an Auteurist history: Jon Burlingame, Roy Prendergast

Among the studies of television music that follow the auteurist or composer-centered priorities of their cinema-music counterparts is Jon Burlingame's *TV's Biggest Hits* (1996). Burlingame's book is a treasure trove of information and historical data on composers of TV theme music during the first fifty years of television. It contains an exhaustive supply of information on composers and television programs, many bits of composer trivia, and a comprehensive account of composers and the television programs for which they composed theme music. The volume is organized by popular television genres, including game shows, daytime soap operas, police and detective shows, medical dramas, westerns, sitcoms, documentaries and news, and cartoons.

The strength of Burlingame's work is the scope of information on the hundreds of composers and television programs, based on meticulous archival work that covers some forty years of television programming. Beyond the compelling thumbnail life histories of these composers and commentary about the theme songs themselves, however, the book provides little historical perspective on television music and avoids any engagement with how these themes function within the whole of a television narrative. Since Burlingame limits his book to television theme songs only—that is, those minute, yet complete musical texts that serve the dual purpose of identifying a television program, while also summoning the viewer to the screen—he does not consider the large library of other television music, namely the narrative cue music, the underscore, the play-on and play-offs of variety shows, or music in advertising.

At the other end of the spectrum is Roy Prendergast, whose take on television music is *auteurist and negative*. In *Film Music: A Neglected Art* (1992), he describes the form and function of television cue music, focusing on Jerrold Immel's music for the program *Dallas* (1979–90). Prendergast comments on the composer's musical "bridges," "bumpers," "act-ins," and "act-outs," all devices used as conventional transitions during television programs. Unlike Burlingame, however, Prendergast believes that television's ephemeral structure actually cheats the composer out of developing any substantial sort of musical expression. Television's constant interruptions and all too brief narrative structures undercut any sense of musical continuity, and Prendergast bemoans the role of the TV composer who is working in the grip of this most unmusical of art forms: "The problems [television] create[s] for the composer are mainly related to time, specifically, having enough time to allow music to achieve some effect in a scene" (Prendergast 1992, 275). He expresses some bewilderment at the musical structure of television, puzzling about these minute musical forms. He regards the true nature of television as a series of constant interruptions of narrative, continually darting from one text to another; and he is disdainful of the viewer who can "tune out" by changing channels, walking away from the set, or simply turning it off in the middle of a narrative. For all of these reasons, Prendergast sees television music as impoverished compared to film. Unlike Burlingame, then, Prendergast does engage music's role *within* a narrative, but dismisses it as inevitably limited and superficial.

1.2 The Successful Television Composer

Both Burlingame and Prendergast try to make the case for an auteurist tradition in television music, even if their focus on composers cannot avoid revealing the medium's limitations. In Burlingame's case, he ends up restricting his readings to themes, ignoring music's role within a narrative text. In Prendergast's case, the music in the entire medium itself is found wanting. When considered from these auteurist viewpoints, TV music *does* look impoverished, and Burlingame's extensive coverage of composers' forty-five-second TV theme music seems somewhat overblown. Television texts *are* ephemeral and brief, so how can ten minutes of a TV score be compared with hours of music in an epic film? In fact, the successful TV composer is one who understands the medium and produces music that adapts well to it. Adapting, however, does not necessarily mean producing a musical artwork with a full-blown tonal and narrative arc, as a film score. Instead, success in TV music stems more from producing effective music that quickly links narrative program (or commercial) semiotically with audience expectations.

One way of looking at the issue is by considering how miniature TV music texts convey nonmusical ideas. Successful TV composers have a knack for creating brief, miniature musical texts that produce discursive musical topics, which in turn serve to communicate to an audience, whether to identify a particular show, or correlate a musical style with a mood, a setting, or an *ethos*, that is, the fundamental underlying character or spirit of a TV show, mutually agreed upon by audience and composer. Nicholas Cook (1998) calls effective TV scoring "composing with styles." For example, "light music," was a catch-all term for early situation comedies from *Leave It to Beaver* (1957–1963) in the 1950s to *Three's Company* (1977–1984), evoking a light comedic and often "wholesome" topic. Composers like Dave Kahn (*Leave it to Beaver*), Frank DeVol (*The Brady Bunch*, *My Three Sons*), and Vic Mizzy (*Green Acres*, *The Addams Family*) excelled at this style on television. Other popular styles also connected with audience expectations. The use of jazz music in the early detective and cop shows like *Peter Gunn* (Henry Mancini), *M Squad* (Count Basie), *77 Sunset Strip* (Mack David and Jerry Livingston), and other shows conveyed "urban suavity" to audiences in the late 1950s and early 1960s.

Those TV music composers who have become auteurs of sorts are those who have successfully manipulated these rhetorical musical topics while also effecting change in musical practices over time. Mike Post, for example, is regarded by many as a TV composer-auteur because he introduced a light rock-style topic for the program *The Rockford Files* (1974): its theme led to a number of imitations, culminating in Jan Hammer's hard-rock theme to *Miami Vice* in 1984. Other composers, such as W. G. "Snuffy" Walden, Mark Snow, and Angelo Badalamenti, are notable due to their ability to set musical styles that correlate with the overall mood of the shows for which they compose. Walden composed the intimate, "hip" score for *thirtysomething*, Snow the vague, mysterious music to *The X Files*, and Badalamenti the postmodern mix of soap opera and Gothic horror in David Lynch's *Twin Peaks*.

1.3 Critique of the Auteur Model for Television Music

Although we may define television music auteurship on the basis described in the section above, a major problem with television music is that the music of many program episodes throughout the 1950s to 1980s featured music by several composers over varying periods of time. Jeff Bond (1999) notes that in narrative television productions, musical cues are often cobbled together using pieces by several different composers in a process known as "tracking." Bond shows how in the original *Star Trek* series, cues were continually recycled, with new cues added as needed. Episodes may use music by a single composer, but many others have as many as four, five, and even six different composers (Bond 1999, 41–55). Such musical practice shifts the role of auteur from the composer to the music editor and director. In the heyday of the large film and TV studio, composers for a particular series were those in the "stable" for the studio or network.

For the *Star Trek* original series, composers included Fred Steiner, Alexander Courage (who wrote the now-famous theme music), Jerry Mullendore, Jerry Fielding, and Gerald Fried. The long-running *Gunsmoke* series (1955–1975) employed composers Lud Gluskin, Rex Koury (who composed the theme), Morton Stevens (who later became music director at CBS and also composed the *Hawaii Five-o* theme), Fred Steiner, Leith Stevens, Nathan Scott, Wilbur Hatch (an early pioneer who had provided music for the *I Love Lucy* show), Leon Klatzkin, Nathan Scott, Lee Van Cleave, and several others who inhabited the stable of the music department at CBS over the years. Authorship may be apparent in most narrative TV theme songs, but in a tracked TV episode, a particular composer's voice may or may not be heard, as the newly composed music goes through an intensive editing process. As Bond shows for *Star Trek*, a composer's work may be augmented by other cue music of an earlier program by another composer. Moreover, a surprisingly great percentage of music composed for television is never heard at all, as cues end up (metaphorically) on the cutting room floor, victims of the music editor's scissors.

A few TV composers have achieved recognition in the popular and scholarly press through their individual work, including some who have effectively integrated music into genre narratives—such as Henry Mancini (*Peter Gunn*), Lalo Shifrin (*Mission Impossible*), or Billy Goldenberg (*Kojak*)—or have innovated by infusing different musical styles that have altered audience expectation, such as Morton Stevens (*Hawaii Five-o*), Mike Post (*Rockford Files, Hill Street Blues*), and Jan Hammer (*Miami Vice*). When viewed from an auteur standpoint, television music may be considered impoverished when compared to film music, but the fact that TV music composers and editors so adeptly communicate with TV audiences reveals that perhaps less can actually be more—as we shall see in considering the second term in the auteur–agency dichotomy of television music.

1.4 The New Television Music Auteur

More recent trends in the auteurist approach to television music have tended to focus on case studies of individual programs. Certain programs broadcast on cable, like *The Sopranos*, *The Wire* (Chare 2011 and Brown 2010), and *Treme* (Ersoff, 2012), have received a great deal of attention in the popular press. Some programs have an almost cult status, such as *Twin Peaks* (1990–1991) and *Buffy the Vampire Slayer* (1997–2003). Animated cartoons like *The Simpsons*, *Family Guy*, and *South Park* have also received scholarly attention. In these and other programs, the musical auteur role has shifted from the composer to the "creator" (that is, the writer, and sometimes director and producer) of the show. For example, Joss Whedon has been hailed as the primary architect of musical design in his series *Buffy the Vampire Slayer* (Leonard 2010; Attinello, Halfyard, and Knights 2010). Whedon is credited with everything from selecting the theme music (by the Santa Barbara–based punk band Nerf Herder) to the composition of the music to the episode "Once More, with Feeling," a parody of stage and film musicals. Whedon's control of music in the series is evident in his commentary to the Buffy DVD:

> We had a composer do a credit sequence for us, a song rather, it didn't really work out and so we went to a few unknown rock bands to see what they could come up with. Alyson Hannigan turned me on to Nerf Herder and … they won the prize. They did a great job. (Whedon as quoted in Hill 2010, 175)

Whedon's auteur status is also evident in research on the musical episode "Once More, with Feeling," where he is compared with musical composers Frank Loesser and Stephen Sondheim:

> Like Stephen Sondheim and others who echo him, Whedon sings a different sort of song in "Once More, with Feeling," and he does so in part by very purposefully playing off the patterns of the Hollywood past. (Sandars and Wilcox 2010, 190)

and:

> Whedon's affection for and knowledge of the American musical are everywhere evident, even if we did not have John Kenneth Muir's admission that he is a "virtual encyclopedia of musical film history." (Bauer 2010, 209)

Although Whedon is a composer (of sorts) who contributed some original music for the show, he is more noted for his selection of pop tunes played by various bands in the series. In this regard, *Buffy* is a successor to an earlier program, *Northern Exposure* (1990–95), in which "creators" Joshua Brand and John Falsey also selected music from a wide range of sources, both popular and classical. The theme music to the program was a newly composed piece by David Schwartz, but the soundtrack of the episodes was populated with music selected by the creators and played diegetically (although usually acousmatically, that is, out of sight) (see Rodman 2010, 266–69, for more on this series). Likewise, Julie Brown (2011) has written on David Kelley's use of music in the series *Ally McBeal* (1997–2002), in which pop singer Vonda Shepard appears in nearly every episode. In the series, it is not so much that Shepard supplies music as the auteur (even though she composed and performs the theme song), but, as Brown points out, it is her appearance in nearly every episode performing a cover of a pop tune that functions as a sort of feminine, postmodern Greek chorus, musically commenting on that episode's narrative theme.

The transformation of the television musical auteur can also be seen in the animated cartoon series of the twenty-first century. In particular, the music in three animated series, *The Simpsons* (1989–) and *Family Guy* (1999–), and *South Park* (1997–) are the products of their creators rather than their theme composers. *The Simpsons* has enjoyed a twenty-plus-year run on American television, due in large part to creator Matt Groening's use of parody and satire of nearly every aspect of contemporary society. Although the series features a theme by master film composer Danny Elfman (see Kutnowski 2008) and episode music by Alf Clausen, the music of the series is noted more for Groening's musical parody episodes, such as the faux musical, "Marge and the Monorail" (a parody of *The Music Man*), and a newly composed musical, "A Streetcar Named Marge" (based on Tennessee Williams's *A Streetcar Named Desire*), as well as numerous intertextual musical quotations. Similarly, Seth McFarlane's *Family Guy* features a theme by composer Walter Murphy and episode music by Murphy and Ron Johnson, but the show is noted more for its often-abrupt shifts to diegetic musical numbers during episodes (see Rodman 2012). Much of the music in the series is big band swing music, a parody of "cool" music of an earlier era. The theme song itself is a reference to the opening of the famous *All in the Family* (1968–1979). In both these series, Groening and McFarlane, like Whedon in *Buffy*, may be considered the new auteurs of television music. Finally, Sean Nye (2011) examines music in the animated cartoon *South Park* (1997 and continuing) as a means of lampooning the intertextual knowledge of its viewers.

2 A Communication Model: Audience and Agency

Another fertile area to view television music is in its agency, a term that refers to music's *functions*: its ability to identify and interact with the television audience. Scholars in film and media studies and communications have worked for decades in theoretical areas that deal with agency, including the areas of narrative theory, gender theory, reader response theory, semiotics, queer theory, and psychoanalysis. Approaches such as these, when applied to music, consider not so much the creative role of the composer as the role of audience reception, and thus can potentially yield insight into how individuals in a particular culture understand the meaning of music in television (and other electronic media) and the aesthetic or commercial uses to which they put that knowledge.

Jim Collins (1992) argues that television music also might be profitably considered in the context of postmodern thought. Unlike film, television really did not have a modernist tradition from which to develop, and from its very inception has been essentially a postmodern medium that embodies certain traits and themes that resonate with conceptions of postmodernism. Collins (and others) have identified themes for postmodernism that include: (1) a continual proliferation of signs; (2) the pervasiveness of rearticulation and appropriation of previously articulated signs, or the foregrounding of intertextual references; (3) subjectivity, *bricolage*, and eclecticism; (4) the commodification of politics and value. From the outset (except in its very early years, the 1930s), television has always produced a continual proliferation of visual, auditory, and musical signs. Broadcast schedules consisted of programs, announcements, commercials, and station breaks, which create a seemingly unending flow of programming through time. An extreme point was reached with the rise of cable television in the early 1980s, when the number of networks proliferated and these and local stations increased their broadcasting to twenty-four hours a day. (This proliferation continues into the twenty-first century, with hundreds of cable channels, compared to the dozens of channels in the 1980s.) The foregrounding of intertextual references has also been a characteristic feature of television, as shows or other segments seek to connect with the viewer in a familiar fashion in the short time available to do so. In this section, I survey work of some key authors who have written on how TV music negotiates through the proliferation of signs and how it helps the commodity function of TV as a whole.

2.1 "Here I Am, Look at (and Listen to) Me": Vying for Attention in the Proliferation of Signs

A fundamental difference between film and TV as media is that the latter provides continuous broadcasting of texts through time. As Raymond Williams describes it, "in all developed broadcasting systems the characteristic organization, and therefore the characteristic experience, is one of sequence or flow. This phenomenon, of planned flow, is then perhaps the defining characteristic of broadcasting, simultaneously as technology and as a cultural form" (Williams 1992, 86). Williams's main focus is the connecting of sequence as programming to the concept of sequence as flow in highly developed broadcasting systems in the U.S. and Britain. Katy Stevens (2010) updates Williams's concept of flow by describing "hum" as the sonic equivalent to visual flow in the TV show *Buffy the Vampire Slayer*.

In a seminal article on television sound, Rick Altman adapts Williams's concept to argue that televisual flow is dependent upon the cultural practice of "household flow," that is, the comings and goings of viewers within their household living spaces. Altman says that the main mediator between the two flow systems is the television soundtrack (Altman 1987, 570). Highly developed broadcast systems are embedded in capitalistic societies where competition for viewers is keen, and where television revenues increase with increased viewership. Since TV channels must compete for viewers, not only with each other but also with distractions in the household, TV sound functions in two primary ways: (1) to identify or define images on the screen (what Altman calls "labeling"), and (2) to call attention to important events on the screen ("italicizing") (573–74). Altman lists other traits of TV sound, but these fall readily under the two generic categories. For example, "sound hermeneutic" is an acousmatic sound source that identifies the location of a character or event on screen, a labeling device. "Internal audience" is the sound of a favorite actor, which has the potential to draw the viewer to the screen, an italicizing device. The "sound advance" is a sound that cues important events to come, usually in the form of applause from a studio audience or applause track—yet another form of italicizing. Finally, "discursification" is sound intended to involve the viewer in some way, such as instant replay in a sporting event, another italicizing device.

As part of the TV sound apparatus, Altman's generic sound functions of labeling and italicizing apply to music as well, but music adds nuances to both. In relation to italicizing, Phillip Tagg ([1979] 2000) has identified an "apellative" function, that is, music's ability to summon the viewer to the screen. This function is usually found in theme music, but is also found in the "bumpers" or "act-ins," that is, music that announces the resumption of a particular show after the commercial messages. (Claudia Gorbman [2004] has referred to this function as "hailing.") Television uses music, like sound in general, to call the viewer's attention to the small screen. More recently, K. J. Donnelly (citing Jeremy Butler) describes the function of sound on television as: (1) capturing viewer attention; (2) manipulating viewer understanding of the image; (3) maintaining televisual flow; and (4) maintaining continuity between individual scenes (Donnelly 2005, 114). Donnelly speculates that music's function in television is primarily conative, a term that by definition refers to a stimulus prompting an action or change, including impulse, desire, volition, and striving. In other words, sound and music attempt to control the viewer (113–15). Music calls us to the set by announcing the beginnings of programs and coaxes us to buy products.

A second significant difference between film music and television music is the extent to which the latter shifts its agency. Theme music pulls the viewer to the small screen, but as programs continue, music is used to convey aspects of the narrative—the setting, the traits and emotions of the characters, the mood of the program, and so forth. This function is still conative—designed to keep viewers watching, but is focused more on the show's narrative action. But then, music helps to transition the viewer out of the narrative and into the realm of commercials. I (and others) labeled these distinctive agencies as interdiegetic, intradiegetic, and diegetic (see Rodman 2010, 53–55). Interdiegetic music is that which operates through televisual flow (transitioning in and out of discrete media units), whereas intradiegetic music is the underscore of programs and commercials. Diegetic music, that is, music that emanates from the action on the set, is also significant. Feature film music displays all of these traits as well, but it usually focuses more on the intradiegetic—providing a musical counterpart to the moods and setting of a film's story.

2.2 "Here's the Story of a…": Labeling Function of Intradiegetic Music

These three television music agencies listed above also contain labeling and italicizing functions. In fact, the efficacy of television music is its multiple or plurisituational status in television, where it can function in several different ways simultaneously. In traditional semiotics, Morris (1946) calls these types of sign vehicles ascriptors. The ascriptive function of television music is that in addition to alerting viewers of goings on on the screen, its labeling function serves to identify the program or evoke moods, settings, and character traits in TV narratives and on commercials. Composers were sensitive to the labeling functions of music even very early in the medium's history. Roger Bowman, a music critic and columnist, also predicted the need for filming television programs rather than relying on live music. In an article for *Film Music Notes* (Bowman 1949), he outlines a list of musical functions for "films in TV," or "spoken dramatic shows on films" (as opposed to live shows and TV musical programs). His list reads as follows:

- The theme: identifying the program as a whole.
- The Wagnerian leitmotifs, or "character themes" heralding or accentuating the approach or presence of a character by use of a theme identified with him.
- Recalling past events by repeating music identified with those happenings.
- Predicting future events by suggestive themes
- Imitating sounds, actions, or characteristics, in musical caricature.
- Building action, or indicating time, place, or unseen action.
- Providing a transition from scene to scene, place to place, thought to thought, period to period.
- Suggesting a blackout or a slow fade-out.
- Showing subjectively the inner thoughts, feelings and meanings of a character or a scene.
- Achieving montage effects with two or more themes or types of music played contrapuntally for special effects or distortions, as in Prokofieff's Lieutenant Kije music.
- Use of music to annotate dialogue.

Though they predate them by nearly forty years, Bowman's eleven functions for television music are remarkably like Gorbman's (1987) list of "seven rules" for the classical cinema. In addition, they already point to Altman's labeling and italicizing, discussed in Section 2.1. Theme music, leitmotifs, musical caricatures (items 1, 2, and 5) all serve as labeling devices, whereas the remainder of the items express the italicizing, or apellative function, calling the viewer's attention to the screen. Bowman's list also tacitly acknowledges the differences between interdiegetic and intradiegetic functions of music on TV, that is, music as it functions within a narrative (intradiegetic), and outside of the narrative in one of the functions listed by Altman and Tagg (interdiegetic).

2.2.1 Philip Tagg

Philip Tagg's *Kojak: Fifty Seconds of Television Music* ([1979] 2000) is a pioneering work on the labeling function in TV music. The book, which originated as a dissertation, deals exhaustively with the theme music to the 1970s-era American police drama in its title. Actually more a study of the signifying power of music in general than it is a work on television music, the volume nonetheless describes and highlights the labeling and italicizing power of theme music in a narrative agency for television. The book methodically lays the groundwork for the analyses of the music by summarizing the role of traditional musicology in the analysis of popular music, citing works on music and affect (especially popular music), and reviewing several models of communication. Taking a single musical text, Tagg puts the theme under his analytical microscope by contextualizing it in terms of traditional musicology, pop music analysis, communications theory, and formal and processive analysis, including "centrifugal versus centripetal" features in the theme's syntagmatic process.

The main feature of Tagg's book is what he calls "musematic" analysis, where he parsesout fundamental units of musical meaning ("musemes") from the *Kojak* (1973–78) theme music. Meaning in this type of analysis is revealed through the association of this music with similar music that came before, either through the pop music vernacular or through traditional Western European art music. Tagg sees the theme of *Kojak* as layered into musematic "stacks" and undertakes to dissect each of these to find their historic origins.

Tagg not only associates musical gestures with their affective precedents but he also aligns the music with the images. In another chapter of the book, he analyzes the quick-edited cuts of the opening images of *Kojak*. He even analyzes Kojak's (actor Telly Savalas's) clothing, appearance, the origin of the name "Kojak," and cites Biblical references relevant to the opening.

The crux of Tagg's analysis is that for music to be meaningful in a television text, it must present an affect with which the viewer is familiar, and these musical affects come from the viewer's musical knowledge. For example, for *Kojak*'s violin ostinato theme (played on a Moog synthesizer), Tagg provides musical antecendents of similar musical gestures from works by Monteverdi, Debussy, Stravinsky, Berlioz, Handel, Rozsa, Gershwin, Ravel, and others. He labels the context of these gestures in the various concert and stage works as "paramusical concomitants," which align themselves very closely with a single particular mood or affect. Though *Kojak* remains a classic in television music analysis, Tagg's work continues at present on his web site (http://www.tagg.org).

2.2.2 Nicholas Cook

While Tagg's monograph describes how musical gestures become conventional discursive labels, Nicholas Cook's *Analysing Musical Multimedia* (Cook 1998) tests the relationship of these labels against audience encoding. Like some theorists before him (Michel Chion, in particular), Cook develops three "models" of multimedia texts based on the relationship between visual image and music. The models are based on metaphor, or the hierarchical binary parsing of the image and music relationship. The first level is "similarity" *versus* "difference." If images, music and other multimedia parameters seem to agree (peaceful images accompanied by peaceful sounding music, for example), Cook calls them "conformant," whereas if there is difference, that difference may be complementary (a state of "contrariety") or may represent a contest (a state of "contradiction"). Conformance falls into three subcategories: *unitary*, where one medium predominates, while the other conforms to it; *dyadic*, where one medium corresponds directly to another; and *triadic*, where two media correspond to yet a third. As an illustration for this last category, Cook describes a Kandinsky play where color and sound correspond to an underlying emotional or spiritual meaning. For the two subcategories of difference, *contest* is a situation where two media compete for the viewer's attention, "each attempting to impose its own characteristics upon the other" (Cook 1998, 103). "Complementation" is where media function within "separate spheres," each having its own intrinsic properties. Cook cites songs with music and lyrics as such an "essentializing" complementarity, even though at times these media could be in a contest for attention.

2.2.3 Intertextuality: Music as Topic

Both Tagg and Cook explore the ability of music to signify and generate referent fields that tap into the intersubjectivity of that music's culture. Musical sounds, rhythms, and timbres at this level become *topoi*, that is, semantic units that are meaningful to the audience in some way, either emotionally or through association with other similar texts in a culture. Here, music takes on an "extroversive" semiosis, or meaning beyond the music itself. Early writing on television music reveals that artists were highly sensitive to these semiotic qualities. Heylbut (1945) describes how early TV composers try to fit music with the mood of a TV or radio program while remaining unobtrusive. Nalle also writes on the effect of music on a television narrative: "Music greatly helps both the writer and director in many ways. It gives tensile strength to the script and camera work. It can enrich and heighten the dramatic line" (Nalle 1962, 121). Nalle continues by describing the effect of music on the actors (playing music for actors was a practice held over from the era of silent films, when music was played for the mute actors to encourage them to emote): "Further, not only does it encourage active participation on the part of the viewer, but also it gives a real 'lift' to those in the cast. Provision is made purposely for them to hear the musical score via studio speakers as they play their parts."

There have been recent approaches to correlate musical styles with television genres. One such comprehensive work was done by Spencer (2008), on many diverse genres, but other works have focused on single genres. Some of the works with the animated cartoon have been mentioned, but within this category is Martin Kutnowski's (2008) close reading of the theme to *The Simpsons*. Work has also been done in science fiction (Donnelly 2012), the horror genre (Donnelly 2005), and Westerns (Lerner 2001). Finally, Rodman (2011) writes on how many TV shows present hybrid genres, and the music to these shows often contributes to generic ambiguity. Shows like *Cop Rock* (police procedural/musical), *Have Gun Will Travel, Shotgun Slade* (Western/detective show), and *Lost in Space* (science fiction/soap opera/comedy) all contain musical scores that frustrate a simplistic categorization of television genre.

3 COMMODITIES: MUSIC AND TV COMMERCIALS

At the heart of the labeling and italicizing functions of television sound and music are their ability to effect a translation into commodity exchange. Essentially, these functions are the same in TV commercials as they are in TV narratives, although the music's agency is now calling attention to the attributes of a product or service rather than characters, plot, or affect of a narrative story. Barnouw (1968) writes that the decision to make television a commercial medium was not a foregone conclusion, but with the public's pent-up desire for consumer goods along with the expansion of consumer goods industries after World War II, the temptation was just too much to pass up (42). The on-air ad, of course, was not new at the time: radio was rife with advertising and sponsorship, and early TV even experimented with ads before mass broadcasting made headway: the first TV commercial is generally taken to be one for Bulova watches broadcast on New York City NBC affiliate WNBT on July 1, 1941.

The trajectory of music in TV ads can be viewed as an evolution from the "jingle" to more generic pop-style tunes. In radio and early television, the primary delivery mechanism of music advertising was the "jingle," a brief musical setting designed to stick in the viewer's memory. Jingle advertising began in the electronic media in 1936 with an ad for Wheaties breakfast cereal that aired on a radio station in Minneapolis. In short order, jingles permeated radio, began appearing in short ad spots during movie theater programs, and eventually were adapted for television, advertising everything from cars to cigarettes to breakfast cereal. The jingle fulfills both of Altman's sound functions in TV: it identifies (labels) a product by providing a semiotic link between the music, slogan, and product being advertised, and it calls attention to (italicizes) the product by either arousing the viewer with exciting/happy music, or by using a particular musical style that appeals to a certain audience.

From the mid-1950s on, the structure of TV commercials was defined by the "Rosser Reeves" approach. In 1955, Reeves became chairman of the board of the Ted Bates advertising agency in New York, and was instrumental in developing the form of early TV jingles. As board chair at Bates, he was committed to making ads that were simple, direct, and focused on the repetition of what he called the "unique selling proposition" or USP. Reeves believed that television ads should state one primary reason why a particular product should be bought or was better than its competitors, and that these reasons should take the form of slogans or, when music was added, jingles. The success of his approach can be measured by the fact that many of his agency's slogans enjoyed great longevity, such as the one for M&M candies that "melt in your mouth, not in your hand." Reeves also argued that entire advertising campaigns should remain constant with only a single slogan for each product. His agency's ad for Anacin, for example, ran successfully for more than ten years, and though it was reported to be grating and annoying by many viewers, sales for Anacin tripled during the period, proving that Reeves' ends justified his means.

Reeves believed that music in television commercials was a most effective way to highlight the USP, especially in jingle form. In an intra-office memo published on September 11, 1950, he described ten traits of the musical jingle. His list is as follows:

- The length of the jingle must not exceed 13 seconds.
- The jingle must carry the whole U.S.P (unique selling position).
- The jingle must carry the name of the product.
- In cases of a new product, the jingle must carry "new product identification," that is, identify what the product is.
- The lyric must be set to a melody.
- This melody must be a new melody.
- This new melody must be singable.
- This new singable melody must be written so that it is singable by one voice.
- A musical gimmick is often effective, like repetition of words, or extension of words ("Good, Good, Good" and "So-o-o-o-o-o-o-o Good").
- There must be no fake scansion, that is, words must fit music following proper, natural accents. (Reeves 1950)

Reeves hired veteran radio and TV composer Harry Sosnik to help compose music for clients at Bates in 1963, just after Sosnik retired as music director at ABC. That same year, Sosnik wrote an unpublished memo describing the process of jingle composing, adapting many of Reeves's ideas about simplicity and efficacy in the lyrics. Thus, Sosnik recommended composing jingles in which the name of the product is prominent, composing the jingle in standard song (A-A-B-A) form so that the name of the product would be heard three times within the A section, and laying out the title and the remainder of the lyrics (the copy) to form the USP. Sosnik also advocated using a single style of music for a particular jingle, "be it a march form, childlike, swing, blues, sweet ballad, strong masculine, pretty feminine as well as many other styles." (Sosnik 1963, 1).

Sosnik's unpublished memo can be viewed as an early "how to" manual for jingle composers, and it was followed by others, notably Woodward (1982). But perhaps the most elegant expression of how to compose jingles is found in two books by Steve Karmen

(1989, 2005), who was a successful jingle composer in the 1970s and 1980s. In addition to describing his compositions, and the process by which he composes, Karmen lists other commercial musical forms such as the "logo," the "donut," and the "tag." Karmen touts his own ads in his book, but also offers some good advice for composing jingles, the guidelines being similar to the Reeves–Sosnik model.

A significant amount of scholarly work emerged on musical commercials in the 1980s and 1990s, both by musicologists and by scholars in other fields. Although this work often echoes Altman's labeling and italicizing functions, some scholars also discuss the importance of memorability and "enjoyability" of commercial music. David Huron (1989) identifies functions of music in advertising, arguing that its primary role is to entertain, while also realizing other functions, such as achieving structural continuity of the text, spurring memorability from the audience, helping target a demographic or psychographic group, or establishing an authorial voice for the ad (Huron 1989, 560). Mark Booth (1990) views the jingle as a form of lyrical proverb, which serves only to reinforce a buyer's already-made decision to purchase an item or to positively reinforce the buyer's purchase. In a 1990 trade journal, Linda Scott (1990) affirms Altman's sound functions by describing music in commercials as adhering to eight principles, all of which have either a labeling or italicizing function: (1) conveying consonance and dissonance; (2) representation of motion; (3) rhythm and repetition; (4) supporting a narrative; (5) forging identities; (6) locating; (7) structuring time; (8) establishing an ethos (Scott 1990, 228–32). More recently, Claudia Gorbman refers to "miniature chunks" of music in commercials as highly concentrated and designed to keep viewers watching: "Television (especially in its more highly segmented forms) and commercial digital media use more fragmentary, rationalized bits of music and much more repetition than do the sustained narrative forms." Clearly, function outweighs any interest in "internal coherence: . . . Music for TV commercials is so patently and concentratedly rhetorical that the commercial often disregards even the most elementary considerations of musical coherence." In this way, music within a television show works in the same way it does in the intervening "commercials, [which] deploy music for its evident cultural meanings in compact and often complex semiotic bonding with image and text" (Gorbman 2004, 17).

Television advertising moved away from jingles and incorporated popular musical styles in the late 1960s. Thomas Frank traces advertising in print and electronic media in the 1960s, claiming that a shift in advertising was due in large part to the shift in culture writ large: "The 1960s were a time of revolution in American business as they were in so many aspects of American life, an era that saw both the rise of market segmentation and a shift from a management culture that revered hierarchy and efficiency to one that emphasized individualism and creativity" (Frank 1997, 25). Frank's observations can be applied to music in advertising, as music in TV commercials shifted from commercially produced jingles to pop-style tunes. An ad for Coca-Cola in 1971 that featured "The Hilltop Song" ("I'd Like to Teach the World to Sing"), a folk-pop-style jingle that featured a scene of hundreds of young people on a hillside, spurred the "cola wars" advertising campaigns (between Coca-Cola and Pepsi). While the song served as a jingle (with the slogan "It's the Real Thing" embedded in the song), the ad is more memorable for its popular musical style, which appealed to the youth market at the time. Arguably, the commercial was entertaining, and the pop music and compelling images of young people created a "soft sell" approach to advertising. Pepsi followed suit with its "Pepsi generation" ad campaign, and eventually other ads followed the pop music boom.

Highlighting the importance of musical style to identify demographic audiences in ads, Armond White (1988) and Leslie Savan (1993) trace the move of TV ads from jingles to pop tunes, as popular musical styles have been used to identify a product with a target audience, a phenomenon bemoaned by Karmen (2005). Though popular music is most often used in commercials, Cook (1998) has shown that classical music has been employed to good effect, especially when the product (such as Mercedes-Benz automobiles) signifies "elite" or "luxurious." Cook points out the significance of musical style in commercials:

> Traditionally, musicians compose with notes, rhythms, and perhaps timbre. Only with postmodernism has the idea of "composing with styles" or "composing with genres" emerged, at least as a consciously adopted procedure. But composing with styles or genres is one of the most basic musical techniques found in television commercials. (Cook 1998, 16)

Cook emphasizes the advantage that musical styles and genres have over traditional musical continuity and development: the former "offer unsurpassed opportunities for communicating complex social or attitudinal messages practically instantaneously." More generally, "commercials often contain music that almost completely lacks "content" as a music theorist would generally define it—that is, distinctive melodic, harmonic, or rhythmic shaping—but incorporates a musical logic based on style" (Cook 1998, 16–17).

I have shown similar results in an ad for luxury cars and pickup trucks, where the background music is a hybrid of "New Age" music and classical musical styles in one case and a hybrid of American rock and country-western music in the other (Rodman 1997, 2010). In the 1990s, these styles would signify trendiness and the upper class for the car but blue-collar earthiness and toughness for the truck. Bob Seger's popular song "Like a Rock" was used to sell Chevrolet pick-up trucks in a long advertising campaign in the 1990s. The song was successful for Chevrolet trucks in part because of Seger's celebrity as an American rock star, but also because the song's stylistic elements—American rock and Country music—appealed to the young, white males who are most likely to purchase pick-up trucks. Tim Taylor (2007) traces the move to pop music a step farther, by noting the ascendance of pop electronica in commercials of the 1980s. He argues that the shift in music is due to what Pierre Bourdieu calls the rise of the "new petite bourgeoisie," a new youth market that displaced the previous one.

In this new, softer sell style of television commercials, music operates within an inner textual artistic surface (the lyrical language of music), but also on an outer pragmatic level that engages human cognition, identifies socioeconomic groups, and performs other extramusical functions. Semiologist Winfried Nöth (1987) calls this phenomenon "masking," where the explicit appeal to buy a product is hidden in favor of extolling its pleasurable aspects. The appeal for commodity exchange of the outer frame has been obfuscated by the "surface text" of the ad—which includes compelling images, sounds, and music—resulting in what Charaudeau (1983) calls a "strategy of occultation." Rodman (2009) and Cook (1998) both argue that music usually extends beyond the frame of commodity exchange to an external semantic frame of ads, where musical styles align themselves with the musical preferences of the viewers. In its ability to operate on several levels, music provides more of a "strategy of imbuement" than occultation. Music often imbues an ad with a semantic frame of aesthetic beauty, pleasure, or humor that not so much hides or masks the conative imperative to buy a product, but rather associates or correlates the product with a feeling or emotional bond.

More recently, Bethany Klein (2010) examines the growing trend of popular music in advertising, from both an aesthetic and business perspective, highlighting the often incongruous status of musician as artist and corporate shill. Other recent works explore the behavioral aspects of music in ads. Aleximanolaki, Loveday and Kennett, (2007) examine how advertisers use music as an implicit recall device, while Nina Hoeberichts (2012) views how music in ads affects consumer attitudes.

3.1 Music as Televisual Commodity

Yet another area of television music worthy of study is diegetic music, that is, performance by musicians on the screen. As important as diegetic music was to early television (live performance by musicians provided hours of inexpensive programming without the need for writers), little has been written about these music performances. From the beginning, variety shows that featured musical performance were prominent, and programs like *Your Hit Parade* and *Kraft Music Hall* provided smooth transitions from radio to TV. In these early years, some musicians were optimistic that musical performances would flourish in the new medium (as they had on radio) and not only provide employment for musicians but also offer high-quality entertainment for viewers. In 1949, for example, John Francis Cooke interviewed veteran bandleader Paul Whiteman, who was confident that television would be a boon for music of all kinds, classical, jazz, and pop (Cooke 1949). All three major American networks (as well as the BBC and other networks in Europe) contributed to this optimism, as they aired symphony orchestra concerts and operas, as well as pop and jazz concerts. Jennifer Barnes (2002) chronicles the rich history of television opera in the United States and the UK, and Michael Saffle (2006) writes about Leonard Bernstein's "Young People's Concerts," broadcast on American commercial television in the 1950s and 1960s. Mortimer Frank (2003) writes on Arturo Toscanini's years with NBC, both on radio and television. A history of diegetic music on television would show a shift from an open format, in which networks featured many kinds of music (classical, jazz, popular), to the eventual hegemony of popular music, at least on popular network television in America.

Musical performances, of course, were central to the musical variety show. The variety show format made the smoothest transition from radio to early television, and most programs were adaptations of existing radio programs. Perry Como transitioned from radio to TV on the *Chesterfield Supper Club*, while Dinah Shore was featured on *The Chevy Show*. Big band musicians who were popular on radio also tried their hand at the new medium, such as the Dorsey brothers with their program *Stage Show* (1954–1956). Wilk (1976) provides an anecdotal history of some of these musical variety shows, some of which evolved into late-night talk shows with hosts such as Steve Allen (himself a jazz musician and composer) and eventually into band leaders' supporting comedian-hosts such as Johnny Carson (*The Tonight Show*), Joey Bishop (*The Joey Bishop Show*), Dick Cavett (*The Dick Cavett Show*), David Letterman (*Late Night with David Letterman*), and Jay Leno (*The Tonight Show with Jay Leno*). Critical histories of the musical variety show remain to be written.

Aside from variety shows, Joan Baxter (2012) has chronicled the trajectory of television musicals from 1944 to 1996. Robynn Stilwell (2003) and Ron Rodman (2010) have investigated the practice of early sitcoms that featured live musical performance. Though a practice not regularly followed, several sitcoms of the 1950s and 1960s featured singing and dancing as interwoven into the plot. Both authors interrogate the relationship of live music with narrative structure in shows like *I Love Lucy*, *The Dick Van Dyke Show*, and *The Andy Griffith Show*, among others. These shows reaffirmed the notion of TV as a musical medium but at the same time constrained the music to be integral to the plot lines. More importantly, these programs laid the structure for the "made-for-TV band" shows such as *The Partridge Family* and *The Monkees*. Marc Weingarten (2000) provides a historical overview of rock music in television. According to Weingarten, *The Monkees* took live music in narrative a step farther by borrowing some of the postmodern film techniques used by The Beatles in their films, and in this sense the show is an interesting link between these techniques and music videos that would be shown on MTV a decade later.

The relationship of pop and rock music to television has been examined by several scholars, including Weingarten, mentioned above. John Mundy (1999) includes a chapter on pop music on TV in his book on film music (Mundy 1999), where he is quick to point out that rock 'n' roll had its beginnings in the same time period that television developed. As a result, Mundy emphasizes the impact that television had on the careers of Elvis Presley, the Beatles, Michael Jackson, and Madonna, with appearances on variety shows (most notably *The Ed Sullivan Show*) by Presley and the Beatles, and Jackson and Madonna in music videos on MTV in the 1980s. Bernie Ilson (2009) provides an inside look at the artists who appeared on *The Ed Sullivan Show*. Also, Michael Shore (1985), Dick Clark and Fred Bronson (1997), and John A. Jackson (1997) have all provided histories of the long-running *American Bandstand*, a daily, and later weekly, fixture on TV that featured popular rock bands of the time. *Bandstand*, and a few other imitating programs (*Shindig*, *Hullabaloo*, *The Lloyd Thaxton Show*, *Soul Train*), were all important as precursors to music videos.

Histories of popular music on television are emerging. Recent works by K. J. Donnelly (2002), Jake Austen (2005), Ian Inglis (2010), and Murray Forman (2012) trace the trajectory of popular music on TV in the United States and the UK, including performance and dance shows from *Bandstand* to *American Idol*. Yet another work, by Katherine Meizel (2011), demonstrates how musical performance and audience participation in *American Idol* align with the myths of American opportunity and democracy.

4 Dancing in the Attraction Factory: TV Music and Music Videos

From the variety show, musical performance on television evolved into the music video. Like TV ads, music videos are distinct from narrative commercial television shows, in that their primary goal is to provide a sounding board to sell the songs and promote the artist. In this regard, music videos are yet another example of italicizing, but instead of drawing the viewer to the screen for a program, the viewer is lured by the performing artist and/or song. As italicizing agents, music videos rarely deal in narrative (although many scholars have persisted in seeking a narrative base to some of these texts). With the beginning of broadcast on Music Television Network (MTV) in 1981, music videos became a hot topic for discussion by media theorists and musicologists. Ironically, though the texts are music videos, most of the writing on them was focused either on visual, narrative, or ideological traits rather than on the music or its relationship to the television medium.

Music videos, as a result, were characterized in a wide variety of ways: they were considered extended commercial advertisements for bands and/or record labels (Aufderheide 1986; Fry and Fry 1986), visual art (Walker 1987), "electronic wallpaper" (Gehr 1983), "digital narratives" (Jones 1988), nihilistic neo-Fascist propaganda (Bloom 1987), metaphysical poetry (Lorch 1988), shopping mall culture (Lewis 1990), post-structural, postmodern texts (Fiske 1986) and Straw (1993), and semiotic pornography (Marcus 1987). The focus on the visual style of videos perhaps reaches its zenith with Reiss and Feineman's *Thirty Frames per Second* (Reiss and Feineman 2000), which is essentially a richly illustrated visual arts textbook.

Marsha Kinder (1984) in particular received much attention for her argument that videos are dream-like narrative structures. Kinder lists the three components of videos as: (1) the images of performers on the screen; (2) the simple or complex narrative carried by the lyrics of the song; and (3) the extra images on the screen that make the video more memorable, providing the spectator with a sort of "prefabricated daydream" (4–5). She then differentiates videos into two typologies: videos dominated by narrative and videos dominated by dreamlike visuals.

As with Kinder's two types, many articles on video in the 1980s and 1990s sought to create taxonomies of the music video. Gow (1992) classifies videos into "performance" and "conceptual" videos, recognizing that there are also "hybrid" forms. Cathy Schwichtenberg (1993) parses videos into three categories: performance, narrative, and conceptual. Perhaps the most famous is Ann Kaplan's in her book *Rocking Around the Clock* (Kaplan 1987), in which she distills videos down to five types based on their styles, three of which roughly correspond with the styles of music, and two based on the visuals. These five types are: Romantic (corresponding to 1960s "soft rock"), Socially Conscious or Modernist (corresponding to groups of the 1960s and 1970s who took oppositional stances), Nihilist (corresponding to heavy metal groups of the 1980s), Classical (adhering to classical narrative structure), and Postmodern (featuring a pastiche of unrelated images that do not seemingly correspond with the music). Kaplan places these in a matrix based on visual style and the Freudian ideological themes of love/sex and authority. For example, the Romantic video treats love and sex in the pre-Oedipal "loss and reunion" theme, whereas the Nihilistic video deals with the theme from a sado-masochistic perspective. For authority, the Socially Conscious treats authority from the "parent" perspective, whereas the Classical adheres to the Hollywood ideology of male as subject and female as object.

Chion (1994) describes the image/music relationship of video as a sort of inverse property from narrative television. He describes the video as a "joyous rhetoric of images," whose paradox is that, rather than a subordinate music correlating with an image (as in narrative film and TV), it is the video image that conspicuously attaches itself to a piece of autonomous popular music (Chion 1994, 166). He also acknowledges that videos are completely different from linear narratives, as they do not involve dramatic time. Like musical motifs in narrative, visuals in the music video are not depicting linear narratives, but rather presenting recurring visual motifs that play on a number of visual themes. Like Goodwin, Chion asserts that video form is based on music and thus visuals are freed from the linearity of narrative.

Chion's poetic description of music videos perhaps comes closest to a realization that in music videos, it is indeed the music that drives the text rather than visual images. This point is also asserted by Andrew Goodwin (1992), who seeks to situate music in videos within a matrix of pop musicology, television studies, the music industry, and cultural meaning. His is perhaps the most comprehensive of writing on music video, acknowledging the complex cultural relationship between television narrative, the music industry as purveyors of commodity, and of cultures of popular music. In narrative film and television, we regard the visual image and dialogue as primary, as the elements that drive the narrative of the text and indicate its beginning, middle, and end. As Chion also notes, in music video these roles are reversed, or inverted, with the musical structure of the pop song driving the "narrative" trajectory of the text, while visuals make up the "index" either shadowing the song closely (like "mickey-mousing" of a film score) or creating the "mood" (as music in film is so often described as doing), or simply providing a visual backdrop.

More recently, Carol Vernallis (2004) describes videos as falling within a continuum of narrative/non-narrative, with most videos *not* telling a particular story, but rather suggesting a vignette, much like Altman's topics of TV narrative. She also discusses aspects of editing, acting, sets, props, costumes, colors, texture, time, as well as the music itself, touching upon how lyrics and music interact with visual, much in the same vein as Cook's multimedia interpretations.

5   CONCLUSION: SIGNING OFF IN THE POSTMODERN

Many of Goodwin's observations on videos apply to television of the twenty-first century. Many current and past television programs are now marketed as DVDs, and music from them as soundtrack CDs or downloadable MP3s. Due to DVR technology, television programs can be viewed at any time by individuals, and so audiences have been fragmented to individuals rather than demographic collectives. This fragmentation of the audience has led to changes in the techniques of italicizing and labeling. One of these changes is the attenuation of theme music and narrative underscore in TV episodes, a trend that began in the 1990s. Theme music was attenuated as commercials were deregulated in the United States, thus shorter themes meant more time for producers to stick in more ads (see Pennington 1995). Another result of audience fragmentation is "narrowcasting" that is, broadcasting to smaller, targeted demo-/psycho-/sociographic groups rather than mass heterogeneous audiences. Fanzines and blogs accompany many shows with a targeted demographic audience, consisting almost exclusively of young people. Goodwin cites the case where music videos have become interdependent with other media (television, recordings, DVD, and even the film industry), where profits and meaning of the music itself relies on its interaction with other media (Goodwin 1992, 29–30; see also Powell 1991). This interdependence thus increases the longevity of a song and video, which then becomes another means of italicizing the text. This trend has expanded to narrative TV shows as a whole, with DVD sets and CDs of popular programs like *Ally McBeal, Glee*, and others. Narrowcasting of the late twentieth century has also been noted by authors writing about narrative TV—Bond (1999) on *Star Trek*, a collection of essays on *Twin Peaks* (Lavery 1995), and two recent books on music in cult classic *Buffy the Vampire Slayer* (Attinello, Halfyard, and Knights 2010, and Wilcox 2005). As television becomes more interdependent with other media outlets, music will play an even more central role in its labeling and italicizing functions, forming the bond between image, sound, and audience.

Another important trend in current television and television music is how it mediates everyday life, or "reality." James Deaville (2006, 2007) has written two insightful essays on the effect of music in the post-9/11 era for television news. Deaville investigates the music industry that provides music to the news media, and defines structures such as "teasers," "promo beds," and "bumpers" that provide topical musical cues to accompany news programs. Through these musical topics, news media can manipulate viewer perception of real-life events. Using the 9/11 tragedy in the United States as a case study, Deaville describes how news networks (CNN in particular) used music in its post-9/11 news stories to relay a message of "fear and anger" to an American audience, while Canadian news services used music to portray "horror and tragedy" (Deville 2007, 43–44). He identifies a "Fear and Anger" motif used by CNN that included "a martial snare drums, a driving string part, and a concluding plagal cadence and bell sound, referencing the drums of attack and war, the urgent, leaping strings of action and danger, the unresolved cadence of open-ended conflict, and the bell of death and of a call to arms" (51). In contrast the CBC network in Canada featured a "generic solemn tone," with synthesized trumpet, bass, and percussion sounding in long tones in G minor (56).

More than ever before, television music is also achieving status in the scholarly press, evidenced by new scholarly work in TV music (see Deaville 2011; Donnelly 2011; Rodman 2010). Following this, the current trend in TV music criticism seems to be to embrace all aspects of analytical discourse. Reeves, Rogers, and Epstein (1996) have commented on the proclivity of post-1980s TV to seek out niche market audiences rather than broadcast to a mass audience, as was the case in the earlier days of TV. This change has led to "cult" TV shows, where audiences of a particular demographic tend to gravitate toward particular shows, most recently "reality TV." Music helps to reinforce this self-selection process, with scholarly descriptions of this cultural identification found in Fiske's (1987) work on *Miami Vice* (music is described in Fiske 1987), Kathryn Kalinak (1995) on the music of *Twin Peaks*, Lawrence Kramer (2002) on *The X Files*, and Rodman (2010) on *Northern Exposure*. Kalinak's take on Angelo Badalamenti's music for *Twin Peaks* describes the loss of specific denotation in its cue music, where leitmotifs meander from character to character. Of course, this is not really a feature unique to postmodern or narrowcast television, as musical cues were repeatedly recycled in earlier TV shows, as Jeff Bond points out in *Star Trek* (1999, 11). K. J. Donnelly calls these "music blocks," a common device where cues are composed with multiple signifiers in mind (Donnelly 2005, 111). Kalinak's article traces the various music styles that are used on the show, ranging from avant-garde jazz to over-the-top Romantic soap opera music. Lawrence Kramer describes a more complicated scenario in *The X Files*, where the theme music (by Mark Snow) conveys a static "antinarrative" that is at cross purposes with the story line, which he describes as "an image of endless nonprogressive movement." (L. Kramer 2002, 189). Rodman writes of the manifold musical styles that permeate *Northern Exposure, blurring* the lines between diegetic and intradiegetic sound, thus creating a postmodern sound kaleidoscope (Rodman 2010, 266).

Although postmodern television music tends to blur the boundaries between narrative and reality, and diegetic and intradiegetic, television music continues to function through its traditional functions of italicizing and labeling. Narrative music operates in the story world of a TV program, while presenting itself to a very real audience who can decode or "buy into" that story world; commercials seek to appeal for commodity exchange directly to this audience (while masking this intent), whereas diegetic music also appeals directly for commodity exchange while masking this appeal through the guise of "entertainment."

Another recent trend in television has been the practice of many programs and commercials to use pre-existing popular music rather than newly-composed music in their soundtracks. Commentaries on popular music on television have emerged (as noted throughout this article), and will continue.

While the form of television music has changed in the sixty plus years of television history, the function has remained the same. Television music still operates through Altman's "labeling" and "italicizing" functions. The ascriptive properties of TV sound and music, that is, music's ability to produce multiple meanings, also remains a fascinating area of research. Television is a medium produced by multiple auteurs that delivers texts with multiple meanings to a diverse audience.

The future of television music scholarship will surely encompass the topics listed above, along with new areas of investigation. Though the work of Tagg and Cook remain seminal, it remains to be discovered how such small music-visual texts can create multiple meanings within a given cultural context. This study of musical meaning in television may be as much an area for cognitive psychology as for musicology, media studies, or culture studies. Also, as the era of media interface continues, a recorded history and interpretation of how music on television intersects with other media, such as the internet, video games, cell phone ring tones, iPod culture and other new technologies will need to be recorded. Finally (but not exhaustively), certain trends in television music should be noted such as, the continuing attenuation of theme and episodic music to TV shows (and the resurgence of these in many HBO series) that has become more and more abbreviated since the 1990s. Will this trend continue, especially with the rise of "reality" TV? These issues along with the rapid developments in an ever-changing electronic media landscape will keep the nascent television music studies area vibrant for years to come.

REFERENCES

Alexomanolaki, Margarit. Catherine Loveday, and Chris Kennett. 2007. "Music and Memory in Advertising: Music as a Device of Implicit Learning and Recall." *Music, Sound, and the Moving Image* 1.1, 51–71.

Altman, Rick. 1987. "Television Sound." In *Television: The Critical View*, edited by Horace Newcomb, 566–584. 4th ed. New York: Oxford University Press.

Attinello, Paul, Janet K. Halfyard, and Vanessa Knights, eds. 2010. *Music, Sound and Silence in "Buffy the Vampire Slayer"*. Aldershot, UK, and Burlington VT: Ashgate.

Aufderheide, Pat. 1986. "Music Videos: The Look of Sound." *Journal of Communication* 36, no. 1: 57–78.

Austen, Jake. 2005. *TV-a-Go-Go: Rock on TV from American Bandstand to American Idol*. Chicago: Chicago Review.

Barnes, Jennifer. 2002. *Television Opera: The Fall of Opera Commissioned for Television*. Woodbridge, UK: Boydell.

Barnouw, Erik. 1968. *A History of Broadcasting in the United States*, vol. 2: *The Golden Web, 1933–1953*. New York: Oxford University Press.

——. 1978. *The Sponsor: Notes on a Modern Potentate*. New York: Oxford University Press.

Bauer, Amy. 2010. "'Give Me Something to Sing About': Intertextuality and the Audience in 'Once More, with Feeling.'" In *Music, Sound, and Silence in "Buffy the Vampire Slayer"*, edited by Paul Attinello, Janet K. Halfyard, and Vanessa Knights, 209–234. Aldershot, UK, and Burlington, VT: Ashgate.

Baxter, Joan. 2012. *Television Musicals: Plots, Critiques, Casts and Credits for 222 Shows Written for and Presented on Television, 1944–1996*. Jefferson, NC: McFarland.

Bloom, Allan. 1987. *The Closing of the American Mind: How Higher Education Has Failed Democracy and Impoverished the Souls of Today's Students*. New York: Simon & Schuster.

Bond, Jeff. 1999. *The Music of "Star Trek"*. Los Angeles: Lone Eagle.

Booth, Mark. 1990. "Jingle: Pepsi Cola Hits the Spot." In *On Record: Rock, Pop, and the Written Word*, edited by Simon Frith and Andrew Goodwin, 320–325. New York: Pantheon.

Bowman, Roger. 1949. "Music for Films in Television." *Film Music Notes* 8, no. 5: 20.

Brown, Adrienne. 2010. "Constrained Frequencies: *The Wire* and the Limits of Listening." *Criticism* 52, nos. 3–4 (summer), 441–459.

Brown, Julie. 2011. "*Ally McBeal*'s Postmodern Soundtrack." In *Popular Music and Multimedia*, edited by Julie McQuinn, 275–303. Aldershot, UK, and Burlington, VT: Ashgate.

Brown, Royal. 1994. *Overtones and Undertones: Reading Film Music*. Berkeley: University of California Press.

Burlingame, Jon. 1996. *TV's Biggest Hits: The Story of Television Themes from "Dragnet" to "Friends."* New York: Schirmer.

Charaudeau, Patrick. 1983. *Langage et discourse: Éléments de sémiolinguistique*. Paris: Hachette.

Chare, Nicholas. 2011. "Policing Technology: Listening to Cop Culture in *The Wire*," *Journal for Cultural Research* 15/1 (January), 15–33.

Chion, Michel. 1994. *Audio-Vision: Sound on Screen*. Edited and translated by Claudia Gorbman. New York: Columbia University Press.

Clark, Dick, and Fred Bronson. 1997. *Dick Clark's American Bandstand*. Darby, PA: Diane Publishing.

Collins, Jim. 1992. "Television and Postmodernism." In *Channels of Discourse Reassembled: Television and Contemporary Criticism*, edited by Robert C. Allen, 327–353. 2nd ed. London: Routledge.

Cook, Nicholas. 1998. *Analysing Musical Multimedia*. New York and Oxford: Oxford University Press.

Cooke, James Francis. 1949. "The New World of Television: A Conference with Paul Whiteman." *Etude* 67 (June): 341–342.

Deaville, James, ed. 2006. "Selling War: Television News Music and the Shaping of American Public Opinion." *Echo: A Music-Centered Journal* 8, no. 1. http://www.echo.ucla.edu/Volume8-Issue1/roundtable/deaville.html, accessed October 23, 2011.

——. 2007. "The Sounds of American and Canadian Television News after 9/11: Entoning Horror and Grief, Fear and Anger." In *Music in the Post-9/11 World*, edited by J. Martin Daughtry and Jonathan Ritter, 43–70. New York: Routledge.

——. 2011. *Music in Television: Channels of Listening*. New York and London: Routledge.

Donnelly, K. J. [Kevin]. 2002. "Tracking British Television: Pop Music as Stock Soundtrack for the Small Screen." *Popular Music* 21, no. 3: 331–343.

——. 2005. *The Spectre of Sound: Music in Film and Television*. London: British Film Institute.

——, ed. 2012. *Music in Science Fiction Television: Tuned to the Future*. Routledge Music and Screen Media Series. New York: Routledge.

Elias, Albert. 1956. "TV Music by Contemporary Composers." *Etude* 74 (November): 22.

Ersoff, Zarah. 2012. "Treme's Aural Verisimilitude". Paper presented at the 38th Annual conference of the Society for American Music, Charlotte, NC, March 14–18.

Fiske, John. 1986. "MTV: Post-Structural Post-Modern." *Journal of Communications Inquiry* 10, no. 1: 74–79.

——. 1987. *Television Culture*. London: Routledge.

Forman, Murray. 2012. *"One Night on TV is Worth Weeks at the Paramount": Popular Music on Early Television*. Durham, NC: Duke University Press.

Frank, Mortimer. 2003. *Arturo Toscanini: The NBC Years*. Montclair, NJ: Amadeus.

Frank, Thomas 1997. *The Conquest of Cool: Business Culture, Counterculture, and the Rise of Hip Consumerism*. Chicago and London: University of Chicago Press.

Fry, Donald L., and Virginia H. Fry. 1986. "MTV: The 24-hour Commercial." *Journal of Communication Inquiry* 10, no. 1: 29–33.

Gehr, R. 1983. "The MTV Aesthetic." *Film Comment* 19, no. 4: 37–40.

Goodwin, Andrew. 1992. *Dancing in the Distraction Factory: Music Television and Popular Culture*. Minneapolis: University of Minnesota Press.

Gorbman, Claudia. 1987. *Unheard Melodies: Narrative Film Music*. Bloomington: Indiana University Press.

——. 2004. "Aesthetics and Rhetoric." *American Music* 22, no. 1: 14–26.

——. 2011. "Foreword." In *Music in Television: Channels of Listening*, edited by James Deaville. Routledge Music and Screen Media Series. New York: Routledge, ix–x.

Gow, Joe. 1992. "Music Video as Communication: Popular Formulas and Emerging Genres." *Journal of Popular Culture* 26, no. 2: 41–70.

Heylbut, Rose. 1945. "The Background of Background Music: How NBC's Experts Fit Music to Dramatic Shows." *Etude* 63 (September), 493–494.

Hill, Kathryn. 2010. "Punks, Geeks, and Goths: *Buffy the Vampire Slayer* as a Study of Popular Music Demographics on American Commercial Television. In *Music, Sound, and Silence in Buffy the Vampire Slayer*, edited by Paul Attinello, Janet K. Halfyard, and Vanessa Knights, 165-188. Alderhshot, UK, and Burlington, VT: Ashgate.

Hoeberichts, Nina. 2012. *The Effect of Music in Television Commercials on Consumer Attitudes*. N.l.: LAP LAMBERT Academic Publishing.

Huron, David. 1989. "Music in Advertising: An Analytic Paradigm." *Musical Quarterly* 73, no. 4: 557–574.

Ilson, Bernie. 2009. *Sundays with Sullivan: How the Ed Sullivan Show Brought Elvis, The Beatles and Culture to America*. Lanham, MD: Taylor.

Inglis, Ian. 2010. *Popular Music and Television in Britain*. Ashgate Popular and Folk Music Series. Aldershot, UK, and Burlington, VT: Ashgate.

Jackson, John. 1997. *American Bandstand: the Making of a Rock 'n' Roll Empire*. New York and Oxford: Oxford University Press.

Jones, Steve. 1988. "Cohesive but not Coherent: Music Videos, Narrative and Culture." *Popular Music and Society* 12, no. 4:15–29.

Kalinak, Kathryn. 1995. "Disturbing the Guests with This Racket: Music and *Twin Peaks*." In *Full of Secrets: Critical Approaches to "Twin Peaks"*, edited by David Lavery, 82–92. Detroit: Wayne State University Press.

Kaplan, E. Ann. 1987. *Rocking around the Clock: Music Television, Postmodernism, and Consumer Culture*. New York: Methuen.

Karmen, Steve. 1989. *Through the Jingle Jungle: The Art and Business of Making Music for Commercials*. New York: Billboard.

———. 2005. *Who Killed the Jingle? How a Unique American Art Form Disappeared*. Milwaukee, WI: Hal Leonard.

Kinder, Marsha. 1984. "Music Video and the Spectator: Television, Ideology and Dream." *Film Quarterly* 38, no. 1: 2–15.

Klein, Bethany. 2010. *As Heard on TV: Popular Music in Advertising*. Aldershot, UK, and Burlington, VT: Ashgate.

Kramer, Jonathan D. 2002. "The Nature and Origins of Musical Postmodernism." In *Postmodern Music/Postmodern Thought*, edited by Judy Lochhead and Joseph Auner, 13–26. New York: Routledge.

Kramer, Lawrence. 2002. *Musical Meaning: Toward a Critical History*. Berkeley: University of California Press.

Kutnowski, Martin. 2008. "Trope and Irony in *The Simpsons* Overture." In *Popular Music and Society* 31 (December), 599–616.

Lavery, David, ed. 1995. *Full of Secrets: Critical Approaches to "Twin Peaks"*. Detroit: Wayne State University Press.

Leonard, Kendra Preston, ed. 2010. *Buffy, Ballads, and Bad Guys Who Sing: Music in the Worlds of Joss Whedon*. New York: Scarecrow.

Lerner, Neil. 2001. "Copland's Music of Wide Open Spaces: Surveying the Pastoral Trope in Hollywood." *Musical Quarterly* 85, no. 3: 477–515.

Lewis, Lisa A. 1990. *Gender Politics and MTV: Voicing the Difference*. Philadelphia: Temple University Press.

Lorch, Sue. 1988. "Metaphor, Metaphysics, and MTV." *Journal of Popular Culture* 22, no. 3: 143–155.

Marcus, Greil. 1987. "MTV–DOA–RIP." *Artforum* 25 (January), 12.

Meizel, Katherine. 2011. *Idolized: Music, Media, and Identity in American Idol. (Ethnomusicology Multimedia)*. Bloomington: Indiana University Press.

Morris, Charles W. 1946. *Signs, Language, and Behavior*. New York: Prentice-Hall.

Mundy, John. 1999. *Popular Music on Screen: From the Hollywood Musical to Music Video*. Manchester: Manchester University Press.

Nalle, Billy. 1962. "Music for Television Drama." *Music Journal* 20, no. 1: 120–121.

Nöth, Winfried. 1987. "Advertising: The Frame Message." In *Marketing and Semiotics: New Directions in the Study of Signs for Sale*, edited by Jean Umiker-Sebeok, 279–294. Berlin: Mouton de Gruyter.

Nye, Sean. 2011. "From Punk to Musical: *South Park*, Music, and the Cartoon Format." In *Music in Television: Channels of Listening*, edited by James Deaville, 143–163. (Routledge Music and Screen Media Series). New York: Routledge.

Pennington, Gail. 1995. "Have TV Songs Sung Their Last?" *St Louis Post-Dispatch*, July 27, 44.

Pool, Jeannie Gayle, and H. Stephen Wright. 2011. *A Research Guide to Film and Television Music in the United States*. Lanham, MD: Scarecrow.

Powell, Rachel. 1991. "Making the Jump from MTV to the Retail Shelves." *New York Times*, April 11.

Prendergast, Roy. 1992. *Film Music: A Neglected Art*. 2nd ed. New York: Norton.

Reeves, Jimmie L., Mark C. Rogers, and Michael Epstein. 1996. "Rewriting Popularity: The Cult Files." In *"Deny All Knowledge": Reading "The X Files"*, edited by David Lavery, Angel Hague, and Marla Cartwright, 22–35. Syracuse, NY: Syracuse University Press.

Reeves, Rosser. 1950. "Memo to Copy Department." Unpublished manuscript (Sept. 11). Madison: Wisconsin Institute for Film and Television Research.

Reiss, Steve, and Neil Feineman. 2000. *Thirty Frames per Second: The Visionary Art of the Music Video*. New York: Harry N. Abrams.

Rodman, Ronald. 1997. "And Now an Ideology from Our Sponsor: Musical Style and Semiosis in American Television Commercials." *College Music Symposium* 37: 21–48.

——. 2009. "Advertising Music: Strategies of Imbuement in Television Advertising Music." In *Sound and Music in Film and Visual Media: A Critical Overview*, edited by Graeme Harper, Jochen Eisentraut, and Ruth Doughty, 617–632. New York and London: Continuum.

——. 2010. *Tuning In: American Narrative Television Music*. New York: Oxford University Press.

——. 2011. "'Coperettas', 'Detecterns', and Space Operas: Music and Genre Hybridization in American Television. In *Music in Television: Channels of Listening*, edited by James Deaville, 35–56. Routledge Music and Screen Media Series. New York: Routledge.

——. 2012. "'Contemporary Cool' as Trope: A Fourth Semiotic Space of American Television Music". Paper presented at the 38th Annual Conference of the Society for American Music, Charlotte, NC, March 14–18.

Saffle, Michael. 2006. "Toward a Semiotics of Music Appreciation as Ownership: Bernstein's 'Young People's Concerts' and 'Educational' Music Television." *Music, Meaning and Media*, edited by Erkki Pekkilä, David Neumeyer, and Richard Littlefield, 115–128. *Acta Semiotica Fennica XXV. Approaches to Musical Semiotics 11*. Studia Musicologica Universitatis Helsingiensis. Helsinki: International Semiotics Institute.

Sandars, Diane, and Rhonda V. Wilcox. 2010. "Not 'The Same Arrangement': Breaking Utopian Promises in the *Buffy* Musical." In *Music, Sound, and Silence in "Buffy the Vampire Slayer"*, edited by Paul Attinello, Janet K. Halfyard, and Vanessa Knights, 189–208. Aldershot, UK, and Burlington, VT: Ashgate.

Savan, Leslie. 1993. "Commercials Go Rock." In *Sound and Vision: The Music Video Reader*, edited by Simon Frith, Andrew Goodwin, and Lawrence Grossberg, 85–92. London: Routledge.

Schwichtenberg, Cathy. 1993. *The Madonna Connection: Representational Politics, Subcultural Identities, and Cultural Theory*. Boulder, CO: Westview.

Scott, Linda M. 1990. "Understanding Jingles and Needledrop: A Rhetorical Approach to Music in Advertising." *Journal of Consumer Research* 17, no. 2: 223–236.

Scott, Tom. 1956. "Music for Television." *Film Music* 15, no. 5: 19–23.

Sherk, Warren M. 2011. *Film and Television Music: A Guide to Books, Articles, and Composer Interviews*. Lanham MD: Scarecrow.

Shore, Michael, with Dick Clark. 1985. *The History of American Bandstand: It's Got a Great Beat and You Can Dance to It*. New York: Ballantine.

Skiles, Marlin. 1976. *Music Scoring for TV and Motion Pictures*. Blue Ridge Summit, PA: Tab Books.

Sosnik, Harry. 1949. "Scoring for Television." *Variety*, January 5, 95.

——. 1963. "Songwriting." Unpublished manuscript (October 6). Madison: Wisconsin Institute for Film and Television.

——. 1982. "The Rise (Radio) and the Fall (TV) in the Importance of Composers." *Variety*, January 20, 100.

——. 1986. "A View from the Podium: a Retrospective from 1924 thru 1967." Revised. Unpublished manucript. Madison: Wisconsin Center for Film and Theater Research.

Spencer, Kristopher. 2008. *Film and Television Scores, 1950–1979: A Critical Survey by Genre*. Jefferson: NC: MacFarland.

Stevens, Katy. 2010. "Battling the Buzz: Contesting Sonic Codes in *Buffy the Vampire Slayer*." In *Music, Sound, and Silence in "Buffy the Vampire Slayer"*, edited by Paul Attinello, Janet K. Halfyard, and Vanessa Knights. Alderhshot, UK, and Burlington, VT: Ashgate.

Stilwell, Robynn J. 2003. "It May Look Like a Living Room…: The Musical Number and the Sitcom." *Echo: A Music-Centered Journal* 5, no. 1. http://www.echo.ucla.edu/Volume5-issue1/stilwell/stilwell1.html, accessed June 23, 2009.

——. 2011. "'Bad Wolf': Leitmotif in *Doctor Who* (2005)". In *Music in Television: Channels of Listening*, edited by James Deaville, 119–142. Routledge Music and Screen Media Series. New York: Routledge.

Straw, Will. 1993. "Popular Music and Postmodernism in the 1980s." In *Sound and Vision: The Music Video Reader*, edited by Simon Frith, Andrew Goodwin, and Lawrence Grossberg, 2–19. London: Routledge.

Sullivan, Jack. 2006. *Hitchcock's Music*. New York and London: Yale University Press.

Tagg, Philip. (1979) 2000. *Kojak: Fifty Seconds of Television Music; Toward the Analysis of Affect in Popular Music*. New York: Mass Media Music Scholars' Press.

——. "Philip Tagg." http://www.tagg.org/, accessed February 6, 2012.

Taylor, Tim (2007). "The Changing Shape of the Culture Industry; or, How Did Electronica Music get into Television Commercials?" *Television and New Media*, 8/235. http://tvn.sagepub.com (accessed January 31, 2012).

Vernallis, Carol. 2004. *Experiencing Music Video: Aesthetics and Cultural Context*. New York: Columbia University Press.

Walker, John A. 1987. *Cross-overs: Art into Pop / Pop into Art*. London: Comedia/Methuen.

Weingarten, Marc. 2000. *Station to Station: The History of Rock 'n' Roll on Television*. New York: Pocket Books.

Westcott, Steven D. 1985. *A Comprehensive Bibliography of Music for Film and Television*. Detroit Studies in Music Bibliography No. 54. Detroit, MI: Information Coordinators.

White, Armond. 1988. "The Pop Solution: Commercials Move from Jingles to Singles." *Millimeter* 16: 89–90.

Wilcox, Rhonda. 2005. *Why Buffy Matters*. London: I. B. Tauris.

Wilk, Max. 1976. *The Golden Age of Television: Notes from the Survivors*. New York: Dell.

Williams, Raymond. 1992. *Television: Technology and Cultural Form*. Introduction by Lynn Spiegel. Middletown, CT, and Hanover, NH: Wesleyan University Press and University Press of New England.

Woodward, Walt. 1982. *An Insider's Guide to Advertising Music*. New York: Art Direction.

PART 5

HISTORICAL ISSUES

CHAPTER 22

···

WHEN THE MUSIC SURGES: MELODRAMA AND THE NINETEENTH-CENTURY THEATRICAL PRECEDENTS FOR FILM MUSIC STYLE AND PLACEMENT

···

MICHAEL V. PISANI

FILM scholarship has demonstrated overlapping traditions between the use of music in the theaters of the late nineteenth century and the application of music to silent film.[1] In his well-known *Stage to Screen* (1949), for example, Nicholas Vardac described Edgar Stillman Kelley's music to the first major stage production of *Ben-Hur* in 1899. "Throughout the performance," he concluded, "music accentuated the episodes and was as carefully prepared and integrated as in the later screen version" (Vardac 1949, 81–82).[2] The "screen version" Vardac refers to, of course, is the 1925 silent *Ben-Hur* directed by Fred Niblo, who came to film directing as an actor from the vaudeville theater.

In this chapter I will make a different comparison, that is, between theater music in the nineteenth century and the practice of musical underscoring in the *sound film*, particularly in film melodramas of the 1930s and 1940s. Rob Dean has related the technique of a musical "sound bridge" in nineteenth-century theater practice to contemporary film scoring in which music is used to camouflage a sudden shift in time or location (Dean 2007, 145–46).[3] There are many such relevant concurrences, and the line of argument pursued here is that the uses of dramatic music in play production in the leading theaters of France, England, and America (and presumably in other countries) are reflected in techniques adopted by major film studios such as RKO and Goldwyn in the early 1930s, and that a stylistic precedent for such film music as Max Steiner's and Erich Wolfgang Korngold's swashbuckling scores for Michael Curtiz, or Franz Waxman's and

Roy Webb's melodramatic and suspenseful scores for Alfred Hitchcock, can be found in the theatrical music for similar nineteenth-century genres.[4]

What has until fairly recently made this comparative investigation difficult has been the apparent disappearance of so much nineteenth-century theater music.[5] Hence, some scholars in both film and theater assumed that much of it was improvised. Those who were able to examine existing source materials determined that a great deal of what was fashioned as dramatic music for plays was thrown out or lost in theater fires. In the 1970s, theater historian David Mayer found several presumed lost musical sources for nineteenth-century play production. He showed that the technique could be understood by examining the stage manager's promptbook and corresponding orchestra parts, the latter annotated by the musicians and played live during the performance of the play. On the whole, however, musical sources remained stubbornly elusive. What seemed most in evidence from the later part of the century were the publications of "melodramatic music" by firms such as John Church, Carl Fischer, and M. Witmark in the United States and Lafleur & Sons in London. These are collections of eight-bar "hurries" and other types of characteristic music fashioned as ready accompaniment to burlesques and pantomimes, music hall and variety vignettes, minstrel shows, amateur stage productions, and other types of popular drama.[6] These resemble the "mood music" books for silent film, and therefore it could reasonably be assumed that theaters had music directors comparable to those in the later movie houses who would piece together appropriate cues from such collections. Though this was sometimes the practice, the assumption accounts for only a small segment of the total picture. The history of nineteenth-century theatrical music is severely misconstrued if only viewed retrospectively through the lens of silent film practice.

In many nineteenth-century theaters, particularly in the production of a new play with the author on hand (and who sometimes even took on one of the roles), music was often selected or composed as part of the staging rehearsals. An actor was expected to develop his or her voice like that of an opera singer. Actors assumed that some lines would need to be delivered "musically," as well as literally "spoken through music," a technique analogous to opera singers finding where their voices fit in with the various colors of an orchestra. Many of the music cues that survive from nineteenth-century theatrical productions reveal this closely developed relationship between stage and orchestra, rather than the appearance of music's having been added at the last minute.

A cue sheet for a sound film—as opposed to a silent film cue sheet—exhibits many similar features. It very often reflects musical choices made during the production or editing process, perhaps even conceived as part of the conception of the film. This was true of isolated cases in silent film, of course, especially in the case of song placement, as Kathryn Kalinak has demonstrated in the early films of John Ford (Kalinak 2007). But in general music arrangers' standard practice for silents was to assemble a cue sheet after the film had already been shot and edited. And of course not all silent films were viewed with their suggested music. Another highly relevant difference between music in a sound and a silent film lies in the fact that music for silent film was often more or less continuous, and a major shift in mood or tempo was generally signaled by intertitles (cue cards). In American sound films from about 1930, however, with the priority given to dialogue, music was occasional, the next cue prompted by some action, change of scene, the introduction of new visual or verbal information, or perhaps even the sudden alteration of a character's psychological viewpoint. Music's intermittent nature in "talkies"—even in musicals or animation—meant that its placement needed to be justified and could be a significant factor in the success or failure of the film. Set off by periods of "no music," music cues in sound film have form; they have a beginning, middle, and end, even if the end is a fade out or interruption. The very act of spotting a sound film for music automatically lends music a highlighting function markedly different from its role in silent film, where, however much structure it may have brought to the film, it needed to be continuous to keep the audience engaged and to offset the odd silence of the characters against the noise and flickering effect of the film projector.

In the nineteenth century, managers often gave their music directors—or collaborated with them to generate—a "music plot" that resembles a cue sheet for a sound film, with specifications for music to start and stop based on sight or text cues. The procedure, however, only partly conveys normative attitudes toward nineteenth-century melodrama. Choices about where to place music just as often reflected the aesthetic sensibilities of individual actors and managers. Not all managers were satisfied merely with giving instructions for "eight bars of *cautious* music" in order to bring some scheming character onstage, nor were all melodramas conducive to such obvious gesturing. To summarize thus far, although the use of music in these three generations of dramatic media is certainly related, it is decidedly not an incremental development, and many more important correlations in the use of music in spoken theater and sound film need to be identified and examined more closely.

A VARIETY OF PRACTICES: *THE COLLEEN BAWN*

Audiences react differently to a stage *versus* a film dramatization, and music sometimes plays a role in these differences. Compared to a nineteenth-century play, a film is a relatively stable product, especially in the 1930s and 1940s. It may contain splices to repair damaged sections or may be reedited in a different version or censored for various types of showings. It may even have a different music or language track dubbed in. Still, the actors, mise-en-scène, shots, and editing most often remain the same. In the silent period, the music may have changed from house to house of course, but once a soundtrack became a locked feature of the product, the film—with some famous exceptions—could be expected to look and sound relatively the same from theater to theater, varying mostly in quality of projection and sound. Not so with nineteenth-century theater. A play could be produced by a traveling troupe with a seasoned cast but local instrumental ensemble, or by a resident stock company with a combination of skilled

and amateur cast with improvised costumes and sets, or by a major professional organization—say, in London or New York—that maintained the highest standards available in the area not only of acting, but also of costume, set design, lighting, and music.
Moreover, a play that was successful in one location might be pirated and produced at
a rival house under far less favorable circumstances, or parodied in yet another house
with interpolated situations, characters, and music, many of these exaggerated for effect.

A good example is found in a play called *The Colleen Bawn* by the Irish-born
American actor Dion Boucicault. It premiered in New York in 1860 with the author in
the cast. Only six months later it opened in London and was also immediately pirated
in several other American and British houses. A few months after Boucicault's production in London, Drury Lane staged a parody entitled *Miss Eily O'Connor*, which featured
added songs and dances and men and women in reverse gender roles (Daly 2007). If
we wanted to know what music was devised for this rather prominent play, we would
need to specify whether we were asking about the production at Laura Keene's Theatre,
which catered to upper-middle-class audiences, or the Adelphi, which was a noted
melodrama house, or Drury Lane, London's unofficial "national" theater, which was also
known for its high-class burlesques and pantomimes. We would also need to acknowledge copies of the play that were made available within a few years for amateur theater
companies. Moreover, vaudeville houses and musical halls often gave "melodramatic
parodies"—thirty-minute versions of famous plays—with exaggerated acting and musical effects. (These parodies are in fact what many people think of today when they think
of nineteenth-century melodrama.) Hence, we may refer to *The Colleen Bawn* as a popular play by Boucicault, but clearly audiences all over the English-speaking world would
have experienced this play differently, with music type and placement contributing to
those differences. We should also note that the play appeared in film versions in 1911 and
1924. A song by one A. Tinker was printed in London to use in the later version. But no
"score" was ever published to accompany a stage version of *The Colleen Bawn*. Songs
and dances did appear, many of them based on well-known Irish tunes and some merely
inspired by the play, not incorporated in it.

Did this mean that there was no official score for *The Colleen Bawn*? Hardly. When
the play opened at Laura Keene's Theater, Thomas Baker led a small orchestra of about
sixteen musicians. They played thirty-three music cues over the course of three acts, as
well as a full-length *Colleen Bawn* overture and entr'actes of various pieces unrelated to
the play. *The Colleen Bawn* cannot be considered a "musical play." It had perhaps three
songs. The rest of the music was action and dialogue underscoring, including a series
of linked through-composed cues for the famous rescue scene at the climax of act two.
Baker's music was copied and used for the London production (where his overture was
published in score and parts). Moreover, an advertisement in the *New York Clipper* of
1864 announced that Baker's "original music" to *The Colleen Bawn* (and other plays)
could be rented from him "for large or small bands" and could be had by calling on the
well-known music director at his address at the Olympic Theatre.[7] Clearly, then, there
was music closely associated with Boucicault's own production of his play, music that
went beyond the mere use of a standard "hurry" or "misterioso"—what in the nineteenth

century was referred to as a "melos"—or the improvised playing of popular Irish tunes. The latter *did* of course appear prominently in the play though artfully woven throughout Baker's original melodramatic accompaniments.

To be sure, the lingua franca of pizzicatos, hurries, and surprise chords that were such a crucial part of the so-called French "Boulevard" and English "Adelphi" melodramas early in the nineteenth century were never entirely abandoned in play production, both professional and amateur. But in the best of circumstances they were adapted to the play at hand or composed anew to be carefully timed to action and dialogue. Most of the prominent British and American music leaders—Alfred Mellon, Edwin Ellis, William Charles Levy, Ferdinand Wallerstein, John Liptrot Hatton, Robert Stoepel, Charles Koppitz, Simon Hassler, William Furst—were classically trained, and the dramatic music composed and published earlier in the century by Beethoven and Mendelssohn still loomed large over their efforts, not to mention the sophisticated examples of pantomime music in French ballet or in the music dramas of Wagner.

Melodrama 1

The technique by which dramatic music for play production developed is, of course, far more complicated than can ever be explained by one article, book, or even series of books.[8] Outside of early opera and the *ballet de cour*, there was often some form of instrumental music to accompany the *commedia dell'arte* in sixteenth- and seventeenth-century Italy, the fairground theaters of early eighteenth-century France, and English pantomime in the last half of the eighteenth century. (If anything, it is the continuous music written for eighteenth-century pantomime, with its mimed action and cue cards, that most closely resembles silent film music.) Of course Shakespeare and other seventeenth-century playwrights specified music in published editions of their plays, often songs or "stage music" such as fanfares and marches. But there is an incident related by John Burgoyne about how David Garrick, the famous eighteenth-century English Shakespearean, introduced soft music into King Lear's reunion scene with Cordelia, such that the audience was moved to tears. Burgoyne added: "I am convinced that under judicious management music is capable of giving [our compositions for the stage] effect beyond what our best authors can attain without it" (1781, xiii). Over the next couple of decades, actors and theatrical managers experimented with music to accompany action, even incorporating the new French technique of *melo-drame* into monologues and passages of dialogue.[9]

Theatrical melodrama—the nonoperatic genre with which music was specifically associated   officially began in postrevolutionary France with Pixérécourt's plays in the last years of the eighteenth century. But by 1820 nearly every theater in London, Dublin, Edinburgh, Philadelphia, New York, and Charleston had adopted the practice of using music to accompany stage action and to add emotion to dialogue sequences (what in film music is often called background or *nondiegetic* music). To theater historians, "melodrama" is a genre traditionally associated with the stage. It is defined more broadly by the *Oxford English Dictionary* as "a dramatic piece characterized by sensational incident and violent appeals to the emotions, but with a happy ending." James L. Smith, writing in 1973, identified three distinct types of stage melodrama: melodrama of triumph (with a fantasy dénouement, and the most common in the nineteenth century), melodrama of defeat (prominent already in the eighteenth century), and melodrama of protest (a criticism of the social ills of industrialization and political oppression). In the nineteenth century, however, even the melodrama of triumph spawned many related subgenres—these included (to name just a few) gothic, blood-and-thunder, military, nautical, brigands, eastern, docudrama, domestic, sensation, cup-and-saucer, drawing room, detective and secret service, even so-called "toga" or "sacred drama." Moreover, historical tragedies by Shakespeare, Schiller, Hugo, and Scribe were most often in the nineteenth century given distinctly melodramatic treatment.

Each subgenre seemed to require a different type or amount of music. In blood-and-thunder melodramas, for example, no principal character could be expected to make an entrance without some kind of characteristic music. Climactic speeches or significant confrontation scenes would likely rely upon music to assist. (The published playtexts for certain genres of plays—blood-and-thunder or sensation—frequently specify "music all through struggle" or include similar indications during stage action.) In drawing-room melodramas—or, toward the end of the century, courtroom drama—such music would have been considered absurd and heavy-handed. Augustin Daly's *Frou-Frou* (1870), for example, was the most famous of the many English versions adapted from Meilhac's and Halévy's French social drama. Though the play was set in the present and involved modern characters, no one could argue from its dialogue and situations that Daly was anything but a dyed-in-the-wool melodramatist. The published playtext, however, specifies only ten music cues, two of them "source cues" (played onstage). Less than two weeks after *Frou-Frou* opened in New York, Fred Williams, Daly's assistant stage-manager, went to Boston to supervise rehearsals of the play at Selwyn's Theatre.[10] The music that Charles Koppitz composed for these performances includes exactly eight cues. The two pieces of stage music are not included in the orchestra parts. This verifies that in a professional theater comparable to the one for which Daly conceived his play no more dramatic music was used than the author had requested. The production materials from Boston tell us that not a note was played to aid the climactic confrontation between Gilberte and her jilting lover near the end of act four (the Venetian act). Apparently, music to intensify this emotional scene was too melodramatic even for melodrama (at least according to Daly, one of its ardent practitioners). What Daly (or Koppitz) *did* do was bring in music only at the very last moment. Gilberte cries "Do not go—I will be your slave—I will love you!" "Wretch!" Sartorys replies, repulsing her. Music begins.

> [Gilberte] faints, still holding his hand. He drags her a few steps, still trying to open her fingers. When he does, she falls across a chair at back. Sartorys starts to go out. At back he stops, comes back, looks at Gilberte a few minutes as if demented and the Baroness enters. Sartorys, without saying a word, points to Gilberte and exits. Curtain.

Without more information, could we possibly have guessed the music correctly? I will wager not. At this music cue an offstage chorus began singing a reprise of the romantic barcarolle that opened the act and thus serves to frame this Venetian interlude of the play. But more importantly, it functioned here as a classic example of *anempathetic* music, music that offset by contrast—and thereby intensified—the violent action onstage.[11] The first known explanation of this theatrical "serio-comic effect of the highest order" was in an unsigned editorial "Music in drama" in *The Stage* (1887), reprinted in Jackson (1989, 204–5). The technique had been used in opera before then, notably in such works as Verdi's *Rigoletto* and *La Traviata*. In film studies the term "anempathetic sound" or "anempathetic music" originated in French film theory and was used by Michel Chion, Claudia Gorbman, and others (see Gorbman 1987, 159–61; Chion 1994, 8–9).

MELODRAMA 2

In the genre of swashbuckler melodrama, the situation regarding music placement was exactly the reverse of social melodrama. John Brougham's *The Duke's Motto*, also adapted from a French original (Anicet-Bourgeois and Féval's *Le bossu*), was given a lavish production at the Lyceum Theatre, London in 1863. Brougham's performing version of the play, not published until 1870, specified only one musical number, a song and dance at the rise of the first-act curtain. The incorporation of songs in the first act goes back to old English licensing laws about melodrama in public theaters. British Parliament established a licensing code for theaters in 1737. Any new theater must apply for a license, which stipulated that plays be "musical," that is, sung, danced, or mimed. These so-called "burletta restrictions" began to be enforced in 1752. By 1832 the restrictions were so broadly interpreted that the authorities left alone theater managers who simply included a handful of songs in every play.

The Duke's Motto is a three-act play with prologue. The promptbook and surviving orchestra parts used in the 1864 New York production show that there was actually a total of seventy-one instrumental cues. Many of these were substantial and not just curtain-raising or scene-change music. In fact, most music indicated for scene-change seemed to last only about three or four measures, so the stage crew at the Lyceum probably moved quickly to avoid delays in the play's dynamic forward motion. Many of the cues are through-composed, and each is identified by a text or sight cue. Actors were used to "throwing cues" at the music director; his job was to synchronize music to action and dialogue. The conductor book—an elaborated first violin part—contains occasional text cues added throughout so that music may be aligned with the stage action.

To understand fully how music was used for just this one title, however, one would need to take into account what was played in the first version at the Porte St. Martin in 1862, Brougham's version at the Lyceum in 1863, the pirated versions given that same year at the Royal Pavilion, Whitechapel (*The Duke's Bequest*), the Theatre Royal,

Manchester (*Blanche of Nevers, or I am Here*), at the New Adelphi in Liverpool (as *I am Here, or The Seven Servants and the Master*), at the Old Bowery in New York (as *The Duke's Device*) or the New Bowery (as *The Duke's Signal*), or at the "official" New York opening of Brougham's authorized version in 1864 at Niblo's Garden, not to mention Henry Byron's 1863 burlesque version—*The Motto, I am All There*—at the Royal Strand Theatre. Given that the melodramatic subgenre here is a swashbuckler, with sword fights and death-defying escapes, all of these versions most probably used some kind of action music. The only music found so far was for Niblo's Garden, and that only because a set of parts had been duplicated for Lawrence Barrett's production that toured many American theaters in the 1870s.[12]

Similar types of melodramas, such as *The Count of Monte Cristo*, *The Corsican Brothers*, and *The Three Musketeers*, also relied upon an extensive amount of action and dialogue music. There were fifty-five music cues in the original French production of *Monte Cristo*, part one, at the Théâtre Historique. Part two, the following night, had thirty-eight. This extensive use of dramatic music in the spoken French theater constituted what Emilio Sala has called a "mise-en-musique," a sonic and communicative space independent of—though interacting with—the mise-en-scène (Sala and Smart 1995, 197). Sala says the orchestra music was a collaboration of three composers, Alphonse Varney, Robert Stoepel, and Sylvain Mangeant. Strangely, an American production of Monte Cristo with the actor James O'Neill apparently had very few music cues, at least as evident among the surviving parts. See a modern edition of this music in McLucas (1994).

The model for the melodrama being thus set, it was often replicated over the course of the century. For Sydney Grundy's adaptation of *The Musketeers* produced by Beerbohm Tree at Her Majesty's Theatre, London, in 1898, Raymond Roze's music included a long overture and thirty cues played over the course of seven tableaux. A few of these are stage or source cues, but most are action and dialogue underscoring, with characters' lines written into the leader's part to help him time the music to the drama. Roze's stage music for *Musketeers* was also used for a run of Grundy's play at the Broadway Theater in New York, and one of the principal "themes" of the score was even published for piano solo as "D'Artagnan's Love Song."[13] We might also note that the music to Tree's version survives, while that for Henry Hamilton's rival production at the Globe with Lewis Waller—by all accounts a far superior adaptation—has not been found.

In contrast, Beerbohm Tree's production of *A Man's Shadow* (Haymarket Theatre, London, 1889)—a contemporary courtroom drama—required only eleven instrumental cues, two of which were source cues to be played onstage during a scene in a hotel lobby.[14] A few cues are repetitions, thus the total number of different musical pieces amounted to only six. According to Tree's aesthetic, music in this type of melodrama was conspicuous by its absence, in stark contrast to the musical bath that enveloped many scenes in *The Musketeers* or Tree's painterly versions of *Hamlet* and *King Henry VIII*. Each of the six original cues for *A Man's Shadow* is of a distinctive character, one an obvious pizzicato "misterioso" and another a tense tremolo. Dialogue underscoring in this play, when used, was emotionally affective, as in the reading of the letter during the trial. The placement of music here is judicious and purposeful. The information in this letter represented a reversal of fate for the protagonist, an attorney who is defending his best friend and who is about to discover that his own wife was indirectly involved in the murder and theft. The tune is a sixteen-bar melos in G major for strings alone. It is stylistically reminiscent of French opera, in the manner of Gounod. The first violins carry the sentimental melody while the lower strings provide a sustained accompaniment. Whoever wrote this anonymous music used it once earlier in the play to underscore an emotional dialogue sequence between Noirville, the attorney, and his friend Laroque. Here it appears again, played quietly while Noirville opens the incriminating letter and is compelled to read it out loud before the jury. Whether audiences would have remembered this melos from earlier is impossible to say. Given the sparse placement of music it should have been fairly obvious once the musicians began to play that they were playing a specific *kind* of music. Hence, its lyrical and sentimental qualities would have served to establish a psychological connection between Laroque's original anguish—his bankruptcy and his fears of the ruin it would bring on his family—and Noirville's anguish at the trial—namely, in bringing this letter to light he implicates his wife and does bring ruin on himself. Clearly, Tree as actor-manager (he played Laroque) would have considered this possible angle. Audiences may not be expected to remember explicit tunes, especially if heard only once before, but they may indeed remember the character of a melody, particularly if that character was unique and the melody first heard in an intense emotional context.

Among the many subgenres of melodrama there were even lighter-themed plays that required very little action and dialogue underscoring. *Masks and Faces*, a sentimental comedy by Tom Taylor and Charles Reade first produced in London at the Haymarket Theatre in 1852, has no music specified in the published playtext. In performance, the small orchestra played only five music cues, three of them for the rise of the curtain to begin each act. Despite the occasionally pathetic emotional charge of the play there was simply very little need for affective music to distract audiences from the "cheerful, fluent, and natural" dialogue.[15] On the other hand, the 1917 celebrity-cast British film version of *Masks and Faces* required wall-to-wall music, not just for mood and to smooth over any jarring editing but for the usual functions ascribed to the use of music in silent film. A hypothetical filmed version of this play in the sound era—say, in 1957—would probably, depending on the aesthetics of the producer and studio, have had little need for music except possibly for the opening and closing and to bridge changes of scene, not unlike the way music was originally used for this stage comedy in 1852.

Sometimes sound effects took the place of dramatic music. In A. P. Palmer's production of *Julius Caesar* at Booth's Theatre, New York, 1875, the orchestra in melodramatic fashion accompanied many of the final scenes on the plains of Phillippi with emotional under dialogue music. But during the entire second act, as the conspiracy against Caesar was formed, the orchestra was completely silent, deferring to offstage thunder of the storm, created in the wings by stage carpenters rolling concrete balls in a see-saw mechanism while other hands raised and lowered a steel-plated "thunder machine" on a pulley. In another instance, the famous rescue from the train tracks in Augustin Daly's

Under the Gaslight at the New York Theatre, Bowery, 1867, there was no music at all. For the "railroad scene" the entire stage crew went into high gear. Offstage could be heard the approaching train whistle against the sound effects of Laura Cortland chopping her way out of the guard house with an ax, escaping just in time to untie Snorkey before the train roared past, the effect created offstage by several wind machines and carpenters drumming on a large sheet of iron.[16] In the orchestra, the musicians' parts read "tacet for train business to end of act."

CIRCULATION OF THEATER MUSIC

When the orchestra music for nineteenth-century plays survives, a good deal of it demonstrates that there were some elements of a common practice—in placement, musical style, chordal effects, instrumentation, and so on. Yet there were some remarkable exceptions and innovations, especially in the major theaters. A lot of mid-century theatrical music, for example, is in easily playable keys. But if a number suddenly appears in B♭ minor—as does Giuseppe Operti's funeral cortège for Julius Caesar in the 1875 production—a unique complexion suffuses the mise-en-musique, like a color medium fit over a floodlight can instantly transform the mood onstage. A great deal of nineteenth-century British and American theater music tends to be fairly uniform in instrumentation: generally flute, clarinet, two horns, a cornet or two, possibly a trombone, and perhaps six to eight strings, and players rarely if ever double on other instruments. But some musical directors could be creative within these limitations, and if a single cello suddenly rang out, or a French horn played a lyrical solo over pizzicato strings, the dynamic relationship between the actors on the stage and musicians in the pit was unexpectedly altered, with actors partly yielding to the drama residing in the music.

Actors, more than anyone, knew the value of good action and dialogue music. It is for this reason that most theater music survives today not in music libraries but in theater collections, once having been among the personal effects of actors. The American actor Frank A. Tannehill, for example, developed a reputation in the 1870s and 1880s playing the heavy (or villain) in David Belasco's adaptation of *The Stranglers of Paris*. When Tannehill toured with this play, he took along a set of sides (actors' parts), his costumes, and a copy of the orchestra parts, so that he could rely on the same music cues from night to night. Timing and affect, both in the delivery of his lines and in the way his villainous part worked with the musical accompaniment, was a crucial aspect of his success as an actor.[17] Similarly, the actor W. J. Florence was famous for his many villainous roles—characters such as Oberreizer in Charles Dickens and Wilkie Collins's *No Thoroughfare* or Bardwell Slote in Benjamin E. Woolf's *The Mighty Dollar*—and the music accompanying these plays was as valuable a part of his collection as were his costumes and promptbooks.[18]

This was probably how much of the theater music in the early and mid part of the century circulated. In the latter half of the century, however, the rise of the stage director entailed more auteur control over production values, of which music became a central and competitive component. Charles Kean in the 1850s used extensive music not only for his much-acclaimed Shakespeare productions, but also for "gentlemanly melodramas" such as *The Corsican Brothers* and *The Courier of Lyons*. A more extreme case was Henry Irving, who, like Michael Curtiz and David O. Selznick in the early sound film era, was very particular about the choice of music used, often turning to England's most prominent composers, keeping on salary as many as thirty-five to forty musicians and insisting on a score tailor-made to the production. For example, to compliment the rich detail in the scenic effects painted by Hawes Craven and the exquisite designs of Ellen Terry's costumes for Katherine of Aragon in *Henry VIII*, Irving generously allowed composer Edward German as many musicians and instruments as he needed to create a similar variety of richness and color in the music. Irving was a master of atmosphere: among his many distinctive effects, he employed an invisible chorus along with orchestra for the magical Excalibur scenes of *King Arthur*.

In America, director-producers such as A. M. Palmer, Daniel Frohman, and David Belasco emulated Irving's high style. Just after the turn of the century, in 1901, while a silent-film pianist was accompanying a Vitagraph one-reeler in a vaudeville house, Frohman was producing a stage version of Dumas's *The Hunchback of Notre Dame* at Daly's Theatre with spectacular scenic and lighting effects and an orchestra of some sixteen musicians playing thirty-four intricately nuanced cues by Frank A. Howson, many of these nearly as long as those Alfred Newman would write for William Dieterle's *Hunchback* (1939) film nearly forty years later.[19] In other words, in 1901, the technology of film music was in its infancy, but the art of stage music had developed to a high degree of sophistication.

Music: Lack of Documentation

One of the problems in gathering data about the effectiveness of theatrical music in the nineteenth century is that few people of the time, either working on the stage or sitting in the audience, seemed to feel it necessary to explain dramatic music, or even to note its existence, unless of course it was inappropriate or there was some mishap between orchestra and stage. Anecdotes of such miscues abound, but genuine descriptions of when dramatic music was effective, like those of Burgoyne a century earlier, are rare and therefore cannot be relied upon to help explain the prominence of action and dialogue underscoring throughout the nineteenth century, particularly in theaters that could afford the luxury of an orchestra. We tend to think of opera or symphonic music in expressive or aesthetic terms, but the use of music to accompany a play was considered by professionals and audiences alike to be almost entirely a technical affair. Although the lack of commentary can be hugely frustrating, it is not so surprising, perhaps, when we think of how few people in the twentieth century paid conscious attention to dramatic music in films. There have been some exceptions to this, of course, evident in the explosion of film music fandom in the last thirty years or so. But in film criticism of the

1930s to the 1960s, music is positioned rather low in the hierarchy of qualities determining a film's effectiveness. It is generally singled out only if there is singing or dancing, in other words if it is onscreen music that takes over a scene and commands the audience's attention.

As a consequence of these functionalist attitudes towards music in nineteenth-century theatrical production, much of it is only now being discovered and identified. Yet clearly there was a great deal of it: one small anecdote must suffice to convey the extant of specially composed scores circulating in the United States. George Bowron, leader of the orchestra at the Columbia Theatre in Chicago in 1887, received the theatrical music for Sardou's *Fedora* in advance of Sarah Bernhardt's arrival there. The melodramatic music struck him as radically different from that accompanying the production of the play associated with Fanny Davenport, which had been given with Davenport's touring company earlier that year. "Bernhardt's score," the leader noted,

> is interspersed throughout with *pianissimo, con moto,* and *andante.* On the other hand, the music of Davenport's *Fedora* is in big black type, and every other bar is labeled *forte* or *fortissimo,* and our trombone-player blew himself into a hemorrhage last January trying to keep up with the rest of the orchestra in the death-struggle in the last act. (quoted in Field 1887, 273)

"Well-made play" though *Fedora* may be, it fits the description of a melodrama, characterized by "sensational incident and violent appeals to the emotions." And yet these two prominent actresses had quite different ideas about the role that music would play in its realization. I also mention this example because it is obvious from this account that some theaters had a system for acquiring, preparing, and adapting special music composed for plays, and a major urban playhouse like the Columbia Theatre was more likely to use existing music for that play than create something new or patch together a score from commercial melos books.

The demands on theatrical music directors were extensive, and there were no doubt many opportunities where recourse to already existing music was necessary in the face of a huge repertoire of plays that a company could produce in one season (not unlike the coordinated efforts of a music staff at a major motion picture studio in the 1930s and 1940s).[20] Writing about the required skills for a theater's orchestra leader in 1919, Edward Dent concurred that the old-fashioned actor may have "wanted a *tremolo* to help him pump up his emotions." To secure a genuine organic unity of music and action, however, the leader

> must be a man of considerable technical skill, and he must also be completely in the confidence of the actor or producer. The musician must be able and willing to pull his work about, to add three bars here or take ten out there...as the stage requires, and to take a pride in doing so with artistic ingenuity. This he can only do if the producer regards him as a collaborator, not as a slave. (Dent 1919, 151)

The list of such collaborators in the nineteenth century is far more extensive than is generally known. Among these, there was composer George Herbert Rodwell with playwrights Edward Fitzball and John Buckstone, Thomas Baker and Robert Stoepel with Dion Boucicault, Edward Mollenhauer with Augustin Daly and Edwin Booth, John Liptrot Hatton with Charles Kean, Arthur Sullivan and Edward German with Henry Irving, Raymond Roze with Beerbohm Tree, and William Furst with Belasco.[21] Rodwell's dramatic musical effects, for example, helped provoke many of the audience shocks for which Fitzball's gothic dramas were infamous.

DEARER THAN LIFE

In the last section of this chapter I would like to compare a stage play and a film produced some eighty years apart. In these two melodramas music is essential to sustaining the emotional intensity. I have chosen an incident in each that, like the letter-reading sequence in *A Man's Shadow* described above, occurs at the crisis of the drama and deals with the protagonist's ultimate disillusionment with a loved one. The play is Henry J. Byron's *Dearer than Life*. The film is Vincente Minnelli's *Madame Bovary* (1949). There are some obvious technical differences, of course, such as the advantages in film of camera focus and the close-up, and the speed at which mise-en-scène may change within a single musical cue. But it is clear that the music in both instances is striving after similar emotional effects and, more importantly, is operating along congruent technical and structural lines.

Dearer than Life was written as a role-stretching vehicle for the comic actor J. L. Toole and was first tried out in Liverpool before an official London opening at the Queen's Theatre in 1868. A few months later, it opened in New York at Wallack's Theatre, and three years later the Boston company at Selwyn's Theatre staged it with G. H. Griffiths in the title role. The music director there was the German-born Charles Koppitz, who composed music afresh for the play. Perhaps he did not have access to the music used at Wallack's or from the London production, or perhaps he did not much care for what he did know of it. Koppitz, though he died relatively young, had a reputation as an expert writer of melodramatic music, which, in those days, was considered a compliment.[22] Besides, the music for the Queen's production was by Wallerstein, and Koppitz had a number of theatrical scores by Wallerstein in the Selwyn music library. There were internal systems in place in the theatrical world for Koppitz to have acquired a copy of the original music to *Dearer than Life* had he wanted it. Perhaps he thought he could do better. A review in the London *Daily News* had observed that the management at the Queen's produced *Dearer than Life* "with some of those lime-light effects and orchestral accompaniments that are generally associated with plays of a more sensational nature" and was critical of the type of dialogue underscoring accompanying certain emotional passages.[23]

The scene I will examine occurs at the end of the second act. The play's central character, Michael Garner, is a middle-aged tradesman who has acquired a comfortable upper-middle-class existence for his wife and only son, the twenty-five-year-old Charley. Though engaged to his pretty and devoted cousin Lucy, Charley has fallen in with a bad lot and he can't seem to hold on to money. At present, he is working in a merchant's office, a job that he hates but which gives him a few pounds to spend gambling away with his friends. His parents do not know it, but he has gotten into terrible debt, such that it could threaten their financial security. In order to prevent detection, Charley has been forging checks and embezzling from his employer. He finally confesses to his father when he realizes that his employer has discovered his activities. Michael urges Charley to flee and awaits the arrival of the employer, who agrees to a settlement to keep the matter out of court. But when Michael and his wife go to the safe where the couple have kept their savings (some of which is intended as a nest egg for Charley and Lucy), they find it has been broken into and the money gone.

The second act opens with a party for the Garners' twenty-seventh wedding anniversary. A friend among the guests has just sung a version of the old Robert Burns' song "The Honest Man" ("A Man's a Man for A' That"), and the mood as the party goes in to dinner is cheerful. Garner takes Charley aside to tell him that he's heard from his employer, Kedgely, who is on his way over. Charley confesses to skimming funds off his employer's account but says he was led to do so by his friend. "Don't let my mother know it," he tells Garner. This is the cue for music no. 11 (see Figure 22.1).[24]

FIGURE 22.1 Charles Koppitz, No. 11 in Leader book to *Dearer Than Life*; MS Thr 554 (6), The Harvard Theatre Collection, The Houghton Library. Reprinted by permission.

During this muted but tender andante, Garner tells his son that he will find some way to avoid her finding out but urges the young man to get away as quickly as he can. Father and son have a brief tearful farewell. Charley runs off, and Garner sinks into a chair, angry and confused. Lucy enters just as Kedgely arrives (music goes out here). In a somewhat tense encounter, Garner tries to fabricate an excuse that somehow he was responsible for stealing the money, but Lucy interrupts him, selflessly suggesting that they can reimburse Kedgely with money saved for their wedding. "The money is here, here!" she asserts, looking around. Meanwhile, Mrs. Garner has left her guests and come to see what her husband's delay is all about. Music cue no. 12 begins (see Figure 22.2).

During this allegro, Mrs. Garner finds Michael opening the safe, arriving just in time to discover that the safe is empty. "Stolen!" Michael says, incredulously. "Nobody knew where it was but you and me and Charley," Mrs. Garner reveals. Garner explodes in grief and rage, "Charley! Stolen by Charley! Oh bitter shame."

This is exactly the kind of situation in a domestic melodrama where actors and managers would have requested musical assistance. The tension has risen to the breaking point, and the fate of the Garners is clearly about to turn irreversibly for the worse. The drama's mounting crisis is reflected musically in no. 12 in the agitated string figures, the interruptions, and the tremolo crescendo. Unlike the tuneful andante, this cue is divided into two sections, distinguished by tempo, texture, and intensity. Section one,

FIGURE 22.2 Charles Koppitz, No. 12 in Leader book to *Dearer Than Life*; MS Thr 554 (6), The Harvard Theatre Collection, The Houghton Library (cue continues beyond example shown). Reprinted by permission.

the opening ostinato rhythm, twice breaks off with an ominous motive played by clarinet and bassoon. The third time, the ostinato continues further, converting into a nervous six-bar tremolo that reaches a climactic point in a sustained diminished seventh chord in the winds. This held chord freezes the tension in a kind of suspended animation for the discovery of the empty safe and Mrs. Garner's and Michael's heightened outbursts. Suddenly, a jolly chorus of "The Honest Man" rings out from the next room—an ironic juxtaposition—and for the final tableau of the characters, the orchestra concludes with a quiet tone of resignation as the curtain falls.

Several inferences about music in mid-nineteenth-century drama can be drawn from this example. First of all, the music in this sequence was not continuous, though given the speed of the rising action at this point in the drama it certainly could have been. Furthermore, the second of the two music cues had several internal changes, dividing it into sections based on musical ideas and tempo that corresponded to textual and visual changes in the drama. The accompaniment provided not just a static agitato but was more modulated, with an ominous motive twice ringing out and occasional pauses for dialogue. The eighth-note ostinato figures, separated by short rests, seem to convey the sense of nervous, shaking hands fumbling with a combination lock. The string tremolo on rising pitches works to intensify the mounting sense of shock and disbelief felt by each of the characters.

Additionally, there is musical and dramatic contrast between these two consecutive cues. These reflect two types of melodramatic underscoring, thematic and nonthematic (or gestural). The first, reflected in cue no. 11, is the standard eight-bar thematic melos that is a common feature of nearly all melodramatically influenced genres. Technically, its function is to promote sympathy. The melody must be played loud enough for it to register on the audience—it returns in act three at the reconciliation—but not so loud as to drown out the dialogue. It can be repeated as necessary until the scene has been played out. This is not the place to elaborate fully on the social history of this musical technique, but I have come to the conclusion that its prominent role in melodrama, which always contains such a strong moral core and message, is partly to maintain and underscore the social order. Though they may be sentimental, such well-balanced tunes are memorable, and their comforting harmonies, so typical of nineteenth-century sentimental popular music, put audiences at ease in their expectations that a higher order is at work. It is precisely this type of melodic euphony that in the 1940s Hanns Eisler railed against in *Composing for the Films*. He complained that it was something "bourgeois culture" had come to expect as "natural" (Eisler and Adorno 1994, 6–8). Its "naturalness" was in effect codified over some 170 years of theatrical practice.

Music cue no. 12, on the other hand, breaks with this social ideal. Its gestural and irregular metrical features suggest anarchy, and this kind of broken musical punctuation is more likely to underscore scenes of conflict in which the social order is threatened. Such cues are more often "through composed," with built-in stop-gaps to help the music director coordinate his orchestra with the developing conflict onstage. Finally, there is an aspect of melodramatic underscoring that unfortunately cannot be discussed here—unlike in the film example to follow—and that is how music and stage action were precisely coordinated, since we have no visual or sound record of the event. We have evidence only for the plan, not for the actual execution.

Madame Bovary

We now turn to Minnelli's 1949 film, based on Flaubert's famous nineteenth-century novel (itself a subgenre of melodrama). Emma Rouault, a young woman from a small French town, marries a country doctor because she thinks that he will take her away from her humdrum life. But he is a simple man with simple needs, while Emma's dreams, fanciful and unrealistic, were shaped by the romantic literature she had read as a girl. Before she realizes what's happening, she starts to look for satisfaction beyond the simple life her husband can give her, and with that her reputation in town begins to crumble.

Miklos Rozsa, the Hungarian-born Hollywood composer, was noted initially for his scores to films set in exotic subtropical locales, then to films noirs and crime melodramas, and finally to historical-Biblical epics. For *Madame Bovary*, he created a number of musical themes and motives, one of the most important representing Emma's longing. The theme is first heard in a cue called "Temptation" (reel 5, part 1) during Emma's intimate scene with Léon Dupuis in the attic. This is a melodic and sonorous string cue that surges with romantic ardor and passion (see Figure 22.3). The theme also conveys deep sadness, a hallmark of Rozsa's tragic style. But in general this musical idea—played three or four crucial times in the film—conforms to the romantic notion of the *thematic* melos: it follows clear musical phrasing and symmetrical patterns. It serves, like Koppitz's no. 11 above, to create audience sympathy with a character and his or her predicament.

As the film approaches its climax, Emma has been led to believe that she is leaving town with the dashing and wealthy Rodolphe Boulanger. He had said he would pick her up at midnight on the mail coach, which will make an unscheduled stop. Emma has gone deeper and deeper into debt and now risks her husband's future security by acquiring on credit the items necessary for her escape. The camera tightens on her face as we see nervous expectation turn to disillusionment, despair, and then humiliation as the coach speeds by her without stopping, nearly knocking her over. Like other men, Rodolphe has been using Emma and playing on her vulnerabilities. The sequence continues directly into the next musical cue. Dejected, Emma returns home to find her husband waiting for her and on the table a basket of fruit with a letter from Rodolphe. After reading his empty farewells, she suffers a nervous breakdown.

Rozsa's cue is titled "The Coach." Though it plays unbroken, it is actually composed, like Koppitz's no. 12, in several distinct sections. Emma has just signed papers for the purchase of the trunks and wardrobe. The merchant L'Heureux says: "The trunks will be waiting in the front of my shop. The coach can pick them up here and your husband be never the wiser." With a cut to a close-up of L'Heureux's hand pulling a trunk, section

FIGURE 22.3 Miklós Rózsa, sketch excerpt from Reel 5, part 1 in *Madame Bovary*; manuscript in the Rózsa Collection, Syracuse University Library, Special Collections. Reprinted by permission.

FIGURE 22.4 Miklós Rózsa, sketch excerpt from Reel 8, part 1 in *Madame Bovary*; manuscript in the Rózsa Collection, Syracuse University Library, Special Collections. Reprinted by permission.

one of cue 8M1 (reel 8, part 1) begins. An asymmetrical motive is full of anguish and angst. Each statement is mirrored, repeated higher in imitation fashion. Section two is marked by an immediate musical change. With the cut to the child's bedroom, the strings play a quiet melancholy theme in G minor while church chimes ring portentously in the background. Emma hugs her sleeping child goodbye. On a cut to Dr. Bovary returning home to the front door and discovering the basket of fruit, section three is marked by another abrupt change: tremolo strings imply tension that builds toward the climax of his potential discovery of Emma's relationship with Rodolphe. At the cut to Emma leaving by a side door, the string tremolo moves sul ponticello (played on the bridge of the instrument), the distortion suggesting both caution and danger in the mounting tension. Section four begins with a cut to a long shot of Emma running up the street towards L'Heureux's shop, with the camera tracking backwards as Emma runs toward it. The anguish motive returns with fuller orchestration and continues to build in volume. Suddenly, the surge breaks off. Over a *subito piano* L'Heureux makes idle chatter ("I hope you like Italy, I've never been there myself") while Emma hears the sound of the coach in the distance (as do we). A driving ostinato rhythm has begun faintly in the lower strings. Woodwinds take over the anguish theme with a shot/reverse-shot set of Emma/L'Heureux waiting and the carriage approaching. The echoing anguish motives build in intensity, as do the sound effects. The musical cue becomes increasingly less melodic and more purely gestural, as Emma's planned escape threatens to topple the social order. When the coach whizzes past, the instrumental agitation resolves to a loud chord, again suggesting a kind of suspended animation, with a close up of Emma shouting "wait, wait!" after the disappearing coach. This chord—a minor ninth chord—is more complex than Koppitz's diminished seventh, but it serves the same purpose, to underline the protagonist's terrible realization, reflected in a few hysterical words (see Figure 22.4).

Emma slowly backs away in confusion and disbelief as the anguish motive returns briefly, this time quickly losing intensity. The cue ends on a cut to Emma returning to her house. There is no anempathetic music as there was in *Dearer than Life*, since the sequence of Emma's breakdown follows immediately in the film. The next cue, "The Letter," is a musical continuation of the previous one, but the cue sheet gives them separate numbers and titles. The conclusion of that cue, when Bovary burns Rodolphe's letter, effectively brings "act two" of the film to a close.

Conclusion

The two examples I chose here should illustrate that many more useful connections could be made between the practice of composing music for the theater—especially for the melodramatic theater of the nineteenth century—and composing for film melodramas. A different comparison I considered making was between Walter Slaughter's music for the 1895 production of *The Prisoner of Zenda* at the St. James's Theatre, London, first with the score prepared by William Axt and Ernest Luz for the 1922 silent version, and then with Alfred Newman's score for the 1937 film. This merits a much larger study than space allows for here. Such a comparison could convey a great deal of information about how dramatic music shaped itself to different media and how in the sound period the need for music to work with dialogue inspired a return to some of the practices of the stage. For those who are fascinated by classic film melodramas of the 1930s and 1940s a great deal could be learned, I believe, by such comparisons. Many allusions could be made, to cite one vivid example, between Rodwell's music for Buckstone's *The Wreck Ashore*, a popular gothic melodrama that ran at the Adelphi Theatre, London, from 1830 to the 1860s, and Franz Waxman's score for Hitchcock's *Rebecca* (1940).

The films I chose as examples in this chapter may seem old-fashioned in the modern sense of filmmaking, since musical styles and genre definitions have changed a great deal since then. And indeed the techniques these melodramas employ, as I have shown, are older still. Nevertheless, it is an open question whether the problems of music interacting dramatically with dialogue and action—and the kinds of solutions directors and composers have come up with over the age—have really changed all that much.

NOTES

1. With the exception of a few scholars who have written about the transitional period of early film and its overlapping traditions with theater—particularly Nicholas Vardac, John L. Fell, and Guy Barefoot—there has been more speculation than precise knowledge when it comes to explaining the theatrical pre-history of film music. Rick Altman's comparisons are more closely based in sources. See Vardac 1949, Fell 1970, Barefoot 2001, Altman 2001, and Altman 2004, 27–72.
2. Though Vardac is on target with *Ben-Hur*, his conclusions about music throughout his book are sometimes unsupportable. He writes that "the haphazard musical practices of melodrama often gave way to a more careful aesthetic discipline in the spectacle plays" (Vardac 1949, 81). My research has shown that many actor-managers' approach to music in their productions, even early in the century, were far from "haphazard."
3. Dean posits many other concurrences between stage and film music—particularly in the area of signification—in his dissertation (Dean 2010).
4. Some scholars have already begun to explore this connection, especially Anne Dhu McLucas (Shapiro [McLucas] 1984), David Neumeyer (1997, 2010), and Robert Dean (2007, 2010).
5. By "fairly recently" I mean that many libraries—particularly theatrical collections—have only just begun to make music associated with nineteenth-century plays available. The Drury Lane Collection at the British Library was acquired and catalogued within the last twenty years. The surprises continue. The Houghton Library at Harvard acquired only in the last two years an important collection of theater music manuscripts from the Boston Theatre and the inventory was prepared as recently as 2010.
6. For example, Charles L. Lewis, *Melodramatic Music* (Cincinnati: John Church, 1882), L. O. De Witt, *Theatrical Budget* (New York: Carl Fischer, 1896), and Al Henderson, *The Witmark Incidental Music* (London: M. Witmark, 1901).

7. "Thomas Baker's Popular Orchestral Music," *The Clipper*, July 9, 1864, 103.

8. Some key studies for music in nineteenth-century play production (that are based on source studies) are Mayer 1980, Sala 1995, Yzereef 1995, and Lamothe 2008.

9. See Aber 1926, Fuhrmann 2001, Garlington 1962, Sala 1995 and 1998, Shapiro [McLucas] 1984, and Wild 1987.

10. Information derived from Clapp and Edgett 1902, 118, and Schaal 1962, 10.

11. The 1938 MGM film based on this play—called *The Toy Wife*—is not commercially available and I was unable therefore to compare how director Richard Thorpe and composer Edward Ward used music in this scene. The film, starring Louise Rainer, was set in New Orleans instead of Paris and Venice.

12. Music from Barrett's collection is at the Houghton Library, Harvard University.

13. Roze 1899, 9–12. This song was published in conjunction with the run of the play in New York.

14. Most of the orchestra parts used for Tree's British productions are in the Theater Music Collection of Sir Herbert Beerbohm Tree, Boston Public Library.

15. Unsigned review of the published play, *The Athenaeum*, November 4, 1854, 1325.

16. See Wilstach 1896, 188.

17. Because Tannehill safeguarded this music, his granddaughter was able to donate it to the New York Public Library.

18. Several of Florence's promptbooks and orchestra parts are in the Houghton Library, Harvard University.

19. Howson's music is in the Burnside Collection of American Theater Music Manuscripts, New York Public Library Research Division.

20. David Mayer and Matthew Scott published one theatrical bandmaster's private folio of *melos* numbers. Alfred Edward Cooper was for many years leader at the City of London Theatre, a playhouse in the poorer east end of the city.

21. Two studies examine Charles Kean's relationship with his music directors and looks closely at music for play production. See Yzereef 1995 and Cockett 2007. David Mayer explores the relationship between Henry Sprake and George R. Sims in Mayer 1976. Jeffrey Richards's biographical study of Henry Irving devotes a whole chapter to Irving's collaboration with composers and music directors, and two further articles explore Irving's use of music in specific plays. See Richards 2005, 241–58; Tetens 2005; and Cockett 2006.

22. From a biographical entry on Koppitz written shortly after his death, see Moore 1876, 77.

23. Unsigned review, *Daily News*, January 9, 1868.

24. Koppitz's orchestral parts for *Dearer than Life* are in the Houghton Library, Harvard University.

BIBLIOGRAPHY

Aber, Adolf. 1926. *Die Musik im Schauspiel: Geschichtliches und Ästhetisches.* Leipzig: M. Beck.

Altman, Rick. 2001. "Cinema and Popular Song: The Lost Tradition." In *Soundtrack Available: Essays on Film and Popular Music*, edited by Pamela Robertson Wojcik and Arthur Knight, 19–30. Durham: Duke University Press.

——. 2004. *Silent Film Sound.* New York: Columbia University Press.

Barefoot, Guy. 2001. *Gaslight Melodrama: From Victorian London to 1940s Hollywood.* New York: Continuum.

Burgoyne, John. 1781. *The Lord of the Manor: A Comic Opera with a Preface by the Author*. London: T. Evans.

Chion, Michel. 1994. *Audio-Vision*. Edited and translated by Claudia Gorbman. New York: Columbia University Press.

Clapp, John Bouvé, and Edwin Francis Edgett. 1902. *Plays of the Present*. New York: Dunlap Society.

Cockett, Stephen. 2006. "Acting with Music: Henry Irving's Use of the Musical Score in his Production of *The Bells*." In *Europe, Empire, and Spectacle in 19th-Century British Music*, edited by Rachel Cowgill and Julian Rushton, 235–248. Aldershot, UK, and Burlington, VT: Ashgate.

——. 2007. "Music and the Representation of History in Charles Kean's Revival of Shakespeare's *Henry V*." *Nineteenth-Century Theatre and Film* 34, no. 1: 1–14.

Daly, Nicholas. 2007. "The Many Lives of the *Colleen Bawn*: Pastoral Suspense." *Journal of Victorian Culture* 12, no. 1: 1–25.

Dean, Robert. 2007. "From Melodrama to Blockbuster: A Comparative Analysis of Musical Camouflage in Victorian Theatre and Twenty-First Century Film." *Intellect* 1, no. 2: 139–152.

——. 2010. "Musical Dramaturgy in Late Nineteenth and Early Twentieth-Century Theatre on the British Stage." PhD diss., Aberystwyth University.

Dent, Edward J. 1919. "The Musician in the Theatre." *Athenaeum* 4662 (September 5): 850–51.

Eisler, Hanns and Theodor Adorno. 1994. *Composing for the Films*. Introduction by Graham McCann. London and Atlantic Highlands, NJ: Athlone Press. Originally published under Eisler's name alone, New York: Oxford University Press, 1947.

Fell, John L. 1970. "Dissolves by Gaslight: Antecedents to the Motion Picture in Nineteenth-Century Melodrama." *Film Quarterly* 23, no. 3: 22–34.

Field, Eugene. 1887. *Culture's Garland: Being Memoranda of the Gradual Rise of Literature, Art, Music and Society in Chicago, and Other Western Ganglia*. Boston: Ticknor.

Fuhrmann, Christina Elizabeth. 2001. "'Adapted and Arranged for the English Stage': Continental Operas Transformed for the London Theater, 1814–33." PhD diss., Washington University, St. Louis.

Garlington, Aubrey S., Jr. 1962. "'Gothic' Literature and Dramatic Music in England, 1781–1802." *Journal of the American Musicological Society* 15, no. 1: 48–64.

Gorbman, Claudia. 1987. *Unheard Melodies: Narrative Film Music*. Bloomington: Indiana University Press.

Jackson, Russell, ed. 1989. *Victorian Theatre: The Theatre in its Time*. London: A & C Black.

Kalinak, Kathryn. 2007. *How the West was Sung: Music in the Westerns of John Ford*. Berkeley: University of California Press.

Lamothe, Peter. 2008. "Theatre Music in France, 1864–1914." PhD diss., University of North Carolina at Chapel Hill.

Mayer, David. 1976. "Nineteenth Century Theatre Music." *Theatre Notebook* 30, no. 3: 115–122.

——. 1980. "The Music of Melodrama." In *Performance and Politics in Popular Drama: Aspects of Popular Entertainment in Theatre, Film, and Television, 1800–1976*, edited by David Bradby, Louis James, and Bernard Sharratt, 49–63. Cambridge: Cambridge University Press.

Mayer, David, and Matthew Scott. 1983. *Four Bars of "Agit": Incidental Music for Victorian and Edwardian Melodrama*. London: Samuel French.

McLucas, Anne Dhu, ed. 1994. *Later Melodrama in America: Monte Cristo (ca. 1883)*. New York: Garland.

Moore, John Weeks. 1876. *Dictionary of Musical Information*. Boston: Oliver Diston. Reprint, New York: Lenox Hill, 1971.

Neumeyer, David. 1995. "Melodrama as a Compositional Resource in Early Hollywood Sound Cinema." *Current Musicology* 57 (spring): 61–94.

——. 1997. "Source Music, Background Music, Fantasy and Reality in Early Sound Film." *College Music Symposium* 13: 13–20.

——. 2010. "The Resonances of Wagnerian Opera and Nineteenth-Century *Melodrama* in the Film Scores of Max Steiner." In *Wagner and Cinema*, edited by Jeongwon Joe and Sander L. Gilman, 152–174. Bloomington: Indiana University Press.

Pisani, Michael. 2004. "Music for the Theatre: Style and Function in Incidental Music." In *Cambridge Companion to Victorian and Edwardian Theatre*, edited by Kerry Powell, 70–92. Cambridge: Cambridge University Press.

——. forthcoming. *Music for Melodramatic Theatre in London and New York, 1780–1900*. Iowa City: University of Iowa Press.

Richards, Jeffrey. 2005. *Sir Henry Irving: A Victorian Actor and His World*. London: Hambledon and London.

Roze, Raymond. 1899. "The Love Song: *The Musketeers*." For piano. *New York Journal and Advertiser, Musical Supplement* (March 26): 9–12.

Sala, Emilio. 1995. *L'opera senza canto: Il mélo romantico e l'invenzione della colonna sonora*. Venice: Marsilio.

——. 1998. "Mélodrame: Définitions et métamorphoses d'un genre quasi-opératique." *Revue de Musicologie* 84, no. 2: 235–246.

——, and Mary Ann Smart. 1995. "Verdi and the Parisian Boulevard Theatre, 1847–9." *Cambridge Opera Journal* 7, no. 3: 185–205.

Schaal, David. 1962. "The Rehearsal Situation at Daly's Theatre." *Educational Theatre Journal* 14, no. 1: 1–14.

Shapiro [McLucas], Anne Dhu. 1984. "Action Music in American Pantomime and Melodrama, 1730–1913." *American Music* 2, no. 4: 49–72.

Smith, James L. 1973. *Melodrama*. London: Methuen.

Tetens, Kristan. 2005. "Commemorating the French Revolution on the Victorian Stage: Henry Irving's *The Dead Heart*." *Nineteenth-Century Theatre and Film* 32, no. 2: 36–104.

Vardac, Nicholas. 1949. *Stage to Screen: Theatrical Method from Garrick to Griffith*. Cambridge, MA: Harvard University Press. Reprinted as *Stage to Screen: Theatrical Origins of Early Film: David Garrick to D. W. Griffith*. New York: Da Capo, 1987.

Wild, Nicole. 1987. "La Musique dans le Mélodrame des Théâtres Parisiens." In *Music in Paris in the 1830s*, edited by Peter Bloom, 589–610. Musical Life in 19th-Century France, Vol. IV. Stuyvesant, NY: Pendragon.

Wilstach, Claxton. 1896. "Light and Sound on the Stage." *Godey's Magazine* 133, no. 794: 183–189.

Yzereef, Barry Peter. 1995. "The Art of Gentlemanly Melodrama: Charles Kean's Production of 'The Corsican Brothers.'" PhD diss., University of Victoria.

....

CHAPTER 23

AUDIOVISUAL PALIMPSESTS: RESYNCHRONIZING SILENT FILMS WITH "SPECIAL" MUSIC

....

JULIE BROWN

IT is inherently difficult to rejoin a silent film with its "original music" and hope to enhance historical understanding. Our notion of "original music" in early cinema needs to embrace practices from cinema's first two decades as well as the more familiar 1920s, and needs to include music played between films and outside cinemas as well as such early accompanying practices as "cue music" (music implied by film images), accompaniment by means of the title or lyrics of popular songs, silence itself, and dedicated song films (where the film is built around a song, the latter available in commodified form as sheet music or piano roll) (Altman 2004). It also needs to embrace the many practices that emerged or were consolidated in the 1910s: cue sheets of various sorts, existing music and photoplay music categorized according to mood and dramatic situation, free improvisation and "special" scores. Most films of the first three decades of cinema did not have "original music" as such, but were subject to one or other of these practices realized in any number of different ways. One can talk in general terms about the various practices that might have been used, but for a given film screening in a given place any number of sonic practices might have obtained. Music was highly ephemeral—geographically particular, realized by variously skilled individuals, and "live," even if that "liveness" was a question of turning on a gramophone player and synchronizing different musical cues on disc in the exhibition space itself.

Of these practices, and with the exception of song films, original, well-cued "special" scores are our best points of access into the question of precise audio-visual alignment during the period of cinema before synchronized sound. Although compiled "special scores" can overlap conceptually with cue sheets, the self-contained, ready-to-go nature of special scores distinguishes them from cue sheets, for which substitutions were standard, even expected. When we hear a live performance of an original special score we not only get to experience something of silent film "as experience," albeit without the broader theatrical experience of the mixed program,[1] but we also get some impression as to how musicians (even directors, in the case of D. W. Griffith, who took a role in the creation of his scores) intended particular sequences to come together with music. The music helps to construct the films and their imagery as historical texts and therefore to promise access to cultural meanings from the time of the first such performances. For this reason, resynchronizations of silent films with "original music" are seductive; they seem to promise an historically accurate glimpse of another audio-visual era. This is especially so when they are mechanically synchronized and made available commercially as DVDs—reproducible audio-visual objects comparable at some level to contemporary sound films. This last assumption is borne out by the number of conference papers one encounters which analyze a silent film score, or the audio-visual effects created by a silent film score, from a commercially released DVD resynchronization.

Yet although "reconstructions" of such scores can be revelatory, they can also be misleading. They certainly represent a small corner of the wider culture of silent film accompaniment and are unrepresentative of the "silent era" as a whole. "Special scores" were initially for "special films" (opera films, historical dramas, films on literary topics), a small corner of the film market designed to appeal to a middle-to-highbrow audience, though by the late 1910s and 1920s they were used more widely for big feature films, especially in the United States, and especially for first-run screenings (Altman 2004, 251–58). But silent films synchronized with their special scores can also mislead textually. Indeed, one might legitimately ask: What *sort* of object can emerge from an attempt to reconcile a film with its original score? Moreover, what is at stake in the making of such a reconstruction? As my way into this topic, I will start with a debate that emerged following a screening of Griffith's *Intolerance* (1916) at the New York Museum of Modern Art (hereinafter, MoMA) in October 1989; in that debate textual, musical, historiographical, broader curatorial, and even ethical matters were all considered to have been at stake. The MoMA "reconstruction" not only forced film archivists and historians to confront the issues of which silent films to restore and how to restore them (Merritt 1990, 370). Usefully for the present purposes, the debate that ensued also brought into focus some of the key, specifically musical issues that anyone undertaking a silent film score reconstruction is forced to confront, and that easily disappear from view once the newly synchronized textual object emerges. They provide a very useful starting point for the more general survey of musical and textual issues that I present here.

THE MoMA RECONSTRUCTION OF *INTOLERANCE*

The screening of *Intolerance* in New York was the result of a collaboration between Gillian Anderson, then of the Music Division of the Library of Congress (hereinafter, LoC), and Peter Williamson of the Film Department at MoMA, with additional assistance from Paul Spehr (LoC) and Eileen Bowser (MoMA) (Anderson 1990). Anderson, one of an international community of silent film score restorers, and someone who has now participated in the resynchronization of nearly forty films, also conducted the score. *Intolerance* was a particularly difficult, and in the end controversial, project. The screening and associated reconstruction were prompted by the discovery of Griffith's personal copy of the instrumental parts and piano/conductor score arranged and composed by Joseph Carl Breil, as well as a scrapbook containing the first frame of every new shot or intertitle in the film in the order designed by Griffith three months before the official premiere, which is when he deposited the book at the LoC for copyright (on June 24, 1916, to be precise). Using these as a "map," those involved in the reconstruction sought to approximate the version of *Intolerance* seen at the first official screening at the Liberty Theater in New York on September 5, 1916. Other sources were the various versions of *Intolerance* in the collection of materials Griffith transferred to MoMA in 1938, an early print dating from 1917, some tinted nitrate footage from late 1916 or early 1917, and a title list from late 1916.

Breil's *Intolerance* is typical of Griffith's "special" scores: it is compiled from existing sources, with some sections specially composed (by Breil); it has a section of music for each major scene, reflecting the mood or action; these numbers generally have a corresponding cue to an action or intertitle, and within each there are numerous other instructions to help the conductor stay in synchronization with the film (Anderson reports there being "119 major sections in the score for *Intolerance*, some of which are divided, yielding a total of 250 smaller sections," as well as 325 action cues [1990, 159]).[2] Despite the score's clear signaling and relatively close cueing, Anderson has acknowledged that she faced many textual and practical problems when reconciling the music with the film. Key among these was the fact that the piano-conductor score seems to have been prepared after the September 1916 official premiere: reviews of the New York performance refer to scenes between two adjacent musical numbers in the score, for instance. The score also bears witness to substantive changes since its creation: pages of music had been added; there were discrepancies between the numbering of instrumental parts and the numbers in the score; some metronome markings had been altered; markings in the score suggesting a repeat had been erased, and so on (Anderson 1990, 160). Nor was it clear when any of these changes were made. In terms of "fit" between the music and various sequences of the film, Anderson reports that sometimes the given metronome markings produced a close fit between music and film in moments, at other times not—which again suggested to her that the score may relate to a completely different version of the film. There was also the oddity that two pieces in the published musical "Selections" from the film were not in the score at all.

The issues that Anderson faced are representative of the complex textualities of special scores, and there are plenty of other potential complications. To start with, relatively few special scores actually survive. In the United States the situation is fortunate. For reasons of copyright, scores put together for big commercial releases are likely to have been deposited at the Library of Congress, though this was usually only the piano-conductor score; sometimes parts were also deposited (Anderson 1988), but often only certain parts (Anderson 2005b, 29–30). In Holland and the UK, by contrast, this practice seems not to have been widespread; the British Library holds only a small number of "special" scores from film production companies. Theodore van Houten makes no mention of legal deposit in his substantial introduction to the catalogue of the Eyl/Van Houten Collection in the Netherlands, and locally produced "special scores" seem to have been equally rare there given the small number that he identifies.[3] Thus, historians might find themselves in a situation of knowing that a special score was produced for a given film, but not being able to find a single surviving copy. Conversely, of the scores that survive, only a portion will have correspondingly surviving films. Moreover, if music does survive, it might do so as a piano-conductor score only, with no instrumental parts or other indication of orchestration (such as existed for *Intolerance*): a reconstruction would necessarily involve the creation of a completely new orchestration that would be, at best, historically informed.

The cueing of action in a special score is another major issue: it might not be as close as in the score to *Intolerance*; indeed, it might be minimal. Hugo Riesenfeld's score for Cecil B. DeMille's *Carmen* (1915), which Anderson has also resynchronized, manifests careful attention to the film in one sense; the problem is that it is imprecise in indicating the process of synchronization. There are frequently no indications of what is happening onscreen at the beginning of a new section of music; sometimes the titles themselves were not correct, and quite frequently the nebulous indication "Play Until Title" is used. This instruction suggests a strategy of playing until the next title appears on the screen, and then suddenly leaping to the new section of music, regardless of where one had reached in the previous piece (Anderson 2005b, 30). By 1925 Ernö Rapée condemned such abrupt shifts as "brutal," an "antiquated" practice no longer found in "first-class theatres," but the very fact that he bothers to mention the technique suggests that it was still fairly widespread even then (Rapée 1925, 14). Even Rapée's preferred solution— arranging some kind of signal to bring the players to a tonic close, preferably using a "dying away effect"—would have been fairly abrupt. Whatever the procedure, it is nevertheless clear that considerable performer/restorer choice is involved in resynchronizing scores such as Riesenfeld's *Carmen*.

Textual complexities such as these are compounded by the numerous contingencies associated with live performance. A surviving "special" score is a very partial indication of how a film might have played live, as Rick Altman has pointed out:

> Even where good fortune has preserved a cue sheet or a score, we rarely know anything at all about the all-important details of any given performance. Was the orchestra visible? How were the musicians dressed? Did they perform the music in vaudeville, melodrama, or Carnegie Hall style? Did they play continuously throughout the film? How did they handle repeats? Did they finish all numbers? Or was the music subordinated to screen action? How closely was the music synchronized with rhythmic movements in the film? Did the orchestra make any attempt to produce diegetic sound effects? Was every show accompanied? Were there variations between performances? Was there music during intermissions? (Altman 1996, 651)

There are many more contingencies. Did the orchestra play through intertitles? Did it play over the opening titles? Did it take a break between individual numbers? Was the "special" score widely used? Critically: At what tempo was the music played? Even if tempi are indicated in the score, did the musicians succeed in playing the music at those tempi?

PERFORMANCE TEMPO VERSUS PROJECTION SPEED

Tempo is all important when bringing together two time-bound media. Although conductors are skilled at knowing more or less how to beat a given tempo indication (in other words, they internalize roughly how to beat, say, quarter note = 80), they are not machines and so might easily start slightly faster or slower in any given performance. In purely instrumental performances, and even in ballet, or vocal or instrumental soloists, there is a sense of ensemble: the performers involved are aware to a greater or lesser extent how fast or slow the others are moving and can adjust accordingly. The same is not true when one element is mechanical. Motor-driven projectors first emerged in 1908 but were not widely used until an explosion in their production in 1915 (Koszarski 1990, 159–61). These projectors may not have had precise speeds—Anderson reports that she has never encountered two projectors with identical film speed—but they were nevertheless motor-driven: once a film is going it will run on mechanically, unless stopped as a result of breakdown, which was all too common. The conductor of a special score must therefore adapt to the film. If he starts a little slow or fast, or does not keep to the required tempo, the effects can rapidly accumulate, immediately affecting the synchronization of the music. The usual way for a conductor to keep closely synchronized with a film in live performance is to make use of, or to add sync points onto the score. As such, indications are often not especially numerous, even on scores that have been well thumbed by conductors, one wonders just how varied individual performances even under the same conductor might have been.

If performance tempo of the music is critical, as noted above, so too is film projection speed. Many of the issues associated with film shooting speeds and film projection speeds over the thirty years of silent film, and detailed by Kevin Brownlow (1990), are clearly illustrated by the *Intolerance* reconstruction. A decision was taken to project the film at the hypothesized speed of 16 fps (frames per second), which was based on speeds most likely to have been used in 1916 and also on how the film looked when projected at that speed (Anderson 1990, 163). This pragmatic solution transpires to have been problematic, however, as Griffith often shot different parts of his films at different speeds. The "Modern" story in *Intolerance* was shot at the old speed (somewhere between 45 and 65 ft. per min, that is: between 12 fps and 17.3 fps) while the other plot lines were shot at the new speed of around 70 ft. per min (18.6 fps) (Merritt 1990, 344). Though it is impossible to know whether projection speeds matched camera speeds, during the preparations for the Liberty Theatre New York screening in 1916 projectionists were reported to have been "kept on call 18 hours per day to rehearse the various speeds required to sync the picture to the sound effects and music" (343). Thus, although Russell Merritt concedes that 16 fps is a fair rate at which to project *Intolerance*'s "Modern" story, he argues that "it would make the other two-thirds of the film drag." (Anderson has also since revised her preferred projection speeds to 16 fps for the "Modern" story and 18 fps for the other three.)[4]

Establishing or hypothesizing film projection speed is one of the most important issues in undertaking a silent film score resynchronization. Sometimes, of course, the music might indicate timings. Published cue sheets are the best known example of this: Brownlow produces a list of American cue sheets dating from 1919 to 1928 with stated camera and film projection speeds from 16 to 24 fps (Brownlow 1990, 284). A score might include similar information: British film organist George Tootell specified "Running speed thirteen minutes per thousand feet" (that is, about 20 fps) in the front of a score he wrote in 1922 to the film *Frailty* (1921) (Chatterton 1922, 79). If projection speeds varied in the one film, the two temporalities could be coordinated while there was still a theoretical potential for give and take between conductor and projectionist because projectors were hand cranked: a 1915 projectionist's handbook declared that "one of the highest functions of projection is to watch the screen and regulate the speed of projection to synchronize with the speed of [the film's] taking" (Brownlow 1990, 286). Yet there is little evidence of routine mutual cooperation between projectionist and conductor. With Griffith's high-end controlling of presentation, we do find him apparently arranging for different projection speeds to be used during screenings of the same film. Likewise, Hugo Riesenfeld claimed to have collaborated with the projectionists at New York's Rialto and Rivoli around 1920 over changes of projection speed during the showing of films, partly in order to make the film fit with his chosen music (Buhrman 1920, 173). I have also found isolated references to this sort of thing in British film trade papers. In 1919 J. Morton Hutcheson, the music columnist with *The Bioscope*, gave out some advice for accompanying the (filmed) prologue to Vitagraph's *The Common Cause* (1919), a film which "shows the reasons for the civilized nations banding themselves together for the common cause of defeating the project of the barbaric Huns." He advises musical directors to "arrange with their operators to run this prologue as slow as possible," which will enable them to play the entire national anthem to the succession of scenes involving Belgium, France, and Britannia (in the case of Britannia, "play Rule Britannia"). If the film is "rushed, then you will only get a few bars of each, and the effect will be very disjointed and spoil the entire effect of a beautifully arranged prologue" (Hutcheson 1919, 27). But these practitioners, who were overtly trying to elevate practices in their respective domains, were most likely the aspirational exception rather than the norm. As Philip Carli has noted, timings on cue sheets can also be misleading. For instance, the timing for the complete film given at the head of a cue sheet might differ from the aggregate timings of the individual cues actually cited on the cue sheet, which immediately raises the question as to whether it is just sloppy addition, or indicates something else (Carli 1995, 308).

There are other timing issues complicating film music resynchronizations. A surviving "special" score by British composer Frederick Laurence for the Soviet film *Morozko* (Father Frost; Yuri Zhelyabuzhsky, 1924) gives no indication of projection speed, but does contain copious pencilled-in details of precise timings of individual cues (see Figure 23.1, below). Alas, other intersecting textual concerns mean that these markings solve few problems when one attempts to resynchronize this score. The problem is that the timings relate to a version of the film that appears no longer to survive: a version that the exhibitor (Capt. J. B. Noel) claimed in his program to have edited and furnished with English intertitles. A comparison of the print at Gosfilmofond and the British score confirms that some cuts and also possible reorderings of footage had been undertaken, especially near the beginning. As neither the English version of the film nor a separate listing of the English title cards is known to survive, a restorer still cannot know whether the title details were shown on the same number of title cards or distributed over a different number. Even if the same number of cards was involved, we cannot know how long they remained on screen; it might have been longer than the Russian originals. This small consideration may be of little relevance to a silent film restoration on its own; however, if a film's intertitles are held on screen even for one or two seconds longer than they had been originally, there is an immediate impact on how an original musical score synchronizes with it. In the absence of a print of *Morozko* with exhibitor Noel's English intertitles and other editorial changes, or any other evidence of how fast the film was run, a resynchronization must rely on an educated guess based on (1) how the music tempi work in relation to the passing scenes and, possibly, (2) how natural the movement of the characters looks (the aesthetic of this film is highly "realist"). I say "possibly" here, because although the realist aesthetic suggests to a modern viewer equally natural physical movement, Brownlow warns that one should not assume that "natural pace" was the preferred or typical goal of film projection (1990, 288–89).

Similar issues attach to reconstructions making use of freeze frames for missing footage. Anderson notes that one of the assumptions that had to be made for the MoMA reconstruction was to leave freeze frames on screen for an average of five seconds. But as she acknowledges, this assumption was not based on any concrete piece of information, but "made after some experiences with the workprint and score" (Anderson 1990, 163). For a live recreation of the British score to *Morozko* with the Russian film print in April 2011, I had to use similar performance-based experience to decide upon the speed at which to project the film (captured on digibeta tape, so not subject to a particular projector). In the absence of concrete evidence as to the original projection speed, I settled on 20 fps as a speed that enabled the marked performance tempi of the sections of music fit reasonably well with the film (though many cuts and alterations had to be made to the music to fit the Russian version of the film); nevertheless, after that single performance I wondered whether a variety of projection speeds might prove more satisfactory, as some sections worked better at this speed than others. Carl Davis has been quite blunt about what he perceives to be the subjectivity of the process of resynchronization.

Discussing his restoration work with Brownlow and David Gill on Henri Rabaud's original score to Raymond Bernard's *Le joueur d'échecs* (The Chess Player, 1927), he said:

> I am often in a situation where I say, "Here is a piece of music where the metronome mark by the composer is clearly indicated. But if I want to trim it so that it meets the next station point, I've got to cut about eight bars." On the other hand, David [Gill] may say, "Well, why don't we keep the eight bars and I'll slightly slow the film down." That sort of stuff. Totally subjective. (Merritt 1991, 170)

As Davis puts it, a well-marked score is "emphatically not" a reliable guide. "You hurt both the film and the music if you're too rigid" (Merritt 1991, 170). Berndt Heller describes similar conflicts arising from the interaction of film length, music length, projection speed and performance tempo in connection with Hanns Eisler's music for Walter Ruttmann's *Opus III* (1924) (Heller 1998, 543).

Timings in a score might nevertheless provide other information for the film historian. The timings in the Laurence score indicate in minutes and seconds how long individual cues might or perhaps even should last, but a dearth of information about Laurence's working method makes it difficult to judge precisely when they were entered and why. Perhaps they were part of a process of calculating how much music was in each cue based on the tempo marking indicated; perhaps they were a note as to how long the corresponding film footage lasted. These timings may not therefore solve all performance questions, and yet they do provide us with a means of calculating how many bars had been deleted under a paste-over. For instance, the music for titles 19–20 is marked "50 seconds"; it comprises 20 measures of 3/4 (simple triple) at a quarter = 120. A page and a half, however, have been cut by pasting over the music with plain paper. Because of the indication of overall timing, we can calculate that about 13 measures have been deleted. (As the music remaining would amount to precisely 30 seconds played at a quarter = 120, 13 bars must have been deleted: 13 measures = 39 beats of 3/4, or about 20 seconds of music.) But these timings might equally indicate other things. Changes to them might refer to editorial changes to the film after the score's initial composition. For instance, the "Introductory titles" music is marked "60 sec," which more or less corresponds to 16 measures of 4/4 time at a quarter = 60 (more precisely it amounts to 64 seconds)—but this 60 was changed to the faster quarter = 80. This change could be explained by the needs of performance—that it became obvious that the initial tempo needed to allow for the "ritardando" in bar 5 and again in the final bar. Alternatively, it could indicate that a small cut was subsequently made in that section of film—see Figure 23.1.

The restorers' choice of both film speed and performance tempi entered into critiques of the MoMA *Intolerance*. Film historian Russell Merritt was one of the critics of the reconstruction (Merritt 1990). For him *Intolerance* is too slow when projected at 16 fps. When projected at variable speeds, current standard prints run about 2 hours 50 minutes. According to his research, on the evening of September 5, 1916, the film lasted 3 hours 10 minutes at most, and evidence from screenings in October and November 1916 equally suggest about 3 hours, all somewhat shorter than the 3 hours 30 minutes

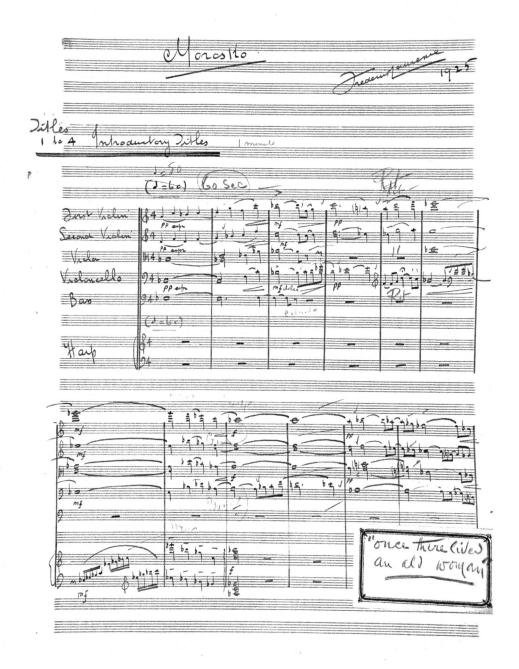

FIGURE 23.1 Opening titles of Frederick Laurence, *Morozko* (1925). By kind permission of Anthony Aynsley Laurence (private collection).

of the MoMA screening. Not only did he feel that the film dragged at 16 fps, he also felt that part of the Breil score dragged at significantly slow tempi, which he likened to playing a 33⅓ rpm recording of "The Ride of the Valkyries" at 28⅓ rpm (Merritt 1990, 344). Merritt's problematizations of *Intolerance's* likely original projection speeds are helpful, but his point about compiled scores that may seem to drag does not take into account historical musical practice. It was not unusual for existing music in compiled scores to be performed with silent film at tempi and in ways that were quite different than the score from which it was excerpted, or than how it was played in concert halls. In North America, adapting performance of written music to changes of mood on screen was an established accompaniment practice from at least as early as 1912 when in *Moving Picture News* Ernst Luz had advocated the "toning method" as a way of adapting music to new expressive requirements (Altman 2004, 263). Performing music at tempi significantly different than their original was an extension of this. Riesenfeld "subjugated" the pieces he chose for his scores and altered tempi as part of this (Buhrman 1920, 171–72). Arthur Roby, music columnist of British film trade paper *Cinema*, wrote in 1921:

> I often hear people grumble because they hear some of their favorite pieces played either too fast or too slow. They forget that a particular piece is put into the programme because it is suitable from a melodic or dramatic point of view.... People must bear in mind that there can be no special tempo for music used in cinemaland. The time, or tempo, of a number may be changed three or four times during its performance to suit the different aspects of the film. (Roby 1921, 36)

One of the starkest examples I have encountered is in a "special" score for Captain J. B. Noel's *The Epic of Everest* (1924), where De Lalo's *Scherzo* has been marked (in what appears to have been the hand of the conductor) "Moderé," in stark contrast to the original "Prestissimo."[5] Such alterations can make a dramatic change on the mood, and, as demonstrated by the case of the Lalo *Scherzo*, the general character and articulation of pieces of preexistent music as we know them in the concert hall, but must be something that the score compilers and conductors were aware of. Thus, sections of a special score, especially a compiled score, might indeed seem to drag (or conversely, to race) and still be presented perfectly in keeping with historical practice—much as Brownlow points out that faster than naturalistic movement on screen was sometimes culturally expected.

PRINTS THROUGH WHICH A FILM IS KNOWN

Textual complexities of the sort identified by Anderson and the inherent problems of bringing together different time-dependent media are two of the difficulties of resynchronizing "special" scores. At the same time, the complex dance of independent temporalities involved in film score resynchronizations needs to contend with a third set of issues. The score will almost certainly come into connection with a film whose scene-by-scene, sequence-by-sequence order is at least partly unknown or unresolved.

For Paolo Cherchi Usai the issue of silent film "versions" is so acute that there is a fundamental ontological problem at the heart of our very discussion. Films undergo a complex history between their first screening and their entry into a moving image archive, and as a result it is difficult to talk unproblematically about a silent "film," as opposed to the "prints" through which the film is known. Any copy has an internal history: "The history of the places where it was shown and kept, and of the people who, with varying degrees of awareness preserved it. It is also the history of the changes that have taken place within the object in the course of time; the history of its progressive self-destruction and, perhaps, of its final disappearance before it could be restored" (Cherchi Usai 2000, 12). The nature of this ephemerality goes far beyond the various imprints that particular performers or directors might have on a musical or opera score. Progressive self-destruction is an inherent property of nitrate film, as indeed is the simple act of showing a film. Actively made internal changes to silent films were also routine: these involved such actions as editing (cutting and reordering scenes) by particular exhibitors or distributors, translating, replacing, shortening, lengthening or adding title cards, or even choosing not to color scenes from a second negative even though advised to do so by a distributor (27). A silent film "is not the same document it was in the past: on the contrary, it is simply one of the many faces the work has assumed in the course of time" (260).

The history of *Intolerance* illustrates this aspect of silent film's ephemerality. Indeed, one of the key concerns expressed about MoMA's *Intolerance* was the decision not only to prioritize one version of the film, but to prioritize a version that Griffith himself soon replaced. Merritt traces the progress of the film from pre-premiere previews through a roadshow around the United States from October 1916 to June 1917. Various previews prompting changes already took place after Griffith deposited his scrapbook at the LoC and before the September screening in New York, which was the stated object of MoMA's reconstruction. After that the film progressed from its differently named and attributed previews, through its roadshow forms, and its eventual splitting into the separate "pocket roadshows" entitled *The Fall of Babylon* (1919) and *The Mother and the Law* (1919), to the chaos that ensued when it proved difficult to fulfill later orders for *Intolerance* because the originals had all been altered in order to make the two shorter films. We should note, however, that once the "tug-of-war" between *Intolerance* and *The Fall of Babylon* and *The Mother and the Law* stopped, Griffith seemed able quite quickly to reconstruct its negative, and according to Merritt "the footage counts remain remarkably consistent" (Merritt 1990, 352). Another, different set of changes took place when the intertitles were cut out and the film was exported to Europe. Griffith had to try to piece it together again. The differences between MoMA's version of *Intolerance* and the one that has generally come down to us emerged essentially from changes that Griffith made in the mid-1920s: for Merritt that version is perhaps the film's "richest, most resonant form," more so than the first official screening of September 5, 1916, used by MoMA (Merritt 1990, 360).

For Merritt, MoMA's foundational decision about the source—or rather, target—text undermined its reconstruction enterprise. He felt that efforts to find a definitive

Intolerance using only a historical spotlight were fundamentally mistaken, as the artist's final word challenges any claims of an original (Merritt 1990, 369). For him MoMA had sought to retrieve "a draft buried under various layers of revision" (370) because the scrapbook in the LoC that had played a large part in its reconstruction shows "still a rough approximation of his preview print," one which although fascinating reveals a film "only partially formed" (342). Rather than take the restorers at their word and read the event as an attempt to re-create an early defining screening of the film, he seems to have understood the MoMA reconstruction as an attempt to present a definitive *Intolerance*. Alternative print candidates for the reconstruction, he points out, might have been the version Griffith reassembled for a tenth-anniversary revival in 1926, which is also the one most commonly circulated, or the version locked into place at the end of February 1917, after Griffith had finished tinkering with it during the various American roadshow premieres, a better notion of "the original." Merritt is not without praise for MoMA's version; he considers its reconstruction of the Babylonian battle sequence to successfully unpack the over-condensed later version; MoMA's "approximation" of Griffith's early design for this battle reveals "a more coherent narrative and a more comprehensive analysis of warfare than do even the longest of the standard versions" (365). Nevertheless, he argues that both aesthetic judgments and archival research need to bear upon decisions as to which text to restore, and in his view there were aesthetically better candidate target texts.

SPECIAL SCORE AS "MAP"

It is difficult to enter into this last aspect of Merritt's critique, as there will always be debate over matters of aesthetic judgment. One of the interesting things about the restoration process is the technique to which it gave rise. In the face of so many candidate prints to work either with or toward, silent film restorers now sometimes turned to surviving special scores as evidence of particular versions of a film. Here the musical score is appropriated in order to resolve certain of the film's philological problems. Reflecting on the ephemeralities of *Intolerance* in her article on the musical reconstruction, Anderson confirmed how their accommodation between sources was forged:

> For the reconstruction of *Intolerance* the implications of all these [musical] changes, discrepancies, and inconsistencies were clear. One could not absolutely depend on the score, even less the parts, for a reconstruction specifically intended to suggest what *Intolerance* was like on the evening of its premiere. Nor could one depend on the copyright frames, because the order and contents of *Intolerance* had been changed after June, 1916. Nevertheless, the music and the copyright frames were all one had to determine the organization of the film at the premiere, and fortunately in many ways the two sources corroborated each other. (Anderson 1990, 162)

For the MoMA performance, "the musical score and the copyright frames became a map to the original version of *Intolerance*" (Anderson 1990, 160). Every shot was assembled in the order as close to that of September 5, 1916, as could be determined, and freeze frames were added where some moving footage was missing.

MoMA's reconstruction capitalized on the fact that because both music and film unfold over time, the cues and instructions in silent film scores now "provide evidence of the film's content and organization in reconstruction work," even though they were originally intended to aid conductors or performers (Anderson 1990, 160). The usefulness of musical scores to film scholarship has since been recognized by others. Those behind the 2010 version of Fritz Lang's *Metropolis* (1927), in the wake of the 2008 discovery in Buenos Aires of previously "lost" footage, have widely publicized the fact that it was the original score to the film by Gottfried Huppertz that laid the template for its marriage of footage from such a wide variety of sources.

Given the many ephemeralities of *Intolerance* and the need to make decisions between competing priorities, it is hardly surprising that MoMA's appropriation of the score as "map," an early venture of this sort, attracted some criticism from film historians. Some found its conflation of different sources a fundamental problem—not only aesthetically, but heuristically—arguing that "it combines and conflates an assortment of artefacts that were generated at various points in the film's early odyssey; telescoped into a single text, each of these elements has been distorted" (Merritt 1990, 338). Both Everson (1990) and Merritt clearly felt that the occasional prioritization of the music had compromised other aspects of the film. For the latter the print was "dragged out to fit a music score originally written for a different arrangement of these shots" (Merritt 1990, 338). Not only that, but the compromise was made with a score to which he argues Griffith appears not to have been committed. Breil's score was not the only one for *Intolerance*: for the April 1917 European debut in London, Griffith had a new score commissioned from A. J. Beard, and used this for the tour around Britain (Merritt 1990, 347). When he produced the 1919 spin-offs, *The Fall of Babylon* and *The Mother and the Law*, he commissioned another score from Louis F. Gottschalk. The existence of multiple "special" scores was not exclusive to *Intolerance*: for instance, Griffith's 1915 *The Birth of a Nation* was initially shown in Los Angeles with a score that was, at least in part, by Carli D. Elinor (under the title *The Clansman*) (Marks 1997, 131–35), while Samuel Rothafel ("Roxy") commissioned a new score for his 1921 revival of the film, essentially declaring Breil's celebrated score out of date (Altman 2007, 218). The fact that there were subsequent scores for *Intolerance* does not of course undermine the interest and usefulness of the first Breil score as an historical document, nor the reconstruction's attempt to recapture a particular moment of the film's existence when that score was used. Nevertheless, the thing that Anderson/MoMA, and subsequently those restoring *Metropolis*, found particularly useful about silent film scores—their ability to point to early versions of a film before the loss, separation, or reordering of footage—was perceived by others, with different priorities, to be a hindrance because of the competing contingencies associated with the two sources.

MoMA's *Intolerance* was not released on commercial videotape or DVD, but we can experience something of the aesthetic of its freeze-frame reconstruction that concerned these critics with the 2010 *Metropolis*. The "restoration" facilitated by Huppertz's score involves quite radical aesthetic jolts in the visual domain, between: (1) almost pristine sequences deriving from an original negative in excellent condition; (2) the rediscovered Buenos Aires footage in 16mm film (that is, with a margin on the left and top of the screen, part of the actual image having been "cut off"), which is in faded and scratchy condition—irreparably so, given that it was transferred to the 16mm stock without cleaning the source print first; and (3) some remaining freeze frames.[6] Nevertheless, the film is essentially now restored to the version closest to the original Huppertz score. For Everson, Brownlow's restoration of Gance's *Napoleon* represents a better approach. It did not make use of freeze frames, only what footage survives, recognizing, in Everson's estimation, "that it was a film and not an archaeological artefact" (Everson 1990, 18). This approach, in which surviving original music is edited to a surviving print, is indeed a common pragmatic solution for such joint restorations, because cutting music to a surviving print leads to an audio-visual result that is usually more acceptable to a film audience, less aesthetically jarring, than one produced by padding out film footage either with freeze frames or (for instance) repeated footage. I will return to this process below.

Music Restoration and Cultural Discourses

An important issue that did not enter into discussions of MoMA's *Intolerance* reconstruction was the contribution that Breil's score made to our understanding of the film. Aside from the role the score played in determining the target film text, commentators tended to focus on questions of its "quality" and "interest." For Merritt, the music "frequently underscores *Intolerance* in startling, disconcerting ways that add immeasurably to an understanding of early audience reactions to the film" (1990, 338). He does not elaborate on what these are in detail, unfortunately, but does note that a split occurred between Breil and Griffith shortly after the film's creation, which suggests that neither Griffith (he replaced some of the music later) nor Breil (he may have resigned, and he definitely wrote a thinly coded article expressing dissatisfaction with his relationship with Griffith) was pleased with the score. Everson seemed happy for there to be "a record of what the original score was like," but finds the score "melodramatic," because it "inappropriately" reused themes from *The Birth of a Nation*. He explains its poor qualities in terms of a lack of musical sophistication on the part of the original audience: "In that pre-radio and certainly pre-TV era, audiences were less sophisticated in their knowledge of music" (Everson 1990, 19). Cherchi Usai is clearly no fan of Breil's original score either, comparing it unfavorably with the music of two other versions of the film issued between 1987 and 1989 (Cherchi Usai 2000, 158–59). One included a new orchestral accompaniment specially composed by Antoine Duhamel and Pierre Jansen for a screening at the Avignon Festival in France of a copy from the collection of American film collector and distributor Raymond Rohauer. The other, with a new score by Carl Davis, was for a Thames Television broadcast involving Kevin Brownlow and David Gill. For Cherchi Usai, the freely created scores by Davis or Duhamel and Jansen are better than Breil's compiled effort.

Although particular concerns were expressed about Breil's undistinguished original contributions to the score, the real issue seemed to be with the fact that it was a potpourri substantially consisting of preexistent pieces of music. Negative responses to compiled scores seem quite common among silent film curators and raise broader questions about music's role in silent film curatorship that I am unable to explore here in full. Suffice it perhaps to contrast Anderson's position as a champion of resynchronized special scores, including scores compiled from preexistent music, with a common critical position against such "potpourris." According to Anderson:

> For a majority of the public, the original score does not become an obstacle to their enjoyment of the film so it usually does not detract from the entertainment value of an early film. But even in those cases where the original score is not to our liking, it was the original accompaniment, and if we are really "restoring" the original work, we must restore all of it, IF (and this is important) our purpose in restoring early films is to allow specialists and the general public to attempt to understand how the original work was and how it functioned, to understand how we got to the films of today. (Anderson 1998, 22; emphasis in original)

By contrast, for instance, someone as historically conscious as Kevin Brownlow asserts that "the problem with using those original old scores is that often the music has become clichéd. It's been played so often on radio and on television that it has simply lost its impact" (Merritt 1991, 168). Carl Davis agrees: "Our view is that if we find an original score that we think is first-rate, as we have with our latest project, Raymond Bernard's *The Chess Player*, we will use it. . . . But Breil turns out—and I would say it frankly—to be a very mediocre composer" (169).

Philip Carli attempts to explain the supposed problem today's audiences have with compiled scores with reference to the music's simultaneous over-canonization, its cliché status, and its tendency to disrupt the feelings of nostalgia that audiences seek in silent film (Carli 1995, 303). He argues that the canonization of the works of the classical repertoire means that audiences tend to approach silent film score recreations, when compiled from preexistent classical works, as if those classical works have remained constant. We do not perceive the same sense of nostalgia in our hearing of the classical music elements of compiled silent film scores as we do when watching the "unavoidably dated" film itself. For him, it is the "sense of nostalgia evoked by the unavoidable visual dating of a film [that] usually helps a naïve audience to bridge the gap of generations, and to attempt, at least, to follow the narrative as it is presented." These classical pieces do not permit of such nostalgic sensibilities because they are too canonized, but equally thought to be "barbarically detached clichés" (304). "There is no auditory cue, with most reconstructed live accompaniments, to invite a naïve modern audience to listen to pastiche scores with any other than 1995 expectations" (305).

Thought-provoking though this notion is that we desire a fundamentally nostalgic experience when we watch silent film, I am not convinced that it is the proper basis for an explanation of our film accompaniment tastes. Arguably, watching silent film is an inherently alienating audio-visual experience, and a score that is as Other as the film is perfectly in keeping with that. To create a score more in line with today's underscoring practices would equally invite a modern audience to listen according to today's expectations. Notwithstanding why Everson and Cherchi Usai feel that compiled scores are in some way alienating in a negative sense, the traits to which they refer are surprising to the extent that they suggest an approach to the music of silent film at odds with their attitude towards film itself. Not only are criticisms that the music is "melodramatic" and "unsophisticated" ones that many people might bring to the music of much mainstream (especially Hollywood genre) film today. They are also charges, along with the statements that the score had "plenty of ambition" but was "not great," that many film-goers unused to silent film might level at all silent films. Back-projecting values formed with reference to Hollywood sound film limits historical understanding. Cherchi Usai argues that we should come to films of the silent era on their own terms, not look back with hindsight conditioned by current cinematic values. He urges that one "must try to imagine the effect of the film when it was first distributed and how that differs from the event you are witnessing," because "the temptation to interpret it according to familiar precepts is strong, at times hard to resist" (Cherchi Usai 1990, 156, 162).

This plea could equally be made on behalf of the music. Notwithstanding the complex performance decisions they can entail and their sometimes unfamiliar musical results, "special scores" have their own interest, and a key value of their live performance is that they allow us better to appreciate silent films as historical artifacts and silent film exhibition as an historical performance practice—certainly potentially. Ultimately, what is at stake here are differing views on silent film curatorship, which, because of the primary interests of the archives preserving the films themselves, has historically been (and remains) in favor of building an audience for the visual artifact. Although they have always valued "film experiences" using celluloid rather than any other mediatized version of the film "content," and also favored live music, the type of live music has not had the same historical attention as has the visual experience of the film itself. Those interested in silent film music and sound might wish to argue, from their own perspective, that such understandable visual biases nevertheless ignore the parallel theatrical history of film screening, a history which recognizes that particular types of music and sounds were integral to the "film experience" from the beginning. What would it be to imagine a festival the aim of which would be to attempt to capture something of the early theatrical experiences of moving picture exhibition, decentering the visual object itself? Rick Altman's "research-driven entertainment" the Living Nickelodeon (2001) is one attempt to explore this question in practice for the US Nickelodeon period.

What none of the responses to Breil's score offered was a reflection on the cultural work it might have been doing, and hence the music's contribution to *Intolerance* in

1916–1917. Films and the music that accompanies them participate in broader cultural discourses, and did so even during the first thirty years of film history when accompaniment practices were more ephemeral. Let us again consider *The Birth of a Nation*. Jane Gaines and Neil Lerner have demonstrated that Breil's motivic material in the score for *The Birth of a Nation* is rich in signifying potential. Being part of the "attractiveness and manner of exhibition" of motion pictures, the music may also have contributed to the Ohio Supreme Court's decision to ban or otherwise cut this controversial film (Gaines and Lerner 2001, 264). They focus on the film's "Motif of Barbarism," which (according to Breil's unfinished essay "On Motion Picture Music") Breil composed after listening to Griffith himself hum some tunes that he remembered "young plantation negroes" sing during his boyhood days on a Kentucky plantation (254). Breil himself claims to have applied this theme to the *description* of the primitive instincts of the blacks, as opposed to directly to the imagery itself, a conceit by means of which Gaines and Lerner suggest that he may have "found a way of distancing his music from certain aspects of the film while at the same time acknowledging the formulaic function of the score." Nevertheless, the theme works as a stereotype, connoting "primitivism" in its repeated notes, stark open octaves, and tom-tom beating underneath a mildly syncopated melody (257); it also potentially embodies the character Austin Stoneman's political ambition (in rising melodies) and unpredictability (in unexpected harmonic turns). Such culturally specific musical connotations have particular textual placements, and reception contexts had the potential to contribute to the inflamed reception of the film. For instance, the presence of the "Motif of Barbarism" in the scene in which Flora Stoneman is threatened by "black" Gus, only to throw herself off a precipice, seems to have inflected reception of the scene and contributed to its becoming widely known as "The Rape of Flora," notwithstanding the fact that no rape takes place. The music seems to have been heard as supplementing the visual narrative in its alignment with the terrifying sexuality of the African (259–60).

Yet the role played by music in *The Birth of a Nation* also highlights the potential for historical film score resynchronizations to become controversial. Music's original role in helping to construct an odious ideology, say, may be an argument for rethinking the scoring, much as in the way that opera productions seek to create new contexts for ideologically controversial operas, or to give even uncontroversial standard repertoire operas new cultural relevance. The ongoing relevance of film, as with any other cultural object, arises as a result of a horizontal expansion of its cultural rootedness. This is an argument for embracing new musical adaptations of silent films, their contemporary cultural appropriation being important evidence of the spread of a film's meaning. One example of this is the receptiveness of Georgio Bertellini to Giorgio Moroder's controversial 1984 pop music rescoring of *Metropolis*, unlike many other silent film enthusiasts at the time. The recent Black History project around the landmark silent film *Within Our Gates* (Oscar Micheaux, 1920), whose curators commissioned a range of twenty-first-century approaches to its exhibition, is another interesting example: the aim was to "rethink the exhibition of politically significant silent films... [i]n order to create a new reception context for a groundbreaking silent film" (Siomopoulos and

Zimmermann 2006, 110). It is also worth drawing attention to the restoration of *The Battle of the Somme* (1916) undertaken by Toby Haggith (2002) of the Imperial War Museum Film Archive. Subsequent to an earlier (1993) War Museum DD Video release, which had an improvised piano accompaniment by Andrew Youdell, for a DVD release in 2008 and earlier associated screenings Haggith commissioned two scores. The first is a recreation for a small ensemble by silent film pianist Stephen Horne, a performance based on a cue sheet that was published in a contemporary film trade paper, but was approved by the War Office's official commercial distributor. Fascinating in itself, this document is nevertheless an early example of audio-visual propaganda, its accompaniment principles being embedded in the historical and ideological moment inasmuch as scenes of war battle, whose brutality we are now fully aware of, are accompanied by upbeat patriotic songs and marches. The second is a new orchestral score by Laura Rossi, which draws on a now familiar harmonic and orchestral vocabulary to read the imagery from a twenty-first-century perspective. Both accompaniments are included on the DVD release. As Haggith has clearly demonstrated with this exemplary undertaking, it is hard to see why a resynchronization of an ideologically problematic film score should not be considered desirable, when the parallel restoration of the film itself is; much is learned.

PRAGMATIC EDITION?

Justifying the "resurrection of dead voices from the past" (Bertellini 1995, 279)—musical in this case—on the basis that it reveals interesting cultural meanings may not necessarily have won the argument over *Intolerance*, however. Even its strongest critics conceded that MoMA's version of the film revealed some aspects in a new light and that it was interesting to historians and scholars. Both Everson and Merritt (by implication) seem to agree that the "freeze frame" technique is useful as a research tool, but that such a resynchronization would need to be considered a "study version" or a reconstruction aimed at understanding the film's original design. Of course, this is precisely how Anderson herself described it: for her, the "freeze frames announce" the fact that the MoMA version was "a scholarly reconstruction, not a restoration" (Anderson 1990, 164). It was "the purpose of MoMA and the LoC... to suggest what the premiere version of this extremely influential film might have been like. It is a hypothetical version based on facts and on best guesses of what might have been true" (164). Given Anderson's clarity on this point, one might justifiably ask: What was everyone's problem?

The perceived problems were not only the sorts of textual and aesthetic concerns raised above about the very status of the resultant "reconstruction"; for some it was the amount of money involved when there was and is so little available for basic film preservation. Some confusion may arise from different understandings of the very term "reconstruction" in connection with an original musical score. Writing about the term in the context of archival work on film itself, Cherchi Usai presents the following distinctions:

> Restoration is the set of technical, editorial and intellectual procedures aimed at compensating for the loss or degradation of the moving image artifact, thus bringing it back to a state as close as possible to its original condition....
>
> Reconstruction is the editorial process through which a print whose appearance is as close as possible to a desired version, considered as authoritative, is created by interpolating, replacing or reassembling segments within the copy and with footage retrieved from other copies. Some segments (such as intertitles) may be newly created by the archive....
>
> Recreation is a strategy aimed at presenting an imaginary account of what the film would have been if some or all of its missing parts had survived. This course of action is taken when material directly or indirectly related to the film is used in order to give an idea of its original concept. (Cherchi Usai 2000, 66–67)

Although these definitions are presented with the caveat that they should be considered "more as a flexible conceptual framework than as a fixed, dogmatically imposed statement on how archival work should be implemented" (Cherchi Usai 2000, 65), it is clear that there is potential slippage between the concepts of "reconstruction" and "recreation", as both allow the possibility of creating materials anew. Various types of "creation" will always be required of musicians when they bring a paper-based score to sonic realization, and so the potential for further slippage between a film archivist or historian's understanding of "reconstruction" and a musician's is equally clear. Indeed these outline definitions pay little attention to exhibition considerations, such as guesswork about projection speed, and questions of music. If we take these definitions as our starting point, however, an attempt to "reconstruct" a historically sourced cue sheet is probably better described as a "recreation" if some of the originally listed music is no longer available. An orchestral performance of a "special" score which survives only as a piano-conductor score may be also be better described as a "recreation," given that an orchestration has to be created from scratch—though this goes straight to the knotty problem of how much "creative" credit is afforded orchestrators and arrangers in the production of film scores even today. What about all those other contingencies stemming from performance tempo, projection speed, precise synchronization, and transition between sections of music? Perhaps the term "performance" is vital to all descriptions of musical realization in relation to silent film "restorations," "reconstructions," and "recreations."

Another perceived problem stems from the considerable resources which go into producing "reconstructions," resources which are especially great if the score is recorded. Given the long, expensive and fraught process, it is perhaps not surprising to find strongly expressed views about use of what are often public resources. Georgio Bertellini has argued that for these reasons the heuristics of all film restoration needs to be read critically (1995, 278). Why that film rather than another? What does one end up with, and why? To what end all this effort? For Bertellini, restorers and archivists—essentially antiquarians who "discover" an object from the past and re-shelve it in their own cultural libraries—need to justify the aims of their "resurrection of dead voices from the past" (279).

The main aims of undertaking to resynchronize a "special score" with a silent film is, as I have suggested, to enhance our historical and broader cultural understanding: of music's role in film exhibition (the forms the music takes, and its potential relationships with the images), and of silent film in general (given music's potential impact on the effect of the film screening). Nevertheless, given the textual complexities associated with both silent films and their special scores, we might usefully think more carefully about what our textual aims are, and how we present what we have done. As Philip Carli has pointed out, the problems arise when such performances are publicized as "authentic" (1995, 307). A good start might be to avoid overstating the status of such resynchronizations. I, for instance, would now describe as "a performance of a reconstruction," or "a recreation", a public performance that was described seemingly more definitively at the time as a "reconstruction" of Frederick Laurence's original score to Yuri Zhelyabuzhsky's *Morozko* which I instigated at London's Barbican Cinema in April 2011.

Equally important might be to take a more flexible approach to exploring the range of possible relationships between film and music. As we have seen, silent films and "special" scores often each have multilayered, palimpsest structures, at once independent of each other and mutually dependent. If exhibited in conditions approaching their originals, they also have competing temporalities; these factors, including other exigencies of the screening and performance event, mean that it will always be difficult to locate "original" audio-visual artifacts, especially in the sense of scene-by-scene audio-visual synchronizations. Unless one were to find a highly cued special score that is also covered in additional conductor markings and happens to marry perfectly with a surviving print of the corresponding film, it is hard to imagine being in a position to monumentalize any resynchronization as representing anything other than one performance of a best guess—which was, in fact, Anderson's stated view of her *Intolerance*. As Carli notes, the degree of creativity required can verge upon "fabrication" (1995, 307); by 1998 Anderson herself acknowledged the limitations of work on historical recreations ("more like hysterical recreations!…history informs my performances"; quoted in Starita 1998, 126). The "palimpsest" qualities of silent film mean that there will be no objective, neutral version of the film, only versions reflecting the particular agenda of those undertaking the reconstruction (Bertellini 1995, 279). If we accept this point, it is worth reflecting on what scholarly work we can do to facilitate access to "historical recreations," if not definitive or "authentic" "reconstructions," involving "special" scores.

Musicians and festival curators need reliable materials. Some sort of critical edition, which facilitates performances of a score with its corresponding film, is therefore a possible first goal. Cherchi Usai argues that the complex nature of film materials typically available and their likely unknown provenances mean that the resemblance of a silent film reconstruction to a critical edition is only superficial. The closest thing to a critical edition in silent film archival work is precisely the sort of "reconstruction" process reflected by the *Intolerance* and *Metropolis* cases: namely, "the editorial process through which a print whose appearance is as close as possible to a desired version, considered as authoritative," possibly by means of "interpolating, replacing or reassembling segments within the copy and with footage retrieved from other copies." For Cherchi Usai, however, these have only a superficial resemblance to a true critical edition, not least because they interrupt the text (2000, 67).

Even if one accepts the argument that a critical edition of an actual film is impossible, the same is not true of a "special" score. It seems perfectly possible to contemplate the creation of a critical edition of the latter, even though musicology has lately become critical of such monumentalizing and canonizing undertakings. The legwork that Anderson describes in chasing up the detail of the original compiled "score" for Charlie Chaplin's *The Circus* (1928) is typical: looking up publishers' plate numbers or copyright information in an effort to identify individual pieces, which in the compiled score might be simply unidentified pages of music excerpted from potentially unfamiliar pieces, and so on (Anderson 1994, 5–7). An even bigger problem, however, is identifying the individual elements in compiled scores that have been copied out in full by a copyist. As one example, Philip Carli described his own activities in the introduction he gave to his recreation (for piano, violin, and percussion) of Albert Cazabon's score to Maurice Elvey's 1926 film *The Flag Lieutenant* on June 8, 2009, at London's Barbican Cinema. Though compiled from a range of elements, including contemporary photoplay music, this score had been copied out in full by hand, and then apparently reproduced and distributed with the film with no acknowledgement of the individual sources. In such cases there are no plate number clues. Such matters of basic identification need to be solved while undertaking the critical work of producing an edition, one that might serve a scholarly and/or performance function. Nevertheless, notwithstanding the potentially long and complicated process, some silent films and some silent film scores are arguably as worthy of a reliable, critically informed version of a "special" score as an opera or a symphony.

Given all the textual issues I have highlighted, the surviving musical materials would ideally be made accessible in such a way as to facilitate multiple synchronizations, thereby proposing not *one* way in which they might marry with the corresponding film, but rather some of the potential ways they might. Traces of the various "authors" will need to be present. The problems attaching to "special" score resynchronization are likely to be less a question of multiple conflicting sources of the music than of conflicts about audiovisual realization, and of conflicts between surviving score and surviving film. These tensions can still be considered in terms of a tension between historically located "authors" (in this case composers and musical directors or arrangers) and the institutions of textual production (in this case performers or conductors) long ago identified by Philip Gaskell (1978). A putative "special" score edition would therefore share many characteristics with an opera score edition. A number of authors and institutions will have a bearing on its possible texts. To be sure, such an edition might also manifest an unwarranted input of resource. Roger Parker has already asked questions about textual fetishism in the production of some music editions, especially opera editions. Given that the latter share some features with silent films, such warnings are pertinent for the putative production of silent film score editions—which would be equally marked by complicated genealogies and the hands of multiple authors, giving rise to a potentially enormous scholarly undertaking if the score were to be undertaken according to established protocols for producing critical editions. For Parker, "The old rules, the old criteria, are, after all, beginning to look like a Sisyphean labor" (2008, 104). How consistent does slurring between instruments need to be, for instance. How textually fetishistic should we be, when performers will take a score and interpret it as they see fit? Is the level of effort expended on some editions worth it? Parker admits that his Donizetti edition is "fast losing pace as its general editors become burdened with other responsibilities and also (perhaps) as their once-prized criteria come to seem in some respects unthinkingly cumbersome" (104). Perhaps it would be appropriate to think through a more pragmatic format for a nevertheless scholarly edition of a "special" score for silent film.

I will not rehearse the critical issues arising from the post-structural turn which militate against the idea of creating "definitive" editions that purport to reveal authorial "intention" and reinscribe an ideology of the transcendent author (Winters 2007, 118–23). Suffice it to say that a silent film music edition would be most useful if it at least manifested the presence of multiple original authors: not only of the excerpts contributing to what are often partly compiled scores (compiled in large part from existing music), but also the hand of the music director who brought the compilation together, the conductors whose traces may be visible on the surviving score, and the film editors whose decisions about the shape of the corresponding film may also have left their mark on the score. It would also be useful to acknowledge the known shapes of the surviving film prints to which the score may need to bend in order to have a life back in performance; this last aspect of the edition would, in effect, reflect the historical impact of chemicals, individual exhibitors, and time itself on "the prints through which a film is known." This latter fact is a key difference between imagining an edition of a sound film and imagining one of a silent film, though even sound films can be subject to editing after release and thus exist in multiple versions; it is also a crucial distinction between a silent film score and a critical edition of an opera.

The elements of an "edition" of a silent film score could have meaning in various forms:

1. As a musical score which is worthy of contemplation in its complete surviving form for evidence of how it might have "fit" with a film that either no longer survives, or that survives in a radically different form. One might glean something about a lost film, or even lost footage, from a score that survives.

2. As a practical performing edition which, as part of its critical apparatus, contains indications as to how the score might potentially be modified to create resynchronization results with the version(s) of the film that actually survive(s). These would be nondestructive indications in the edition itself that also leave room for individual interpretation.

3. As demonstration digital resynchronizations with digital copies of the surviving film prints, creating concrete audio-visual objects of contemplation. These would manifest a reasonable range of possible ways in which the film's and the music's temporalities might coincide, given other textual constraints. Ideally an

interface would be developed permitting scholars (and potentially other users) to experiment with nondestructive alterations to the film and score.

What I am suggesting, therefore, is that in order to serve as a useful resource for the live performance of "original music" with a film, such a critical edition would need to find a way of combining potential performance suggestions with the scholarly apparatus of a regular critical edition. I am also suggesting that the resource should acknowledge the multiplicity of ways in which music and surviving prints might come together, and further acknowledge a reasonable range of possible frame-by-frame synchronization scenarios. The latter will be multiple, but not infinitely variable, which is why, despite their complexity, such resynchronizations would yet prove useful scholarly resources.

Many editorial decisions will need to be made to enable a surviving "special" score to be usable with surviving prints. Cuts and repeats might (in most cases will) need to be made in order for the score to synchronize with particular surviving film prints; it would therefore make sense for a critical edition to include suggestions as to where these cuts might be, and why, while not making them in a way that is irreversible. In order to decide upon such cuts and/or repeats, editors may use as models other cuts already made by the composer/arranger and surviving as markings or paste-overs on the score; equally, they may simply be solutions suggested (nondestructively) in order to solve the real problem of there being too much music for a particular surviving print. In this way, the "special" score critical edition would seek to encourage performance and interpretive possibility, in the spirit of an opera edition, rather than the notion that there is a definitive work to locate or that the edition itself has located the definitive resynchronization, or film "work."

Archivist Cherchi Usai is right to point out that issuing a silent film with a soundtrack synchronized to it (especially on DVD) creates a very different film object from the original; one misses not only the slightly flickering quality of moving film images projected with light passing through film (for real purists, ideally through original nitrate film, though few now have the privilege of experiencing this), but also the experience of live music created in the space of exhibition itself. By mixing the music to emerge from speakers, carefully synchronized with the moving pictures after multiple takes and studio editing to the degree of accuracy that reflects film score synchronization in mature sound films, the music assumes a very different status. For him, experiencing a silent film digitally is a priori inferior to experiencing the original. Nevertheless, as Cherchi Usai also points out, restoration cost is a very real concern for those in silent film archives. If one of the key values of resynchronizations of original "special" scores is scholarly: namely, the possibility of experiencing an approximation of original music with a film print, then one needs to acknowledge that quite a lot of useful work can still be done with digital resources, in the same way that a lot of useful work is achieved by listening to recordings of music primarily conceived for live performance, even though there are key differences between a recording and a live performance.

Thus far I have been describing the work that scholars, performers, and restorers might do with materials presented for flexible use, including mock-ups of more than one possible historical recreation. One might even contemplate a time in future when an Internet-based "mediathèque" will create online resources which would enable people to experience a recreated version of a silent film whose frame-by-frame musical synchronizations approximate to what might have been heard at the time, even if via a digital version of the film with a digital version of its original score. With "mediathèque" I am referring to that section of a film archive that is concerned with public access to "content," as opposed to the original artifacts themselves, and I am alluding to the absorbing attempts to draw distinctions between such terms as "archive," "museum," "cinémathèque," and "mediathèque," and to define "film experience" and "film curatorship" under the new digital dispensation. This discussion appears within a book-length series of conversations by the four film archivists Paolo Cherchi Usai, David Francis, Alexander Horwath, and Michael Loebenstein (2008; on "mediathèque" see esp. 15–16). I should add that these four writers resist thinking about film as "content" as opposed to "experience."

Music technology has brought us to a position where, using music software such as Sibelius, one can produce quite reasonable mock-ups of orchestral scores at a fraction of the cost of a real orchestra. Film editing software such as Final Cut Pro enables one to experiment, nondestructively, speeding up and slowing down the "projection" (playback) speed of a film; it also allows cuts to be made in which nothing is lost of the film; the linked software Soundtrack Pro allows one to synchronize music with the film—again, permitting nondestructive experimentation with musical placement (cueing), tempo, and cuts and editing. Although such computer aids currently require some expertise, the Online Chopin Variorum Edition (http://www.ocve.org.uk), which enables users to try out different versions of Chopin's multitexted scores, holds out the hope that an equally simple user interface for playing around with the complex temporalities and synchronized textualities of silent film scores is possible. Variants might be programmed: one might choose to run a film at 18 fps/19 fps/20 fps/21 fps etc. and for each of these film speed options one might be able to choose various synchronization possibilities, depending on the nature and state of the score and surviving film prints. None of these would substitute for live performances at public screenings, nor for commercial DVD releases involving an orchestra that has been recorded playing a recreation of an original score. Of course, in an ideal world even commercial DVD releases, or at least DVDs released by archives, could make use of such digital mock-ups for DVD Extras, or "remixes" of the orchestral performance, thereby affording audiences the possibility of hearing different synchronization solutions to a film whose main feature track is accompanied by real instruments. The Imperial War Museum's DVD of *The Battle of the Somme* manifests one aspect of this. But one might imagine audio versions of DVD extras such as those for *Final Destination 2* (2003), a Warner Bros. B horror movie, where you can not only see the Director's Cut with the missing scene seamlessly spliced in, but make up your own Director's Cut (Cherchi Usai and others, 2008, 30).

The possibility of approaching a film and its music in the spirit of performance, and experimenting with the various contingencies, would enable us to avoid one of the fundamental problems of DVD "reconstructions": namely, that newly synchronized reconstructions of silent films with their music—in practice, "historical recreations"—are easily reified as a copy of *the original film*. The many compromises and educated guesses involved in the recreation process, stemming from silent film's and silent film music's ephemeral natures, are lost in this process.

Notwithstanding these undoubted difficulties, I and many other silent film music historians and practitioners firmly believe that exploring in practice, or in virtual practice, musical and other sonic aspects of early film exhibition can enhance historical understanding. I am eager to promote the value of resynchronizing silent films with their original music, if known, but only if the ephemerality of the cultural form is acknowledged and accommodated by referring to "performances" of the film or "historical recreations" of the score, and preferably—in the case of DVDs—by making creative use of available new technologies. To do otherwise would be to create, especially in commercial DVD releases, concretized exemplars of sonic practices that were diverse and often textually fluid. It would be to repeat in a slightly different guise the mistakes of medieval music studies, much of whose performance manifestations Daniel Leech-Wilkinson (2002) has recently called invention rather than reconstruction. Philip Carli has already pointed to parallels between the historical performance movement and the enterprise of film restoration, particularly in the case of efforts made towards "authentic" film accompaniment (1995, 306ff.). Even if one were to set out with definitive reconstruction in mind, the sources themselves quickly explode any such preconceptions, and many of the best practitioners, including Carli himself and Anderson, already acknowledge the contingencies involved. Limited restoration budgets, and the conflicting agenda of music historians and film archives (and their commercial DVD production arms), make it hard to realize such high aspirations in practice. But if we were able to experience early films with a series of possible synchronizations we may by proxy learn something about ephemeral historical modes of accompaniment and also about possible audio-visual textualities and their cultural and historical meanings. By stressing the spectrum of synchronization possibilities that "special" scores can afford, I hope to have added something to debates about the ephemeral matter of live musical accompaniments of film prior to synchronized sound. Ultimately, I would like to see all silent films with surviving scores to be available to scholars in a form that would enable listener choice: all the cues available, but—within the individual constraints defined by the individual text—to have the flexibility to perform a range of possible synchronizations of these texts. High aspirations indeed.

NOTES

1. The high value that some film curators attach to the question of film "as experience" is clear in Cherchi Usai, and others 2008.
2. For a detailed account of Breil's score for *The Birth of a Nation*, see Marks 1997, 109–66 and 198–218.

3. The most substantial British collection that I have identified to date is the deposit in the British Library of seven piano-conductor scores (no separate parts) compiled by Herbert H. Hainton and distributed by the Ideal Film Renting company in 1915: g.1435.(1–7.). On the Netherlands, see Houten 1992.

4. While this chapter was in press, Anderson read a paper entitled "D. W. Griffith's *Intolerance* (1916): Revisiting a Reconstructed Text" at the conference *Music and the Moving Image VII*, New York University, June 2, 2012.

5. This score is held in the University of Cambridge Library, Manuscripts Collection.

6. See the 2010 DVD release, *The Complete Metropolis*; the different types of footage are also available for viewing on the commercial website: http://www.kino.com/metropolis/ (accessed August 5, 2011). See also the website of the Murnau Stiftung: http://www.metropolis2710.de/en/restoration.html (accessed August 5, 2011).

BIBLIOGRAPHY

Abel, Richard, and Rick Altman, eds. 2001. *The Sounds of Early Cinema*. Bloomington: Indiana University Press.

Altman, Rick. 1996. "The Silence of the Silents." *Musical Quarterly* 80, no. 4: 648–718.

——. 2001. "The Living Nickelodeon." In *The Sounds of Early Cinema*, edited by Richard Abel and Rick Altman, 232–240. Bloomington: Indiana University Press.

——. 2004. *Silent Film Sound*. New York: Columbia University Press.

——. 2007. "Early Film Themes: Roxy, Adorno, and the Problem of Cultural Capital." In *Beyond the Soundtrack: Representing Music in Cinema*, edited by Daniel Goldmark, Lawrence Kramer, and Richard Leppert, 205–224. Berkeley: University of California Press.

Anderson, Gillian B. 1984. "The Thief of Bagdad and Its Music." *Institute for Studies in American Music Newsletter* 14, no. 1: 8–10.

——. 1988. *Music for Silent Films, 1894–1929: A Guide*. Washington, DC: Library of Congress.

——. 1990. " 'No Music Until Cue': The Reconstruction of D. W. Griffith's *Intolerance*." *Griffithiana* 13, nos. 38–39: 158–169.

——. 1994. "The Circus." *Sonneck Society Newsletter* 20, no. 2: 5–9.

——. 1998. "Preserving Our Film Heritage or Making Mongrels: The Presentation of Early (Not Silent) Films." *Journal of Film Preservation* 57: 19–24.

——. 2005a. "A Consummation and a Harbinger of the Future: Mortimer Wilson's Accompaniments for Douglas Fairbanks." *Film International* 13: 32–39.

——. 2005b. "Geraldine Farrar and Cecil B. DeMille: The Effect of Opera on Film and Film on Opera in 1915." In *Carmen: From Silent Film to MTV*, edited by Chris Perriam and Ann Davies, 23–35. Amsterdam and New York: Rodopi.

——, and Philip C. Carli. 2005. "*Intolerance*. Music." In *The Griffith Project*, vol. 9, edited by Paolo Cherchi Usai, 75–80. London: BFI Publishing.

The Battle of the Somme. DVD. The War Office. 1916; London: Imperial War Museum, 2008. SN6540.

Bertellini, Georgio. 1995. "Restoration, Genealogy and Palimpsests. On Some Historiographical Questions." *Film History* 7, no. 3: 277–290.

Bowser, Eileen. 1990. "Some Principles of Film Restoration." *Griffithiana* 13, nos. 38–39: 172–173.

Brownlow, Kevin. 1990. "Silent Films: What Was the Right Speed?" In *Early Cinema: Space, Frame, Narrative*, edited by Thomas Elsaesser with Adam Barker, 282–290. London: BFI Publishing. Originally published in *Sight and Sound* 49, no. 3 (1980): 164–167.

Buhrman, T. Scott. 1920. "Photoplays De Luxe." *American Organist* 3, no. 5: 157–175.

Carli, Philip C. 1995. "Musicology and the Presentation of Silent Film." *Film History* 7, no. 3: 298–321.

Chatterton, Julia. 1922. "Music, Song and Dance." *The Musical Standard*, August 26, 79.

Cherchi Usai, Paolo. 2000. *Silent Cinema: An Introduction*. Revised and expanded edition. London: BFI Publishing.

——, David Francis, Alexander Horwath, and Michael Loebenstein, eds. 2008. *Film Curatorship: Archives, Museums, and the Digital Marketplace*. Vienna: Österreichisches Filmmuseum: SYNEMA, Gesellschaft für Film und Medien and Pordenone, Italy: Le Giornate del Cinema Muto.

The Complete Metropolis. DVD. Directed by Fritz Lang, 1927; Kino International, 2010. DVK6902.

Davis, Blair. 2008. "Old Films, New Sounds: Screening Silent Cinema with Electronic Music." *Canadian Journal of Film Studies/Revue Canadienne d'Études Cinématographiques* 17, no. 2: 77–98.

Everson, William K. 1990. "Intolerance." *Films in Review* 41, nos. 1–2: 16–20.

Gaines, Jane, and Neil Lerner. 2001. "The Orchestration of Affect: The Motif of Barbarism in Breil's *The Birth of a Nation* Score." In *The Sound of Early Cinema*, edited by Richard Abel and Rick Altman, 252–268. Bloomington: Indiana University Press.

Gaskell, Philip. 1978. *From Writer to Reader: Studies in Editorial Method*. Oxford: Clarendon Press.

Haggith, Toby. 2002. "Reconstructing the Musical Arrangement for *The Battle of the Somme* (1916)." *Film History* 14, no. 1: 11–24.

Heller, Berndt. 1998. "The Reconstruction of Eisler's Film Music: *Opus III, Regen* and *The Circus*." *Historical Journal of Film, Radio, and Television* 18, no. 4: 541–559.

Houten, Theodore van. 1992. *Silent Cinema Music in the Netherlands: The Eyl / Van Houten Collection of Film and Cinema Music in the NederlandsFilmmuseum*. Buren: Frits Knuf.

Hubbert, Julie. 2005. "The Music from *More Treasures from American Film Archives*, 1894–1931." *Moving Image* 5, no. 2: 154–157.

Hutcheson, J. Morton. 1919. "Music in the Cinema." *Bioscope*, 24 April, 27.

Kleiner, Arthur. 1972. "The Re-Creation of a Lost Masterpiece: Edmund Meisel's Score for *Potemkin*." *American Film Institute Report* 3, no. 1: 6–7.

Koszarski, Richard. 1990. *An Evening's Entertainment: The Age of the Silent Feature Picture, 1915–1928*. New York: Charles Scribner's Sons.

Lanchberry, John. 1997. "Recreating the Music for *The Birth of a Nation*." *Griffithiana* 60/61: 30–31.

Leech-Wilkinson, Daniel. 2002. *The Modern Invention of Medieval Music: Scholarship, Ideology, and Performance*. Cambridge: Cambridge University Press.

Marks, Martin Miller. 1997. *Music and the Silent Film: Contexts and Case Studies, 1895–1924*. New York: Oxford University Press.

Merritt, Russell. 1990. "D. W. Griffith's *Intolerance*: Reconstructing an Unattainable Text." *Film History* 4, no. 4: 337–375.

——. 1991. "Opera without Words: Composing Music for Silent Films. And Interview with Carl Davis, Kevin Brownlow and David Gill." *Griffithiana* 14, no. 40–42: 168–181.

Online Chopin Variorum Edition. http://www.ocve.org.uk/about/description.html (accessed June 26, 2011).

Patalas, Enno. 2002. "On the Way to *Nosferatu*." *Film History* 14, no. 1: 25–31.

Parker, Roger. 2008. "*Manon Lescaut*: La Scala 1930." *Opera Quarterly* 24, nos. 1–2: 93–106.

Rapée, Ernö. 1925. *Encyclopedia of Music for Pictures*. New York: Belwin. Reprint, New York: Arno Press, 1970.

Roby, Arthur. 1921. "Cinema Music." *Cinema News and Property Gazette*, 450 (26 May), 36.

Siomopoulos, Anna, and Patricia Rodden Zimmermann. 2006. "Silent Film Exhibition and Performative Historiography: The *Within Our Gates* Project." *Moving Image* 6, no. 2: 109–111.

Starita, Angela. 1998. "Sounds of Silents: Scoring Silent Era Horror Films: The Debate between Restoration and Reinterpretation." *Cinefantastique* 30, nos. 7–8: 99, 101–103, 126.

Tsivian, Yuri. 1995. "Dziga Vertov's Frozen Music: Cue Sheets and a Music Scenario for *The Man with the Movie Camera*." *Griffithiana* 54: 92–121.

Vlada, Petric. 1977. "Silence Was Golden." *American Film* 2, no. 10: 64–65.

Walker, Elsie M. 2005. "When Past and Present Collide: Laura Rossi's Music for Silent Shakespeare (1999)." *Literature/Film Quarterly* 33, no. 2: 156–167.

Winters, Ben. 2007. "Catching Dreams: Editing Film Scores for Publication." *Journal of the Royal Musical Association* 132, no. 1: 115–140.

······································

CHAPTER 24

PERFORMANCE PRACTICES AND MUSIC IN EARLY CINEMA OUTSIDE HOLLYWOOD

······································

KATHRYN KALINAK

THE practice of film music has always been a global one. As cinema exhibition made its way around the world, radiating out from its origins in the United States and western Europe, music was there to accompany it, materializing within days, weeks, or months of film's arrival. Sometimes that accompaniment took the form of recorded music played through phonographs or other similar devices. More often it took the form of live performance: a pianist or small musical ensemble was typical. But whatever form musical accompaniment took, it was wedded early to film, a marriage that has sustained itself over the course of film's history around the globe.

Early on, phonograph recordings played an important role in both peep-show devices, such as Edison's short-lived Kinetophone, and projected image systems, such as Oskar Messter's Biophon, Leon Gaumont's Chronophone, and, slightly later, Cecil Hepworth's Vivaphone, and Kazimierz Prószyński's Photophone. In fact, in many places around the world phonographic technology would have been as novel as the moving images themselves. Edison's Kinetophone, a peep-show device outfitted with a phonograph, cylinder recordings, and ear tubes, enjoyed a brief run in the United States around 1895, offering filmed musical performances loosely fitted to phonograph recordings. By 1896, Kinetophones appeared as far away as Nizhny Novgorod, Russia.

Messter's system had a longer shelf life. In 1903 in Berlin, Messter synchronized a gramophone and a film projector and began producing short, four- to five-minute films to exploit his new technology: these were adaptations of operettas and operas, such as Wagner's *Lohengrin* (1907) or performances by cabaret stars. Within a decade, nearly 500 theaters were outfitted with Messter's sound system. Other enterprising individuals throughout the world devised ways to produce phonographic sound in accompaniment to films, in both peep show and projected formats. Phonographic accompaniment could be heard in places as disparate as England, Belgium, Poland, the Czech territories, Iran, Mexico, and Australia. In Iran, phonographic accompaniment enjoyed a long history, lasting well into the 1920s. As late as 1929, Luis Buñuel and Salvatore Dalí's avant-garde classic *Un chien andalou* was famously accompanied at its Paris premiere by phonograph recordings of tangos and Wagnerian opera.

These systems were hounded by problems, however. These include the phonograph's limited capacity for amplification; the fragility of cylinders and, later, phonograph recordings; the restrictive length of phonograph recordings, which necessitated repeated changing during screenings of longer films; and problems in synchronization. Although some, like Messter, appear to have solved at least some of these obstacles, amplification in particular remained a problem as audiences for films grew and larger theaters were built to accommodate them. In Prague and possibly in other places, oversized phonographic horns were used to boost the sound. But ultimately phonographic sound was difficult to deliver reliably, and it proved inadequate as a long-term solution.

Live music proved to be the more durable form of accompaniment around the globe during the silent era. The first projected images in the United States and western Europe depended upon live music so it should come as no surprise that screenings throughout the world gravitated to the same format. Live musical accompaniment materialized in places as diverse as England, Sweden, Denmark, India, Iran, Japan, China, Hong Kong, Australia, New Zealand, Mexico, and Brazil.

DIVERSITY OF EARLY PRACTICES

As central to the experience of watching films as music was becoming, there were no clear standards in place to guide accompanists in the choice of music. Different practices for the production and reception of musical accompaniment developed around the world. In the United States, accompanists gravitated first to popular music, while in western Europe, the preference was for art music. But in many countries around the globe, indigenous music, both traditional and popular, was the music of choice. One such example is prerevolutionary Russia, where accompanists often chose Russian traditional music and paid no attention to whether or not such music was appropriate for a given film. According to newspaper accounts of the era, Russian audiences seem not to have minded. Music would prove a powerful medium of cultural transmission in the silent era, relying upon and reinforcing the distinct national musical idioms at accompanists' disposal.

In India, the Lumière's projected films were first shown in Bombay (now Mumbai) in July 1896. Although the first screenings were likely silent, live music quickly appeared. By August, musical accompaniment was noted by the *Times of India*. India has a long history of theater and musical performance, a history that saw tremendous growth in the nineteenth century. Thus a ready supply of indigenous music was at hand for accompanists, who sometimes also served as lecturers (the term for those people who narrated the film for the audience before intertitles became the common practice). Sometimes singers would lecture in song form. Foreign films (usually from England) were generally accompanied by English music, often on Western instruments such as the piano and violin. But Indian films would be accompanied by indigenous music— rāgas and folk tunes performed on traditional Indian instruments such as the tabla (drum), sarangi (similar to a bowed lute), and harmonium. This last instrument, a Western invention, had been redesigned for Indian music and allowed for the production of a drone.

In Iran, films were initially the province of the upper classes and royalty. In 1904, the first cinema opened in Tehran screening foreign films imported from the West and utilizing Western-type music and instruments, usually piano and violin. Phonograph recordings from the West were also popular and remained so throughout the silent era, a reminder that in many places around the globe live musical accompaniment and phonograph recordings were both utilized. Cinema-going experienced a series of fits and starts in Iran, with cinemas opening and closing throughout the silent era. Eventually cinemas opened for lower-class audiences and here a different musical practice developed: indigenous Persian music played before, during, and after screenings. At the Grand Theatre in Tehran, it was a live orchestra that was positioned in front of the stage; at the Cinema Iran, it was recorded music played through speakers positioned below the screen.

In Japan, film had arrived, in various forms, by 1897. There is evidence that at least some of these early films were accompanied by music: local exhibitors would position bands on barges near screening venues to hail customers and to provide background music. Soon the musicians would be positioned behind the screen so as not to compete with the *benshi*, stars of the Kabuki stage who interpreted the new medium for the audience through elaborate lecture/performances. In fact, the *benshi* grew so powerful that musical accompaniment deferred to them, the musicians not playing when the *benshi* was speaking. (And many film historians point to the *benshi* as the reason sound film came so late to Japan—it was opposed by *benshi* who were firmly entrenched in silent-film exhibition.)

Many of the first Japanese-produced films were of musical performances. In 1899, films of dancing geishas appeared in a vaudeville-style variety show in Tokyo, where it is very likely that the pit musicians accompanied the films. By 1908, theaters devoted exclusively to film had appeared with full orchestra and live singers. Junko Ogihara has documented an interesting parallel development: films shown in the United States to Japanese-American audiences also featured *benshi* and traditional Japanese musical accompaniment (Ogihara 1990). This tradition was so powerful in Japanese neighborhoods in Los Angeles that exhibitors continued to screen films in silence with *benshi* and Japanese musical accompaniment until 1935, almost eight years after sound films were first heard in Los Angeles.

Musical accompaniment in Japan, as in India, was dictated by a film's country of origin: foreign films exported from the West were accompanied by Western music (opera was a popular choice) and Western instruments such as the piano and violin, while Japanese films were accompanied by indigenous music played on Japanese instruments such as the shamisen (a three-stringed banjo) and taiko drums. In practice, however, these traditions often mixed with Western and Japanese instruments at the same performance.

Throughout Asia, music would surface in accompaniment to film. The first screenings in China took place in Shanghai in 1896. By 1897 musical accompaniment was noted by newspapers. The first Chinese films were recreations of performances from Chinese opera: *Dingjun Mountain* (1905), produced in Peking (now Beijing), and *Stealing a Roast Duck* (1909), produced in Hong Kong. *Dingjun Mountain* was reported to have been shot with live music on the set so it makes sense that the operatic source was used to accompany screenings of the film.

In Korea, the first public film screenings were of Western films, probably in 1903 or 1904. By 1908, newspapers were reporting the presence of the *byeonsa*, the Korean name for the Japanese phenomenon of the *benshi*, who were to become a prominent feature of Korean silent cinema. It is not known whether the earliest film screenings were accompanied by music but by the time that the *byeonsa* were established, bands would provide musical accompaniment in alternation with the *byeonsa*. (Apparently this did not always go according to plan.) The first locally produced Korean film is often cited as *The Righteous Revenge* (1919), which combined live theatrical performances with filmed images. It seems likely that since musical accompaniment was already established as part of the movie-going experience in Korea, it would be a part of these hybrid films as well.

In South America, indigenous music also played an important role very early on. In Brazil, as in Japan and China, the first locally produced films were of musical performances. *Dance of a Man from Bahia* (1899) captures the performance of a local dance and it is hard to imagine that screenings of this film did not utilize the music of Bahia, an Afro-Brazilian community where the samba originated. In fact, throughout the silent era Brazilian filmmakers captured musical performances and exploited Brazilian musics. A popular genre was the *fitas cantatas*, filmed operettas with live singers positioned behind the screen.

As the moving image was nearing the end of its first decade of existence, musical accompaniment to moving images was not yet a standardized practice, either in the United States and western Europe or abroad. Some films screened in silence. (In prerevolutionary Russia, for instance, musical accompaniment did not catch on until the 1910s.) But most films had some kind of musical accompaniment, whether it was phonographic or live music or both. That accompaniment differed from country to country and even within countries. Indigenous films were generally accompanied by indigenous music, foreign films with Western music. When accompaniment was live, it could be provided by a lone musician such as a pianist, a small ensemble, or even in this early period, a full orchestra (as in Japan). Accompaniment could be continuous or intermittent, improvised, or originally composed. A common thread is indigenous music, both traditional and popular, which proved a staple for accompanists around the world.

Increasing Standardization

During the second decade of film's history, musical accompaniment began to move toward more standardized practices and functions. Music was no longer a secondary consideration, arbitrarily chosen or haphazardly performed. Accompaniment became an accepted and expected part of the screening experience, with music chosen to fit the images. Continuous music became the norm and live accompaniment gradually replaced phonograph recordings. Above all, theater owners began to tout the quality of musical accompaniment as a marketing tool to attract audiences.

Music's functions became standardized as well, coalescing around the presentation of appropriate moods and emotions. In many places around the globe, conventions borrowed from Western music developed as a kind of shorthand in the creation of moods and emotions: tremolo strings for suspense, pizzicato strings for sneakiness, dissonance for villainy. And these conventions could be heard even when Western music itself was not utilized. In fact, mood music became so embedded in the musical practices of the era that it began to be played on the set as motivation for cast and crew.

The standardization of musical accompaniment was facilitated by a number of institutions and practices. Trade publications began addressing musical accompaniment, advocating high standards in the selection and performance of music. Studios, such as Gaumont in France in 1907 and Edison in the United States in 1909, began circulating appropriate musical selections for their films. Called cue sheets, these lists of musical suggestions could include actual quotations of music, detailed timings, and even directions for coordinating music and image. Cue sheets were an early attempt to police the content and quality of musical accompaniment and they often traveled with a film as it traversed the globe. There is evidence of cue sheets exported from the West traveling as far as China.

Cue sheets depended upon musical encyclopedias, which developed at about the same time. These encyclopedias contained inventories of music, some culled from art and folk music repertoires and some originally composed, exhaustively catalogued by mood, emotion, and narrative situation. One of the most influential was the *Kinothek* series, published in Berlin, by the Italian composer Giuseppe Becce. The first of these volumes was published in 1919 and contained original compositions with titles such as *Threatening Danger (Andante Dramatico)*, *Wild Chase (Allegro Vivace)*, *Tragic Moments (Andante Mosso)*, and *Happy Ending (Andante Largo)*. Musical encyclopedias circulated and were produced worldwide. In prerevolutionary Russia, for example, Anatoli Goldobin and Boris Azancheyev published *Accompanying Cinematograph Pictures on the Piano* (1912).

Originally composed musical scores would soon emerge as an important phenomenon. Although original scores were written as early as the 1890s, the trend can be traced to the influx of art-music composers to the film industry in the early twentieth century. In France, Camille Saint-Saëns scored *L'assassinat du duc de Guise* (1908); in Russia, Mikhail Ippolitov-Ivanov wrote music for *Stenka Raza* (1908); in Italy, Piero Mascagni composed for *Rapsodia satanica* (1915). These scores, for the most part, did not accompany films outside their country of origin. Sometimes foreign films would have original scores created for them in the countries where they arrived: composer Theófrastos Sakellarídis, for instance, scored the Italian import *The Nine Stars* in 1917 for Greek screenings. By the 1920s, composers were routinely commissioned to produce original music for big budget, high profile films around the world: in France, Darius Milhaud for *L'inhumaine* (1924), Arthur Honegger for *La roue* (1923) and *Napoleon* (1927), and Erik Satie for *Entr'acte* (1924); in Germany, Gottfried Huppertz for *Metropolis* (1927) and Edmund Meisel for the Berlin premiere of Soviet filmmaker Sergei Eisenstein's *Battleship Potemkin* (1925); in the Soviet Union, Meisel for *October* (1928) and *The Blue Express* (1929) and Dmitri Shostakovich for *The New Babylon* (1929); in Greece, Manólos Skouloúdis' for *Daphnis and Chloe* (1931); in Argentina, José Ferreyra for his own *La muchacha del arrabal* (1922); and in Iran, Ebrahim Moradi for his own *Bolhavas* (1933). Related to these is the unusual case of Teinsoke Kinugasa, who composed a score for his silent film *A Page of Madness* (1926) when it was rediscovered and rereleased in 1975, almost fifty years after its initial release.

Issues in Research

A history of film music as a global phenomenon, such as the one I have sketched here, is at best provisional and tentative. There are many difficulties. Much of the earliest musical accompaniment to moving images (and this is true globally) was ephemeral: lost to time, or never written down in the first place. Even in the rare instances where actual scores have survived, they can be difficult to interpret in terms of how and when the music might have accompanied a series of images. Even the term "accompaniment" can have a variety of meanings during the period.

Reconstructing the history of film music is dependent upon surviving related sources: newspaper accounts of film screenings, reviews, first-hand accounts of musical accompaniment, trade publications, cue sheets, film-music encyclopedias, and how-to manuals. Even some of these sources, especially first-hand accounts, are rare and all of them can be subjective and even unreliable. Caution is always in order.

Unfortunately, access to these types of resources is limited by the time and money it would take to unearth the materials, not to mention the required fluency in the languages. Thus, in writing this history, I have relied upon scholars who have done this spade work. Although there is now a growing body of work on the global practice of film music, much of it is focused on the sound era; scholarship on the silent era is just now beginning to come to light. The journal *Film History* has been a beacon here. Scholars writing histories of national cinemas outside Hollywood have also begun to attend to music, such as Yuri Tsivian in his *Early Cinema in Russia and Its Cultural Reception* and Mary Farquhar and Chris Berry in their "Shadow Opera: Towards a New Archeology of the Chinese Cinema," in the anthology *Chinese-language Film: Historiography, Poetics,*

Politics. Indeed the history of film music itself is beginning to be written and global practices in the silent era have been highlighted in a few of these: Tatiana K. Egorova's *Soviet
Film Music: An Historical Survey*; Martin Marks's *Music and the Silent Film: Contexts
and Case Studies, 1895–1924*; and Mervyn Cooke's sweeping *A History of Film Music*.

The lack of primary resources globally has left gaping holes in our knowledge of
accompaniment in the silent era as it was practiced around the world. I would like to end
here by highlighting one topic that begs for further research: the role of popular music.
A key element of musical accompaniment, popular music nevertheless chafed against
the growing standardization of musical practices for silent film. As cue sheets and musical encyclopedias developed, which customized accompaniment for specific films or for
particular narrative and emotive situations, popular music, which often bore little relationship to the images other than a title, was increasingly understood as a problem. In
the United States, the Hungarian émigré Ernö Rapée crusaded against the use of popular
music in silent-film accompaniment through his various positions at several New York
cinemas in the 1920s. He was not entirely successful in his quest—audiences liked hearing popular tunes and they were not afraid to make their feelings known at screenings.
In addition, when sound film transformed the industry in the late 1920s and 1930s, film
producers gravitated to popular music, filling the soundtracks of a new genre, the musical, with popular songs, but also inserting popular songs into films no matter what their
genre or subject matter. This use of popular song became central to sound film globally
with indigenous popular songs filling the soundtracks of films produced in countries
such as Mexico, the Soviet Union, China, Hong Kong, India, Iran, and Egypt.

Studies on the impact of race and ethnicity on film reception in the United States
have shown that popular music was sometimes used as an expression of subcultural
tastes, practices, and values. Mary Carbine's research on African American cinemas in
Chicago, for instance, reveals that although films screened there had been produced
for white audiences, the musical accompaniment was jazz, played by black musicians
who privileged the music over the film and gave their musical performance free rein
(Carbine 1996). Here a form of popular music, jazz, functioned transgressively, interrupting the film's hold over the audience, becoming a site of cultural struggle.

It would be valuable to know much of this transgressive potential was tapped in other
places around the globe, especially where indigenous popular musics played so important a role: Brazil, India, China, Hong Kong, Japan, and Iran. Indigenous popular music
functioned, of course, as an expression of national identity, especially in indigenous
films, but there is evidence to suggest that some foreign films were also screened with
indigenous music in Japan, in India, in Iran, and perhaps many other places globally.
One striking example of the effects created by culturally idiosyncratic practices is the
early Japanese film entrepreneur Toyohiro Takematsu, who screened films while providing his own voiceover mistranslation, thus transforming films, no matter what their
original politics, into examples of his own socialist views. Something similar happened
in Korea during the Japanese occupation. When police were not present at film screenings, the *byeonsa* would inject criticism of the Japanese as part of their narration. More
research into what happened when foreign films were screened with indigenous popular

music might yield fascinating and crucial insights into the extent that musical accompaniment transformed moving images, translated them, or even challenged them in the way that voiceover narration could and apparently sometimes did.

Music functioned as a cultural interface throughout the silent era in a way quite different from the sound era. Although studios attempted to control the music that accompanied their films through cue sheets and original film scores that circulated with the films, these resources were often ignored: by cinema owners, who hired their own musical directors to create unique accompaniments; by accompanists, who did not want their hands tied by a preprogrammed score; and by audiences, who asserted their own musical tastes and thus influenced theater owners and accompanists in the creation of musical accompaniments. In the sound period, music came under the firm control of film producers, who hired the composers and had final control over the scores. Silent-film accompaniment functioned differently with the power over accompaniment dispersed over a number of individuals such as theater owners, musical directors, influential accompanists, and even audiences. Thus music in the silent era had an impressive power to interact with moving images in ways not controlled by films or their producers. To what extent did musical accompaniment around the world tap this potential to function transgressively as a medium of critique, particularly of the West, where so many of the foreign films screened globally were produced? Only with further research can we hope to find answers.

BIBLIOGRAPHY

Abel, Richard, and Rick Altman, eds. 2001. *The Sounds of Early Cinema*. Bloomington: Indiana University Press.

Carbine, Mary. 1996. "The Finest Outside the Loop: Motion Pictures Exhibition in Chicago's Black Metropolis: 1905–1928." In *Silent Film*, edited by Richard Abel, 234–62. New Brunswick, NJ: Rutgers University Press.

Cooke, Mervyn. 2008. "The 'Silent' Cinema." In *A History of Film Music*, 1–41. Cambridge: Cambridge University Press.

Egorova, Tatiana K. 1997. "Music and Silent Cinema." In *Soviet Film Music: An Historical Survey*, translated by Tatiana A. Ganf and Natalia A. Egunova, 3–13. Amsterdam: Harwood.

Farquhar, Mary, and Chris Berry. 1995. "Shadow Opera: Towards a New Archeology of the Chinese Cinema." In *Chinese-Language Film: Historiography, Poetics, Politics*, edited by Sheldon H. Lu and Emilie (Yueh-yu) Yeh, 27–51. Honolulu: University of Hawaii Press.

Film History. (1987–). See especially 14, no. 1 (2002): Special Issue on Film Music.

Gallez, Douglas W. 1976. "Satie's *Entr'acte*: A Model of Film Music." *Cinema Journal* 16, no. 1: 36–50.

Kalinak, Kathryn. 2010. "A History of Film Music I: 1895–1927." In *Film Music: A Very Short Introduction*, 32–50. New York: Oxford University Press.

King, Norman. 1996. "The Sound of Silents." In *Silent Film*, edited by Richard Abel, 32–44. New Brunswick, NJ: Rutgers University Press.

Marks, Martin Miller. 1997. *Music and the Silent Film: Contexts and Case Studies, 1895–1924*. New York: Oxford University Press.

Ogihara, Junko. 1990. "The Exhibition of Films for Japanese Americans in Los Angeles During the Silent Era." *Film History* 4, no. 2: 81–87.

Rapée, Ernö. 1924. *Motion Picture Moods, for Pianists and Organists*. New York: Schirmer. Reprint, New York: Arno, 1970.

——. 1925. *Encyclopedia of Music for Pictures*. New York: Belwin. Reprint, New York: Arno, 1970.

Robinson, David. 1990. "Music of the Shadows: The Use of Musical Accompaniment with Silent Films, 1896–1936." *Le giornate del cinema muto, Pordenone. Supplemento a Griffithiana* 13, nos. 38–39: 1–19.

Tsivian, Yuri. 1994. "The Acoustics of Cinema Performance." In *Early Cinema in Russia and Its Cultural Reception*, translated by Alan Bodger, 78–103. London: Routledge.

Zamecnik, J. S. 1913. *Moving Picture Music*, Vol. 1. Cleveland: Sam Fox.

CHAPTER 25

PERFORMING PRESTIGE: AMERICAN CINEMA ORCHESTRAS, 1910–1958

NATHAN PLATTE[1]

ORCHESTRAS serving theatrical and commercial venues in the early twentieth century provided employment for many, but the work was not always satisfying. Writing in the *Los Angeles Times* on January 28, 1917, Edwin Schallert complained that "the bane of the orchestral musician's career as far as his advance in work of higher class goes is his inability, for financial reasons, to avoid the drudgery of café and theater playing." But Schallert also saw improvement on the horizon: "Of late, however, there has been a certain degree of artistic compensation in this extraneous employment, which is probably showing its beneficial influence now, in the opportunity for the musician to play in the orchestras for big feature pictures."

Unfortunately, the good fortune that Schallert describes lasted only a decade, through the short-lived era of the picture palace. Traditional symphonic orchestras have accompanied "silent" and sound films for more than a century, but the transformation in the late 1920s from a live, performing ensemble in the theater to a recorded, bodiless entity in the sound film contributed greatly to the orchestra's subsequent neglect. Once reviewed by press critics and touted in theater advertisements, the orchestras for silent cinemas were perceived as both a cultural boon for audiences and an economic stimulus for theaters and symphonic players. "The time has come," averred Victor Wagner (1926, 42), "when the motion picture theater orchestra is receiving universal recognition as an organization of artists who are working to achieve and maintain a high standard in a distinct art." In the same year Hugo Riesenfeld wrote that "he musician today is in demand as he never was before. Think of the army of them necessary to man the orchestras in our 18,000 film theatres." The year 1926, however, also saw the first feature-film deployment of Warner Bros.' new high-fidelity synchronized sound system, Vitaphone, a

development that marked the beginning of the end for orchestras in moving picture theaters. By the early 1930s, most theaters had disbanded them. A few hundred symphonic
musicians in Hollywood now fulfilled a service previously provided by thousands across
the country. The press and audiences paid little attention to these recording orchestras
that they frequently heard but rarely—if ever—saw. In 1948, Lawrence Morton would
observe: "Hollywood's musicians are perhaps the most productive workers in the world
today. About 450 of them serve a weekly audience of 80 million people.... These men
and women... certainly deserve more honor than they get."

The history of the American movie orchestra from its emergence in the 1910s through
the fall of Hollywood studio orchestras in the late 1950s reveals that these ensembles
contributed considerably more to cinematic culture than background music for sound
films. Movie orchestras also announced and sustained American cinema's status as
prestigious, middle-brow entertainment, they helped theaters and production studios
to distinguish themselves from the competition, and they promoted new technologies
and formats. Often, movie orchestras fulfilled these tasks in performances outside the
feature films they accompanied, during those (admittedly brief) times when the orchestras themselves occupied the limelight. With the exception of concerts given by movie
orchestras in the silent era, these occasions have received little attention from scholars. These performances of prestige, in which orchestral concerts bolstered theaters' or
studios' cultural cachet, are the focus of this chapter.[2] Analysis and contextualization of
these events show how movie orchestras brought the symphony to the cinema, and how
they changed critical perceptions of both in the process.

THEATER ORCHESTRAS OF THE SILENT ERA

As Gillian Anderson has noted, "orchestral forces had been available for silent film
accompaniment since the moving pictures were first presented in vaudeville theaters"
(1987, 259), but orchestral accompaniment remained a rare and typically ineffective performance practice in motion picture theaters until the mid-1910s. Most theater managers kept only a pianist, organist, or violinist, who might be joined by a drummer. Select
theaters occasionally featured ensembles, but self-described "large orchestras" in 1912
Nickelodeons consisted of just four to twelve musicians (Altman 2004, 289).

Musical standards varied widely from theater to theater, and contemporary accounts
suggest that some ensembles presented more in the way of liability than service. William
McCracken, for example, began his letter to the editor of *Moving Picture World* (January
28, 1911) with this lament: "But oh! Such torture as we were obliged to suffer while in that
place was indescribable," and then detailed the shortcomings of the six-piece orchestra,
whose members were "there all right, but very little music was rendered, for they never
started to play to a picture until it was almost over, and when the end of the picture
appeared they shut off the music abruptly"; furthermore, "when a comic picture was
on the screen; they did not play at all [but instead] got up and scattered through the

audience." McCracken, who praised a solo pianist at one theater over the substandard orchestra he describes here, was not alone in his evaluation. Many commentators felt that orchestras were more prone to inadequacy, as they required more organization, rehearsal time, and collective talent than a solo pianist. Too many theater managers and music directors were simply not interested or vigilant enough to ensure satisfying results. Clyde Martin, a theater pianist and columnist for *Film Index*, also found superior musical accompaniment at a cheap theater with a good pianist and drummer after being disappointed by the tacit orchestra at a more expensive theater: "It is the same old story every place you go, an orchestra either plays long andantes and waltzes, or they sit and watch the picture " (*Film Index*, December 10, 1910). Rick Altman's observation that "when orchestras were mentioned [in the trade presses], it was most often to decry their uselessness for accompanying motion pictures" serves as an important reminder that orchestras did not emerge as preferred cinematic accompaniment until after many critics had written them off (Altman 2004, 290).

The construction of picture palaces in Manhattan and other urban centers starting in the mid-1910s, the advocacy of exhibitor Samuel L. "Roxy" Rothafel, and the release of longer, more ambitious films drastically changed the role and status of cinema orchestras (Anderson 1987, 259; Altman 2004, 290–95). D. W. Griffith's *The Birth of a Nation* (1915) was particularly important in this regard. Both Anderson and Altman emphasize the importance of orchestral music in its exhibition. Altman even notes that when the film toured the country, advertisements promised audiences a large orchestra, even in small towns not accustomed to enjoying one at their local movie theater (Altman 2004, 294).

Devoted to facilitating the upward mobility of cinema from cheap amusement to theatrical entertainment, Rothafel demonstrated music's potential to increase a theater's competitive edge. Music performed by a well-rehearsed orchestra, he argued, would draw middle and upper class clientele and justify higher prices. But Rothafel's goals were more ambitious than just providing "suitable music." His theaters, orchestras, and the films that soon played on the screens marked a new style of cinematic exhibition that intertwined film's established mass appeal with the trappings of economic privilege and elitism. His theaters overflowed with sonic and visual excess. The Roxy Theatre in New York marked the pinnacle of his efforts when it opened in 1927. Among its spectacular features and amenities were a "vast marble Grand Lobby rotunda, with its two-story crystal chandelier and enormous round carpet,...elaborate ladies' and gentlemen's lounges and a vast auditorium seating 5,920, richly decorated in eclectic Renaissance style." The music department, which "boasted four conductors, including Erno Rapée and Charles Previn, also the chorus master," was treated equally well: "both orchestra pit and stage had hydraulic elevators, as did the three organ consoles, [there] were comfortable dressing rooms, rehearsal facilities, a vast music library, and Roxy's office" (Dorris 1995, 88).

At this establishment and in other theaters large enough to afford such orchestras, elaborate musical programs supplemented the showing of films (Altman 2004, 291). Overtures and other orchestral selections, such as individual movements from

symphonies, began the programs and usually featured familiar, nineteenth-century repertoire. At Rothafel's Rialto Theater, for example, Hugo Riesenfeld conducted Wagner's
Overture to *Tannhäuser*, Tchaikovsky's *Capriccio Italien*, Liszt's *Les Preludes*, Rossini's
Overture to *William Tell*, and other nineteenth-century warhorses (Anderson 1987, 274).
Operatic selections, movements from concertos, and other musical numbers rounded
out the programs, which could become so long—and were promoted so heavily by their
theaters—it "almost became a case of the tail wagging the dog" (Hubbard 1985, 429–30).

Theater advertisements regularly billed the orchestras and their conductors, and the
performances were reviewed in the press. The *New York Dramatic Mirror*, for example,
supplemented columns on film music with reviews of musical programs featured at
movie theaters: "The Rivoli set overture came back last week in the shape of the second and last movements of Tschaikowsky's Fourth Symphony. The orchestra and Erno
Rapée had to respond to the burst of applause that greeted the rendition of this work"
(March 8, 1919). May Johnson of the *Musical Courier* also made weekly rounds to major
New York movie theaters to report in more detail on featured repertoire, soloists, and
exceptional orchestral musicians. In a review dated July 12, 1923, she observed that "The
overture [at the Capitol] was the second Hungarian rhapsody, with an original violin
cadenza specially written by David Mendoza, associate conductor. This cadenza was
played by Eugene Ormandy, concertmaster, with impressive mastery." The language
with which she characterizes Ormandy's playing is indistinguishable from that of a concert review: "This young man has become a fine player in the last two years. His tone is
of notable breadth and quality, his musicianship excellent, and he plays with a surety of
intonation that many a more famous colleague might envy him."

Johnson's role as music critic at a movie theater is an unusual one, made all the more
striking by her comments on the films: "The musical program [at the Rivoli], one is
sorry to say, had to take secondary place, not because it fell below the usual standards,
but for the simple reason that all were very much absorbed in the film" (*Musical Courier*,
August 9, 1923). Not all—or even most—orchestras merited the attention of serious
music critics, however. After visiting a smaller theater, Johnson reflected: "The conductor…noticeably had difficulty in controlling the tempi and keeping a semblance of
co-ordination. It only takes a performance like this on the part of an orchestra to make
one appreciate the excellence of these large Broadway theaters, where the organization has been held together for years with the same conductors and the same players"
(*Musical Courier*, October, 4, 1923).

Although most commentators, like Johnson, tended to focus on the orchestras of the
Manhattan picture palaces, William Clune's and Sid Grauman's musical investments in
Los Angeles were arguably more impressive, in part because of their impact on a city
with fewer established musical organizations. William Clune helped institute orches-
tral accompaniment in Los Angeles theaters by hiring an eight-piece orchestra for his
Broadway Theater in 1910 and hiring a larger (and much praised) ensemble for the
Temple Auditorium in 1914. Four years later, Sid Grauman's theater orchestras grew in
size and prominence to quickly become a major component of the city's music scene.
In early 1918, over a year before the Los Angeles Philharmonic held its first rehearsal,

Grauman's Million Dollar Theatre had permanently engaged a thirty-piece orchestra directed by Rudolf Kopp and the Theatre's opening featured a special performance by the orchestra with coloratura soprano Lina Reggiana. By August of 1919, Kopp's replacement, Arthur Kay, had begun performing what would nowadays be called pops concerts before films. Reporting on the upcoming event, Edwin Schallert assured readers that the "Grauman orchestra is sufficiently large to permit of the presentation of a large repertoire of musical compositions" (*Los Angeles Times*, August 7, 1919). (By then the orchestra had approximately thirty-five members.) Fearful that this trend might damage the city's nascent symphonic ensembles, music critic Jeanne Redman warned patrons that musicians were turning to theater orchestras for better pay and leaving the city's symphony orchestra, where a position "is more an honorary title than a steady employment" (*Los Angeles Times*, June 8, 1919). "Does the public understand," asked Redman, "that Arthur Kay, who has been first cellist, and even substitute conductor of the Boston Symphony Orchestra, is conducting at Grauman's?" In spring of 1920, Kay received permission from Grauman to embark on an independent series of Sunday morning concerts with a newly enlarged orchestra of seventy-five players. "One of the most imposing bodies of instrumentalists ever assembled for concerts in a theatre devoted primarily to photoplay entertainment," noted Schallert (*Los Angeles Times*, May 20, 1920). The first concert, which "played to a very large audience," received a thorough and positive review from a newly supportive Jeanne Redman, who now heralded the Grauman orchestra as a credit to the city. She also noted (and praised) members of the Los Angeles Philharmonic seen among the orchestra (*Los Angeles Times*, June 7, 1920). The program featured Wagner's Overture to *Tannhäuser*, "Irish Melody" and "Shepherd's Hey" by Percy Grainger, the Adagio movement from Dvořák's "New World" Symphony, and the third movement from Tchaikovsky's Fourth Symphony. By mid-summer, Schallert proclaimed the Grauman Symphony Orchestra to be one of the city's most vibrant musical institutions:

> Those who have watched the orchestral concerts at Grauman's during the past year have come to realize that it needed only the proper scheme of reaching the public to rouse a more widespread appreciation for music. Practically every one of these affairs have drawn a capacity attendance. Enthusiasm has reigned at the concerts. The audiences have demonstrated their highest approval of this form of diversion and this in the height of the summer season, when melody and harmony are generally sent on a vacation.
>   …It is not at all impossible that a third symphony orchestra…may be the result of the progress which Arthur Kay and his men have made…. The personnel is chiefly made up from the present membership of the Philharmonic and Los Angeles Symphony orchestras. It is shown that both of these bodies have co-operated in various ways, because they recognize that the move is essentially beneficial to their interests. Mr. Kay's orchestra is playing to a public that is not ordinarily reached by the symphony concert, and he is creating a desire on the part of this public to hear the other organizations…. While our picture theaters will never become symphony concert halls…the effort which they are putting forth will exercise and influence…. They are making opera and symphonic music popular—something that probably could never have been accomplished in the broader sense without their aid. (*Los Angeles Times*, July 25, 1920)

Nor were Grauman and Kay alone in their efforts, as Schallert was quick to add: "Practically all the larger houses are now making a feature of melodic entertainment. The California Theater offers an ensemble chorus, the Kinema, at various times has staged tabloid versions of opera, while the Victory has been having a great success with a group of soloists." In a city with fewer musical opportunities than New York, the orchestras of Los Angeles's movies theaters had quickly assumed an integral role in the city's cultural life.

For the latter half of the 1910s and into the 1920s, Grauman, Roxy, and other metropolitan film exhibitors continued to support large cinema orchestras as a means of distinguishing their theaters as sites for entertainment that was simultaneously prestigious, edifying, and accessible to the masses. As we noted above in the case of Los Angeles, orchestras not only improved the cinematic experience, they also contributed positively to cities' cultural life beyond the theater. The shift in moviegoers' taste away from pianists to the previously vilified orchestra is especially vivid in a column by Emerson Whithorne (*Musical Courier*, August 5, 1926), in which he reports that he "had occasion to see a feature film run off twice in an afternoon at one of New York's leading emporiums of the silent drama. During the first presentation the orchestra played a tolerable accompaniment to the screen drama; but what was my amazement to hear the organist perform an entirely different score at its second showing." The critic was not impressed by this effort at originality: "I have no doubt that the musical director having gone forth to an early dinner, the organist let his fancy roam and gave what he in turn considered a superior accompaniment to the picture. The urge to self-expression is strong in all of us."

Emulating the impressive results achieved at these larger theaters now became the primary goal, regardless of the size of one's theater. Smaller cities could never afford seventy-five member orchestras, but the pursuit of this ideal created great opportunity for orchestra musicians. Drawing from columns printed in *American Organist*, Gillian Anderson emphasizes the high financial priority exhibitors placed on their house orchestras: "The pit orchestras in 1929 at the best houses cost between $3,000 and $10,000 a week. At the Roxy Theater the bill was between $15,000 and $20,000 a week.... By 1926 the musicians in the Broadway houses were earning $83 a week, in the vaudeville houses $63 a week" (Anderson 1987, 65). The pay was exceptional, but hours were long. Labor historian James Kraft writes that in 1925, "most theater musicians performed seven days a week during 'seasons' that ranged from 30 to 52 weeks depending, in the days before air conditioning, on location." In addition to performing every day of the week, "musicians performed between five and seven hours [daily], typically divided between one or two evening shows and an afternoon matinee. Orchestras [also] had to rehearse, and rehearsals lengthened the work day" (Kraft 1994b, 71).

Despite the taxing lifestyle, theater orchestras in the late 1910s and 1920s provided employment for tens of thousands of musicians and made orchestral music a regular part of the moviegoing experience in many cities. Rick Altman refers to these years as the "golden era of silent film music," in part because the construction of film scores improved considerably. But these years also mark the golden era of the cinema orchestra in the twentieth century; never again would orchestras playing for moviegoers receive such extended coverage, praise, or performance opportunities.

Vitaphone's Possibilities and Perils

When Warner Bros. unveiled its new Vitaphone sound system in New York on August 6, 1926, the gala event was introduced by a filmed speech from Motion Picture Producers and Distributors of America president Will H. Hays who proclaimed, with many a dramatic pause: "The motion picture…is a most potent factor in the development of a national appreciation of good music. That service will now be extended as the Vitaphone shall carry symphony orchestration to the town halls of the hamlets." (Hays 2011).

To prove his point, a film of the New York Philharmonic performing Wagner's overture to *Tannhäuser* (*Overture: Tannhäuser*, 1926) opened the program, clearly imitating the practice of preceding a film with an orchestral overture that had been a popular pick at picture palaces on both coasts. A musical program of recital pieces, operatic excerpts, and novelty performances followed, again in keeping with the practice of Broadway's theaters. The feature of the evening, *Don Juan* (1926; starring John Barrymore) had no dialogue, but it did have a synchronized orchestral score performed by the New York Philharmonic (the soundtrack also included a few sound effects). Thus, Vitaphone's premiere offered little more than a canned performance of music offerings similar to those heard at Roxy's theaters. There were, however, three significant differences. First, the performers were more renowned. Associate conductor Henry Hadley and the New York Philharmonic, singers Giovanni Martinelli and Marion Talley, violinists Efrem Zimbalist and Mischa Elman, and even the Metropolitan Opera chorus contributed to the evening's entertainment. The New York Philharmonic was certainly not a theater orchestra, but it functioned in that role for this film by providing the overture and recorded musical accompaniment, thereby assuring a level of musical prestige beyond even that of Rothafel's theater orchestras. Second, the performances were replicable and distributable; pending the licensing of Vitaphone technology, theaters in the "town halls of the hamlets" would soon be able to enjoy the very same music. Third, the audiovisual experience of watching an orchestra perform *on film* altered audience members' perception of the orchestra, a factor commented upon by critics. Mordaunt Hall noted that "During the exhibition of this subject the screen scenes swayed from those of the whole body of musicians to small groups as each instrumental choir took up its work" (*New York Times*, August 7, 1926).

Viewed today, the "swaying" scenes appear rather jolting. One camera is stationed as though in the audience, at a distance far enough to fit all 107 members of the orchestra within its frame. Shots from this camera are interspersed with medium shots from a second camera that occasionally pans in a bumpy fashion across members of the orchestra. The operator of this roaming camera had not been prepped on the score, however, so that in one shot he swings the camera hurriedly across the orchestra in search of trumpets and trombones carrying the melody. Such lapses were not missed by the anonymous reviewer from the *Musical Courier* (August 12, 1926), who, like Mordaunt Hall, was nonetheless impressed by the film's audio quality and visual structures: "This was something decidedly impressive, the reproduction of the music being far the best yet produced, the only possible criticism being that the bass end of the tonal spectrum does not quite achieve its proper value in quantity. The reproduction of tone colors, however, is perfect." Not only audio quality but also synchronization drew the reviewer's praise: "The coordination of the picture of the playing orchestra and the music is startlingly impressive." Image editing also enhanced the presentation, as "long shots showing the complete orchestra at work, were made alternating with close-ups showing the various orchestral groups."

As the leading article of the issue (a picture of conductor Henry Hadley adorned the journal's cover), the *Courier* review conveys excitement and a sense of occasion; its critique of the evening's musical content is one of the most detailed and insightful records of the evening. The reviewer was less enchanted with Hays's speech—"a good comedy act, for Mr. Hays had evidently been instructed to make, for the sake of the camera, as many gestures as possible, in an address loaded from beginning to end with bromidic platitudes"—but largely agreed with its message on orchestral possibilities. The reviewer noted that "the orchestra accompaniment [for *Don Juan*], which had been recorded for the Vitaphone by the New York Philharmonic, Henry Hadley conducting, was the most effective part of the whole evening's demonstration." The recorded soundtrack permitted some improvement on typical exhibition practices. For example, "there is no break-up after the first ten minutes of the picture, to see all the rest accompanied by organ which, even in the hands of an expert player, is an unsatisfactory substitute." In addition, "there are no orchestra players and conductors to disturb the line of vision with their movements and their going and coming."

The *Courier* reviewer was not alone in thinking that Vitaphone would primarily serve smaller theaters. Hugo Riesenfeld, one of Roxy's premiere conductors, would similarly remark that "it is not probable that the Vitaphone will ever entirely replace the orchestra, but it does make it possible for certain films requiring the finest musical accompaniment to be shown in places where there is no orchestra available" (1926, 61). As it turned out, the success of Warner Bros.' Vitaphone system—and the eventual dismissal of live musicians from movie theaters—would be prompted less by the New York Philharmonic accompanying *Don Juan* than by the voice of Al Jolson in *The Jazz Singer* (1927).

Although most film historians agree that it was this later film and not *Don Juan* that marked the tipping point toward sound films, the Vitaphone premiere with the New York Philharmonic, nevertheless, proved more influential for the future of movie orchestras. First, it facilitated the carryover of orchestral accompaniment from silent to sound film by reaffirming the orchestra's contribution to drama and—perhaps more compellingly—cinematic culture and prestige. Second, it linked the symphony orchestra with cinematic innovation and improvement, much in the same way that Roxy's and Grauman's orchestras had heralded a new style of movie exhibition set in lavish movie palaces.

If Vitaphone helped establish orchestral accompaniment in sound film, the advent of mechanically reproduced sound also initiated the rapid decline of orchestras for silent film. Alexander Walker notes that "the U.S. Bureau of Labor Statistics has estimated that in 1928 some 20,000 musicians were in the employ of movie theatres across the country: during the next two years alone, fifty per cent of them were sacked" (1979, 67). The orchestras did not go quietly, and Preston J. Hubbard (1985) and James Kraft (1994b) have documented extensive campaigns fought by the American Federation of Musicians to preserve the jobs of movie theater musicians across the country. At best, the unions only delayed the inevitable by two years. A sound system could be expensive, but the cost of installing one was still less than the cost of supporting an orchestra. Sound films also drew bigger audiences, thereby diminishing box office returns for silent films and the musicians that accompanied them (Kraft 1994b, 78–80).

Yet if the late 1920s witnessed the swift devastation of most movie theater orchestras (a circumstance only made worse by the Great Depression, which closed many theaters), those left standing remained longer than might be expected. As Kraft notes, "as late as 1933, the Paramount, Pantages, Chinese, and Mayan theaters in Hollywood still had sixteen-to-eighteen piece orchestras, while smaller houses such as the Orpheum, Manchester, and Million Dollar employed four-to-eight piece bands" (1994a, 269). In January 1931, the characteristically extravagant Rothafel supported a series of benefit concerts for unemployed musicians that featured his theater's 125-member orchestra augmented by seventy-five out-of-work instrumentalists. *Musical Courier* critics praised these concerts, and Rothafel even received a medal from the music division of the Federation of Women's Clubs. Reflecting on Rothafel's support of symphonic music in movie theaters, one critic mused on his civic contributions, no doubt aware that such performances would not continue much longer: "When Roxy opened his magnificent picture palace not quite four years ago he installed a first class symphony orchestra in it, engaged eminent conductors, and ever since has been giving hundreds of thousands of people each year the opportunity of hearing the best music at minimal prices of admission." Given that a minority of these cinema patrons could afford to attend symphony concerts or operas, the critic argues that "Roxy is instilling in the masses an understanding of and a love for the best there is in music" (*Musical Courier*, January 24, 1931).

Hollywood Studio Orchestras on Film

Despite the auspicious beginning with Hadley and the New York Philharmonic, the sight of a performing orchestra in American sound films became a rare phenomenon before long, with preference instead going to popular dance bands and vaudeville performers. The New York Philharmonic did make a second Vitaphone short of a performance of the overture to *William Tell* in 1926, and another handful of orchestra film shorts were made in 1926–1927 with the "Vitaphone Symphony Orchestra" conducted by Herman Heller. In 1935 Warner Bros. considered an orchestral short for the studio's prestige film, Shakespeare's *A Midsummer Night's Dream* (1935). As executive producer Hal Wallis noted, a filmed orchestral performance would have recalled the studio's prestigious Vitaphone shorts of the late 1920s, but the project was scrapped and viewers instead watched music director Erich Wolfgang Korngold perform at the piano as part of *A Dream Comes True* (1935), a short devoted to behind-the-scenes work (Platte 2011, 226–33). This shift from orchestra to composer-arranger reflected Hollywood's broader treatment of film music in the classical sound film era. Critical commentary focused increasingly on prominent composers: Max Steiner, Alfred Newman, Dimitri Tiomkin, and Miklós Rózsa, among others. With few exceptions, public discourse ignored studio orchestras. By the late 1930s, when a small company titled Symphonic Films, Inc., produced a series of filmed orchestral performances with Frederick Feher as conductor, the genre seemed to have run its course.

The practice of featuring orchestral music apart from the feature film itself, however, did continue in a limited fashion. Films that received roadshow tours in large cities before general release often carried musical supplements: namely, a recorded orchestral overture that played before the main titles, usually while the theater's lights were up and the curtain was closed. As roadshow exhibitions typically included intermissions, entr'acte music and even exit music could also be added in a similar manner. These overtures and entr'actes featured music from the film's score as opposed to concert-hall works. In all of these cases, the playing of orchestral music around, rather than during, the film offered additional exposure of the film's original themes and, to a limited degree, the uncredited orchestra members. In lieu of their planned orchestral film for *A Midsummer Night's Dream*, for example, Warner Bros. included a prefilm overture recording instead. Later the studio indulged in live performances at Hollywood premieres, with Korngold conducting the studio orchestra in specially arranged overtures for *Juarez* (1939), *The Private Lives of Elizabeth and Essex* (1939), and *The Constant Nymph* (1943) (Carroll 1997, 282).[3]

Although prefilm overtures preserved at least something of the historical practice of preceding feature films with orchestral music, the use of original themes from the film's score had the effect of reinforcing the film composer's contribution and underplaying the musicians, who remained—with the rare exception of the live Korngold performances—confined to the soundtrack and invisible to the audience. MGM offered an intriguing alternative in the 1950s when it released six film shorts of its studio orchestra. Audiences in 1953 no longer expected a classical overture before the main feature as they had in the 1910s, 1920s, and early 1930s, but the studio's films from 1953 and 1954 hearkened back to this practice, even featuring similar repertoire (see Figure 25.1).

Earlier in his career, MGM's music director, Johnny Green, had himself participated in live performances at movie palaces. Reminiscing on his days as conductor at a Brooklyn movie palace he remarked, "It was tremendous training, and then, of course, the golden moment for an apprentice conductor was when he was allowed to do the Overture on the 5 o'clock show" (Bernstein 1976, 312).

The MGM films marked a twofold celebration. On the one hand, they commemorated orchestras' historic relationship with cinematic exhibition, technology, and prestige. On the other, they elevated MGM's orchestra as a distinguishing facet of the studio. By rendering the orchestra through a particular visual aesthetic and emphasizing orchestral members, the films projected MGM's corporate identity through the image of a performing orchestra, an idea closely related to Rothafel's and Grauman's uses of orchestras to

Title (Premiere Date)	Conductor	Film Director	Paired Feature Film
Capriccio Italien (3 June 1953)	Johnny Green	George Sidney	*Julius Caesar*
Merry Wives of Windsor (22 December 1953)	Johnny Green	George Sidney	*Knights of the Round Table*
Poet and Peasant Overture (3 March 1954)	Alfred Wallenstein (director of the Los Angeles Philharmonic)	George Sidney	*Rose Marie*
M-G-M Jubilee Overture (15 June 1954)	Johnny Green	George Sidney	*The Student Prince*
La Gazza Ladra (15 July 1954)	Johnny Green	Charles Vidor	*Seven Brides for Seven Brothers*
Strauss Fantasy (8 September 1954)	Johnny Green	Vincente Minnelli	*Brigadoon*

FIGURE 25.1 The six films of the MGM Concert Hall

distinguish their theaters. But whereas the orchestras of the picture palaces could be seen and heard in person on a daily basis, the MGM films offered an enticing glimpse of an otherwise invisible studio orchestra, revealed on film through an attractive lens of artifice.

In addition to alluding to silent-era prestige, the MGM films also served to promote new technology. Just as the New York Philharmonic short had helped introduce sound film in 1926, the MGM films helped sell emerging cinematic formats. The first film of the series, a performance of an abridged *Capriccio Italien* (1953), featured stereophonic sound (Rózsa 1982, 161). Stereo had been introduced in commercial cinema with another orchestra film—Disney's *Fantasia* (1940)—but did not catch on in theaters until it was reintroduced by studios in 1953. The orchestra proved especially effective in demonstrating the technology: Tchaikovsky's penchant for opposing choirs of strings, brass, and woodwinds emphasized the soundtrack's new spatiality, with the source of sound correlated aurally with players' onscreen positions.

The five remaining films revealed a still more ambitious agenda. They were printed in Technicolor and featured a recent widescreen format: CinemaScope, which expanded the screen to almost twice its standard width. The MGM orchestra also received a new "concert hall," its chief distinguishing characteristic being color: a dazzling pink. The image of tuxedoed and black-gowned musicians performing against the raucous shade ensured that audiences would never mistake MGM's orchestra for any other ensemble performing anywhere else. By then it was a distinction worth making, as MGM had competition.

Later in 1953, 20th Century Fox's *How to Marry a Millionaire* opened with a performance by the 20th Century Fox studio orchestra conducted by its music director, Alfred Newman. Shot in color, CinemaScope, and stereophonic sound with a seventy-three-piece orchestra, the performance challenged MGM's previously released *Capriccio Italien* in orchestra size and production values. Newman first conducts *Street Scene*, a composition originally written by him for a 1931 film of the same title. He then turns to face the camera, shrugs a bow, and strikes up the next selection: the opening credits music for the main feature.[4] When Charles Emge interviewed Newman about this unusual beginning, the director ignored MGM's *Capriccio* film and focused instead on the promotion of his own house ensemble. "Chances are," hypothesized Newman, "very few people ever noted the extraordinary work of our Russ Cheever (soprano sax) or John Clyman (trumpet), though I have featured them quite a bit in underscores. When audiences actually see them it will be different" (*Down Beat*, September 23, 1953).

By December 1953, Johnny Green and the MGM Symphony were back in theaters: in color, CinemaScope, stereophonic sound, and with a substantially larger orchestra of some ninety members. Instead of a short title sequence introducing the orchestra and its selection, an announcer introduces the group in the manner of a radio broadcast. It is telling that an early version of the announcer's script read "We are about to hear and see a performance of the ever popular Overture to 'The Merry Wives of Windsor.'" This statement sets the repertoire selection first, but the revised text emphasized continuity across films, as though the orchestra shorts comprised a subscription series: "We're about to hear and see *another* performance in the MGM Concert Hall." MGM's publicity department also played up the distinction between Alfred Newman's performance with the 20th Century Fox Orchestra, which was part of a feature film, and MGM's stand-alone short, *Overture to The Merry Wives of Windsor* (1953), the first of its kind to be filmed in CinemaScope, a point duly ballyhooed in newspaper ads.[5]

Visual style is another major difference between the two studio's orchestral films. Though vastly superior to the bumbling camera in the New York Philharmonic's *Tannhäuser*, the 20th Century Fox performance is nonetheless filmed in a perfunctory, unimaginative fashion. In the most elaborate shot of the film, the camera trucks around twice on what appears to be a triangular track, moving sideways across the front of the ensemble and then backwards and forwards. The orchestra members are viewed from a distance and the camera never passes beyond the conductor into the orchestra. The spectator occupies the position of a restless audience member, shifting from seat to seat but never actually entering the orchestra's ranks or viewing the conductor from the musicians' perspective. Not surprisingly, Bosley Crowther of the *New York Times* curtly dismissed the performance as "static, pretentious, and dull."

MGM's *Capriccio Italien* and *Merry Wives of Windsor* were directed by George Sidney, best known for his musicals, including *Annie Get Your Gun* (1950), *Show Boat* (1951), *Kiss Me Kate* (1953), *Pal Joey* (1957), and *Bye Bye Birdie* (1963). He had already directed scenes featuring instrumental soloists and orchestras in *Bathing Beauty* (1944), *Anchors Aweigh* (1945) and *Holiday in Mexico* (1946). Sidney went uncredited in the orchestra films, but his style is evident in the editing and motion of the camera, which characterize these films visually as cousins of the celebrated genre of MGM musicals. Sidney's contribution is at times charmingly simple, such as his playful introductions of Johnny Green, who might appear in front of the orchestra through a crafty lap dissolve or in a dramatic

FIGURE 25.2 Johnny Green conducts to an offscreen cello section at the opening of *The Merry Wives of Windsor* (1953).

cut. While the spectator watches musicians enter the stage and tune in the film of *Merry Wives of Windsor*, for example, Green is absent; he is revealed through an abrupt cut, as though he had just appeared magically. As he begins conducting, the camera shot excludes the orchestra musicians from the frame and focuses only on Green's hands. The camera angle suggests he is conjuring sound from thin air (see Figure 25.2).

Sidney's editing alternately divides and unites sections of the orchestra in visual terms that correspond with musical phrasing and orchestration, a technique that Eric Monder (1994, 18) also discerns in Sidney's feature-length musicals. For example, in *Merry Wives*, Sidney structures the opening passage as a single shot to give visual expression to an extended musical passage. As the cellos and violas play an ascending, lyrical line (mm. 2–10), the camera rotates slowly left across the section while pulling back and up to reveal the woodwinds, who engage in an alternating dialogue with the lower strings. A firm cadence sets the camera in motion again (m. 17), turning gently in a counter-clockwise direction to reveal the entire violin section, now carrying the melody the cellos had originally introduced. As the violins rise in tessitura, the camera crane slowly ascends, pulling the spectator upward as though to suggest a drift towards reverie. If Green was introduced as a wizard, the spectator is now given the vantage point of a god, looking down upon conductor and orchestra (see Figure 25.3). When the lyrical episode concludes, Sidney punctuates the shift to *poco più animato* (m. 32) with a cut. Every motion of the camera—laterally and vertically—in this minute-long shot is motivated by orchestration and register, an expression of musical texture through three-dimensional camera movement. In passages like these, Sidney's work calls to mind Marcia Citron's observations on filmed opera: "[The camera] is a powerful tool [that] guides what we see and how long we see it. In this way it controls not only the content of the image but its rhythm. This suggests a close connection with the rhythm of the music, and the manipulation of this relationship can lead to interesting results" (Citron 2000, 12).

FIGURE 25.3 The spectator looks down upon conductor and orchestra in *The Merry Wives of Windsor* (1953).

In other films, Sidney's musicovisual logic goes still further. In the *Poet and Peasant Overture* (1955), with guest conductor Alfred Wallenstein of the Los Angeles Philharmonic, the director is careful to give the spectator opposing perspectives of the orchestra for a reprised passage of music. In the first, the orchestra's shift from a melancholy waltz to a driving orchestral tutti is viewed through an extremely high angled shot that mischievously obscures the violins as they navigate a thorny passage (mm. 192ff.). When the section is reprised, Sidney balances the visual composition by positioning the camera on the opposite side of the orchestra. When the technical passage for violins returns (mm. 295ff.), the camera trucks toward the players, providing the visual gratification of frantically fiddling violinists that had been withheld previously.

Alfred Newman of 20th Century Fox had hoped his orchestra's performance of *How to Marry a Millionaire* would help audiences identify and appreciate individual orchestra members. Unfortunately, the spectator is never afforded a view of these exceptional performers at close range. In contrast, Sidney's direction of the MGM films draws the audience in close for repeated shots of pillar members of the orchestra, especially concertmaster Lou Raderman and Phil Memoli, longtime principal oboist and something of an unofficial orchestra manager (see Figures 25.4 and 25.5). Other featured members include flautist Arthur Gleghorn, trombonist Si Zentner, and clarinetist Gus Bivona, and, of course, maestro Johnny Green himself. Sidney's attentive camera treats these individuals like movie stars, a suggestive parallel that links the studio orchestra—a veritable army of generals—with MGM's famously large arsenal of screen stars.

George Sidney did not direct all the MGM Symphony shorts. The *Strauss Fantasy* (1954) was done by Vincente Minnelli, a more celebrated director of MGM musicals whose credits include *Cabin in the Sky* (1943), *Meet Me in St. Louis* (1944), *An American in Paris* (1951), and *Brigadoon* (1954). The results, somewhat unexpectedly, are less satisfying. Apparently not at all intrigued by musical structures or symmetries, Minnelli reveals more interest in oddities of orchestral performance. He tracks the camera

FIGURE 25.4 Concertmaster Lou Raderman plays a solo in the *MGM Jubilee Overture* (1954).

urgently toward trumpeters as they blow on their mutes before inserting them in their bells. At other times he abruptly inserts close-ups of Johnny Green shushing certain sections of the orchestra. Granting that Sidney's approach is anything but restrained, there is still a musical sensibility and economy in the editing of his visuals that is largely absent in Minnelli's direction.

Green later claimed that the MGM Symphony films represented one of his most important undertakings at the studio (*Los Angeles Times*, March 13, 1958). Louis B. Mayer had appointed Green as music director in 1949 because—as Green related—Mayer "wanted the greatest music operation in the history of the entertainment business" (Bernstein 1977, 349). One of the new music executive's first actions was to replace almost half the salaried musicians in the orchestra. The shake-up angered many, but it also gave Green a strong sense of connection with the orchestra that now recorded MGM's scores. An accomplished songwriter, arranger, composer, and conductor, Green often regretted that the studio's administrative duties reduced his time for conducting

FIGURE 25.5 Phil Memoli enjoys a medium shot in *Poet and the Peasant Overture* (1954).

and composing. When columnist Ted Hallock decried Hollywood film music, reporting that Green could barely conduct beyond a "businessman's bounce," Green was livid and vented his anger in a follow-up issue (*Down Beat*, May 4, 1951). Just behind the cover photo of a smiling Green with MGM star Jane Powell, the headline seethed: "Hallock 'A Barefaced Liar', Says Johnny Green." On multiple occasions in the column Green protested that Hallock's criticisms were "a false reflection upon my abilities as a conductor" (*Down Beat*, June 1, 1951). The orchestra films, then, were a very personal affair for Green; they afforded him the opportunity to present himself (and to represent the studio) in a musical and not merely administrative capacity; at the same it allowed him to show off the orchestra's abilities to an audience of millions.

It is easy in retrospect to regard these films as light fare. The pink stage, swooping camera, "ever popular" repertoire, and even Johnny Green's conspicuous silver watch chain may strike one as an undesirable mingling of Hollywood hype and symphonic pretension. The constructed nature of the films may also trouble purists. The single uninterrupted performance depicted onscreen, after all, is a far cry from the actual contents of the soundtrack: a cobbled assortment of short takes recorded in another location by an augmented studio orchestra that—if the daily music reports are accurate—was still smaller than the extra-augmented orchestra shown onscreen. (Daily music reports indicate that the recording session for *Jubilee Overture* (1954) had eighty-five members; *Poet and Peasant*, eighty; *Strauss Fantasy*, eighty-five; and *Merry Wives*, seventy-five.) In other words, these films do not deliver an authentic performance of MGM's day-to-day studio ensemble: instead, they serve up an MGM production fancifully depicting the MGM "Symphony Orchestra," featuring regular members performing alongside "guests."

Yet for all their whimsy, the films reveal that which is otherwise invisible: the remarkable musicians of the studios. James Decker, a french-horn player who played in the Columbia studio orchestra during this era, noted this double-sided quality when he remarked that "We all thought it was very corny," yet confided, "I was able to get a copy of all of the films and give a video tape…to Jack [Cave, MGM's longtime principal horn player,] after he retired." For Decker and other musicians, the films' silliness did not negate their personal significance.

Indeed, they proved timely. In the spring of 1954, less than a month after Johnny Green accepted an Oscar for *The Merry Wives of Windsor* film, RKO became the first major studio to disband its staff orchestra. After a disastrous labor strike four years later, studios were no longer obliged by the AFM to maintain staff orchestras, an issue that resembled in circumstance, if not scope, the AFM's doomed attempt to save movie theater orchestras at the end of the 1920s (Wierzbicki 2009, 183–86). Many studio musicians had worked as freelancers in the years leading up to the strike, but the new arrangement made freelancing the only option, a notoriously stressful employment scheme that persists to this day. The MGM Symphony films did not revolutionize or save the studio orchestra system, yet they succeeded on their own terms, promoting the studio's orchestra while articulating MGM's unique production aesthetics through a combination of musical and visual virtuosity that included glamour along with genuine insight. At the same time that the films hearkened back to the orchestral performances of silent-era picture palaces, the structuring of these performances through imagetrack editing brought to the surface a particular form of musico-visual dialogue in which the musical gestures of sitting musicians acquired kinetic energy through the motion of the camera through space. In other words, the films challenge viewers to think critically about the way in which visual editing interprets orchestral performance, whether one is observing orchestras in narrative films like Hitchcock's *The Man Who Knew Too Much* (1956), televised broadcasts of Leonard Bernstein's Young People's Concerts, or the Berlin Philharmonic's digital concert hall.

CONCLUSION

Though orchestral scores continue to play an important role in certain genres of American cinema, they no longer characterize a particular theater's exhibition style or studio's soundtrack. If the staff orchestras of the studios were visible to the public only through exceptional projects like the MGM films, then the ad hoc orchestras that accompany films today lack even a name or affiliation by which to identify themselves. Only films that boast soundtracks recorded by independent symphony orchestras, such as the London Symphony Orchestra in the *Star Wars* sextet (1977–2005) or the London Philharmonic Orchestra in the *Lord of the Rings* series (2001–), offer some vestige of the historical use of an orchestra's name (as opposed to merely orchestral music) to enhance a film's prestige.[6] Yet the sound of the symphony orchestra has remained a surprisingly stable factor in the cinema soundtrack. Whether performing in the pit, on the soundtrack, or even in the picture itself, cinema orchestras over the past century have offered moviegoers an opportunity to engage with orchestral music beyond the concert hall. Even if they occupy an unusual cultural niche, it is nevertheless clear that closer study of the cinema orchestra's influence on the composition and performance of film scores stands not only to change our views of film music but also enrich our understanding of the orchestra in American culture.

NOTES

1. The author gratefully acknowledges Edward Comstock (Cinematic Arts Library, University of Southern California), who provided archival materials central to this study.
2. This essay is concerned with the orchestra in the context of a history of cinema exhibition in the United States during the first half of the twentieth century. An equally important thread in the symphony orchestra's history during that time played itself out on the East Coast, where radio and record companies formed their own full-time orchestras, mostly in the 1930s, and maintained them into the 1950s.
3. Thorough study of the pre-film overture remains to be done; the practice receives only occasional comment in the secondary literature (see, for example, Long 2008, 68–72).

Analysis of these overtures has also been inadvertently complicated by their presentation on DVDs, in which the overture is often paired with a still or publicity image related to the film, an addition not based in historical practice. The construction of these overtures in relation to their parent film scores also varies widely across productions. MiklósRózsa, for example, describes composing pre-film overtures in his memoirs (Rózsa 1982, 161), but in some cases the music editor compiled the overture by splicing together excerpts from cues recorded for the film. As soundtrack historian Ray Faiola has discovered, some overtures were not even heard during a film's initial roadshow tour, but were instead constructed by editors for subsequent re-releases, as happened with *King Kong* (1933) (Ray Faiola, personal communication with author, 8 August 2011).

4. For more on Newman's *Street Scene* and its use across multiple films, including *How to Marry a Millionaire*, see Malsky 2008, 105–22. Malsky notes that the orchestra performance "even evoked the live-performance codes of first-run silent movie exhibition—more keenly felt because this CinemaScope premiere was held in exactly such a movie palace" (106).

5. Like Green at MGM, Newman conducted in several more orchestra shorts over the following year, including Tchaikovsky's "Waltz of the Flowers" from *The Nutcracker*, Tchaikovsky's Symphony No. 4, finale, Borodin's "Polovetzian Dances" from *Prince Igor*, and Haydn's Symphony No. 45 ["Farewell"]. These films are not commercially available.

6. More recently, select soundtrack albums have instead listed orchestra members in the liner notes, thereby giving individual musicians due acknowledgement.

BIBLIOGRAPHY

Altman, Rick. 2004. *Silent Film Sound*. New York: Columbia University Press.

Anderson, Gillian B. 1987. "The Presentation of Silent Films, or, Music as Anaesthesia." *Journal of Musicology* 5, no. 2: 257–295.

Bernstein, Elmer. 1976. "A Conversation with John Green: Part I." In *Elmer Bernstein's Film Music Notebook: A Complete Collection of the Quarterly Journal, 1974–1978*, 303–315. Sherman Oaks, CA: Film Music Society, 2004.

——. 1977. "A Conversation with John Green: Part II." In *Elmer Bernstein's Film Music Notebook: A Complete Collection of the Quarterly Journal, 1974–1978*, 341–357. Sherman Oaks, CA: Film Music Society, 2004.

Carroll, Brendan G. 1997. *The Last Prodigy: A Biography of Erich Wolfgang Korngold*. Portland, OR: Amadeus.

Christlieb, Don. 1996. *Recollections of a First Chair Bassoonist: 52 Years in the Hollywood Studio Orchestras*. Edited by Anthony Christlieb and Carolyn Beck. Sherman Oaks, CA: Christlieb Products.

Citron, Marcia J. 2000. *Opera on Screen*. New Haven: Yale University Press.

Dorris, George. 1995. "Léo Staats at the Roxy, 1926–1928." *Dance Research* 13, no. 1: 84–99.

Faulkner, Robert R. 1985. *Hollywood Studio Musicians: Their Work and Careers in the Recording Industry*. Lanham, MD: University Press of America.

Hart, Philip. 1973. *Orpheus in the New World: The Symphony Orchestra as an American Cultural Institution*. New York: W. W. Norton.

Hays, Will H. 2011. "Will B. Hays Introduction to Vitaphone." Special feature, *Don Juan*, directed by Alan Crosland. DVD. Burbank: Warner Bros. Archive Collection).

Horowitz, Joseph. 2005. *Classical Music in America: A History of Its Rise and Fall*. New York: W. W. Norton.

Hubbard, Preston J. 1985. "Synchronized Sound and Movie-House Musicians, 1926–1929." *American Music* 3, no. 4: 429–441.

Kraft, James P. 1994a. "Musicians in Hollywood: Work and Technological Change in Entertainment Industries, 1926–1940." *Technology and Culture* 35, no. 2: 289–314.

——. 1994b. "The 'Pit' Musicians: Mechanization in the Movie Theaters, 1926–1934." *Labor History* 35, no. 1: 66–89.

Kaufman, Louis, with Annette Kaufman. 2003. *A Fiddler's Tale: How Hollywood and Vivaldi Discovered Me*. Madison: University of Wisconsin Press.

Liebman, Roy. *Vitaphone Films: A Catalogue of the Features and the Shorts*. Jefferson, NC: McFarland, 2003.

London, Kurt. 1936. *Film Music*. Translated by Eric S. Bensinger. London: Faber & Faber.

Long, Michael. 2008. *Beautiful Monsters: Imagining the Classic in Musical Media*. Berkeley: University of California Press.

Malsky, Matthew. 2008. "Sounds of the City: Alfred Newman's 'Street Scene' and Urban Modernity." In *Lowering the Boom: Critical Studies in Film Sound*, edited by Jay Beck and Tony Grajeda, 105–122. Urbana: University of Illinois Press.

Monder, Eric. 1994. *George Sidney: A Bio-Bibliography*. Westport, CT: Greenwood.

Morton, Lawrence. 1948. "The Music Makers." *Film Music Notes* 7, no. 3.

Platte, Nathan. 2011. "Dream Analysis: Korngold, Mendelssohn, and Musical Adaptations in Warner Bros.' *A Midsummer Night's Dream*." *19th-Century Music* 34, no. 3: 211–236.

Riesenfeld, Hugo. 1926. "Music and Motion Pictures." *Annals of the Academy of Political and Social Science* 128 (November): 58–62.

Rózsa, Miklós. 1982. *A Double Life: The Autobiography of Miklós Rózsa*. New York: Wynwood.

Smith, Catherine Parsons. 2007. *Making Music in Los Angeles: Transforming the Popular*. Berkeley: University of California Press.

Wagner, Victor. 1926. "Scoring a Motion Picture." *Transactions of the Society of Motion Picture Engineers* 25 (September): 40–43.

Walker, Alexander. 1979. *The Shattered Silents: How the Talkies Came to Stay*. New York: William Morrow.

Wierzbicki, James. 2009. *Film Music: A History*. New York: Routledge.

Index

Page numbers followed by *t* or *f* indicate tables or figures, respectively. Numbers followed by "n" indicate notes.

CPSIA information can be obtained at www.ICGtesting.com
Printed in the USA
BVOW04s1232140916

461750BV00010B/9/P